D1572609

The publisher gratefully acknowledges the generous support of the Authors Imprint Endowment Fund of the University of California Press Foundation, which was established to support exceptional scholarship by first-time authors.

The publisher also gratefully acknowledges the generous contribution to this book provided by the AMS 75 PAYS Endowment of the American Musicological Society, funded in part by the National Endowment for the Humanities and the Andrew W. Mellon Foundation.

Frontier Figures

CALIFORNIA STUDIES IN 20TH-CENTURY MUSIC

Richard Taruskin, General Editor

Frontier Figures

*American Music and the Mythology
of the American West*

———

Beth E. Levy

*for Rachel
in friendship*

Beth E. Levy

UNIVERSITY OF CALIFORNIA PRESS

Berkeley   Los Angeles   London

University of California Press, one of the most distinguished university
presses in the United States, enriches lives around the world by advancing
scholarship in the humanities, social sciences, and natural sciences. Its
activities are supported by the UC Press Foundation and by philanthropic
contributions from individuals and institutions. For more information,
visit www.ucpress.edu.

University of California Press
Berkeley and Los Angeles, California

University of California Press, Ltd.
London, England

Library of Congress Cataloging-in-Publication Data

Levy, Beth E. (Beth Ellen), 1972–
   Frontier figures : American music and the mythology of the American
West / Beth E. Levy. — 1st ed.
      p.   cm. — (California studies in 20th-century music ; 14)
   Includes bibliographical references and index.
   ISBN 978-0-520-26776-3 (cloth : alk. paper) — ISBN 978-0-520-26778-7
(pbk. : alk. paper)
   1. Music—United States—20th century—History and criticism.
2. Legends—West (U.S.)—History and criticism. 3. West (U.S.)—
Social life and customs—20th century. 4. West (U.S.)—History—
1890-1945. I. Title.
  ML200.5.L49 2012
  781.5'9—dc23

                                      2011038214

Manufactured in the United States of America

20   19   18   17   16   15   14   13   12   11

10 9 8 7 6 5 4 3 2 1

In keeping with a commitment to support environmentally responsible
and sustainable printing practices, UC Press has printed this book on
50-pound Enterprise, a 30% post-consumer-waste, recycled, deinked
fiber that is processed chlorine-free. It is acid-free and meets all ANSI/
NISO (Z 39.48) requirements.

To my parents,
David and Lynne Levy

CONTENTS

ILLUSTRATIONS

ACKNOWLEDGMENTS

For decades, artists and thinkers have approached the American West with a mixture of nostalgia and excitement–as if simultaneously returning home and embarking on an adventure. So perhaps it should come as no surprise that I have found both comfort and challenge in writing this book. I have had many companions along the way, and it is my heartfelt pleasure to thank them for their wise guidance, their practical assistance, and above all their camaraderie.

As this book took shape first in the form of a dissertation, I owe significant thanks to those who guided its first stages. First, my committee of readers. I feel the warmest and most profound gratitude to my adviser, Richard Taruskin, whose enthusiastic support and careful reading have informed and enlivened this project from the start. His influence continues to inspire me toward a scholarship that has both musical and moral force. I am also grateful to Katherine Bergeron for her generous advice and for knowing the right questions to ask; to the late Michael Rogin, whose insights into American cultural history have left their mark on each of my chapters; and to Kerwin Lee Klein for his insights into the American West and the writing of history. Research support at the dissertation stage was provided by the Andrew W. Mellon Fellowship Foundation, the American Musicological Society, the Townsend Center for the Humanities, Phi Beta Kappa (UC Berkeley Chapter), and the Music Department and Graduate Division of the University of California, Berkeley. More recently, the University of California Office of the President and the University of California, Davis, College of Letters and Sciences have provided fellowship and grant support during crucial phases of research and writing.

To my faculty colleagues at the University of California, Davis, I want to express my sincere thanks for their unflagging interest in my work and their commitment to creating an exceptional environment for research. I have also appreciated the contributions of graduate students in my recent seminars (on nationalism, music in the 1930s, and music in the West). I have benefited immensely from financial support and the intellectual companionship of colleagues at the UC Davis Humanities Institute in a faculty research symposium on California Cultures, and at Harvard University's Charles Warren Center for Studies in American History. For expert editorial feedback, I owe serious debts to Richard Crawford, Denise von Glahn, and many other readers—anonymous and otherwise. My thinking about Copland has evolved in productive conversation with Elizabeth Bergman, Jessica Burr, Jennifer de Lapp, Carol J. Oja, and Howard Pollack, and on matters Californian with Leta Miller, and the late Catherine Parsons Smith. And for a delightful variety of writing advice, moral support, and good company, it is my great pleasure to thank Ardith Allen, Laura Basini, Mark Clague, Robert Fallon, Danielle Fosler-Lussier, Sandra Graham, Alyson Knop, Tanya Lee, Nathaniel G. Lew, Klára Móricz, Joel Phillips and Peter Schmelz.

The West is a big place and its archival materials are scattered widely. In addition to the army of mostly anonymous librarians (past and present) who collected and catalogued old concert programs, letters, the residue of "community pageants" and the like, I am especially grateful to the Interlibrary Loan staffs at UC Davis, UC Berkeley, and Harvard University; to the Oral History of American Music project at Yale University (especially Vivian Perlis and Libby van Cleve) and the University of California's Regional Oral History Program; to the Denver Public Library and the New York Public Library for access to isolated collections; to Patricia Harris for permission to use materials related to her father Roy; and to Ellen Bacon and Jon Elkus for assistance with the Ernst Bacon papers.

For more extensive assistance with archival research, I am grateful to David Coppen and the Special Collections staff at the Sibley Library, Eastman School of Music for their help with the Arthur Farwell Collections; to Jim Quigel and the Cadman Collection at the Historical Collections and Labor Archives, Special Collections Library at Pennsylvania State University; to Suzanne Lovejoy and Richard Boursy for access to the Virgil Thomson Papers at Yale University's Irving Gilmore Music Library; to David Sigler and Renee James at the Roy Harris Archive (California State University, Los Angeles); to Stephen M. Fry at the University of California, Los Angeles, Music Library and to Timothy A. Edwards and the staff at the UCLA Music Library, Special Collections; and to Wayne Shirley and Wilda Hess for their help with the Copland Collection at the Library of Congress.

I should also like to thank many members of the University of California Press for their support, expertise, and encouragement, chief among them Mary Francis, whose editorial eye and gentle understanding of authorial psychology were crucial to this project's completion. I am grateful to Eric Schmidt for technical assistance, to Jacqueline Volin for her responsiveness to many queries, and to Mary Ray Worley for her exceptionally careful copyediting. A special word of thanks goes to Sam Nichols for his painstaking and good-humored typesetting of music examples.

Four sections of this book present revised versions of material published elsewhere. A précis of the material that grew into chapters 1 and 3 appeared as "'In the Glory of the Sunset': Arthur Farwell, Charles Wakefield Cadman, and Indianism in American Music," *repercussions* 5, nos. 1–2 (1996): 124–83. Portions of chapter 8 were previously published in "'The White Hope of American Music'; or, How Roy Harris Became Western," *American Music* 19, no. 2 (2001): 131–67. Material on Aaron Copland covered primarily in chapter 10 was included in "From Orient to Occident: Aaron Copland and the Sagas of the Prairies," in *Aaron Copland and His World,* ed. Judith Tick and Carol J. Oja (Princeton, NJ: Princeton University Press, 2005), 307–49. Finally, an expanded treatment of chapter 13 has been published as "The Great Crossing: Nostalgia and Manifest Destiny in Aaron Copland's *The Red Pony*," *Journal of Film Music* 2, nos. 2–4 (2009): 201–23.

Finally, my oldest, deepest, and most cherished debt: to my family—my parents, my brother, Benjamin, and many others. I know they will recognize in this book the souvenirs of many shared road trips and the imprint of many lively conversations. I thank them for their unfailing support and their love beyond words.

ABBREVIATIONS

AFC   Arthur Farwell Collection, Sibley Library, Eastman School of Music

CC   Nicolas Slonimsky, "Roy Harris: Cimarron Composer," unpublished manuscript (1951), Roy Harris Collection, California State University, Los Angeles

CCLC   Copland Collection, Library of Congress

EDC   Evelyn Davis Culbertson, *He Heard America Singing: Arthur Farwell, Composer and Crusading Music Educator* (Metuchen, NJ: Scarecrow Press, 1992)

HP   Howard Pollack, *Aaron Copland: The Life and Work of an Uncommon Man* (New York: Henry Holt and Company, 1999)

OH   UCLA Music Library Special Collections; Oral History Interviews, UC Regents; typescript (1983) in the Bancroft Library, University of California, Berkeley

Perison CWC   Harry D. Perison, "Charles Wakefield Cadman: His Life and Works." (PhD diss., Eastman School of Music, University of Rochester, 1978)

PR   Paul Rosenfeld, *An Hour with American Music* (Philadelphia: J. B. Lippincott, 1929)

RHC   Roy Harris Collection, California State University, Los Angeles

VPAC1   Aaron Copland and Vivian Perlis, *Copland, 1900–1942* (New York: St. Martin's, 1984)

WJ   Arthur Farwell, *"Wanderjahre of a Revolutionist" and Other Essays on American Music,* ed. Thomas Stoner (Rochester, NY: University of Rochester Press, 1995)

Introduction

The Course of Empire

Facing west, from California's shores,
Inquiring, tireless, seeking what is yet unfound,
I, a child, very old, over waves, towards the house of maternity, the
land of migrations, look afar,
Look off the shores of my Western Sea—the circle almost circled;
For, starting westward from Hindustan, from the vales of Kashmere,
From Asia—from the north—from the God, the sage, and the hero,
From the south—from the flowery peninsulas, and the spice islands;
Long having wander'd since—round the earth having wander'd,
Now I face home again—very pleas'd and joyous;
(But where is what I started for, so long ago?
And why is it yet unfound?)

—WALT WHITMAN, LEAVES OF GRASS

The turn of the twentieth century came early to America. Still a young country by international standards, the United States seemed determined to celebrate its coming of age in 1892–93 with a cluster of events marking the four-hundredth anniversary of Christopher Columbus's fabled transatlantic voyage and so-called discovery of the New World. They culminated in the 1893 Chicago Columbian Exposition, also known as the Chicago World's Fair. Drawing on a pointedly diverse range of natural and human resources, the exposition was meant to reinforce the idea of American exceptionalism and to display America's growing centrality on the world stage. For the Columbian moment was not just a convenient anniversary. By backdating the birth of the nation from the revolution to the age of exploration, these commemorations aligned the United States not only with the civic republicanism of the founding fathers, but also with the increasingly relevant issue of empire and its relationship to America's own westward expansion.

The Gay Nineties at home coincided with unprecedented aggression abroad. Following the 1890 massacre at Wounded Knee and the effective end of the Indian

1

wars, the Spanish-American War, with America's interventions in Cuba and invasion of the Philippines, placed the United States at the heart of a new colonial network. When Americans directed their attention east, they saw the Old World crumbling under the weight of its own history. When they looked south, they saw a tropical paradise virtually untouched by history. When they looked west, they saw history in action. This book attempts to hear the traces of this last, "western" history in the lives and works of classically trained musicians during the first half of the twentieth century.

Between the Eastern Seaboard and the Pacific coast, where the American frontier seemed to fall off the edge of the world, lay a continent in flux. The rhetoric of "Manifest Destiny" furnished Americans with images and metaphors through which to understand their status as a twentieth-century imperial power: natives, savages, and Indians; scouts, pioneers, and settlers; mavericks, cowboys, and gunfighters. This mythology is so fundamental to the telling of American histories and the construction of American identities that its presence even in the rarefied realms of music should not be surprising. Far more remarkable is the variety of projects that these frontier figures could be made to serve. Western imagery was at once a natural and strategic choice for projects both romantic and modern, individualistic and communal, nostalgic and progressive.

Taking as its point of departure the geographical imagination of the nineteenth century's Columbian year, this book embarks on its own voyage of discovery, navigating waters that are sometimes familiar and sometimes uncharted. Like any ship's captain, I have selected one route among many, tracing a current that may seem relatively narrow: American art or "classical" music as practiced by a handful of influential composers between 1900 and 1950. En route, this current commingles with and gains momentum from many others—the dime novel, the community pageant, the popular song, and the Hollywood film score, to name a few. At the outset, I choose to dock for a while in 1893, to take on board some of the themes that will sustain our westward journey, and to ponder their relationship to the world-historical vision captured in the most famous line of Bishop George Berkeley's poem "America or the Muse's Refuge: A Prophesy": "Westward the course of empire takes its way."

THE DVOŘÁK DEBATE

Between May and December of 1893, composers and audiences participated in one of the landmark debates in American musical history. The presence of Antonín Dvořák at the National Conservatory in New York City sparked intense discussion about European expertise and the appropriate use of folk sources. Dvořák was hardly the first composer to experiment with American folk idioms. Yet he is still among the most famous to have done so, and in the 1890s his words carried the weight of continental authority. Although the Czech composer was hired as an exponent of the German tradition à la Brahms, he knew what it was like to work on the periphery of Europe's musical centers. He had learned the importance of inventing and marketing a provincial style that could win cosmopolitan acceptance. He admitted the importance of regional and racial difference, and he recognized that musical nationalism and gestures toward authenticity were deeply intertwined.

Less than a year after his arrival, Dvořák issued a proclamation that would quickly overshadow his status as a disciple of Brahms: "I am now satisfied," he told the readers of the New York Herald, "that the future music of this country must be founded upon what are called the Negro melodies."[1] Not all shared Dvořák's unequivocal assessment. When pressed by the editor of the Boston Herald, Boston's musical elite tended to take exception to the notion that "plantation" or "slave" songs were the best basis for distinctively American music. As Joseph Horowitz has shown, there was a distinct difference between the enthusiasm that cosmopolitan New Yorkers mustered for their adopted son and the skepticism, verging in some cases on hostility, with which many Bostonians greeted their Bohemian guest. To Harvard's John Knowles Paine, it seemed "a preposterous idea to say that in future American music will rest upon such a shaky foundation as the melodies of a yet largely undeveloped race." George Whitefield Chadwick stated flatly that "such negro melodies as I have heard . . . I should be sorry to see become the basis of an American school of composition." Benjamin Lang, too, begged to differ with Dvořák's claim. And he made a polite request: "I wish that Dr. Dvořák would write something himself, using themes from these plantation songs. Such an act would set an example for our American composers."[2]

As Lang may well have known, Dvořák had already committed himself to exactly such a project: his Symphony in E Minor, "From the New World" (1893). Much has been written about the aftermath of its premiere; the critical posturing threatened to engulf the symphony, and subsequent reverberations still shape its reception by raising questions about racial authenticity and national or regional identity. Shortly before the first performance, Dvořák complicated the answers to these questions by revealing that the middle movements of the symphony had grown out of his fascination with Longfellow's Song of Hiawatha and its romantic re-creation of Indian lore.[3] The rich confusion of ethnic implications that resulted may account in part for the symphony's enduring status as a turning point in American music history.[4] Here was a Slavic composer, employed as a representative of the Germanic tradition, publicly committed to the incorporation of African American melodies and inspired by (faux) Native American legend.

James Huneker was one of the first to weigh in on the symphony's value and its racial mixing: "When the smoke of criticism has cleared away it will be noticed, first, that Dr. Dvořák has written an exceedingly beautiful symphony; secondly, that it is not necessarily American, unless to be American you must be composite. The new work, thematically considered, is composite, sounding Irish, Slavic, Scandinavian, Scotch, negro, and German."[5] More enthusiastic critics, such as Henry Krehbiel, William J. Henderson, and even H. L. Mencken, noted the work's hybrid character as one of its chief virtues. Henderson, for example, praised the main melody of the slow movement: "It is an idealized slave song made to fit the impressive quiet of night on the prairie. When the star of empire took its way over those mighty Western plains blood and sweat and agony and bleaching human bones marked its course. Something of this awful buried sorrow of the prairie must have forced itself upon Dr. Dvořák's mind."[6] Whether Henderson had in mind the grasslands of Iowa (where Dvořák had spent part of the previous summer) or the vast expanses of the Far West (a rather more likely site for bleaching human bones), his words suggest that the "New World" Symphony's New York appeal was enhanced by its openness—its ability to accommodate every critic's favorite stripe of Americana.

By contrast, as Horowitz points out, members of the Boston intelligentsia retained a mixture of skepticism and indignation when their turn came to review Dvořák's symphonic effort. Spurred by the influential writings of Philip Hale, Boston readers learned to ridicule this supposedly "American" product as a hodgepodge of foreign elements—Scotch snaps, "negro airs," and "primitive" gestures—that were all too typical of cosmopolitan New York. William Apthorp included in his response a brief excursus: "Our American Negro music has every element of barbarism to be found in the Slavic or Scandinavian folk-songs; it is essentially barbarous music. What is more, it sounds terribly like any other barbarous music."[7] Far from being a source of delight, the symphony's interpretive slipperiness functioned as a red flag to the Brahmins, for whom such hybridity was at best unrefined and quite possibly dangerous. Nearly twenty years later, Hale lamented that, even though he had presented ample evidence that the symphony expressed "the state of a homesick soul," other critics would not abandon the idea that the "New World" was based "for the most part, on negro themes, and that the future of American music rests on the use of congo, North American Indian, Creole, Greaser and Cowboy ditties, whinings, yawps, and whoopings."[8]

American composers participated in this debate with words and music. The most conservative composers fervently wished to partake of what they saw as the universal "mainstream," populated by German masters, not regional ones. Paine protested: "The time is past when composers are to be classed according to geographical limits. It is not a question of nationality but individuality, and individuality is not the result of imitation—whether of folk songs, Negro melodies, the tunes of the heathen Chinese or Digger Indians, but of personal character and inborn originality."[9] Many of Paine's compatriots, however, were at least a little interested in creating a national music, whether according to Dr. Dvořák's pre-scription or by some other means. Like Dvořák, they favored the tried-and-true European model for creating a national music: injecting indigenous elements into conventional contexts. But unlike the Czech composer, they recognized that this was no simple proposition in the multiethnic United States.

As Dvořák's American sojourn wore on, his position became more circum-spect. He stood by his preference for "the so-called plantation melodies and slave-songs," but admitted that "it matters little whether the inspiration for the coming folk-songs for America is derived from the Negro melodies, the songs of the Cre-oles, the red man's chant, or the plaintive ditties of the homesick German or Nor-wegian. Undoubtedly, the germs for the best of music lie hidden among all the races that are commingled in this great country."[10] As an outsider, Dvořák could afford to base his selection of folklore on personal inclination rather than politi-cal agenda or family heritage. Here he was not bound by the rigid dictates of sup-posed national or racial authenticity that had complicated his creation of a Czech musical identity.[11] It hardly made a difference whether his information about Native American life came from Longfellow, Buffalo Bill, or the Kickapoo Medi-cine Show, nor did it matter whether his exposure to African American music came courtesy of Stephen Foster, from his students' recollections, or from his pe-rusal of the American press. The theme of his slow movement could still become the ersatz spiritual "Goin' Home," and Dvořák's secretary could still maintain that the subtitle "From the New World" had been added as an afterthought, "one of his innocent jokes."[12]

For Dvořák's American contemporaries there was more at stake. They knew that any type of folk borrowing would bring with it pressing questions of authen-ticity. And they knew that not all folk music was created equal. To Amy Beach it was self-evident that biographical justifications for borrowing were necessary or at least highly desirable:

> To those of us of the North and West there can be little if any "association" con-nected with Negro melodies. . . . We of the North should be far more likely to be influenced by old English, Scotch or Irish songs . . . than by the songs of a portion of our people who were kept so long in bondage. . . . If a Negro, the possessor of talent for musical composition, should perfect himself in its expression, then we might have the melodies which are his folk-songs employed with fullest sympathy, for he would be working with the inherited feelings of his race.[13]

Beach put this philosophy into action almost immediately with her "Gaelic" Symphony (1894–96), which quotes Irish-Gaelic folk songs. As Adrienne Fried Block has observed, she may have learned from Dvořák's example, for some of her later works also borrow Native American themes. She steered clear of black America, however, for reasons that she readily confessed:

Without the slightest desire to question the beauty of the Negro melodies . . . or to disparage them on account of their source, I cannot help feeling justified in the belief that they are not fully typical of our country. The African population of the United States is far too small for its songs to be considered "American." It represents only one factor in the composition of our nation. Moreover, it is not native American. Were we to consult the native folk songs of the continent, it would have to be those of the Indians and Esquimaux, several of whose curious songs are given in the publications of the Smithsonian Institute. The Africans are no more native than the Italians, Swedes, or Russians.[14]

Indian melodies at least had the virtue of indigenousness; moreover, for many Americans, the imagery associated with the native "noble savage" was more appealing than the minstrel show stereotypes of the "plantation darkey." Though Edward MacDowell opposed the creation of a specifically American style, after the tremendous popularity of his "Indian" Suite, he observed that "the stern but at least manly and free rudeness of the North American Indian" was a worthier inspiration than "the badge of whilom slavery."[15] Such were the continental divides between New York and Boston, between cosmopolitan and provincial, between races, colors, and creeds.

THE TURNER THESIS

Less than six months before Dvořák's premiere, and about eight hundred miles west, the nation's foremost American historians, meeting at the Columbian Exposition in Chicago, witnessed another key moment in American cultural history when young Frederick Jackson Turner delivered his address "The Significance of the Frontier in American History." Though the speech went virtually unremarked by its original audience, it quickly became a fundamental document in American historiography, marking a move away from narratives centered on military or political heroes and shaping the nascent discipline of western history for decades to come. No matter how vigilantly later historians have revised the factual premises of Turner's hypothesis, it has retained its narrative power.

Turner's address, famed for its rhetorical and social-scientific authority, began with a statement that placed the western frontier at the center of America's conduct and character. Responding to an 1890 census report which stated that the "frontier line" separating civilization and wilderness was no longer a viable concept for analysis, Turner proclaimed: "This brief official statement marks the closing of a great historic movement. Up to our own day American history has been in a large degree the history of the colonization of the Great West. The existence of an area of free land, its continuous recession, and the advance of American settlement westward, explain American development." He asserted that "the peculiarity of American institutions" resulted from "the fact that they have been compelled to adapt themselves to the changes of an expanding people—to the changes involved in crossing a continent, in winning a wilderness."[16] In other words, the frontier was both a convincing reason for American exceptionalism and the best assurance of its continuation.

If Dvořák's "New World" was populated by Negroes and Indians, Turner's belonged to men of European extraction. They made up the successive waves of settlement that washed across the North American continent—from the Appalachians, to the Midwest, to the Great Plains, the Rockies, and beyond. The Indian trader prepared the way for the rancher and the small farmer, whose families and commercial support systems eventually coalesced into frontier towns. The promise of available land drew families of different classes and backgrounds; unnecessary European habits were abandoned as unpragmatic; democracy was renewed. The changing frontier thus functioned as what Turner called "the line of most rapid and effective Americanization." At first, the wilderness shaped the settler into a less-than-noble savage: "Before long he has gone to planting Indian corn and plowing with a sharp stick; he shouts the war cry and takes the scalp in orthodox Indian fashion." Gradually, though, the fertilization of Old World roots in a New World environment bore uniquely American fruit: "The advance of the frontier has meant a steady movement away from the influence of Europe. . . . And to study this advance, the men who grew up under these conditions, and the political, economic and social results of it, is to study the really American part of our history."[17]

More recent historians have disagreed about whether Turner saw the frontier as a line of expansion into the empty West, or a line of conflict along which Euro-Americans met and conquered indigenous tribes. As Kerwin Lee Klein has observed, "One could read pre-Columbian North America as the historical landscape of savagery or the wild space of nature. Frontier history swung back and forth on this hinge, revealing alternate worlds, pasts, and futures."[18] Turner himself had stated at the outset that the frontier is "the meeting point between savagery and civilization," and that each phase of westward expansion was "won by a series of Indian wars." Yet the potent phrase "free land" and Turner's frequent references to the natural obstacles of the American wilderness soon gained lives of their own. It was all too tempting for Turner's readers to let romantic depictions of Anglo ingenuity and perseverance in the face of a hostile landscape override the human toll of westward expansion. Though tragic depictions of defeated and "vanishing" tribes often took pride of place in the arts and anthropology, it was heroic Anglo advance under the banner of Manifest Destiny that captured most historians' imaginations. According to Klein, "More and more, wilderness displaced savagery as the frontier scholar's antagonist of choice and a simple agon replaced Turner's dialectic."[19]

In one of Turner's earliest essays, "The Significance of History," he famously stated: "Each age writes the history of the past anew with reference to the conditions uppermost in its own time."[20] Given this philosophy of history, we might ask what contemporary conditions Turner himself was responding to when he chose to begin his speech with the census figures heralding the closing of the frontier. Why did his thesis emerge at the exact point when the frontier line could no longer ensure the future development of American democracy?

The explanatory power of the Turner hypothesis was enhanced by its appearance when the time was ripe for retrospect. Indeed, there is nothing new in grounding theories of national identity in the process of looking backward. Dvořák knew this as well as anyone, and even his most inclusive recipe for musical Americanness was liberally seasoned with nostalgia. The plantation song (even when recreated by Foster), Native American lore (especially as depicted by Longfellow), and the "plaintive ditties of the homesick German or Norwegian" were not modern musical currency at the turn of the century. In the United States, where historical memory forms a more reliable basis for cohesion than race, American identity has always depended on the specious clarity of hindsight to blur the rough edges of ethnic and class tensions. Among representations of America, the landscapes of the American West are particularly susceptible to suffusion by nostalgia. The penetration of unspoiled nature, the supposed disappearance of Indian tribes, and the unrepeatability of westward expansion—all these conjure a sense of loss no less palpable than the exhilaration of pioneering advances. Those historians who took Turner's thesis as gospel, and the legions of artists and thinkers whose efforts were colored by its endorsement of Manifest Destiny, could never fully escape its twinning of progress and nostalgia.

Perhaps only a historian of Turner's generation, the first for which the strife of the Civil War would have been barely a memory, could step so decisively away from viewing North-South sectionalism as the crucial topography of U.S. history: "The true point of view in the history of this nation is not the Atlantic coast," he announced, "it is the Great West. Even the slavery struggle . . . occupies its important place in American history because of its relation to westward expansion."[21] As a defining episode in the nation's character, westward expansion had undeniable advantages over civil war. It had direction, and it had a resolution that a majority of Americans could comfortably consider a victory. The frontier calculus could generate many useful images: hard-won advances against hostile nature or the embrace of Mother Nature, the glory of the successful Indian fighter or a world-historical pathos that consigned Native Americans to extinction. In every case these pictures were preferable to the bloody battlefields that set brother against brother and nearly shattered the Union.

There is a second, more specific way in which Turner's thesis responded to the demands of its time and place. Gathered together under the auspices of the Columbian Exposition, the more attentive members of the American Historical Association might have predicted where Turner would finally anchor his exploration of American identity: "Since the days when the fleet of Columbus sailed into the waters of the New World," he declared, "America has been another name for opportunity, and the people of the United States have taken their tone from the incessant expansion which has not only been open but has even been forced upon them." The cadence that closed Turner's march of history balanced American exceptionalism against the westward movement of universal history as charted by Hegel and others, according to which the riches of the Orient yielded to the glories of Greece, the grandeur of Rome, and the rise of modern Europe. In Turner's eyes, the American frontier experience continued this westering process: "What the Mediterranean Sea was to the Greeks ... the ever retreating frontier has been to the United States directly, and to the nations of Europe more remotely."[22] From the Far East to the Far West, America's Manifest Destiny was the world's westward expansion, the crowning achievement of the age of imperialism. In Klein's words: "West, even as a particular arid region of the United States, always also harks back to 'The West' as a cultural tradition from ancient Greece to modern Europe. And since Americans have frequently claimed for themselves a privileged place in the course of history, the West is crucial to understanding history in the abstract. The frontier was not just the place where civilization and wilderness made American democracy, it was the ragged edge of history itself, where historical and nonhistorical defied and defined each other."[23]

Dvořák was understandably less concerned with American exceptionalism than was Turner, but he still situated the United States at a unique moment in the steady (westward) progress of history. Columbus and colonialism figured in Dvořák's "New World" as well. There was no concealing the historical coincidence that linked the composer's arrival in the United States with the "discovery" of America. On the contrary, at a ceremony welcoming him to New York, Colonel Thomas Wentworth Higginson gave an oration entitled "Two New Worlds: The New World of Columbus and the New World of Music." Though his English was less than fluent, Dvořák probably got the drift, and Michael Beckerman has suggested that the memory of this speech might have given his symphony its famous subtitle.[24] In light of the heightened colonial awareness surrounding his visit, Dvořák might also be understood as an agent of cultural imperialism, spreading German theory and practice to eager American pupils. As Richard Taruskin has argued, the National Conservatory employed its Czech guest "not as a Bohemian or nationalist but as master of the unmarked mother tongue," German symphonic writing.[25]

The controversial pronouncements Dvořák made upon arrival were also secondhand European methods, Old World wisdom about manufacturing national identity in music through reliance on folk roots. In the multicultural United States such teachings were at best difficult to realize, and at worst destined to perpetuate their creators' exile to the awkward periphery of the Teutonic "mainstream." More often than not, composers' responses to this imported philosophy exhibited an Americanness far more complex than the assertion of blood ties or the celebration of shared historical experiences. Their selection and manipulation of source materials reflect their views on race, class, and the power relations among American population groups. In short, their music encodes the same tensions and resolutions embodied in the nation they represented.

THE WILD WEST

While Frederick Jackson Turner spoke from inside the hallowed halls of the Columbian Exposition's numerous congresses, another version of the West took shape outside the fair gates—one that exposed westward expansion's processes of conflict and conquest for all to see: Buffalo Bill's Wild West. Of course I am not the first to point out this conjunction. Richard Slotkin, Louis Warren, Frederick Nolan, and Richard White, among others, have observed that while intellectuals were discussing the West, Buffalo Bill was reliving it for a paying crowd.[26] Representing William "Buffalo Bill" Cody's return to the States after years of European touring, the appearance of his Wild West show at the exposition had the character of a homecoming celebration; 3.8 million tickets were sold for its six-month stand near the Midway Plaisance.

Though never called a show by its creators, the Wild West was nonetheless exiled from the neoclassical structures of the so-called White City because of its commercial associations—its emphasis on animals and acrobatics linked it to the circus. Yet it made visible the same rhetoric of racial and industrial progress that animated the fair as a whole.[27] In its depictions of man mastering nature and its impressive deployment of the still noteworthy technologies of electricity and locomotion, the Wild West displayed not just a rustic frontier but a modern marvel whose import went beyond mere entertainment. According to business manager Nate Salsbury, the Wild West "is something of which intelligence, morality, and patriotism approve, because it is history not vaudeville."[28]

The Wild West staged the ethnic and ecological confrontations of the frontier in highly dramatic fashion, and it quickly grew into what cultural historian Richard Slotkin has called "the most important commercial vehicle for the fabrication and transmission of the Myth of the Frontier."[29] With origins in modest frontier theatricals, spiced with melodrama and stunts, it was patterned in part on the serialized chapters of the dime novel (the genre that made Cody literally a legend in his own time) and in part on the unfurling of wilderness landscapes and historical events on the traveling panorama shows that were so popular in the mid-nineteenth century.[30] By 1887, under the influence of New York dramatist Steele MacKaye, the structure of the show had coalesced into a "drama of civilization," tracing the development of frontier life through four "epochs": from the

Primeval Forest to the Prairie to the Cattle Ranch and the Mining Camp, the last of which included a terrific cyclone replicated by wind machines and the famous attack on the Deadwood Stagecoach. The Wild West was designated "America's National Entertainment," and by the late 1880s, it was thrilling the capitals of Europe, in effect replacing the minstrel show as America's most prominent popular culture export.

As its relegation to the Midway Plaisance suggests, the Wild West would always have to battle those who saw it as cheap or disreputable. Yet in this fight it could mobilize powerful resources that have continued to support western art and literature: a pretension to historical authenticity, an emphasis on real or imaginary audience participation, and a tendency to read the national or even the international into the regional. Historians have long noted that Buffalo Bill's own authenticity was a matter of much debate. His storied biography was intertwined with the dime novels of Ned Buntline and Ingraham Prentiss, spiced with tales of Pony Express riding, gold digging, buffalo hunting, and Indian fighting that were as much fiction as fact. Cody was already being portrayed as a character in frontier-themed plays before he took to the stage himself, and once he did, he joined a host of Buffalo Bill impersonators who continued to play at the boundary of history and myth.[31] The Wild West's merging of truth and tall tale might itself be considered "western," as Warren writes: "In the popular mind the West *was* an artful deception, a place to be explored with the same methods, and often the same level of enjoyment, as any humbug. In ways long underappreciated by historians, frontier ideology reinforced popular eagerness to play this game. After all, the border between settlement and wilderness was not only the meeting point of civilization and savagery. It was also where the West—whatever that was—met the printing press, the artist's canvas, and the lithograph machine."[32]

Although the spectacle was meant to offer universal lessons about valor and skill, western heroes had particular advantages over regional icons. Like Edward MacDowell's "rude" but "manly" Indians and Turner's intrepid frontiersmen, they could symbolize the nation's most distinctive virtues while eliding the most divisive event in American history. As Warren observes, part of the Wild West's appeal depended on "projected amnesia" about the Civil War.[33] For all their educational aspirations, Cody's press agents would have been the first to admit that the Wild West was much more than a history lesson: instead, it allowed audience members to participate in westward expansion. Elite spectators were treated to a stagecoach ride complete with an ambush, and even those watching from the stands were invited to wander through a "real" Indian encampment and to imagine themselves repelling the savage "Attack on the Settler's Cabin" that was the show's typical closing act.

With its gripping defense of home and family, the Settler's Cabin episode reinforced an ethos of domestic protection as the primary purpose of western heroism.

Yet many scholars have noted that Buffalo Bill's frontier imagery was transferred easily and often to other kinds of conflict, both national and international. Historians have often called attention to the cowboy and Indian stereotypes permeating contemporary understanding of the struggles between capital and labor that culminated in Chicago's Haymarket Riot of 1886 and the Pullman Strike of 1894. Richard Slotkin has noted the enormous range of cultural and political contexts that Americans have understood through the figures of "savage war."[34]

Occasionally the Wild West itself made such interpretations all but explicit. Its famous reenactment of "Custer's Last Rally" is a case in point. As Warren has pointed out, Custer episodes rarely figured as the climax of the show. Whenever Custer was evoked, however, the arena atmosphere was especially charged by the presence in the show of Indians who had actually fought at the Battle of the Little Big Horn in 1876, and by the long-established (though largely fictional) intertwining of Cody's and Custer's biographies. Mere days after learning of the general's defeat, Cody claimed to have taken "The First Scalp for Custer" in a furious battle with the Cheyenne Yellow Hair. (Whatever its dramatic background, the violent act was real, and the resulting scalp traveled with Cody for years, forming one of the Wild West's most durable, if controversial, attractions.) Roughly a decade later, Cody was playing Custer to Madison Square Garden, flanked by a posse of cowboys better rehearsed, and more uniformly Anglo, than Custer's regiment had ever been.[35]

The Wild West had not toured in the United States since 1888, and upon arriving in Chicago, it sported a new name befitting both its new international reputation and the American West's continuing status as the leading edge of a global westward march. Now dubbed "Buffalo Bill's Wild West and Congress of Rough Riders of the World," it featured Cossacks as well as cowboys, Arabs, gauchos, Magyars, and the military horsemen of other lands (see figure 1). In Warren's words, "The Congress of Rough Riders of the World reinscribed America's frontier history not just as racial conflict, but as the *last* of the many conflicts in the east-to-west march of white civilization."[36]

Imperial overtones became stronger still as the United States approached the Spanish-American War. A billboard of 1898–99 asked potential Wild West spectators to contemplate American history "from the primitive days of savagery up to the memorable charge of San Juan hill," and in fact Cody staged the "Battle of San Juan Hill" instead of "Custer's Last Fight" in 1899.[37] Slotkin writes, "This substitution of an imperial triumph carried off in 'Wild West' style, for a ritual re-enactment of the catastrophe that symbolized the end of the old frontier, completes the Wild West's evolution from a memorialization of the past to a celebration of the imperial future."[38]

The undisputed hero of the San Juan Hill charge was Theodore Roosevelt. Historians have long observed that Roosevelt's vision of the West was deeply

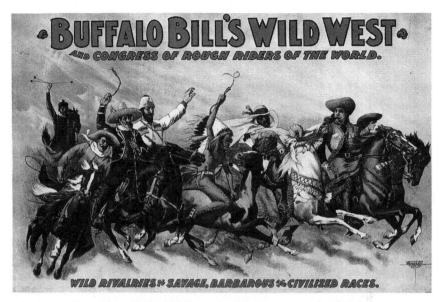

FIGURE 1. The intermingling of "Savage, Barbarous and Civilized Races" on the international stage in Buffalo Bill's Wild West, circa 1896

connected with his national and international aims.[39] Given the latter-day fame of his Rough Riders—a volunteer cavalry that crossed social and racial lines— many have assumed that Buffalo Bill named his famous "Rough Riders" after Roosevelt's. In fact, the reverse seems to have been true, though Roosevelt at times disputed the link. Even if the shared moniker were mere coincidence, there is little doubt that Cody's and Roosevelt's Rough Riders had much in common. As Slotkin puts it, Cody "performed as myth and ritual the doctrines of progressive imperialism that Roosevelt promulgated as ideology."[40] Associating the West with competition, self-reliance, democracy, and the advance of civilization, both Roosevelt and Buffalo Bill shaped popular understandings of the West that were potent enough to seem relevant for more than a century, and flexible enough to meet new cultural needs. This book bears witness to the costume parade of western heroes who, by turn, became imperial conquerors, self-made men, Depression-era outcasts, and emblems of Cold War individualism.

FRONTIER FIGURES

The metaphorical richness of the frontier myth and the manifold identities of the western hero found expression in every cultural sphere, including classical music. This book thus lies at the intersection of three frontiers: the musical frontier opened by American composers' search for a national identity, the historical frontier pioneered by those seeking the roots of the American character in the American West, and the cultural frontier enacted by those who celebrated the West's potential for colorful and commercial exchange. In the watershed carved out by the confluence of the Dvořák debate, the Turner thesis, and Buffalo Bill's Wild West—the intersection between American music, American history, and the mythology of the American West—there is much fertile ground. And while the line of westward expansion across North America has unique and powerful symbolic content, it was in reality only one frontier among many. In the chapters that follow, we will also see figures negotiating with the frontiers represented by new technology, political and demographic change, and large-scale shifts in aesthetic sensibility. Every frontier is, by definition, a site of hybridity and exchange, and therefore a likely site for transformation.

During the first half of the twentieth century, as western imagery became ever more prominent in the visual arts and popular culture, American composers also turned to the West for inspiration. On their westward journey they carried a sometimes unwieldy load. They were burdened and encouraged by a changing sense of responsibility toward audiences and toward what they perceived as the "progress" of art. They shouldered among their equipment a small arsenal of European conceptions of nationalism and a catalog of stereotypically western figures already rendered familiar by artists in other media—Henry Wadsworth Longfellow and James Fenimore Cooper, Frederic Remington and Charles M. Russell. Increasingly as the century progressed, they also had at their disposal the documents of early ethnography and western history and the glossy simulacra of the tourist trade.

Composers were no more interested in the impossible project of defining "the West" than were their counterparts in literature or painting. But they contributed to the ways the West was imagined, responding to its landscapes and inhabitants as Americans always have, by idolizing, exaggerating, and stereotyping. In short, they made myths. When they incorporated western images, texts, or folk melodies into their scores, composers invited audiences to listen for the frontier and to imagine themselves as participants in its history. The resulting music forms the soundtrack of Manifest Destiny, marked by symbols that are usually easy to recognize but not always easy to interpret. Rather than a comprehensive history of composers' engagement with western Americana, in this book I offer thematically related case studies, while a string of reluctantly omitted chapters stretches to the horizon in my mind's eye. I hope that my choices have allowed me to suggest the complex negotiations that composers made between the intricacies of their individual biographies and such sweeping historical phenomena as world wars, economic fluctuations, and the entertainment revolutions caused by radio and film.

From the Boston Tea Party to the Boy Scouts, images of Indians have been central to the manufacture of American identity.[41] At the turn of the century, composers usually turned to Native American materials if they wished to give their works a western flavor. Parts 1 and 2 treat Arthur Farwell and Charles Wakefield Cadman, showing how these dissimilar composers—one a patriotic ideologue, the other a sentimental songwriter—shared assumptions about Indian music and about Native Americans as "disappearing tribes."[42] As the forced relocation of Native Americans drew to a close, many American composers seized the chance to build a national music based on the readily available European model for national musics: injecting indigenous elements into conventional contexts. Farwell's most important achievement (the founding of the Wa-Wan Press in 1901) was but one branch of a lifelong agenda that included original works based on indigenous sources, grassroots organizations for composers, and elaborate community pageants. Throughout these varied endeavors, he embraced a vision of the West as unique in its potential for musical and cultural revitalization. By contrast, for Cadman, western folklore functioned more like other types of exotica.[43] He minimized the importance of anthropological accuracy and disavowed overtly political messages. He made only modest claims to any kind of personal identification with these "foreign" sources—yet he was more engaged than Farwell was in the political struggles of the Indians who collaborated with him. He was also more successful than Farwell in his relationships with the musical institutions of his day, and many of the conventions employed in his dramatic works are reflected or deflected in other works on western themes: Arthur Nevin's *Poia*, Mary Carr Moore's *Narcissa*, Victor Herbert's *Natoma*, and George Gershwin's *Girl Crazy*.

Like early ethnographers, these composers walked a fine line between sympathetically portraying Native American life and propagating racial stereotypes. Echoing frontier historians before and after Turner, they had a tendency to treat natives and nature as a single entity—an unspoiled geography to be admired or a fearsome obstacle to be conquered. Their fascination with Indian tunes was genuine, but their music also encoded a celebration of westward expansion and the supposed disappearance of Native American life in the face of white civilization. No less than Buffalo Bill, they could celebrate Indian heroes without disrupting the tragic trajectory of the "dying race." While Farwell depended upon American Indian songs and symbols in pieces such as his *American Indian Melodies* (1901), he relied heavily on musical techniques that emphasize the foreignness of the material he borrowed. And while Cadman's opera *Shanewis* (1918) explores (doomed) interracial love, his cantata *The Sunset Trail* (1927) is a blatant eulogy for the living. In instrumental works, these composers overrode the Indians' own creative agency by altering borrowed melodies or disregarding original contexts. In their texted music, emphasis on Indian identification with the land suggests a metaphorical collapsing of the human, Native American presence into the distinctive western landscape.

As if recapitulating an episode in western history, Indian music began disappearing from concert music during the late 1920s, when American composers seemed to lose interest in the "noble savage" and instead turned their attention toward the pioneering settler and the western cowboy. In part 3, "American Pastorals," I touch on two treatments of Carl Sandburg's prairie poetry, the first by the Chicago-trained Leo Sowerby (whose tone poem of 1929, *The Prairie*, continues a European tradition of instrumental landscape painting), the second by the émigré Lukas Foss (whose choral paean on Sandburg's text was penned in 1944, almost immediately after he arrived in the United States). Two chapters are devoted to Virgil Thomson's score for the Depression-era documentary film *The Plow That Broke the Plains* (1937), and Ernest Bacon's 1942 opera *A Tree on the Plains*, with libretto by Paul Horgan. Both of these scores place (traditionally African American) blues and (supposedly Anglo American) folk song in service of a skewed opposition between unscrupulous or irresponsible urban life and disadvantaged but wholesome farming families. Despite their different media, each exposes a distinctly twentieth-century vision of the disruptive "machine in the garden," fracturing the traditional identification between proper land stewardship and political or personal maturity.

Thomson's nostalgic treatment of Americana—from the 1928 *Symphony on a Hymn Tune* to *Pilgrims and Pioneers* of 1964—forms the basis for his contentious claims of insufficiently acknowledged influence on his colleague Copland. Whether his score for *The Plow That Broke the Plains* represents the first use of a cowboy song in large-scale classical composition depends on the definitions of "large-scale," "classical," and "composition." (Farwell could have made the same claim with his arrangements of "The Lone Prairie" in the 1910s.) But there is no question that Thomson's work situates him at the beginning of a shift in the relationship between the "folk" and "classical" repertory and in the type of folklore composers favored. Using published folk song collections, composers like Thomson, Elie Siegmeister, Ross Lee Finney, and Morton Gould brought cowboy melodies into classical symphonies, choral works, and ballets not long after the "singing cowboy" rode onto the Hollywood scene. The familiar tunes and simple harmonies of cowboy songs allowed them to enter the popular repertory in ways that Native American tunes could not, providing American composers with a link between the populism of the 1930s and a new western mythology. Moreover, in the cowboy's bravado—independence and good humor, but also aggression and alienation—America found heroic qualities that could sustain it through both the military conflicts of the Second World War and the ideological conflicts of the Cold War. In parts 4 and 5, I investigate this new mythology as revealed in the music of Roy Harris and Aaron Copland.

In Harris's case, turning to cowboy song was a logical extension of the strategies that had brought him to the center stage of American musical life by the mid-1930s. Western images shaped his early career by providing a rich vein of metaphors in his critical reception and scenarios for his programmatic works. Creative self-fashioning solidified his claims on western folk song, framing it as his artistic inheritance and thus imbuing his pieces on western themes with an aura of "authenticity." In the "Western Cowboy" movement of his *Folksong Symphony* (1940), he took care not to disturb the singable qualities, consonant harmonies, and regular phrasing of the traditional cowboy songs he borrowed. Referred to as the "white hope" of American music, Harris bore a mantle of musical and moral authority when he approached cowboy song that relied heavily on his Anglo heritage and rural upbringing. He invited concertgoers to hear autobiography in his western works.

As a second-generation immigrant living in Brooklyn and a prominent exponent of self-consciously modern music, Copland relied on alternative sources of prestige when meeting the challenges of Depression-era Americanism. His engagement with western Americana came in reaction to specific commissions and to the new audiences provided by radio and other mass media. The public appeal of cowboy tunes helped win unexpected nationwide acclaim for a composer who might otherwise have been marginalized on the basis of his Russian-Jewish heritage or his homosexuality. As if capitalizing on his personal distance from the aggressively heterosexual masculinity of the stereotypical western hero, Copland chose to modify and distort many of the cowboy songs he incorporated into his ballets *Billy the Kid* (1938) and *Rodeo* (1942), placing them in contexts full of abrupt juxtapositions and humorous surprises. But his turn toward western folklore also coincided with a move away from the African American materials that had characterized much of his earlier music, suggesting that even in its musical guises America's fascination with the West was in part a nostalgic escape from the burden of contemporary racial tensions.

LEGACIES OF CONQUEST

In the past, a scholarly preoccupation with the overarching category of "Americanism" has often obscured specific decisions that composers have made about what could and should sound American. Experiments with western Americana carried a racial message very different from pieces that mixed jazz and classical idioms. Similarly, borrowing a Native American melody had different social implications from quoting a cowboy song—not only because of the ethnic associations of the material but also because of cowboy tunes' presence in the mass media. Musical manifestations of the West remain entangled with questions of national identity, but the sheer variety of methods and motivations for turning westward reminds us to question the usefulness of homogenizing labels for region and nation. It was perhaps inevitable that the American West should provide an impetus for this reevaluation. No region of the country is so relentlessly plural in population and connotations, and none has been crossed by so many contested frontiers. There are both musical and methodological reasons for exploring the places where America's music, geography, and mythology meet.

Although my case studies can stand alone, the book is intended to be more than the sum of its parts. As this project has unfolded, I have been pleasantly surprised at the connections that have emerged from comparing composers whom patterns of historiography have often separated and distinguishing between those whom historians have often lumped together. Of course, there are biographical links among my protagonists: Harris studied with Farwell; Copland's first teacher studied with Dvořák; Farwell and Cadman viewed each other as distant rivals, while Thomson, Harris, and Copland began their careers as colleagues and friends despite their different backgrounds. The musical corollaries of these straightforward facts stretch further afield. Copland's and Thomson's flexible treatment of cowboy song resembles Cadman's "idealization" of Indian music, while Harris followed in Farwell's more cautious footsteps. Such observations suggest that we might identify "cosmopolitan" and "provincial" schools of borrowing, the former characterized by cavalier freedom and a desire to mix folk materials into international or modern contexts, and the latter committed to preserving local references, often as a means of resistance to a perceived mainstream.[44] Even when composers relied on the same folk sources, their individual definitions of creativity and authenticity gave them wildly divergent career trajectories. While Farwell is recognized as a progressive figure in the history of American music, Cadman is often dismissed as merely commercial. More striking still is the gulf that has opened up between Copland's and Harris's reputations—a gulf widened by changing opinions not just about musical style, but also about race and patriotism.

Above and beyond my attempt to bring together stories that might prove mutually illuminating, the case studies I have selected reflect an important shift in the imagery composers chose to associate with the West—from Indians at the turn of the century to pioneers and cowboys during and after the Great Depression. I believe this change mirrors transformations in American society occurring as the nation moved through war, economic fluctuation, and demographic upheaval. In Harris's and Copland's cowboy compositions, the maverick individual came to the forefront, and the western landscape receded to become a picturesque backdrop for the adventures of its human inhabitants. This represents an intriguing reversal of earlier depictions in which Native Americans disappeared into the landscape. Like Turner's successive waves of frontiering, these different character types depend on the land in different ways. It is hardly surprising that, during a half-century of sweeping alterations in the demography of the West, artistic imagery reflected changing relationships between people and nature. American music thrived on such complexities.

Examining the shift from Indian to pioneer to cowboy imagery, my book traces a move from orient to occident—a westward migration that recalls not only the forced removal of Native Americans to reservations, but also the world-historical vision that drove imperialism from the Old World to the New. Early in the century, composers using Indian themes relied on strategies that had much in common with orientalism.[45] They depended upon an exaggerated separation between observer and exoticized object, and their stances often verged on voyeurism. During the 1930s and 1940s, when composers incorporated pastoral tropes and cowboy tunes into classical music, their strategies had been transformed by the alchemy of the West. They depended upon a false identification between observer and commodified object, and their intentions were often masked by mass media. The same processes that allowed Copland to convert his Russian-Jewish heritage into a convincingly pastoral populism also allowed American consciousness to move westward—away from regions where the indigenous was inescapably foreign and into regions where hybridity was inescapably native.

But the celebration of cultural mixing has a darker side as well, for the manufacturing of populism could have unexpected costs. In his study of Jewish immigrants' appropriation of blackface minstrelsy, Michael Rogin noted the extent to which the popular culture of the United States reinforced the patterns of colonial exploitation: "In yet another permutation of American exceptionalism, our national culture rooted itself—by way of the captivity narrative and the frontier myth on the one hand, of blackface minstrelsy on the other—in the nationally dispossessed."[46] Mining the musical resources of minority populations may have solidified a national identity based on frontiers of cultural exchange, but in America—as in other nations—it also carried the moral weight of empire. This book aims to interpret that legacy.

PART ONE

Arthur Farwell's West

The book was open at a hymn not ill adapted to their situation, and in which the poet, no longer goaded by his desire to excel the inspired King of Israel, had discovered some chastened and respectable powers. . . . The air was solemn and slow. At times it rose to the fullest compass of the rich voices of the females, who hung over their little book in holy excitement, and again it sunk so low, that the rushing of the waters ran through their melody like a hollow accompaniment. . . . The Indians riveted their eyes on the rocks, and listened with an attention that seemed to turn them into stone. But the scout, who had placed his chin in his hand, with an expression of cold indifference, gradually suffered his rigid features to relax, until, as verse succeeded verse, he felt his iron nature subdued, while his recollection was carried back to boyhood. . . . His roving eyes began to moisten, and before the hymn was ended, scalding tears rolled out of fountains that had long seemed dry.

—JAMES FENIMORE COOPER, *THE LAST OF THE MOHICANS*

The Wa-Wan and the West

THE RAGGED EDGE OF HISTORY

If on the afternoon of 27 April 1919, you found yourself seated at the Greek Theatre on the campus of the University of California, Berkeley, you would have witnessed and most likely been asked to participate in *California: A Masque of Music*. With musical numbers and libretto crafted by Arthur Farwell and personnel recruited from the ranks of the Berkeley Music Department, the masque places a toga-clad personification of California in the company of the muses: "California! 'tis a name Worthy of Apollo's nine; 'tis music's self / Soft syllabled upon the silent air." Only six of the nine muses grace the stage, but California seems destined to join their number if she can pass the musical "tests" set forth by Apollo and the Spirit of Ancient Greece. Having produced the requisite instrumentalists from isolated corners of the outdoor amphitheater, California musters her forces for the final test: choral song. "From hill, from canyon, shore and fragrant grove, / From city, vineyard, white Sierras' snows, / With summons far I call you to this shrine / . . . O noble children of our Western world."[1]

Springing as it does from the mouth of California, "our Western world" is a deliberately ambiguous phrase, and this ambiguity lies at the heart of Farwell's West. If early twentieth-century California represented the endpoint of westward expansion in the United States, the golden reward of America's Manifest Destiny, it also occupied a special spot on the continuum of "Western civilization." Though mythological, the masque is set explicitly in "the present," and it privileges symbolic meanings over strict adherence to chronology. In the first scene, for example, three groups are conjured up in turn to sing Farwell's own arrangements. Each chorus features a tune transcribed by an ethnologist, and each setting reflects the tension that would forever mark Farwell's approach to the West: on the one hand, a scientific emphasis on anthropological fact; on the other, a subjective identification bordering on rapture:

> "First let the [inserted: red] race speak, whose plaintive strain / Charms the divinities of wood and plain." *(The division of the chorus on one side, accompanied by the orchestra, sings the "Bird Dance of the Cahuillas")*

> "The black race now, redeemed from slavery's smart, / Pathetic-humorous in its artless art." *(The division of the chorus on the other side sings the "Moanin' Dove")*

> "Last the bold race who bore across the main / To California's shores, romantic Spain."

> *(Both divisions of the chorus together sing "Chata cara de bule.")*[2]

This gradual introduction of ethnic groups reflects something other than actual demographic data. While it might make historical sense to give Indians pride of place, the Spanish settled California long before there was a substantial black population—let alone an English-speaking, spiritual-singing black population. Instead, it is tempting to see in this ethnic procession Farwell's implicit judgment about the relative usefulness of each group's music to the task at hand: ensuring that the western United States could take up the artistic mantle of ancient Greece.

For Farwell, Indian song represented a uniquely valuable resource and a necessary starting point in the creation of "a new art-life" for America—a project in which black music occupied an explicit but historically uncomfortable middle ground. While Farwell recognized the spiritual as a resource for the community singing movement, he preferred to speak of "Spanish folksongs" whose value was in his eyes "beyond all power to estimate or predict."[3] Therefore, in the masque, it is "romantic Spain" who eventually ascends to stand beside California and the muses.

But this is not where Farwell's *California* masque ends. After the choral groups unite and ascend the stage, they perform music that emphasizes the union of diverse populations and draws the largely Anglo audience into Farwell's vision: a medley of university fight songs, followed by "Hail California." The Spirit of Ancient Greece reminds California that song holds the key to national cohesion. The chorus responds with Farwell's wartime anthem "Our Country's Prayer," sparking an on-stage discussion of religion. The Spirit of Ancient Greece invokes Almighty Zeus, but her plea goes unanswered. Instead, the audience is invited to join California's chorus, singing praise, in Farwell's words, to "the God that IS." All present rise and sing an amply foreshadowed "Battle Hymn of the Republic."[4] By the end, the regional has been subsumed into the national and even the supranational through the invocation of a larger, vaguely Christian world. The western vantage point seems all but forgotten. Yet its human and natural resources were crucial at every step of the way.

The same might be said for Farwell's career. His early and most influential years were almost wholly identified with Indian-inspired material and the Wa-Wan Press (1901–11). At midcareer, his involvement with the community chorus movement, initiated during World War I and reaching its height during his years in California (1918–27), placed him on the front lines of a national campaign. By the 1940s, Farwell was inclined to express himself in polytonal experiments and ruminations about creative intuition that bear no regional references. While the composer's later projects seem to leave the West behind, their outlook remained consistent with his Indianist aesthetic and his community chorus work. Indeed, I aim to show how deeply and purposefully intertwined these visions were.

A "NEW ART LIFE" FOR AMERICA

Although his attitudes toward Indians would never completely slough off their skin of exoticism, Farwell found in Indian ritual a valuable example of the power of music to unify and sanctify a community. He chose to name his signature achievement, the Wa-Wan Press, after an Omaha ceremony of unity and coming-of-age; under its banner he wished to bring together American composers and to celebrate their new artistic maturity.[5] Farwell founded the press in Newton Center, Massachusetts, two years after returning from his European studies and finding no ready publisher for his scores. As he remarked in his "Letter to American Composers," "Either American composers must inspire some one else to build up this work or they must do it themselves."[6] The latter was evidently the easier project. Farwell's unwavering commitment earned him repeated encomiums from the start. The critic Lawrence Gilman hailed the press in 1903 as "probably the most determined, courageous, and enlightened endeavor to assist the cause of American music that has yet been made."[7] During the decade before its copyrights were ceded to G. Schirmer, the press issued vocal and instrumental pieces by some thirty-seven composers, usually young and often unpublished, among them Henry Gilbert, Edward Burlingame Hill, Harvey Worthington Loomis, and Arthur Shepherd, not to mention Farwell himself.[8]

Throughout his life, Farwell described the Wa-Wan enterprise as a challenge to mainstream commercialism. "Salability," he recalled in the 1940s, "had nothing to do with the matter whatsoever."[9] Yet his idealism always went hand in hand with a certain defensiveness. Midway through the press's third year, Farwell answered potential detractors: "The Wa-Wan Press does not represent itself as a collection of masterpieces. It does not aim to be that which critics praise. It does not propitiate the gods of traditional culture. It does not seek to elevate the masses. It respects no coterie. It does not attempt to 'cover mediocrity with a

cloak of patriotism.' It is not a financial scheme masquerading as a 'noble cause.'"
Instead of stating what the Wa-Wan was, Farwell emphasized what the Wa-Wan
did: namely, to foster American composition, which he called "the goal, the core,
the very grail of life."[10] Though he denied being a "nationalist," Farwell wanted to
cultivate specifically American art with "convincing qualities of color, form, and
spirit from our nature-world and our humanity."[11] Evaluating the press's first
year, he noted that the Wa-Wan already exhibited a character "different from
that of the music of other lands," stating that its works were "independent of old-
world prejudices, yet remembering old-world victories."[12]

Farwell's anti-European stance soon grew stronger. In 1902, he argued that
the main hindrance to a "new art-life" for America was the overwhelmingly and
exclusively German influence on the nation's musical institutions, an obstacle "so
large that it is difficult to see": "since our national musical education, both public
and private, is almost wholly German, we inevitably, and yet unwittingly, see everything through German glasses. . . . Therefore the first correction we must bring
to our musical vision is to cease to see everything through German spectacles,
however wonderful, however sublime those spectacles may be in themselves!"[13]
Farwell's resistance to things German had its exceptions, especially when he could
point to the presence of folk influences (which he usually could): Thus, "Beethoven
demonstrated, and Wagner both insisted and demonstrated, that the greatest music must eventually arise from a Folk." And again, "No one has penetrated more
deeply than Wagner himself, the nature of the folk-spirit, nor drawn more freely
from the wealth of folk-expression."[14]

Folk-based efforts were always an important part of Farwell's plan, and often
a point of contention with his critics. At times, he defined folk song narrowly. In
preparation for a lecture tour, he explained that "only the songs of Stephen Foster, George Root and a few scattering songs, such as 'Dixie,'" could properly be
called American folk song (WJ, 140–41). More often, however, folk expression
was so broad and pervasive a category for Farwell that even original art music
could fall under its purview. He noted that "the folk" have "no monopoly" on the
creation of folk song: "The composer of culture, prompted by new feelings in a
new land, and untrammelled . . . by obsolete or alien traditions, will accomplish
the same end upon another plane, and, so to speak, create folk-song of a second
degree."[15] Divested of the "obsolete" and "alien," the American composer would
of necessity turn inward, both psychologically and geographically.

SPIRITUAL ARTIFACTS

Farwell framed the close relationship between folk and art music in terms of
historical inevitability. For him, the incorporation of Native American influences into American music was not a matter of choice, but simply a matter of

time. Nowhere was this more apparent than in his ideas about Indian music and its "assimilation" according to what he called "the natural law . . . of the impossibility of annihilating race spirit," namely, "When one race conquers, absorbs, or annihilates another, the spirit, the *animus* of the destroyed race invariably persists, in the end, in all its aspects, —its arts, customs, traditions, temper, —in the life of the conquering race."[16] That same year (1903), in an essay for a wider audience, Farwell explained: "Because we have conquered them, mingled with them (to an extent not dreamed of by the dwellers in our Eastern cities), have been thrilled in turn by the land which thrilled them, we will inevitably have inhaled great draughts of their splendid optimism and faith, their freedom of spirit and largeness of feeling, and their power to appropriate nature's teeming stores of energy. This is not only a poetic but also a scientific fact."[17] The thrill of the land, facilitated by the subjugation and relocation of its original inhabitants, was for Farwell both necessary and sufficient to inspire a truly American art.

What those Eastern city dwellers could not imagine, Farwell believed he knew from personal experience. Even in the frankly midwestern context of his youth, Farwell found a combination of spiritual and physical proximity to Indian life.[18] As he put it in 1909,

> The Indian, his life, customs, romance—in books or in real life—constitute a world in which every American boy revels at one time or another. I had lived in an Indian village on Lake Superior, seen the Sioux in strange sun dances, and heard the impressive speeches of the old priests. On my father's hunting expeditions, we had been taken into the great woods by Indian guides; and I had seen Sitting Bull in captivity and had heard of his exploits. . . . To this day I never see an Indian, especially an Indian on horseback, even in a "Wild West Show," without a tingling thrill coursing up my spine, such as I experience from the climaxes of certain music. (WJ, 77–78)

It was convenient for him that late nineteenth-century Minnesota harbored its fair share of Indian mystique, but Farwell also considered "playing Indian" to be a birthright of American boyhood. Moreover, his language reveals that, for him, the experience of seeing Native Americans in the flesh always had at least as much to do with aesthetics as with anthropology.

Despite these formative experiences, Farwell's initial approach to Native American music was hesitant. Alice C. Fletcher's modest tome *Indian Story and Song from North America* was the catalyst in his Indian adventures. Farwell took to heart her suggestion that these "aboriginal songs" (harmonized by John Comfort Fillmore) could become "themes, novel and characteristic, for the American composer."[19] Farwell happened upon the collection around the time of its publication in 1899, and by 1901 he had completed the ten pieces included in *American Indian Melodies,* nine of which took their melodies directly from Fletcher.[20] In fact, his setting of "The Old Man's Love Song" so resembles Fletcher's printed page that at first glance it is difficult to say whether it qualifies as a new composition at all (see example 1). Farwell was strictly faithful to Fillmore's choice of key signature, meter, and rhythmic notation, adding only expressive and dynamic markings.

As if to compensate for his literal borrowing of melodic material, Farwell dramatized his account of the impact Fletcher's book had on him. At first, he was more impressed by the strength of Indian stories than by the beauty of Indian song. In his 1902 article "Aspects of Indian Music," he described his frustration with Fillmore's harmonic settings, which he considered "too general in character to bear out the special significance of the different melodies."[21] After a summer of ruminating on Wagnerian mythology, he "picked up the book of Indian songs again":

> This time, however, I did not play these melodies over on the piano, with the elementary harmonies with which they had been provided. Divesting them of these harmonies, I sang them, as actual songs, softly to myself, taking pains to carry out the rhythms exactly as indicated. Here was a revelation! The melodies took on a new meaning. Primitive as these songs were, each now appeared to be a distinct and concentrated musical idea. . . . Nothing was more natural than to take advantage of the situation. In fact the combination of circumstances fairly called out for action of some kind. (WJ, 79–80)

With a combination of religious fervor and good business sense, Farwell framed his vocation as an opportunity but also a calling to "take advantage" of his newfound Indian sympathies.

As Farwell described it, his "insight into the Indian character" depended both on his own emotional investment in the material and on a strict adherence to what might be considered the sacred texts of his experience; he internalized the melodies and carried out the rhythms "exactly as indicated." But if Fletcher became his Bible, Fillmore was a false prophet who could not or did not want to allow Indian song the "heightened art value" that Farwell was sure it possessed. The chief point of contention was harmony. Farwell owned a copy of Fillmore's book *The Harmonic Structure of Indian Music,* but he seems to have gone out of his way to subvert Fillmore's theoretical principles.[22] His harmonic choices veer instead toward the Wagnerian. In Farwell's setting of "The Old Man's Love Song," the third beats of measures that Fillmore had allowed to float unperturbed over tonic G-major chords have become almost spasmodic, clutching not at the expected D–F♯ but slipping instead to C♯–E in bar 1 and C–E♭ in bar 2 before settling uneasily on the C–E that rests against the open fifth drone (G–D) of the left hand. Farwell enlivened what Fillmore had left static, first through bass arpeggiation (bars 7–8) and then with a striking diminished seventh chord (bar 9). He explained:

EXAMPLE 1A. "The Old Man's Love Song," as harmonized by John Comfort Fillmore, mm. 1–9 (from Fletcher, *Indian Story and Song*, 1900)

EXAMPLE 1B. "The Old Man's Love Song," as harmonized by Arthur Farwell, mm. 1–9 (Wa-Wan Press, 1901)

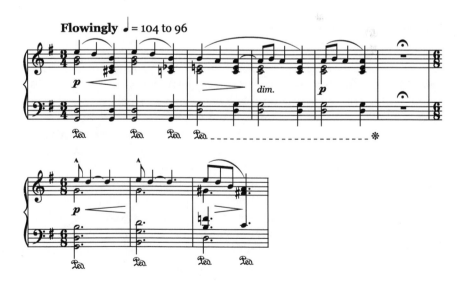

"We are driven to chromatics and modern effects in harmony in order to represent those various feelings characterizing, for the Indian himself, the various emotions underlying the different songs."[23]

Significantly, Farwell's ideas about the Indian worldview came not from adult contact with actual Native Americans, but rather from personal intuition (heavily influenced by the harmonic norms of his favorite composers) and isolated immersion in the song as artifact. Farwell was not exactly lacking in ethnological scruples. To a greater extent than many of his Indianist colleagues, he warned against "the folly of any attempt to produce great results without including the religious, legendary or life significance underlying the songs. Any attempt on the part of composers to use the mere notes of the melodies detached from their generating ideas, will lead only to a barren reproduction of the old musical forms, disguised with new colors which have in themselves no vitalizing power."[24]

But Farwell's means of coming to understand the songs was decidedly not ethnographic. He minimized the importance of face-to-face contact and empirical observation. He emphasized instead the sufficiency of what was already, so to speak, in white possession: the melody as fixed in notation and the text translated into English. In this light, Farwell's assertions about Native America's role in the development of American music gain unmistakable overtones of imperialism: "The hunger of art growth in a new country is never appeased until every available source of new art life, and especially folk-expression, has been seized upon and assimilated. . . . Materialistically, America is sufficiently conquered. We have wrested a living from the soil from East to West, and now we must wrest from it its treasure of poetry."[25]

"DAWN," "HURAKAN," AND THE LIMITS OF ETHNOGRAPHY

Farwell capitalized on his own investment in "The Old Man's Love Song," producing versions for solo voice (1908) and a cappella chorus (1901, 1937). Shortly after finishing the piano miniatures of 1901, he crafted a more extended piano piece whose title, "Dawn," is taken from the song's epigraph: "With the dawn I seek thee." Farwell cited this new work as evidence that "we have a distinctive and beautiful folk-song, born of life amidst our own forests, prairies, and mountains, which may form a worthy basis for musical art-works of larger dimensions."[26] He framed this development as a natural step in the evolution of any national music, listing among his predecessors the ancient Greeks, Josquin, Bach, Beethoven, Dvořák, Grieg, Tchaikovsky, and above all Wagner. Compared with any of these composers, however, Farwell placed a greater value on fidelity to the tunes he borrowed. "Dawn" presents a strictly sectional structure (see example 2). "The Old Man's Love Song" appears verbatim over a changing background of accom-

EXAMPLE 2. Excerpts from "Dawn," mm. 1–3, 32–34, 65–67 (Wa-Wan Press, 1902)

panimental figurations in measures 1–40 and 65–82, and a contrasting middle section is based on an unidentified Otoe melody (bars 41–64).[27] A gradual thickening of the texture leads to sonorous chords and an apotheosis of sorts, but repetition and reverence for the source text overwhelmed Farwell's grandiose hopes, as the composer himself seems to have admitted in a carefully couched disclaimer: "It is with no desire to forestall criticism that we state plainly our attitude toward this work, which is regarded as an essay, a reaching out into new fields, and therefore, but a partial attainment of what it is hoped to gain eventually."[28]

Other piano solos from 1902 bear out Farwell's more ambitious aims: "Ichibuzzhi," which expands on one of the pieces in *American Indian Melodies,* and a new work called "The Domain of Hurakan." Like "Dawn," "The Domain of Hurakan" concerns itself with questions of creation and rebirth. But while "Dawn" depicted the tranquility of an old man's reverie, "Hurakan" offers a stormier picture as befits its namesake, a Mesoamerican wind god, whom Farwell linked to "cosmic and elemental feelings and impulses."[29] "Hurakan" represents a significantly freer and more elaborate treatment of melodic material. One portion of a Vancouver game song is detached and used to begin the central nocturne section, which is otherwise devoted to newly composed material using motives derived from the other borrowed themes: a Pawnee game song and a Navajo "night chant." Fletcher herself praised "Hurakan" as "large and masterly . . . American in scope and feeling," and Lawrence Gilman called it "a fantasy conceived in the spirit of the Indian creation-myths, a finely vigorous and notable achievement."[30]

A critic for the *Musical Courier* observed that despite being a piano piece, "Hurakan" "aimed for orchestral effects," and Farwell seems to have agreed.[31] He orchestrated the work in 1910 and before one of its performances appended an extensive program note, justifying the work's "rhapsodic" character with a fanciful program:

> A traveller, at night, enters an Indian lodge near the Pacific. Within, in the glare of the firelight, he sees a company of Indians singing and swaying in the animated rhythm of the game. As he watches them their ceaseless motions seem to represent to him the eternal wash and play of the waves of the ocean, and he remembers the ancient legend which tells that "Hurakan, the mighty wind, passed over the waters and called for the earth." The traveller goes out into the night and walks along by the seashore, beyond the sound of the revellers. He hears the murmurings of the sea, and far-off melodies come to him—the sound of the wind over the water, or the distant crying of sea birds—dim sounds which die away at last into nothingness.[32]

It requires no great leap of imagination to identify the traveler with Farwell himself: a visitor, an observer, distant and alone. As it happens, his narrative program mirrors almost exactly Fletcher's prose introduction to the "Vancouver Game Song" in *Indian Story and Song.*[33] In both cases, the perspective is frankly a white one, yet with Farwell, this frankness is complicated by a deeply felt belief in his own capacity to channel "Indian spirit." An anthropological residue adheres to Farwell's story—the "game" of the game song and the "night" of the night chant remain. But these features now justify a psychological response, not an anthropological one.

Indeed, apart from the transcription work discussed below, anthropology was rarely the goal of Farwell's engagement with Native America. In the introduction to the Wa-Wan's publication *Traditional Songs of the Zuñis,* by the controversial arranger Carlos Troyer, Farwell makes explicit his views on the limitations of ethnography. "We have tried four methods of approach to the Indian," he writes: "First, by fighting him; second, by seeking to convert him; third, by treating him as a scientific specimen; fourth, by offering him the hand of fellowship." Of these methods, the first yielded only "wounds, torture and death, and the material for a little superficial romance," and the second was stymied by bigotry and mis-understanding. But the third method, the scientific method, was equally unsuc-cessful: "By the third process we have filled the shelves of great museums with rare and valuable objects, all carefully labeled, and the museum libraries with books learnedly written by scientists for scientists. It is wonderful work, but there is an aristocracy, a free-masonry about it all, that constitutes an almost impassible barrier between it and the America [sic] people."[34] Though better than soldiers or missionaries, museum makers preserved knowledge of Indian lifeways in forms that common Americans could not access or understand. Farwell's outlook was both loftier and, in a way, more realistic in its solipsism: Indian folklore had nothing to offer unless it could be made relevant to a contemporary worldview. As he put it in 1903, "Only where Indian life and American life meet at the shrine of the universal, will living art be born."[35]

Perhaps to Farwell's surprise, the Indian predilections of the Wa-Wan Press caused more consternation among his critics than his anti-German fulmina-tions. Some critics attacked the very notion of incorporating Indian song into art music. In his first anniversary issue, Farwell countered with the matter-of-fact observation that his "'Indian Melodies' have made quicker and more universal appeal, and have earned a larger demand than anything we have yet published."[36] Later, with the benefit of hindsight, and the candor of old age, he admitted that "the Indian music, because of its novelty, became a powerful weapon of propa-ganda; it enabled me to reach large numbers of people. Indeed I could not have made this national campaign without it."[37]

More difficult to stifle was the perception that the Wa-Wan Press had singled out Indian music as the *only* viable path to America's new "art-life." First of all, there was the "Wa-Wan" name and logo. In the white heat of Farwell's engage-ment with *Indian Story and Song,* the "Wa-Wan" rubric had seemed not only apt but prophetic. As he recalled in 1909, "I was so filled with enthusiasm over the Indian music ... that nothing but an Indian name would do. Had I foreseen at that time that such a name would mislead people as to the broadly American aims of my undertaking, I would probably have chosen otherwise."[38] Farwell pointed out time and time again that folk-based works were only one branch of American composition. But he was on shaky ground when he claimed that all folk materials were equal in the eyes of the press. Indians did hold a special status in the Wa-Wan's pages, especially during the early years. Thanks to the contributions of Farwell and his associates, especially Loomis and Troyer, the number of Indianist works published grossly outnumbered the total of all other folk-based pieces combined. An early brochure described "quarterly publications of American compositions and the Indian music," and the back cover of Wa-Wan issues regularly carried a concise statement of purpose that singled out Indian lore. Sometime in early 1906, Farwell made one and only one change to his mission statement, replacing "the melodies and folk-lore of the American Indians" with "the melodies of American folk songs."

THE CONTINENTAL DIVIDE

Farwell was generally adamant in his insistence on national unity over sectionalism. At the end of the press's third year, he clarified: "Ordinarily, there are easterners, westerners, northerners, southerners, Bostonians and what not. . . . How, then, can any of these reasonably be expected to grasp, even with faint animation, the central vivifying principle of the Wa-Wan, which is forgetfulness of section in the unifying spirit of the whole?"[39] Yet Farwell also felt that the western United States held a special potential because of its open-minded citizens and its distance from cosmopolitan Europe. During his first visit to Los Angeles, Farwell conveyed his enthusiasm to Wa-Wan readers: "We must reckon with the west. The Great Word of the west has not yet been spoken in art,—when it arises, many traditions must fall. Here the mind is overwhelmed by the vastness of nature's plan. . . . Already there are many . . . Botticellis in the rough, scattered about these deserts and Edens of the west."[40] Comparing contemporary America to an ancient Greece in which overcivilized Athens required renewal from its own West (Sicily and Corinth), he wrote: "History is repeating itself. . . . Again we have the vast, vague, significant west, and the self-centered and consciously cultured east. And the culture of the east is in part borrowed from Europe, as the eastern culture of Greece was in part borrowed from the Orient." Thankfully, the distinguishing features of the western landscape ensured that America's renaissance would be unique. "The Rockies, the plains and the Pacific," Farwell continued, "will afford another stimulus to the creative mind than the Isles of Greece."[41]

Farwell himself found this stimulus first in Indian music and then in western peoples and places. The narrative of his artistic awakening, including the four "western tours" he undertook between October 1903 and March 1907, survives in slightly eccentric form under the title *Wanderjahre of a Revolutionist*, published in weekly installments by *Musical America* during May and June 1909.[42] By the spring of 1903, he recalled, he was already nurturing "an ardent desire" to see the Far West for three reasons: to observe "the musical conditions of the whole country at first hand"; to give "a broad trial" to his newest compositions based on Native American themes; and "to get out into the Indian country, and hear the Indians sing" (WJ, 95).

Though Farwell sometimes cited Indians' presence in every American state as a reason for their universal appeal, especially when he wished to distinguish Indian music from black or Hispanic music, he more often associated Indians with the West—the Plains, the pueblos, or the reservations to which many tribes had already been removed. Indians may have had a ghostly presence in Farwell's native Minnesota, but he knew that his chances of hearing Indian music depended on his getting out west. The prospect of closer contact with Native American people was certainly an enticement, but Farwell already considered himself something of an Indian aficionado. In fact, the expertise he had manufactured in this area was precisely what made his westward travel possible—an irony that was not lost on the composer himself. He noted that the means of financing his trips was, "curiously enough, the very thing disparaged by such critics as had noticed it . . . namely—the Indian music. . . . I realized that in the making of this Indian music I had forged the wings by which I could fly out of my Eastern prison" (WJ, 95–96).

Farwell called each of his four ventures a "western tour"—perhaps because each circuit extended as far as California, or perhaps simply because each involved travel beyond the cultural spheres of Boston and New York. The first trip took him from coast to coast with stops in upstate New York, his native Minnesota, Chicago, Kansas City, and Denver; he spent Christmas week at the Grand Canyon before continuing on to the West Coast for the month of January. Farwell made sure to hit cities where he had relatives or friendly contacts, and numerous music clubs and civic groups responded favorably to his advance publicity.

Ever effusive, Farwell devoted special energy to capturing the thunderous impact of the landscape during his first trip. Having reached his native state, he took a stand on the banks of the Mississippi to exclaim: "How vastly these great scenes exceed in space and grandeur anything which may be witnessed upon the Rhine! . . . What great unwritten music lingers about these dreaming lands!" (WJ, 98). By the time he reached New Mexico, he was clearly, exultantly, on unfamiliar ground:

> Going over the Great Divide, and into New Mexico for the first time, it is hard to believe that these strange infinite stretches of opaline desert, mesa-grit and mysterious, are part of the same old United States that we have always known. A dweller of the East, the Mississippi Valley, or the Northwest suddenly dropped down into this extraordinary region would certainly think himself nowhere except in Egypt, or possibly on Mars. And the strange beings that came crowding up to the train at stopping places—no one familiar with the Sioux or any of the Middle Western tribes would take this unfamiliar race at the first glance for Indians. . . . At the pueblo of Isleta, near Albuquerque, I first had the opportunity of seeing these

strange and picturesque desert dwellers in the midst of their native surroundings, and of casually hearing a few of their songs. (WJ, 101–2)

On the rim of the Grand Canyon, Farwell finally found himself at a loss for words when he "arrived at the edge of the world":

I had often wondered what it would be like to die and wake up on the other side, or to be Beethoven, or Wagner, or Dante. But such slight experiences are engulfed in the great one of that first glimpse into the incredible other-world of the Grand Canyon of Arizona. One cannot write about this place. There is no word, no phrase, no description that does not belittle it, unless we go to the Apocalypse. . . . I sat there watching the lights and shadows play and change over the strange distances and depths of this wonderworld, and heard the unwritten symphonies of the ages past and the ages to come. (WJ, 102)

Farwell's tours were motivated by curiosity and the anticipation of modest financial gain; it quickly became apparent, however, that the chief advantage of his sojourns would be the personal contacts he made along the way. Everywhere he went, he found supportive women and like-minded men, and he expressed his appreciation of the region's receptiveness in a variety of newspaper pieces, perhaps most explicitly in Portland, Oregon, where an unnamed interviewer quoted the composer's opinion that "American ideals are purer in this section of the country, too, for one does not find so much European alloy in them, and individuals are not afraid to think for themselves and express what they think in plain terms."[43] Farwell's regional emphasis was not lost on his western (or midwestern) audiences. Under the headline "Western Genius to the Fore," one Minnesotan reported: "It is satisfying to our Western pride to note that out of a dozen names mentioned by Mr. Farwell as among the best of the American composers, at least a half are Western men."[44] Farwell was likewise proud to have sparked East Coast interest in "western musical expressions" (WJ, 128). Here and elsewhere, Farwell's "West" encompassed anything that was distant—literally or metaphorically—from the European past.

The lecture component of Farwell's first trip was devoted to a tripartite presentation usually titled "Music and Myth of the American Indians and Its Relation to American Composition." Most of what Farwell said on the topic can be pieced together from tour publicity and the copious review articles Farwell collected at almost every stop on his western journey and pasted into an extensive but deeply redundant scrapbook held in the Arthur Farwell Collection. Many of these clippings seem to paraphrase his lectures quite closely, and the substance of the lecture-recital changed very little from city to city. On the 1903–4 circuit, Farwell usually led with a report on the state of composition in America, paying particular attention not only to "Indian racial expression," but also to popular music, ragtime, and cowboy song. The talk's next section was illustrated with excerpts drawn mostly from the *American Indian Melodies* and grouped into three categories: "elemental or cosmic songs," "songs of human expression," and "songs of the superhuman." It explained "the Indian's place in American life and thought," the "indestructibility of race spirit," the worship of "the Great Mystery," and the "inseparableness of story and song."[45] Almost every documented lecture ended with a selection of "original compositions developed from Indian themes" that expanded in tandem with the Wa-Wan's catalog of Indianist scores.

As Michael Pisani has ably demonstrated, "Indian Music Talks" were more than a passing fancy during the early twentieth century. Farwell seems to have pioneered the genre, but he was soon joined by many others, often frank imitators of his lecture-recital format.[46] Several singers adopted portions of his program, but apparently they felt free to do the talking themselves if Farwell was not in town.[47] Among composers, Loomis, Cadman, Troyer, and Thurlow Lieurance took lecture-recitals on the road. Yet Farwell's presentation seems to have carried especially strong anthropological authority because of his association first with Alice Fletcher and later with Charles Lummis. The earliest versions of his "Western Tour" brochures declared this kinship using the words of New York critic Henry Krehbiel, who wrote in 1902: "Miss Alice C. Fletcher has found a sympathetic companion in Mr. Arthur Farwell . . . who has made the first sustained attempt to infuse [Indian melody] with poetical significance and emotion by means of harmony." Fletcher's own, private endorsement would soon follow. Shortly before Farwell set out on his lecture circuit, she declared to Farwell's mother, Sara, "how impressed I am with the progress your son is making. . . . His trip this Autumn will surely do him and the country good."[48] Contemporary newspapers frequently exaggerated Farwell's ethnological expertise and especially his work with Lummis, often blurring the line between transcription and fieldwork, claiming that he lived for years "among the Indians."

Just as Farwell did, Charles Wakefield Cadman made sure that his "American Indian Music Talk" sported a veneer of anthropology. He mentioned Fletcher in the first paragraph of his descriptive brochure and took care to point out that the performance of the "Omaha Tribal Prayer" by Cadman's singer-collaborator Paul Kennedy Harper had earned "the unqualified approval of Francis La Flesche, a son of Chief Joseph of the Omaha Tribe."[49] Yet other passages in Cadman's brochure and the structure of the talk itself emphasize musical appeal more than cultural awareness. "Musical history, psychology, and ethnology are touched upon lightly," the brochure states. Given the popularity of his *Four American Indian Songs*, Cadman's credentials rested more with the list of venerable singers who had already performed his music than on the scholarly sources for his tunes. Like Farwell, Cadman offered simple transcriptions before moving on to more elaborate scores—generally works by MacDowell, Troyer, and Farwell, all outnumbered by pieces by Cadman himself. But unlike Farwell, who grouped his numbers on the basis of their content, Cadman took a decidedly "musical" approach. He opened with the same "Old Man's Love Song," but immediately after it, he played an excerpt from the first movement Beethoven's "Appassionata" Sonata, op. 57 (to illustrate some shared facet of melodic construction). He juxtaposed his own idealization of "The Mother's Vow" with portions of Grieg's *Peer Gynt Suite* and Tchaikovsky's *Symphonie "Pathétique."* In perhaps the most credible of his three comparisons, one that he actually learned from Fletcher and La Flesche, he followed the "Omaha Tribal Prayer" with a "Gregorian Chant of the 7th Century" and a "Mohammedan Call to Prayer," each harmonized by Cadman himself. He wrote to La Flesche: "We sang the three religious songs first *unaccompanied* and as they would be heard in their native environment with afterward a simple harmonized accompaniment. This convinced the audience that *all music* really had its genesis in the same emotional root—springing from the same soil—and when they caught this fact—the bond of sympathy was established and the enjoyment and appreciation keen. It was most gratifying."[50] From start to finish, Cadman aimed to explain Indian music and make it more accessible through productive comparisons with more familiar music.

By contrast, Farwell's emphasis on the particularity of Indian music is striking. In his eyes, its value lay not in its similarity to established classics, but in the departures from European tradition that it could enable. He proclaimed that Indian music "springs from, and interprets in new colors, the 'great mystery,' . . . to which refreshing source American life is leading us back from the artificialities and technicalities which have latterly beset European culture."[51] While Cadman might have adapted his format to deliver a "Negro Music Talk" or even a "Persian Music Talk" with equal ease, for Farwell, only Native America carried the "cosmic," "human," and "superhuman" powers to revitalize American music. He wanted audiences to recognize Indian ideals (not Indian sounds) as familiar: "love of nature, reverence for its great invisible powers, freedom of spirit, self-reliance and stoical courage, dignity, elemental breadth of nature, intrinsic spiritual worth." Without an understanding of the common humanity of the Indian (whose myths Farwell believed to be entirely transparent to any sympathetic mind), the progress of American art would falter: "We shall not know what Indian mythology has for us, and for the aggregate expression of the west, until we know all that the Indian has dreamed."[52]

WAR AND PEACE

Implicit in Farwell's fervent, if imaginary, identification with the Indian is an effort to counteract some of the more egregious stereotypes that had long colored white views of Native life. Pisani counts among these "bloodthirsty warriors or traitorous scouts . . . occasionally a noble chieftain or a dark, mysterious maiden . . . the murderous thief, the idler and drunkard, or the embittered 'half-breed.' "[53] Farwell considered it a source of satisfaction that his *American Indian Melodies* had already brought to life alternative images of Indians, "to supplant the tales of scalps and tortures which have constituted heretofore nearly the whole stock in trade of his European reputation."[54] As Pisani has demonstrated, these stereotypes circulated in the United States as well as in Europe; but Farwell nonetheless offered a valuable corrective. His selection of "Wa-Wan" as a motto reflects this, for it memorializes a ceremony of "peace, fellowship, and song" that Farwell attempted to explicate in a new lecture-recital for his second western tour (see figure 2). In contrast to the piecemeal presentation of the original Indian Music Talk, Farwell here attempted to recreate an entire ritual, and thus to present Indian music in its most meaningful form: "These ceremonials mark the culmination of Indian racial expression; they focus and crystallize for us the inmost meanings of Indian racial life, exactly as the Greek drama preserves for us the great central truths of Greek civilization."[55] Compressing a multiday event into a single evening, Farwell nonetheless sought to retain its ritual structure and, by extension, an aura of communal experience that foreshadows his later work in pageantry and civic singing.

More than anything he could play or say, Farwell felt that with his own Wa-Wan ceremony, he could draw audiences into an experience that would yield insight into "the Indian character." He observed: "The ritual is not someone's idea or explanation of the Indian's view of the world and of life, but is that view revealing itself . . . speaking for itself in the very music which the Indian himself conceived and employed in the enacting of those scenes."[56] This lecture-recital featured roughly a dozen tunes transcribed by Fletcher and Fillmore in their *Study of Omaha Indian Music,* and eight of these tunes found their way into a new piano suite that Farwell titled *Impressions of the Wa-Wan Ceremony of the Omahas* (1906): "Receiving the Messenger" (no. 33 in Fletcher/Fillmore), Nearing the Village" (no. 34), "Song of Approach" (no. 35), "Laying Down the Pipes" (no. 38), "Raising the Pipes" (no. 39), "Invocation" (no. 42a), Song of Peace (no. 42), "Choral" (no. 41).[57] Apart from switching the placement of no. 42 and no. 42a, and moving the "Choral" to a valedictory position at the end of the cycle, Farwell replicates the music as it occurs during the ritual action: the formal delivery and acceptance of sacred pipes representing peace and prosperity.

As he did in the *American Indian Melodies,* Farwell preserves most of the essential aspects of the tunes as he found them in print, keeping Fillmore's key signatures in five of the eight pieces. Apart from the occasional elision of measures that reiterate the final note of a phrase, Farwell relies on repetition of whole tunes or multiple phrases rather than developing motives or inventing related melodic material. The overall effect, however, is rather more elaborate here than in the earlier piano miniatures. Several of the pieces involve introductory or closing gestures that expand on the borrowed melody, usually in the form of a partial

TWO LECTURE-RECITALS

I. MUSIC AND MYTH OF THE AMERICAN INDIANS
and its Relation to American Composition

SYNOPSIS:

PART I. The "Great Mystery." Gods, heroes and men. Music,—mythical, legendary and personal. Rendering of simple pianoforte transcriptions of traditional Indian songs, preceded by brief word-pictures of corresponding scenes from myths and legends to which they are related, as follows:

Elemental or Cosmic songs: The Approach of the Thunder God; Inketunga's Thunder Song.

Songs of Human Expression: The Old Man's Love Song; The Mother's Vow; Song of the Leader; Choral.

Songs of the Superhuman: Song to the Spirit; The Ghost Dance.

PART II. The present moment in the development of American music. The demand for music characteristic of America. The "Margin of the Un-German." Popular music. Music of Negroes, Indians and Cowboys. New Inventions of American Composers. Survey of contemporary work for American composition.

PART III. Presentation of original compositions in larger forms, developed from Indian melodies and myths.

Dawn.
    "With the Dawn I seek thee."

Ichibuzzhi.
    "The enemy comes and calls for you, Ichibuzzhi."

The Domain of Hurakan.
    "Hurakan the mighty wind passed over the waters and called forth the earth."

Note. The above program is substantially the same as that given during the 1903-4 Western Tour, and is to be preferred as a general introduction to Indian Music. It is subject to change in accordance with the development of the work.

FIGURE 2. Publicity for Arthur Farwell's "western tours." Courtesy of the Arthur Farwell Collection, Sibley Library, Eastman School of Music

TWO LECTURE·RECITALS

II. THE WA-WAN CEREMONY OF THE OMAHAS
An entirely new lecture-recital

Music receives its highest significance with the Indians as the foremost and most indispensable element in the great tribal ceremonials. These ceremonials mark the culmination of Indian racial expression; they focus and crystalize for us the inmost meanings of Indian racial life, exactly as the Greek drama preserves for us the great central truths of Greek civilization. In them the incidental and ephemeral details fall away, leaving to us that which remains eternal as a revelation of the true inward spirit of Indian life. In other words, the ritual is not someone's idea or explanation of the Indian's view of the world and of life, but is that view revealing itself in the scenes of the ritual,—speaking for itself in the very music which the Indian himself conceived and employed in the enacting of those scenes.

"Wa-Wan" means "to sing for someone," and is the name given to a ceremonial of social relationship, in which the symbolistic "Pipes of Fellowship" were formally presented by a man of one family or tribe to a man of another. In the actual observance it occupied a number of days, and sometimes involved the traversing of hundreds of miles. The Wa-Wan, which has already passed from actuality to tradition, is of singular poetic beauty and suggestiveness; it touches many of the finer ethical points of Indian life, and contains many songs of exceptional value.

These melodies have been transcribed for the piano, and when presented with a descriptive account of the ceremonial, give not only a broad and varied idea of Indian Music, but also an insight into the deeper life of some of the most important tribes.

Among the songs of the ceremonial thus transcribed are, On the Way, Receiving the Messenger, Nearing the Village, Song of Approach, Laying Down the Pipes, Raising the Pipes, Choral, Around the Lodge, Prayer for Clear Weather, Final Dance, and many others. Examples of Pawnee and Otoe Wa-Wan music are also given.

Address: American Recital League, The Wa-Wan Press
NEWTON CENTER, MASS.

FIGURE 2 *(continued)*

reprise or an echo—an effect that Pisani finds crucial to the popular history of Indianism.[58] The third vignette, "Song of Approach," bears this type of rhetorical frame. Like most of the melodies Farwell favored, the tune is pentatonic, linking it in early twentieth-century parlance to "primitive" musics from around the world and allowing for a variety of harmonic realizations. Fillmore's setting clearly assumed a key signature of A♭; Farwell instead assumes the minor mode, and although he raises the melody by a half step, its notes occupy the same lines and spaces on the musical staff that they did in Fillmore's harmonization, yielding the peculiar result that Farwell's borrowing looks more faithful to Fillmore than it actually is.

Farwell's opening gesture (now E–F♯–E instead of Fillmore's E♭–F–E♭) is stretched for dramatic effect and made to accommodate a flamboyant arpeggiation of chromatic harmonies before being echoed at a lower register and in a simpler guise (see example 3). His initial harmonic progression might be understood as a move from a seriously altered supertonic seventh chord (G♯–B–D–F♯, but with B♯ replacing B♮) to the tonic F♯ minor, which itself has been transformed into a seventh chord by the E♮ dictated by the pitches of the borrowed melody. The impact, however, is purely coloristic. The sense of a tonal center arrives first with the bass tremolo in measure 3 marked "in imitation of Indian drum," and from this point on F♯ functions as a pedal, sounding in some register on almost every quarter-note beat until the rhapsodic figuration of the opening returns to close the piece. For this entire time (mm. 6–33), the accompaniment throbs a double-drumbeat figure comprising an eighth note followed by a sixteenth note— substituting length for strength in an approximation of the typical STRONG-weak articulation of the Plains tribes.

It is easy to imagine Farwell's *Impressions* evolving over the course of his western tour as he would have had ample chance to tinker with each setting until he was pleased with the result. In one of the earliest analytical studies of the composer, Edgar Lee Kirk in fact gave Farwell's lecture recitals credit for his fluency at the keyboard.[59] Not surprisingly, the composer favored a more psychological explanation for the relative elaborateness of his Wa-Wan miniatures:

> The pianoforte sketches based upon this ceremony have been called "Impressions" since they depend, in feeling, largely upon early memories of the Indian of the west. . . . They aim to reflect in some measure the peaceful nature of the ceremony, the quiet and the breadth of the prairie, and to serve as an introductory insight into certain lesser known phases of Indian life. Peace, fellowship, song,—these gifts of the Great Spirit shall not pass with the Indian, and may long remind us of the efforts and deeds through which he sought to attain them.[60]

Though the sad fate of the Indian might already have been sealed, Indian gifts could still be handed down to future generations. Farwell considered himself in

EXAMPLE 3. "Song of Approach," mm. 1–18 (Wa-Wan Press, 1906)

a position to transmit this legacy because he had grown up on native soil: "It is not without powerful influence upon after life [*sic*] to spend the impressionable years of childhood and youth there upon the very ground where so lately, and so remote from the thought of the outer world, were enacted the scenes and performed the deeds of a romantic and heroic epoch."[61]

"Peace, fellowship, song"—though Farwell was forceful in articulating these themes, they were not necessarily what audiences wanted to hear. Among the dozens of newspaper reviews that Farwell collected while on tour, few convey anything about audience reaction. A bevy of headlines show the variety of ways in which audiences understood and misunderstood Farwell's message: "The Mental and Emotional Life of the Indian," "Myth and Song Inseperable [*sic*]," "Much Music in Indian Songs," and "Weird Singing Enraptures Women." One observer considered the Omaha setting "The Song of the Deathless Voice" to be "very much like 'My Old Kentucky Home,' without the 'weep no more my lady.' "[62] The question of reception was particularly thorny where Farwell's ideas bumped up against long-standing traditions of western-themed entertainment. In an anecdotal passage from Farwell's travelogue, he relished having been mistaken for a Wild West show of the Buffalo Bill variety while visiting Kinsley, Kansas:

> A stray cowpuncher, in search of a lively time, read the legend "American Indians" on a placard in the village street announcing my lecture-recital, and determined to take it in. He paid his quarter without asking any questions, like a good sport, and went into the little church where the event was about to begin. Leaning over the back of a pew, he timidly touched a man in the audience on the shoulder and said, "Say, is dis a show?" Being assured that it was, he took a seat and attended carefully; but after waiting vainly for half an hour for the scalping, or at least a little shooting to begin, he slid quietly out into the night in search of more thrilling adventures. (WJ, 100)

Farwell frequently had to contend with widely held prejudices about the West, and it should not be surprising that he also found ways to turn these stereotypes to advantage. For example, he added a "Navajo War Dance" to his catalog in what he claimed was a calculated response to public opinion that his works celebrating the "quaint, poetic, and picturesque aspects" of Indian life were insufficiently "savage": "Evidently I must reform and do something really Indian," he wrote in 1909 (WJ, 123). For melodic material, Farwell chose "something to make your blood curdle and your hair to stand on end" (EDC, 384). In fact, Farwell wrote two Navajo War Dances and, as Thomas Stoner has pointed out, the two are often confused. Both are tripartite, featuring two borrowed melodies deployed in vigorous outer sections and contrasting midsections. The more famous of the two (in common time with a key signature of E major) is usually referred to as "Navajo War Dance No. 2." It was written sometime in 1904, revised and labeled op. 29 circa 1908, and revived in the 1940s by John Kirkpatrick, who published his own edition and programmed it frequently.[63] Together with "Pawnee Horses," it remains one of Farwell's most compelling works, and yet its origins are somewhat mysterious.[64] Given the work's popularity, it is surprising that Farwell never divulged his source tunes. Perhaps this is because both war dances seem more at home in the solo recital than the lecture-recital.

More than any of his earlier works, the "Navajo War Dance No. 2" makes liberal use of small-scale repetition not just as a background feature but as an engine that can be manipulated to create momentum—as if Farwell's belated acknowledgment of the "savage" Indian freed him to explore rhythmic and textural considerations, not just melodic or harmonic ones. In the outer sections of the piece, the ostinato overwhelms the melody in its claim on the listener's attention. The serpentine bass line unsettles the texture, at least at first, when its not-quite-chromatic sequences of pitches is still surprising. During the first section, the figuration from bar 1 (D♯–C–D–C–C♯–C–C–B) or bar 2 (D♯–C–D–C–C♯–C–B–F♯) appears in every measure that is not interrupted by a full stop in the melodic phrasing (see example 4). By bar 24, when the repetition becomes less literal, the ostinato has been so well established that a few pitch alterations have little effect on the impression of constancy.

The "Navajo War Dance No. 2" is emphatic, but circularity on many levels renders its violence curiously impotent. The motoric ostinato goes nowhere: the focal note, E, can be heard on almost every beat except at points like measure 6, where both melody and accompaniment come to rest on B in a type of primitivist half cadence. The gradual thickening of texture that gives momentum to each section is undermined by the melody's modular phrasing, which dictates abrupt halts that remain startling even after repeated hearings. The third section rises to a climax no higher than the first, and although a sequential extension (m. 50) helps prepare the listener for an ending, the possibility remains that the piece will double back on itself yet again.

Until the original tune comes to light, it is difficult to say whether the "exotic" features of the "Navajo War Dance No. 2" came from Farwell's pen or from the borrowed melody. Alas, no reviews seem to have survived from his 1907 performance in Logan, Utah, where Farwell "held forth for American music in the Mormon Tabernacle, and tried a Navajo War Dance on the elect" (WJ, 144), but composer Benjamin Lambord recognized in 1915 that the piece represented an extreme for Farwell in its "barbaric crudity," noting that the composer had "renounced almost all defined harmony, preserving only the vigorous rhythm of the dance in the bold intervals of the Indian melody."[65] If the "barbaric crudity" was unusual for Farwell, the particular manner of his harmonic renunciation was not. Chromatic harmonies seem to have been the norm for Farwell, but both of his war dances exploit melodic chromaticism to excess. The other Navajo War

EXAMPLE 4. "Navajo War Dance No. 2," mm. 1–6 (ed. John Kirkpatrick, New York: Music Press, 1947)

Dance begins with an off-kilter chromatic scale that rumbles through the piano's lowest register.

As initially published in the folk collection *From Mesa and Plain* of 1905, this less famous war dance is immediately followed by Farwell's other lasting contribution to the repertoire of Indianist piano miniatures: "Pawnee Horses," which the Bostonian composer and violinist Charles Martin Loeffler called in 1949 "the best composition yet written by an American."[66] Here we find chromatic activity of a different persuasion. The beginning, middle, and end of the piece feature a three-bar passage saturated with half steps that are designed to confuse harmonic perceptions, not to intensify the motion toward or away from a tonal center (see example 5). Although the pillar pitches for the key of C major (the tonic C and the dominant G) sound together in the opening chord, they are immediately dispersed into mutually exclusive groups as all twelve chromatic pitches are aligned and divided to present both of the available whole-tone scales, spelled G F E♭ D♭ B A and A♭ F♯ E D C B♭.

For several years Farwell had advocated French and Russian models as a counterweight to America's overwhelmingly German musical life, and in "Pawnee Horses" we have evidence that he took his own advice, employing one of Debussy's favorite scales to make a pointed departure from common practice harmony. While the downward trajectory of these framing bars may be linked to the typically descending phrases of Native American melody, the accompanying sense

EXAMPLE 5. "Pawnee Horses," mm. 1–9 (Wa-Wan Press, 1905)

of harmonic free fall has its roots in a resistance to the patterns of tension and release dictated by Wagnerian and post-Wagnerian harmony. Like each of the tritones in the French augmented sixth chords that Farwell so enjoyed, the whole tone scale divides the octave into equal parts, eschewing a single center in favor of a cosmic democracy of pitches. The power of C and G to solidify a tonal center is dissolved in a downward spiral of intervals that achieves a not-quite-equal division of the octave; extracting the notes played by the right thumb yields a near cycle of minor thirds starting with a fall from B to G♯ to F but slipping down a half step before the last minor third can sound (E–D♭ replaces the expected F–D).

In overall form, "Pawnee Horses" is simpler than either war dance. Once the tune gets under way, in the middle register at the pickup to bar 4, much of the mysterious atmosphere evaporates. A♭ takes its rightful place as an upper neighbor to the dominant G and ostinato figuration hammers home G and C almost exclusively. The two statements of the melody are separated and brought to a close by reprises of the whole-tone opening (mm. 15–17, 25–28). Farwell may have intended the regular structure and accompaniment of "Pawnee Horses" as foils for a melody that he considered "so complex and difficult in its rhythm as to render it virtually impossible as a song to be sung by any known singer except an Indian" (WJ, 124). In effect, however, the ostinato figures transfer the striking directionlessness of the whole-tone opening to rhythmic and harmonic realms.

Like the war dances, "Pawnee Horses" is built on drones and the reiteration of small rhythmic cells. In this case, however, the constant motion suggests an environment free from human intervention: "There go the Pawnee horses," the epigraph reads, "I do not want them,—I have taken enough." Two discrete layers of accompanying material surround the melody, but they take no notice of its stops and starts. The implied fade-in (soft accompaniment followed by "well pronounced" melody) and literal fade-out suggest that the listener has been privileged to catch a glimpse of nature in transit—not a dance of "savages," but the running of animals only barely tame, as Farwell states: "The melody carries the rhythm of the gallop and the spirit of the scene as only an Indian would have conceived it" (WJ, 124).

This last assertion points to the central paradox of Farwell's Indianism: the impossible claim of complete spiritual identification with borrowed material. The war dances show that he was not immune to contemporary stereotypes about native savagery, and some of his piano miniatures engage with the conventional icons of Indian removal—the "defeated warrior" and the "vanishing race." But Farwell's desire to serve as a conduit for "Indian spirit" was so fused with his self-image as a pioneer for American music that such sunset themes are outnumbered in his oeuvre by works that emphasize peace, dawn, and rebirth.

INDIANS AGAIN

After 1901, Indian music was never absent from Farwell's professional life, and in fact it haunted his reputation in ways that he came to resent. By the end of his life, he could state flatly: "It is in fact a matter of regret to me that my Indian works are being brought to performance more widely than my very greatly numerous other works, not based on folk themes of any kind."[67] Yet Farwell surely knew that he was partly responsible for his lingering Indianist associations, as he continued to adapt his earlier piano works to new formats. One of the earliest such arrangements was *Three Indian Songs* (1908), in which Farwell adapted three excerpts from his *American Indian Melodies*.[68] Farwell described these songs as his response to the false but potentially profitable impression that he was a popular songwriter: "As I had never written an Indian song in my life except to transcribe literally and publish a little one-page 'Bird Dance Song' of the Cahuillas, I felt that if I was to make this shadowy reputation secure, the quicker I could write some Indian songs the better" (WJ, 170). As if to stamp the set with his superior ethnological expertise, particularly since he was now operating on Cadman's home turf, he selected one melody from each category in his Indian Music Talk: the cosmic "Inketunga's Thunder Song," the human "The Old Man's Love Song," and the superhuman "Song of the Deathless Voice." Unlike Cadman's sentimental fare, these were meant to be "striking modern vocal developments, boldly Indian," replete with Indian names and vocables. For each song, Farwell included English lyrics (some paraphrased from Fletcher) translating the original into the more conventional language of unrequited love and stoic death.

Farwell also made choral arrangements of four of the pieces included in *American Indian Melodies,* and they became favorites at Westminster Choir College in the late 1930s and 1940s.[69] Despite his grumbling, these and a second installment of four choruses gave particular satisfaction to Farwell in his later years. He wrote to his daughter Sara in 1946: "Toscanini heard [the Westminster Choir] do my *Navajo War Dance* and said something to the effect that it was the best American composition he had heard. He wanted to orchestrate it, but found that as written for the voices it won't transcribe rightly for orchestra! I guess I'll make an independent orchestration . . . and show it to him."[70]

There are only two exceptions to this pattern of recycling and rearrangement, and each one shows Farwell returning to the familiar ground of Indian material when trying out a new form or genre. First, in 1914, he sketched "Indian Fugue-Fantasia" for string quartet (arranged for piano in 1938 but never published). In Evelyn Davis Culbertson's words, it is "more *Fantasia* than *Fugue*," but it does come complete with augmentation, inversion, and a contrapuntal strictness unusual for the composer (EDC, 513). More important is Farwell's single-movement string quartet of 1923, *The Hako,* which represents his last and by far his longest original essay on Indian themes.

Farwell had once believed that with his 1906 *Impressions of the Wa-Wan Ceremony* he had taken Indian melody "about as far as it will go in modern music" (WJ, 138–39). *The Hako* tests this hypothesis by taking a very similar ritual as the basis for a much more intricate work. Like the Wa-Wan of the Omaha, the Pawnee tribe's Hako ceremony is a protracted ritual of unification between two different tribes or clans within a tribe—one led by a man designated as the "Father" and the other led by the "Son"—whose symbolic actions are meant to ensure peace, prosperity, and the procreation of children. Both ceremonies were recorded in great detail by Fletcher, and both invest power in sacred objects created during months of preparation.[71]

The crucial difference between Farwell's *Impressions of the Wa-Wan Ceremony* and *The Hako* is a matter of form. In the earlier work, the outlines of the Indian ritual itself provided a loosely unifying framework for a series of otherwise self-sufficient miniatures. In *The Hako,* the work unfolds along the lines of sonata form as understood in the nineteenth century, complete with introduction, exposition, development, recapitulation, and coda. Commissioned by the Los Angeles–based Zoellner Quartet, *The Hako* represents Farwell's first claim to unify western melos with the elite genres of "western" classical music.

Inserting Indian melodies into a canon so hallowed by European masterworks was no easy task, as the composer seems to have recognized. Although the work won an honorable mention at the 1926 Ojai Valley Chamber Music Festival and was performed on both coasts, Farwell was still uncertain of its success. As he wrote to Arthur Cohn (of the Dorian and Stringart Quartets) in 1935, it remained to be seen whether *The Hako* could be "pulled through by a vigorous and convincing performance, whether with time and understanding of its Indian implications, it will at last carry the day—or simply, whether I have set out to do too much with a string quartet."[72] Farwell was anxious that the players should instill the performance with the proper "Indian spirit." To this end, he offered some instructions:

> Certain things must be brought to [the quartet's] interpretation before it has even a chance of proving itself, e.g. the immensely reverential spirit of the Indian in general, and his immense dignity, and the unction with which each syllable is taken in his singing. Specifically, I might speak of the reverential attitude of the chanted prayer of the priests which forms the greater part of the introduction . . . [and] the dignity of the processional . . . where the held note of 1st vl. indicated the flatness of the plains, the 2nd vl. the swaying of the feathered stems, viola the inevitable drum, cello the priests' chant. . . . In short the work has to be dramatized, and dramatized with an intelligent and sympathetic understanding. The hearer should feel "here is something real, purposeful, expressive, going on, even if I do not yet understand the full meaning behind it."[73]

In Farwell's view, the composer alone could go only so far. Responsibility was shared with performers, who must adopt the proper mindset, and especially with listeners, who must cultivate the proper respect for the work's spiritual import.

Farwell did not shy away from programmatic links between his score and the ritual that inspired it. The swaying of feathers, the drum, lightning, thunder, the

EXAMPLE 6A. "The Hako," Seventh Ritual, Part 3 (from Fletcher, "The Hako," 1904)

woodpecker and the owl—all these are meant to be audible in the quartet. More complex are the moments when ritual meanings and formal functions intersect. At the opening, for example, the priests' invocation coincides nicely with the evocative material and harmonic freedom of a sonata form introduction. Above and below a drone on E, first violin and cello intone a pentatonic melody "like a pulsating chant"; Farwell holds fast to the original tune for five measures before the drone is transferred to the bass lines and the other voices rise upward exactly as the ceremony would suggest: "like a prayer" (see example 6).[74]

The exposition and development sections instead suggest two kinds of tension between the melody of the American West and the norms of "western" classical music. While the episodic introduction presented an "exotic" surface meant to signal "Indianness," those themes that are most crucial to the working out of the conventional sonata form exposition are couched in late-romantic harmonies that threaten to overwhelm any impression of the indigenous. In the development section, by contrast, Farwell's reverential attitude toward his borrowed melodies seems to overwhelm his ability to create momentum. The section begins with the dignified "processional" Farwell described in his letter: a complete statement of the introductory priests' chant (in its original key) is played out against the lovely "swaying" countermelody in second violin before undergoing the expected fragmentation (see example 7). At points, Farwell works with segments small enough to be called motives, but more often entire measures or pairs of measures are preserved, resulting in an overly regular pacing. This was, after all, one of Farwell's first large-scale compositions, and while it bears traces of

EXAMPLE 6B. Farwell, "The Hako," mm. 1–17 (ed. Ron Erickson, San Francisco: Erickson Editions, 1997)

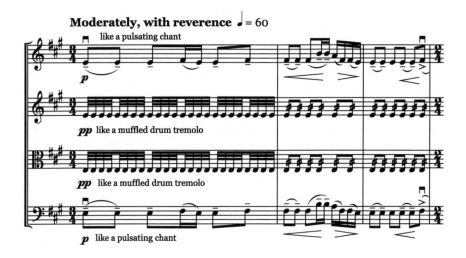

inexperience with the genre—particularly in its unrelentingly four-voice texture—it also reveals much stronger traces of what he had already absorbed from his work with Indian music: namely an impulse to preserve as he encountered it (i.e., in western notation) melodic material that he recognized as sacred.

Farwell's attempt to reconcile the music of the West with the genres of western music proved more difficult than he might have imagined. Like the partici-

EXAMPLE 6B *(continued)*

pants in the Hako ceremony, he was concerned with cycles of renewal, inaugu-
rating a "new art-life for America," or sparking a spiritual awakening through
Indian song. Most of all, it was the moment of frontiering that captured his imagination. Understanding this aspect of Farwell's westward gaze sheds some light on
the enthusiasm he mustered for the grassroots projects (community choruses and
historical pageantry) that occupied him after the demise of the Wa-Wan Press.

EXAMPLE 7. "The Hako," mm. 243–55

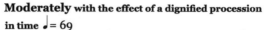

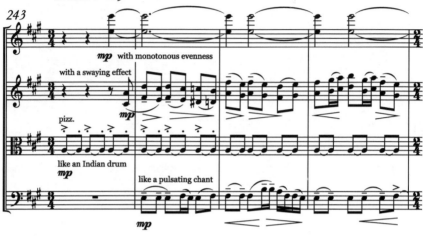

It also helps explain his tendency to see even his best efforts as works-in-progress. In 1906, he prefaced his *Impressions of the Wa-Wan Ceremony of the Omahas*:

> When all is said, when all is done that can be done today to crush or to obliterate the race that dwelt in this land before us, there still remains a dignity, a vastness, a freedom, in our memory of the Indian of the plains, an investiture of heroic circumstance, which seems destined to haunt us until it be accorded at last a full and adequate measure of artistic expression. Such an art, stripped of every detail of

EXAMPLE 7 *(continued)*

modern civilization, surcharged with the elemental forces of earth and sky, and the passions and deeds of heroic and primal men, may not be for the cities of the east. But it is not impossible that such a development may arise in the west.[75]

While the historians who followed Turner grappled with the uncertain consequences of the final chapters of westward expansion, Farwell, whose frontiers were largely figurative, could instead paint an ever-receding horizon—one whose natural and human resources were inexhaustible.

2

Western Democracy, Western Landscapes, Western Music

A VOICE IN THE DESERT

On his western sojourns, Farwell saw himself as an evangelist bringing the gospel of good American music to such remote locations as Kinsley, Kansas. But he also returned to the East in evangelical mode, ready to discourse about Indians and to spread the word about composition in the American hinterlands. Although Farwell functioned as a prophet, for many of his western adventures Charles Lummis was actually the one who prepared the way. Travel writer, ethnographer, architect, librarian, activist, and antiquarian, Lummis was a formidable figure in the culture of Southern California. In January 1904, when Farwell's Indian Music Talk brought him into Lummis's orbit of influence, he was apprehensive, as he explained in his *Wanderjahre:*

> Now, there is a man in Los Angeles who keeps a sort of fatherly eye on all the Indians of the Southwest, Californian, Arizonian and New Mexican. . . . he also keeps an eye on the artistic and intellectual developments of Los Angeles, and edits a magazine, *Out West,* containing a "Lion's Den" department, in which the lion, which is the man in question, eats up all intruders, and has a special relish for easterners. . . . I bore with me from the East an introduction to this dread monster, but had not the opportunity to present it until after my recital. (WJ, 104–5)

Lummis proved if not tame at least friendly. More important, he introduced Farwell to a practice of ethnography and transcription that, while idiosyncratic by today's standards, involved extended sessions with individual informants and the most sophisticated available technologies of recording and reproduction.

Lummis's interest in Mexican and Hispanic song predated his acquaintance with Farwell by many years. In 1892, he told the readers of *Cosmopolitan* that he had already collected "several thousands of these quaint ditties" and that the process had been "no small labor":

> There was but one way to get an air. A phonograph would have scared off my bashful troubadours, even if it could have caught—as no portable phonograph yet devised could catch with its varying register—the unique movimiento which is the heart of that music. I had to sit by the hour before crackling adobe hearth or by the ruddy campfire, singing each song over time and time in unison with my good-natured instructors, until I knew the air absolutely by heart—and not only the air, but the exact rendition of it.[1]

Lummis eventually acquired his own phonograph, and as prime mover of the Southwest Society, he secured funding in 1903 from its parent association, the Archaeological Institute of America, to purchase a better Edison machine. Over a period of several years, Lummis recorded—in musicologist John Koegel's estimation—more than five hundred wax cylinders preserving roughly 150 Indian songs (in two dozen languages) and at least twice as many "Spanish Californian" songs—the only major collection of Hispanic field recordings made in the United States before the 1930s. Lummis had a keen ear but little musical training. Now, in Farwell's enthusiastic company, he hatched a plan to make his entire collection available in standard musical notation.

Soon after Farwell's first Los Angeles lecture recital, he received an invitation to visit Lummis in his famous "den," El Alisal, a Spanish-style castle of a home that Lummis designed and built, mostly by hand, using materials salvaged from or modeled after pueblos, missions, and especially the ranchos and haciendas of the Californio population—with additional support from telegraph poles donated by the Santa Fe Railroad in recognition of Lummis's role as a spokesman for the "See America First" campaign. In this evocative setting (later the headquarters of the Historical Society of Southern California), Farwell "swam in the musical atmosphere" of "the suave or vivacious songs of the Spanish settlers and the weird, somber, and mysterious songs of the dwellers of the desert" (WJ, 111). According to the legendary hospitality of El Alisal, meals were followed by group singing and listening to wax cylinders. Less than two weeks after his arrival, Farwell was dabbling in transcription and observing recording sessions with Ramon Zuñi and Procopio Montoya, the two Indians Lummis had brought to Los Angeles from Isleta Pueblo in New Mexico.[2]

As cultural historian Martin Padget points out, Lummis's "advocacy of the Southwest" involved cultural preservation on many different fronts: "the preservation of threatened manhood, the consolidation of Anglo racial identity, and the conservation of both natural and cultural resources."[3] While at Isleta, Lummis came to love the tribes of the Southwest as uniquely civilized, gentle, and hospitable. He compiled a still-unpublished dictionary of the Tiwa (Tee-wahn) language and founded the Sequoia League in 1902 to fight for Indian rights. Although he had worked with the noted archaeologist Adolph Bandelier for more than five years, journeying as far as Peru in the early 1890s, Lummis preferred what he called "Catching Our Archaeology Alive," a form of activist scholarship for which the body of wax cylinders was both tool and artifact.[4] When Lummis undertook his own lecture tour, he found that his recordings won friends for the Southwest Society, and he was eager to make the music more widely available.

After Farwell left Los Angeles, only six weeks elapsed before he received a letter from Lummis proposing that he spend the summer of 1904 "out West" doing transcriptions. "Deep in my consciousness," Farwell recalled, "where I heard the strange chants of Ramon and Procopio echoing and echoing, and voices and guitars in the *patio* ringing, I saw again those vast and alluring strips of Arizonian desert, fraught with uplifting inspiration and bigness" (WJ, 116). After much effort, Farwell secured a two-hundred-dollar stipend from the American Archaeological Institute and arranged for his second lecture tour to arrive in Los Angeles by mid-July to begin his months of transcription work.[5]

Several things made this experience unusual. First, while the atmosphere at El Alisal rang with living voices, the bulk of Farwell's work was isolated, involving little contact with singers. Whether he liked it or not, Farwell's transcribing took shape as a process of repetition and internal assimilation for the purposes of reproduction—in other words, a process resembling his work with the printed songs in Fletcher's books. Second, when he did make "live" transcriptions, Farwell's informants usually visited him in familiar domestic settings. Most of Lummis's cylinders were made at his own home or at a handful of Hispanic estates— his singers included Manuela Garcia, Rosa and Luisa Villa, the del Valle family, Rosendo Uruchurtu, and Adelaida Kamp—and the actions of each side were dictated more by the rules of courtesy and hospitality than by scientific pretensions. Among Lummis's Spanish-speaking friends, these rules were mutually understood. But for the Indians, the situation was much more problematic.

Ramon Zuñi and Procopio Montoya were Lummis's key Indian informants and also his household help, performing tasks that ranged from doing construction work to serving breakfast. They were probably the first Indians with whom Farwell spent any substantial amount of time, and it was the memory of their voices that inspired him to dedicate his summer months to the Lummis collection. Farwell recalled that Lummis had to exert all his persuasive power to induce the shy "Indian boys" to sing their religious songs. Ramon, who had been in the Lummis household longer, finally acquiesced and, "taking up an Indian drum, began in low tones a very insistent rhythm." The phonograph was quickly pressed into action, but it "required coaxing and a prolonged council of war between Ramon and Procopio." Once Lummis played back the recording, "Procopio's face darkened . . . and he hastily retreated to a far corner of the room." (WJ, 109).

Given these difficulties, Farwell remained optimistic, but not blindly so, about the possibility of faithful transcription. Under the heading "Not Difficult Work," he told a reporter that his work was "mere recording, not harmonizing." For this project, he continued, "they want the irregularities recorded; the correct rendering—supposedly correct—may be put in the foot notes; an accurate record as sung is the first consideration." He continued: "Even when the tune, as sung by some absent-minded old brave, perhaps, is irregular and therefore puzzling, the rhythm swings one into comprehension, and enables the transcriber to read the tune aright."[6] Farwell could see that the process of cross-cultural extraction was in some ways a painful one. Still he attempted to grasp the resulting raw materials, making them his own just as thoroughly, and through the same process that had infused his rereading of Fletcher's texts—a spiritual identification no less potent for its use of the phonograph as medium.

THE MULTIETHNIC WEST

Perhaps the most striking thing about Farwell's transcription work was that it brought him into contact with the music of diverse groups in quick succession. Rather than immersing him in one new cultural context, it presented him with a smorgasbord of ethnic options. Already, his western tours had introduced him the music of the Zuñi (courtesy of Carlos Troyer); to western painter Maynard Dixon (friend and protégé of Lummis, who helped spark Farwell's interest in cowboy song); and to ethnographic photographer Edward S. Curtis (famous for his compendium of Indian portraits).[7] Now in the living room of El Alisal, at a work station he called "the museum," Farwell immersed himself in the songs of Spanish California, heard stories of Lummis's Peruvian adventures, and came to appreciate regional differences among Indian tribes.

The productive jostling of ethnic groups left its mark on Farwell's oeuvre as early as 1905, when the Wa-Wan Press published in quick succession his vocal collection *Folk-Songs of the West and South: Negro, Cowboy, and Spanish-Californian* and his piano miniatures *From Mesa and Plain: Indian, Cowboy, and Negro Sketches for Pianoforte*. Together with his 1909 *Wanderjahre*, these sets represent Farwell's *Années de Pélérinage*, and they illustrate his comparative geography (example 8). Farwell found the "The Bird Dance" of the California Cahuilla tribe (later used in his *California* masque) among Lummis's wax cylinders, and he experienced it as distinctly different from the Omaha melodies Fletcher had published.[8] Unlike his earlier arrangements, this one preserves more of the original performance practice, rendering it more anthropologically accurate yet more "foreign" sounding

EXAMPLE 8. Excerpts from *Folk-Songs of the West and South* (Wa-Wan Press, 1905)

"Bird Dance Song," mm. 1-4

"The Lone Prairee," mm. 3-7

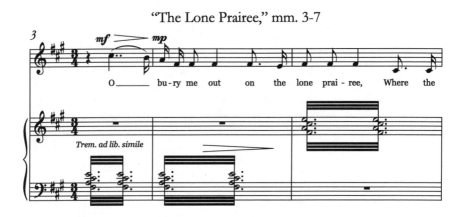

to Anglo audiences. Marked "low and tremulous, flute like and in obvious imitation of low weird bird-tones," the score identifies its "Indian" singers with primeval nature.[9] The tune itself is marked by circular flutterings and unexpected transposition of melodic fragments, as if the singer (or singers) had accidentally slipped upward in register—an impression reinforced by the evocation of sliding pitches, marked "a mere quaver of the voice, not a distinct triplet." Though pedal tones on G and D would appear to ground the melody in the tonic and dominant of western tonality, signs of foreignness reinforce the song's power as incantation, outside the realm of intelligible speech.

EXAMPLE 8 *(continued)*

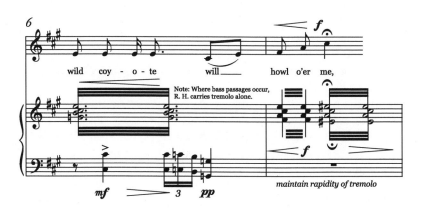

"Las Horas de Luto," mm. 1-7

Moderately slow, with pathos.

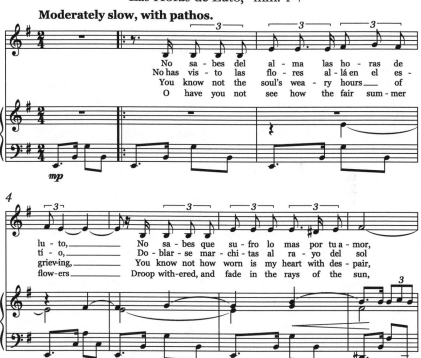

By going West, Farwell did get to "hear the Indians sing," but he did not need to travel to hear black music. Farwell understood and embraced (with some ambivalence) the ubiquity of ragtime, calling it "our indisputable native folk-song" and ratifying its popularity (if not its musical substance) by deferring to the wisdom of the people. "We must not blame the honest American for preferring ragtime to the German masterwork," he wrote; "it is more his own."[10] Despite ragtime's winning syncopation, which he happily linked to Indian song, Farwell gravitated instead toward the spiritual, producing two arrangements for *Folk-Songs of the West and South* and one for *From Mesa and Plain*.[11] All seem tame by comparison to the "Bird Dance Song," "Pawnee Horses," and the "Navajo War Dances." In "De Rocks a-Renderin'," vocal ornaments are confined to a pair of grace notes and a passing tone; for "Moanin' Dove" (better known by its third verse "Sometimes I feel like a mudderless chile"), Farwell included the instructions "ingenuously, crooning," and provided a static, rocking accompaniment. In both cases, the tone is elegiac rather than vigorous, and unlike the "Bird Song," no footnotes are required to understand or perform the dialect texts.

Farwell's Indian arrangements purchased local color at the price of intelligibility; his spiritual settings proved more familiar yet (for him) less compelling. But in cowboy song and especially in "Spanish-Californian" themes, he saw a chance to combine western character and broad appeal. Farwell would appear to be the first composer to make a classical setting of a cowboy song. Like all western claims, this one is contested, but it gains credence from the difficulty Farwell had both in finding the relevant tunes and in crafting convincing accompaniments. Having acquired the melody from his Wa-Wan colleague Henry Gilbert, Farwell included a setting of "The Lone Prairee" in his *Folk-Songs of the West and South*. Today the text and tune are well known under many titles ("The Dying Cowboy," "The Dying Ranger," etc.), but in 1905 some now-standard features had yet to crystallize. Farwell cites as the opening line, "Oh, bury me out on the lone prairee," noting in a footnote that some sources give "not" for "out." In addition, the metrical disposition of the tune in Farwell's setting differs from most subsequent ones in making the downbeat of his triple meter coincide, rather sensibly, with "bury" and "lone" (instead of "not" and "-ree," as Roy Harris and Aaron Copland would do three decades later).

Of greater import is Farwell's uncertainty about how best to preserve and accentuate the song's unusual features. He recalled in 1909:

> With the accompaniment of this song I had a vast deal of difficulty, providing for the necessary rhythmic license of the melody, the free and easy way of singing it which alone could preserve the effect of the song as heard on the plains; to do this without interrupting an accompanying effect which should suggest the continuity, the unbroken loneliness of the plains, was a knotty problem. It was finally solved . . . by a species of compound tremolo which alone could represent the constant limitless plain, while the melody should go its own characteristic way.[12]

Two pairs of open fifths make up the most stable sonority in the piece, a shimmering F♯-minor seventh chord from which added-note harmonies radiate outward, always preserving at least two of the focal pitches: F♯, C♯, A, and E. Unlike the Indianist double drumbeat, the strumming of guitars, or the iconic clip-clop of the dusty trail, Farwell's compound tremolo evokes landscape, not movement—the cowboy is swallowed up in the prairie. A different version of "The Lone Prairee" tune forms the central section of Farwell's untexted "Prairie Miniature" in *From Mesa and Plain,* and again, the setting seems idiosyncratic in retrospect. While the framing sections are lively and matter-of-fact in their progress, the middle section begins with a mysterious (funeral?) march. Staccato articulations and an off-kilter oscillation of fourths give way to an instance of romantic excess: a soft but dramatic glissando.

Two years before publishing these settings, Farwell observed: "The cowboy songs which have come to our notice are free from Indian, Negro, or Spanish influence, and are among the most stirring and poetic folk-songs we have heard."[13] Gauging this poetic appeal is not easy, however, for Farwell did not speak often about the cowboy. He was surely aware of the cowboy figures who worked together as a team to defend the Deadwood stagecoach in Buffalo Bill's Wild West—to which he made intermittent references throughout his career. He knew the western novels of Bret Harte, and it would have been hard to miss the gunslinging cowboys who circulated so widely in the dime novels of his youth. Yet Farwell's settings suggest an isolated and introspective cowboy, one whose charisma is more visionary than jocular or violent. His scores also remain ambiguous about the racial identity of America's cattlemen. Wa-Wan composer Benjamin Lambord described the minor mode and Scotch-snap rhythms of "The Lone Prairee" as "peculiar to negro music." He continued: "Its outstanding ethnic character, if it has any, is, however, Irish. It is not improbable that the cowboy song should have acquired a certain tone from the Indian, though a generous admixture of the Celtic idiom is most certainly to be expected from the racial character of its cast."[14] Only Spanish America is absent from Lambord's list, yet Hispanic influence might also be heard in the melodic doubling at the sixth that Farwell employed in the central section of "Prairie Miniature."

What Farwell himself did choose to say about cowboy song concerned its preservation. "It is becoming more and more difficult to get these songs, which ought to be saved before it is too late," he wrote in 1908 to J. L. Hubbell, a friend of Maynard Dixon.[15] There are unpublished cowboy materials among Farwell's papers, and he compiled a typescript listing thirteen songs for which he had acquired both texts and at least partial melodies, seven texts still lacking melodies, and four titles about which nothing else was known. His plan was to make "a complete collection of cowboy songs, words and music," beginning with what he had "obtained in my sojourn in the west," but the collection never came to fruition.[16]

If Farwell borrowed his rhetoric of preservation from Alice Fletcher and Charles Lummis, he also let them guide his decisions about folk repertories, preferring Indian and Hispanic song. Black music and cowboy song were more than passing fancies, but they were almost always approached through multiethnic sets like *Folk-Songs of the West and South* and *From Mesa and Plain*. By contrast, Farwell's engagement with Hispanic music received more sustained attention—first via the Lummis transcriptions and then from Farwell's activities in the community music movement.

Farwell published only two "Spanish California" songs during the period he spent under Lummis's roof: "Las Horas de Luto" and "La Cara Negra." In light and lively fashion, each one echoes Farwell's recollection of the after-dinner music at El Alisal: "The guitars rang out with magic which can be imparted only by Spanish fingers and song after song, in inexhaustible array, floated or danced upon the air" (WJ, 108–9). Accordingly, Farwell abandoned his usual chromatic palette in favor of triadic *habañera* bass lines, spiced with modal mixture and the occasional diminished chord, but generally straightforward in harmonic function, as Koegel has observed. Rather than providing a poetic accompaniment (like the prairie tremolo), Farwell aimed for greater transparency, arguing that artistic subtleties "belong not to folksongs in their primitive presentation, but to developed musical artworks based upon them."[17]

It is curious that Farwell himself never attempted such a "developed musical artwork." In contrast to his varied engagement with Indian material, he seems to have found "Spanish California" song either unmalleable or impossible to dissociate from its texts. Nevertheless, he seems to have felt the same sense of "ownership" regarding Hispanic material that he felt with other folk materials, and for roughly the same reason: these songs belonged above all to "American soil." It was conquest that made them fair game for interracial borrowing, or so he told the readers of Lummis's *Out West* in 1904. Here Farwell identified three processes that had generated America's "undeveloped musical resources." First was "racial inheritance, natural genius, Anglo-Saxon, Teutonic or otherwise." Second was a process of "racial accretion" that Farwell attached to "the folk music of the negroes—the plantation song," which he inexplicably identified as "a derivative form originally from the Spanish." Third came the "territorial acquisition and consequent racial accretion," which gathered up the many musics of Native America. And finally, "the characteristic songs of the cowboys, railroad makers, voyageurs, sailors, etc., all of which must be hauled into court and tried before American musical growth will be satisfied. Also there are the folk-songs of Mexico, qualified by Spanish influence as they must be, yet which cannot but exert a powerful influence of the musical life of our Southwest."[18]

In Farwell's eyes, as American composers emancipated themselves from the European masters, all the music of the land they now occupied would find a similar freedom. But ensuring this greater liberty required the proper perspective. Farwell declared:

> Let the composer stand on the bluffs overlooking the Mississippi. Let him ask himself, an intruder, what those men must have felt, who through generations inherited that wonderland and the freedom of it. Let him study and learn what they thought and felt and sung. Then let him look for himself—and sing. . . . Who cares any longer if his song be Indian or American? If the truth is to be known, in that song, which the future is reserving for us, the Indian, the American, the European, the African, all, will live again in a universal expression which will be the collective voice of America's world-wide humanity.[19]

LISTENING TO AMERICA

In his essay "Toward American Music," Farwell exhorted: "There must be a willingness on our part to be, in our imaginations or our sympathies, at a moment's notice, a cowboy ranging the plains, a Southern planter taking his leisure or his slave at work, an Omaha chief watching the approach of the Thunder god."[20] Although this approach effectively glosses over racial difference, it could never fully escape the grip of nostalgia. The composer struggled mightily, however, to chart a way forward, first in a more aggressively polemic lecture recital and second through his involvement in the community music movement. So serious was Farwell's demeanor that he issued a warning to prospective audiences wishing to hear both his old standby, the Indian Music Talk, and the new lecture recital: "The first, while being educational in a marked degree, is also distinctly an entertainment," he explained. "The second, while not being without entertaining features, is primarily an earnest discussion of the uppermost questions in American musical development." In Farwell's mind these questions were "Is a national musical art desirable for the United States of America? What is 'American spirit' in music? Have we any American folksongs? Shall folksongs enter into a national musical art?" and finally, "What shall we do?"[21]

As a "national" program meant for a "western" tour, the lecture advertised a wide variety of examples, "many of them the result of Mr. Farwell's musical explorations in the far west and south-west."[22] In addition to playing "German, Russian, Scandinavian, and French music," Farwell included two of his spiritual settings. The rest of his illustrations came from Indian or western sources, including one Spanish Californian song, his two cowboy pieces, and no fewer than nine Indianist scores. While he resisted defining American music by "any particular style or type," he argued that if a composer "sings of the Mississippi, it must be incapable of being mistaken for the Rhine." Farwell had faith that a "national American music" would be identifiable "by nothing else than its *freedom* of manner and spirit," to which portion of his typescript Farwell appended a crucial clarification in ink: "which means virtually, freedom from the known European methods."[23] Hand in hand with this freedom came a democratic spirit that Farwell found in the community chorus and the community pageant.

From the 1910s through the 1920s, Farwell was increasingly involved with what he called "the movement for community music," which he considered the only antidote for a proliferation of artistic ills that he enumerated for the Music Teachers National Association: "the shams, artificialities and pretences of our social and professional music world, the exploitation of musical art for private gain . . . the attention given to all manner of sterile and degenerate musical outpourings of modern Europe, the ignoring of the greater part of the sincere and beautiful music that is being produced in this country, the coteries that spend money upon musical nothings for their own entertainment while the people go hungry."[24] From 1910 until 1913, Farwell was Supervisor of Municipal Concerts in the city parks of New York, where he had moved in 1909 to write for *Musical America*. Here he began a systematic campaign for free concerts of "good music" and biweekly amateur chorus meetings called "sings." In 1911, he staged his first successful Fourth of July celebration, which by 1912 had ripened into plans for a full-fledged community pageant under the influence of America's pioneer pageant master, William Chauncy Langdon. The first president of the American Pageantry Association and the director of the 1911 Pageant of Thetford (for which Farwell had served as musical adviser), Langdon defined the historical pageant as an episodic, locally generated drama, in which "the place is the hero and its history is the plot."[25]

Bolstered by his connections both with Langdon and with pageant master Percy MacKaye (whose father had helped stage Buffalo Bill's Wild West), Farwell's involvement in community music reached a highpoint in 1916. The New York City Community Chorus concluded its inaugural season with the spectacular Song and Light Festival, and Farwell collaborated with MacKaye on a gargantuan pageant in celebration of the tercentenary of Shakespeare's death, *Caliban by the Yellow Sands,* which filled New York City's Lewisohn Stadium for fourteen performances involving, by Farwell's count, five thousand community actors, a five-hundred-person chorus, and a one-hundred-piece orchestra.[26] With the U.S. entry into World War I, Farwell's activities gained government approval as the War Department enrolled him in an officer's training camp to develop a plan for army group singing. Farwell was soon proclaiming "international democracy through song," as reported by the *Los Angeles Times* under the title "Kaiser's Defeat by Singing Army Seen."[27] Farwell's rhetoric of democracy was already a rhetoric of "western" democracy. While he remained in New York, this rhetoric persisted in tension with his proximity to the bastions of music education and concertizing in the European mold. Once he moved to California in the summer of 1918 it would slip easily into a valorization of the trans-Mississippi West as the most American part of America.

CALIFORNIA

Farwell acquired his community music credentials in the East; he then brought these skills west to California communities that were eager to employ him. After six weeks of teaching summer school at UCLA (where he also organized and conducted a community chorus), Farwell was invited to spend a year as head of the music department at UC Berkeley, filling in for Charles Seeger while the latter was on leave. Farwell took charge of singing for the University's Student Army Training Corps. He led public singing in local movie theaters, and (after delays necessitated by the 1918–19 flu epidemic) founded the Berkeley Municipal Community Chorus. In addition to producing a very successful postwar Fourth of July pageant called *The Chant of Victory,* Farwell presented extension lectures outside the university with such titles as "Musical Government by the People," "The People's Music Drama," and "Shaping America's Soul through Song." One local newspaper commented, "It was only the Spirit of priesthood that could have sustained Mr. Farwell's enthusiasm for Community Music through four of the five lectures in the face of the small audience . . . But it was as apostles of this new-est (and oldest) faith that his listeners received his message."[28] Indeed Farwell must have gained a following rapidly, as he was elected president of the San Francisco chapter of the Music Teachers National Association less than six months after his arrival in the Bay Area. Immediately upon the completion of his year-long term at Berkeley, he was invited to Santa Barbara—not on the basis of his skills as a teacher or as a composer per se, but because of his proven enthusiasm for community music on the West Coast.

In an article dated 1919 in the *Berkeley Times,* an anonymous reporter took pride in proclaiming that "since his first visit to California in 1904, it has been [Farwell's] intention to become a Californian, but his work and engagements in the East have made it impossible until now. He is animated by an intense belief that because of climatic conditions and freedom from older traditions, the Pacific Coast is destined to become the scene of the greatest developments of the community chorus and the community pageant and music drama, and he will now devote himself wholly to the promotion of this movement on the coast."[29] The reporter's words must be taken with a grain or two of salt—any intention on Farwell's part to relocate westward in 1904 is at best unclear. Nevertheless, Farwell's experiences in California transformed his career in two important ways, intensifying his interest in what he called "Spanish Californian" songs and inter-twining his ideas about community spirit and the natural landscape.

Spanish Californian songs were a centerpiece of Farwell's community chorus activity, particularly in Santa Barbara. *Musical America* described them as the "novel feature" of a concert involving three thousand singers and featuring works by Handel, Haydn, Wagner, and Gounod, as well as Farwell's own "Prelude and

Chorale, Joy! Brothers, Joy!" and the "Entrance and Processional of Country Folk" from his *First Pageant Suite*. The song sheets he prepared for his Californian community choruses are peppered with such titles as "Peña Hueca," "La Golondrina," and "La Noche Está Serena," and Latin themes also infiltrated his pageants as, for example, in *La Primavera*, produced in Santa Barbara in 1920. Some in the Santa Barbara area encouraged Farwell to collect and transcribe those tunes still remembered by the city's oldest Hispanic residents. Mary Louise Overman, perhaps a chorus member or just an appreciative listener, visited two elderly ladies (including a descendent of Governor Pico), attempted to transcribe a melody, and tried to arrange for Farwell to make a visit of his own. Farwell in turn asked his choristers to alert him of any "Spanish songs" known to them.[30]

Farwell's papers also suggest that he planned a semicomprehensive but unfinished catalog of Spanish American song, just as he had for cowboy tunes fifteen years earlier. As Koegel has meticulously shown, Farwell transcribed almost three hundred Spanish-language items from Lummis's collection for preservation and study. Farwell and Lummis's report to the Archaeological Institute in 1905 stated that of the three hundred songs, roughly half were ready to be engraved.[31] Yet their collaboration eventually bore a different kind of fruit. Their academic publication foundered—probably, as Koegel suggests, due to lack of funds and each man's habitual overcommitment. Instead, the public came to know these melodies in Farwell's harmonizations, first through his folk song sets and his incidental music for Virginia Calhoun's dramatization of Helen Junt Jackson's novel *Ramona* (1905); next through Farwell's community sings and pageants during the 1910s and early 1920s; and finally in the 1923 volume *Spanish Songs of Old California*.[32]

Early in their collaboration, Farwell and Lummis had earmarked about fifty tunes for what Farwell called a "popular song book" with piano accompaniment. Despite his plans to devote a Wa-Wan issue to a dozen such settings, only fourteen of the Spanish California songs saw publication outside of Farwell's early folk song sets.[33] And even these might never have seen the light of day had it not been for the community music movement. Farwell explained in 1922: "Now that I am living here on the Coast, where I have been active in song movements of the people, the matter has come forward with great vitality. . . . These same Spanish songs (for which I wrote accompaniments) which I taught the people by rote, as they are unpublished, became one of our most enjoyed and important features of the chorus, and a source of unfailing delight to the thousands who attended our Sunday 'sings' at the Plaza del Mar."[34] According to Koegel, Farwell and Lummis approached four other publishers before deciding to issue the arrangements themselves, enabled by a five-hundred-dollar loan from one of the Southwest Museum benefactors. More than forty-five hundred copies were printed by 1925, earning the composer modest royalties and exciting interest from composer F. S.

Converse in Boston, Carl Sandburg of Chicago, and publishers of books for schoolchildren in California and Texas.

Farwell believed that Spanish California songs had given community music a "new lease [on] life" because of "their power to animate and thrill the people." He wrote in the foreword to *Spanish Songs of Old California:* "The great present need of the community song movement is to enlarge its scope, to escape from the old ruts and to find new songs of the right kind which the people will take delight in singing."[35] In the spirit of Lummis's "Catching Our Archaeology Alive," Farwell linked material preservation and musical revitalization. Lummis himself was even more dramatic. In his own preface to the song book titled "Flowers of Our Lost Romance," he began with an elegy to "old California, 'Before the Gringo Came,'" praising the region's cultural inheritance from "Mother Spain" and "Step-Mother Mexico." "For 38 years," he wrote, "I have been collecting the old, old songs of the Southwest. . . . It was barely in time; the very people who taught them to me have mostly forgotten them or died, and few of their children know them. But it is a sin and a folly to let such songs perish. We need them now!" Lummis echoed Farwell's urgency and his notion that Hispanic song could transform the community music movement:

> There is nothing in the world that could be so "good for what ails us"—the unrest, the social dyspepsia, the de-humanizing and de-homing, the apartness that comes by multitudes—as to Get Together and Sing Together. It brings a marvelous psychological "thaw," even in a crowd of strangers—and a wondrous welding in a crowd of friends. And for that, these old Spanish songs have, in Mr. Farwell's splendid Community Choruses, become fully as great favorites as their Saxon kindred, "Suwanee River," "Old Kentucky Home," "John Brown's Body," and all that roster of deathless memory.[36]

Lummis's pointed "Saxonizing" of Foster's most famous minstrel songs suggests what was at stake in the composition of the ideal western community. For most of his career, Farwell wrote of race in the best transcendental tradition—tolerant of difference but resigned to the fact that "progress" might consign certain races to the past. But in 1926, at the height of American nativism, in the midst of the eugenics movement, and a mere two years after the Johnson-Reed Act slashed European immigration to its lowest levels in U.S. history, Farwell's less liberal attitudes surfaced when he argued for the unique artistic potential of the Southwest, where Anglo-Saxon pioneers had superimposed themselves upon "Spanish and Spanish-derivative" populations. "Consider the racial bearing of the matter," Farwell wrote in a series of essays for the *Los Angeles Times.*

> Welcome as is the leaven of the better element of the "foreign" races in the life of the United States, it remains a fact, interpret it as you like, that the "American" of the Southwest is from the old pioneering colonial stock, north and south, which

created our nation and gave it its original characters. . . . It remains that this stock, as it is found in the Southwest today, is practically without the incumbrance of the hordes of more or less unassimilable aliens admitted by the insufficiently restricted immigration of the past, which constitutes one of its most difficult problems in so many other sections of the country.[37]

Farwell's multiethnic West was not without its racial hierarchies. Was it accidental that two of the Spanish California songs he chose for his community chorus work—"La Cara Negra" (The Black Face) from *Folk-Songs of the South and West* and "Chata Cara de Bule" (Darling, Snub-Nosed Face) from the *California* masque and *Spanish Songs of Old California*—make reference to physical markers of racial difference? Yet the Hispanic population offered the possibility of revitalization without miscegenation. The Californios were valuable not just because of their history in settling the West, but also because they offered a civilized, European counterbalance to British formality and reserve: "They are Latins, for which we Anglo-Saxons, emotionally stiff-jointed by comparison, should be profoundly grateful. And they come from the Latin country least known and understood today, most mysterious and alluring in its charm." Given that Spain's allure has always been tied up with its proximity to Africa and the Arab world, and given that Farwell welcomed what he saw as California's "continually increasing attention to things oriental," the composer's words suggest that in fact the tension between white and nonwhite "elements" was precisely what made the frontier so fertile a site for musical and social experimentation.

THE MARCH OF MAN

In addition to focusing his attention more keenly on Hispanic song, Farwell's California years attuned him to new opportunities for civic arts sponsorship. In Pasadena, he was the recipient of the Composer's Fellowship of the Pasadena Music and Arts Association, which provided a reasonably generous stipend, stipulating only that Farwell continue his creative work while living in the city. Renewed for three successive years, it allowed the composer to draft and complete *The Hako* and to engage in a host of other, nonlucrative endeavors. He took as a pupil the budding composer Roy Harris, guiding his studies in harmony and counterpoint in 1924–25 and engaging in wide-ranging discussions of aesthetics and society. He also composed music for pageants, often on ecumenically Christian or spiritual texts, such as the *Pilgrimage Play* (retelling the life of Christ) and a grassroots *Gesamtkunstwerk* called *The Grail Song*.

Neither the religious nor the Wagnerian tones of Farwell's pageantry were accidental. On the contrary, his very first pageant-style work in New England treated a Judeo-Christian theme, *Joseph and His Brethren* (1912); his holiday masque *The Evergreen Tree* (1917) was meant to be an "American *Messiah*"; and he led Easter morning "sings" in the Hollywood hills. He considered the community music meeting to be a type of "service" in both senses of the word: an activity for the common good and an event akin to a liturgical celebration.[38] As for Wagner, we have already seen how Farwell invoked the master's example when discussing folk-based composition. He had visited Bayreuth in 1897 and was one of America's strongest champions of the Wagnerian conductor Anton Seidl.[39] During the 1910s, Farwell also came to share Wagner's understanding of Greek drama as a model for a communal art. He described the pageant and masque as American "music dramas," purposefully opposed to opera, "presenting aspirational concepts of the highest racial significance, having the aspect of a ceremonial for the community at large, and involving the participation of the people."[40]

For all his Wagnerian tendencies, however, Farwell's *Festspielhaus* was emphatically outdoors. Back in 1904, during his second "western tour," Farwell had witnessed one of the so-called Grove Plays of San Francisco's elite Bohemian Club. He made a repeat visit to the grove in 1910, and again during his California years, and he carried impressions of the club's redwood forest ceremonies with him for the rest of his life. Farwell's New England pageants had generally been staged outside or in open-air stadiums, in keeping with the ideals articulated by Percy MacKaye and other famous pageant masters. Once in California, however, Farwell made the western landscape a prominent factor in his dramatic work.

In Farwell's eyes, California was blessed not just with a climate conducive to outdoor concerts, but also with a wealth of natural amphitheaters. After contributing music for a 1921 pageant-drama called *California: The Land of Dreams*, staged in the Yosemite Valley by the California Federation of Women's Clubs, Farwell was moved to advocate a regular, "utterly uncommercial" "festival drama," which would "light a torch to brighten the new civilization of the West" (EDC, 206–7). He came closest to this sort of project that same year with *The Pilgrimage Play*, an open-air extravaganza championed by Christine Wetherill Stevenson and staged in the hills above Los Angeles. Farwell and Stevenson were both involved in the emergence of the famous Hollywood Bowl as a regular concert venue.[41] Stevenson was actually one of the Bowl's first underwriters, but as musicologist Catherine Parsons Smith has shown, she withdrew her support and set up camp in the next canyon over once it became apparent that the larger Theater Arts Alliance in charge of the Bowl was more interested in concert-giving than in her sacred dramatic fare. For his part, Farwell led community singing at the Bowl as early as 1919, and he remained close to the woman known as the "Mother of the Bowl," Artie Mason Carter, an avid supporter of the Hollywood Community Chorus, which was directly inspired by Farwell's rhetoric about the chorus as a musical embodiment of western democracy.[42]

In 1924, Farwell found a Bayreuth to call his own in the San Bernardino Mountains east of Los Angeles, on Big Bear Lake. Here Farwell's friend, pianist and composer Fannie Charles Dillon, convinced the real estate developers of a resort community called Fawnskin to help finance a massive outdoor stage-space, complete with colored light projectors and performance areas scattered over a quarter mile of forest and extending up to points along the canyon rim (some 450 feet above the audience). Farwell became an enthusiastic promoter and artistic director, christening it the "Theater of the Stars," in a striking echo of the Hollywood Bowl's concert series "Symphonies Under the Stars," inaugurated in 1922.

Although the "Symphonies Under the Stars" continue into the twenty-first century, Farwell's theater suffered a precipitous decline, and Farwell's own involvement lasted but a single season, reaching its dramatic climax in September 1925, with *The March of Man*, a masque in which the spirits of the natural world (each illuminated by a different colored light) are threatened by greedy captains of industry and careless vacationing revelers. Farwell wrote the text and the music, he served as stage manager, and he performed some of the musical numbers. He also appeared as the masque's central character: the Seer, a benevolent Man whose arrival (foretold by the World Soul) comforts the fearful tree and rock spirits, and whose intervention (together with a spectacular storm scene) saves them from the manmade threats of axe, forest fire, and dynamite—each of which invites its own special effects. Pacific Coast critic Bruno David Ussher was clearly impressed by the superimposition of nature and technology:

> Hidden behind firs, in a little shed, before a cleverly constructed switchboard, bending over an elaborate lighting chart, someone turns the lever of the dimmer and the glow that revealed world-soul or rock-spirit . . . recedes into the ground, mysteriously as it has come. The conflict between nature and man proceeds. Flames rise, voices of wind and fire hiss. An axe pounds dully, till the crashing fall of a great tree before the eyes of spectators punctuates another chapter in this realistic symbol pageant. Where is another theater where the audience sees a tree felled and remaining on the stage until the last lights are dimmed?[43]

Little of the music for the masque has survived, and Ussher indicates that at least one portion of the incidental music was by Ernest Bloch, not by Farwell himself. The annotated production copy of Farwell's typescript indicates "soft music," "string music," or "music of the night" for the nature spirits and notes that the young revelers "[burst] in . . . singing a popular song to jazz instruments." The only score Farwell preserved was his own climactic Prayer, uttered by the Singer, an invisible voice sent by the World Soul to herald the dawn and to proclaim man's potential for union with the divine. The ecstatic text is matched by rapturous harmonies generated by chromatic voice-leading and a tendency to modulate by thirds. Although the Engineer with his dynamite claims to represent the progress of civilization, the true and transcendent march of man must, of course, be led by the Singer.[44] According to Farwell's stage directions, "Coinci-

FIGURE 3. *The March of Man*, cast photo. Courtesy of the Arthur Farwell Collection, Sibley Library, Eastman School of Music

dent with the last three notes . . . three consecutive rays of light are seen to flash upward in a zigzag course, like inverted lightning . . . a celestial choir bursts forth from the height, while the last upward flash, as it were, ignites at the same place a heavenly light which grows, as the chorus continues, to a stupendous illumination of the entire horizon."

It is hard to know precisely how this came off in production. Newspaper articles and the community's own magazine, *Fawnskin Folks,* show the theater's famous lighting effects at the revelatory moment marked by the entrance of the celestial choir. Photos capture the company in costume (see figure 3). Farwell stands as the central figure, sporting a turban and flanked by dryads, hamadryads, engineers, and an array of musicians. His wife, Gertrude (a noted pageanteer), appears as the World Soul, placed above with arms uplifted in the prophetic attitude of a "Wagnerian Erda."[45] The critical reception that survives is dominated by the testimonials Farwell collected in an ill-fated attempt to sustain the Theater of the Stars into a second season. Charles H. Gabriel Jr., writing for *Musical America,* contrasted its open spaces with the shallow and fashionable foyers of the city concert hall, and Ussher called the production a "great pageant-music drama of the future . . . of which Richard Wagner has written, in which stage, chorus in the sense of the Greeks i.e., a singing-acting chorus, light and orchestra, form one grandiose unity." Ussher further predicted: "Drama and opera, cramped so long into the apple-box shaped stage, with its silly mechanized, dimensionally limited spaces, will give way to a music-dramatic rebirth which will restore to art its holiness as in ancient Greece."[46]

In the end, then, Farwell's West was not really the "Wild West" of cowboys and Indians at all. It was meant to transcend that West—and yet not to replace it entirely. For the distinctly American West was present in the Spanish California melodies of the community chorus and especially in the thematic use and manipulation of the western landscape, whose personification and protection are central to the plot of *The March of Man*. In fact, these two western emphases are so pronounced that they seem almost to have erased the Indianist references that were so important to Farwell's earlier career. Perhaps it is not surprising that community choruses took more readily to Hispanic song than to Farwell's Indianist arrangements, which, despite the composer's protestations, always sounded (and still sound) "exotic." More telling is the absence of Native America in *The March of Man*. Actual and fictional Indians did make frequent appearances at Fawnskin, and the opening gala week of the Theater of the Stars was set to coincide with what Fawnskin promoters called the "Big Pow Wow." This Big Pow Wow, acted by Indians, included its own "outdoor play" in which a warlike tribe adopts a white man and promptly cedes its land to him. In a manner that would probably have pleased Fawnskin's real estate developers, *The March of Man* rewrites this parable about custodianship of the land for an all-white cast. The future history of Farwell's frontier would be written by whites, not in conflict with the diverse peoples of the West, but in battles about mastery and good stewardship over the land itself.

GOD'S COUNTRY

Farwell's love of landscape predated his experiences in the Far West. He frequently recalled the midwestern hunting and fishing trips of his Minnesota boyhood and teenage summers spent in the mountains of New England. He also relied on the healing power of nature during subsequent times of mental or moral crisis. He spent a week of walking in the White Mountains of New Hampshire before taking his "National Music Talk" on tour; he retreated to Saratoga to regain his health in 1907; in 1914, Farwell's friend, pianist Noble Kreider, even took him to Bermuda to recuperate after a disastrous attempt at writing incidental music (now lost) for a Broadway play (EDC, 590–91). As we have seen, the imposing geography of the western United States hit Farwell with the impact of a religious revelation. It was only fitting that, following Lummis's lead, he called the region "God's Country."

Why, then, does Farwell's catalog during the Wa-Wan years contain so little instrumental nature painting? One answer is that he was preoccupied with folklore. Another is that the miniature forms he preferred were ill-suited to the landscapes he found most impressive. Among his early works, only the piano suite about the Finger Lake region, *Owasco Memories* (1899, published 1907), offers up loosely geographical titles. In 1911–12, he attempted a slightly more expansive evocation of the White Mountains, a sonata-form movement called "Symbolistic Study no. 6—Mountain Vision," which he framed as a struggle between "the depths of failure and despair" and "the joyousness of tramping over the mountains in the crisp autumn air." Though he aimed to suggest "the boldness of the mountain scenery, and the mystery of its distances," his program was psychological, even autobiographical. These were mountains on a human scale.

By contrast, the topography of the West did not enter Farwell's oeuvre for more than two decades. Until his final years in California, all of his western works would be based on folk materials. In 1930, however, Farwell tried to capture a more rugged mountain range in his piano suite *In the Tetons*. The outer movements ("Granite and Ice" and "The Peaks at Night") announce their western majesty, with widely spaced, crashing dissonances, spiky chromatic lines, mysterious harmonies, and slow pacing meant to suggest the sublime. The most human and perhaps the most interesting movement is "Arduous Trail," which Farwell chose to subtitle "Humoresque." The protagonist seems to be on foot—the 4/4 meter is marchlike, not galloping—and his trudging progress is twice halted for a moment of nature appreciation, marked by a footnote: "Leaning against a tree, breathing, and listening," first to birdsong and then to the sounds of a brook. Fixing this attitude of contemplation is a quasi-whole-tone chord (D♭, E♭, F, C♭ with added A♭; then A♭, B♭, C, G♭ with added E♭) uttered in soft contrast to the otherwise unrelenting F minor. Ultimately, *In the Tetons* bursts free from the confines of the piano suite with a pendant piece called "Big Country" that presents eleven pages of rushing octaves.[47]

The grandiose programmatic impulses that Farwell had to rein in for the piano suite burst out in the large-scale score *Mountain Song*, which faced no generic constraints. Farwell completed the project in 1931 and later called it "probably much the greatest work which I have produced for the people's musical movement, and one of the chief works of my life." Some seven years earlier, he had begun sketching a massive choral-orchestral work based on his recollections of northern California's High Sierras.[48] In keeping with his ideas about community music and ritual, Farwell labeled this piece a "symphonic song ceremony," and in an apt analogy, he compared it to the chorale prelude of Reformation Europe. Farwell wrote his chorales first and then crafted an orchestral setting that would heighten the meaning and anticipation of the choral passages. The strong implication of audience involvement is matched by the work's spiritual aim. "We live mostly on the flat country, without the emotions which such scenes inspire in us," Farwell related. "I have sought to bring the inspiration of these great mountains . . . to the many who cannot reach them and participate in their beauty and grandeur."[49]

Out of necessity, Farwell wrote his own texts, alternating between elaborate choral-orchestral movements and movements for choir with simple accompaniment:

Introduction and chorale of the mountains

1. From the Heights
2. Depth of Pines; Chorale of the Forest
3. Azure Lake; Chorale of the Lake
4. Crags; Chorale of the Crags
   Interlude: Mystery, for Strings
5. Dawn and Day; Chorale of the Mountains

The rhetoric resembles that of *The March of Man* in its invocations to the "Lord God of the Mountain," in whom "we shall rest and be whole," and to "the Soul" that it may rise to "far horizons [that] in orient splendor gleam." Yet in *Mountain Song,* the peaks also speak, attempting to bar the seeker's path and to shield "the dread height's mysteries" from human corruption. In the end the chorus asks the God of the Mountains to "Smite us with vision, / Gird us with power!" for the coming hour of transfiguration.

Farwell spent considerable effort trying to work out a sufficiently transcendent musical language, and his sketches bear witness to this labored genesis with pages of notes on voice leading and discarded harmonic progressions. The most revealing of these sketch pages outlines one aspect of Farwell's basic plan: "Begin with chromatic and carry out by systems of equal intervals, all half steps first bar, all whole steps second, all minor thirds, etc." While I have not found this pattern literally in the pages of the score, the residue of Farwell's intervallic experimentation is everywhere apparent. Take, for example, the opening of "Crags," which Farwell tidied into a piano-vocal score presumably for some never-realized performance (example 9). Farwell's harmonic choices had always been highly chromatic, and his favorite chord was the French augmented sixth (which itself combines two tritones, each of which bisects an octave). Here, however, Farwell seems in search of a chromaticism that could be as much structural as coloristic. He juxtaposes chords whose roots are separated by tritones: C and F♯ at the opening of line 1; G and D♭ at the opening of line 2. Still basically functional, the F♯ triad in effect resolves to G-minor in bar 2, but by bar 4, Farwell's penchant for chromatic motion has pushed the G down to G♭ (related by tritone to the opening C).

Equal divisions of the octave are rare but not unprecedented in Farwell's work. Recall the dispersed whole-tone scale in the framing material of the piano miniature "Pawnee Horses." By contrast, in "Crags," tritones organize entire passages of

EXAMPLE 9. Farwell's piano arrangement of "Crags," from *Mountain Song*, mm. 1–7 (courtesy of the Farwell Collection, Sibley Music Library, Eastman School of Music)

score and chromaticism is pervasive. In transferring chromaticism from the background to the foreground of his landscape painting, Farwell found sonorities that were distant enough from conventional harmony to sound otherworldly. During the 1920s, Farwell had also experimented with modal scales outside the major-minor system, not in evocation of any folk music, but in homage to Ancient Greece and in the related belief that the modes had an otherwise unspecified "application to the requirements of community music."[50]

Farwell believed that *Mountain Song* and works of similar scope might be a vehicle for the wholesale "naturalization" of musical experience. In his correspondence with Harris in 1931, Farwell argued that new genres like the "symphonic song ceremony" offered salvation from the damning compromises of the concert world. As he envisioned it, "This work doesn't belong to any department of our present set scheme of things, and may have to wait a good while for a presentation. Attendance ... might become one day almost like a Nature Ceremony—something quite apart from the life of the symphony hall." While works like the *Wa-Wan Ceremony of the Omahas* and *The Hako* attempted to envelop white audiences in Indian ritual, *Mountain Song* aimed at something more transformative. Farwell explained the stages of this process: "I believe we were true and right to absorb our primitives—Indian and negro—as part of the immense blend of the future race here. Then, in the midst of this chaos and confusion, *I* have felt strongly that the next thing to do is to go to our own greatest American aspects of *Nature*."[51] With the shift from "primitive" folklore to future-oriented nature-painting, Americans of color, overtaken by modernity, would vanish into colorful and timeless landscapes.

Indeed, folklore all but disappears from Farwell's oeuvre in the 1930s, with the not inconsiderable exception of his arrangements of earlier scores. Having moved in 1927 to take up a new teaching position at Michigan State University, Farwell busied himself with large-scale forms, teaching obligations, and the typesetting of his music using a handcrafted lithograph printing press. But even when he returned to the American West for inspiration, as in his Piano Quintet of 1937, he renounced melodic borrowing. The Quintet is based on materials Farwell jotted in his sketchbook during his early western tours. Farwell admitted that the quintet might display "something of the loneliness of the plains and the ruggedness of the mountains." Yet he was careful to emphasize that he had used "no American folksongs whatsoever" in the score.[52] The opening pits a pentatonic melody suggesting F-major against B-major harmony, showing that the composer's fascination with tritones remained. Ron Erickson (violinist, publisher, and a student of Harris) rightly compares this gesture to the Scherzo of Dvořák's "American" Quartet.

In the midst of this harmonic and motivic richness, two moments stand out as vestiges of Indianist practice—yet each brings some alternate interpretation to the fore. In the opening movement, the bridge between the first and second themes of the sonata form includes a sudden change in texture, heralded by a return to the quintet's opening motif at bar 122. After this declarative phrase, percussive fifths in the piano reverberate with such steady familiarity that it is easy to hear a double-drumbeat instead of the written triple meter (example 10a). But these are diminished fifths, not perfect ones; they carry the symmetrical perfection of the tritone, not the pulsing of an Indian drum. Another kind of harmonic stasis characterizes the quintet's second movement—as if all the drones of Farwell's early scores had come to rest in a single extended gesture (example 10b). Although the composer would later allow that this movement projects the "desert moods" of the quintet as a whole, his program note states that he conceived this movement "by listening to a large Chinese gong struck softly but continuously, and noting the musical effects arising from the overtones."[53] On the one hand, this reference to Asian percussion suggests that Farwell's western wandering finally took him to a place where East met West. On the other hand, the gong's reverberations reveal Nature in a way that is not folkloric but material. The space he evokes is not the emptiness of the Great Plains but the unfolding fullness of a single pitch. Here

EXAMPLE 10A. Piano Quintet, first movement, mm. 128–36 (ed. Ron Erickson, San Francisco: Erickson Editions, 1997)

EXAMPLE 10B. Piano Quintet, second movement, mm. 7–18

Nature is not merely symbolized in the metaphorical perfection of the interval cycle but *embodied,* audible in the fundamental sounding of a naked tone.

THE DECLINE OF THE WEST?

Farwell's Piano Quintet was a logical choice for programming at the Depression-era Composers' Forum-Laboratory concerts in 1939. Not only was it his most recent chamber work, but it also reflected his Americanist leanings in an evocative rather than a literal way. And it had none of the overblown prose that critics from the 1930s forward have chosen to overlook. The monumental *Mountain Song,* in which Farwell invested so much labor, has never been heard in anything close to its seventy-two-minute totality. Two of its chorales were sung during the 1940s at a celebratory concert in the composer's natal state of Minnesota, and the string movement "Mystery" was excerpted for performance by none other than Roy Harris. Yet Harris's planned performance never happened, and he took the time to tell Farwell why:

> I rehearsed your work meticulously with my string quartet and had planned to put it on a nationwide broadcast, but your letter gave me such a worry that I would not do you justice according to your spiritual ideals that I decided I had better not do it. . . . I found your work a very sensuous piece, which indicates to me that I really missed the whole spirit of it. I found it very Wagnerian and very sensuous in

texture—beautiful, delicate and extremely pantheistic, exactly the opposite of what your letter said, so I fear I am too much of a barbarian. I will have to do some more rugged work of yours I guess. (EDC, 679–80)

The letter from Farwell that caused Harris's chagrin does not seem to have survived, but we can surmise that—despite their many affinities—the two men (born more than a quarter century apart) heard *Mountain Song* with distinctly different ears.

It is clear from Farwell's copious writings and lectures that he felt himself out of sync with his contemporaries—a critic both of long-established institutions and of what he heard from avant-garde or "ultramodern" circles. In most cases, Farwell was able to frame his loneliness as a virtue, casting himself as a pioneer or prophet. The force of repetition necessary to maintain this stance over three decades can be felt in his many forecasts of musical progress, his rhetoric about new audiences and "new epochs," and his reversion to the metaphor of new days dawning—from his piano fantasy "Dawn" to *The Hako* string quartet to *Mountain Song* and beyond. Fittingly, Farwell chose to sign Charles Lummis's guest book at El Alisal once with an incipit of the "Old Man's Love Song," and again with the text "up with the break of day."

It does not take an especially astute observer to note that Farwell was better at beginning projects than at continuing them: the Wa-Wan Press, the community music movement, the Theater of the Stars . . . each was hailed as the birth of a new era, and all were relatively short-lived. Financial and family considerations kept Farwell on the move, and he could at times be autocratic—shutting out the opinions of the fellow workers needed to sustain his projects.[54] Yet there is also a sense of impatience and perhaps even desperation in Farwell's grasping at a string of idealistic ventures, none of which could be achieved in a single lifetime. It was, after all, an "Old Man's Love Song" that Farwell so often chose to cite.

What, then, gave Farwell such confidence in the future? For a man who had suffered so many disappointments, so many grand plans unfulfilled, Farwell's optimism is little short of astonishing. Its roots seem to lie in the intensely visionary experiences he had as a young man and in his understanding of history. He was deeply influenced by German historian Oswald Spengler, whose eccentric and magisterial *Der Untergang des Abendlandes* (Decline of the West) posited a cyclical view of human history, marked by a succession of eight epochs (Egyptian, Chinese, Classical, etc.), each of which followed an organic life cycle of birth, growth, maturity, decay, and death. Writing amid the chaos of World War I in Europe, Spengler saw only the crumbling of contemporary, or "Faustian," civilization. Farwell, however, had long seen the decay and stagnation of European institutions as a portent of America's coming of age. His most extensive treatment of Spengler, in a talk called "The Music Teacher and the Times," includes corrective subsections titled "Exceptional Position of America" and

"American Musical Supremacy," which grafted Spenglerian wisdom onto exist-ing ideas about westward expansion.[55] In a related talk titled "The Artist as a Man of Destiny," he made the distinction between Old and New Worlds explicit: "For those of us who entertain a large measure of respect for Spengler's methods and conclusions, but who [are] inhabitants of a new continent and members of the new and irrepressible Yankee race, and hence [are] the possible [crossed out: probable] forerunners of a new culture, there remains still another attitude . . . which looks to the artist as priest in a new order of life."[56]

The priests of the new order were few but not necessarily far between. As we shall see, Farwell did not hesitate to appoint Harris the "protagonist of the time-spirit" and hero of the "western race-soul." Though such public statements were perhaps cryptic, privately Farwell made sure that Harris knew what he had in mind: "You and I, and a good many others in this country are born out of the soul of America," he wrote.

> The proto-soul of a new race—a race worthy of a new continent. . . . We are the forerunners of another breed, a breed that bears within it a spiritual germ worthy of generating one day a new "Great Culture" of the world. The discovery of Amer-ica, the pouring in of the races of the world, a new and broader nature world, a new absorption of the primitive (negro and Indian)—in short, a new continent. . . . It is unthinkable that such a new continent and new race as this can remain and be a mere tail to an old-world world-view that has had its day.

"Your letter makes me feel that you haven't *really read your Spengler,*" Farwell chided, after receiving Harris's despondent missive about the cultural bank-ruptcy of the concert hall: "Western civilization . . . is defeating itself at a terrific pace. A new spirit in the world will have to defeat it. And that spirit will not arise on the now depleted soil of the senescent Occidental culture in its original Euro-pean home. It will appear somewhere else."[57]

Though Farwell briefly entertained the notion that the next great world cul-ture would appear in Russia—"which is not *Europe,*" he explained to Harris—there was really little doubt that the fertile soil he had in mind could be found in the American West. Farwell's series of articles for the *Los Angeles Times* "The Riddle of the Southwest" (1926) was devoted to showing that the region was uniquely equipped for this mission. "A new race, a new culture and civilization, a new glory of human achievement—a veritable new spirit of life—is coming to birth in South-ern California!" Following Whitman's "Facing West from California's Shores," Farwell argued that this birth was enabled by geography: "Eternal Walt, himself humanity, has started in the dimness of time westward from Asia, the cradle of races, has circled the world, has come at last around to the Pacific, and now faces home again looking over the waves."[58]

Yet even so powerful an influence as geography was dwarfed in Farwell's mind by the human factor, the determining influence in the destiny of the West: "It comes before us with the force of a conviction, almost from racial considerations alone, that the proper conditions for such an achievement exist here in Southern California and the Southwest generally as nowhere else in the United States." Just as the "greatness of Greece arose in considerable part from the fact of a new race being created by the various and divergent hordes," he wrote, so the citizens of California represented an "admixture . . . not such a one as the 'melting pot' ordinarily implies but the one which is caused by the intermingling of the different aspects of the original sturdy stock, the direct descendants of the Atlantic colonists, north and south . . . and their indirect descendants coming from localities farther to the westward."[59] These were, of course, the men and women whom Farwell aimed to reach through the recreation of music as ritual, whether Indian rituals like the Wa-Wan and the Hako, or the new ceremonial forms of the community pageant. More than passive recipients of an evening's entertainment, the western audience represented for Farwell a force of living history. "What people these Westerners are," Farwell told a newspaper reporter from Portland back in 1904; "how wide awake! They seem to catch ideas so much quicker than Eastern people do—or at least they grasp and absorb them in a different manner than I have been accustomed to seeing. . . . There is not such a thing as a comparison between a Pacific Coast audience and a Boston audience. One might say of Boston that it is hermetically sealed. That expresses the whole situation there, I think. With New York—well, New York is a whirlpool; but the West is open and free-minded, ready to absorb and learn—but at the same time it is critical."[60] More than distinctive geography or climate, more than Indians or cowboys, it was the intrepid western audience that Farwell believed would generate the greatest potential energy: in imitation of ancient wisdom, the gathering of this artistically engaged community would ensure that western music remained ever the music of the future.

PART TWO

Western Encounters

Charles Wakefield Cadman and Others

The sunset beams played around her hair like a halo; the whole place was aglow with red light, and her face was kindled into transcendent beauty. A sound arrested her attention. She looked up. Forms, dusky black against the fiery western sky, were coming down the valley. It was the band of Indian shearers. They turned to the left, and went towards the sheep sheds and booths. But there was one of them that Ramona did not see. . . . It was Alessandro, son of Pablo Assis, captain of the shearing band. Walking slowly along in advance of his men, he had felt a light, as from a mirror held in the sun, smite his eyes. It was the red sunbeam on the glittering water where Ramona knelt. In the same second, he saw Ramona. He halted, as wild creatures of the forest halt at a sound. . . . As he gazed, his senses seemed leaving him, and unconsciously he spoke aloud: "Christ! What shall I do!"

—HELEN HUNT JACKSON, *RAMONA*

3

Encountering Indians

"ONCE UPON A TIME RECENTLY"

Farwell never wrote an opera. Nor did he complete a full-fledged music drama in anything approaching a Wagnerian sense. While his preference for the miniature surely dissuaded him, turning to opera would also have seemed at odds with his vision of the community pageant as the real "music of the future." His scripts feature souls and seers, but few lovers, villains, heroes, or sidekicks. Farwell's was not a comic muse. Yet his closest approximation to a conventional stage work bears the title *Cartoon, or Once Upon a Time Recently*. Completed in 1948, it relies on spoken dialogue to advance its quasi-autobiographical story line. The music includes many of Farwell's earlier patriotic anthems and folk arrangements, as well as a parody of European modernism ("Pierrot's Lunacy, or The Blight of Spring"). The central character, "Americus," an aspiring composer, is spurned by the robber-priests of the Temple of Europus but beloved by "Columbia" and urged by a statue of Beethoven to study folk song. Accordingly, Americus sets out from the corrupt eastern metropolis of "Philabostoyork" for points west. Thanks to the hospitality of the Spanish Californians and the warlike tendencies of the Indians (who agree to follow Americus only after he promises to transcribe their songs for posterity), Americus wins the day.[1] With his newfound power, Americus wrenches the plot of *Cartoon* out of its slide toward operetta and thrusts it into a more typically Farwellian mode, calling upon all assembled to perform a "New World Ceremony." The Indians' "wild war dance" incites the crowd to overthrow the idol of Europus, replacing it with an "Uncle Sam" bedecked in red, white, and blue regalia and hailed by choral acclamations about "America's musical message to the world in the age to be." Individual characters recede into a national or universal background; millennial overtones prevail.

These world-historical themes, so characteristic of Farwell's music and writings, are much harder to find in other composers' western scores. As we shall see, western stage works have usually structured their conflicts around ethnic tension, not spiritual unity; they have featured strongly delineated heroes and villains rather than vaguely symbolic or allegorical ones. While Farwell emphasized the *import* of frontiering—its place in grand, evolutionary schemes—others more often chose to depict the *process* of frontiering with its inevitable scenes of discovery and conflict. As the historian Patricia Limerick has observed: "Western historians, like Western people throughout the centuries of contact between formerly separate worlds, have been desperate for categories in which they could place these perplexing 'others' whose existence made life unmercifully complicated. . . . Minorities and majority in the American West occupied common ground— literally. . . . Each group might have preferred to keep its story private and separate, but life on the common ground of the American West made such purity impossible. Everyone became an actor in everyone else's play."[2] Scenes of dramatic encounter littered the western landscape long before such scenes were worked out in literary or movie westerns. Only minor adaptations were required to bring them to the stage, and even these adaptations sometimes had to be hidden behind a veil of ostensible historical accuracy.

With occasional excursions, I have chosen to focus attention in Part 2 on Charles Wakefield Cadman, Farwell's contemporary and by far the most popular Indianist of his generation. Cadman's frontier music dramas operated with a ready-made cast of characters meant to evoke real people and places. But they also relied on centuries of operatic practice that placed more importance on the suspension of disbelief than on the pretense of realism. In fact, as I aim to show, Cadman's works illustrate very powerfully the tensions at the heart of so many American westerns: between "tall tales" and "true-to-life" stories, between the desire for dramatic effect and the impulse toward verisimilitude.

Like Farwell, Cadman experienced Alice Fletcher's *Indian Story and Song* as revelatory, toured the country with an Indian Music Talk, and felt strong ties to the community music movement. Each made a name for himself by way of Native America, and each protested mightily (and ineffectively) when Indian-inspired pieces threatened to overshadow later scores that were pointedly free of borrowed material. In the end, however, Farwell's and Cadman's reputations diverged as critics chose to exaggerate the differences between the idealistic composer and the commercial songwriter. Cadman was most proud of his symphonies and sonatas, and if Farwell did not write "popular songs," it was not exactly for lack of trying. Yet both men contributed to this critical schism even as they suffered its effects.

Farwell joked wryly that it was a good thing the Wa-Wan Press had rejected Cadman's lucrative *American Indian Songs*: "Had they been accepted, this ideal enterprise for the 'publication of unsalable American compositions' might have become a financial success and I might have become a business man."[3] Cadman, in turn, considered Farwell something of a fanatic. After his exclusion from the ranks of the Wa-Wan, Cadman railed against Farwell's rigidity. "Ideals are all right," he complained to Francis La Flesche, "but they must not be *too visionary* or impractical."[4]

If Farwell offered up a visionary West—philosophical and introverted to the point of idiosyncrasy—Cadman represents an extroverted West, pragmatic in its aims and material in its rewards. In a sense, Farwell and Cadman exemplify precisely the two types of speculation that drove America's westward expansion: the abstract ideal of Manifest Destiny and the concrete exploitation of natural resources. As we have already seen in our survey of Farwell's career, these two goals overlap, but one often surpasses the other. In Cadman's case, profit was a brighter touchstone than prophecy. These two modes of future-oriented speculation are echoed by two ways of viewing the past, one mythic and the other realist. Living at the turn of the century, Farwell and Cadman knew that western history was simultaneously remote and close at hand. Farwell wrote letters to aging cowboys, and Cadman lived for a time on an Indian reservation, but both were caught up in rhetoric that placed the true West beyond reach. As the subtitle of *Cartoon* suggests, their western history was a history in which the "once upon a time" of legend bumped up against the "recently" of the newsroom. While Farwell grafted western history onto world history, Cadman chose to dwell on its more immediate effects, as communicated through the faux-realist language of verismo. While Farwell vied with Wagner, Cadman embraced Puccini.

"IDEALIZING" INDIAN SONG

Cadman's engagement with Indianism was briefer and later than Farwell's. Not interested in organizing a "new art life for America," Cadman was content to participate in established American musical institutions. He was carried to fame on the voices of Irish tenor John McCormack (who championed his first hit song, "At Dawning") and American soprano Lillian Nordica (who sang "From the Land of the Sky-blue Water" all over the country after Cadman had caught her attention with a glowing review titled "Woman of Iron").[5] Cadman never needed to start his own publishing ventures; on the contrary, even after respiratory problems spurred his move from the Midwest to the dry air of Denver in 1911, half a dozen East Coast publishers continued to clamor for his songs, piano pieces, and high school operettas.

While Farwell took full advantage of print media to spread his ideas on Americanism, nationalism, and Indianism, Cadman did so much less frequently. Glimmers of historical insight crop up in Cadman's opinion pieces, but he wrote only one sustained scholarly article, "The 'Idealization' of Indian Music," which appeared in *Musical Quarterly*, under the editorship of Oscar Sonneck. Written in 1915, well after Cadman's royalties had set him on the path to self-sufficiency, it aims both to justify Indianist borrowing and to distance him from Farwell, Loomis, Troyer, and the Wa-Wan contingent. Cadman invoked the Russian nationalists, noting that "the lilt, the life, and the love of the strange and elemental peoples that make up the great Russian Empire" have been adequately captured by those "whose veins are without a drop of blood of those wild tribes." All the more, Cadman argued, were composers of the American West justified in exploiting the natural resources of their region: "If the old life and unconquerable spirit of the red man were not wrapped up in the history of this continent, how strange that would be! One cannot live in the Great West without sensing it and thinking how it would 'sound' in terms of rhythm and melody. The composer feels the very pulse of it in his contact with the awesome cañons, the majestic snow-capped ranges and the voiceless yet beautiful solitudes of the desert."[6]

Cadman praised MacDowell's "Indian" Suite as more than "a mere ethnological report set to music," and he observed (pointedly, given Farwell's preference for piano miniatures) that "Indian music is essentially vocal. . . . the themes do not lend themselves successfully to piano music and little success has been achieved in this direction. Such attempts generally savor of 'salon music.'"[7] Cadman feigned to undercut his status as Indianist role model, explaining that he had adduced examples from his own pieces only at the request of the editor and not because he wished to set out "a criterion for others to follow." Despite this disclaimer, however, he did not shy away from offering advice: "Above all, if the composer has not something to *express musically,* aside from the thematic material he employs, if he can not achieve a composition that is aurally pleasing and attractive, it is better that he abstain from the idealization of Indian themes. Music, interesting music and *good* music first, color afterwards, should be the watchwords for those who experiment with folk-themes.[8] Cadman noted further that "only one-fifth of all Indian thematic material is valuable in the hands of a composer." The chosen material must be "attractive in its simplicity," inherently melodic, and "fairly good in symmetry." Such melodies, he wrote, "are pure gold." Once the appropriate material had been selected, Cadman advocated a flexible approach, claiming that "the potentiality of a folk-theme is in direct ratio to the ability of the composer to idealize it."[9]

In comparison to his vehement assertions about the priority of artistic quality, Cadman's advice about learning Native American culture is unimpressive. Though he conceded that the "idealizer" would need to "exercise intimate sympathy" in order to achieve "*rapport* with the native mind," his language suggests that he himself found such sympathy elusive: "One should, if possible, be in touch with the Indian's legends, his stories and the odd characteristics of his music, primitive though they may be, and one should have an insight into the Indian's emotional life concomitant with his naïve and charming art-creations. And while not absolutely necessary, a hearing of his songs on the Reservation amidst native surroundings adds something of value to a composer's efforts at idealizing."[10] Whether his characterization of the reservation as an Indian's "native surroundings" indicates a willful self-deception or an awareness of the rapidly changing realities of Native American life, Cadman recognized a great gulf between creativity and anthropology. Moreover, he was prepared to view this critical distance as an aid to the idealizing process, not a hindrance.

"FROM THE LAND OF THE SKY-BLUE WATER"

Though Cadman may have been reluctant to serve as Indianist ambassador, he was a natural choice after the immense success of his *Four American Indian Songs*, op. 45, completed in 1908 and published the following January.[11] In retrospect, it seems strange that it took him so long to respond to the Indianist call. He had already shown a penchant for New World colors in his youthful operetta *La Cubanita*. His friend and fellow Pittsburgher Nelle Richmond Eberhart (who penned the text for "At Dawning" and supplied prefatory verses for Cadman's 1906 *Prairie Sketches*) had worked for a time on an Indian reservation in Nebraska. She prefigured the romantic thrust of Cadman's Indianism in her text for his song "The Tryst" (1904), which relates the story of a lovesick brave keeping vigil on the prairie for a maiden called Shanewis.

Given his theory that the majority of Indian melody was not "suitable for harmonic investment," Cadman needed a substantial library of sources. In addition to Fletcher, he consulted Theodore Baker's *Über die Musik der nordamerikanischen Wilden* (1882), Frederick Burton's *American Primitive Music* (1902), Natalie Curtis's *The Indians' Book* (1907), and various volumes of Frances Densmore. At the beginning, however, Fletcher was clearly the key figure, not only because of her interest in American composers, but also because of her ties to Francis La Flesche. The son of an Omaha woman and a French trader, La Flesche became Fletcher's most important informant, the coauthor of her work on the Omaha, and, strangely, a member of her family after she adopted him in 1891.

Cadman had probably already begun his first attempt at "idealization" by the time he wrote to Fletcher asking permission to "use the melodies you have gathered in their 'native state' and also with my own adaptations, guided by your

knowledge and with a full appreciation and *public acknowledgement* in the preface." Fletcher blessed the project with alacrity and with a recommendation that
he send the resulting suite, *June on the Niobrara,* to the Wa-Wan Press. Cadman
complied, despite his misgivings. On one hand, he respected Farwell enough to
consider Farwell's approval as proper recompense for his efforts—or so he told
Fletcher: "I would sacrifice *all* remuneration in order to have him get it out." On
the other hand, Cadman asserted his originality: "I have never seen or heard much
music founded upon Aboriginal themes, save some of Farwell's efforts and Mac-
Dowell's *Indian Suite,* so I am not influenced by any set method or treatment. . . .
I wanted to be *uninfluenced* so far as I could."[12]

Far from being a manifesto for the future of American music, Cadman's songs
fall into the same exotic mold as his works on Persian, Hindu, and Japanese
tunes, the "authenticity" of which is carefully and prominently footnoted in each
case.[13] Although Cadman told Fletcher that "I endeavored to preserve the spirit
of your Indian themes, deviating as little as I possibly could from the primitive
melodies," in reality his adaptations are extremely free, especially when compared with Farwell's.[14] The first of the four songs, "From the Land of the Sky-blue
Water," exhibits radical changes to both text and tune. According to Eberhart
family lore, Nelle "wrote the lyrics to the Omaha melody by imagining a fasci-
natingly beautiful girl, part Sioux and part French, whom she once saw cross the
Niobrara River in a canoe to attend a leap-year dance and whom she imagined to
have been taken captive from Minnesota—or 'land of the sky blue water.'" Cadman was reported to have employed a similar blend of memory and imagination:
"Charles had been practicing his organ music for Sunday . . . when he went into a
small room off the big cold church to get rid of some of the numbness in his fingers by the cheerful open fire. As he sat there alone watching the sunlight on the
stained-glass window opposite, he suddenly thought of the theme of the love
song, and going to the small upright he quickly started the rippling bars of the
introduction . . . after which the harmonies fell in place."[15] Like Farwell, both
Eberhart and Cadman emphasized the role of intuition in their creative processes, perhaps to counter to the fact that the material itself was borrowed, not
original.

A comparison of Cadman's score and the Omaha melody reveals no inconsis-
tency with the story of the song's creation. Apart from the flageolet introduction,
the first two lines of the first stanza, and the first line of the second stanza, the
tune is flexibly coaxed into newly lyrical and periodic phrasing. Most other
phrases draw not on the original melody, but on the rhythmic profile that Cadman provided for the first phrase of his setting and the distinctive SHORT-long
accent of the accompanying rhythmic ostinato (examples 11a, 11b). The text paints
a stereotyped image of the defeated hero, or in this case, heroine: "From the Land

EXAMPLE 11A. "Be Thae-Wa-A*n* (Love Song)," opening phrase (from Fletcher, *Omaha Indian Music*, 1893)

He tha ho ha he ah hae   ha hae   he ah hae__ ah hae__ha ho ho he__tha hae

of the Sky-blue Water, / They brought a captive maid; / And her eyes they are lit with lightnings / Her heart is not afraid! / But I steal to her lodge at dawning, / I woo her with my flute; / She is sick for the Sky-blue Water, / The captive maid is mute." Already a prisoner, subject to the wooing of the lover's flute, she is unable—or perhaps unwilling—to speak for herself.

The balance between "authentic" Indian material and romantic stereotype is even more precarious in the last of the four songs, "The Moon Drops Low." After a brief introduction, the singer enters with a line that is faithful to the Indian melody for its first phrase, but quickly becomes freer, relying to a certain extent on motives drawn from the original tune. The piano accompaniment is again a near ostinato, liberally peppered with inverted-dotted figures and departed from for rhetorical effect. The words blatantly reinforce that invidious cultural construction, the living Indian as the last of a dying race: "Our glory sets like the sinking moon; / The Red-Man's race shall be perished soon; / Our feet shall trip where the web is spun, / For no dawn shall be ours, and no rising sun."

Not content to let the text alone depict the vanishing race, Cadman has provided a musical equivalent for the process of resignation to fate. As the second stanza closes, the singer arrives forcefully on a D♮ suspended above the C♯ pedal that continues until the end of the song (example 12). The power of this moment, however, is immediately eroded. The D quickly capitulates to C♯, and the piano figuration descends until the singer returns with a final statement of the already repeated text, "no dawn for us and no rising sun." Exhausted by its futile resistance, the vocal line is now reduced to near-stasis, hovering on members of the tonic, C♯-minor triad until it finally expires in a wordless "Ah—." It can hardly be surprising that, some years later, La Flesche apparently told the composer that this song was "not representative of the way an Indian sees himself."[16] That had, after all, never been the point.

EXAMPLE 11B. "From the Land of the Sky-blue Water," from *Four American Indian Songs*, mm. 1–19 (Boston: White-Smith, 1909)

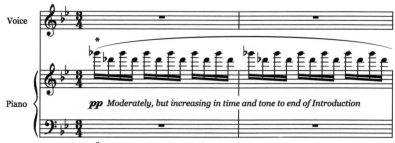

* Flageolet Love Call of the Omahas

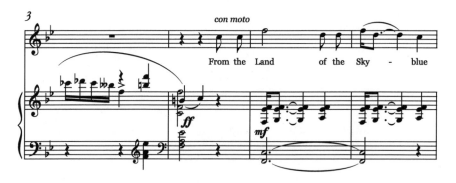

The unrequited Indian lover and the dying Indian warrior: these were the twin icons of Cadman's Indianism. He often began his Indian Music Talk with a rendition of "The Old Man's Love Song"—unaccompanied in the lecture recital's early years and in Farwell's arrangement beginning around 1913. Each half of the talk moved toward its own culmination: the first, a demonstration of Omaha

EXAMPLE 11B *(continued)*

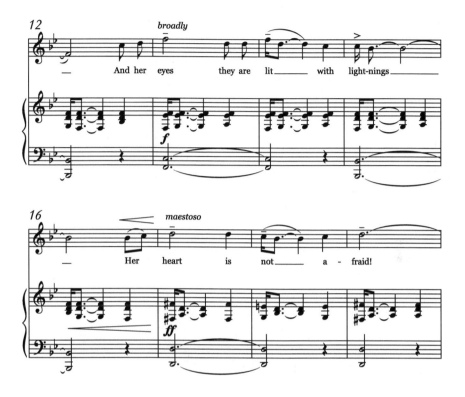

flute calls, which Cadman was soon able to illustrate with his own "authentic" instruments; and the second, "The Moon Drops Low," functioning as a sort of eulogy.

The solitary brave who graces the title page of Cadman's popular op. 45 plays on a similar ambiguity of associations (see figure 4).[17] He represents a vision of Native America that was stylized and open to interpretation. Sun and moon merge in the lover's night/dawn song. The human figure itself melts into the natural surroundings: Where do his leggings meet the surrounding grass? Which is his thigh and which is the ground on which he sits? Most important of all, who is this Indian? Perhaps it is the lover who fails to woo the maid from the "Land of Sky-blue Water." Perhaps it is the first-person narrator of Cadman's third song ("Far Off I Hear a Lover's Flute"), who cries out: "Why do I hate the crying flute / Which happy lovers play? / Ah! far and white my loved one walks / Along the Spirit Way!" In either case, the Indian is bereft—robbed by conflict, migration, or death—with no potential for romantic union or procreation. In this

EXAMPLE 12. "The Moon Drops Low," mm. 29–40

sense, the cold racial logic of "The Moon Drops Low" seems merely to exaggerate the lover's frustration; both point toward extinction.

CADMAN, LA FLESCHE, AND *DAOMA*

The highlighting of song in Cadman's lecture recital reflects his aesthetic priorities, as well as the input of tenor Paul Kennedy Harper, Cadman's first important singer-collaborator. Harper was the most visible, but he was not the only contributor to the Indian Music Talk. Working behind the scenes were Fletcher and La Flesche. Indeed it was in preparation for his talk that Cadman first asked to

EXAMPLE 12 *(continued)*

The vocal part may end *here* * if desired,
but the ending as written is more characteristic.

meet them face-to-face, calling on them when he passed through Washington, DC, in mid-August 1908. Impressed by the composer's songs and his plans for the upcoming lecture tour, La Flesche returned the visit in late November, when his travels brought him to Pittsburgh. Not long afterward, he suggested that Cadman and Eberhart create an opera based on his adaptation of a Sioux legend. They accepted at once. For Eberhart, the project represented an extension of the dramatic, even melodramatic "scenes" that she readily sketched when Cadman asked her for a song text or a prefatory lyric; for Cadman, it was a chance to join his trademark Indian material and his lifelong ambition: grand opera. For all

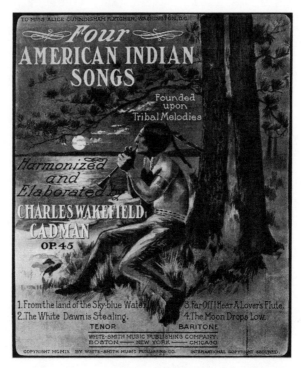

FIGURE 4. The cover of the sheet music for Cadman's *Four American Indian Songs,* op. 45 (Boston: White-Smith, 1909)

three, the project involved an unusually close collaboration, well documented in correspondence that extended from the time La Flesche completed the scenario in March 1909, through the summer months when Eberhart was working on the libretto, and well into 1910–12, while Cadman wrote and revised the score.

Although it is not clear whether Cadman knew it at the time, Indian operas were in the air when he sat down to write the ill-fated opera *Daoma,* later called *The Land of the Misty Water,* revised as *Ramala,* and never performed. In fact, Pittsburgh was the unlikely leading edge of a wave of Indian operas, beginning with Arthur Nevin's *Poia* (given a concert performance in Pittsburgh in 1907), and continuing with Victor Herbert's *Natoma* (1910). Cadman took note when Berlin's Königliches Oper picked up *Poia* for its 1909–10 season. "What do you think of Nevin's big piece of luck?" he wrote to Fletcher in June 1909. "I do hope his opera will prove successful, for a failure would likely put a damper on *ours,* don't you think? . . . I hope it makes a big hit."[18] Though the libretto for *Daoma* was well under way before Nevin's work appeared in Berlin, most of Cadman's composing happened after *Poia* had received a fiasco of a premiere in April 1910.

Poia could thus serve as both model and cautionary tale. Several years elapsed between the summers Nevin spent on the Blackfeet reservation in Montana and his work on the opera.[19] By contrast, Cadman's pilgrimage to "Indian country" took place with the opera project distinctly in mind and with La Flesche on board as musical adviser and guide. More important, while Nevin's approach was firmly Wagnerian, *Daoma* was to be a grand opera that would be "purely Indian" in its material—"ethnologically as well as artistically right," as Cadman put it.

What could count as "purely Indian"? This was a matter of some debate, even among the collaborators. As Harry Perison has shown, Cadman first evaluated musical material on his own and then worked with La Flesche to select appropriate melodies. In late summer 1909, Cadman followed La Flesche to the reservation at Walthill, Nebraska, where he spent several weeks helping make wax cylinder recordings, transcribing relevant tunes, and photographing Indian rituals.[20] Eberhart argued that the opera need not confine itself to Omaha song. Apparently still unaware of *Poia,* she wrote: "There will probably not be a market for more than *one* Indian opera and as a *grand opera* in three acts is a large undertaking would it not be best to use the finest of all melodies, making the opera national, as you might call it, instead of tribal?" On this point La Flesche seems to have prevailed as the opera incorporated only Omaha melodies and the closely related Pawnee melodies that Fletcher included in her book *The Hako.*[21]

In most other instances, however, La Flesche's input was trumped by the composer-librettist team. When he objected to overly lyrical moments in the battle sequence of Act 2, Eberhart retorted, "Of course no Indian would sing [an aria] at such a time, neither would a man of any other nationality, but grand operas are never true to life."[22] For his part, Cadman later confided to Eberhart his rather low opinion of La Flesche's musical advice after he had been stung by La Flesche's critique of the opera's storm scene. "To tell the truth I think it was above his head," Cadman rationalized. "It is very ultra modern . . . and also is not very Indian (ethnologically and scientifically). I told him he had not heard enough modern stuff and was not a musician or rather not enough of one to comprehend the orchestration in its full significance. He looked sort of shocked but had to admit my statement. . . . We dropped the subject."[23]

Disagreements of this sort and a lengthy hiatus necessitated by Cadman's ill health, together with an emphasis on ritual rather than dramatic action, may account for the lopsided structure of *Daoma,* one of the best explanations for its failure to reach the stage. The first act contains the least action and the most set pieces: fully ten of the opera's fifteen discrete arias or ensembles occur in this portion of the work, devoted to Aedeta's and Nemaha's discovery that they both love the maiden Daoma, their vow of friendship, Daoma's inability to choose between them, and their departure for war against the Pawnee. The action unfolds primarily in recitative, the least congenial medium both for Cadman (who was denied his trademark lyricism) and for Eberhart (who burdened her dialogue with archaisms and other stilted verbiage). Act 2 gives Daoma two arias in quick succession as she overtakes the encamped warriors and requests an impromptu wedding to Aedeta. She remains onstage during an offstage battle and anxiously greets the returning Nemaha, who attempts to convince her that her husband is dead, when in fact he has been captured. The melodramatic Acts 3 and 4 show the rescue, the lovers' return to the Omaha village, and the discovery that Nemaha was responsible for the treachery against his rival. Against cries for vengeance and pleas for mercy, Nemaha stabs himself. Thus the action establishes what Perison identifies as the dominant theme in Cadman's operas: "the swift and violent punishment of deceit or betrayal of friendship for the sake of love."[24] The impetuous Nemaha falls victim to his passions, while the more spiritually inclined Aedeta survives.

More than Cadman's later operatic projects, *Daoma* relies on leitmotifs for coherence and, to a lesser extent, for characterization. In his correspondence with La Flesche, Cadman made clear that his models were Italian. "I have used the rigorous 'modern' innovations in harmony," he explained. "However, I am emphasizing MELODY and while my 'working out' will hinge on the modern I shall follow the style of the Puccini and Post-Verdian School."[25] While working on Act 1, Cadman reviewed the Hammerstein Grand Opera Company's performance of *Tosca* and wrote to La Flesche: "The joy of seeing it and the object lesson in operatic construction and color was incalculable to me. I got many points."[26] Yet in terms of plot, *Daoma* departs from grand opera conventions. For one thing, it lacks a clear conflict between love and duty; to decide between her two lovers, Daoma instead trusts to the mysterious workings of a game of chance. The faithful lovers survive, and their happiness is chastened, not secured, by Nemaha's self-inflicted retribution. Perhaps ironically, it is Cadman's treatment of the Omaha chorus that most recalls Verdi or Puccini. The only excerpts from the opera to achieve national broadcast (under Leopold Stokowski, no less) were the "Spring Dance of the Willow Wands" from Act 1 and the "Processional Dance of Sacrifice" from Act 3, numbers that could easily find counterparts in *Aida* or *Turandot*.[27] As bearer of local color and arbiter of morality, the tribal chorus could be both "operatic" and "purely Indian."

The arias presented a much greater potential for stylistic confusion. How was Cadman to unite Indian melody, Italianate gestures, orchestral leitmotifs, and (if possible) something of the simple tunefulness that had made him such a successful songwriter? Daoma's Act 2 arias show all these elements jostling one another uneasily. The act opens with an introduction rich in leitmotifs, chiefly Nemaha's gapped-fourth fragment and Aedeta's syncopated circling figure, presented over a steady, pulsing bass. As the curtain rises, a chorus of warriors intones in octaves the melody of "The Moon Drops Low" from Cadman's *Four American*

EXAMPLE 13. "I have come here alone," from *Ramala* (originally *Daoma*), opening (courtesy of the Cadman Collection, Historical Collections and Labor Archives, Special Collections Library, The Pennsylvania State University)

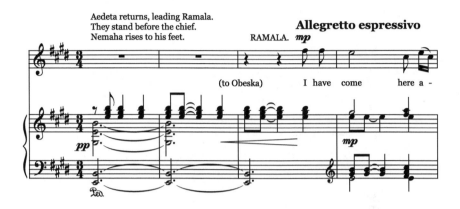

Indian Songs. In this operatic context, a new chromatic countermelody and a double-drumbeat accompaniment depersonalize but do not erase the foreboding associated with the well-known popular song. A sentinel announces Daoma's approach with the unaccompanied delivery of an "authentic" melody ("Hu-bae Wa-a*n*"). By contrast, Daoma's brief entrance aria, "I Have Come Here Alone," opens over an accompaniment that lingers on E major for more than five bars (example 13). Three measures of borrowed melody give way to free paraphrase. Leitmotifs and quotation fall by the wayside, leaving behind a mixture of Indianist rhythms (the inverted accent at "pure") and expressive chromaticism ("Scorn me not with

EXAMPLE 13 *(continued)*

disdain"). If this is verismo, it is verismo slightly unhinged by its encounter with Native America.

The longer aria that follows, "I Have Followed My Love," mirrors "I Have Come Here Alone" in scansion, sentiment, and gesture, but it is given the character of a cabaletta by its lively and utterly un-"Indian" accompaniment. When this excerpt won $150 in prize money from the National Federation of Music Clubs in 1911, the three collaborators were so buoyed by the early success that they began to discuss the distribution of future profits. Yet *Daoma* never reached the stage. When the opera was submitted to the Boston Opera Company, it was rejected as "dangerously untheatric," despite the intercession of Cadman's friend, soprano Alice Nielsen.[28] In an effort to capitalize on the "Land" and the "Water" of their well-known song, Cadman and Eberhart renamed the opera *The Land of the Misty Water,* but after it was again rejected in 1913 by the Chicago Opera Company, Cadman took more aggressive steps, dedicating an "Indian song" to director Giulio

Gatti-Casazza's wife, Alda, before submitting the opera unsuccessfully to the Met in 1914. One more attempt to bring *Daoma* to performance involved hiring the young designer Norman Bel Geddes to create watercolor mock-ups of costumes and scenery and even a portable stage in miniature—all to no avail.[29]

Cadman's commitment to verismo undermined the distinctiveness of his borrowed material. At the same time, the quasi-anthropological constraints of a "purely Indian" opera meant that stylistic plurality would not help delineate the principal characters—none is "more Omaha," "more Wagnerian," or "more Italian" than the others. Cadman thus inherited the difficulties of using borrowed materials while receiving no assurance that his quotations could enrich his audience's listening experience except in the vaguest of ways. Who, apart from Fletcher or La Flesche, would recognize that the tune cited at the beginning of Daoma's declaration of love was actually taken from a lament sung after the death of a warrior? If this choice was meant to foreshadow Aedeta's death, its irony would surely have gone unperceived.[30] In addition, as Cadman was quick to admit, the opera project was plagued by poor timing. Not only had *Poia* been a flop in Berlin, but the very next year Victor Herbert's *Natoma* received only lukewarm reviews. F. S. Converse's *The Pipe of Desire* (1905) achieved little success when it finally reached the Met in 1910; his 1911 score *The Sacrifice* did better in Boston, but even this did not work to Cadman's advantage, for when he sent the libretto of *Daoma* to the Boston Opera Company, impresario Henry Russell quickly objected: "Oh, I see you have the 'sacrifice' idea again! Can't you Americans write a plot without *that?*"[31]

Perhaps the most telling reason for *Daoma*'s failure was that its chief dramatic conflicts took place behind the scenes. In a literal sense, the battle between tribes occurs offstage, as does the near-fatal treachery of Nemaha. Metaphorically speaking, the cross-cultural tensions between Cadman, Eberhart, and La Flesche found no counterpart in the "purely Indian" love triangle and no audible resonance on stage. In addition to their quarrel over the storm scene, Cadman and La Flesche faced major misunderstandings about assigning proper credit for their ethnographic and creative work.[32] The most serious incident occurred in 1911, when the *Christian Science Monitor* gave Cadman sole credit for secretly recording an Osage ceremony, when in reality he had merely transcribed cylinders that La Flesche recorded with the participants' consent. Cadman's name was omitted from La Flesche's subsequent Report to the Bureau of American Ethnology, and the two men never collaborated on fieldwork again.[33]

It is hard to say how Cadman's career might have unfolded had *Daoma* been a success. Its trials and tribulations did not immediately dampen his enthusiasm for Indian material. On the contrary, the public still responded warmly to his Indian Music Talk, and the royalties from the *Four American Indian Songs* (together with a flurry of arrangements) were encouraging. He completed a collection called *Idealized Indian Themes* for piano in 1912 and dashed off a second quartet of songs titled *From Wigwam and Tepee* in 1914. In 1917, he published excerpts from his incidental music for Bel Geddes's *Thunderbird,* together with a new defense of idealization. Yet he would never again attempt an evening-length opera.

GO WEST, YOUNG MAN . . .

Equally profound, though indirect, was the impact that *Daoma* had on the geography of Cadman's career. When he began *Daoma,* he was a Pennsylvanian following in the footsteps of Victor Herbert and the Nevin brothers. By the time the score was finished, Cadman had lived in New Mexico, done fieldwork in Oklahoma and Nebraska, purchased a vacation home (christened "Daoma Lodge") in Colorado, and set his sights on California. *Daoma* took him first to Europe, where Act 2 served as his laboratory for the study of orchestration with Luigi von Kunits. The rigors of the six-week trip wrecked his already fragile physique. Upon his return, a benefit concert was arranged to send the ailing composer to the Presbyterian Sanatorium in Albuquerque, where all strenuous activities (including operatic composition) were strictly off limits, at least during the first phase of his stay. After he recovered, Cadman made his home in Denver, and in 1916, when its mile high winters proved too severe for his respiratory system, he moved to Southern California, where he would remain for the rest of his life.

The American West had long been a symbol of good health and clean living, as the writings of Theodore Roosevelt and others attest. Charles Lummis built on this rhetoric when he disparaged the "poor, anemic East" and reminded Farwell of the West's potential to foster and reward masculine strength: "Come out where the iron is, set up your forge, put the strong men outdoors to swing your hammers for you, and forge your brands."[34] For Cadman, the healing powers of the West were very real. The West was the site of his recuperation from sicknesses ranging from tuberculosis to the vaguer maladies of nervous exhaustion and stomach ailments. "I simply cannot live very happily or *physically well* in the *East,*" he wrote in 1919. "I *have* to be here where my health is always good, and where I can best do my work."[35]

But Roosevelt's and Lummis's words about the quintessentially masculine West must have resonated somewhat differently for Cadman, whose homosexuality was secret from the public at large but abundantly clear to his friends. In 1911, for example, he wrote to the Eberhart family about his unmarried status with a poignant combination of shame and resolve: "When I analyze my true feelings I find there is something lacking in me as a human being. I then get ashamed of myself,—but the next minute I feel defiant and rebellious and say 'No I will in spite of the Inferno BE YOUNG, FEEL YOUNG AND STAY SINGLE.' Good Lord how I run on with this nonsense!"[36] Writing more than twenty years later, Cadman remained ill at ease with what he called his "weak body and certain tendencies I will have till I go to my grave but which I have managed to 'manage' pretty darned well up to a certain point." He continued: "If the public knew ALL [that] certain people know (and respect) theyd probably label me with the undesirables but as I say I have learned to control many things and I HAVE been as decent and good about everything and to those in my life whom I sincerely love and who love ME and so what the public doesnt know, I dont care a fig about."[37]

Indeed the paying public would have gained little insight into Cadman's sexuality from his scores. No same-sex relationships figure in his oeuvre, and although many of his Indian ballads focus on frustrated love, other hit songs indulge the most conventional expressions of romantic happiness. Cadman's private life did not make him especially sensitive to the marginalizing effects of stereotype; on the contrary, of all the composers treated in this book he had perhaps the deftest hand at sketching racial and gender difference in broad strokes.

Given the near invisibility of homosexual allusion in Cadman's voluminous output, it is striking that one of the few songs that does seem ripe for homo-erotic reading sets a poem by Charles Farwell Edson called "The West," the first of Cadman's *Three Songs of the West*. Beginning and ending on B♭, the opening phrase ("Oh boundless, beautiful, lonely west") arcs downward to the E♭ of "boundless" and back up to "west," gathering up its lonely, minor-mode coloring on the G♭ of "beautiful," poignantly supported by the only complicated harmony in the otherwise diatonic phrase. The twinning of boundless freedom and beautiful loneliness is echoed by the poem's closing quatrain, which offers up an ecstatic paean to love that transcends societal niceties: "Living, loving without pretense; King of the world you be!" Emerging out of tonal uncertainty, Cadman directs his energies toward a cadence in G, which is deflected deceptively to B♭ (as dominant of E♭), and then reinforced by a twofold repetition of "King of the World!"

In between these framing stanzas, we find a species of age play well suited to the West, with its robust heroic types and its emphasis on youth and renewal (example 14): "Infinite mighty young-old free . . . Full of silence of mystery. . . . Cradled in finite joy . . . Man-like and strong, you boy!" Cadman mirrors the falling octave (from C to C) of the word "mystery" with a rising C♭-C♭ at the phrase "you boy," set in the shadowy key of F♭. The West that Cadman here embraces is definitively masculine, but alluringly uncertain; the connotations of purity or simplicity that so often attach to C♮ are here undone by enigmatic chromaticism, while the more unusual C♭ functions as a the dominant of F♭ (straightforward to the ear, but masked by Cadman's peculiar notation).

The poet Charles Farwell Edson was a music patron and composer (apparently no relation to Arthur Farwell). He embraced a mystical type of Christianity, and his son was a scholar of classical antiquity. His West thus had multiple meanings. Given that the last the final song in *Three Songs of the West* features a

EXAMPLE 14. "The West," mm. 13–18, 28–33 (Boston: White-Smith, 1916)

"wild coyote's long-drawn wailing note," the trans-Mississippi West seems the strongest connotation. Yet the "West" of ancient Greece lingers in the background, calling to mind other evocations of California as an "American Athens," where public democracy and personal (perhaps also sexual) freedom went hand in hand. By and large, however, if sexuality played a role in Cadman's life as a

EXAMPLE 14 *(continued)*

composer, it affected his choice of professional associates more than his subject matter. He was equally at home with men's clubs like the Bohemians or the Up-lifters and with the women of the MacDowell Club. He served as musical mentor, and probably more, to the young pianist Edward Earle; and his Violin Sonata was written for Sol Cohen, with whom he retained close personal ties.[38] While it cannot be said for certain, it seems likely that Cadman's sexuality also affected where he chose to settle. Southern California on the cusp of World War I probably offered a greater variety of socially acceptable lifestyles than Cadman had found farther East. Whatever the reason, he left Colorado for more hospitable climes in 1916.

FROM TSIANINA TO *SHANEWIS*

Although Cadman's time in Denver was brief, it transformed his career by bringing him into contact with Tsianina Redfeather. Born in 1892 on a ranch assigned to the Creek tribe in what is now Oklahoma, Tsianina and her siblings attended the Indian Government School in Eufala. An adept piano pupil, she caught the attention of the first Congresswoman to serve the new state, Alice Robertson, at whose expense she was sent to Denver. According to her autobiography, *Where Trails Have Led Me,* her piano teacher there discovered her voice by chance and recommended her to John C. ("Jack") Wilcox.[39] As it happened, Wilcox was a friend of Cadman's, and less than a month after Tsianina entered his studio, he alerted the composer that he had taken a promising Indian girl under his wing.

Accustomed to hearing his songs among the encore selections of such seasoned singers as Nordica and McCormack, Cadman was skeptical about Tsianina's undeveloped voice. Nonetheless, he agreed to let Wilcox arrange two trial engagements of the Indian Music Talk for Denver-area music clubs featuring the young Indian girl. To Cadman's delight, the program went over beautifully: "The singer was for once the star of my Indian talk," he wrote to Eberhart in May. "I was tickled to death for it means a lot to see that she can do the stunt. You don't know the ATMOSPHERE it adds to the vehicle. People went crazy over her. I realise that it is on account of her lovely personality and winning way and her '100% Indian' nature that helped the thing out, yet I must say that vocally she was more than adequate."[40] A reporter in Rocky Ford, Colorado, observed: "Tsianina has the fine, strong beauty of the aristocrats of her race—a voice that is haunting, appealing—and more than anything else, Indian. Always in her tones there is a plaintive note, the echoing faraway bird-like call of the voices of the primeval forest. The Indian songs she sings proudly, tenderly, sometimes sorrowfully, with a wistful note of pitying love for a vanishing race."[41]

During the 1913–14 season alone, the pair presented Cadman's Indian Music Talk more than twenty-four times, traveling through all parts of the Midwest, as far east as New York and Boston, and westward to Arizona, California, and Oregon. By 1924 (despite a significant interruption during World War I), the cross-cultural duo claimed to have performed in more than five hundred cities.[42] According to Tsianina, she received half of the total fee for each appearance, and she chose her own songs, favoring Frederick Burton's Ojibway arrangements. With less space devoted to the piano, Farwell's works slipped off the program, but songs by Wa-Wan composers Troyer and Loomis remained. Far more significant than these changes, however, were the new meanings that accrued to the talk, meanings that framed Cadman as both friend and benefactor of the Indian.

Cadman was a generous contributor to the cause of Indian welfare when his budget allowed. In 1910, for example, he gave a benefit performance of the Indian Music Talk that raised more than a hundred dollars for the Omaha Indian Reservation Hospital, directed by La Flesche's sister. Moreover, he conceived of his musical idealizations as a type of missionary work to foster appreciation of Indian culture and as "part of a larger 'movement' to better the lot of 'our poor red brethren.'"[43] For all this work, La Flesche was a key source of authority. But in the person of Tsianina, Cadman found a visible symbol of interracial symbiosis and of the potential, even the necessity, for "idealization" or "improvement" through the institutions of white civilization. Tsianina's youth and Cadman's prominence conspired to create strong overtones of white beneficence that were rarely questioned in the press. Cadman's financial situation in the mid-1910s was haphazard, and Tsianina's revitalization of the Indian Music Talk was the composer's saving grace; yet in the eyes of the public, Cadman was in charge, "allowing" the Indian Princess to choose her own repertory and costume—white buckskin with colorful beadwork and moccasins.

Tsianina's presence also deepened the significance of the talk in complex ways. Reviewers who had commented on the earlier lecture tours tended to focus on its entertainment value, Harper's "delightful" voice, and the "weird" melodies that the composer had uncovered. When Tsianina took the stage, however, the political import of the event was clearer from the start. Reviewers were intrigued by her posture and costume, her skin color and facial features. But many also attempted to identify Tsianina with the warriors and maidens of Eberhart's now-famous texts. When the duo performed in Chicago, one critic commented on the discrepancy between the artistic evocation of a "dying race" and the fact that Tsianina herself was very much alive: "She is aborigine and so charmingly so, that when the composer announced that the theme of *The Moon Drops Low* was no longer true because the latest government reports showed that the Indians were increasing, the spontaneous burst of applause was a direct compliment to the singer and her race."[44]

Had Tsianina merely renewed Progressive Era interest in the Indian Music Talk, her importance in Cadman's biography would be secure. But as luck would have it, she was also the inspiration for what became, after the *Four American Indian Songs,* the composer's most famous work: *Shanewis (The Robin Woman).* After the failure of *Daoma,* Cadman was reluctant to try another opera on an Indian theme. Yet Wilcox and other Denver musicians prevailed upon him and Eberhart to create a dramatic vehicle for both Tsianina's voice and her life story. The result was a one-act opera requiring only five solo singers and chorus, completed in roughly four months. Though conceived to be suitable for community groups—and perhaps, if successful, as a stepping-stone toward a performance of *Daoma*—this modest opera became the composer's next big success.[45] While the wartime cancellation of German productions must be credited for the prestigious premiere of *Shanewis* at the Metropolitan Opera on 23 March 1918, it was performed again on 28 March, 5, 10, and 15 April, and three more times in 1919, thus becoming the first American opera produced by the Met to remain in the repertory beyond a single season.

La Flesche had provided a mythic scenario for *Daoma,* but Tsianina's own past would shape the new opera: the young Indian soprano, her generous white patroness, and reservation life in Oklahoma. Even the title character's name is, according to most sources, a rough transliteration of Tsianina (chee-NEE-nah).[46] Given the story's biographical origins, Cadman felt that he had to remind Eberhart of the difference between the real Tsianina and the fictional Shanewis: "I had hoped that you would carry out the tragic ending, with the Indian girl either killing herself or being killed or else stabbing the false lover in a passion or frenzy at the revelation of his perfidy. That would give an opportunity for BIG MUSIC and dramatic music. I fear you are thinking too much of Tsianina's own characteristics and *her* life and story of her career rather than the *manufacturer* of a plot that will be grand operish!" And in the same letter:

> Tsianina said you felt the tragic ending or the killing or being killed business was not "Indian" or "civilised Indian" for this age and day and therefore you felt we could be TRUER in our conception by not doing it. That may be ethnologically true and may be consonant with Tsianina's *own character* but I have never at any time associated this plot of hers with *her life story* save ONLY the opening which is that drawing room scene and the fact of her having a "benefactress." Outside these two TRUE events I had pictured the whole plot in the nature of a tragedy or melodrama such as one thinks of and associates with the grand opera stage.[47]

Instead of becoming a celebrated recitalist, or a spokesperson for Indian contributions to the arts, the character Shanewis becomes one member of a predictably ill-fated love triangle.

In the opera's first part, Shanewis sings for guests of her patroness, Mrs. Everton, and unwittingly inspires Lionel (the fiancé of Mrs. Everton's daughter Amy) to fall hopelessly in love with her. Shanewis is unaware of Lionel's betrothal and eager to return his affections; yet she insists that he first accompany her to Oklahoma, to see if reservation life will cool his ardor. After Lionel and Shanewis steal away to the pow wow scene of the opera's second part, Amy and Mrs. Everton follow remarkably close behind, arriving just in time to precipitate the tragic denouement. When Shanewis learns of Lionel's engagement to Amy, she renounces him and prepares to lead a life of solitude in the forest. But as Lionel prepares to return to Amy, Philip Harjo (who has harbored a secret love for Shanewis), kills Lionel with a poison arrow, which legend has dedicated to the punishment of perfidious white lovers. Already removed from *Daoma*'s rituals by its modern setting, *Shanewis* soon left behind its own realistic trappings, veering instead into melodrama. Like Cadman's "idealization" of Indian song, the dramatization of Tsianina's story is meant to ensure effective communication with a white audience. But while Cadman molded Indian tunes to emphasize their familiar features, operatic convention required that Tsianina and her people become more exotic, prone to superstition and violent ends.

Even the title character, by far the most sympathetic and complex of Cadman's Indian roles, is introduced in ways that frame her as exotic. The audience at the Metropolitan in 1918, assembled for the performance of *Shanewis* (the opera), would have found itself immediately mirrored by the audience onstage at Mrs. Everton's soiree, eagerly awaiting the debut recital of Shanewis (the character). Because the opera is entirely without subplots, conversation must focus on the imminent arrival of Mrs. Everton's curious protégée.

The preparation for Shanewis's arrival is threefold. First the chorus of spectators wonders about her costume and appearance ("At least 'twill have the charm of novelty"). Then Mrs. Everton sets the scene, reminding her guests to "hear her with kindness":

> Remember she is no alien nightingale
> Fostered by tender sea-born zephyrs
> In balmy climes where the charmed air
> Exhales a golden melody.
> She is a native forest bird
> Born of our mighty wilderness,
> Warmed by our fervent sun,
> Taught by our free winds and leaping canyon waters
> A strange primeval song of ancient intervals.

Last, the betrothed couple comment on the strangeness of the occasion, and Amy shows Lionel the fateful photograph that sparks his love for the Indian maiden ("So straight, so tall, so lithe and slender! / Years ago, in Arizona, I saw a face like hers, / With the same proud eyes, / The same white, flashing smile"). As the chorus calls for quiet, the music also signals the soprano's imminent arrival with a striking interpolation of chromatically descending, tritone-related triads. Finally, Shanewis, in beaded costume, enters onto a staged stage.

When Shanewis begins her aria, "Spring Song of the Robin Woman," the orchestra falls silent, and she is accompanied only by the pianist visible onstage. The opening of her melody is modified from a Cheyenne Swinging Song, collected by Natalie Curtis. Predictably enough, the tune is altered to provide periodic phrasing and predictable melodic goals. But Shanewis's difference does not melt away as Cadman "idealizes" her melody. Instead, it is accentuated by the pianist's persistent hammering on open-fifths and eventually on parallel chords over a drone pedal (example 15). The Ojibway canoe song (borrowed from Frederick Burton) that serves as encore to the "Spring Song" features a more conventional,

EXAMPLE 15. *Shanewis,* "Spring Song of the Robin Woman," mm. 1–16 (Boston: White-Smith, 1918)

waltzlike accompaniment instead of a double-drumbeat, but the alternation in meter (between 6/8 and 9/8 bars) creates a rhythmic profile that both Cadman and Tsianina claimed were extremely difficult for non-Indian singers. Only in Shanewis and Lionel's love duet does the soprano break completely free of Indianist references, suggesting that Cadman turned to these tropes primarily when their colors serve the dramatic function of emphasizing the exotic.

EXAMPLE 15 *(continued)*

hum-ming birds,   Come un - to this   bar-ren land.   Hear   the   wa - ters

glid - - - - - - ing

"AN AMERICAN OPERA!"

Cadman may have employed as many as twenty "genuine Red Indian themes" in the opera.[48] Nevertheless he was keen to label *Shanewis* an "American" opera rather than an "Indian" one:

> The composer does not call this an *Indian* opera. In the first place, the story and libretto bear upon a phase of present-day American life with the Indian in transition.

As it is not a mythological tale nor yet an aboriginal story, and since more than three-fourths of the actual composition of the work lies within the boundaries of original creative effort (that is: not built upon native tunes in any way) there is no reason why this work should be labelled an Indian opera. Let it be an opera upon an American subject or if you will—an American opera![49]

In keeping with this view, Cadman and Eberhart suggested that opera companies might wish to choose costumes representing "the various phases of America in the Making": Queen Isabella of Spain, Evangeline (presumably Longfellow's), John Alden, and Pocahontas for the four leads, and a chorus including Sir Francis Drake, Leif Ericsson, Lincoln, Emerson, Susan B. Anthony, Betsy Ross, Salem Witches, Quakers, Franciscan Monks, and Rip van Winkle![50] Clearly the authors were willing to forgo ethnographic "correctness" in favor of symbolic potential.

The framing of Shanewis's story as an "American" one has serious implications for the interpretation of Act 2, which is set on the reservation. Many reviewers commented on this colorful crowd scene, complete with ice cream and balloon vendors, a chorus of high school girls, and even (in name only) a "jazz" band. The critic for *Musical Courier* delighted in the novelty of the tableau but betrayed an alarming willingness to take it as an accurate representation of Native American culture: "The second scene, a summer powpow [*sic*] in Oklahoma, was undoubtedly true to life, with its tepees, its dilapidated Ford in the background, and the lemonade and peanut stands with their tawdry red, white, and blue bunting. . . . The first act was played in modern evening costume. The Indian costumes of the second act . . . were quaint and attractive."[51] The stage directions call for "full-blood Indians and half-breeds in ceremonial, mongrel or modern dress and white spectators in holiday attire." Each group has its own music, ranging from the cries of the vendors and the unison singing of the Indians, to the lovers' operatic lines and the diatonic harmonies of the white crowd. In fact, the opera differentiates so meticulously that the "half-bloods" selling lemonade are explicitly separated from the "Indians":

> *Indians:* The Sun walks in the south Whence come all light and brightness; But now he goes to the west Where dwells the end of all. So we forsake our ceremonies, So we cease from singing.
>
> *Toy-Balloon Vendors (Boys):* Balloons, balloons, just like the American flag!
>
> *Lemonade Vendors (Half-Bloods):* Lemonade! Ice-cold lemonade, very refreshing in the heat.
>
> *Spectators:* See the handsome man with the pretty Indian maid; I wonder is it a flirtation? The crops are looking fine, but we need more rain, we need more rain. This wind is destructive; the soil is dry! 'Tis growing late!
>
> *Jazz-band of eight young people:* Za za za za . . .

Ice-cream Cone Vendors: Ice-cream cones! ...
   Indians: The drums grow silent, The dance is over!
Spectators: The sun is sinking fast!

       ...

   Indians: Yo ho ho Hi yo ho hi yo ho ...

The pow wow is a multiethnic event, but one in which society is strictly segregated, reinforcing one of the opera's morals: the inevitable doom of interracial mixing. Amy remonstrates with the faithless Lionel: "(*earnestly*) I plead for you and for our unity of blood. Each race is noble when the line is clear, but mingled bloods defile each other; It is the law."[52]

As in Mrs. Everton's drawing room, the spectators at the pow wow are prominent and Anglo. They watch and offer comments—"Pow-wows are picturesque and quite unique; This has been a splendid show, a gala week"—again inviting the audience watching the opera to identify with the voyeurism of the onstage spectators. As they leave, Lionel starts to follow them. Shanewis stops him, crying out, "No, there's one more song!"—in effect, announcing the arrival of the opera's most "authentically Indian" moment just as her own appearance was presaged by Mrs. Everton and company (example 16).

The footnote in the score is telling: "This is an Osage Indian ceremonial song and is used by permission of the U.S. Bureau of American Ethnology." Carefully separated from the preceding mélange of activity, the melody is unidealized, sung in vocables, and accompanied only by gourd rattles, timpani, and lower strings. Such an approach, apparently contradicting Cadman's usual "idealizing" aims, was evidently not so unusual in his stage works. In the foreword to his piano arrangement of the unproduced incidental music he wrote for Norman Bel Geddes's play *Thunderbird,* Cadman explains: "In the play ... I used the above Blackfeet Indian tunes in their *native state,* without altering a single note. . . . making no attempt at harmonizing the melodies. All my 'idealizing' such as you find in this piano score was indulged in at the fall of the curtain or between the acts. In this way the audience hears the tunes in 'native form' and later with the 'white man's harmonies.'"[53] Cadman implies that idealization can be separated from representation, but his distinction holds true only to a certain small degree. For Cadman, "representation" involved emphasizing difference (the Osage song, or the Blackfeet tunes in "native form"), while "idealization" aimed to assimilate (the "Spring Song," or Shanewis herself). But in reality, the processes by which these two effects are achieved are startlingly similar, especially in their use of framing devices. As the curtain falls, the "white man's harmonies" merely replace the white man's gaze.

Strangely, the aspect of *Shanewis* that Cadman believed would ensure the opera's Americanness—its modern setting—also represents its most pointed fidelity to Tsianina's biography. It would have been easy enough to place her in a

EXAMPLE 16. *Shanewis,* entrance of the "Old Indians"

*Note: This is an Osage Indian ceremonial song and is used by permission of the U.S. Bureau of American Ethnology

mythic past of Indian princesses and warrior braves. Instead, Eberhart and Cadman selected an interracial population and contrasting geographic settings: Mrs. Everton's Southern Californian salon and the Oklahoma reservation. One might argue that this aiming for Americanness explains the geographical stretching of the plot from the relatively narrow compass of Tsianina's upbringing (Oklahoma and Denver) to one that covers the entire United States (Oklahoma childhood, New York schooling, Los Angeles society). But the real Americanness of *Shanewis* lies in the title character's pronouncements about U.S. history. After Lionel's infidelity is discovered, Shanewis denounces white treatment of Native America: "For half a thousand years/Your race has cheated mine/With sweet words and noble sentiments." She continues: "Your ships infest our rivers,/Your cities mar our hills./What gave you in return?/A little learning, restless ambition,/A little fire-water,/And many, many cruel lessons in treachery!" This passage represents the opera's most successful exercise in integration. At the very moment when Shanewis's words call attention to antagonism between races, her music performs the opposite task, mixing Indianist and Euro-American elements with unusual freedom (example 17).

Like the passages discussed above, Shanewis's monologue is framed, though its frame is more "western" than "exotic." After Lionel interrupts her recitative, she counters, "Be silent! Let me speak," while a descending melodic sequence leads to V of B minor, complete with *rallentando* and vocal line falling from dominant to tonic in an emphatic, cadential gesture worthy of any Italian opera. In this instance the monologue's function as conventional dramatic climax offsets some of its political implications. As Shanewis offers the opera's most racially charged statements, she simultaneously steps into the role of the outraged soprano, diminishing the specific impact of her words. At the moment when she might be most crucially heard as a Native American voice, Shanewis is even more powerfully linked to the operatic heroines of other nations, Lakmé, Aida, and perhaps Carmen.

A similar sort of balancing can be found between the melodic and harmonic styles of Shanewis's arioso. Its hexatonic melodic fragments and inverted-dotted figures are clothed in harmonies that are pure Puccini. Like a mirror image of the Caucasian singer Sophie Braslau, who sang the title role in elaborate buckskin costume, Shanewis's monologue presents its exotic elements in distinctly Italianate garb. This aspect of Cadman's harmonic language was not lost on his contemporaries; a reviewer for *Musical Courier* described *Shanewis*'s love duet in terms which could also be applied to the monologue: "While there is absolutely no reason for charging Mr. Cadman with plagiarism, it is evident that he realizes that Puccini is the most effective writer for the musical stage today, and has accordingly taken the Italian for a model." The *Evening Sun*, commenting both on the opera's harmonic idiom and (obliquely) on its racially charged setting, called *Shanewis* an "American Madama Butterfly."[54]

EXAMPLE 17. *Shanewis,* opening and closing of the title character's monologue

Although Cadman gave Shanewis's monologue special attention, most reviewers did not mention it at all. This willingness to overlook the politically charged monologue text reflects a more general indifference to any of the social or cultural information encoded in the opera. Of the reviews I have seen, only one moved in this direction, remarking on the sharp contrasts in the score: "a tragic overture to a merry scene," an intermezzo that was "light and gay by way of prelude to a swift

EXAMPLE 17 *(continued)*

5 mm. after 114

What gave you in re-turn?_____ A lit-tle learn-ing,

rest-less am - bi - tion, A lit - tle fire___ wa - ter, And

ma-ny, ma-ny cru - el les-sons in treach - er - y!

and sombre conclusion"; "The double contrast was intentional, it was clever, and it worked like yeast in the dough. Under the sparkling froth of a society in which moved and sang an Indian girl of today, there could be felt the dark current of past dealings with the Red Man."[55] While the review wishes to dissociate the "Indian girl of today" from the "dark current of past dealings with the Red Man," Shanewis recognizes no such separation of past deeds and present injustices; on the contrary, her monologue exposes Lionel's betrayal as one episode in a series of ugly acts that are but poorly covered by the mantle of Manifest Destiny.

THE ROBIN WOMAN AT THE HOLLYWOOD BOWL

Shanewis readily links Lionel's betrayal with decades of white duplicity, but she also recognizes her own ambivalent "modernity." As she rejects the legendary vengeance of bow and arrow, she questions Progressive Era thinking about racial progress: "Am I too civilized or too weak?" The published synopsis states that she recognizes "the evolutionary distance" separating her from her ancestors. She struggles to reconcile past and present identities. Yet her uncertainty is but a shadow of the complexities that faced Tsianina. Both before and after Cadman had mangled her biography in order to achieve "grand operish" effects, she had been forced to speak both for the timeless "Indian" and for twentieth-century Native people coexisting with white society.

The Metropolitan premiere brought this tension into high relief. Confusion swirled in the newspapers about the opera's degree of fidelity to Tsianina's life story, and audiences in the lobby mistook her for the soprano assigned to sing the title role.[56] Some on the Metropolitan staff felt that her presence onstage would enhance the production, and this pressure increased after the intended Shanewis, Alice Gentle, fell sick. Tsianina was confident of her ability to convey "the feel of Indian rhythm" and the proper pantomime rowing motions for the famous "Canoe Song," but she declined the title role: "The opera would be a Metropolitan premiere and the story was based on my life . . . for me the responsibility was staggering."[57]

While Tsianina did not consider herself ready to face the New York critics in 1918, there was little question that she would eventually sing Shanewis. This assumption had been key to the work's conception in Denver, and plans were soon afoot for a West Coast performance. The San Carlo Opera Company of San Francisco tried and failed in 1920.[58] The California Opera Company announced its intent in 1921, but Shanewis never materialized. In 1924–25, a much publicized Hollywood Bowl production (with Tsianina in the title role) was announced, rehearsed, and abandoned due to internecine conflicts between the Bowl Association and Cadman's financial backers. Tsianina finally sang Shanewis in December 1924, in two Denver productions that were paired with Cadman's "operatic cantata" *The Sunset Trail*. But Cadman had to wait until June 1926 to see *Shanewis* staged in California, after his supporters rallied decisively to the cause. In November 1925, Cadman's agent, L. E. [Lyndon Ellsworth] Behymer, incited a grassroots campaign for a Hollywood Bowl production, and local pride won the day.

By the time *Shanewis* reached the Bowl, two important changes had taken place. First, the story of *The Robin Woman* had gained a following through excerpts presented in recital and so-called operalogues, semistaged productions usually hosted by music clubs.[59] A similar spirit of informality extended to the Hollywood Bowl, where high society liked to exercise its "communal feeling" through mammoth Easter sunrise services and Farwell's celebrated "sings." Given that the "Clubs and Civic Organizations of the Southwest" served as cosponsors for the show, it makes sense that Cadman's crowd of singers and extras expanded to fill the outdoor stage. While the Met had preferred more realistic costuming, the Hollywood Bowl production followed Cadman and Eberhart's suggestion that the principal singers and the chorus in Act 1 should be costumed to depict "outstanding characters in American History." Cadman himself made a guest appearance as Shanewis's onstage accompanist, reinforcing the cast's emphasis on community participation and masquerade.

As the status of *Shanewis* was altered through its informal network of dissemination, Tsianina's reputation underwent a complementary transformation. The idea that she might sing the opera's title role during the Met's second season was quashed in part by General Pershing's call for volunteers to entertain American soldiers stationed in Europe. Tsianina embraced this mission, boosting morale and even putting together a show called "Indians of Today and Yesterday" with Native American soldiers. She was back on American soil in time to make a forty-three-stop tour with Cadman during the 1919–20 season, and she brought with her a new sense of self-worth. In her own words, "At the beginning of my career with Mr. Cadman I had a feeling it was all his, that the honor all went to him. I now agreed that he had done a lot for Indian music, but that the Indian had done a lot for him, too."[60]

In keeping with the newfound confidence of the Indian Princess, the demography of the cast for *Shanewis* underwent a visible change for the Hollywood Bowl production. The Mohawk baritone Os-Ke-Non-Ton sang the role of Philip Harjo, which was expanded with him in mind. The producers also invited Indians from ten reservations in Arizona to dance during Act 2. Curtain calls thus featured around one hundred actual Indians (instead of a handful of painted "redface" Indians drawn from the Metropolitan Opera chorus). The publicity for the production emphasized the Indian and Hispanic history of the amphitheater itself, describing the West Coast premiere as "another glorious chapter of musical history in the Southwest" set to transpire "at the foot of Cahuenga Pass, near

FIGURE 5. *Shanewis* at the Hollywood Bowl. Courtesy of the Cadman Collection, Historical Collections and Labor Archives, Special Collections Library, the Pennsylvania State University

El Camino Real, the King's Highway of a past generation, where the Indians rested enroute to and from the pueblos of Los Angeles and Santa Barbara, in the Hollywood Bowl." In this context, Mrs. Everton's seaside bungalow underwent an ethnic relocation, becoming "the Spanish patio of a home in Santa Monica." Her former parlor was thus pulled partially outdoors into the picturesque twilight. Similarly, for the pow wow, only a few scattered tepees were required to transform the California stars into the night skies over Oklahoma (a couple of prominent palm trees notwithstanding).

The Hollywood Bowl production of *Shanewis* displayed a heightened awareness of its own "Indianness" from start to finish. As the pow wow scene dwarfed Mrs. Everton's patio, so Lionel (played by Texan tenor Rafaelo Diaz) was now outmatched by Harjo as a potential love interest. More striking still was an interpolated Indian "invocation." Tsianina described the overall effect: "Indian tepees covered the hills behind the platform. Indians on horseback rode down the trail. To the right of the stage was a campfire with Yowlache, a Yakima Indian, in breach [*sic*] cloth and with arms outstretched singing in a gorgeous baritone voice, 'Wah-to-ho—Rise, Arise. Life is calling thee.' It was a stunning picture."[61] Although the printed program labels this invocation as an introduction to the pow wow scene, Tsianina remembered it happening just before the overture. In either position, this number constitutes a significant reframing: here the Indian is indigenous, emerging out of the natural landscape. It is Mrs. Everton and her fancifully costumed guests who seem out of place.

All in all, the Hollywood Bowl production was infected with a spirit of pageantry not unlike that which motivated Arthur Farwell's nearly contemporaneous "Theater of the Stars." Rehearsals for *Shanewis* were not yet under way in the Bowl when Farwell's *March of Man* graced the outdoor stage at Fawnskin, yet the two productions were separated by less than nine months. Farwell and Cadman were apparently on cordial terms during Farwell's California sojourn (1918–27), as Cadman on occasion expressed his regret at missing a chance to visit with Farwell under Charles Lummis's roof at El Alisal.[62] No evidence survives to suggest that Cadman heard *The March of Man,* and Farwell left behind no written impressions of *Shanewis.* But if any of their mutual friends—Lummis, Artie Mason Carter, or a host of community music makers—did make the trek between the Hollywood hills and the mountains of San Bernardino to hear both works, they would have witnessed in dramatic fashion how each composer chose to interact with his Californian setting and how each mobilized his vision of the West.

When Farwell appeared as the Seer in *The March of Man,* he presided over an ecological spectacle with Wagnerian overtones and little ethnic import. Despite their "jazz instruments," his careless vacationers are as Anglo as the white-clad World Soul. Although Farwell and Fawnskin advertised strong attachments to Native America, in *The March of Man* such connections were at best atmospheric; whatever communion it might have offered between white and Indian was spiritual, abstract, and mediated by the awesome power of nature. By contrast, in *Shanewis,* the outdoor air of the pow wow is but a backdrop for human and musical conflict: the layering of so-called jazz, faux-Indian chant, and operatic recitative; the juxtaposition of Osage ceremonial song and Italianate love duet. While Farwell cast himself as the prophet in a drama of messianic revelation, Cadman impersonated himself (as Tsianina's accompanist) in a drama of historical encounter.

4

Staging the West

Cadman's was a scenic imagination. Before his career came to an end in the 1940s, he had written operas or operettas set in Puritan New England, Arizona, California, the upper Mississippi Valley, Mexico, Cuba, and Japan, as well as pageants for Colorado and Portland and a small assortment of film music. With or without Indian characters, these works offer variations on the theme of encounter: between cultures, between lovers, and between man and nature. Cadman's high school operettas, like his vast quantity of pedagogical piano miniatures, were written more or less on demand for publishers eager to meet a market for "good" and useful music. Designed to be immediately accessible, these works traffic in stock figures, offering a valuable index to early twentieth-century associations between people, places, and sounds. By extracting the western highlights of this catalog and organizing them into a "scenic tour," I depart in this chapter from the chronology of Cadman's career to address his treatment of the varied musical ecosystems of the West and to allow brief side trips into the works of his near contemporaries.

Before we embark on our tour, it will be worthwhile to address one important feature of Cadman's dramatic practice in its Indianist context: the tendency to articulate threatening or violent emotions through ethnically "marked" material and to assimilate happy sentiments into more conventional, often loosely Italianate, musical gestures. When *Shanewis* was performed as part of Denver's 1924 Music Week, it shared the bill with Cadman's newly expanded cantata, *The Sunset Trail,* to which the published score appends an explanatory subtitle: *An Oper-*

*atic Cantata Depicting the Struggles of the American Indians Against the Edict of
the United States Government Restricting Them to Prescribed Reservations.* With a
libretto by Denver resident Gilbert Moyle, *The Sunset Trail* is one of Cadman's few
Indianist works independent of Eberhart. As was the case in *Daoma,* no white
spectators intervene to justify a distinction between familiar and exotic idioms.
Instead, Cadman's score links unmarked music (typically diatonic and function-
ally harmonic) to supposedly universal feelings and uses the hallmarks of Indianism (pentatonic passages, ostinati) to signal moments of racial difference.

At the close of the piece, for example, tenor Redfeather staggers mortally
wounded onto the stage and, with his beautiful Wildflower, briefly recalls music
from their earlier love duet—operatic music at its least exotic. In the passages
that follow, however, Cadman gradually moves to unfamiliar harmonic ground
as the Old Man exclaims, "We have heeded a false prophet!" and eventually to stasis
as the Chief states, "Thus are we punished!" An interlude of open fifths prepares
for a final reprise of a choral outburst invoking the "Great Spirit" in stacked pentatonic lines. In the space of fifty bars, Cadman provides enough unmarked music
for a convincing love duet and enough exoticism that the defeat of the Indians, at
the hands of an invisible white army, can be accomplished with minimal moral
qualms.

The same pattern may be seen in modified form in one of Cadman's high
school operettas, *Indian Love Charm* (1932), whose title refers to a totem stolen
from "the Red Chief" by "the White Chief" in retaliation for the abduction and
(accidental) death of his white daughter. A young brave is thus deprived of romance, and he journeys far and wide to recover the love charm. Uncharacteristi-
cally, this Indian woos and wins a lover, after the deity Manitou takes pity on him.
Cadman makes liberal borrowings from flageolet calls in the introductions and
opening phrases of numbers devoted to love and longing. Once the falling fourths
and iambic rhythms have sent up their musical smoke signals, however, they dis-
sipate into the unmarked language of Cadman's sentimental songs. By contrast,
the choral cries for vengeance are tomahawked home with declamation in parallel intervals and pentatonic melodies over unwavering double-drumbeat accompaniment. Less substantial, but equally characteristic, is Cadman's *Naranoka,* an
eight-movement song cycle/cantata of the composer's later years. Again, the unmarked Indian lover is defeated by the marked Indian warrior, and a violent
death cuts short the tribe's hopes for the future. Thus the "good Indian" traits of
love, loyalty, and closeness to nature are dissociated from those Indians doomed
by warmongering and superstition.

Interestingly, Cadman also articulates this pattern in the "Indian Duet" he
wrote specifically for Tsianina and Chief Yowlache in 1928. Titled "The New Trail,"
its first half is devoted to memories of the native past. Introduced by Cadman's
signature flageolet stylizations, the mezzo-soprano enters over a pulsing perfect

fifth in the bass. The atypical triple meter of this "drum" becomes duple at the moment where the singer turns nostalgic: "Ah, the lodge is forsaken, the old days are gone." The drumbeat fades away with the onset of chromatic harmonies, and when the baritone joins in, providing the texture of a love duet, the only remnant of Cadman's Indianist vocabulary is an overemphasis on the downbeats (weighted with two sixteenth notes). The pattern is repeated, but this time transformed into the vision of a new Indian future: "Let the old be remembered, a race proudly run, While our faces are turned to the dawn and the sun!" Here, even the word *race* appears strangely diverted from its expected "racial" meaning into a more generic figure of speech. The Indian lovers purchase their survival through a shedding of racial traits. They turn instead to look East.

THE FOREST PRIMEVAL

If *Shanewis* was anomalous for its present-day setting, it was also unusual among classical scores for its depiction of Indians on the plains (Oklahoma) and in the coastal Far West (California). In keeping with the towering figure of Hiawatha, the novels of James Fenimore Cooper, and the stage sets of German romanticism, the majority of U.S. composers' Indians appeared in woodland works, whether the timberland of the Rocky Mountain region or (more typically) the forests of New England and the Upper Midwest.

Heroes may climb mountains and settlers may farm the plains, but the forest belongs to natural magic.[1] In this sense, the forests of the Rockies and the Sierras are not so very different from Fenimore Cooper's Hudson River Valley and Thoreau's wooded Walden—or, for that matter, from the sylvan realms of the Brothers Grimm or Shakespeare's *A Midsummer Night's Dream*. Latitude, longitude, and tree species would seem to matter little in the face of the forest's potential to dislocate societal norms. For colonial and antebellum America, the forested places of New England and the Upper Midwest served as a narrative nursery for characters and themes that would be transferred to the American West after the Civil War: the scout, the captive, the outcast, and the wanderer. Among these characters must also be counted the descendants of Hiawatha, whose very name carries within it the throbbing double-drumbeat of later Indianist imitators. Michael Pisani has discussed in rich detail Hiawatha's lasting appeal as the hero of symphonic poems, sheet music, and cantatas; moreover, he has shown how tropes drawn from Longfellow and, by extension, from the Upper Midwest quickly spread through the whole interwoven fabric of Indianism regardless of their geographic appropriateness.[2] The staying power of the supernatural Hiawatha helped fix the forest as a favorite setting for all things Indian.

The linking of Indian action and the mythic forest reached a high point in Arthur Nevin's *Poia*. The composer and his librettist, Randolph Hartley, set the three-act opera in "the far Northwest"—an accurate reflection of its origins in Blackfeet lore, as collected by Walter McClintock. Brought West by his work as a photographer and land surveyor, McClintock had settled with the tribe on their reservation in Montana and recorded many wax cylinders. Although he specified in his proposed scenario that the stage setting should depict "an Indian camp upon the prairies, with its picturesque lodges and the snowcapped Rocky Mountains for a background," *Poia*'s forests also teem with the nocturnal sounds and symbols of German opera, as passed from Hoffmann and Weber to Wagner and Humperdinck. In fact, as it unfolds, *Poia* comes to resemble *Parsifal* ever more strikingly. The second act—in which the scarred hero (Poia) wanders in the wilderness on a quest to heal the wound he bears for the sins of his people— opens *geheimnisvoll* in a world of mysterious woodland murmurings. Healed and newly equipped with an enchanted flute, Poia returns to save his tribe and to redeem his beloved Natoya, whose beauty has been defiled by her inane laughter at Poia's plight and her association with the savage Sumatsi. Begging Poia's forgiveness, Natoya throws herself in front of Sumatsi's knife; her death achieves transfiguration as the Sun God raises Natoya and Poia to the stars.

Cadman, too, wrote his share of woodland works, including his Hiawathan piano miniature "Wah-wah-taysee (Little Fire-fly)" (1912) and portions of his historical pageant *The Father of Waters* (1928). Consider, in addition, *Daoma* with its "Dance of the Willow Wands" and its climactic rescue scene, in which the forest shadows externalize the heroine's distress. Even in *Shanewis*, despite the genteel California salon and the dusty Oklahoma reservation, the opera's most famous excerpts, "The Spring Song of the Robin Woman" and especially the "Canoe Song" return us to a woodland world.[3] Shanewis herself, at the moment when she retreats into a life of solitude, resolves to disappear among the trees—"Into the Forest, Near to God I Go (Indian Lament)"—a topographical alternative that is not exactly convenient to its original Oklahoman setting and still less so for the Californian productions that moved the pow wow scene to the deserts of Arizona.

Cadman's longest forest idyll, discounting *Daoma*, was the three-act operetta *Lelawala: The Maid of Niagara* (1926), with libretto by George Murray Brown— not to be confused with Henry Hadley's cantata, *Lelawala: A Legend of Niagara* (1898). In the earlier score, Hadley's chorus tells of the maiden Lelawala, who sacrifices herself to appease the "Thunder Waters" and end the famine afflicting her tribe. In Cadman's tale, however, a variety of subplots push the story to a happy ending, in which the practice of Christian forgiveness that Lelawala has learned from a white missionary indirectly saves her from a watery end and a sacrificial canoe is repurposed for a nonviolent matrimonial ritual.

Although the operetta is eventually infiltrated by white characters, they enter late and alien to the established atmosphere. Indeed almost the entire first act is given over to Indian action, starting with the choral proclamation "We Are the

Tribe . . . We roam the forest," and continuing with a recitation of "The Legend of Niagara" by Lelawala's father. Following in quick succession are a perfunctory love song, a duet called "Silent the Forest," and the chorus "Lelawala Has Been Chosen," responding to her conviction that by sacrificing herself to the "Thunder Waters" she will preserve her tribe from destruction by the warlike Delawares. Only after fifty pages of piano-vocal score does a non-Indian character take the stage.[4]

Of course it is the scout Eagle Eye who leads the way with his quasi-Indian moniker (reminiscent of Cooper's "Hawkeye") and his backwoods dialect. Alone in his familiarity with Indian ways, he is the only white character who has any real impact on the unfolding plot: he rescues Lelawala and her white friend Mabel after they are captured by Lelawala's frustrated lover, Shungela. Yet even this crucial intervention suggests the operetta's overriding concern with Indians, for it modifies the racial makeup of the familiar "captivity narrative" to make the Indian maiden the target of the kidnapping; Mabel is taken along merely as her companion.

Like Mabel, all the white characters except for Eagle Eye function mainly as foils for the Indian principals. Only the Indians are at home in the forest—a dramatic fact that is conveyed musically as well. More than two-thirds of the operetta's numbers are sung by Indians, and apart from a love-song vocabulary that is more or less common to Indian and white lovers alike, the Anglo interpolations seem distinctly out of place. "Why, father," Mabel exclaims after she and Lelawala have been rescued from Shungela's encampment; "what moment could be more fitting for a minuet than *right now,* when we have safely returned from our adventure." The Indians answer with a dance of their own, moving to the music of "We Are the Tribe." While the white characters provide comic or romantic relief, the Indian chorus is fully naturalized.

THE GOLDEN TRAIL

If some of Cadman's lighter Indianist works are only vicariously "western"— through their use of character types that moved easily from eastern forests onto western ranges—other productions invite us to Arizona, San Juan Capistrano, Utah, or Sonora, sometimes in quick succession. Such is the case with *Trail Pictures,* a suite that Cadman composed at the MacDowell Colony in 1934, scoring it for "augmented orchestra, including xylophone, sleigh bells, Indian drum, and wind machine."[5] In the orchestral manuscript, the movements extend westward from "Stars over the Hills (New Hampshire)," to "The First Snow (Pennsylvania)," to "Cheerful Indian (Oklahoma)," and the mysterious "Red Rock Gnomes (Colorado)," before returning to Arkansas for a rousing fiddler-finale ("Evening in the Ozarks"). In practice, the composer omitted and reordered movements to suit the occasion. Nonetheless, when speaking with a reporter in Portland, he conveyed his original intent to chart a westward course that stretched all the way to the West Coast—farther than the finished suite would actually reach. "My Indian and folk lore work is a closed chapter, except for incidental music," Cadman claimed. "Now I am trying to express contemporary life. Gershwin and Carpenter have admirably expressed the contemporary America of the drawing room and cabaret, but I want to go outdoors. . . . That is why I have been writing 'Trail Pictures,' which will be given its world premiere soon by the Sacramento symphony orchestra. In 'Trail Pictures' I depict the life on the road from New Hampshire to Pennsylvania, to Arkansas and Oklahoma on out to California."[6] Direction was everything in *The Sunset Trail* (where sunset serves as a metonym for the West and a metaphor for death) and in "The New Trail" (in which the Indian lovers turn East to find their future). For non-Indians, however, whimsy and romance seem to be the guideposts for travel through the postcard pieces of Cadman country.

It would appear that Cadman's plans for an "Oregon Trail" Symphony never transpired, but he did complete one homage to travel and discovery: the *Pageant of Colorado,* slated for seven performances in May 1927 at the Denver City Auditorium. The poetic text, by Lillian White Spencer, takes the idea of travel as its structuring principle, dividing the history of her native state into three epochs, which *Musical America* described as follows: "'The Coming of the Runner,' representing the triumph of the Red Indian over the brown cliff dweller; 'The Coming of the Horse,' depicting Coronado's quest for the Seven Cities of Cibola; and 'The Coming of the Wheel,' showing the settling of the West by white pioneers."[7] Clearly, in this ever-accelerating march of civilization, the footman differs from the horseman or the wagon master not just in mode of transportation, but also in skin color.

The pageant also contained a prologue and interludes that trace the more or less militant progress of civilization: from a Stone Age family to a "March of the Indian Tribes" featuring nine tribal groups, a "March of the Explorers," and so forth. The interlude that follows Epoch Three is called "The Golden Trail," and it commemorates the "discoverers," "the gold rush," and "the march of the cowboys," not to mention the children of Denver, who scatter gold confetti. According to the Denver *Evening News,* the pageant culminated with "the discovering of the gleaming yellow metal, and on up to that crowning achievement of the 'red state' when the backbone of a great continent was pierced and the East and West made one."[8] The epilogue hails David Moffat, a railroad and mining engineer (here called "the Empire Builder"), who spent a personal fortune laying tracks in and out of Denver to facilitate commerce from the Rockies to the West Coast.

Like many Progressive Era community pageants, Cadman's *Pageant of Colorado* made visible the diverse populations drawn to the West in search of fame and fortune. Its final tableau shows the maiden Denver surrounded by a motley crew of explorers, pioneers, miners, and cowboys. The music seems to have matched the diversity of the crowd, according to the *Evening News:* "Eerie warwhoops split the air, weird chants, tribal dances—all woven into an absorbing story of high adventure and romance. Come the picturesque trappers, the gold seekers, the yelling cowboys firing their six shooters, and then those men of vision who built a towering city on the plains at the foot of the great peaks and drove their iron engines over the divides." Cadman's "rollicking prospectors' chorus," "Pike's Peak or Bust," won special praise from *Musical America,* as did the impressive finale, in which all of the pageant participants reprise the alma mater refrain of the "Song of Colorado," which proclaims Colorado "holiest and best . . . Queen and Mother of the West."

Although Cadman himself was unable to attend, the *Pageant of Colorado* assembled a cast of more than fifteen hundred citizens, many of whom were, according to the local press, "descendants of dauntless souls who crossed the perilous plains and who invaded a wilderness to serve a mighty empire."[9] The empire in question was partly a religious one. Yet as the plot turns to the Anglo pioneers, commercial motives come to the fore that were latent in the Cliff Dwellers' arts and crafts and Coronado's quest for the cities of Cibola. The quasi-legislative Proclamation in the Pageant program book makes much of modern Colorado's entrepreneurial spirit.[10]

It is no accident, then, that the *Pageant of Colorado* ends with a "Ballet of the Golds," which celebrates the region's rich natural resources: Forest Gold (timber), Black Gold (coal), Gray Gold (oil), Fairy Gold (the beauty of the hills), Green Gold (vegetables), and the like. The ballet thus diffuses the commercial impulse, realizing profit potential in a wide range of western commodities and averting the possibly negative boom-and-bust connotations of the metals mine. Yet by linking each natural resource to the *ne plus ultra* of western adventure, gold, the pageant still manages to capitalize on the excitement of prospecting and to validate an economy based on the "right of first discovery"—an ethic far removed from Farwell's in *The March of Man.* Though Cadman's pageant personifies the same species of rock and tree spirits, "Stone Gold" and "Forest Gold" do not fear the engineer or the tourist; on the contrary, they hail the "Empire Builder" precisely because he can extract them, uproot them, and bring them to market.

As the *Pageant of Colorado* carries us along the "golden trail" toward the "golden West," it also opens up common ground with other works more specifically devoted to the strange bedfellows brought together by the lure of the western mine. Operating outside the "mystic time" of the pageant, the characters we meet at operatic mining camps tend to announce their identities and to act in accordance with their "type." Take Puccini's *Fanciulla del West,* for example. The "Preliminary Note" printed in the English libretto states that "people coming from God knows where, joined forces in that far western land." In turn, the plaintive Jim Larkens sings of his homesickness for Cornwall; the shifty Australian Sid cheats at cards and is almost hanged; the generous but hot-tempered Sonora insults Sheriff Jack Rance with the epithet "yellow face" (*faccia di cinese*); the simple servant Wowkle delivers some of her opening song in Indian vocables (to which her mate Billy Jackrabbit responds, predictably, "Ugh"); and the duplicitous José Castro (identified in the English libretto as a "greaser") misleads Sheriff Rance and the *ragazzi* ("boys") concerning the whereabouts of the bandit Ramerrez.[11]

Except for Ramerrez, Castro, and the Indians (who sing only in Act 2), these diverse participants are united in the opening set piece "Che faranno I vecchi miei là lontano" (What are my folks doing back home, far away), which emphasizes both the transience and the foreignness of the mining camp. The number is introduced by the itinerant singer Jake Wallace, who appeared in blackface at the premiere but was merely a wandering "minstrel" thereafter. As Allan Atlas and Annie Randall have pointed out, Jake's ballad was adapted from a Zuni melody that Carlos Troyer arranged for the Wa-Wan Press; stranger still, the bandit Ramerrez sings material drawn from an African American cakewalk.[12] This conflation of American types (black, Native, outlaw) notwithstanding, it is the miners' collective nostalgia that suffuses the scene, lending a it distinctly Old World melancholy. Sheriff Rance is the least nostalgic, but even he exclaims: "What a cursed place, this golden West!"

The peculiar gender balance of the mining camp disrupts familial structures, placing Minnie as the lone soprano-mother-lover figure. One would think that gold would hold an equally powerful potential to upend social hierarchy. Yet this possibility seems to have held little interest for Puccini, Belasco, or any of the men charged with turning his play into a libretto. They treat gold primarily as an intensifier for questions of character: it is the tangible sign of what the community stands to lose to the gang of bandits and the objectification of everything that has been entrusted to Minnie's protection. According to the miners' moral compass, luck is as much a virtue as hard work, but abandoning the rules of fair play can have dire consequences, as Sid's narrow escape confirms. Once Dick Johnson is unmasked as a thief, it seems only natural that he should also be a murderer. How much more radical, then, is Minnie's act of redemption, when she cheats at cards to save Johnson's life.[13]

A similar but simpler moral economy guides Cadman's operetta *The Golden Trail,* in which the miners operate on the periphery of a convoluted domestic drama devised by George Murray Brown, who also wrote the lyrics for *Lelawala.* The widower Don Carlos Alvarado is traveling south to Sonora with his daughter Barbarita, who is in love with the valiant Pony Express rider Smiling Charlie. Stationed at the foothills of the Sierras, the Golden Trail Hotel makes room for them even though the dashing Don Pedro Carranza has taken up residence with his entourage and despite the fact that a wagon train of westward moving emigrants is expected to arrive at any moment. In contrast to Puccini's score, there is no homesickness whatsoever at the Golden Trail Hotel, only the excitement of multicultural encounter.

Unlike *Fanciulla*'s miners, Don Carlos and the emigrants travel as families, and much of the first act is devoted to highlighting their cultural differences. The Hispanic characters are divided between the respectable Spanish Alvarado family and the Mexican Don Pedro (a.k.a. the singing bandit Murietta). Like *Fanciulla*'s prostitute, Nina Micheltorena, he only pretends to be Spanish, but he does so poorly; when hotel proprietor Mike O'Rourke asks his guests how they wish to eat supper, Don Alvarado replies "a la *Espagnol*," while Don Pedro suggests "a la *Mexico*"—to which the freckled orphan emigrant Tad protests "Ala*bama!*"

When the emigrant Hurd family appears on the horizon (just after the bandits have sneaked off with the miners' gold), they sing a lusty march called "The Golden Trail": "From farthest east to farthest west, Across the desert sand,/O'er mountain height, we toil with might, A bold and dauntless band." The Anglo travelers match Spanish serenades with square dances. But even before their wagon train arrives on the scene, there is a diverse "American" presence. The oddest man out is certainly Montmorency Puddington, whom hotel proprietor Mike O'Rourke describes as a "tenderfoot.... From *Bawston* and now my pardner. Also, house-maid, waitress, gardener, book-keeper and utility man." Set apart by his effeminacy and his ambiguous social class, Monty is the chief source of comic relief—standing in sharp contrast to western locals like Trapper Joe and a band of Gold Creek miners who take the stage to sing a parody of Stephen Foster's "Oh, Susanna." Although its imitation banjo strumming may evoke the black-and-white imagery of the plantation south, in this arrangement (as in many other western settings), gold has displaced black or white as the primary color referent.[14]

Given the stark differences sketched between the families moving on the "golden trail," it is all the more remarkable that the operetta ends with not one, but two Anglo-Hispanic couples: the predictable union of Barbarita and Smiling Charlie and the utterly unexpected engagement of Monty to Carmela, Queen of the Mexican Dancers. Monty and Carmela never have the chance to sing together, but Barbarita and Charlie share music that reflects Cadman's attitudes toward their union. Their "Betrothal Dance" is labeled a tango in the vocal score, and it comes complete with *habañera* rhythms, frequent motion in parallel thirds, and the indication that, if Charlie and Barbarita do not wish to dance, "this number may be performed *entirely* by Mexican Dancing Girls." Attentive listeners may hear a softening of the *habañera* profile, however, particularly as the number progresses (example 18). It is frequently overlaid with rhythmic patterns that Cadman considered characteristic of a fiddle tune or frontier square dance. Downbeats subdivided into an eighth note plus two sixteenth notes muddy any audible lingering on the tango's all-important dotted eighth. Hereafter, and particularly when she sings of love, the Spanish Barbarita will employ

EXAMPLE 18. "Betrothal Dance (Tango)" from *The Golden Trail,* mm. 1–15 (Cincinnati: Willis Music Co., 1929)

NOTE: If preferred, this number may be performed *entirely* by Mexican Dancing girls; half of them dressed in male attire.

the unmarked "Anglo" style of Cadman's sentimental ballads, unsullied by even the whiff of a corporeal *habañera.*

The implied absorption of Spanish into Anglo becomes more explicit in an optional tableau that may be inserted immediately after the "Betrothal Dance." Here, without warning, the allegorical figure of Columbia emerges out of an otherwise normal choral reprise of the "Golden Trail." Speaking with a fervor worthy of Farwell's dramatic masques, she reveals the true historical importance of Charlie and Barbarita's engagement: "*(Gesture to the emigrants, L. H.)* My children of the east, you are winning in the golden lands of the west, *(Gesture to Californians, R.H.)* My children of the west, you are winning the best blood of the east. *(Unfurls flag and holds aloft)* Under one flag! Forever one people! *(Here, while Columbia waves Stars and Stripes, piano or orchestra strikes up and plays one verse of 'America.')*" Charlie and Barbarita celebrate a melting-pot marriage, meant not just to signal Charlie's graduation from pony express rider to family man, but also to mark the maturation of his United States through the fruitful union of eastern blood and western land. The riches of the West—literally the gold dust of the suspicious miners, figuratively the Alvarado family jewels—thus become a betrothal gift to those Anglo men who seize their destiny as discoverers.

MISSIONARY WORK

The miracle of the western mine lies not just in its veins of ore, but also in the way its treasure is hidden from view. To discover its riches requires a certain amount of speculation and often a leap of faith. As the real action of Manifest Destiny was bound up with experiences of pilgrimage and conversion—from the stalwart Puritans to the Mormon migration—so the rugged trails and desert expanses of the West offered a backdrop for strenuous spiritual endeavor. Taking their place alongside the all-purpose Protestant churches that came to dot the plains and the solitary homestead corners where pioneer women observed designated "prayer hours" with distant fellow believers, the most dramatic sites for religious encounter in North America were surely the Spanish missions. Here the theological disparity between Franciscan Padres and Indian neophytes was matched by looming battles among world powers for dominion over the western lands of Texas, New Mexico, and California.

The conflicts of colonization are part and parcel of mission-themed texts, whether they are set in the Southwest—like Helen Hunt Jackson's widely read novel *Ramona* (1884)—or the Northwest, the location of Mary Carr Moore's historically inspired grand opera *Narcissa*. The 1847 massacre of Marcus and Narcissa Whitman and their Presbyterian converts made a gripping tale, and some survivors still lived in the Seattle area when Moore's opera was premiered there in 1912. Moore recalled: "The stirring romance and martyrdom of the Whitmans . . . interested me beyond measure. It seemed that someone should commemorate the lives of these noble patriots."[15] According to Catherine Parsons Smith and Cynthia S. Richardson, Moore first urged Farwell or San Franciscan Henry Hadley to try their hands at an operatic rendition; after they refused, she turned to her mother, an accomplished writer, for a libretto.

Sarah Pratt Carr and her daughter chose to call their opera *The Cost of Empire*, and for good reason. In her foreword to the 1912 piano-vocal score (published by Witmark thanks in part to Farwell's endorsement), Sarah Pratt Carr stated that "missionary passion is the theme of the opera, with patriotism as a second motive scarcely less powerful." When the curtain rises, the U.S. claim to Oregon Territory is contested by the British; in Act 2, we meet the Englishman McLoughlin, whose American sympathies cause him to lose his job with the Hudson Bay Company; and in Act 3, Marcus prepares for a dangerous midwinter trek to Washington, DC, to urge the U.S. government not to cede the Columbia River valley. An ensemble number foreshadows his success. Against an orchestral "Star-Spangled Banner," the settlers proclaim "Our country's flag, the glory of the Lord," while the Natives mutter "Woe, the Indians' fate is sealed" and McLoughlin admits "My doom comes with the morrow, my state is gone."[16] In the end, however, the victorious outcome of Marcus's geopolitical "mission" places his religious mission in peril, for it is "a cowardly American" who murders the friendly Indian Elijah, thus giving the bellicose Indians led by Delaware Tom an excuse to avenge themselves against the Whitmans. In the end, McLoughlin is the only Anglo to survive; yet it is the wailing of the Indian women that brings the opera to its close. Delaware Tom may have won the battle, but the Indians are destined to lose the war.

While territorial conquest is never far from the surface of Narcissa, Christian conversion is ostensibly the Whitmans' goal, and religious themes inflect the opera in several ways. Perhaps predictably, the Christian Indians sing differently from the non-Christian ones. As Smith and Richardson observe, "The two most colorful character roles in the opera belong to unfriendly Indians." By contrast, the convert Elijah sings an innocuous ballad to his beloved Siskadee before departing to explore California. Despite the Act 2 war dances and the final massacre, both Moore and her mother were outspoken about their attempt to depict Indian life with sympathy. The foreword to the score reads: "Misunderstood, defrauded, outraged, his relations with Americans make that chapter in our history one of growing shame. No plea of the 'destiny of the white race' can ever wipe out the infamy. The Whitmans least of all people deserved their martyrdom; yet according to Indian ethics—probably as good as any in the sight of God—their lives paid only a just debt."[17]

While religious identity helps shape the music of Narcissa, the pace of religious ritual seems also to have shaped its narrative, as a critic for Musical America noted: "There is a solemnity and dignity pervading the whole which never loses its grip. . . . Strangely enough, there is not a single incident in the action of the play worthy of the name, until the climax." Indeed, Smith and Richardson have pointed out that the first act of Narcissa, in which the missionaries are commissioned to leave upstate New York, was occasionally performed on its own as a cantata.[18] The later action at the mission is more varied, but there are few extraneous subplots, few emotional arias, and no carefully engineered scenes of confrontation. One audience member testified: "I have twice witnessed the Passion Play in Oberammergau, and this opera . . . approaches nearer to that than anything else I have ever witnessed." The critic for Musical America concurred: "It would seem as if 'Narcissa' is destined to be featured in historical pageants, instead of becoming part of popular operatic repertoire."[19]

The missionary work that stood the best chance of joining "the popular operatic repertoire" was not Narcissa but Natoma, Victor Herbert's much-vaunted effort at historical Americanism.[20] Composing at almost precisely the same time, Moore and Herbert arrived at their grand operas from different directions: Moore came by way of the cantata, while Herbert was undergoing a very public conversion from operetta to more "serious" fare. As might be expected, *Natoma* relies on love triangles, local-color choruses, and stock character types. Still, Herbert could not sidestep the question of "authenticity." He described his use of Indian themes in terms quite similar to Cadman's: "I have composed all of *Natoma*'s music, at least the greater part of it, out of fragments of Indian music, which I have collected and studied for some time past. However, I have pursued none of these melodies to their logical conclusion. If I used Indian music with all its original intervals and cadences it would become very monotonous, and so, of course, I have adapted it."[21]

Herbert's tunes came by way of his librettist, Joseph Deighn Redding (attorney, composer, and creator of several "Grove Plays" for San Francisco's Bohemian Club). Redding also drew on historical sources to justify his much-maligned libretto and his multifaceted understanding of its title character.[22] As servant and bosom friend of the Spanish debutante Barbara de la Guerra, Natoma is demure, watchful, and charming. In service of the plot, however, she becomes a creature of conflicting impulses: as the would-be lover of the "Americano" Paul, she is Barbara's unrequited rival; when accused by the crafty Castro of abandoning her Indian heritage, she is a haughty princess: "You half-breed," she cries. "Don't touch me! You are no Indian!" When Castro later challenges her to the ancient (and apocryphal) "Dagger Dance" amid the Spanish dances of the fiesta, she drops her civilized mien and stabs the Spaniard Alvarado when he attempts to kidnap Barbara.[23] Yet, in the end, Natoma is transfigured almost without explanation into an obedient and cloistered devotee of the Catholic Church.

In *Narcissa*, the plot replicated the missionaries' westward journey from their home church in New York to the Whitman Mission. But in *Natoma* the mission is present from the opening. In Act 1, all anticipate Barbara's return from the mission's convent school. The Act 2 celebration, dance, and murder of Alvarado occur under the shadow of the church's facade, outside in the Spanish plaza—a colorful marketplace of piping shepherds, Mescal-drinking guitar players, fruit vendors, and whip-cracking vaqueros. Act 3 transpires within the mission itself. As we are drawn into the ceremonial presence of the mission, its figurehead, Father Peralta, also grows in stature. In Act 1, he is courteous, even obsequious, to Barbara's father, Don Francisco. He remains invisible during the climactic events of Act 2 until Natoma's stabbing of Alvarado incites the crowd against her. At this point, Paul shouts "To the rescue!" But it is actually Father Peralta who silences the mob with the imperious words "Hold, hold, nomine Christi!" From this moment onward, Peralta towers over all the opera's other characters. Natoma drops her bloody dagger and falls at the padre's feet while he intones "Vengeance is mine saith the Lord!"

Up to this point, much of *Natoma*'s action has unfolded in song and dance. But once the action moves inside the mission, an atmosphere of religious ritual prevails. Alone on the altar steps, Natoma might be expected to offer up a prayer. Yet the childless heroine instead sings a lullaby—a peculiar choice, but one that prepares the way for Father Peralta, who calms and converts the refugee in his sanctuary by appealing to her childhood memory of the mutual affection between her and Barbara. At the padre's signal, an onstage organ begins to play, monks open the mission doors, and the church fills with congregants as the sun slowly sets. Candles are lit and nuns (anachronistic, as convents did not appear in California until after the missions had been secularized) sing "Te lucis ante terminum." The pantomime action overlaid on their sacred song looks for all the world like a wedding procession. According to the stage directions in the score, Paul and his fellow officers occupy one side of the aisle; Barbara and her father, the other. Then "NATOMA steps slowly down toward the main aisle. She walks down main aisle, reaches the pews where PAUL and BARBARA are seated, pauses, and turns facing altar. BARBARA and PAUL, as though under the spell of some controlling power, come into aisle and kneel in front of NATOMA, who takes the amulet from off her neck and places it over BARBARA's shoulders. She then turns and continues down main aisle to cross-aisle, then turns and walks between the kneeling nuns up cross-aisle to open door of convent garden." The mission has swallowed up all the principal characters: Paul and Barbara in a mystic, Anglo-Hispanic marriage, Natoma in the chastity of the convent. While the region's future population might spring from the young lovers, the church doors close upon Natoma, burdened as she is by her inexplicable but apparently inevitable regression to savagery and murder.[24]

The librettist Redding described the opera's symbolic treatment of race: "To me Natoma is somewhat allegorical in that she epitomizes the pathos and heartache of the disappearing race as against the influx of the Aryan tribes. Again the work shows that two characters are virtually obliterated: the devil-may-care and romantic Spaniard and the Indian."[25] The fiery Alvarado dies by the native dagger, leaving the elderly Spanish men (Father Peralta and Don Francisco) to live out their days in peace. Meanwhile, with Father Peralta as presiding magician, Natoma performs the vanishing act expected of her as "the last of her race." What's more, with her final gesture she cedes her birthright (as represented by the abalone amulet she received from her father) to Barbara, and by extension to Paul. Already decorated with the Castilian lace she inherited at her coming of age, Barbara now wears the tokens of both East and West, civilized artifact and natural emblem. And as for Paul, while his status as an "Americano" (stationed on a ship called the "Liberty") at first set him apart from the Californian community, he becomes at the last its *pater familias*.[26]

Cadman heard *Natoma* in 1911, and *Shanewis* may reflect some lessons learned from Herbert's free treatment of Americana; in fact, at least one critic seems to have confused the two "Indian operas" in retrospect.[27] *Natoma* also bears comparison with Cadman's later mission operetta, *The Bells of Capistrano,* completed in 1928 on another text by George Murray Brown. Replete with an Indian serving girl, Spanish maids, Anglo lovers, and lively cowboys, it also unfolds in the shadow of a mission, but in the manner of any good operetta, it steers its cast of characters out of tragic circumstances into carefully coupled happiness and good fortune.

More than Moore's or Herbert's scores, *The Bells of Capistrano* deals explicitly with matters of real estate. The Rancho Ortego belongs to Ramon but is heavily mortgaged to the villainous Jake Kraft, who has convinced some disgruntled Indians to rustle the Rancho herd, thereby ensuring bankruptcy and foreclosure. The mission attracts guests to the Rancho, including "eastern scientist" Professor Anderson and James Alden, who (in apparent homage to preservationist Charles Lummis) has been commissioned to restore the crumbling California missions. Alden's daughter Marian happens to be in love with Ramon, and Professor Anderson's students happen to fall in love with Ramon's sisters. (The Indian girl Noneeta loves Lone Eagle, and Professor Anderson's sister Laura is destined for the cowboy Billy Burns, leaving no female unattached.) A prophecy has circulated that if the damaged mission bells were to ring again, the Indians' stolen lands would be restored. More mysterious still, the last padre died with a secret on his lips—something about a treasure. *The Bells of Capistrano* thus treats its mission as a locus of superstition and material wealth more than spiritual enlightenment.

Like *Lelawala* and *The Sunset Trail, The Bells of Capistrano* presents a conflict between Christian teachings and Indian legend, here represented by Posé, who convinces his people that by stealing the Ortegos' cattle they can fulfill the will of the gods. It is no surprise that Posé preaches an outdated wisdom, joining the ranks of stereotyped medicine men who lead their tribes doggedly toward racial oblivion. But in Cadman's operetta, Christianity too seems to be past its prime. Alden is at the mission to restore, not to worship, and Ramon welcomes his custodianship because "the elements are playing havoc with the ruins." Instead of the comforting presence of Narcissa or the imposing figure of Father Peralta, the mission at Capistrano is inhabited only by memories, nostalgically recalled in the operetta's title song over a fabric of rolling, tolling triads (example 19): "Oh sweet and sadly chiming / The vesper bells are calling, / Across the dark'ning plain . . . Ring out, ring out, O sweet toned bells, / Wake mem'ries old again." Though the building may be threatened, fond memory will restore the mission and its social hierarchy of priests and neophytes. Right up to its closing vaudeville-style tagline ("Ah, those olden, golden Spanish Bells!"), this number places the mission in its proper time and place: the long-gone days of Spanish exploration as seen against the dwindling light of sunset.

EXAMPLE 19. *The Bells of Capistrano,* refrain of title song (Chicago: H. T. FitzSimons Co., 1928)

Like the mission itself, the Ortego family is threatened by the passing of time; Ramon is the "last male descendent of an old Spanish family," and he seems incapable of acting to preserve his ranch. It is the foreman, Billy, who stirs the cowboy to pursue the cattle rustlers, while Ramon sighs: "Who can fight against such enemies! It almost seems that the old curse is coming true." Ramon's virtues are

EXAMPLE 19 *(continued)*

generosity and hospitality. His misguided gallantry almost costs him the chance to court Marian, as he does not wish to burden her with a bankrupt lover. By contrast, the practical cowpoke Billy pursues his love with clear-sighted competence and no beating around the bush. Ramon's "Serenade" is affecting, but Billy is the instigator of action.

If Ramon and Billy represent conflicting brands of western masculinity, Prof. Anderson and Mr. Alden bring the authority of eastern learning to the rancho in its hour of need. Alden restores the bells just in time to fulfill the prophecy. And when Marian discovers that one of the mission paintings conceals the map to a lost mine, it is Anderson (conveniently "an authority on mines") who certifies its profitability. In addition to the professor and the preservationist, however, there is another species of "eastern" masculinity that proves crucial to the denouement: the Chinese servant Gow Long. Gow Long is a pantomime role, and he appears with recognizable "yellow-face" props: a long pipe (presumably for opium) and a laundryman's basin. Like his cousins in comic relief, he serves as bumbling porter and clumsy dancer—he participates in the cowboy number "I'm Ridin' Down to Mexico" without ever leaving his washtub.

Ultimately all these forces conspire to bring Act 3 to its happy end. Posé orders the Indians to keep watch inside the mission church, to see whether Kraft or Ramon will fulfill their respective promises to restore the native lands. Noneeta has explained to Marian about the prophecy, and both agree that everything depends on the ringing of the newly restored bells. Hard on the heels of Ramon's announcement that all will share equally in the wealth of the mine, Marian finds that the mission is occupied by suspicious Indians who bar all entry. Nonetheless, the bells ring out seconds later, and after the requisite confusion has subsided, cowboy Billy discerns the cause: "Gow Long is your miracle man who rang the bells!" Noneeta concurs: "The gods have used Gow Long to fulfill their prophecy."

With this startling turn of events, both Indian prophecy and mission religion are definitively abandoned. The prophecy is fulfilled, but utterly demystified— fulfilled, but through the mechanics of comedy, at the hands of a Chinaman. What's more, the "miracle" of the bells does not satisfy the characters' needs. Instead it is the future development of the mine that will ensure their happiness. Ramon restores land to the Indians and marries Marian; and the Ortego sisters reaffirm their love for the Anglo students, implying a total of three Anglo-Hispanic weddings. Billy and Laura are presumably united as well, but an emphasis on cultural mixing remains as the uneducated cowpoke woos the professor's daughter. These and other examples suggest a telling contrast: while the Indian West was won by conquest, the Hispanic West was won in romantic fashion—through force of love and sanctity of (inter)marriage.

OLD CALIFORNIA: FIESTA AND RANCHO

It practically goes without saying that, after the discovery of the mine and the ringing of the mission bells, the newly expanded Ortego family holds a fiesta. A necessary feature of *Natoma,* the fiesta also played around the edges of *The*

Golden Trail (with its dancing girl Carmela and its singing bandit Murietta). The fiesta topos appears fully formed in two of Cadman's other operettas: *South in Sonora* (1932, libretto by Juanita and Charles Roos) and *Meet Arizona* (1947, George Murray Brown). *South in Sonora* is Cadman's most fully "Latin" operetta, and the action unfolds mostly at the rancho owned by Don Ricardo Gomez. The plot yields a bevy of mixed couples—always Anglo men and Hispanic women—thanks to a group of "College Boys" from Texas who behave more or less like a glee club, singing on cue a reprise of "Mexico, My Mexico," the sentimental ballad "Dreaming," and the rousing "By the Rio Grande." Though the boys are ostensibly present to study "practical mining," their real function is to provide partners for Don Ricardo's five daughters. As elsewhere, the keynotes of the fiesta are love and dance: smoldering passions, entrancing bodies, and music spiked by *habañera* rhythms and thrumming accompaniments.

The main obstacle to a five-wedding finale lies with Don Ricardo's second daughter, Catalina, who speaks but does not sing. She is ugly. What's worse, she has been to college in the States. As her sister Paquita puts it, "She is strong-minded and she don' like men! She believes in 'Women's Rights' which is something she have learned in those United States of yours!" Paquita's distress is magnified by her father's decree that none of the younger daughters may marry before Catalina does. Despite Don Ricardo's old-fashioned ways, a happy ending is engineered through the girlish mischief of the sisters, the Texas stubbornness of the College Boys, and the democratic wherewithal Catalina absorbed at school: after a local bandit is tricked into marrying Catalina, she manages his successful campaign for the Mexican presidency.

Feminism is not the only point of conflict between Mexico and its neighbor to the north. The gallantry of the Spanish men is accompanied by the threat of violence, and both the bandit and Don Ricardo place great stock in costume and the trappings of wealth. They are fooled by the disguised bride only because each places such importance on the "priceless Gomez wedding veil" that shields the impostor Catalina from discovery. The Mexican government is also portrayed as unstable. The proper president is deposed by an easily bribed bandit, and government surveillance stifles dissent. "Hush, Papa mio!," Paquita cautions. "The very walls have ears." By contrast, the College Boys' native state of Texas is aligned with Mexico only for the purposes of romance (in the love song "By the Rio Grande"). When action is required, they rally effectively under the banner of the Lone Star State ("Fear Not, for we are Texas born") and associate themselves with Kansas and the American Midwest.

Cadman's *South in Sonora* involves a familiar mix of western settings. Yet no one is concerned with cattle, there are no cowboys, and no serious interest in mining is required. The fiesta takes precedence over all. The same cannot by said for Cadman's tenth and last operetta, *Meet Arizona,* subtitled *A Dude Ranch*

Operetta. Here the Hispanic characters are mostly exotics imported for comic relief: the fiery Carlotta, the henpecked Antonio, and the weeping maidservant Maria. Carlos has a somewhat more dignified role, befitting his status as fiesta manager. But unlike *South in Sonora,* which poked fun at the incomprehensibility of English slang, *Meet Arizona* takes pains to make its Mexican characters sound as foreign as possible, including such polite footnotes as "Please pronounce it Maý-he-co." The fiesta itself is largely incidental to the plot, which offers only a loose revue-style framework within which individual characters are in turn invited to sing or dance on the slightest pretext.

With the move from "rancho" to "dude ranch" comes a change in racial and thematic hierarchies. The crucial alchemy no longer lies in the mingling of Anglo and Hispanic blood, but in the confrontation of eastern and western "types." Domineering Aunt Lavinia, grand dame of the East, has come to Arizona "to be wild and wooly." Amateur actor Tom Wilder arrives on the scene just in time to impersonate Arizona Tom, an ex-sheriff known for his tall tales. The big-hearted Corral Boss Cappy serves as a foil for the tenderfoot Bertie, whose only memorable line is "When East meets West I'll bet on Vermont." The conflicted meeting of East and West is best represented by Vermonter Lettie and her ranch-bred cousin-by-adoption, Larry, whom all manner of plot devices push toward marriage. Alongside this Anglo crowd, the Hispanic characters are tangential; in fact, "the romantic cowboy," Rennie, says as much to Emily, the dudine he fancies: "Our Mexican help live in a little world of their own," he explains, and Emily agrees: "And a rather excitable world. Oh, Rennie, I'm just going to love Arizona. Everything is so *different.*"

As Emily, Rennie, and the other characters would surely expect, ethnic and regional differences between the musical numbers are clearly marked. Lettie sings of Vermont's "Green Mountain Boys" while the chorus performs vocal "drum rolls." On either side of her song are Arizona Tom's tall-tale number, "You Can Put it Down as True," and Carlos's announcement of the next day's fiesta, replete with Hispanic markers. Act 2 opens with a musical revue staged for the benefit of the dudines: a cowboy duet ("Old Mule"); a song from Arizona Tom "sung with nasal tone, in Hill-Billy style"; an "Indian Song"; and a four-part Serenade, "Fair Flower, Lolita," sung by a "chorus of Mexicans." Only one character effectively blurs the boundaries between races and types: Tonita Sunrise, "modern, educated, and of remote Indian descent." More like Tsianina Redfeather than most of Cadman's Indian characters, she sings her "Love Song" but then vanishes from the story until the surprise announcement of her engagement to Arizona Tom.

Interestingly, the only dialogue between Tom and Tonita reveals them both to be adept at impersonation. Tom recognizes Tonita, apparently from their days on the stage. He calls on her to "remember our show in Los Angeles," and she inquires about his disguise:

> *Tom:* I'm impersonating Arizona Tom. Why the *Pocahontas* outfit?
>
> *Tonita:* I am to sing an Indian song to the guests tonight, in the costume of my *ancestors.*
>
> *Tom:* Ancestors?
>
> *Tonita:* Yes, Tom, a long way back. *Tonita* is really Indian.
>
> *Tom:* I thought it was Spanish.
>
> *Tonita: (stepping back and gracefully posing as an Indian maid, with head held high)* Tonight I shall be *Tonita Sunrise,* Indian Princess.

Tonita's performance as Indian Princess would appear to be a racial masquerade while Tom's invokes region or class, but both are driven by the desire to entertain. Tonita's performance is musical, but Tom's involves tall tales and an eccentric western dialect, for which the writers of the synopsis felt an apology might be in order: "If the grammar employed by CAPPY and ARIZONA TOM strikes one's ear as not what one would expect to hear at the best finishing schools, let us accept it as a brave attempt to impress Easterners as they feel Easterners want to be impressed concerning the 'wild and wooly' West. Let them keep their romantic illusions!"

Like so many western stories, *Meet Arizona* concerns itself with land and inheritance. In practical terms, the plot turns on a lost will. Once discovered, it deeds the ranch to Larry and Lettie on the unreasonable but easily satisfied condition that they fall in love. More figuratively, the story sets out a continuum of attachment to the West. For the locals, the landscape inspires a genuine affection inseparable from its economic potential. The operetta's eponymous anthem is, in essence, the marketing jingle of the Dude Ranch. "Most of these dudines are from back-east Vermont," cowboy Rennie announces. "Let's give them our good, old 'Meet Arizona' song, boys." The refrain extols the local tourist attractions ("colored canyons," "sunrise on the sage," etc.), and the verse is meant to entice: "Come on out and get acquainted; This old State will treat you right." The targets of this public relations campaign respond with varying degrees of seriousness, ranging from a naive embrace of exotic color (exemplified by Emily and the dudines) to a more tangible desire for change and adventure. Aunt Lavinia's cowgirl clichés are echoed by a "yipping" chorus of ranch hands, but Lettie sings a more earnest "March Song" that recounts her westward journey with triadic lines, dotted rhythms, a stomping tonic-dominant accompaniment, and a statement of intent: "I want to love your golden West."

As the operetta's romantic leads, Larry and Lettie are required to transfer their love of landscape to one another. Perhaps this is why the production's most striking tribute to the western land issues not from the mouth of a cowboy or a dudine but instead from the Mexican fiesta-impresario Carlos. He begins: "In my contree we have what you call *deep respect* for the land. We Mexicans like the *tortilla* ver' much. But where tortilla without *corn*? An' where corn without *soil*?

(widespread gesture of hand) So, I will recite to you, *"I Am the Land!"* Dropping his dialect entirely, Carlos continues:

> I am the land that takes the seed.
> And shapes it for man's every need.
> As light and rain impartial fall,
> My bounties flow to one and all.
> I care not who may till or sow,
> My largess makes the plant to grow.
> I take no sleep, I take no rest;
> I nurse all races at my breast.

The ensemble joins in, *maestoso,* taking an unlikely patriotic cue from the Mexican entertainer. Cowboys and city slickers, dudes and dudines, servants and tourists are united in this hymn to a Mother Earth, whose generosity turns humankind into one fertile family, cross-pollinated by ethnic and cultural heterogeneity.

More than most of Cadman's operettas, *Meet Arizona* plays on the self-conscious performance of racial and regional identity: Aunt Lavinia wants the chance to play cowgirl; the operetta's villain turns out to be an escaped felon disguising himself as a ranch manager; Tom Wilder, already an actor by trade, has no trouble adopting the persona of a Wild West sheriff; and Tonita Sunrise knows just how to assume the posture of an "Indian Princess," no matter what her actual background might be. Even Lettie and Larry seem to understand that certain behavior is expected of them as representatives of their respective regions. This performance-of-performance is hardly unusual in the realm of operetta or, for that matter, in opera. For all their ubiquity, however, these performative moments are not merely piquant plot devices. There is, as always, the pleasantly reflexive irony of watching a fictional audience see what we can also see. But in plots so charged with identity politics, much more is at stake.

Western dramas by Cadman and others invite us to consider a relatively recent history of national expansion, political conquest, and economic development by watching the interaction of distinct character types. Sometimes the invitation is explicit, as when the spirit of Columbia descends to bless the East-West union of Charlie and Barbarita in *The Golden Trail.* More often it is implicit, as when Gow Long effects the happy ending in *Bells of Capistrano,* tacitly asserting a vision of the West Coast as the eastern edge of the Pacific Rim. As each production disrupts or reinforces our assumptions about behavior appropriate to "the Spaniard" and "the Mexican," the "medicine man" and the "educated Indian," the "city slicker" and the "ranch hand," it also alters our understanding of western history. When can love cross ethnic or class lines? What lies in store for characters who transgress regional or cultural boundaries? Who inherits the land and its riches? Such questions have been complicated by the pervasive idea that western land held the power to shape a uniquely "American" identity through a kind of instant evolution. Instead of arising from climatic or demographic factors working slowly over generations, the "typical American" was to emerge in a matter of years thanks to the accelerating influence of the frontier. The catalyst for this rapid reaction was encounter.

HOLLYWOOD AND THE "NATIVE" COMPOSER

If the ironic tone of *Meet Arizona* seems at odds with Cadman's earlier operettas, we must remember that approximately twenty years had elapsed between the "Dude Ranch Comedy" and Cadman's first successful operetta, *Lelawala*. Much had happened in his life and even more had happened in his sometime hometown, Hollywood, California. Cadman's last two decades brought local prestige and national frustration. Lee Shippey of the *Los Angeles Times* saw in Cadman's output of the 1920s "a number of operettas which are extremely popular in high schools—so popular that it would be hard to estimate his influence on the musical taste of the rising generation."[28] But few East Coast critics would have agreed, and Cadman himself may have blushed at this acclaim for works written to order. The national recognition Cadman received was almost exclusively confined to his Indianist works. Like Farwell, he saw his reputation tied to music that he now considered passé. In California, Cadman's popularity was such that the Pacific International Exposition at San Diego chose to celebrate "Cadman Day" on 4 September 1935, but even here, his erstwhile Indianism held sway. The festivities were held at the Exposition's "Indian Village," and newspaper photographers delighted in the ceremony by which Cadman was made an honorary Indian chief. In 1934 and again thereafter, Cadman spent part of his summer at the MacDowell Colony, but he found the experience somewhat daunting. He wrote to Eberhart in 1937: "These guys here . . . are steeped in TRAINING (even the kids are)."[29]

Meanwhile, in and around Hollywood, two seismic changes had altered the musical landscape during the years leading up to World War II: the explosion of the film industry and the arrival of émigré composers fleeing fascism. By 1933, the dual impact of the Depression and the synchronized soundtrack decimated the area orchestras and concentrated economic opportunities in the hands of movie studios. Over the next ten years, greater Los Angeles became home to dozens of transplanted European composers, many of whom brought in their wake modernist tendencies far bolder than anything Cadman or the Music Club circuit would ever embrace. Cadman responded to each of these changes.

Cadman's earliest evocations of California reflected an emphasis on the Christian community characteristic of the Hollywood Bowl. Shortly after his arrival, he wrote "God Smiled Upon the Desert (A California Poppy Song)" to a text by Elizabeth Gordon (1917). Though cataloged with his secular songs, a footnote reminds us that it "may be used effectively as a Sacred Solo," and its musical idiom indeed aims for the ecstatic with gently syncopated, harplike rolled chords. Cadman dedicated the third movement of his piano suite *From Hollywood* to his mother and their shared Hollywood bungalow at "Sycamore Nook," with its "tall Tapers of Yucca,—those 'Candles of the Lord.'" The religious tone here is merely a foretaste of the final movement, "Easter Dawn in Hollywood Bowl," which spreads its bell-tolling chords over three staves and more than five octaves to evoke "One gigantic Group Soul! . . . Assembled there in the eternal unquenchable Spirit of Democracy,—to celebrate the Symbol of Eternal Life,—an annual homage to the White Christ."[30]

While the silver screen had made Hollywood a household word even in the 1920s, many residents, including Cadman, believed that natural beauty and civic-religious fervor were the community's real claims to fame. In fact, Cadman's sentiments are echoed quite precisely in the rhetoric of a peculiar little book called *Hollywood as a World Center,* by Perley Poore Sheehan. Published by the Hollywood Citizen Press only a year after Cadman's suite *From Hollywood,* Sheehan's monograph deals in an occult geography that places Hollywood at a worldwide crossroads comparable to ancient Byzantium: "It likewise was a place of hills, of fertile seas, blue skies. Its geographical position as to Africa and Europe was like that of Los Angeles as to the two Americas. Also *it faced Asia*" [emphasis in the original].[31] Though he was primarily a screenwriter and secondarily a novelist, Sheehan here acted as chamber of commerce booster, reserving his highest praise for the community music movement and the Hollywood Bowl, which seemed to make "the ancient wish" of the Oberammergau Passion Play "come unbelievably true." Still more extravagantly, he claimed that the communal feeling sustaining the Bowl sprang from "a new race, an evolving religion, the first stirring of a civilization that will mean not only the coming of a Golden Age like that of Ancient Greece but a second and universal Advent."[32]

In addition to quoting Dane Rudhyar at considerable length, Sheehan devoted six pages to Ferdinand Earle's photodrama on the Rubaiyat of Omar Khayyam, for which Cadman had written incidental music. He discussed the weekly "sings" of the Hollywood Community Chorus, and although he does not mention Farwell by name, Farwell nonetheless returned the compliment in the second installment of his three-part series, "The Riddle of the Southwest," written for the *Los Angeles Times.* Here he built on the conceit that "a New York friend" who is visiting the Southland has perceived a special racial potential in the region's populace:

> They are from every State in the Union but more especially from the Middle West and Western States . . . all pure American stock; people who, pushed by the intense European invasion, migrated beyond the Alleghenies and Appalachians, retaining all the old-time virtues of the race, but shedding many of the old-time narrownesses and intolerances, then migrated into the regions beyond the "Father of

Waters" and the "Big Muddy," and finally across the Sierras and the Rockies to the Pacific Slope, where, as Perley Poore Sheehan so well puts it "the Aryan race is making its last stand."[33]

Sheehan took time to praise Hollywood's multiethnicity, calling the movie studio an "intimately cosmopolitan place." But Farwell was right about Sheehan's preoccupation with the ever-westward-moving Aryans. The first full page of his text proclaims the rise of Hollywood to be "the culmination of ages of preparatory struggle, physical, mental, and spiritual. In brief, we are witnessing the last great migration of the Ayran race. This is the end of the trail."[34]

Farwell left California in 1927 for his new job at Michigan State University, but Cadman remained in the area long enough to see Hollywood's putative position as the Aryan "last stand" seriously imperiled not just by a general increase in nonwhite population, but more specifically by the arrival of composers like George Gershwin and Arnold Schoenberg. The writing was starting to appear on the wall even in Sheehan's era; he spoke of a "degraded Orientalism that has oozed into [films] from above," thanks to the "so-called leaders of the industry," whom he compares to "war-profiteers." Though not explicitly anti-Semitic, Sheehan's rhetoric evokes familiar stereotypes about the "oriental" Jew. It also carries a strong strain of racial determinism that would be intensified in Los Angeles during the 1930s. As Catherine Parsons Smith has observed, "The nativism that had been one aspect of the old Progressive movement . . . now, as the émigrés from Hitler gathered in Los Angeles, seemed uglier than ever."[35]

One example of musical xenophobia in Depression-era California can be seen in the Society of Native American Composers. In the late 1930s, Cadman, Mary Carr Moore, and composer-pianist Homer Grunn convened to discuss the best means of bringing American music to the attention of "conductors, most of whom are foreigners." Building on their earlier efforts under the auspices of the Cadman Creative Club, they organized the California Society of Composers (CSC) and produced two festivals that Smith identifies as among the first in Los Angeles to be devoted to American music.[36] The CSC was musically conservative, as were its founders, and Smith astutely observes that their conservative-modernist stylistic spectrum was readily mapped onto a native-alien axis. Out of fear that "their own interests would be swamped in a sea of international-oriented ultra-modernism," they disbanded the CSC and reorganized with an explicit requirement that members be "native born."[37] They sought support from a roster including Amy Beach, Howard Hanson, Carl Ruggles, and Charles Ives, who lent the society his support until rumors began to circulate that the society was "pro-fascist" and he pointedly withdrew.[38] The society reached its greatest prominence when it sponsored the entire 1940–41 season of the Los Angeles Federal Music Project Orchestra, including a performance of Cadman's new "Pennsylvania"

Symphony. Californians were impressed, but a reviewer for *Modern Music* in New York grumbled that the Society of Native American Composers' programming so far had been "very depressing, the usual program featuring items like the *Symphony* by Charles Wakefield Cadman about which the less said the better."[39]

Cadman felt these conflicts deeply. He was no modernist, but he was also no fascist. He was appalled by the "repugnant" policies of Nazi Germany, and he resigned very publicly from the American Music Committee of the 1936 Olympics—the only member to do so.[40] But Cadman did feel a certain need to make a stand against stylistic invasions, especially when the financial stakes were high.

In 1929, Cadman was on the verge of "breaking into" the movies, having received a six-month thirteen-thousand-dollar contract from the Fox Film Corporation. He quickly became disillusioned by the studio's lack of interest in producing a film version of *Shanewis,*[41] but while under contract, he found himself engaged in a debate that the *Los Angeles Examiner* covered with military glee: "The war lords in the imbroglio are Charles Wakefield Cadman, famous composer with the William Fox Studios, and Dimitri Tiomkin, pianist-composer for the Metro-Goldwyn-Mayer organization. Cadman advocates the classics and Tiomkin jazz, and war, therefore, is brewing." Cadman's view was paraphrased thus: "The motion picture industry would gain neither dignity or respect from the encouragement of jazz . . . a shallow and soulless mode of musical expression." Surprised by the fierce reactions that ensued, he tried to backpedal, but he soon found himself in hot water again, this time after attacking movie studios who chose their theme songs for commercial, not dramatic reasons. The results, he claimed were "emasculated" soundtracks, "'spotted' with cheap and vulgar songs."[42]

For Cadman, the movies were both an impetus to composition and a threat. He moved from Hollywood to La Mesa (near San Diego) in 1929, citing his disillusionment with a city that was "selling solitude at so much per front foot."[43] Although the *Hollywood Citizen* continued to regard him as a local boy, Hollywood no longer represented for Cadman the site of grassroots communion. Instead, in his 1938 operetta *Hollywood Extra,* we find that a fully operational studio system has lured the meek but talented Irene away from her home town, Hopetown, Maine. From the moment she arrives, Irene is thwarted by the conniving Rita Lupa, whose director-husband consigns Irene to the "extras" instead of making her a star in the Goldenrod Motion Picture Company's new film about the abducted daughter of an Algerian sheik. Fortunately, Irene's countrified guardian, "Uncle" Abner, arrives to set things straight. Charmed by his rural ways, the studio head, Isaac Goldenrod, arranges a new tryout for Irene and promises to shoot a picture called *Uncle Abner* on site in Hopetown complete with quilting bees and baked bean suppers. Hollywood lucre is redistributed to Hopetown; and the "oriental" atmosphere of the Algerian picture is replaced by something more homespun and wholesome.

Both *Meet Arizona* and *Hollywood Extra* play on themes of regional distinction, bifurcating the United States on an East-West axis for comic effect: the tenderfoot learns to love the desert, the Hollywood movie mogul waxes nostalgic for a New England he has never known. But it should be noted that the two works suggest quite different things about where the "real" or "native" American spirit may be found. At the Arizona dude ranch, it seems a foregone conclusion that the Vermonter Lettie will drop her eastern sophistication and become a true cowgirl, while in Hollywood it seems as if the pendulum has swung a bit too far—one must look back toward the Eastern Seaboard to rediscover America.

Given this regional conundrum, and given his conflicted views about Broadway, one wonders what Cadman would have made of George Gershwin's *Girl Crazy* (1930, filmed in 1932 and 1943)—a far better known "dude ranch comedy" than his own *Meet Arizona* would ever be. Cadman admired Gershwin. Yet it must have been startling to Cadman and to many other self-styled westerners to see cowboys doing crossword puzzles and dudines dancing to "I Got Rhythm." Like *Meet Arizona*, *Girl Crazy* is an East-meets-West love story, though this time it is New York playboy Danny Churchill who ventures west, not to find love or adventure, but rather to pacify his father, who is disgusted by his philandering. Of course Danny finds and falls for the only girl in Custerville, the postmistress, Molly Gray, and while she might be credited with his conversion to monogamy, there is no sense in which Danny becomes a "westerner." On the contrary, he manages almost single-handedly to transform dusty Custerville into an upscale dude ranch qua nightclub, complete with dancing girls and a chorus line. Like Danny, Gershwin himself was preparing to move west to California as he finished the show. Fortunately for both of them, the institutions of the eastern metropolis proved easy to transplant; as Robert Kimball and Alfred Simon put it, "*Girl Crazy* was about as Western as West End Avenue." In Howard Pollack's words, Gershwin "made the West his own."[44]

Even before Custerville gains its chorus line, matters of local color in *Girl Crazy* are treated with at least a pinch of salt. Charles Schwartz called it a "rib-tickling satire on the Old West," noting that its signature number, "Bidin' My Time," was "drawlingly sung by a group called The Foursome, as four lazy, tired cowboys. . . . But, lethargic or not, they doffed their hats with reverence whenever 'West,' the word sacred to all self-respecting cowboys' hearts, was spoken."[45] In the Broadway show, the curtain rises on a "lonesome cowboy" who sings about taking his "gal" back to the "Rancho X Y Z" and then disappears, never to be heard from again. This number was omitted or obscured in the film versions, leaving the barbershop "Foursome" as the main representatives of cowboy culture. Where Cadman would have used folklore (or at least fakelore), the brothers Gershwin refer to the cowboy crooners of stage and radio.

Although it was composed and adapted for the silver screen fifteen years before Cadman finished *Meet Arizona, Girl Crazy* has a far more "modern" sound. Its idiom can still be heard on Broadway, and at least two of its tunes survive today as jazz standards: the ballad "Embraceable You" (a Charlie Parker favorite) and above all "I Got Rhythm," whose famous reincarnations defy cataloging here.[46] The show is famous not for its local color and certainly not for its plot (which even the authors considered subpar), but for its position at a nexus of jazz, Broadway, and Hollywood: it helped launch Ethel Merman's career, solidified Robert Russell Bennett's credentials as a "jazzy" orchestrator, and sported a pit orchestra manned by Benny Goodman, Glenn Miller, and Gene Krupa. *Girl Crazy*'s "swing" is not an especially western swing, yet it is so thoroughly woven into the fabric of the show that—even though the cast troops down to Mexico for a spell and despite a reference to Helen Hunt Jackson's *Ramona* in the number that returns them safely to Custerville—there is nary a *habañera* rhythm to be heard.

It should come as no great shock that the Big Apple and the California orange grove bore such different fruit. Despite their contrasts, however, comparing Gershwin and Cadman also reveals continuities in the dramatization of the West. *Girl Crazy, Meet Arizona,* and indeed all of Cadman's western operettas take racial and regional difference as axiomatic. There is no more important factor in their various plots. Yet these works also explore the ways in which different identities can be "performed," adopted, or masked as a means of escape, intrigue, romance, or sheer fun. *Girl Crazy* makes the most of masquerade. Danny, of course, plays cowboy; at one point he also plays cowgirl. The most elaborate costume changes are reserved for Gieber Goldfarb, the New York taxi driver who drives Danny out to the ranch and then stays on as sheriff. Gieber was played by the famous Jewish vaudevillian Willie Howard, who was meant to be recognized. He disguises himself as an illiterate Indian, is mistaken for a certain "college educated Indian," and, after failing to communicate with that educated Indian in any other way, finds that they can both speak Yiddish![47] Tellingly, when Gieber first encounters the Custerville cowboys, he assumes that they are Hollywood actors, hired for a movie western.

Although not as radically as the Gershwin brothers, Cadman also thematizes performance and impersonation, most obviously in *Meet Arizona,* but in other productions as well. Consider the veiled Spanish beauties of *South in Sonora,* the square dancing emigrants of *The Golden Trail,* any number of Mexican bandits disguised as upstanding citizens, and even Gow Long with his washtub pantomime. Recall *Shanewis,* with its singer-heroine moving freely between the white parlor stage and the Indian pow wow. As Tonita, Shanewis, and Tsianina herself make plain, once we acknowledge that regional and racial identities can be performed instead of inherited, we must entertain some productive confusion over what it means to be "native."

Cadman began and ended his career best known for his understanding of Native Americans and "native" America, respectively. His work reflects the entire spectrum of early twentieth-century tensions about whether the true West was to be found in indigenous peoples, trail-blazing pioneers, or modern western cities, like Hollywood. That Cadman was not immune to the appeal of Farwell's world historical West is clear enough from his *Pageant of Colorado* and his Hollywood Bowl experiences. Yet he located most of his western works in down-to-earth places where recognizable characters could interact. He placed these characters on frontiers, borderlands where encounter is inevitable and claims to "native" status can always be contested. All who take the western stage are strangers in these parts.

PART THREE

American Pastorals

Presently we saw a curious thing: There were no clouds, the sun was going down in a limpid gold-washed sky. Just as the lower edge of the red disc rested on the high fields against the horizon, a great black figure suddenly appeared on the face of the sun. We sprang to our feet, straining our eyes toward it. In a moment we realized what it was. On some upland farm, a plough had been left standing in the field. The sun was sinking just behind it. Magnified across the distance by the horizontal light, it stood out against the sun, was exactly contained within the circle of the disc; the handles, the tongue, the share—black against the molten red. There it was, heroic in size, a picture writing on the sun. Even while we whispered about it, our vision disappeared; the ball dropped and dropped until the red tip went beneath the earth. The fields below us were dark, the sky had sunk back to its own littleness somewhere on the prairie.

—WILLA CATHER, *MY ÁNTONIA*

5

West of Eden

PRAIRIE IDYLLS

Given Cadman's geographic imagination and his substantial catalog of operas and operettas, it is striking that none involves a farmer, a homestead, or a family of settlers. The emigrant Hurds in *The Golden Trail* intend to put down roots once their journey is done, but when we meet them they are still traversing land that is pointedly not their own. The Ortego family of *The Bells of Capistrano* rely on their land for cattle grazing, but they do not till the soil. The impassioned recitation "I Am the Land" by the Mexican fiesta maker Carlos rouses a certain agricultural reverence among the cast of *Meet Arizona*, yet this feeling is short-lived and foreign to the everyday workings of the dude ranch. The figure of a "thresher" does make a brief appearance in one of Cadman's pedagogical piano sets, but it is included as the "characteristic" component of the suite; the farmer is observed rather than personified, as if he were a curious feature of the landscape itself.[1]

Cadman did write a handful of "prairie pieces," but these generally identified the Great Plains with the Indian past, not with an agricultural present.[2] Only in 1939–40 did he approach a recognizably "pioneer" theme, and this came by way of his "Pennsylvania" Symphony, which had roots in Cadman and Eberhart's discarded plans for an opera about the steel industry. After an Indianist first movement titled "Forest Primeval," and a climax depicting the confluence of the Ohio, Allegheny, and Monongahela Rivers, the second movement, "Pioneer Spirit," featured "homespun Americanism," "the building up of the Valleys and the HINT . . . of industry and the coming of great industry, but through [all] a wholesome homelife and the joy of living, maybe a bit of the old time quadrilles and dance tunes."[3]

When the "spirit" of the second movement became rather lighter than Cadman had anticipated—involving barrel organ sounds and reminiscences from his own childhood—the "pioneer" idea infiltrated the first movement instead. Cadman wrote to Eberhart that he wanted "at least a suggestion of SOMEBODY human living in all that 'sylvania' wilderness." Privately, Cadman described his desire to reflect "those old settlers who were full of religious feeling . . . Quakers, Scotch Presbyterians, fanatical but practical Methodists like MY ancestors."[4] In the more public forum of the Chicago Symphony Orchestra program notes, one can see an eight-bar ersatz hymn labeled the "pioneer theme" and can read (in words attributed to the composer) of Cadman's own Anglo-Saxon lineage.[5] The symphony garnered a certain amount of national attention at its Los Angeles premiere; NBC deemed it worthy of coast-to-coast broadcast, and after at least six more Californian performances, the work was heard throughout the Midwest and apparently also in Santiago, Chile.[6] Yet the *Modern Music* critics were unimpressed, and Eugene Ormandy never followed up on his interest in bringing the work to Philadelphia. Cadman complained: "I have been told FIVE times so far by conductors that doing a symphony 'laid' in one state of the U.S. has NOT made for ready acceptance."[7]

Despite its lack of East Coast success, Cadman's "Pennsylvania" Symphony marks some telling changes in American composers' understanding of pioneer and pastoral imagery that began in the late 1920s and lasted through the Great Depression and after. While Cadman's earlier prairie pieces were landscape paintings of bygone days, in the symphony, he touched on many of the themes that I will treat in the pages to come: the intertwining of industry and Anglo-Saxon pioneering, the religious connotations of the pastoral, and a significant confusion about the extent to which this particular "pioneer" experience could represent a broader "American" experience.

Many Americans had long felt a need to recoup the idea of progress without recourse to the factory, or at least with a clearer sense that "progress" might have its downside. Without disregarding the late nineteenth-century "antimodernism" outlined by the historian H. T. Jackson Lears, I argue that these ideas arose with special force for the generation after Cadman, in part because of the widespread conviction that the Depression had proved the bankruptcy of industrial capitalism, and in part because the machinery of agribusiness that enabled farming in the Far West also threatened deeply entrenched American ideals about the family farm. In the end, the real dangers of the prairie came not from the "lurking Indians" and buffalo ghosts of campfire tales, but from the very present forces of weather, technology, and the real estate market.[8]

All the works treated in part 3 of this volume can be considered pastorals in the broad sense outlined by the cultural historian Leo Marx: their "controlling theme is a variant of the conflict between art and nature—nature being represented by an idealized image of landscape."[9] Yet each piece also disrupts its landscape painting by placing the figure of the pioneer in its foreground or background. Cadman's early pioneer figures passed quickly over the short-grass prairies in order to reach the golden treasures of the Far West. The pioneer figures of this chapter and the two that follow, however, are intent on putting down roots in a new "Garden of the World." They are neither tourists nor travelers, but settlers, and the residue of their pioneering progress fertilizes the American pastoral landscape with regional and political significance.

No piece is "western" merely by virtue of its exploration of the relationship between man and nature. American pastorals may be simply rural or grounded only in fantasy. In this chapter, I will explore the pastoral soundtracks of two distinctly midwestern works: one by Leo Sowerby and one by Lukas Foss, both inspired by Carl Sandburg's poem "The Prairie." Like Virgil Thomson's soundtrack for The Plow That Broke the Plains, each departs from Arcadian pastorals by making conflict a central theme. And taken together, they can be seen to chronicle the impact of technological "progress" on western land that was, despite all previous mythmaking, not very well suited to the family farm. The tensions that shatter the operatic households of Aaron Copland's The Tender Land, Douglas Moore's Giants in the Earth, and Ernst Bacon's Tree on the Plains suggest that even a healthy crop of folk song cannot sustain domestic harmony in the face of personal and national maturation. No matter how pastoral, these prairie landscapes were not idyllic and never timeless. In this chapter and the two that follow we will see their fruits discovered, cultivated, threatened, and remembered.

THE MACHINE IN THE GARDEN

Although the examples in this chapter date from the twentieth century, the ideals they manipulate were inherited from centuries past. Even before presiding over the Louisiana Purchase, Thomas Jefferson was the great architect of agrarian America—providing a social blueprint for the new nation: a republic of family farms stretching gradually westward and thereby escaping the evils of the dehumanizing factory and the overcivilized salon. In his classic study The Machine in the Garden (1964), Leo Marx observes that, beginning in the late eighteenth century, "the cardinal image of American aspirations was a rural landscape, a well-ordered green garden magnified to continental size. Although it probably shows a farmhouse or a neat white village, the scene is usually dominated by natural objects: in the foreground a pasture, a twisting brook with cattle grazing nearby, then a clump of elms on a rise in the middle distance and beyond that, way off on the western horizon, a line of dark hills. This is the countryside of the old Republic, a chaste, uncomplicated land of rural virtue."[10] As geopolitical landscape painting, this arrangement was nothing new, and Marx takes pains to uncover its Old World roots: first in the bucolic atmosphere of Virgil's eclogues, and second in the English pastoral tradition that peopled the early modern imagination with whole hosts of shepherds and shepherdesses.

Linking these pastoral images is their position between the city and the wilderness—what Marx calls the "middle landscape," neither savage nor civilized. Citing the French critic-cartographer-farmer J. Hector St. John de Crèvecoeur, he notes that the American farmer's demesne is bounded by Europe's "oppressive social order" and "the dark forest frontier." Jefferson, too, saw the American nation poised between an Old World to the east and an undiscovered country to the west, meaning that, in America, the pastoral was not just a "symbolic setting" but "a real place located somewhere between *l'ancien régime* and the western tribes. Moreover, it is a landscape with figures, or at least one figure: the independent, rational, democratic husbandman. . . . He is the good shepherd of the old pastoral dressed in American homespun."[11] With a new costume, a more serious association with agriculture, and a little less emphasis on livestock, Jefferson's yeoman farmer can occupy the same middle ground as Virgil's shepherd.

However appropriate this particular topos was for the eighteenth century, the nineteenth century exerted several pressures on America's pastoral imaginary. There had always been a hint of dissonance between the Old World and New World types. Marx says as much in a telling footnote that contrasts the "the typical American hero" and the pastoral shepherd. The shepherd is satisfied with a "sedentary life"; he has little interest in exploration, hunting, or other such strenuous pursuits. By contrast, Marx notes, "our heroes do confront the true wild, and they often become hunters."[12] The proximity of wilderness and the remoteness of the market economy required a new strength, self-sufficiency, and capacity for action. Over the course of the nineteenth century, the wilderness would be beaten back and the market would extend its reach westward with the railroads, yet the American plainsman would never revert to the Old World shepherd's life of ease. Instead, the image of the pastoral hero, the central figure of America's middle landscape, would be permanently grafted onto the mythology of the pioneer.

The overlaying of these two figures (the shepherd and the pioneer) brought several interrelated changes in mythological apparatus. First and most important, it imbued the pastoral landscape with a sense of direction—literally westward, or metaphorically "upward" to a better future. In both life and literature, as Henry Nash Smith has shown, westward migration often meant a move from indentured servitude to independence. With the so-called closing of the frontier in the 1890s and the ever-quieter beckoning of "free land," relocation began to seem like an exhausted alternative. Yet the idea of pioneering progress survived because it could denote equally the acquisition of greater tracts of land, the conquest of new markets, or the bringing of formerly barren land under the control of new agricultural technology: dry farming, irrigation, and the plow. Regionally speaking, the imagery of the agrarian West, the fabled "Garden of the World," drew strength from comparisons with plantation life in the antebellum South. Smith explains: "The fiction dealing with the plantation emphasizes the beauty of harmonious social relations in an orderly feudal society. . . . Such symbols could not be adapted to the expression of a society like that of the West . . . where rapidity of change, crudity, bustle, heterogeneity were fundamental traits."[13]

As the pastoral landscape was imbued with a sense of westward or future-oriented direction, the pioneer became a warrior. Having claimed a homestead, he still had to fend off western foes (Indian attackers or encroaching wilderness), but he did so from a new position of responsibility: as a landowner and, more often than not, as a family man. Ownership brought with it an appealing rhetoric of man and nature in symbiotic relationship. Yet the responsibility of family brought with it an even greater harvest of metaphorical riches. As Smith observed, "The master symbol of the garden embraced a cluster of metaphors expressing fecundity, growth, increase, and blissful labor in the earth, all centering about the heroic figure of the idealized frontier farmer armed with that supreme agrarian weapon, the plow."[14] It requires only a delicate interpretive leap to move from the fertility of the fields to the growth and prosperity of the family. In literature and myth, America's pastoral heroes were not free-loving nymphs and swains, but the nuclear families memorialized by Willa Cather, Ole Rölvaag, and Laura Ingalls Wilder. In this respect, the stereotypical pioneer retained the connotations of the contented shepherd and yeoman farmer, but expanded them to wield greater historical force: he became a shepherd not just of livestock but also of future generations; he sowed the seeds not just for wheat or corn but for civilization itself.

QUIET ON THE WESTERN FRONT

No single factor can be pinpointed as catalyst for the transformation of Cadman's peaceful prairie into a place of greater tension and struggle. Nonetheless, World War I seems to have played a decisive role. In its tumultuous wake, the Great Plains became a site of geopolitical significance. Willa Cather takes note of this in *My Ántonia* when her narrator explains that the neighboring cornfields "would enlarge and multiply until they would be . . . the world's cornfields; that their yield would be one of the great economic facts, like the wheat crop of Russia, which underlie all the activities of men, in peace or war."[15] Government propaganda proclaimed more succinctly: "Wheat will win the war!" Before 1914, there was nothing particularly "American" about farming; after 1917, the farmer was recognized as a heroic American type, with tools and virtues that set him apart from those who cultivated the soil of other nations.

Cadman was too old to serve in World War I, and his ill health would in any case have disqualified him from active duty. Farwell, for his part, brought his expertise on communal singing to the Army Officers Training Camp and led patriotic song fests in New York and California. But for those younger men who did their marching in France and Flanders, fields of corn and wheat would never sound the same. One such musician-soldier was Leo Sowerby, and his tone poem *The Prairie* will serve to exemplify both the features of an older tradition of musical landscape painting and a prairie newly figured as a site of struggle.

Sowerby was born in Grand Rapids, Michigan, and educated in Chicago, where he thrived as an organist and became perhaps the best-known composer of the Midwest, championed by conductor Frederick Stock.[16] He volunteered for the army, and his musicianship moved him quickly up the ranks and out of the stables at Camp Grant, where he had been assigned to curry the mules. In the words of his colleague Burnet Tuthill, Sowerby "was shipped off to France in the summer of 1918 as bandmaster and second lieutenant."[17] After he was mustered out in February 1919, he rejoined Chicago's musical life without missing a beat. Yet he apparently recalled the army often and with pleasure, stating that "the experience influenced his whole life, and that through it he learned to live with people."[18]

Like many composers of his generation, Sowerby was drawn to France even before the war. In June 1914, after one Boston reviewer noted the influence of Debussy on his harmonic language, Sowerby himself affirmed his Francophile leanings by declaring d'Indy "the greatest living composer." After the war, critic W. L. Hubbard thundered a prediction that "America Will Lose Its Greatest Composer If Sowerby Goes Abroad," stating: "To study with Vincent d'Indy or any other teacher over there would be to put a veneer of French manners and methods upon him which would ruin him."[19] As it happened, Sowerby did return to Europe—but not to Paris. In 1921, he became the first recipient of the new Rome Prize of the American Academy; the following year, he was joined by Howard Hanson, whose friendly influence dovetailed with that of Frederick Delius and Percy Grainger to instill in Sowerby a love of England so strong that he was known to some as "the Handel of Lake Michigan."[20]

Before traveling to Rome, Sowerby had penned several works featuring Anglo folk music, but the first work he wrote in Rome, *From the Northland*, was inspired by his 1919 visit to the Great Lakes. As its title suggests, there are hints of Hiawatha about the score. Without borrowing Indian song, the first movement, "Forest Voices," invokes the magical atmosphere of Indianist forests, and the final movement echoes Longfellow directly in its title, "The Shining Big Sea-Water." Particularly in "The Lonely Fiddle-Maker," Sowerby's stance is nostalgic: "It speaks as through a mist, of the long ago, when he fiddled and fiddled as the simple country folk danced the reel at time of harvest."[21]

Immediately upon his return to the States, Sowerby was commissioned by Paul Whiteman to compose two works of more modern Americana: an overture called "Synconata" and a "jazz symphony" named "Monotony." Inspired by Sinclair Lewis's novel *Babbitt,* the latter score reflects Sowerby's opinion that "jazz is a truly

American product . . . [that] has certainly taken hold of the people, and therefore deserves a goodly amount of respect."[22] Sowerby's argument here is well aligned with that of poet and fellow-Chicagoan Carl Sandburg, for whom Sowerby provided more than twenty harmonizations featured in the *American Songbag* (1927).[23]

Sandburg was especially fond of Sowerby's Cello Concerto built on the "Irish Washerwoman," and he used it as the jumping off point for a remarkable paragraph in his *Songbag* Introduction:

> [Sowerby] took a favorite folk piece of American country fiddlers, a famous tune of the pioneers, and made an interesting experiment and a daring adventure with it. He was a bandmaster during the World War. Then later he is found doing a happy-go-lucky arrangement for Paul Whiteman's orchestra; it may be an exploit in "jazz" or possibly a construction in "the new music." . . . He is as ready for pioneering and for originality as the new century of which he is a part. One other definite thing is that he does not prize seclusion to the point where he is out of touch with the People. Not "the peepul" of the politicians, nor the customers of Tin Pan Alley, but rather The Folks.[24]

With a deft touch, Sandburg acknowledges Sowerby's attraction to an array of Americana types, while still distancing him from the cheap eclecticism of the politico-commercial creatures of Washington and New York.

THE MIDDLE LANDSCAPE

Just as Sandburg was putting the finishing touches on the *American Songbag,* Sowerby was drafting *Prairie,* an orchestral tone poem based on an excerpt from the poet's *Cornhuskers* collection. The *Prairie* preface reads: "Have you ever seen a red sunset drip over one of my cornfields, the shore of night stars, the wave lines of dawn up a wheat valley? / Have you heard my threshing crews yelling in the chaff of a strawpile and the running wheat of the wagonboards, my corn-huskers, my harvest hands hauling crops, singing dreams of women, worlds, horizons?" Sandburg hallows the middle landscape of corn and wheat, insistent that natural abundance can be well managed by tools of human invention, and both sides of Sandburg's pastoral economy—man and nature, the artificial and the organic—find expression in Sowerby's tone poem. Following critic Burnet Tuthill, many have classified the composer's melodies into two rough types: "tunes" that have "a rhythmic verve and snap"; and longer-breathed melodies that are "wandering, perhaps even meandering."[25] In *Prairie,* however, there is a purposeful ambiguity about which melodic type should be associated with Nature and which reflects the mind of Man.

Nature would seem to have the upper hand in the tone poem's persistently nondirectional motives. The opening, "somber and slow," crawls and wavers,

EXAMPLE 20. Sowerby, *Prairie*, mm. 35–47 (Boston: C.C. Birchard & Co., 1931)

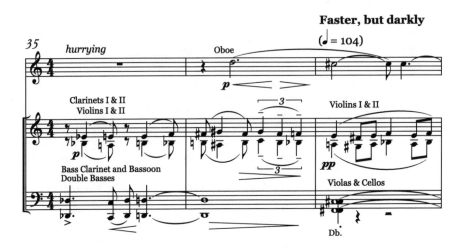

usually by half steps. Loosely contrapuntal on the page, the passage nonetheless has the Debussyan sheen of parallel voice-leading until the syncopated timpani enter to offer some metric undergirding. By measure 31, the brass have acquired an unmistakably military tone, scored in open fourths and fifths and bolstered by clangorous percussion. This is in turn quashed by the gently circling chromaticism that starkly reasserts itself at bar 37, where the strings initiate a near ostinato composed of twenty-two consecutive half steps constrained within the compass of the minor third between D♯ and F♯ (example 20). Floating above this serpentine material is an oboe solo, *Prairie*'s first candidate for a traditionally

EXAMPLE 20 *(continued)*

pastoral tune. Though akin to the reedy shepherd's pipe in tone color, this melody is infected by the coiled-up chromaticism of the underlying ostinato and a syncopation that seems more ruminative than folklike, denatured, or renatured, by the circling fragments underneath.

This passage is typical of the pastoral, not just in its woodwind timbres but also in its playing around the edges of ostinato procedures that, to the dismay of Daniel Gregory Mason, were pervasive in Sowerby's work. Mason critiqued Sowerby's "glib diffuseness, which ends by turning all of his streams of thought (often sparkling fresh at their source) into stagnant fens wherein all landmarks disappear."[26] *Prairie* does suffer from an absence of distinguishing features or, rather, from the fact that figuration tends to accumulate through repetition and to disappear unceremoniously when its service is complete. The circling half steps of example 20 have their say in measures 37–53, but their oppressive presence here does not ensure that they will appear again later. Instead, Sowerby has other repeated patterns in store, including a variety of closely related figures that begin winding their way through the texture at measure 86 (example 21). More prominent still is the ostinato work that begins in bar 123, where a descending tetrachord creeps through the strings and celesta in a manner worthy of Sibelius while solo English horn spirals above and a bass pedal tone sounds the fundamental pitch below or moves in slowly grinding counterpoint with the upper strings (bars 123–35, 138–45, 299–312).

In the austere outer sections of *Prairie*, only a few passages stand out to relieve the incessant circling and, perhaps unsurprisingly, the most important of these involves an echo. Together with the ostinato or drone accompaniment, the melodic echo is one of the best-established hallmarks of the pastoral topic. As Leo Marx observes: "In the pastoral economy nature supplies most of the herdsman's needs and, even better, nature does virtually all of the work. A similar accommodation with the idealized landscape is the basis for the herdsman's less tangible satisfactions: the woods 'echo back' the notes of his pipe. It is as if the consciousness of the musician shared a principle of order with the landscape and, indeed, the external universe. The echo, a recurrent device in pastoral, is another metaphor of reciprocity."[27] For composers of the eighteenth and nineteenth centuries, this reciprocity was most typically personified in the relationship between shepherd and shepherdess or, in sacred works, between soul and savior. But as these echoes are themselves echoed in twentieth-century scores, they often seem to reverberate in ways that are attenuated by nostalgia, distance, or desolation.[28]

To initiate his echo (bar 88), Sowerby chose a solo trumpet and an augmented triad built on E♭, sounding a call to arms that stretches the traditional major triad ("nature's chord") by raising the fifth of the chord from B♭ to B♮. The upper octave of this fanfare is likewise altered by a half step (lowered, in this case to D) to amplify the sense of distortion and to create a harmonic dissonance as this

EXAMPLE 21. Sowerby, *Prairie,* mm. 86–93

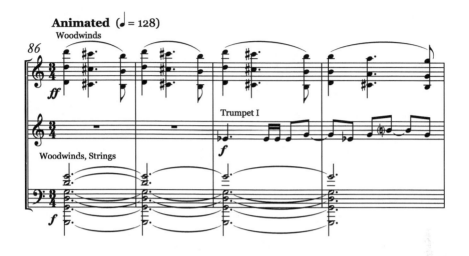

highest pitch is sustained while the echo enters underneath on E♭. Two muted trumpets answer the call, repeating the augmented triad but adding a timbral distortion to the tonal-harmonic one. The same fanfare figure appears without an echo in measure 119, and again in measure 277, each time marking the end of a section. As was the case in the melancholy countryside Berlioz conjured for his

Symphonie fantastique, the unanswered echo signals incompleteness, but here the association tends more toward unresolved struggle than unrequited love.

Sowerby's *Prairie* is no Arcadia; or, it is an Arcadia liberally inscribed with the memento mori "Et in Arcadia Ego." Death and discord lie just below the surface. In fact, almost all of the tone poem's references to human action are military or mechanical, despite the composer's folk credentials. Dance rhythms are few and far between; the pentatonic melodies and repeated phrases of folk music are entirely absent. Instead, the tone poem sports a full brass complement, together with snare drum, bass drums, kettledrums, and all manner of cymbals, bells, and the like. The buildup to bar 152 is distinctly military in tone, and one of the last ostinato passages of the score (mm. 232–54) uses measure after measure of plodding quarter-note triplets followed by two quarter notes to suggest an inexorable, marching advance.

In the end, even these military moments seem restrained in comparison to the riotous music that Sowerby reserves for the harvesting crew. After almost ten minutes and more than 160 measures of circling, the spring is finally wound and the tone poem unleashes its momentum: the threshers leap to life. With music marked "fast and machine like" at quarter note equals 192, the strings chug like an engine under the clangorous brass. Soon the roles are reversed as strings and bell intone a melody that is almost singable but more or less drowned out by the pure whir of pistons and gears, as if the spiraling figures of the opening have at last tightened and come into focus, now revealed to be the cogs of a giant machine. Sowerby's energetic laborers would probably have pleased Sandburg, who spoke earlier in his prairie poem of pioneers: "the laughing men who ride iron . . . the worker in flint and clay, the singing women and their sons a thousand years ago marching single file the timber and the plain."[29] But if the women or the workers' dreams are singing, as the poem suggests, they sing of the machine, not the garden.

As a twentieth-century "Garden of the World," Sowerby's *Prairie* has the mythic features of a paradise lost. Its innocence has been irrevocably disrupted; its resident serpent is fully audible in the spinning of harvesting machinery and the bluster of military brass. There is more than a measure of celebration in this loss of innocence: the acquisition of knowledge, of techne, of joy in labor. Yet the exuberant mood of the harvesters quickly collapses, absorbed into the stillness of the prairie. This was the chief impression left on a reporter for *Time* magazine, who summed up the tone poem's vast expanse by stating that the sections of the symphonic poem "follow one another in succession without break or special line of demarcation." At the end of this continuously receding horizon of themes, the piece turns back on itself to recall "the hush and perhaps monotony of vast stretches of farm . . . whose beauty mid-westerners too seldom appreciate."[30] Sowerby and Sandburg (both midwesterners) appreciated the prairie and used it to explore a middle landscape that was not just geographical but stylistic. If there is a radical component in *Cornhuskers,* it lies in Sandburg's rapport with the vernacular: small-scale sing-song patterns and the easy rhetoric of the speechmaker. As for Sowerby, Chicago audiences would never call him "conservative," and New York critics would not suffer him to play the "ultramodern." Frankly impressionist in style, Sowerby's *Prairie* records his ambivalence about musical, agricultural, and technological "progress."

SANDBURG'S PRAIRIE

Sowerby's *Prairie* takes Sandburg's text seriously, but flexibly—with no melodic quotations and few direct references apart from the threshing machinery. Yet it manages to capture something of the poem's multivalence on two fronts. On the one hand, the poem suggests the insignificance of time passing: "To a man across a thousand years I offer a handshake. I say to him: Brother, make the story short, for the stretch of a thousand years is short." On the other hand, "The Prairie" is intensely future-focused: "I speak of new cities and new people. I tell you the past is a bucket of ashes. I tell you yesterday is a wind gone down, a sun dropped in the west."[31] Related to this contrast in attitude toward time is a contrast in poetic point of view. The outer sections of the poem speak with a human, masculine voice: "O prairie mother, I am one of your boys." For the most part, the inner sections personify the land, inviting us to listen for the voice of the prairie itself (or, as the poem would have it, "herself"): "I am the prairie, mother of men, waiting." Sowerby also contrasts timeless prairie and time-bound working men, but he inverts Sandburg's order of things. The manmade music of the threshing machinery is engulfed by the static music of the outer sections, as though the mechanical residue of pioneering had been swallowed up by forces operating outside of human history.

Sandburg's poem is more optimistic than this. Like other Progressive Era figures, he extended the rhetoric of pioneering to areas of inquiry that survived and perhaps even facilitated the supposed "closing" of the American frontier. When asked to speak at Knox College in his hometown of Galesburg, Illinois, he responded with "Youth and Pioneers: An Ode," in which he compared the pioneers of "chemistry and physics" and the "pilots of the night air mail" with the restless western pioneers and "the pony-express riders of the old days." Sandburg queried: "Because the frontier with the free land is gone, are we to lose the word 'pioneer'?"[32] Sandburg sat on the cusp of nostalgic reverence for the agricultural pioneer and the refiguring of a pioneer better suited to labor in the modern fields of science and industry.

Sowerby spoke little about the pioneer per se, and he measured folk-based composition using a squarely romantic rhetoric of race and sincerity. In his 1927 article "The Folk Element—The Vitalizer of Modern Music," he wrote: "The world admires, not the eclectic who can adopt anyone's language, but the man who speaks that which is deep within his own soul, and which reflects the imaginings and the very being of his race."[33] In later chapters, we shall see how a similar rhetoric was adopted and adapted by Roy Harris to explain such pieces as his *Farewell to Pioneers*. But this was not the only option for America's would-be pastoralists. As Sandburg's words suggest, it was possible to give the pioneer distinctly "contemporary" features—to identify the pioneer not as the emblem of a largely Anglo phase of westward expansion, but as a less agricultural and more generally heroic type. We will see this impulse at work in Aaron Copland's music, but first let us examine another treatment of Sandburg's "Prairie," a cantata by Lukas Foss—a composer for whom the "native soil" and race soul rhetoric that often attached to Sowerby's scores was completely out of place.

LUKAS FOSS ON THE PRAIRIE

Prodigy, pianist, composer and émigré, Lukas Foss would eventually embrace the "eclectic" practices that Sowerby took such pains to repudiate. Born Lukas Fuchs in 1922, he fled with his family from Berlin to France in 1933 after Hitler came to power. Four years later, they arrived in the United States as part of the latest transatlantic wave of westward immigrants searching for religious tolerance and opportunity. After studying piano and conducting at the Curtis Institute, Foss apprenticed with Serge Koussevitzky in the first class to convene at what would become Tanglewood; he played piano for the Boston Symphony Orchestra, became a pupil of Hindemith, and quickly found himself a fellow at the MacDowell Colony. As luck would have it, his residency coincided with one of Charles Wakefield Cadman's trips to Peterborough. Cadman reported back to the readers of the *Pacific Coast Musician*: "Among the young modernists is one Lukas Foss, Jewish French-German boy about 22, who has been in the United States five years.... A modest, sweet kid who has made an ideal [MacDowell] colonist—fine mentality, innate culture, and much personal charm. His setting of Sandburg's 'The Prairie' has some grand moments in it, quite individual and rhythmically fascinating; tuneful in many places, and some fine choral writing."[34] Cadman's apparent fondness for Foss did not make it easier for him to classify his young "Jewish French-German" colleague, upon whom the alleged American melting pot had barely begun to work.[35] Foss himself stated simply: "I was born in Berlin, raised in Paris, but I came here when I was barely fifteen, and I consider myself completely American."[36] Foss became a naturalized citizen in 1942, the same year he began *The Prairie*, and he later described this work as "American, almost popular at times."[37] Foss was at home with a wide range of vernaculars, and it would be strange not to find Anglo-Americana among them. He returned to American themes in his setting of Mark Twain's *The Jumping Frog of Calaveras*

County (1950), the bicentennial work *American Cantata*, and the guitar concerto *American Landscapes* (1989), which sports moments of sheer bluegrass. But interpreting these elements in and on *The Prairie* carries special importance because of the composer's youth and because of the wartime tensions that inevitably colored such categories as "native" and "foreign."

In his praise for *The Prairie*, Cadman left out (perhaps pointedly) the most obvious influence on Foss. Cadman was not on particularly good terms with Aaron Copland in the 1940s, but the young Foss met and idolized Copland at Tanglewood. Virgil Thomson's review of the premiere links Foss to Copland merely by innuendo.[38] In 1945, Donald Fuller observed: "The opening, undeniably effective, proclaims his debt to Copland, but later he has much to say on his own." Irving Fine concurred, writing that "the influence of Copland is strong, especially in the opening measures, but it can be overestimated, for Foss's writing is more contrapuntal and has not achieved Copland's transparency."[39] More specifically, Fine continued: "There has been much nonsense heard lately about Foss's desire to be 'one of the boys,' to be known as an indigenous American composer. Some time before he started his magnum opus, *The Prairie*, his attitude toward musical expression was undergoing a change. He had conducted Copland's *Billy the Kid* suite during the 1941 session of the Berkshire Music Center and was ready for a new influence anyway. It was natural that Copland and cowboy Americana should fascinate this intensely lyrical young composer."[40]

Fine's statement raises two kinds of questions: What made Foss's fascination with Copland or with the cowboy seem so inevitable? And how was it that the "cowboy" should become the dominant figure in *The Prairie*, a work with no references to cattle? The lure of cowboy song, and its presence in *Billy the Kid*, will be treated later, but here it is worth observing that "The Open Prairie" section of Copland's ballet has more in common with Sowerby's ostinato-laden naturepainting than it does with Foss's setting of "The Prairie" (example 22). Foss recalls instead the declamatory style of Copland's *Piano Variations* or the *Fanfare for the Common Man*, complete with trumpet timbres at the outset. Unlike Sowerby's fanfares, which were heard as if from a distance, Foss's tenor narrator himself intones the fourths and fifths that span the octave A–E–A above added-note chords that give forceful punctuation to his words. Thanks to Sandburg's text, Foss's statements of identification with life on the prairie were more direct than anything Copland would ever attempt: "I was born on the prairie and the milk of its wheat, the red of its clover, the eyes of its women, gave me a song, a song and a slogan."

Foss seems to have encountered Copland's *Billy the Kid* and Sandburg's poem almost simultaneously. He recalled: "Shortly after I left Europe and emigrated to this country as a boy of fifteen, I fell in love—with America. At nineteen I read Sandburg's *Prairie* and immediately started to set it to music. A colleague looked

EXAMPLE 22. Foss, *The Prairie*, movement 1, mm. 1–13 (New York: G. Schirmer, 1944)

at the sketches. 'Why are you trying to write so American?' I wasn't. I was in love. I had discovered America." It is noteworthy that Foss "fell in love" with an America hundreds of miles west of where he lived. "Carl Sandburg's poem *Prairie* (from *Cornhuskers*) is young and enthusiastic. So was I," Foss later recalled.[41] In his exuberance, Foss felt free to engage with the text as if he himself were the poet: "Once I choose a text I become extremely involved in it. The text must be just right for me, and right for me at that time in my life. . . . I like to 'play' with a text, combining, omitting, dividing into sections, exchanging the order of paragraphs or verses.[42]

From Sandburg's multisectional poem, Foss devised seven movements (nine sections) lasting roughly fifty minutes in performance:

I.	"I was born on the Prairie"	Tenor Solo
II.	"Dust of men"	Chorus—Soloists
III.	"They are mine"	Alto Solo—Chorus (with Soprano Solo in the Introduction)
IV.	"When the red and the white men met"	Chorus
V.	"In the dark of a thousand years"	Bass Solo—Male Chorus
	[possible intermission or moment of silence inserted here]	
VI a.	"Cool prayers"	Chorus
VI b.	"Prairie girl"	Soprano Solo
VI c.	"Songs hidden in eggs"	Soprano and Alto Duet
VII.	"To-morrow"	Chorus—Soloists

While most of the movements set contiguous lines or sections of text, "Dust of men" and "They are mine" involve substantial omissions, and "They are mine" combines sections that are far removed from one another in the original. Foss wrote: "The order of these sections is not always true to the order of the poem. Add the many omissions and one will appreciate the hesitance, even fear, with which I approached the poet whose permission had to be secured. To my amazement, Carl Sandburg wrote: 'You have revitalized the old poem.' He wrote to his publishers: 'Give the young man a break. It seems he has approached the music in the same sporting way in which I wrote the poem.' "[43]

All in all, Foss chose to set 120 lines of Sandburg's 215, adding a one-line reprise ("They are mine") to round out and reiterate the title of the movement that suffered the most textual alteration.[44] No doubt some of Foss's omissions were necessary for reasons of economy: omitting the thirty lines after the text for movement V, and the thirty lines between those that end movement III and those of movement VIc allowed Foss to keep his cantata under one hour in length. But aspects of these long cuts, and other, shorter deletions, suggest that Foss was also interested in modifying Sandburg's prairie to fit his own vision.

Keeping in mind the mechanical moments of Sowerby's score, and Marx's governing metaphor of "the machine in the Garden," it is noteworthy that the first substantial passages Foss chose to omit from Sandburg's text involve railroads: first, an account of "the overland passenger train" with its hissing pistons and cursing wheels; and second, a description of the headlight of the Pioneer Limited train crossing Wisconsin. Given his relatively recent immersion in English, Foss may have chosen to omit some colorful phrases simply because they seemed unnecessarily obscure: coonskin caps, "chinooks let loose from Medicine Hat," and many of the details related to corn and cornhusking. But the downplaying of machinery also suggests that Foss valued a pastoral mode that was more nostalgic than Sowerby's or Sandburg's, a prairie closer to Jefferson's American Arcadia. Along these lines it is not surprising that, although he retained references to "railroad cattle pens," "smokestacks [that] bite the skyline with stub teeth," and "the flame sprockets of the sheet steel mills," Foss declined to set the stanza that Sandburg devoted to the slaughterhouse, which ends with the grizzly injunction "Kill your hogs with a knife slit under the ear. / Hack them with cleavers. / Hang them with hooks in the hind legs."

Perhaps the most telling pattern in Foss's deletions is the erasure of geographical specificity, in marked contrast to Sandburg's litanies of place names. Within the text of the first movement, the only omitted phrase is the one that includes proper nouns: "Here between the sheds of the Rocky Mountains and the Appalachians." In movement II, Foss retains an allusion to World War I, "I fed the boys who went to France in [the] great dark days," but cuts the subsequent battlefields: "Appomattox is a beautiful word to me and so is Valley Forge and / the Marne and Verdun." In movement III, Foss passes over lines naming "Towns on the Soo Line, Towns on the Big Muddy," "Omaha and Kansas City, Minneapolis and St. Paul," "Towns in the Ozarks, Dakota wheat towns, Wichita, Peoria, Buffalo." Foss sought to universalize the prairie, idealizing the landscape without limiting it to the places Sandburg had known and loved. Cultural references to the Fourth of July, skyscrapers, and "a thousand red men," situate Foss's text firmly within the United States, but the remarkable fact remains that France is the only place he calls by name.

In a related move, Foss skips over two stanzas of poetry that mention American songs: "You came in wagons ... / Singing *Yankee Doodle, Old Dan Tucker, Turkey in the Straw,*" and a series of three parallel statements that end with the titles of spirituals or popular songs. It is easy to imagine the mature Foss taking advantage of such moments for musical quotation and parody, but in *The Prairie,* he let such invitations fall by the wayside. Although his score has more folksy moments than Sowerby's did, Foss made sure his audiences knew that he had borrowed "no native tunes."[45] The youthful composer instead followed his own recipe of stylistic and generic ingredients. As critic Richard Dyer puts it, "*The Prairie* is a work of paradoxes. ... it is populist in its reach, but the compositional resources are those of high art, romantic in its attitudes and effect, neo-classical in its disciplines."[46] *Time* magazine was more direct, noting in 1945 that "Foss's music is far from Sandburg's prairie: it is modern, glittering, sophisticated, plainly rooted in Europe. Critics were somewhat baffled by the cantata which mixed Foss champagne with Sandburg cornbread."[47]

THE PRAIRIE PARADOX

From the start, Foss acknowledged a twofold purpose for the cantata: it should represent something "native" to the United States and yet should transcend a narrowly geographical understanding of the prairie. He called Sandburg's poem "a new expression of an old faith drawn from the native soil. The protagonist, simply, is the prairie, but through this poem the prairie grows until it becomes the symbol for the all-embracing principle of growth itself."[48] Foss thus skirts the question that Leo Marx suggests had eluded generations of pastoralists before him: how much growth can the pastoral landscape sustain before it loses its "happy balance of art and nature"? Marx writes that "no one, not even Jefferson, had been able to identify the point of arrest, the critical moment when the tilt might be expected and progress cease to be progress."[49]

After the score of *The Prairie* was published, Arthur Berger complained good-naturedly that "*The Prairie* . . . is already a familiar affair. The repetitiveness of its motives, the recurrence of its melodic devices (e.g. the syncopated third at phrase-endings), made it familiar, in fact, after the first performance."[50] Irving Fine also singled out for mild critique Foss's "propulsive ostinati, repetitions and frequent squareness of phrasing."[51] Writing in 1945, Fine saw these features as typical of Foss's recent music, but they clearly also recall the pastoral works of Sowerby and earlier composers, and Foss himself had no desire to hide this fact. "The opening movement," he wrote, "speaks of the prairie as we are accustomed to visualize it. The author, in a pastoral tenor solo, sings of open valleys and far horizons and the music breathes fresh air. After this pastoral introduction, a fugue."[52] In keeping with the complexity of its program, however, each of Foss's traditionally pastoral traits—drones and harmonic stasis, ostinato and motivic repetition, even echo effects—bear multiple interpretations.

Foss reserved his first and last movements for the human storyteller and the inner ones for the voice of the prairie. As the opening measures suggest, Foss kept a careful eye out for recitative-like moments in which the solo narrator (a tenor, like those of the Bach Passions) could deliver his text over sustained chords, usually including the pitch A. The static harmonic underpinning of the opening measures acquires a more conventionally pastoral sound in bar 26, where octave A's recall a bagpipe drone, sounding underneath the reedy lines of an oboe melody. The tenor's next entrance (m. 38) echoes the oboe line, but ties its melody to poetry of nature: "Here the water went down, the icebergs slid with gravel, the gaps and the valleys hissed, and the black loam came, and the yellow sandy loam." Already an analogy is suggested between the birth of the narrator and the genesis of the prairie, forging a link between natural and human events. Is it coincidental, then, that the émigré Foss singled out for extra repetition Sandburg's mention of migration? "Here the grey geese go five hundred miles and back with a wind under their wings honking the cry for a new home."

Sandburg's text suggests a fairly clean break between the human voice and the voice of the prairie. Foss acknowledges this division, but he blurs the boundaries between man and nature in part by suggesting that the first two movements do not represent separate worlds but instead are linked in the manner of a prelude and fugue. Over a backdrop of bustling counterpoint, the chorus of the second movement ("Dust of Men") recites text that might be considered the prairie's own catechism: "I am here," "I am dust of men," "I am dust of your dust." Even at a molecular level, man and the landscape are here indistinguishable.

Also contributing to the confusion of human and natural impulses is the only movement Foss himself described as "folk-like." Devoted to the same text that Sowerby chose for his epigraph, "They are mine" consists of a recitative duet for alto and soprano soloists followed by a da capo aria for alto, with choral interjections. Open-fifth drones in the winds set the stage for melodies that are plausibly "folk-like," not by virtue of quotation or repetition but because of their pentatonic flavor. Yet the poetry springs not from some imaginary folk singer, but from the mouth of the prairie herself, personified by the two female soloists. The division (or multiplication) of the prairie voice into a duet helps forestall the danger of assigning too personal a psychology to the prairie voice, who speaks so tenderly of "my cornfields" and "my threshing crews." In case this vocal duplication is not enough to carry the point, Foss also calls for the two soloists' voices to be echoed by a third, offstage chorister at the word "horizons" (example 23a). The textual invocation of a visual vanishing point is thus given an aural counterpart that seems to emerge independent of perceived human agency.

The offstage echo ushers in the aria proper, which contains the only dancelike material in the entire cantata. The open-fifth drone sounded subtly by bassoon and horn at first sets up a more raucous open-string evocation of folk fiddling at bar 81 with woodwind melodies chattering away on top (example 23b). Although the passage is short, it operates in the best of rustic traditions and shows that, like generations of composers before him, Foss assigned pastoral connotations to the woodwind timbres. This is most obvious in the triptych of movement VI ("Cool prayers," "O prairie girl," and "Songs hidden in eggs"), which in the composer's words form "a lyrical intermezzo . . . held together by a dreamy little shepherd's lay, a nostalgic woodwind refrain of the prairie."[53] Of course, the reciprocity of the shepherd's pipe accounts for only half of the woodwinds' pastoral potential; the other half involves the evocation of birdsong. In movement VIc, "Songs hidden in eggs," alto and soprano lines overlap one another in imitation of the mockingbirds whose "follies of O-be-joyful" are immediately rendered more directly by clarinet and company.[54]

The metamorphosis of women's voices into birdsong has a substantial concordance in classical mythology, but this allusion to the antique pastoral is rare in the

EXAMPLE 23B. Foss, *The Prairie*, movement 3, mm. 81–89

cantata as a whole. Far more often, Foss concerns himself with Sandburg's twentieth-century vision of history, in which even the most potent signs of technological advance are witnessed by the prairie as if from a great distance. In the cantata's brief and rather ponderous depiction of industry (movement V), a quasi-ostinato bass line in 5/4 and 7/4 measures grinds relentlessly, undergirding references to grain elevators, flame sprockets, and steel mills. Likewise, in movement IV ("When the red and the white men met") the pounding of a low C pedal conjures up an atmosphere both "Indian" and funereal but also carries listeners through the moments when "a thousand red men cried" and "a million white men came" with little pause for sentimentality or pathos. Even before *The Prairie* turns its attention to the growth of midwestern cities, the impersonal churning of history depersonalizes the cantata's references to war and peace ("I last while wars are fought, while new wars arise"). In contrast to the sustained military topos of Sowerby's prairie, Foss passes over the "great dark days" of World War I quickly. His ostinato links his transatlantic soldiers to the discordant militia-work of trumpets and drums but also, through a recurrence of related ostinato material, to the geese who move according to the annual cycles of the prairie world.

As suggested by Foss's program note, the controlling metaphor of growth is diffused through *The Prairie* in such a way that it is hard to distinguish between human and geological "progress" and even harder to tell when this "progress" will fold over onto itself in cyclic fashion. With the cantata's last movement, even the

EXAMPLE 24. Foss, *The Prairie*, movement 7, mm. 349–54

passage of time is drawn into this prairie conundrum by Sandburg's closing lines: "I am a brother of the cornhuskers who say at sundown: To-morrow is a day." In keeping with the theme of renewal—and with the poetic return to a human narrating voice—this last movement opens with a recollection of the fanfaring trumpets of the prologue. The solo tenor reidentifies himself as a son of the prairie, and a compressed set of echoes (mm. 70–77) marks the shift from his recitative to the choral proclamations that fill the remaining 342 bars of the score. From unified declamation, Foss gradually splinters the final text into fragments of just a few words, assigning them to a welter of overlapping voices. Anchoring the perpetual breaking of new days is a series of pedal points, some lasting just a few bars, others unifying stretches of forty measures or more (mm. 196–235 [on A]; mm. 291–332 [on D]). When the pedal points lapse, their function is generally taken over by rhythmic ostinati, plodding at first but accelerating along with the stringendo of verbal disintegration; a climax is reached at "an ocean of tomorrows" where words and days lap like waves at the shore (example 24).

The cantata as a whole is profoundly end-oriented. "Tomorrow" lasts nearly twice as long as any of the other movements except for the da capo third movement. In Foss's own description, "everyone joins in the final hymn to the future, expressing the healthy and sunny optimism unique to this country."[55] For Arthur Berger, however, Foss's "sunny" optimism also had a darker side. Though he considered Foss "guiltless of such insincere designs on his listeners," he nonetheless wrote that "the young composer has inherited some of the rhetorical tricks which sprang, in their originators, from a concert with audience persuasion."[56] Indeed, Foss's tendency to isolate and repeat bits of poetry that reference human speech ("I speak," "I tell you," "who say at sundown") solidifies the feeling that "To-morrow" is music for a great, vocal army on the march. If Foss's optimistic peroration draws upon the rhetoric of propaganda, however, it does so in a distinctly pastoral context. The mottled antiphony of his shouting crowd is the endgame of all the echo effects in *The Prairie*. Although Sandburg's final line ("Tomorrow is a day") was spoken by the human narrator, the choral climax identifies the forward-looking slogan with the land itself, which answers back with the reciprocity that Leo Marx identified in the echo moments of literary pastorals. After iteration and reiteration, the text fragments seem to emanate from a source no longer human: perhaps mechanical, perhaps natural—either the machine or the garden.

6

Power in the Land

"PIGEONS ON THE GRASS, ALAS"

Foss's cantata reinforced the idea that the prairie has a voice of its own. But in his sixties, the composer looked back with a more introspective understanding of the prairie allure. "*The Prairie* is still a favorite work of mine," he told Vivian Perlis in 1986. "I'm not ashamed of it even now . . . it did a lot for me." He further recalled: "I felt like a refugee, but then a refugee learns to call anything his home, wherever he is. So America very quickly became my home, and I am sure Aaron had something to do with it, and Carl Sandburg. . . . My *Prairie* is very Coplandesque . . . I fell in love with America and why did I fall in love with America? It wasn't just the landscape obviously. It was people like Aaron."[1] Yet the "Coplandesque" was not the only source for impressions of rural Americana, and as many have observed, it was not the first. Among those with a claim to the right of first discovery, Virgil Thomson was perhaps the most vocal.

Thomson's vocabulary for America's middle landscape was made up primarily of Protestant hymn tunes. According to Steven Watson, Thomson linked the American hymn tunes in his oeuvre not just with childhood experience but with a certain kind of rootedness: "When you reach down in your subconscious, you get certain things. . . . When Aaron [Copland] reaches down, he doesn't get cowboy tunes, he gets Jewish chants. When I reach down, I get southern hymns or all those darn-fool ditties we used to sing: 'Grasshopper sitting on a railway track.'"[2] In the mid-1930s, Thomson rightly considered himself a pioneer in the incorporation of Americana into classical music. Later famous for his role as music critic for the *New York Herald Tribune,* Thomson did some of his earlier "heralding" from the composer's pulpit. His *Symphony on a Hymn Tune* (1926–28) gave him a claim on Americana that he felt an increasing need to protect from urban interlopers.

As chance would have it, these themes are subtly interwoven in Thomson's first and most famous treatment of the plant family that he would later memorialize in the grasslands of his documentary film score *The Plow That Broke the Plains* (1936) and the orchestral movement *Wheat Field at Noon* (1948). In Gertrude Stein's play-libretto *Four Saints in Three Acts,* which Thomson began setting in the late 1920s, she indicated: "Make it pastoral. In hills and gardens."[3] Yet even after he had finished the music some years later, Thomson had little sense of how their "Opera to Be Sung" might be staged; the work of crafting a "plot" was largely left to Thomson's friend Maurice Grosser, who directed the first production. One of the few passages for which Stein actually did intend specific narrative content is the Vision of the Holy Ghost that St. Ignatius experiences near the beginning of Act 3. For her incarnation of the Holy Ghost, Stein replaced the serene dove with its gawky, urban cousin: "Pigeons large pigeons on the shorter longer yellow grass alas." Whether short or long, the grass is yellow, suggesting that the Holy Ghost descends either out of season or onto a lawn seriously marred by overuse. The chorus conjectures that "it was a magpie in the sky," but this move merely substitutes its own set of unholy connotations: a shallow attraction to shiny objects and a tendency toward theft.

Although Stein sets the scene in a "Monastery garden with . . . a bare Spanish horizon and an empty sky," the associations of her text are urban. Thomson's music follows suit. Part of what makes this passage so fetching is its jaunty contrast to the chantlike lines that fill the rest of the score.[4] He does not choose here to recall the four-square phrases of Protestant hymnody or the vocal inflections of the Negro spiritual. Thomson's pigeons move neither to the nursery rhyme tunes of Sunday school song nor to the high, heavenly strains that affirm their fall to earth. They flutter instead to music that resembles nothing more than a cabaret song, complete with a chorus of male backup singers.

Although Stein linked the birds in the Luxembourg Gardens to the imagery of Annunciation, Thomson seems to have preferred the Pentecostal moment— perhaps because he recognized that the creation of musical Americana required a certain kind of "speaking in tongues." Thomson understood the appeal of stylistic costuming. His love of Erik Satie, his own midwestern je ne sais quoi, even the cellophane garb that enveloped the black cast of *Four Saints*—all these suggest a fascination with ironic surfaces that short-circuit any attempt to penetrate an "authentic" interior. Nadine Hubbs has commented on "the extent to which Thomson's diatonic idiom could evoke a distinct religiosity even while maintaining an extraordinary blank-screen quality, subject to its viewers' projections," and she has argued persuasively that this "interpretive pluralism" was a crucial factor not just in the Stein settings, but in his music more generally.[5]

Even when Thomson's travels in the Basque region coincided with the final stages of composing *Four Saints*, Thomson made a point of lingering on the French side of the border until the score was complete. In July 1928 he crossed over into Spain and found the landscape reminiscent of Texas.[6] Yet the opera sounded neither Texan nor Spanish (leaving aside a couple of Latinate Montmartre tangos). "The music evokes Christian liturgy," Thomson later wrote. "Its local references, however, are not to Spain, which I had never seen, but rather to my Southern Baptist upbringing in Missouri."[7] In keeping with his interest in the musical "subconscious" and his Stein-inspired practice of "automatic writing," Thomson looked inward for his musical material. And whether he saw before him the neatly manicured lawn of a city park or the grasslands of middle America, Thomson heard with keen ears the perpetual tread of the popular—sometimes fertilizing, sometimes corrupting—upon things sacred.

AFTER FLANDERS

Like other composers of his generation, Thomson solidified his birthright while in France—a fact that he liked to advertise. It is common knowledge that World War I helped make France the destination of choice for U.S. artists and entertainers. Those with pastoral leanings, including Sowerby, found there both an established school of musical landscape (sometimes seascape) painting that was easily adaptable to the waving grass of the American plains and an interest in the primitive, "collective" past that could serve as an antidote to Viennese psychologizing. Sowerby's midwestern "impressionism" suggests a parallel between the rippling waves of *La Mer* and the swirling grasses of his tone poem *Prairie*. Thomson's iconic hymn-singing saints exemplify the impersonal principles of primitivism with a certain neoclassical nonchalance. Unlike many of their Parisian counterparts, however, Thomson and Sowerby did not look outward toward exotic borderlands but rather gravitated inward toward a midwestern middle landscape that could be autobiographical as a matter of fact, without the fervor of emotional expressionism.

In the 1940s, Thomson explained: "During my second twenty years I wrote in Paris music that was always, in one way or another, about Kansas City. I wanted Paris to know Kansas City."[8] As Steven Watson has observed, Kansas City was itself poised on the brink between East and West: "By the turn of the century, the bustling city lay at the edge of eastern culture's reach. The starting point of the Santa Fe and Oregon trails, Kansas City mixed the brassy independence of a frontier town with the amenities of culture, touring Wild West shows, religion, and open vice."[9] According to biographer Anthony Tommasini, Thomson recalled seeing "cowboys and Indians hanging around the railway station."[10] Yet the composer would also gain an experience of the arid West from a less likely source: his National Guard and army service during World War I.

It was a source of great chagrin to Thomson that his entire military service during the Great War was performed stateside: training with the Army Medical Corps at Camp Doniphan in southwestern Oklahoma, with further work in radio telephony and aviation in New York and Texas. Watson describes Thomson's weeks in Oklahoma as providing the composer's "first taste of close living in a community where erudition counted for little." Thomson wrote to his friend Alice Smith (great-granddaughter of the Mormon prophet Joseph Smith): "Living in such intimacy with fellows is bound to be an experience."[11] He craved privacy and found the landscape both exhilarating and bleak, as he conveyed to his sister, Ruby: "The mountains to the west are beautiful, just freckled with trees, and the rest of the reservation is perfectly bare, that is, bare of trees." In the section of his autobiography titled "My World War I," he called the camp "a desert paradise of sun and dust, high winds, and hard ground . . . and the dust storms, which penetrated everything—your clothes, your shoes, your gloves, your fur-lined goggles—blew just as hard in cold months as in others."[12]

Thomson had enlisted in large part because of a "yearning toward novel experience."[13] Disappointed when the armistice was signed before his ship set sail, he reached France under distinctly postwar circumstances: as a member of the Harvard Glee Club on tour in 1921. Carol Oja has written about Thomson's Harvard years, noting both the emphasis on early music in the Glee Club repertory and the Francophile predilection of his chief mentors, Archibald Davison, Edward Burlingame Hill, and S. Foster Damon.[14] Lingering after the Glee Club's departure, Thomson got his first taste of Nadia Boulanger's tutelage and immersed himself in Parisian musical culture. When he returned to Harvard, Thomson nurtured a lively interest in France. In 1925 he made his way back to Paris, where he would retain an address until the installation of the Vichy government made it prudent to return home. In 1940, Thomson took up his new post at the *Herald Tribune,* and critic Samuel L. M. Barlow reintroduced him to the readers of *Modern Music* as a "trans-Atlantic liaison officer," a laborer for the cause of "fundamentally democratic music," one who "reposes comfortably on the bosom of the eighteenth century," although his subject matter is "curiously homegrown." Barlow concluded: "Thomson moves, unexpectedly but decorously, across the musical skyline like a baroque covered wagon. More unexpectedly, there's a pioneer inside."[15]

HOW FIRM A FOUNDATION

The pioneering stance that Barlow identifies has two chief musical components: one readily accepted and one more contentious. While Thomson is universally acknowledged as a master in setting the English language, his claims to have "discovered" musical Americana have always been controversial.[16] Certainly, composers like Farwell with his "Lone Prairee" (also arranged by Charles Martin Loeffler) had made small-scale settings of Anglo Americana while Thomson was still a child. Even with Charles Ives relatively unknown, Amy Beach had created large-scale works with borrowed folk materials, and George Whitefield Chadwick had experimented with the recreation of Anglo Americana independent of actual borrowed tunes. Nonetheless, Thomson helped prepare the way for a number of his closest colleagues, including Copland. Writing in 1929, Paul Rosenfeld reserved special praise for a new symphony that had "the quaintness of a Currier and Ives print." He continued: "The symphony is pervaded by a mysterious feel of the American soil and past; and with the organ pieces suggests that in Thomson, too, the eclectic may eventually make way for the earth-born."[17]

The symphony that Rosenfeld had in mind was the idiosyncratic *Symphony on a Hymn Tune,* which occupied Thomson both before and after *Four Saints.* An outgrowth of (or perhaps a rebellion against) his position as a young church keyboardist, the symphony was a proving ground for the techniques that he would bring to his documentary film scores: quotation spiked with "wrong note" doubling, contrapuntal combinations of tunes, and a mélange of sacred and secular, "high" and "low." Like *Four Saints,* whose title vastly underestimates the number of saints in question, the *Symphony on a Hymn Tune* actually treats a much broader swath of Americana, as musicologist Michael Meckna observes: "Thomson cuts and pastes bits and pieces of the hymns, as well as marches, cowboy songs, and dance hall melodies, all of which suggest the broad spectrum of American life."[18] The same creative collage would characterize *The Plow,* and especially *The River,* which in fact takes the final movement of Thomson's symphony as the soundtrack for the last half reel of film.[19] Even the thematic confrontation between the pastoral and the mechanical—a crucial feature of *The Plow*—is in a way foreshadowed in the symphony, as its second movement ends with the wistful depiction of a passing locomotive. Thus, once more the "machine" rears its head and is subsumed in the garden.[20]

Though his prior evocations of saints and Sunday school may seem far removed from the gritty realism of the documentary film, Thomson had in fact acquired many of the musical tools he would use in collaboration with director Pare Lorentz well before the two men met. In his youth, Thomson had filled in playing piano and pipe organ for "silent" films.[21] By 1933, he had even done some theorizing about the role of musical quotation in film, maintaining that diegetic music (music that the characters can also hear, or, in Thomson's words, music used "as part of the drama") could yield even more potent effects: "The quotation of familiar hymns or popular tunes to accentuate or to comment a [sic] situation is of course an old and very useful device. Here the music becomes more than tune. It speaks its name. It is present on the stage."[22] In Thomson's documentary film scores, there are few characters to

EXAMPLE 25. Thomson, *The Plough That Broke the Plains,* Four Pieces for Piano, "Prelude," mm. 1–16 (New York: G. Schirmer, 1942, 1980)

make or hear diegetic music. Yet each tune or genre he alludes to "speaks its name" with historical and often ironic significance.

In the middle of the first sequence of *The Plow,* the well-known "doxology" tune, "Old Hundred," asserts itself as part of the "Prelude" in two stately phrases for a wordless woodwind chorale.[23] Many listeners no doubt supplied for themselves the familiar words of thanksgiving for blessings received—a text greatly at odds with the film's images of devastation. Further interpretive layers arise from the material that frames "Old Hundred" (example 25). In the opening nine measures and again at the end of the "Prelude" a melody unfolds over a steady four-square drumbeat. The parallel fourths recall Thomson's evocations of medieval organum, but the pulsing drum, together with the gentle syncopation and descending melodic contour, may suggest, as Neil Lerner has argued, "invisible Indians." Lerner calls our attention to the voice-over narration later in the film: "By 1880 we had cleared the Indian, and with him, the buffalo, from the Great

Plains, and established the last frontier." As Native Americans are never depicted on screen and never mentioned again in the narration, he observes, "this subtle musical presence exaggerates their otherwise conspicuous visual absence."[24] Whether the ominous ostinato is understood to reflect the uncanny emptiness of the landscape, a ghostly echo of the Indian Wars, or simply the tattoo of impending disaster, the message is substantially the same: on the Great Plains, the would-be settler (presumably Protestant) has come to a place of danger.

FARM SECURITY AND THE DOCUMENTARY IMPULSE

Pare Lorentz was not a filmmaker when he took on *The Plow*. He was a film critic with an interest in politics. He attracted government attention through personal connections, an article about the Dust Bowl in *Newsweek,* and his book *The Roosevelt Year* (1933), which was originally intended as a news film, but given the lack of funds, took shape instead as "a picture book in the form of a newsreel" instead. Armed with this book as a gift, he set out for the office of Agriculture Secretary Henry Wallace, to plant "the seed of [his] idea about photographing . . . the New Deal."[25] Not long after, Lorentz was summoned to work for the new Resettlement Administration (RA), later renamed the Farm Security Administration. From the start, the RA was a creature of Roosevelt's New Deal, funded by the Works Progress Administration (WPA) and led by polymath economist Rexford Guy Tugwell, who counted among his staff John Franklin Carter, Roy Stryker, and the photographers Walker Evans, Carl Mydans, and Dorothea Lange.[26] Tugwell was raring to go, and when he prompted Lorentz for a subject, the director had a ready answer: the Dust Bowl. Lorentz had been trying to find backers for a film about the Great Plains. This vision was finally realized in *The Plow,* the first government film to be widely distributed to the public, shown in almost 20 percent of the nation's fourteen thousand theaters. According to *Time* magazine's May 1936 account, President Roosevelt himself was "brimming with enthusiasm" over the film. He suggested an unprecedented screening before a joint session of Congress, but his plans were thwarted partly because neither chamber was equipped for "sound cinema" and partly because of "Republican opposition."[27]

Although he was a novice in the director's chair, Lorentz quickly developed firm ideas about the documentary genre, which he preferred to call "the factual film" and whose potential he pointedly opposed to that of the movie industry: "Hollywood doesn't know anything about the United States," he told the readers of *McCall's* in 1939.[28] More important than geographical verisimilitude was the documentary genre's attempt to capture "realities of great social significance." Lorentz did not belabor this point, but it was taken up and amplified in the discussion guide that the U.S. Film Service produced and circulated along with the film reels. This fascinating document hails *The Plow* as "the first documentary production to cover the facts of American life and dramatize events and conditions without resorting to any boy-meets-girl motif." While acknowledging that the documentary ought to sound a "persuasive note" (in contrast to the merely "objective" aims of the newsreel), the *Study Guide* explains:

> [Lorentz] wrote a scenario showing what has happened to the grasslands of the West at the hands of plowmen pioneers.... They "shot," or filmed, scenes in the Panhandle of Texas, and in Nebraska, Wyoming, Montana, Oklahoma and California. No actors were used, although a number of native plainsmen appeared in the picture. It is an important attribute of documentary films that actual people and actual places rather than stars and stage sets are used to portray the social and economic lessons of the film. The plains people showed great natural talent and dignity in their difficult sequences.

Lest anyone miss the point, the following page states: "It must be emphasized that ... *real* people in *real* places portraying a *real* problem were depicted."[29] In response, Thomson would create a soundtrack with a liberal smattering of "real" tunes.

Thomson was well aware that Lorentz had not gone looking for him in particular. "I was not the first one he had interviewed; Copland, I know, and Harris, I think, he had already not got on with." In fact, Thomson seems to have been the twelfth man on Lorentz's list by the time the two met for lunch in January 1936, but as Thomson recollects in a chapter of his autobiography called "Show Business for Uncle Sam," they quickly saw eye-to-eye:

> Our conversation went like this. He first explained this film, asked could I imagine writing music for it. My answer was, "How much money have you got?" Said he, "Beyond the costs of orchestra conductor, and recording, the most I could possibly have left for the composer is five hundred." "Well," said I, "I can't take from any man more than he's got, though if you did have more I would ask for it." My answer delighted him. "All those high-flyers," he said, "talk nothing but aesthetics. You talk about money; you're a professional."[30]

Whether Lorentz wanted Thomson's clear-eyed pragmatism, his ability to work to deadline, or merely the assurance that he would not interfere with the film's aesthetic (or political) stance, once the team was in place Thomson and Lorentz worked together well and closely, as indicated in their correspondence and in Thomson's recollection of the filmmaking process.

Building on the work of documentary film historians Robert L. Snyder and Richard D. McCann, Neil Lerner has presented the most detailed analysis of the music for *The Plow*, including the manuscript materials that chronicle its genesis.[31] Lorentz had begun filming in September 1935, based on an outline approved by Tugwell and John Franklin Carter (head of the RA information staff). By the time he engaged Thomson, he was almost done with a rough cut of the film and had specific ideas about musical cues. In this and his other films, Lorentz exercised broad authority over the soundtrack. He had studied music for ten years and had even entertained the idea of becoming a music critic. His contract with Thomson grants that "selection of thematic material, popular songs, sound effects, and the general score, wherever it is reasonably and physically possible, is to be under [Lorentz's] direction and supervision."[32]

Despite Lorentz's controlling hand, Thomson felt that he had considerable input in the later stages of the process, as he described in correspondence with Snyder. After getting Lorentz's approval for the basic musical materials, Thomson elaborated each section to fit the rough cut of the film. He played through a piano arrangement while the film was projected and only then turned to matters of orchestration. The soundtrack was then recorded, and, Thomson says, Lorentz recut the film to fit the orchestral score.[33] Only after the synchronization of music and image was complete did Lorentz introduce the spoken narration. For the voice-over, Lorentz hired his friend Thomas Chalmers (a baritone whose career at the Metropolitan Opera was curtailed by injury), but strangely, Chalmers only heard Thomson's score and did not see the film itself before recording the narration, in which Lorentz aimed "to use a minimum of words and to reiterate them in rhythm with the music wherever possible."[34]

Thomson composed the score in less than a fortnight, and he justified his rapid progress not just on the basis of his vaunted professionalism, but because of his life experience: "The music of *The Plow* had poured forth easily," he wrote. "I knew the Great Plains landscape in Kansas, Oklahoma, New Mexico, Texas; and during the War I had lived in a tent with ten-below-zero dust storms. I had come to the theme nostalgic and ready to work. . . . The subject, moreover, was highly photogenic—broad grasslands and cattle, mass harvesting, erosion by wind, deserted farms."[35] Though Thomson described his attitude as "nostalgic," this is only part of the story; operating in tandem with the film's political argument, the score offers its own commentary on the people and places of the plains.

LANDSCAPE OR PORTRAIT

Though the script for *The Plow* was not as widely acclaimed as that for *The River* (which James Joyce called "the most beautiful prose I have heard in ten years" and Sandburg counted "among the greatest of the psalms of America's greatest river"), Lorentz's words were still powerful.[36] When he was later assigned to review his own film, Lorentz modestly described it as "a brief history of the Great Plains from the time of the first cattle ranches to the present day," with two clear objectives: "one, to show audiences a specific and exciting section of the country; the other, to portray the events which led up to one of the major catastrophies [*sic*] in American history—to show, in other words, the Great Drought which is now going into its sixth year." Though uncomfortable extolling his own handiwork,

Lorentz praised his photographers, Ralph Steiner and Paul Strand, for taking "some of the most beautiful pictures ever made for any production," and he was no less complimentary of Thomson's work, calling it "the best musical score ever composed for an American movie."[37]

The plot of *The Plow* is captured accurately enough in the subtitles Thomson included in the full score: Prelude, Pastorale (Grass), Cattle, Homesteader, Warning, War and the Tractor, Blues (Speculation), Drought, and Devastation.[38] But to understand the project's epic ambitions, we must turn again to Lorentz, who dropped his critical reserve in order to explain that the film "tells the story of the Plains, and it tells it with some emotional value—an emotion that springs out of the soil itself. Our heroine is the grass, our villain the sun and the wind, our players the actual farmers living in the Plains country. It is a melodrama of nature— the tragedy of turning grass into dust that only Carl Sandburg or Willa Cather perhaps could tell as it should be told."[39]

Rather than celebrating the rancher, the farmer, or even the Resettlement Agency, Lorentz was adamant in considering the grass itself as embattled heroine. Right from the outset, Lorentz's words scroll across the screen to proclaim: "This is a record of land . . . of soil, rather than people—a story of the great Plains; the 400,000,000 acres of wind-swept grass lands that spread up from the Texas panhandle to Canada . . . A high, treeless continent, without rivers, without streams . . . A country of high winds, and sun . . . and of little rain . . . [ellipses in the original]." He echoed these themes incessantly in the instructions he sent to Thomson: "The title will be printed over grass—a wash drawing of pioneers going across the horizon." And later: "Grass will start with dark close-up, grass slightly waving. Will dissolve into a series of panoramic shots with grass waving more and more—will dissolve finally with close shot, grass waving mightily. The dialogue will point out that grass country has high winds and a great deal of sun and no water." From Thomson he requested "a Peer Gynt pastorale" to evoke "the beginning of the world," calling to mind both the Garden of Eden and a characteristic silent film cue for rural utopia.[40]

In contrast to Lukas Foss's erasure of prairie place names, *The Plow* describes in detail the geography of the plains. Immediately following the credits, an animated map names and locates the region. Informative though they may be, the prologue and map do not make for gripping cinema. Thomson filled the void with an austere fugato whose intertwining lines (as Lerner suggests) mimic both the animated line-drawing of the map and the interwoven blades of buffalo grass that filled the undisturbed prairie. What follows is not exactly "a Peer Gynt pastorale," but it serves the purpose. Under the subtitle "Pastorale (Grass)," Thomson indulges in leisurely woodwind counterpoint; the triadic flute melody is treated in spare two-part imitation (example 26). While there are no bagpipe drones or twittering trills, it is easy enough to connect the consonant, contrapuntal un-

EXAMPLE 26. Thomson, *The Plow That Broke the Plains,* "Pastorale (Grass)," mm. 1–12
(New York: Mercury Music Corp., 1942)

folding with the intricate perfection of untrammeled Nature. It is axiomatic to
the film that mankind can only disrupt this harmony.

Thomson's polyphony of grass and Lorentz's insistence on the prairie heroine
depersonalize the film in ways that may have aided its distribution but undercut
its message. From the beginning, Lorentz and the RA were dogged by completely
justifiable charges of propagandizing. *The Plow* was released during an election
year, when FDR's New Deal was embattled by the twin specters of socialism and
inefficiency. Hollywood's mistrust of government meddling hampered Lorentz's
efforts to acquire stock footage. To make matters worse, his cameramen were
avid and very public leftists. According to Lorentz, Paul Strand and Leo Hurwitz
went "on strike" in protest of the film's insufficiently anticapitalist stance.[41] As

Scribner's Magazine told the story, "They wanted it to be all about human greed and how lousy our social system was. And he couldn't see what this had to do with dust storms."[42] Lorentz thus felt beset from the right and the left—no wonder he chose the impassive grass as his heroine.

Lorentz's elimination of dialogue and professional actors can also be linked to his desire for distance from Hollywood's business as usual. A publicity brochure from the RA clarifies: "Film depicts story of the land with people as background. Land is dramatized; quite the reverse of usual motion-picture technique."[43] According to the *Baltimore Sun,* "There is more serious drama in this truthful record of the soil than in all the 'Covered Wagons' and 'Big Trails' produced by the commercial cinema." W. L. White told the readers of *Scribner's* that "voice, music, and pictures made the rape of 400,000,000 acres more moving than the downfall of any Hollywood blonde."[44] These contrasts are pointed, but Lorentz retained his fondness for panoramic landscape shots even in feature films. When called upon to review Nunnally Johnson's adaptation of Steinbeck's *The Grapes of Wrath* (1940), he argued that the movie slighted the land itself and that, particularly in passages without action or dialogue, the production "needed a movie director." This may seem a strange injunction for a film directed by the soon-to-be illustrious John Ford, and Lorentz actually praised Ford as the man "who, by virtue of going to Zion Park [*sic*] in Utah to photograph his outdoor sequences in *Stagecoach,* made a Western action picture into a thing of beauty." In the case of *The Grapes of Wrath,* however, Lorentz's own vision of the Dust Bowl was obviously still uppermost in his mind. Calling for greater attention to "skies and brown land and, most of all, wind," Lorentz suggested that the filmmaker "needed only to have written 'drought' and then left it to the director to re-create the feeling of those dusty plains tilting from Oklahoma clear up to Canada with their miserable huts and busted windmills. In fact, he needed only to have gone to the panhandle of Oklahoma and Texas and western Kansas and the Dakotas and eastern Colorado and said: 'Photograph this—here is where they came from.'"[45]

PEOPLE ON THE PLAINS

Although Lorentz clearly drew greater inspiration from the panoramic sweep of the land than from the wind-chiseled features of the plainsmen, his team took some human interest shots that rival the more famous Farm Security photographs of Dorothea Lange. After all, the *Study Guide* pointed out, "the Great Plains area means life": "It means Indians, white men, cattle herding, railroads, General Custer, Sitting Bull, Little Big Horn River, the rush into Oklahoma, the lure of free land. An endless wealth of material, the 'Opening of the West,' perhaps the most romantic, colorful period in American history. Having 'conquered' the West, man now attempted to 'conquer' the natural resources he found there."[46]

Among the film's human images are a dusty baby playing on a rusty plow, children braced against the sun or running to escape a dust storm, and above all the Texas farmer Bam White (whom Lorentz paid to plow on camera). According to *Literary Digest,* the seventy-two-year-old Bam was "a wiry blunt-speaking plainsman, whose life and prophecies curiously matched the tone of the film." Yet, as a reviewer for *Variety* pointed out, Bam and his neighbors "aren't called upon for any histrionics other than staring at sky or whittling sticks to indicate complete resignation to fate."[47] Indeed, it is remarkable how often the film obscures the people it aimed to help: cowboys are dwarfed by vast herds and open spaces; farmers are barely visible riding atop their tractors; families are enveloped in dust—their feet more memorable than their faces; Okies are concealed in their sad parade of automobiles.

It was perhaps inevitable that Thomson's soundtrack would emphasize the human element more frequently than the image track does. According to the *Study Guide,* Thomson "based his music for THE PLOW on native American cowboy airs and familiar American folk music." *Literary Digest* let it be known that "Mr. Thomson went back to the basic plains themes for his music in the picture, and wove in the old cattle and dirt-farmer songs. There is a brief period of authentic war music (as opposed to Tin Pan Alley war music) and each dust-storm scene has a thematic hymn which runs through the picture." Copland praised Thomson at greater length in a lecture at Columbia University: "You get an earthy and rather American quality by the fact that the music is rather thinly orchestrated, depending mostly on a tune that Thomson either borrowed from some native source or invented in the style of a native folk-tune."[48]

Shortly after receiving Lorentz's commission, Thomson took himself to the New York Public Library, where he checked out Sandburg's *American Songbag,* as well as five other volumes: *Cowboy Campfire Ballad, Folk Music of the Western Hemisphere, Lonesome Cowboy, Songs of the Open Range,* and *Songs of the Saddle.* Lerner's detective work, confirmed by materials in Thomson's papers, suggests that he actually took his borrowed western tunes (usually including their key signatures) from Margaret Larkin's collection *Singing Cowboy* (1931).[49] Lorentz had asked Thomson to use some "herding songs." At one point he had also planned to pepper the otherwise placid narration with a second voice rattling off cattle prices, but in the end the pastoral vision held sway. He described instead the undisturbed "paradise" of the early cattleman, an "uncharted ocean of grass," telling Thomson, "The grass and cattle sequences run almost four minutes without cues—this is a very long time for panoramic motion pictures and the audience should feel the endless horizon of grass—the vastness of Nature minding its own knitting."[50]

Lorentz envisioned the cowboy operating in a preindustrial Eden, before fences sprouted in the prairie soil, and before the shadow of the slaughterhouse

FIGURE 6. The Grasslands, film still from *The Plow That Broke the Plains*. Courtesy of the George Eastman House

fell upon the cowboy image. Thomson's medley of cowboy tunes seems likewise to float free of these darker undercurrents. A variant of "Old Paint" (or "Houlihan") enters with a strumming accompaniment that sets the English horn quotation in relief, speaking a gentle 3/4 against the melody's 6/8 meter—instead of loping, it waltzes (example 27). "The Cowboy's Lament" enters over the same comforting oom-pah-pah, but with a syncopated rhythmic profile all its own (Thomson marks it first "Fancy Free" and then "High wide and handsome"). Only with the entry of "Git Along Little Dogies" is the metrical play resolved into a clearly duple meter. All the "herding songs" feature major keys, and all are repeated with changes in scoring that are gently colorful, not distracting.

As if taking to heart the processes outlined by Frederick Jackson Turner in his famous frontier thesis, the homesteader succeeds the cowboy on screen as the narrator proclaims: "The railroad brought the world into the plains . . . new pop-

EXAMPLE 27. Thomson, *The Plough That Broke the Plains*, "Cowboy Songs," ("Houlihan," "Laredo," and "Git along, little dogies") mm. 1–12

ulations, new needs crowded the last frontier. Once again the plowman followed the herds and the pioneer came to the plains. Make way for the plowman!" In true Turnerian fashion, the *Study Guide* notes: "People moved into the dry Western Plains slowly. During the latter part of the nineteenth century cowboys and stockmen invaded the plains and helped drive out the Indians. . . . the cowboys drove these herds northward across the plains, which at that time were crossed by no fences and cut up by no farms. . . . Gradually, however, the pressure for more free land grew in the east, and farmers, rather than stockmen, began to push into the plains region."[51] Hollywood footage shows covered wagons jolting into action for a land run, right in line with the familiar equation of westward expansion and the progress of civilization. The *Study Guide* called this episode "part of the great sweep of empire . . . a spectacular race of covered wagons into territory just being opened by the Federal Government." Yet Lorentz's frontier thesis takes its meteorology far more seriously than Turner's did: "High winds and sun . . . /a country without rivers and with little rain. / Settler, plow at your peril!" The settler may be more "civilized," but the cowboy represents a "higher" stage in the natural history of the plains, a better symbiosis between man and nature.

In contrast to the leisurely insouciance of Thomson's cowboy songs, the home-steader's good cheer is short-lived and interrupted by moments of foreboding. A distorted fanfare (not unlike those in Sowerby's *Prairie*) announces a change of scene after the cattle are herded into pens and the screen melts into footage of an approaching wagon train. The jangling strains of "Walking John" and "Idyho" last a mere thirty seconds while the covered wagons lurch across the screen like children's toys. The pioneers themselves are largely hidden from view, and their progress seems giddy, colored with strumming banjo, woodblock, the toy tim-bres of xylophone and piccolo, and whirling wagon-wheel figurations in the winds and brass. The hammering of the first fence post into hard ground brings the music to a halt, as Lorentz had requested: "The entire sequence is one of great exuberance except for the definite dramatization of the first plow—at which mo-ment the music should pause—introduce the warning of 'plow at your peril' and should continue warning . . . the plow is the villain."[52] When the homesteader's music resumes, it is uncannily mechanical. Celesta and glissandi in strings and brass mirror the reapers, whirling out of balance with the rhythms of nature. Whether villainous (in Lorentz's eyes) or heroic (as Willa Cather described it in *My Ántonia*), the plow magnified man's impact on the land.

TRACTORS, TANKS, AND ALL THAT JAZZ

In a move that would have pleased Leo Marx, the "Homesteader" sequence of *The Plow* ends with the smoke of a passing locomotive slicing across the screen—a visual parallel to the action of the plow on the grasslands. The machine has en-tered the garden, and it rides roughshod over the middle landscape while a ratchet sound gradually emerges from the background music. The plow and rail-road tipped the balance from fruitful progress toward degrading industrializa-tion. In the argument of the film, however, the real point of no return was reached in the 1910s-20s, with the dovetailing of two related corruptions: war-time overproduction and rampant speculation.

Given Thomson's thwarted attempt to fight for the Allies during World War I, he must have taken some delight in what the *Study Guide* called "one of the most exciting sequences ever put on the screen," "War and the Tractor." In fact, the *Study Guide* seems to have shared Thomson's romantic idealizing of the Great War: "Tractors move in fateful procession over the hill. Tanks on the battlefield rush toward the camera . . . a parade of soldiers passes down the avenue as crowds shout before the flag-bedecked buildings. It's war! War with all its fervor and excitement and restlessness."[53] Lorentz himself was only slightly more circumspect: "The first time the mass tanks come over hill we are in the middle of our own war frenzy—'Win the War with Wheat'—'plant that vacant lot'—newspaper headlines—grain boats and guns in a dissolve sequence which leads finally, into another appearance of the tractors over the hill, which builds to a gigantic roar of machinery and guns and fades into the final victorious parade of bayonets and tractor blades."[54] Instead of beating swords into plowshares, the film turns plowshares themselves into weapons.

Lorentz's cross-cutting of tractors and tanks is justly famous, and many have linked it to the documentary work of Eisenstein and other Soviet filmmakers.[55] This was the most expensive sequence in *The Plow*, as the director himself had to hire a squad of farmers to drive their tractors in military formation.[56] It also provides perhaps the clearest support for Thomson's contention that Lorentz recut some film sequences to fit his music. Though solo snare drum and assorted bugle calls serve as the only musical background for explosions, screaming headlines, and the like, other film cuts correspond to the regular phrases of the tunes that Thomson borrowed: "Buffalo Skinners," "Mademoiselle from Armentieres," and "Brown Eyed Lee." Military and musical cadences coincide. If "Mademoiselle" with her "Hinky-dinky parlez-vous" conjures up images of doughboys soldiering, the other two songs bring us back to the film's real battleground: the plains.

Thomson liked to discount folk song texts as irrelevant to his decisions about film scoring—even going so far as to suggest that he selected the tune "Mississippi" to underscore flood scenes in *The River* for solely musical reasons.[57] His claim holds water for "Brown Eyed Lee." Here, martial dotted rhythms and an opening melody that rockets up through the major triad seem to provide some musical common ground between the cowboy and the soldier. But comparing "Buffalo Skinners" with the western songs that appear in the "Cattle" sequences suggests at least some underlying consciousness of the text.[58] The "herding songs" that accompany the cowboy as he rides into the unspoiled prairie are either cheerful ("Git Along Little Dogies"), adventurous ("The Cowboy's Lament"), or evocative of the close cooperation between men and animals ("Old Paint"). By contrast, the Buffalo Skinner is a worker under contract, railing against his ill treatment by a dishonest employer. It is the boss whose bones are left to bleach in the prairie sun while the cowboys escape from wretched exploitation: "Go home to our wives and sweethearts, tell others not to go, / For God's forsaken the buffalo range and the damned old buffalo."[59] The moment one considers the cowboy as just one cog in the larger industrial spinning out of capital versus labor, the romance of his gritty loneliness evaporates. The text of "Buffalo Skinners" offers a similar substitution of realism for romance.

For Lorentz and other New Dealers, the ultimate fall from grace—the mother of all WPA projects—was the stock market crash of 1929. The salience of this event may be the best explanation for the prominence in *The Plow* of the film sequence Lorentz first called "The Brokers and the Grasslands" and later titled "Speculation." No one doubts that land speculators were a key factor in transforming America's bread basket into a Dust Bowl, but *The Plow* also implicates the excesses of the so-called jazz age more generally: a ticker tape machine spouts a frantic stream of stock receipts until it crashes (literally) to the floor; glimpses of a black drummer pounding out "hot" jazz mark the climax of the scene.

The union of land speculation with other symbols of the "roaring twenties" was in large part Lorentz's work. This episode relies heavily on the stock footage that he obtained after his cameramen were effectively out of the picture. Because of the enmity that had grown up between Lorentz and the Hollywood studios, he had only a limited number of reels at his disposal. Nevertheless, the frenzied jazz drummer remains a striking choice. Jazz had been part of Lorentz's imaginary soundtrack for this scene from the very beginning. One of his initial memos to Thomson reads: "Music should start with high clarinet—opening of Bugle Call Rag or St. Louis Blues is jazz feeling I have in mind—and go into jazz sequence—even if it does seem hackneyed lets [*sic*] see how it sounds."[60] Again Thomson wrote more or less to order, even adding "Blues" to Lorentz's scene title. A high clarinet lick saunters in over a softly throbbing rhythm section consisting of tom-tom, wood block, cymbal, and low strings (example 28). Muted trumpet sighs its response before English horn answers the clarinet's call and alto saxophone enters with a more rhythmically elaborate line reminiscent of Dixieland.

Although the instrumentation of this passage is absolutely in keeping with the generic associations Lorentz desired, it also functions in context as a corruption, even a perversion of the bass ostinati and pastoral upper woodwinds of happier days. Though it is prefaced by a distorted fanfare signaling that all is not well, the music seen in example 28 first underscores images of waving grass almost identical to those of the earlier Pastorale. Some time elapses before the dissonance between music and image begins to resolve in a shared crescendo of activity: printed bills of sale are churned out almost "in time" to the clockwork of the rhythm section. At rehearsal number 24, high saxophone and wah-wah muted trumpet enter out of kilter with their surroundings, gradually increasing in volume only to drop again to a stage whisper. The push to a real climax does not begin until rehearsal number 30, where "brassy" sforzandos fasten onto the syncopated rhythm—a dotted-eighth note followed by an eighth note tied to a half note—that both Lorentz and Thomson identified with the Charleston. The Charleston rhythm coalesces underneath footage of night harvesting—more evidence that the farmer now operates out of sync with the natural order of things. At a preliminary stage, Thomson linked the Charleston with the first appearance of the on-screen jazzman; his sketches labeled this passage "Jazz Menace." But in the film itself the drummer's memorable visage does not enter until the final ten

EXAMPLE 28. Thomson, *The Plough That Broke the Plains*, "Blues," mm. 1–12

seconds of the three-minute scene. Despite this long period of jazzy preparation, his appearance still has a certain shock value. He is the grinning stunt double for the invisible land speculator.

Like the rest of the film, "War and the Tractor" and "Blues (Speculation)" show Lorentz's deep involvement in shaping the musical profile of *The Plow*. The composer's prerogative emerges not at the level of borrowed tunes but in matters of musical texture and structure. In Thomson's hands, the musical-industrial complex of war and jazz represented a distinctly different kind of danger than droughts or dust storms. While the results of these meteorological threats were exacerbated by human activity, they were in essence natural, cyclical, and recurring. Thomson chose for them circular melodies and contrapuntal action related to that of the original "Pastorale (Grass)." By contrast, the music of soldiers, brokers, and jazzmen grows by accretion and crescendo. As the film's mechanical threats are cumulative and irreversible, they can only end in military explosion or economic implosion.

PLOW AT YOUR PERIL

The rapid intercutting of the "Negro drummer" and plummeting ticker tape machine is followed by an even starker juxtaposition: the bleaching bones of dead cattle against a background of parched earth. In Lorentz's explication, "the final crash is leading into complete inactivity and sterility. What I mean is, the end of this sequence is the end of the world."[61] With the exhaustion of the fertile grasslands we have reached the antithesis of pastoral fecundity. At this moment, before we ever see the migrating Okies, the film has reached its denouement. Edwin Denby, writing for *Modern Music,* indicted *The Plow* for exactly this reason:

> The trouble is that the weight of the film—the most space, best build, heaviest shots—center around the exploitation of the land that collapsed with the crash of '29. The boom is the big thing pictorially. When the drought comes, the most thrilling pictures are over. . . . This misproportion has made the film longwinded and confused. Worse than that it has turned the story into a nostalgic fairytale of boom times, evading the real issue: Fellow citizens in misery, what can we do for them. Unfortunately, the *Plow* is smug.[62]

When Denby saw *The Plow* in 1936, it had a three-minute epilogue lauding the RA. By 1939, when the film was withdrawn from circulation by the Farm Security Administration, this epilogue had been removed. From an artistic standpoint, no one was sorry to see it go. Its animation and camerawork were painfully clumsy. Denby considered it "tacked on the end"; *Scribner's* compared it to the Hollywood "happy endings" that Lorentz claimed to detest; and many other reviewers singled it out for critique.[63] As an artifact of propaganda, however, *The Plow* is seriously crippled by the excision of its only direct references to the New Deal. Only in the epilogue was the RA mentioned by name (along with the Soil Conservation Service, the Civilian Conservation Corps, and the Forest Service).[64] Only here did the film include images of government programs working to restore the land and to provide relief for farmers. Film critic Frank Nugent (also a favorite screenplay writer for John Ford) raised an unusual note of praise for the epilogue in his *New York Times* review: "It contains a few short glimpses of the model homesteads on workable land in which some of the drought-stricken farmers and their families have been resettled. The epilogue might have been arrant flag-waving. But it is not."[65] For many others, however, "model homesteads," cooperative grazing associations, and Soil Conservation Districts smacked of socialism.

Lorentz's description of the epilogue shows his intent to balance the machinery of destruction with the machinery of modern, sustainable agriculture: "Short flashes of house-building: tree-planting; sod-stripping and, finally, huge machine on plains re-seeding barren land will go off in distance, fading into dark, windy, close-up of grass—or dead tree at sunset."[66] With or without its modest epilogue, *The Plow* quickly seemed too bleak for government work. A report to the House Appropriations Subcommittee in December 1939 stated: "Because they feel that the conditions have changed for the better since the picture was shot, the areas concerned want their story brought up to date. New maps, animations, and titles will be made when money is available."[67] Planned revisions fell victim to short attention spans and shorter budgets, leaving the scenes of "Drought" and "Devastation" to linger instead in the mind's eye.

Thematically and structurally, these closing scenes recall or reverse the film's Arcadian opening. "Drought" echoes the material of "Grass (Pastorale)," now in a minor key, before trailing into reminiscence motives both textual ("a land of little rain") and musical—from "Blues (Speculation)" and the "Prelude." And after the dust storm itself, the final sequence, "Devastation," returns to the music of the "Prelude," adding a tango-inspired coda to take the Okie migrants into California. As a negative counterpart to the lively, waving grasses of the "Pastorale," Lorentz conceived the drought sequence as a "slow march of feet in sand. . . . They are supposed to represent 7,000,000 farmers, the Democratic party and motherlove." Thomson's sketching marginalia indicate that he latched on to Lorentz's plan to alternate dusty boots and newspaper headlines ticking off the drought years of the early 1930s.[68] In the film, the footsteps appear only briefly, yet their steady trudging, together with the reminiscences in the underscoring, highlights the passage of time.

Shots of windmills, dust devils, and the worried face of a farmer return us to the present moment just in time for the dust storm, which is relatively short-lived on screen (just over two minutes) and mostly characterized by a dissonant antiphony of open-fifth alarm calls, racing trills answered by heart-thumping chords, and mimetic scurrying figures that move in and out of sync with shots of horses, men, and children running for cover. In keeping with Lorentz's emphasis on the land as protagonist, the dust gets more screen time than the Okies do. Reviewers were particularly struck by the dust-choked homes: dust drifting against doorways, dust filtering in through the cracks of closed windows, dust filling up an empty fireplace. The RA expected all those watching *The Plow* to understand this "black blizzard" as a current event—the film footage was almost as up-to-date as a newsreel. "Most of the people in the United States are aware that something is wrong in the Great Plains," the *Study Guide* observed in 1938: "Perhaps they still remember the days in 1935 when yellow clouds of dust from the area just east of the Rocky Mountains palled the sky all the way to the Atlantic Coast. . . . Newspapers have shown them farmers praying for rain, buildings and fences buried in drifted soil, and the ragged bands of refugees who streamed westward from the burned-out farmlands of the plains during the drouth years of 1934 to 1936."[69]

As Lorentz saw it, the limited budget and "skeleton staff" of *The Plow* made it impossible to do justice to the Dust Bowl tragedy: "You will not see the full horror of the dust storms," he wrote, "a horror that drove men to kill their cattle because they could not stand their ceaseless bellowing, the horror of children choking and dying of dust pneumonia."[70] Nevertheless some legislators from the afflicted areas protested mightily. According to one congressman, *The Plow* was so insensitive to the accomplishments of his fellow South Dakotans that it "would make his state Republican forever." Representative Eugene Worley from Oklahoma, himself a Democrat, threatened to punch the head of the RA, calling the film "a libel on the greatest section of the United States" and complaining that "the cameraman selected isolated spots."[71] But another resident of the Texas Panhandle, Mrs. R. L. Duke, weighed in with words of gratitude:

> The only criticism I could offer was that you did not have the worst things that happened out here; people dying from dust pneumonia, cows being shot and BLACK dusters. What I want to say about this picture is this: you told the truth and a lot of Chambers of Commerce flew up in the air. . . . I have lived in this country since 1900. I have seen my country go from the country of Parkman's *Oregon Trail* to sand dunes. I have seen this country in the happy time 1900–1914. I am afraid I will never see it again in the happy time.[72]

In her closing words, Mrs. Duke identified the narrative crux of *The Plow*. Return to the "happy time" was impossible. If the intrepid plainswoman read her Parkman in one of its later editions, she would have known that the historian considered his 1846 "tour of curiosity and amusement" to be itself a relic of times gone by. In 1892, for an edition illustrated by Frederic Remington, he admitted, "He who feared neither bear, Indian, nor devil, the all-daring and all-enduring trapper, belongs to the past, or lives only in a few gray-bearded survivals. In his stead we have the cowboy, and even his star begins to wane."[73] What, then, lay in store for the plains? And for its people?

In light of such questions, the film's final image seems deliberately ambiguous: the silhouette of a bird's nest in a dead tree. Artfully mirrored by a tenuous major ("Picardy") third in Thomson's underscoring, the empty nest suggests a desolation that still hints at new life.[74] Particularly after the omission of the epilogue, however, this symbolism seems hollow in comparison to the havoc wrought by the dust storm. The film presents no viable future for the plains—no return to the prairie past and only one escape from the present Dust Bowl: further, desperate westward migration.

PILGRIMS AND PIONEERS

As hearth and home are abandoned in *The Plow*, the hymn "Old Hundred" is also undone, set in a melancholy minor mode to the wavering breath of a feeble harmonium. It would appear that Lorentz's suggestion to include the venerable doxology actually sprang from the ironic potential it held for this sequence of desolation, not from its appropriateness to a vision of the early, fertile prairie. While there is no mention of hymnody in his instructions for the opening sequences, he wrote of the dust storm: "While I originally had a scene to go with it I still would like you to think seriously of introducing organ tones and a few measures of 'old hundred' or some other hymn—with the church service heard over the wind."[75] Given Thomson's preoccupation with hymn tunes in 1936, it is hardly surprising that he took "Old Hundred" to heart as a crucial symbol in *The Plow*. (It is perhaps more surprising that Olin Downes identified the tune as "Ein Feste Burg" in his *New York Times* review.)[76] If this salient quotation was first conceived alongside scenes of destruction and then transplanted, along with the ominous timpani ostinato, to the unspoiled prairie of the prelude, then Thomson may be credited with shaping our perception of *The Plow* in several important ways.

First, the doxology solidifies the film's status as a meditation on the care and keeping of natural resources. Second, because the melody marks sequences devoted to both the virgin prairie and the devastated hearth, it unites the film's human figures across generations, helping underscore its allegorical treatment of people. *The Plow* is not so much about Bam White, Tom Joad, or the iconic woman captured in Dorothea Lange's Migrant Mother, so much as it is about "the Settler." Finally, as the only borrowed tune to recur at different points in the film, "Old Hundred" carries some weight in defining precisely who these settlers were: Anglo Protestants akin to those who brought this tune across the Atlantic in the first place. After "clearing the Indian," they took up the challenge of the Homestead Act, to improve the land and bring it into cultivation. At one point, Lorentz's script actually read "white man, you plow at your peril" instead of "settler, plow at your peril," but in the end he trusted the pictures to speak for themselves.[77]

In Thomson's mind, the connection between religiosity and agricultural life seemed natural enough: "Farmers my people were, all of them," he wrote in his autobiography, "with an occasional offshoot into law, divinity or medicine, rarely into storekeeping, never into banking. Baptists they were too, and staunch ones. I do not know when it got started in Virginia, this business of their being always Baptists."[78] Although the farmers on the plains operated considerably farther west than Thomson's forebears, they are introduced to us as fellow citizens of the country church. How strange, then, that Thomson ushers them offstage to the rhythms of a *habañera* (example 29). Scholars have puzzled over this choice. Joseph Horowitz, for one, notes that "the final parade of cars, fleeing bankrupt farms, was wickedly coupled with a catchy habanera"—evidence of the film's "blithe eclecticism, its informality and humor." Lerner considers it one of many "typically modernist ironies . . . subverting traditionally highbrow and lowbrow forms."[79] Perhaps the rhythmic motto here functions as a sign of exhaustion or fatalism; buffeted by ill winds, the embattled farmers pack up and depart in a

EXAMPLE 29. Thomson, *The Plough That Broke the Plains*, "Finale" ("We're Goin' to Leave Ol' Texas Now"), mm. 98–110

line of automobiles that was choreographed for the film crew with the help of Dorothea Lange.[80]

In his instructions to Thomson, Lorentz described the "Devastation" sequence with the phrase "They are literally leaving old Texas," apparently referring to the western folk song "Leaving Old Texas." Although closely related to the famous "Oh Bury Me Not on the Lone Prairee," its lyrics do not record the lament of a dying cowboy; instead they speak of abandoning the grasslands: "I'm going to leave old Texas now, / They've got no use for the longhorn cow, / They've plowed and fenced my cattle range, / And the people there are all so strange." This cowboy chooses to go south, and other variants take "The Trail to Mexico" as their title.[81] Steinbeck later included "Leaving Old Texas" among the song repertory of the Okies in his 1939 novel *Grapes of Wrath*, not just because of its name but also because he associated it with something ancient, calling it "that eerie song that was sung before the Spaniards came, only the words were Indian then."[82]

Though he could not have known Steinbeck's work in 1936, Thomson at the very least took Lorentz's words to heart. (Steinbeck may have as well—both *The*

Plow and Lorentz's film *Ecce Homo* were acknowledged influences on *Grapes of Wrath*.) On the reverse of Lorentz's typescript instructions, Thomson penciled in a list of relevant images in a column on the left: "trailer disappearing," "2 cars arrive in Cal.," "line of cars on high-way," and so forth. The right-hand side reads "fugue" and "leaving Texas." The fugue in "Devastation" is identical to the one that closes the "Prelude," but "leaving Texas" is a coda that marks the migrants' arrival in California. He also penciled "I'm goin' to / to [*sic*] leave Ol Texas now" next to "feet walking through sand" in the drought sequences and he subtitled the finale of the piano suite drawn from *The Plow* (including the material of the prelude and the tango coda) "We're Goin' to Leave Ol' Texas Now."

To my ears, no part of *The Plow* quotes directly from the source tunes for "Oh Bury Me Not" / "Leaving Old Texas," but there are some suggestive details.[83] First and foremost, the textual reference to Mexico might help justify the idiosyncratic pairing of Okies and the *habañera*. In his article "Swing Music," Thomson identified its characteristic pattern with the label "Tango. Enter the Latin influence."[84] A casual conflation of Mexico and California under the "Latin" rubric is all that Thomson would have needed to justify his tango. More speculatively still, the prevalent poetic meter of "Oh Bury Me Not"; / "Leaving Old Texas" (short-short-short-LONG) may be obliquely or subliminally related to the melodic figure in example 29, drawn from the fugue subject that appears in the "Prelude" and "Devastation" sequences. If any of these associations hold true, then "Leaving Old Texas" might be considered the theme song of *The Plow*. Its rhythms fill the long opening and closing sequences; its text describes the Okies' plight; and the Charleston of the "Speculation" sequence bears its rhythmic motto (which Thomson once described with the caption "Jazz takes a tango accent").[85]

The film script made a valiant effort to link the Dust Bowl refugees with the pioneers of log cabins and land runs. "On to the West!" the narrator proclaims. "Once again they headed into the setting sun." The *Study Guide* joined the cause, forcing the Okies into the costumes of an earlier age: "Once again they headed West. Last year in every summer month 50,000 people left the Great Plains and hit the highways for the Pacific Coast, the last border."[86] But Thomson's score gives the lie to these characterizations. Hearth and home may well be Baptist, but the harvest gypsies move to a different kind of music. There is a disjunction between the psalm-singing settlers of "Old Hundred" and the tango-inflected migrants (let alone the jazz-happy speculators). Simply put, the Okies were the wrong kind of pioneers. Vacating their homesteads, they presented a conundrum for latter-day theorists of westward expansion. Although they were moving in the proper direction, they had no Manifest Destiny to fulfill.

7

Harvest Home

Thomson's oeuvre is remarkably free of cityscapes. Perhaps the most important near-exception lies in the ballet he wrote for Lincoln Kirstein's Ballet Caravan, *Filling Station*. Here, a gas station attendant vies for attention with two truck drivers, a highway patrolman, and a gangster. Kirstein created some vaudeville-style dancing for the 1937 premiere, including a ragtime "Big Apple" number. Yet the atmosphere is distinctly suburban; in Thomson's words, the ballet aims "to evoke roadside America as pop art."[1] Thomson's evocations of urban spaces—factories, skyscrapers, and the like—occur almost exclusively in his film scores, where they present an antithesis to more pleasant, rural scenes.

Thomson's tangos notwithstanding, how is it that one of America's most urbane composers wrote so little "urban" music? The same is true for Sowerby, but not for Foss and certainly not for the composer whose pastoral soundscapes remain among the best-loved works of American music: Aaron Copland. During the late 1920s and early 1930s, Copland made a name for himself in large part through works that were readily associated with urban spaces: the jazzy suite *Music for the Theatre* (which alludes to "Sidewalks of New York") and the stony *Piano Variations* (which critic Paul Rosenfeld likened to skyscrapers). A mere decade later he would be known for his evocations of western and rural life—a shift that has caused such lasting consternation that critic Wilfrid Mellers felt compelled to comment: "The folksy vein of Copland's ballets is not an evasion of the steel girders . . . of the Piano Variations: for he sees the prairie as symbol of the irremediable loneliness of big cities, the hymn as the symbol of the religious and domestic security that urban man has lost."[2] For Thomson, the explanation was rather simpler: having heard and admired Thomson's Americana works, Copland followed suit. Thomson made his most trenchant case in retrospect, in *American Music Since 1910* (1970). Citing in particular *Four Saints, Filling Station,* and his soundtracks for Lorentz, Thomson concluded: "My vocabulary was, in the main, the language Copland adopted and refined."[3]

Thomson's resentment of Copland's success did not develop overnight, and it was almost always mixed with a healthy dose of admiration. One case in point is the ambivalent musical portrait Thomson sketched on 16 October 1942: "Persistently Pastoral: Aaron Copland." Here Thomson's irritation seems very close to the musical surface, which features nineteen measures of triadic melody, spiraling aimlessly around G major, followed by a thirty-measure canon at the octave and nearly two pages of marching in place. Thomson thought enough of this material to reuse it in his film score for John Houseman's documentary film about the American electoral process, *Tuesday in November* (1945); nevertheless, it is easy to agree with Neil Lerner's conclusion that this glib miniature might be interpreted as "an indicator of Thomson's growing animosity toward his more successful colleague."[4]

When composing the portrait in 1942, Thomson must have had in mind Copland's two "cowboy ballets"—*Billy the Kid* and *Rodeo.* These and Copland's other treatments of the Far West will be treated in later chapters, but strictly speaking they are not "pastoral" scores in the sense outlined above. The ballets are rural and western but, apart from Agnes de Mille's brief soliloquy in *Rodeo,* neither devotes much attention to the symbiotic relationship between man and nature. Copland's film score for Steinbeck's *Of Mice and Men* comes much closer to the traditional pastoral, with its threshing machines and Lenny's dream of raising rabbits and living "off the fat of the land." Copland's own celebrations of the middle landscape emerge during and after World War II: the ballet *Appalachian Spring* (1944), extended passages in the Third Symphony (1942–46), and the opera *The Tender Land* (1952).

Written while Martha Graham still had a Civil War–era scenario in mind, Copland's "Ballet for Martha," soon to be known as *Appalachian Spring,* employs luminescent triads, sparkling woodwinds, and a Shaker tune wholly in keeping with the pastoral ethos described above. Thomson could not help but be impressed: "The style is pastoral, the tone . . . blythe [sic] and beatific." With folklore and open intervals, Thomson continued, the score "evokes our sparse and dissonant rural tradition rather than the thick suavities of our urban manner."[5] *Appalachian Spring* even features a revival preacher, who acts as the shepherd of his "flock" of followers but who also dances to the most militant music in the score. In the Third Symphony, Copland undertook a more systematic alternation between military and pastoral topoi not unlike those of Sowerby's *Prairie.* With

The Tender Land, however, we find articulated a crucial aspect of American pastorals that Sowerby, Foss, and Thomson did not fully explore: namely, the significance of the pioneer family in the winning and losing of the West.

From its earliest phases, the stakes of westward expansion were symbolized by families moving across the plains. The salient stories of the wagon train and America's iconic "captivity narratives" all involve the separation or reunion of families, and Buffalo Bill knew that there was no better way to close his Wild West than with a successful defense of the settlers' cabin against external threats (sometimes Indians, sometimes outlaws). Against internal threats, however, the mythic settler family proved less resilient. In Copland's *Tender Land,* for example, the family is frustrated and fragmented.[6] Square dancing and hymn singing exert a powerful cohesive force, yet the community disintegrates in a storm of suspicion after two strangers arrive looking for farmwork, igniting accusations from the neighbors and self-discovery for the teenage heroine. Douglas Moore's Pulitzer Prize–winning *Giants in the Earth* (1951) provides a parallel case. Based on Ole Rölvaag's classic 1928 novel *Giants in the Earth: A Saga of the Prairie,* the story was suggested and adapted by Norwegian-American Arnold Sundgaard.[7] Rölvaag's tale acknowledged the multiethnicity of the pioneer experience; Irish immigrant farmers rival the Scandinavian protagonists more than nomadic Indians do.[8] More than this, the story identified the frontier family as both crucial and fragile: for these pioneers, simple pleasures can barely compensate for the pent-up pressures of isolation.

ON NATIVE SOIL

Idealized as the bearer and bulwark of civilization in a new land, the frontier family is besieged by threats from within and without. This is certainly true of the characters that populate Ernst Bacon's opera *A Tree on the Plains* (1942), with libretto by western writer Paul Horgan. Though less famous than the regional operas of his pupil Carlisle Floyd, Bacon's *Tree on the Plains* chronicles a long day in the life of a farming community on the high, arid plains of New Mexico. The settlers are close kin to the Okies who move through *The Plow That Broke the Plains,* but here they have put down roots that are clearly symbolized in the title and the plot. Traditionally associated with strength and stability, the "tree" of this opera is a more complex symbol. A sentinel in the background, it represents the loneliness of pioneering; in some ways, it takes the place of the family patriarch, whose funeral organizes the first act. Yet in this drought-stricken time and place, the tree depends on human cultivation, and the sacrifices required to nurture it become a flash point for family conflict.

Though he never lived there, Bacon knew the Great Plains as a traveler, having crisscrossed the country several times in the course of his career. Born and trained in Chicago, he vacationed with his family in the Sierras.[9] At age thirty, he returned to take up residence in California, teaching at the San Francisco Conservatory, founding the Carmel Bach Festival, and in 1935 becoming director of the Works Progress Administration's Federal Music Project in San Francisco.[10] His decade in California (1928–38) was sandwiched between stints at the Eastman School of Music and Converse College in South Carolina. He taught for almost twenty years at Syracuse University but moved back to California, settling in Orinda (east of Oakland), where he lived until 1990.

Always an avid reader and writer, Bacon made a name for himself on the basis of his songs.[11] His favorite poets were Emily Dickinson and Walt Whitman, but Carl Sandburg, the "poet of Chicago," ran a close third. Bacon included in his longest song collection a setting of Sandburg's "Omaha," whose "red barns and red heifers" echo the themes of *Cornhuskers:* "Omaha the roughneck feeds armies . . . Omaha works to get the world its breakfast." Bacon claimed that his arrangement of "The Buffalo Skinners" featured "tune and words personally from Carl Sandburg"; he circulated the anecdote that Sandburg had mistaken one of his own scores for a folk song; and later in life he penned a tribute to the poet, recalling a shared road trip to see redwood trees in Yosemite.[12] Sandburg helped inspire Bacon's attention to geography and Americana. Yet the dreamy nature painting and electric intimacy of *A Tree on the Plains* seem more closely linked to Dickinson. Among his more than sixty Dickinson songs, the aphoristic "To Make a Prairie" is especially memorable. A quiet, contrapuntal opening suggests the interweaving of prairie grasses, while Dickinson states the required ingredients of her prairie recipe: one clover, one bee, and revery. Bacon gives away the poet's punch line with an expansive exhalation on the word *revery* before stating the truth of the matter with a sly wink and some gentle dance rhythms: "the revery alone will do, / if bees are few."

While Sandburg and Dickinson inspired songs and miniatures (for the most part), Bacon found in Paul Horgan a partner for more ambitious projects. He and Bacon met in upstate New York while Bacon was in Rochester, and they corresponded about many projects, including a symphony based on excerpts from Horgan's Pulitzer Prize–winning book about the sources and history of the Rio Grande. As early as 1932–33, Horgan registered the hope that they might collaborate on an opera. Horgan admired Bacon's down-to-earth seriousness and his devotion to literature. Shortly before the 1934–35 concert season, he anticipated with relish but with no great optimism the notion that Bacon might become head of the Stanford University Music Department: "Do tell me of the late developments in this project. I have a gloomy presentiment that Charles Wakefield Cadman is the average California image of the composer."[13]

For his part, Bacon found himself in sympathy with Horgan's interest in regional history and dialect. Much of Horgan's writing is set in the Southwest, he was a close friend of New Mexico painter Peter Hurd, and he was later on the board of the Santa Fe Opera. Given Horgan's and Bacon's concerns about the centralization of cultural capital in a few East Coast cities, there is no small irony in the fact that the score for *A Tree on the Plains* was commissioned by the League of Composers in New York, a city against which Bacon would register increasingly belligerent complaints over the course of his career. "New York is not the United States," Bacon wrote in an essay called "Native Soil." "It is mainly a beach-head for Europe and a banker for America."[14] Elsewhere he praised regionalism as "a national many voiced fugue—where all sections are equal before the Lord—where the winter wheat of Kansas, the grass mountain of Calif., the brick red rivers of Carolina are equal at least to Central Park, N.Y."[15]

In the opera, Horgan aimed to tell a story that would be modern, not nostalgic. He delivered the scenario to Bacon, saying "it is a contemporary scene, western, and I want it to use both symbolic simplicities of timeless experience and the modern, jazzy, religious, social folk idioms which our radio and movie and revival audiences know so thoughtlessly." Horgan continued: "Naturally, the *story* is very slight. But if people and doings are truly enough seen, it does not take earthquakes and abdications and murders to make drama, or stage-kindle . . . about this kind of place-and-people." In fact, Horgan hoped his characters could be not just "truly . . . seen," but also truly heard. He wanted Bacon to convey the idiosyncrasies of western speech as powerfully as possible. To this end he borrowed some recording equipment and recited his lines in a manner intended "to test the flavor of the words."[16] While Bacon clearly made strategic use of the idioms that the librettist had suggested, it is somewhat harder to say whether he took Horgan's heightened declamation to heart. In any case, he agreed with the writer's aims, calling it "unfitting" that American singers, "from an athletic, spacious, experimental, resourceful, democratic, room-for-all, 'catch as catch-can' land such as ours should have to imitate the speech and gestures of the Italian."[17]

Bacon likened Beethoven and Handel to Sequoia trees; he was a close friend of western photographer Ansel Adams and, together with his sister Madi, a fierce advocate for the Sierra Club. He took his botanical metaphors seriously. In one of his many updated aphorisms, he explained: "They say we are a new nation, not ready yet to sing its own song. But only the mixture of peoples is new, and the ground we stand on. We are neither Englishmen nor Indians; rather we are the old world, removed to new soil."[18] This was Bacon's middle landscape, and one of its distinguishing features was the prevalence of human and botanical transplants. "In transplanting a tree from one land to another," he wrote, "the purpose is to have the tree serve the new land and not the new land serve the tree."[19]

LIVING DRY

Many operatic settings feature atmospheric phenomena that mirror the psychological states of the protagonists with impending storms, for example, used to mirror growing tension. In *A Tree on the Plains,* this situation is reversed, or at least complicated, as the characters find themselves fighting the sun, suffering under a devastating drought that wracks an already arid land. Western writer Wallace Stegner observes: "Aridity, and aridity alone, makes the various Wests one. The distinctive western plants and animals, the hard clarity (before power plants and metropolitan traffic altered it) of the western air, the look and location of western towns, the empty spaces that separate them . . . those are all consequences, and by no means all the consequences, of aridity."[20] No less than the emblematic wide open spaces, the necessity for communal oversight of natural resources springs directly from the scarcity of precipitation.

The inhabitants of *A Tree on the Plains* know that they are living in what Pare Lorentz called "a land of high winds and sun, and of little rain." They identify with the tree entrusted to their care, but for different reasons. The hired-hand Lou describes the nourishment he gets from the soil, and the farmer's daughter Corrie (the object of Lou's eventually requited love) protests that she is drying up on the desolate farm, just like the dying tree. The deceased grandfather, too, used the sapling to make sense of the hardships brought upon him by the Dust Bowl and the harsh indifference of economic institutions, as Pop recalls: "He used to say only when it blew breezy / Did the little tree have a chance to toughen its limb!"

The single tree, the isolated house, the lonely road—all are intensified against the empty backdrop. Horgan's prologue for the opera points out:

> This is a play about the people and the hours of one of those little pine board houses that you may see on the plains of the Southwest, standing at the barely perceptible dome of a long rise in that land of level horizons and the most vast of skies. Human possessions seem like signals of life there; and out of all proportion to their value, can carry weight of dignity for what they may mean to their owners: a roof, a tree, a windmill, a barrel to catch the rain in when there is any, a fence that might break the drive of windstorms and sand.[21]

Like the title tree, the clapboard homestead is almost always visible on the stage. Yet all of the action of the opera takes place outdoors: "the great circle of the plains, domed by the sky." In the yard, Lou nails together a coffin and hopes for a new life with Corrie; running into the sunlight and "tak[ing] the sky in her gesture," Mom emerges from the house to vent her grief; after an orchestral "essay on the power of the sun," Buddy comes back from college, full of city stories, and he argues with Lou over Corrie's future. Their conflict is mirrored in the bickering of their dust-choked neighbors, who recall the droughts of years past and dream of the easy life in California. When a summer thunderstorm brings "blessed relief," no one goes inside. Instead they sing and dance to the rhythm of the rain.

Though Buddy's college is reasonably close by (he hitchhikes home just in time for the funeral feast), it represents three things that are lacking on the farm: water, jazz, and nightlife. When Mom sings of her love for green things and flowers, Buddy thoughtlessly describes "the way it is in town" with hoses, faucets, running water, irrigation ditches, and city swimming pools until his mother is driven to tears. Buddy's experience also stands in sharp contrast to the long-suffering neighbors who complain of dying cattle, dried-up rivers, and parched nightmares about "choking . . . on dry dust." Collectively, they imagine moving to Los Angeles, where unending ocean waves would surround "Chewing Gum Island" and fill up "Listerine Bay."

The presence or absence of water separates town and countryside, the reality of the high plains and the fantasy-land of California. It also marks the major turning points in the plot. The opera begins with a death and ends with a marriage, but in between these rites of passage, the climactic thunderstorm and a jovial bathing scene are two of the most important set pieces, and each unites a community that had been on the verge of disintegration. The neighbors stop fighting and join hands to celebrate the downpour, and the collected rain is recycled as Buddy showers his antagonist, Lou, with pails of bathwater. Together these two scenes also highlight the two most potent forces for relief and cohesion in this western community: religion and folk song.

SPIRITS AND PLACES

No factor unites the characters of *A Tree on the Plains* more obviously than religion. Horgan titled the first section of the opera "God and Death," and by beginning with a funeral scene, he gave Bacon ample opportunity to evoke Protestant genres. Mom and Pop speak with the emotive, Amen-saying intensity of a revival meeting. When Mom comes outside to greet the neighbors, her sorrow explodes in an aria saturated with half steps. The libretto calls it "a seizure by tongues": "And the dry wind has blowed through my green thoughts / Amen . . . / And the harvest that came no matter what the year was like / Amen / Was the harvest of death cuttin' down the child and the old man, both, / Amen." Pop functions as a preacher—in fact, his aria is labeled a "Sermon." There is even a local "Jeremiah," who aptly performs his prophetic and peace-making roles: "O trouble," he laments. "The earth of my fathers is dry, / The dirt is powder to my fingers, / The sun is a fiery plow." The Christian aura surrounding these key figures also colors the chorus, which performs a wide spectrum of congregational behavior from the staid to the ecstatic. Chorus members can be relied upon to answer "Amen" to Pop's and

Jeremiah's homilies. They also sing an "Amen chorus" in strict fugal counterpoint and hymns (e.g., "Hymn to Evening") in chorale textures clearly modeled on Bach—with some harmonic updating. Their final "Hallelujah" chorus seems to partake equally of gospel and oratorio. While preparing a revised version (finished in the 1960s, and premiered by San Francisco City College in 1991), Horgan wrote to Bacon, requesting that the finale be "a glory in the highest Handelian dimension—though of course the idiom must be yours entirely."[22]

Among the most important choral numbers are two "revival" hymns: "The Last Train" at the funeral and the "Rain Jubilation" that welcomes the storm. In the first instance, the cortege gradually transforms itself into an onomatopoetic locomotive. One mourner sounds the call "as if improvised," and the choral response coalesces into an internal refrain: "Alleluia, all aboard." Strongly reminiscent of the funeral scene in Act 2 of *Porgy and Bess,* the chorus chugs through repetitive fragments of text, and the vowels of its final "Alleluia" are stretched into an imitation train whistle, complete with vocal and instrumental glissandi. More thoroughly integrated into the action is the "Rain Jubilation," which begins as a rather straight-laced hymn (free of counterpoint, syncopation, or any invitation to dancing) but gradually accelerates with the storm: "Wind sky and air hurrying past, dust, all shrieking, and the wind airs across the crowd, blowing the women, and there is a free sort of movement like dance among them all. . . . They have created the people's-rhythm, the jollity of the clapped hands and the rocking house." Whatever their ecumenical mix, this choir keeps its distance from the institutional church. There is a bona fide "Reverind" in the script. He makes a brief appearance shortly after Corrie consents to marry Lou, but his music is comic and undignified compared to Pop's or Jeremiah's. His entrance cue is the sound of a car motor, and the quirky march that accompanies his arrival on the scene is marked, in one source, "corny throughout." The true religion of *A Tree on the Plains* is grounded in the local and the land. It arises out of Grandfather's ashes, Pop's earthy sermon, Mom's love of flowers, and even the sound of the locomotive speeding past.

If *A Tree on the Plains* reinforces the association between Protestantism and proper pioneering, it only exaggerates a thematic strand present in many American pastorals. Whether they feature swords beaten into plowshares or hymns of gratitude for nature's bounty, artistic depictions of the Great Plains are so saturated with biblical imagery that it is tempting to seek some musical reflection of the etymological fact that "pastoral" care is provided equally by farmers/shepherds and ministers. One might even trace a lineage of pastoral scores stretching back to Corelli's "Christmas" Concerto, the "Pastoral Symphony" of *Messiah,* and other musical manger scenes. The shepherds who visited the Christian Nativity fulfilled their biblical function in part because they operated at the fringes of mainstream civilized society. They emphasized the universality of the incarnation. By contrast, the works described here suggest more varied missions for the pastoral characters of American music.

Thomson was keen to extend the umbrella of Baptist Sunday School over his scores both before and after "Old Hundred" made its appearance in *The Plow That Broke the Plains*. In addition to the *Symphony on a Hymn Tune* and the "white spirituals" of his film score for *The River*, he fashioned a more austere, ersatz hymnody for *Pilgrims and Pioneers*, drawn from his score for John Houseman's movie *Journey to America* (a single-reel history of immigration for the New York World's Fair in 1964). For Lukas Foss, the religious associations of *The Prairie* were more generic than nostalgic: chantlike melodies, recitative narration, chorale preludes, and vocal counterpoint strongly reminiscent of the Bach cantata or the Handelian oratorio. Strange to say, the Episcopal Church musician Sowerby created the most secular of the prairie scores described above. Military and mechanical topoi make his counterpoint much more redolent of human effort than Foss's fugues (which seem to stake a particularly musico-historical claim) or Thomson's, in which an organic order thrives unperturbed by commerce or jazz. Bacon, too, set his Protestant pioneers in an environment where market forces pose a variety of imminent threats, but he did so in a context leavened by a distinctly ecumenical outlook.

UNPAVED ROADS

In light of the pervasive religiosity of *A Tree on the Plains*, one might interpret Lou and Buddy's bathing scene as a casual baptism—the absolution of their violent impulses in a wash of holy water. To overcome their former conflict, however, they eschew religious imagery in favor of folklore. The storm brought an end to their fistfight, but their reconciliation is realized only later when, in easy alternation, they deliver verse after verse of "Frog went a-Courtin'." It is mildly ironic that this should be the song of choice, for the marriage it recounts ends in tongue-in-cheek tragedy: Miss Mousie is eaten by a tomcat, Master Frog is swallowed by a snake. It is the music, not the text, that gives communal force to the scene. The call-and-response between Buddy and Lou spills out into the community and washes over the boundaries of folk music into an eclectic array of musical genres, as indicated by Horgan's instructions: "The various instruments characterize the different actors in the little folk-tale, and in solo flights call on jazz, hymn, vaudeville vamp, as well as the resources of the classical orchestra." Presumably of his own accord, Bacon superimposes the "Frog went a-Courtin'" tune and an old-time "Chicken Reel," perhaps to satisfy his more contrapuntal musical ear or to reinforce a more distinctly rural setting.

Early in his career, Bacon preferred a broad definition of folk music, not limited by race or region. In 1934, he praised American composers because "instead of studying the latest Parisian fashions at the Boulangerie, the atrocities of Berlin, and the supposed propagandists of Moscow," they were "beginning to respect their own folk songs, their much-damned Puritan heritage, their great Puritan literature, their negroes, cowboys, hill-billies, Creoles, lumberjacks, their workmen, their own provincialities, and their musical extremes such as stolidity on the one hand and jazz on the other."[23] While he was prepared to consider the pilgrim, the ranch hand, and the jazzman on equal footing, Bacon grew gradually more insistent about the importance of regional specificity.

In 1951, Bacon sketched his thoughts on geographical influence in the preface to an orchestral suite called *From These States (Gathered Along Unpaved Roads)*. Like a classic pastoralist, he placed the influence of the land above and before the manifestation of national, regional, or ethnic identity: "Do not the vista, the altitude, the humidity, the vegetation, the crops, the desert, the sea-coast, the fertile inland valleys, the characteristic sky and clouds, the temperature, wind and rainfall—all affect the people's song no less than their national, racial and cultural heritage? Indeed these very factors of the land determine in large measure the strains of the people that choose to live in one section rather than another."[24] Even granting Bacon's questionable assumption that cultural groups were free to inhabit whatever geography they innately preferred, the proposition is still a peculiar one for a nation of immigrants, who had been (as Bacon put it) "transplanted" to the New World. According to this place-driven logic, the appropriate way to begin questions about the "authenticity" of folk expression is not "who" but "where."[25] Eventually, Bacon simplified his stance, allowing all song to be measured on a single, clearer axis: commercial distribution. According to this scale, the music of rural communities would always come out on top.

Bacon's emerging ambivalence about folklore is already on display in *A Tree on the Plains*. The spiritual richness of its hardscrabble characters fits hand in glove with his views on the musical virtues of the pioneer. "Pioneering entails isolation," he wrote, "as in the farms, the lumber camps, the fisheries, the ranges, the mining camps, the frontier armies, the rivers, the prisons, the religious settlements. . . . While we may not minimize the price, we should know that *poverty too is a preserver* and a friend to song. Prosperity means intercommunication and the leveling of regional differences, with its organized and sophisticated entertainment."[26] The threat of encroaching commerce is already well established, even in the Dust Bowl era of the opera. It can be no accident that the neighbors, when they yearn for the beachside glamour of Los Angeles in "Chewing Gum Island," sing out their desires in a "deliberate habanera" rhythm. As was the case for the migrating Okies of Thomson's *The Plow That Broke the Plains,* the Latin tinge here signals the allure of California and a pointed contrast to the varied hymn styles and square dances that seem more "native" to the frontier community.

The *habañera*'s remoteness at once constitutes and limits its power. It is a passing fancy, not a pressing danger. But the opera also invites us to interpret stylistic contrasts that are more fraught because they lie closer to home. Immediately following "Frog Went a-Courtin'," the neighbors gather to watch a little girl, Shirley, do a ragtime tap dance. According to the libretto, "the tune is a jaded, out of focus (discordant) satire on jazz tunes."

> *A Woman:* She breaks your heart, jazzin what she don't know anything about!
>
> *Another Woman:* She'll know, soon enough.
>
> *A Man:* Honey, don't you *ever* do that for a boy, less you *mean* it.

Pop intervenes to praise all manner of joyfulness as a gift from the divine, but he also steers the music toward an evening hymn that returns the crowd to its congregational demeanor. One might identify Pop's liberality with the composer's. "Folk song is Nature in music," Bacon wrote. "Like the wilderness, men need it, at times, to recover their musical humanity."[27] Ragtime could be justified by its popularity, but in the world of the opera it still presents an invidious point of comparison. While "Frog Went a-Courtin'" draws the community together in contented joy, Shirley's tap dance exposes its fissures and appetites. If folk song grows from close ties to the land, jazz suggests instead sex, commerce, and the unsavory combination of the two.

THE VIRGIN AND THE DYNAMO

Corrie and Buddy represent opposing paths for the frontier family: one with deep ties to the land, the other eager to escape it, one attuned to the life around her, the other intoxicated by modern technology and jazz. Because she is the only character to undergo a change of heart during the opera, Corrie's decision to remain with Lou, to "dream his child upon the land," constitutes in some way the moral of the story. At the outset, in Horgan's words, "her heart is set on city ways, and she dreams of luxuries." The text of her first song flits about store windows, street lights, and beauty parlors, while she prances around an imaginary microphone. The score offers a saccharine parody of radio commercials. Human attachment is trivialized. "When you hear the chime," an orchestra player intones through a loudspeaker, "it will be exactly love o'clock."

With her brother home on the farm, Corrie's temptation grows more concrete. Buddy tells exciting stories about "the college boys" and has at his fingertips the persuasive power of jazz, which is so closely associated with his character that it anticipates his first stage entrance. When Lou upbraids him for rudeness, he responds with "an insolent fillip on clarinet," and when he talks of getting

Corrie off the farm to work in a sweet shop and have a good time in town, he "plays an insinuating line on the clarinet" over Lou's angry protests. As the neighbors return from the funeral service, Buddy executes an "obscene little skirl," sidestepping Mom's embrace and "piping in self-ecstasy, squeezing his shoulders together, and dancing away in little steps until he has quite finished his jazz seizure." While the adults keep their distance, Corrie is intrigued, and she eventually joins Buddy's "Night-Time Music" with its "cheek-to-cheek swing." Bluesy chromatic inflections reach their climax in the vocal glissando that punctuates Buddy's most direct appeal to Corrie's emerging sexuality: "Hot time! Make money. Good kids. Jazz-azz-azz! [wordless slide] Boy! Would they go for you." Finally brother and sister join in scat singing: "Bi-d'yi, d'yi, da-dee, d'd'd'd'-do, do, do."[28]

According to Bacon's grim logic, there would be little hope for Corrie in an urban environment where all pure things face the contamination of the market. She would suffer the same fate that he later outlined for unspoiled folk song, which he saw being driven "into the arms of the juke box." Bacon wrote: "We can safely predict that the age of our folk song is coming to an end, a victim of communication, highways, and electricity, and all the enemies of isolation, and finally the appetite of commerce and its immodest mistress, advertising."[29] In the end, however, Corrie achieves salvation—not through the precepts of religion, but through the force of nature. Only when she and Lou are held spell-bound in the thunderstorm does she yield to him, and their much-awaited love duet is sanctified not by the neighbors (and certainly not by the reverend), but by a most unusual mockingbird (example 30a).

Although Lou is the romantic lead, it is Buddy who emerges with the most strongly etched character, and not just because he knows jazz. From entrance to exit, he is associated with mechanized transportation and fast living. As a hitch-hiker, he flouts conventional morality—drinking himself sick in one man's truck, necking with the daughter in another's backseat, and shirking his share of the work when a tire blows out. Even on the farm, he is associated with machines. In his second solo number, Buddy and his clarinet mimic an "idling windmill" after it has creaked to life in the wake of the storm. Amid his absent-minded singing, Buddy is roused by the whir of a distant transport plane, and he launches into an excited catalog of technical data: "Douglas twin-motor / He prob'ly goes over this time every evening / El Paso to Denver / Six hours and fifty minutes." As Horgan puts it, "He is possessed; the music portrays this; he joins his hands like planes and flies with them, swoops and banks, curves and returns; he dances; he is flight." The text of the aria, too, pantomimes an airplane in action; it is peppered with fourteen different vocal imitations of motors, guns, takeoffs, and landings. The music is similarly motoric, generated out of circling accompaniment figures with no melodic content of their own (example 30b). Buddy is intoxicated not

EXAMPLE 30A. Bacon, *A Tree on the Plains*, "Lou and Corrie," mm. 1–10 (courtesy of Ellen Bacon)

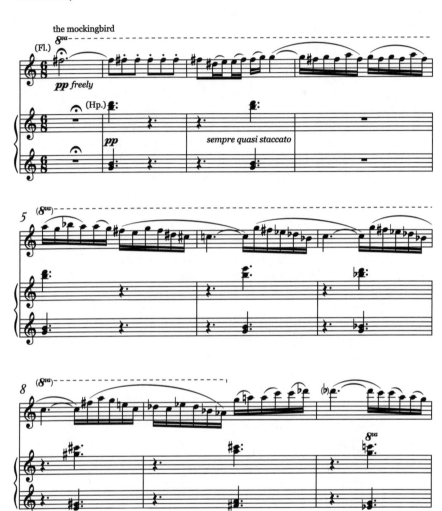

just by flight, but by acceleration. He exclaims: "My granpa walked, / My papy rode, / And me, I can fly."

In *A Tree on the Plains*, the garden has been overrun with machines that are both necessary and destructive. This is the West's catch-22. Traversing its wide-open spaces, Buddy must rely on the highway system to get home from college, but the call of the open road lures him away. Radio advertising stokes desires

EXAMPLE 30B. Bacon, *A Tree on the Plains,* Buddy and "The Transport Plane," mm. 68–83

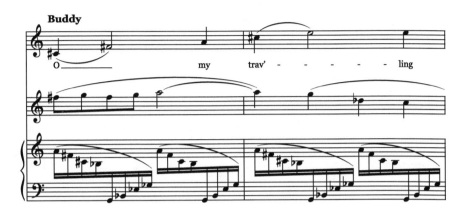

beyond the bare-bones subsistence that the land can support. The plow is rendered useless in the grip of drought. Even the windmill seems to whirl with double-edged swords—a tool of irrigation sufficient only to hold out false hope for the family farm. In the logic of the opera, technology disrupts the natural order of things. And yet, how striking it is that Bacon chose to represent his machines and his garden with fundamentally similar music. As example 30 shows, the birdsong that sanctifies Corrie's love for Lou is crafted from the same type of scale that Bacon used to depict the "transport plane"—an eight-note scale of alternating whole steps and half steps that scholars today call octatonic.

(spoken) "Sergeant, is this my ship?"

Bacon never described his opera as octatonic, but in fact many of its numbers use one of the three possible octatonic scales: (C–D♭–E♭–E–F♯–G–A–B♭), (C–D–E♭–F–F♯–G♯–A–B), (D♭–D–E–F–G–A♭–B♭–B).[30] The composer was well aware of the distinct harmonic and melodic possibilities arising from different scales, and he relished the internal symmetries that the octatonic and other "equipartite" scales could provide. In his theoretical treatise "Our Musical Idiom," written when he was not yet twenty years old, he attempted an exhaustive taxonomy of some 350 scales, and he returned to these tables periodically during his lifetime, mostly obviously in his geographical organ suite *Spirits and Places*. The movement devoted to "Rattlesnake Bar, California, Gold Country," for example, involves "indiscretions to an 8-tone scale (Liszt, Rimsky-Korsakov, Bloch)."[31] While associations between specific scales and topography remain elusive in the organ suite, the opera allows us to conjecture that Bacon's octatonicism was most strongly associated with the divine clockwork of nature, the whirring gears of modern technology, and isolated moments of human awe in the face of these overwhelming forces.[32]

Octatonic pitch collections accompany a wide range of moods and actions in *A Tree on the Plains,* but they seem most prominent in the interludes that mark the opera's progress through the day. In the prelude, which suggests the early morning "shimmer of the plains," Bacon's bass line first falls through a diminished seventh chord (E♭–C–A–F♯) with chromatic motion above; it then rises through the same octave range, but fills in the gaps between notes to form an octatonic scale (F♯–G–A–B♭–C–D♭–E♭–F♭) in the low register, supporting chords drawn from the same scale (example 31). In "The Heat of the Plains," which separates morning and noontime, the orchestra makes a mosaic of octatonic fragments over which Lou speaks about the drought. When Lou moves from speech to song, his pitches are chosen more freely, but the first and last phrases of the vocal line reflect the orchestra's octatonic predilections. "Before the Rain" features octatonic oscillations and cymbal riffs that shadow the windmill creaking to life. And to depict "The Plains at Night," Bacon relied on half-step sighing figures ("Night wind. The mill going softly.") that stretch but do not rupture the primarily octatonic fabric.

Of the opera's short landscape paintings, only "Moonset/Dawn" is more or less free from octatonic material. Nonetheless, human characters have the last words and the last music. After Buddy leaves his family behind, rushing into the night at the call of another plane motor, the ensemble number "Morning after the Rain" returns to the folkloric mood of "Frog Went a-Courtin,'" with triadic melody and a backup chorus of tenors and basses calling cattle to pasture. The very last chorus, which Horgan called Handelian, resembles an oratorio finale in its choral "Halleluias." While the distinction is far from absolute, Bacon's allusion to folk and religious genres (with clear tonal centers) reinforces an opposition

EXAMPLE 31. Bacon, *A Tree on the Plains*, Prelude, mm. 1–14

between the human music of grief and celebration and an impersonal musical environment full of whirling rotors and waving grass. Although it makes unlikely bedfellows of airplane propellers and octatonic mockingbirds, *A Tree on the Plains* is fundamentally pastoral, not just in its setting but also in its charting of the changing relationships between the natural and the artificial and in its strained hope that a balance between them can be maintained in perpetuity. "Nature," Bacon wrote, "will finally harmonize anything. Even the most presumptuous billboard will in time acquire some grace, when the lichen, the weeds, the trees and fields take over."[33]

THE COMPOSER AS ECOLOGIST

In an obituary tribute to Bacon, Paul Horgan wrote: "A sort of pedal point that resonated throughout Ernst's life was his deep love for the natural world in all its great elements. . . . With his instinct for understanding secrets of the land, he would have made a brilliant geologist."[34] Bacon could indeed be called a geologist, or more accurately, a geographer; dozens of his pieces bear place names as their titles, and he wrote a letter to the editor describing the "honorable science" of geography: "It is orientation; it is multiplied environment; it is river courses, cities, deserts, mountain ranges, ocean currents, forests, minerals, tides, islands, continents, populations, nationalities. . . . It is where we live."[35] Better still, Bacon might properly be considered an ecologist, concerned with the politics of preserving native nature from outside threats. This fact was not lost on his contemporaries. Roy Harris called Bacon's writings "a penetrating analysis of the forces and factors which threaten the natural development of the musical life of our people," and *Time* magazine described *A Tree on the Plains* as "a signpost that opera is turning from an exotic plant into a wayside flower." Perhaps most telling is the praise bestowed on Bacon by Ansel Adams: "You are like a clear dawn wind in the midst of the foul smogs of contemporary cultural decay." Bacon in turn called Adams "my oldest friend in the West" and memorialized to him in the elegy *Remembering Ansel Adams*.[36]

Bacon's ecological impulse shaped his attitude toward folk music, which he saw as corrupted by commerce and conserved by poverty. It shaped his stance on musical traditions more generally, as he wrote in his "Notes on Style": "Some people have called me 'eclectic,' which says in essence, that I honor my musical ancestry; that I do not have to break laws to be relatively independent."[37] The laws of music were for Bacon deeply linked to the laws of nature, not by a facile organicism of motivic relationships but by a scientific awareness of the intricate interrelationships between flora, fauna, and habitat.

Perhaps there is even an ecological component to Bacon's octatonicism, with its compositional economy of reuse and recycling. For that matter, one might tease out some ecological strands in Virgil Thomson's contrapuntal evocation of "Nature minding its own knitting," and interestingly enough, Thomson's longest evocation of waving grain shares Bacon's aim: to preserve and maintain an internally complex stasis through contrapuntal or cyclic rotation. Thomson explained: "*Wheat Field at Noon* is a landscape piece," a set of "free variations or developments of a theme containing all twelve tones of the chromatic scale arranged in four mutually exclusive triads" presented in such a way that all twelve-tones are continuously sounding, "a harmonic continuum that is static because it is acoustically complete."[38]

Thomson did not fancy himself an environmentalist, but Bacon did. Particularly as he grew older, he cranked out dozens of letters to the editor registering his outrage on subjects ranging from mandatory retirement to the interstate highway system. He reserved his most trenchant critique for what he called "sound pollution." In an untitled essay the composer railed:

> There is no worse pollution today than noise. Its victims are not primarily land, water or sky—but humans, indeed all humans subjected to it, whether they know it or not. Apart from the terrible engines of war, the worst offenders are the gas engine and music (I mean music spewed electronically into the streets, homes, stores, offices, factories, restaurants, even lakes, resorts, camps, even some wilderness areas and mountains, deafeningly and amazingly loud in dance halls, dives, etc., inescapably in TV and Radio and vastly overused in movies). What the gas engine cannot reach, music will.[39]

Calling to mind camping trips disturbed by loud rock music and the "jazz bath" of modern shopping, Bacon proposed a species of conservation as the only possible solution. He wrote to the magazine *True West* that the cross-country trips of his youth bore little relationship to the modern interstate, with its "discordant signs, shops, and gas stations, each screaming in self-praise. The inevitable exclamation is blanketing the land, though somewhat de-decibelized in mountain areas." Speaking of the burgeoning of water-hungry Los Angeles, Bacon observed: "The entire West beckons to population problems in the future and cannot be permitted to 'pioneer' recklessly henceforth. In short, to save the True West, it will need protection, as we have learned to give the grizzly and the beaver."[40]

The pioneering that Bacon invokes is more complex than the simple, steady march of civilization that Crèvecoeur and Jefferson envisioned for agrarian America. As Wallace Stegner has pointed out, the ideal of the family farm was so powerful that it was extended, with tragic consequences, into areas where the climate could sustain only a very different kind of farming. Putting down roots in such soil is a precarious business. The westward moving farmer is the protagonist of countless covered wagon novels, and yet, Stegner writes, "these are novels more of motion than of place, and the emigrants in them are simply farmer-pioneers on their way to new farms. They have not adapted to the West in the slightest degree. . . . The farmer's very virtues as responsible husband, father and home builder are against him as a figure of the imagination. To the fantasizing mind he is dull, the ancestor of the clodhopper, the hayseed, and the hick."[41]

These placid pastoral attributes help explain the rise of the gunfighter as America's favorite western hero in the 1930s and 1940s. But, as Stegner's own writings show, the geography of the American West also changed the farmer, and those changes are reflected in the prairie scores of Sowerby and Foss, Thomson and Bacon. Explicitly or implicitly, their pioneers operate in an environment of crucially limited resources. While Sandburg's prairie boys might see themselves secure in nature's bounty, in fact they are hired hands, organized into the threshing crews required to operate the machinery made necessary by western agribusiness. In Thomson's and Bacon's hands, the farmer-pioneer is thwarted both by nature itself and by the machinery that seemed to hold the best promise for a pastoral future.

All these works dramatize in one way or another the problems (political and aesthetic) of transposing the pastoral idyll onto the American frontier. The heroism of their twentieth-century pioneers typically resides in their struggle against nature, not their ability to live in balance with it. They work in a world where progress has already veered toward destruction and where efforts toward conservation have a special relevance: these frontier figures are at once the agents of violence against the natural order and the first victims if the balance tips too far. On the frontier, the recovery of a precarious pastoral balance requires an impulse not just to conservation, but to restoration—to the reversal and erasure of pioneering progress. In the end, it was not just the intrusion of the frontiersman into the Garden of the World that gave an American flavor to the pastoral mode. It was the land itself, and the abiding historical paradox that America's Garden of Eden was also its Land of Canaan.

PART FOUR

Roy Harris

Provincial Cowboy, White Hope

Most famous in our Western annals and Indian traditions is that of the White Steed of the Prairies. . . . He was the elected Xerxes of vast herds of wild horses, whose pastures in those days were only fenced by the Rocky Mountains and the Alleghenies. At their flaming head he westward trooped it like that chosen star which every evening leads on the hosts of light. The flashing cascade of his mane, the curving comet of his tail, invested him with housings more resplendent than gold and silver-beaters could have furnished him. A most imperial and archangelical apparition of that unfallen, western world, which to the eyes of the old trappers and hunters revived the glories of those primeval times when Adam walked majestic as a god, bluff-bowed and fearless as this mighty steed. . . . Nor can it be questioned from what stands on legendary record of this noble horse, that it was his spiritual whiteness chiefly, which so clothed him with divineness; and that this divineness had that in it which, though commanding worship, at the same time enforced a certain nameless terror.

—HERMAN MELVILLE, *MOBY DICK*

8

How Roy Harris
Became Western

LOG CABIN COMPOSER

"Born in a log cabin on Lincoln's birthday in Lincoln County, Oklahoma"—this is the inevitable and emblematic opening of any biography of Roy Harris. From the beginning of his career until the present, these phrases have encapsulated crucial aspects of the composer's life: his humble but self-sufficient beginnings, his association with the rural West, and his almost magical ability to represent anything and everything genuinely American. This was indeed the stuff that myths were made of, and in Harris's case, fact and fancy were quickly entangled in a journalistic and autobiographical web.

Even before Harris returned from his Parisian studies in 1929, he was the subject of intense critical activity. The eagerness with which his efforts were received in print allowed characterizations about his life and works to crystallize rapidly. By 1935, Aaron Copland could accurately report that "a considerable legend has already grown up around his log-cabin origins and early life as a truck driver," and in the same year, *Time* magazine could include under the heading "Log Cabin Composer" a concise restatement of virtually all the components of the Harris myth.[1] John Tasker Howard looked back at the impressive expectations Harris faced: "When he first appeared on the scene, in the late 'twenties, he seemed the answer to all our prayers. Here was a genuine American, born in a log cabin in Oklahoma, like Lincoln, tall, lanky, rawboned, untouched by the artificial refinements of Europe or even the stultifying commercialism of cosmopolitan New York; a prophet from the Southwest who thought in terms of our raciest folk-tunes. Small wonder that we called him the white hope of American music."[2]

All the familiar ingredients are present here: a pinch of American history, a respect for geographic generalization, a healthy dose of physical masculinity, a dash of good humor, and a significant statement of racial identity with pronounced religious overtones. It would take a special kind of man to undertake this messianic mission: together, Harris and his critics made sure he fit the bill. They were successful during the 1930s. But in the end, the critical conviction required to sustain this mythmaking enterprise faltered. Already in 1941, Copland preferred to present the Harris myth in a more questioning light: "One has been conscious of a persistent attempt to relate the Harris personality to the open prairies and the wooly West—to picture him as a kind of boy-pioneer composer." Copland repeated almost verbatim his earlier assertion about Harris's legendary "log-cabin origins and his early life as a backwoodsman," but he now felt compelled to add, "Actually, Harris grew up in a small town in the environs of Los Angeles."[3]

Of all the individuals treated in this study, Harris was the most profoundly affected by his association with the American West. And, as Copland's evocation of an urban Los Angeles suggests, the meanings of this association changed over time. Along with the prominent composers of his generation, Harris went questing for musical Americanness, and for many years he seemed uniquely equipped to tackle the task at hand. First and foremost, Harris truly was a Westerner. No matter how the fluid boundaries of the West were construed, Harris's Oklahoman birth and Californian childhood placed him safely within its wide open spaces and gave him particularly easy access to certain wellsprings of American self-identification. During the decades after World War I, when the measure of artistic Americanness was still calculated as a function of one's distance from European models, Harris had special symbolic connections to that mainstay of American exceptionalism, the western frontier. In addition, because his father was a farmer, Harris could and did invoke agrarian ideals. Harris thus had biographical access to two of this country's most powerful national myths: the United States as a confederation founded upon self-sufficient agricultural enterprise and America as the triumphant realization of westward expansion and Manifest Destiny.

Invocations of the American West are so common in Harris's music, writings, and critical reception that even attributes not necessarily attached to his westernness took on a vaguely western glow, helping him turn potential professional liabilities into assets. Harris's isolation from East Coast musical centers became symbolic of his distance from cosmopolitan and commercial forces. His late start in formal composition and his rocky relationship with Nadia Boulanger bolstered his subsequent claims to artistic independence. Furthermore, Harris's humble origins and artfully cultivated candor (not to mention his commitment to diatonic harmonies and predominantly melodic writing) enhanced his ability to achieve that highest of all Americanist desiderata: a plausible sense of sympathy with the American people, however defined—as actual audiences or as imaginary "folk."

In part 3, I explore how these tropes shaped Harris's earliest and most successful decades and reflect briefly on his precipitous decline. After examining the role of the West within the cycle of critical reception and self-fashioning that accompanied his rise to prominence, I turn to a number of Harris's works on western themes to show how a rhetoric of westernness influenced his decision making at every level. Though certain general associations with westernness may have influenced a very wide range of Harris's works—for example, through his theories of folklike and "autogenetic" melodic construction—much more can be gleaned from the programmatic works that deal explicitly with western expansion, such as *A Farewell to Pioneers* (1935) and *Cimarron* (1941), and especially from his manipulation of cowboy songs in works like the *Folksong Symphony* (1940) and *American Ballads* (1945). As we shall see, the contradictions of the mythic cowboy shaped Harris's life both in fact and in fantasy; and while the popular appeal of the cowboy spurred his rise to fame in Depression-era America, the reinterpretation of cowboy characteristics in light of Cold War politics just as surely contributed to his fall from grace.

PROVINCIAL SON

Serendipity and selective memory gave Harris the perfect pedigree for a western hero. By the time Harris had reached national prominence and had begun to think about recording some of the formative experiences of his childhood and early career, a mythology had already grown up around him that, while based on biographical truth, also demanded a certain conformity to legend. By midcentury, a loose collection of anecdotes—delightfully and repeatedly recorded in an unpublished biography of 1951 and a series of rambling oral history interviews conducted in 1962, 1966, and 1968–69—had solidified into a Harris hagiography preserved by the composer himself and by his dwindling legion of followers.[4] Determining the precise percentage of fact and fiction in these accounts may no longer be possible, but in the end, that may be less important than recognizing how thoroughly the two became enmeshed: the older man's recollections of the younger man's preoccupations, goals, and ambitions show not only what wonderful raw material Harris's mythologizers had to work with, but also how thoroughly Harris himself had absorbed their clichés.

The legend runs as follows: Harris's father participated in one of the last land rushes that opened Oklahoma, then Indian Territory, for white settlement. There the family endured illness, hardship, bad weather, and occasional visits from impoverished Indians during the five years after Harris's birth in 1898. With money won in a rare bout of gambling luck, they then moved farther west in hopes that Harris's mother would recover her health. In Covina, California, they set up a small farm, first planting potatoes and later fruit trees. Rural life was quiet and isolating, but the Harrises cooperated with their neighbors, bartering for supplies and joining together for special occasions (such as when the family acquired the community's first piano). Harris excelled at both music and sports—the former in private and the latter in public.

The experiences of these years provided a vein of imagery that Harris frequently mined when articulating his aesthetic philosophy or elucidating his creative processes. As we shall see, agricultural language also permeated Harris's ideas about melodic construction. In the oral history interviews, after four decades of intervening successes and failures, Harris described at length the importance of his boyhood on the farm:

> I was born into a family of farmers. Farmers don't talk very much, the ones that I've known anyhow. They sit around the table, have dinner and very little is said. That doesn't mean that they are not thinking, but they are thinking in other terms. They are not thinking in the conventional word terms. They are thinking in terms of the essence of things. . . . This is because they don't see people very much. They are with animals, plants, the seasons and all that has to do with nature. I think, in a way, that is a wonderful and fortunate beginning for a person who is going to become a composer. This is because music is not a word language, but a time-space language. (OH, 2–3)

Though vague, Harris was quite consistent in this aspect of his musical metaphysics: despite his considerable activity as a critic and lecturer, he often labeled his commitment to composition as a turning away from words. Furthermore, this aesthetic turn relied upon instinct, inwardness, and a faith in organic processes. When asked to speculate on the sources of his creativity, he maintained: "I think that it is a natural function for a naturally creative person to be creative. I think if he examines it too much, he'll destroy it. My farmer's background would say, 'Digging up the potatoes to see whether or not they're growing'" (OH, 41).

With their anti-intellectual stance, Harris's musings place him firmly in line with nineteenth-century romantic aesthetics. In their twentieth-century context, however, they also helped Harris distinguish himself from some of his modernist colleagues. He took great pains to illustrate the roots and results of this distinction, locating the fundamental difference between a truly creative artist and a mere "arranger" explicitly as a function of one's placement with respect to the rural-urban divide: "I've often wondered how a city boy has time. I suppose he finds it somehow, but I've often wondered. I had so many hours all through the spring, summer and early fall in California. . . . I sometimes feel it would be very difficult for someone to be a good composer if he grew up in a very busy society. I don't think you would become a creator, but an arranger or a kind of journalist dealing with others' ideas which already existed. I think it's very, very important that young composers not be in big cities just for these reasons" (OH, 3, 4–5).

Though Harris tactfully admitted that he might be "all wrong about this," he spoke with authority and with obvious, if unnamed, targets. Eclectic, urbane, and well known for their music reviews, Copland and Thomson were two of Harris's most prominent foils. Directly and indirectly, Harris contrasted his own rootedness with what he viewed as typically urban posturing and creative bankruptcy. For him, the creative impulse was introverted, personal, and instinctive, requiring only sincere individual commitment and the peace and quiet of the countryside.

Although in the above passage, Harris's "city" is an abstract one, and although Harris's rural Covina was only a few miles from what was even then a burgeoning urban Los Angeles, "the city" for Harris (as for Farwell) almost always meant New York or Washington, DC. Thus, many of his celebrations of the rural also carry a pro-western message. In the oral history interviews, Harris explained his distrust of these eastern cities with varying degrees of civility. Not only were they too closely tied to Europe; they also represented a dangerous and even anti-American centralization of power: "I don't feel that all the wealth and power of a hundred and eighty-five million people should be vested in a hundred and eighty-five people in one square mile in Washington or one square mile in New York City. . . . I think it should be broken down and scattered out all over the country" (OH, 82–83). More specifically, he noted:

> New York exerts great influence, I think, on Washington, and vice versa. New York is the culture center, I suppose we would have to say, of the nation. In fact, I will go even farther and say that one square mile in New York City controls the mores of the nation. The whole mass media business is pretty well controlled in New York City. That is one of the reasons why it's so difficult to live out West. (OH, 397)

Here and elsewhere, New York represents the forces of standardization, commercialism, and conformity. These were evils to be resisted, and for Harris the West was the primary site of such resistance. Like countless other artists and intellectuals, and like the mythic cowboys he celebrated in his music, Harris found in the West both a freedom from the Eastern Seaboard and a freedom to redefine Americanness in ways that reflected his own talents and aspirations.

ENCOUNTERING THE COSMOPOLITAN

Although Harris made his identification with the rural West seem inevitable, he could have chosen other paths. There were more cosmopolitan influences in his background, but unlike Thomson, Harris chose to minimize their importance or, in some cases, to dismiss them altogether. Harris's earliest musical training was understandably provincial. After learning to play the piano from his mother and studying organ and clarinet with musicians in the Los Angeles area, Harris had a sporadic undergraduate education that was interrupted by his stateside service in the American Expeditionary Forces during World War I. During one of his semesters at the University of California, Berkeley, after the war, he made his initial attempts at large-scale composition resulting in an incomplete work for chorus and orchestra. Alfred Hertz, conductor of the San Francisco Symphony, suggested that Harris take the manuscript to Albert Elkus, a prominent Bay Area composer and teacher, but the latter was not encouraging to the late-blooming composer.

At last, when Harris was twenty-seven, encouragement, professional guidance, and long-lasting friendship came from Arthur Farwell, former Indianist (now Americanist) crusader. Harris had taken lessons from Fannie Charles Dillon, Farwell's friend and later associate in the founding of the Theater of the Stars, and she seems to have introduced the two men.[5] As Harris's biographer Dan Stehman confirms, it is not clear exactly what kind of compositional instruction Harris received while working with Farwell (1924–25), yet, as we have seen, the older composer's influence is undeniable.[6] They shared a mystic, missionary zeal and an unabashed commitment that the West was ripe for spiritual battle against the commercial and cosmopolitan forces that they saw dominating American musical life. Perhaps ironically, it was in part thanks to Farwell that Harris began to break free from the limitations of his provincial youth. Farwell helped Harris make professional connections, recommending him as a music critic to the *Los Angeles Illustrated News* and helping him secure a position teaching harmony at the Hollywood Conservatory, which enabled him to quit his job as a dairy truck driver. Farwell also provided introductions to such influential patrons as Artie Mason Carter (cofounder of the Hollywood Bowl) and Alma Wertheim, who would eventually finance Harris's study in France. By 1926, with Farwell's blessing, Harris had composed an orchestral Andante that won him an East Coast premiere under Howard Hanson and a visit to the MacDowell Colony. There he would meet the young Aaron Copland, who promptly encouraged the less experienced composer to follow his example by studying with Nadia Boulanger in Paris. Harris set sail almost immediately.

How did Harris survive his three-year adventure in the early twentieth-century's cosmopolitan mecca? First of all, Harris chose to live outside the city, in the small village of Juziers (where Copland had also lived for a time), with a landlady whom he befriended by helping her pick cherries (OH, 302–3). In retrospect, Harris had a matter-of-fact explanation for this decision: "I suppose one of the reasons was that I was originally a country boy; I was brought up that way, and Paris was very strange to me. It seemed to me very superficial when I first arrived. You know, all the little horns with their squeaks way up high and everybody running around and talking very, very fast. All that sort of thing. It seemed very far away from the kind of burly thing that I had been brought up in" (OH,

314). With no desire to play the American in Paris, Harris maintained a physical separation from the metropolis. He resisted urban life and sought out solitude. This pattern can also serve as a metaphor for his resistance to Boulanger in particular, and to musical modernism more broadly. Though Harris's reactions against these cosmopolitan forces probably grew more colorful as he remembered and recounted them years later, their resonance with early critical assessments suggests that retrospective idealization was not alone in manufacturing the enduring characterization of Harris as a loner or maverick. His American reception immediately after he returned from France in 1929 relied heavily on the idea that Harris remained mysteriously untouched by Boulanger's teaching and contemporary trends in composition; consequently, depending upon one's critical stance, Harris the "autodidact" appeared either freshly original or desperately lacking in technique—or often both.

Harris's time in Paris might be expected to resemble that of Copland, Piston, Sessions, Thomson, and the other American composers who studied there early in the twentieth century. Indeed, his departure is symptomatic of American composers' need to study abroad, and his destination is consistent with the general reorientation from German to French models in the wake of the First World War.[7] Yet Harris was emphatic in distancing himself not only from his colleagues in the "Boulangerie," but even from its revered pedagogue. Writing in 1939, Harris framed his outright resistance to Boulanger as a product of his own immaturity, but he still refused to admit that her guidance might have shaped his compositional output: "Had I known then what I subsequently learned, my first year would not have been such a fiasco. . . . I was like the rookie who came to France to win the war. I would not take it easy, settle down. I was all for immediate action. I rejected Boulanger's formal teaching of counterpoint, harmony, solfeggio. And she had the patience of an angel. She called me her autodidact and allowed me to go my own way."[8] A few years later, as Nicolas Slonimsky was working on his still unpublished account of Harris's early career, the composer apparently offered his biographer a more vehement, third-person account of his own unhappiness under Boulanger's tutelage:

> The first year in Paris was torture to our composer. He was worried and disappointed. He disagreed violently with his great teacher. He came to get *knowledge* and *discipline*. She preached both. But her knowledge was a detailed cataloguing of what had already been done; her discipline, a Royalist-Catholic negation of spontaneity. She taught the doctrine of conservation—the tailor-made article designed from any material to meet the needs of the time and place. He was in search of the machinery with which to release and harness the wild horses within him.[9]

Boulanger is presented as competent but authoritarian, the proponent of a stifling aesthetic that denied composers the opportunity to express their innermost feelings. The political overtones present in this passage grew even stronger by the time of the oral history interviews, in which Harris mentions Boulanger's subsequent connections with Franco and Mussolini, and her admiration for the clipped gardens of Versailles (OH, 207–9), which he found dreadfully comic. Harris's "wild horses" could hardly feel at home in such a realm.

The musical counterparts to Harris's personal friction with Boulanger are more complex. Harris and Boulanger agreed on the importance of tradition and of understanding music history, and together they charted a course of study based on the examination of past masterworks including chant, Renaissance polyphony, Bach, and Beethoven. Harris's ideas about organically unfolding melody may also have been derived in part from Boulanger's emphasis on la grande ligne, though he never (to my knowledge) admitted this possibility. In addition, the angel and the autodidact shared a deep concern with the working out of musical form. In this case, however, Harris claimed a fundamental difference between his own organic approach and Boulanger's more constrained formalism. In the oral history interviews, after praising Boulanger's exacting standards and her honesty with her pupils, he continued in a less complimentary vein:

> On the other hand, because she was such a formalist, she depended too much on the codification of traditional formulas. I remember when she asked me to bring my first lesson. She asked me to write some melodies so she could see what my melodic materials were, whether or not I had melodic talent. I brought her a whole book full of melodies in one week. She looked them all through and said, "With this book, I could make a great career." Well, she was quite wrong, of course, because she thought, and I think she does think, that, if you have materials, you can make a suit of clothes. But a suit of clothes and a symphony are not the same thing. A symphony has to have a kind of new impetus all the time. The same impetus has to be in there driving for the whole work that was able to invent the materials for the work. It has to be there all the time. It's not just that here I give you this seed, and out of this seed grows a tree. (OH, 213)

Here, Harris's critique invokes the same connotations that he used to denigrate the city composer: the "journalist," the mere "arranger" of other people's ideas, equally adept at piecing together commercial music for New York or producing made-to-order scores for Hollywood. Harris positioned his own "organic" forms against the idea of form as a sterile container for melodic material, explicitly connecting his own dynamic forms with what he called "autogenetic" melody, in which the parts of a melodic line were carefully interrelated so as to achieve an impression of organic growth.

In Harris's version of music history, composers who failed to achieve interesting and original forms were either lacking in creative talent or suffering under misplaced musical priorities. Looking back on the aesthetics prevalent during and after his time in Paris, Harris recalled an unhealthy emphasis on dissonance at the expense of attention to form and melody: "We had a long period which I called modern academic. You could take the most obviously dull melodies and put them in the most square melodic designs with very little formal development, just boxlike pieces. But, you could make them very dissonant, and that made it modern. Of course, we've grown out of that pretty well because it was too easy to do" (OH, 112). Harris considered dissonance both aesthetically unsuccessful and profoundly at odds with nature. He chose a less traveled path: "I concentrated harmonically on the development of modern consonance, exactly the opposite of the way most of them have been concentrating on dissonance. . . . I felt the greatest part of music was a consonant thing, and of course, this was supported by my philosophical attitudes, that nature keeps the world in perpetuity through coordination, not through disorientation. I'm sure I'm right about it. Even the physicists say that" (OH, 288–89). Clinching his argument with a not-quite-deferential bow to the hard sciences, Harris aligned himself with the powerful thesis that art should be "natural." He posited a kind of natural truth in consonance—what he liked to call an "*a priori* value"—that informs much of his harmonic writing, particularly his practice of scoring chords so that they are reinforced by the overtone series.[10]

Hand in hand with the Keatsian equation of beauty and natural truth came the more strident assertion that composers who did not share Harris's unpopular proclivities were false in some way, either to their own better judgment or to their audiences. Harris's convictions about the proper hierarchy of musical elements allowed him to dismiss, for example, Stravinsky's *Rite of Spring*. In the 1960s, he related his initial reaction to the work: "Melody was poor, there was hardly any harmony; it was all orchestration and rhythm and dynamics. . . . What happened was that music was really doing exactly what we were doing in our marketing: it was all going into packaging. You see? Very few people have agreed with me" (OH, 286). With this single gesture, Harris advocated a surprising reversal of conventional modernist wisdom: lyrical melody and consonant harmony, so often linked with sentimental pandering to the general public, here became the tools that would save music from the perils of the marketplace that had driven Stravinsky to rhythmic and orchestral extremes.

Harris charged Stravinsky with a grave but common crime: cheapening a work's content by striving for sensational effects. Harris did not venture to attribute the scandalous premiere of the *Rite of Spring* to the high standards or artistic integrity of its audience members, but he was a firm believer in the infallible wisdom of the popular audience. "If we create an indigenous music worthy of our people," he opined, "it will make its way swiftly and unfalteringly."[11] He had great faith that good pieces (including his own) would be both successful and in demand. What else could have led him—well before the height of his popularity—to the shockingly confident decision that he would write only on commission? Harris's diatonic musical language, his avoidance of dissonance, his reliance on Americanist imagery, and (especially after 1940) his commitment to writing works that could be performed by amateur or school groups—all these elements gave his music a market value that he felt obliged both to advertise and to rationalize. His concern for profit was rendered respectable by his widely publicized view that composers were to be socially useful and should thus be valued (and paid) as other professionals were. Harris's pursuit of popular acclaim thus blurred the boundaries between idealism and materialism. This strategy might have set him apart from the more esoteric modernists of the 1920s, but it put him right at home in the left-leaning politics of Depression-era America.

BECOMING WESTERN

From Farwell, Harris learned the rhetoric of the provincial and received his first exposure to the cosmopolitan; with Boulanger in Paris he experienced the cosmopolitan and dedicated himself to the provincial. But it seems that both the provincial and the cosmopolitan camp—the Wa-Wan contingent and the Boulangerie—agreed that his works presented a departure from existing artistic trends. By the time he returned to the United States in 1929, he had firmly established in his own mind, and in the minds of many others, his striking difference from his colleagues: Harris was not urban or cosmopolitan; he was not a typical Boulanger pupil; he was not interested in the dissonances or intricacies associated with musical modernism; he was not Schoenberg, and he was not Stravinsky. It would have been difficult, however, for Harris to build a reputation entirely from these negative definitions, and in fact he quickly acquired another label, more potent in its connotations and its intangibility. During the 1930s, Harris became western. Through a series of catalytic events, Harris was enthusiastically and openly identified with the American West. The chief vehicles of this change were a 1932 article and his *Symphony 1933*, each of which linked Harris both directly and indirectly to the West. Whether calculated or accidental, the strategy was successful. Although at age twenty-five he had barely begun composing, by age thirty-five Harris was nationally famous and well on his way to international recognition. The confident, independent, practical character of the Westerner was reaching a new popular high point. American literature had celebrated the West for decades. Now Hollywood too began turning out western heroes by the dozen: singing cowboys, taciturn trailblazers, maverick sheriffs, and honorable outlaws. Once Harris was convinced that he was at home in these parts, his western attributes were embraced and exaggerated by critics, mentors, colleagues, conductors, friends, and most importantly by Harris himself.

Earlier reception of Harris foreshadowed the critical turning point. Copland, who had introduced Harris to Boulanger, also introduced Harris to the readers of *Modern Music* in 1926 as one of "America's Young Men of Promise."[12] After describing Harris as "a Californian" who had been "engaged in one form or another of manual labor so that he is seriously handicapped by his late start in music," Copland continued in a more conciliatory vein: "But on the other hand, he was born with a full-fledged style of his own. Harris is a child of nature with a child's love for his native hills and a child-like belief in the moral purpose of music."[13] The acknowledgment of self-sufficiency and connectedness to nature affirmed ideas that Harris propagated as well; the suggestion that Harris was immature or naive may have been more difficult to swallow, but this too would prove characteristic of the critical reception that followed.

Three years later, in a longer and more influential treatment of the emerging composer, Paul Rosenfeld, one of the most significant modernist art critics at the time, greeted Harris as an "awkward, serious young plainsman" and "one of the chief potentialities of American music; perhaps of modern music altogether."[14] No longer stamped as a Californian, Harris was reidentified as an Oklahoman—a state farther east but more vividly "western" because of its frontier history. Harris appeared in a chapter along with Horatio Parker, and both were supposed to embody "traditional, probably Scotch-Irish, musical norms" (PR, 117); nevertheless, Rosenfeld's most evocative descriptions of Harris and his music rely on the imagery of the American West. To illustrate his view that Harris's melodies tend to meander "atonally" without obscuring certain implicit tonal centers, Rosenfeld selected a striking metaphor: "This gives his melodic conduct a certain irregularity and looseness, makes it affect one like the sight of a body reeling from side to side, staggering a little and yet never actually losing its balance. Cowboys walk in that fashion, extremely awkwardly and extremely lithely; and so personal a piece as the scherzo of Harris's sextet brings to mind nothing so much as the image of a little cowboy running and reeling about on the instruments, toppling but never falling."[15]

To forestall concern about the apparently casual slip from the Celt to the cowhand, the two were promptly reconciled in Rosenfeld's observation that most cowboy songs have a direct lineage in Scotch-Irish folk song. With this potential dilemma safely out of the way, Rosenfeld introduced another new theme in Harris criticism—one which the composer may well have recalled when formulating his own views on folk music. "No doubt," Rosenfeld wrote, "Harris heard the peasant tunes preserved by his stock all through his childhood. No doubt, they are inextricable elements of his picture of life" (PR, 120–21). Rosenfeld proclaimed that western folk song was Harris's legitimate inheritance through blood and soil: familial roots and rural upbringing. Yet he also suggested that even if Harris had not been born in cowboy country, his style would probably have evolved along similar lines. "The ubiquity of the Scotch-Irish melodies," he stated, "doubtless merely speeded the inevitable process" (PR, 121). If Harris had harbored any doubts about his individuality or his national role, Rosenfeld's sheer certainty would surely have helped dispel them.

As early as 1929, then, critics had begun to cast Harris's association with western America as innate, and Harris had no desire to escape what had been framed as inescapable. On the contrary, he rushed in to help shape his own manifest destiny. Not long after Rosenfeld's words were published, Harris received a much more substantial statement of support in the article Arthur Farwell submitted to *Musical Quarterly* (1932). For better or for worse, Farwell's article announced Harris's arrival to the musical world with the fanfare, "Gentlemen, a genius—but keep your hats on!" and a lengthy analogy to Schumann's famous welcoming of Chopin.[16] But while Chopin was probably not complicit in Schumann's rather grandiloquent proclamation, Harris definitely played a role in the manufacture of Farwell's critical salvo. According to Evelyn Davis Culbertson, Harris exerted his influence in determining the article's content and organization, offering quotations about himself, making suggestions about which themes to emphasize, and providing favorable citations from sources including both John Tasker Howard's *Our American Music* (1931)—an earlier version of the essay cited at the opening of this chapter—and an excerpt from Rosenfeld's 1929 article (EDC, 274–75). The correspondence between Harris and Farwell during the fall of 1931 provides concrete evidence that Harris was intimately involved not just in outlining but even in writing some of the critical discourse that shaped the rest of his career. "Arthur," Harris prodded in September, "what did you decide to do about an article concerning your friend and pupil—having kept his string quartet and symphonic reduction—lo these many moons?" (EDC, 270). A month or so later, Harris suggested that such an article should emphasize his commitment to "classic" values and his unusual formal expertise: "Again I think it well to say that the form is so lacking in repetition, so constantly reconstituted in melodic line, rhythm etc. that the casual observer will not hear or feel its organic continuity—especially those who have been trained to think of form as a series of sequential mosaics—a pattern of easily discernible characteristics turned inside out and upside down" (EDC, 272–73). Farwell's statement shows Harris's influence: "Form, in the general musical mind of the present period, has degenerated to the obvious, to a mere sequence and juxtaposition of musical blocks, a pattern of easily discernible figures, easily discernible even where the themes have been turned inside out and upside down to present a simulacrum of 'development.'"[17]

Harris also wanted Farwell to emphasize his aversion to "programmatic tendencies," and again the older composer dutifully took the hint. Harris wrote that he had "eschewed Programmatic tendencies from the first at a time out West when all the rage was Programmatic—Debussy, Strauss and early Stravinsky" (EDC, 273). Farwell recast the idea thus: "As a youth in the West he eschewed programmaticism and its allied divagations at a time when these ideas were rampant in the musical life about him."[18]

Significantly, in the above citation "out West" became "the West" of Harris's childhood. This was more than a slip of the pen. At a later point in the sequence of letters, probably in early October, Harris commented: "I hope that you will stress the Western influence as opposed to the Eastern European influence" (EDC, 272). In keeping with Farwell's conflation of the American West and the West of Western civilization, the meaning of the word *western* is ambiguous in Harris's request: it could refer to Western Europe or to the western United States, taking in either case Stravinsky and his treatment of Russian folk music as its probable foil. For much of the article, however, the American West is clearly the intended point of reference. The article repeatedly invoked Harris's biographical westernness, and its conclusion traced the composer's path to Paris and welcomed his westward homecoming: "Leaving his original West, he went abroad to steep himself in technical resources. Now he feels the urge to go back and identify himself again with the Western earth-rhythm, the Western social consciousness, to refresh and reinforce his original vision and integrate it with his newly gained expressional resource."[19] In Farwell's portrait, Harris was not merely or accidentally western, but purposefully western. Having explored the European options, he chose to return to his roots. Moreover, Harris's "original vision"—presumably predating any Parisian influences—was large enough to subsume anything he might happen to have learned while abroad.

What allowed Harris's European experiences to be so readily dismissed? It was, Farwell suggested, a matter of recognizing the importance of Harris's formative years and acknowledging his true "teachers." This proved particularly important when coming to terms with Harris's melodic writing: "If we would get at the melodic rationale of Harris, we must throw over every melodic convention, and follow him to his early life in the West. There are his teachers of melody—the broad horizon, the long undulations or the craggy lines of mountain contours, winding streams, and the gracious curvature of tree branches. This is not fiction, but fact, and the melody of Harris, as well as much else in his music, is not to be understood without a recognition of it."[20] With a certain admirable modesty, Farwell allowed elements of the western landscape to dwarf his own pedagogical role, wisely deferring to one of the few avenues of instruction open to the legitimate autodidact: learning from the land. Farwell here relied on one of the oldest and most potent tropes ever to shape statements of American identity in the arts. As we have seen, imagined inspiration from the western landscape has traditionally held a power to obscure contradictions and to make the complicated seem simple. Like Thoreau or Whitman, like Kit Carson or Buffalo Bill, Harris had a legendary closeness to the land that seemed to be both cause and effect of his special abilities, at once the inner source of his creative strength and the outward manifestation of his worthiness to wield such strength.

As one of Harris's first mentors, Farwell made plain his high hopes—expectations which even Harris found daunting on occasion (EDC, 275). But underlying Farwell's enthusiasm was something stronger than a teacher's pleasure in the pupil's success; like many paternal figures, he rediscovered in Harris what he himself had once hoped to become. In the 1910s and early 1920s, when Farwell organized his projects to reform the "art-life" of the United States, his idealism often appeared naive. Farwell's fascination with the West was sincere enough, but his calls for action came at the wrong time and had to rely on musical examples that the public found either trivial or esoteric. These difficulties were eclipsed by Roy Harris's brilliant arrival. Although Farwell's attempts to ground his own attitudes with western rhetoric may have sounded forced at the turn of the century, they seemed realistic and captivating when applied to Harris during the Great Depression. With a nationwide, government-sponsored network disseminating images of self-made men and populist propaganda, provincialism and regionalism became mainstream. In this context, Harris's western heritage and emerging mythic stature gave Farwell free rein to indulge in colorful speculation, and he rose to the occasion, offering his own précis of Harris's special role: "We have had musical sensations *ad nauseam* during the past twenty years, which may have added to the gaiety of nations, but which have pointed no path onward. . . . But Harris is not a sensation. He is a product, a first-fruit perhaps, of a deep rebellion of the general human soul, though more especially the Western American soul. . . . It may be that he will prove to be the protagonist of the time-spirit."[21] With typically Farwellian mysticism, he charged Harris with a mission that was not merely musical. Whatever metaphysical historian Oswald Spengler's idea of the "time-spirit" might have meant to Farwell or his audience, its protagonist was surely engaged in something more important than spinning shapely melodies, even if those melodies were temporarily its most potent sign. And while Farwell could not successfully act as a spokesman for his own time, Harris could.

"BIG SYMPHONY FROM THE WEST"

The first unmistakable signals that Harris had leaped to the center of American musical life came with his *Symphony 1933*. Given the kind of advertising Harris's associations with the West had recently received, it is not surprising that the rhetoric of westernness infiltrated both the way Harris described the symphony's conception and the critical reception of the work (though not necessarily in that logical order). The story of the work's origin provided one of Harris's most cherished anecdotes. It exists in numerous variants, and the most detailed is one of the last. In an oral history interview from 1966, he related his initial interaction with Serge Koussevitzky during the spring of 1933 and the circumstances that led the conductor of the Boston Symphony Orchestra to commission a symphonic work from him:

> Koussevitzky said, "Copland has told me about you (I know you anyhow from Nadia Boulanger), but Copland says that you are the American Moussorgsky."
> You see? And we had a laugh about it.
> He said, "You must write me a symphony."
> So I said, "What kind of symphony do you want?"
> And he said, "Oh, I want a big symphony from the West."[22]

This account is plausible enough, especially considering that Farwell's (or Rosenfeld's) recent western characterizations may have been echoing in the background. There is a certain aptness, too, in the Harris-Musorgsky analogy in that both have often been portrayed as autodidacts. The friendships between Copland, Boulanger, and Koussevitzky are well known; furthermore, according to Stehman, Koussevitzky would probably have seen Harris's earlier score, *American Portrait*, when it was entered in (but then withdrawn from) a competition that the conductor helped judge.[23] But the story of the symphony commission is curiously absent from any sources predating 1951, indicating that the composer either kept his exchange with Koussevitzky strangely private for almost two decades or else recollected (or developed) it sometime after the fact. Indeed, the striking coincidences between the language of the anecdote and the wording of some of the publicity surrounding the premiere suggest that in the end it made little difference whether the composer shared the conductor's words with certain favored critics or whether he later fashioned their words into a more compelling, autobiographically enriched formula.

Harris's anecdote would have been right at home, for example, in Nicolas Slonimsky's article for the *Boston Evening Transcript* of 24 January 1934, just two days before the work's premiere. Slonimsky provided nearly two full columns of biographical background and musical description under the headline "From the West Composer New to Bostonians." His readers, the potential audience for the upcoming concert, could have memorized some of the familiar themes: Harris's pioneer parents and his early days on the farm, the difficulty of preserving a "native idiom" amid "European syntax," and the achievements of a composer whose "inspiration is derived from the nature about him." "His music is born not invented," Slonimsky opined. "It reflects not the European ready-made manufacture, but a free and somewhat mysterious firmament of America."[24] So great was the European threat that Slonimsky even felt compelled to reframe Harris's growing interest in medieval and Renaissance music as a lesser-known aspect of his all-American style. After discussing Harris's harmonic language, he dismissed the argument that references to the church modes might reflect Harris's interest in older music (which was unfortunately European): "Ascetic intervals that suggest monastic origin, are reflective in an American composer, of the spacious Western deserts. Harris is not a poet of the city and does not take interest in 'depicting the age of machinery.' In his music he is always a Westerner; his rhythmical verve reflects the dry energy of the mountain air; his melodic line is heliotropic."[25]

The preconception that Harris was characteristically western seems to have been the primary motivation for linking the *Symphony 1933* and the West. There is nothing in the symphony that requires a western interpretation. In fact, Harris took almost all of its material from earlier sketches and compositions. This borrowing may have been a necessity given that he had only a few months to complete the entire score (and copy the parts) for Koussevitzky's rehearsals in the fall, but it does raise questions about the anecdote regarding its commission. The bulk of the third movement, for instance, consisted of reworked material from a previous symphonic effort, the *American Portrait: 1929*. That work celebrated what the composer considered generally American features—its movements were titled "Initiative," "Expectation," "Speed," and "Collective Force"—but lacked any specifically western references.[26] Harris's own description of the 1933 symphony also adhered to these relatively abstract attributes: "In the first movement I have tried to capture the mood of adventure and physical exuberance; in the second, of the pathos which seems to underlie all human existence, in the third, the mood of a positive will to power and action."[27] All of these traits were advantages for the western hero Harris was becoming, but none was geographically determinate.

If the music of *Symphony 1933* displayed nothing that had to be read as western, it nevertheless contained much that could be so interpreted, especially in the first movement's two main themes (example 32). The aggressive, upward-thrusting first theme, played by unison horns, sets the symphony's predominantly brassy tone, and the blaring final cadence makes sure that listeners remember it. The movement also features the percussion prominently; timpani solos mark its opening and many subsequent structural points, and other instruments follow suit by punctuating rather than accompanying melodic lines, resulting in a coarseness that many critics understood as an American vernacular. In addition, Harris juxtaposed sections with abrupt discontinuities in textures and instrumentation, and he constructed long passages using easily audible, propulsive ostinati, a technique favored by Farwell and the Indianists—not to mention Stravinsky.

Among the specific passages ripe for a western interpretation, two examples should suffice. In one of the episodes following the first main theme, we come across an unexpected patch of metrical irregularity with a suddenly faster pulse. Nervous woodblock and marcato upper strings appear off-balance, first anticipating, then echoing, then anticipating brass interjections that will only later take shape as a melody. For reviewers who wanted or expected a western work, the mental leap from this kind of asymmetrical rhythm to Slonimsky's "dry en-

EXAMPLE 32. *Symphony 1933*, first movement, mm. 11–23, 174–94 (as it appears in Dan Stehman, "The Symphonies of Roy Harris: An Analytical Study of the Linear Materials and Related Works" [PhD diss., University of Southern California, 1973], 1062–63).

ergy of the mountain air" or Rosenfeld's reeling cowboys would not have been too hard to make. If such critics then began listening for Farwell's "gracious curvature of tree branches" and "craggy . . . mountain contours"—or if they were simply curious to learn how a heliotropic melody might behave—they could have found no clearer confirmation than the movement's lyrical second theme, as shown in example 32. It traverses a wide range in a sparse soundscape, soaring over an undulating brass motif and utterly indifferent to the contrapuntal fragments in the lower voices. The melody relies on the quarter-note triplets that characterize most of the movement's main themes, but it achieves a completely different mood through a casually wandering chromaticism and a contour built of arched figures variable in duration.

The critics may have waited until after the performance to write their reviews, but Slonimsky and others had already suggested what direction their figurative language should take. The pump had been primed, in other words, and the premiere unleashed a veritable flood of biographical allusion and botanical metaphor. At the very least, reviewers commented on the symphony's propulsive rhythms—its "rugged, driving sincerity," its "breadth and vigor," its "important and forceful expression." Critic Moses Smith summed up, "The symphony speaks the American language. This music is virile. It has a destination."[28] Henry Taylor Parker of the *Boston Evening Transcript*—a critic whose initials and acerbity inspired the epithet "hard-to-please"—identified the symphony's "destination" as a western one and proposed geographical reasons for the symphony's appeal. In an effulgent review, whose opening sentence described Harris as a "composer of music from the West," Parker waxed rhapsodic:

> For Mr. Harris's symphony is unmistakably American—American of the Far West that nourishes itself rather than of the East that naturally and inevitably draws from Europe a part of its esthetic sustenance; less still of that nondescript Middle West lying somewhat inertly between. The new symphony is American, first, in a pervading directness, in a recurring and unaffected roughness of speech—an outspoken symphony. . . . In the second place, Mr. Harris's symphony is American in the nature of its rhythms, the scope of its melody. . . . They seem to derive, besides, from the West that bred Mr. Harris and in which he works most eagerly—from its air, its life, its impulses, even its gaits.[29]

Whether or not Parker knew of Rosenfeld's prior attention to Harris's cowboy gait and Farwell's framing of the western landscape as the source of Harrisian melody, this review illustrates that, at least for some, Harris's westernness had become an article of faith.

At the midpoint of his review, Parker had offered a bit of wisdom: "Those that like to define a composer by his environment will discover Western origins ad libitum." But not everyone was interested in playing that critical game. Most notably, when Koussevitzky took the symphony to New York the week after the Boston premiere, it faced a much cooler crowd. The work was a qualified success, but critics expressed more serious doubts. The abruptness and rough edges that had seemed "virile" in Boston now left Harris open to charges that his music was crude, awkward, mechanical, or overly episodic. Olin Downes led the tide of skepticism from his post at the *New York Times*. He paraphrased earlier critics' observations about Harris's "earnestness and determination," but failed to see how the work represented more than an unripe essay at symphonic development. "Much has been written in recent years about Mr. Harris," Downes noted. "There are not lacking those who see in him a present white hope of American music." Downes reintroduced Howard's ringing reference to Harris as a "white hope" only to disagree with it. Instead of sharing Howard's optimism, Downes labeled the symphony "fussy," "academic," and "immature." Even more damning, he maintained that "the rhythms and figures of the 'Sacre' haunt pages of the first movement." The work was not merely unready, but also derivative, and Downes—perhaps overcome by the desire for a snappy ending—closed his review by calling Harris's symphony "an American ineptitude."[30]

The discrepancy between Boston's reactions and New York's proved to be one of the most dramatic and far-reaching aspects of the symphony's critical reception. A week after the performance, Arthur Mendel's response to Downes appeared in the *Times* along with a detailed rebuttal. A similar controversy greeted Harris's second symphony only a few months later; Irving Kolodin, writing for *The New Republic,* took a position similar to Downes's and was promptly attacked by two Harris supporters.[31] At the height of this journalistic showdown, according to Slonimsky's unpublished biography of Harris (another work which Harris seems to have had a hand in crafting[32]), the composer and some of his friends determined that they should respond "by an appeal to the Vox Populi." They are said to have reprinted the Downes and Parker reviews side by side and distributed them to libraries, journalists, and other musicians, "so the people could decide."[33] Through the entire controversy, Harris and his symphony remained in the news; thus, his national reputation was spread and reinforced through a debate in which westernness was one of the key terms. Readers were asked to choose sides: was Harris "an American ineptitude" or a western hero? It did not take long for the public summarily to reject the former view. In 1934, just after Koussevitzky recorded the *Symphony 1933* in Carnegie Hall for Columbia Records, Harris signed his first major publishing contract with G. Schirmer. In 1935, RCA Victor commissioned and recorded his concert overture, *When Johnny Comes Marching Home,* and Harris began organizational work for the Composers' Forum-Laboratory of the Works Progress Administration. During the mid-1930s, Harris raked in commissions as fast as he could fill them—from the Boston Symphony (via Koussevitzky), the League of Composers, Columbia Records, RCA Victor Records, Elizabeth Sprague Coolidge, and the Columbia Broadcasting System.[34] By 1936, he had garnered enough popular support to win first place among American composers in a nationwide poll conducted by CBS, and in 1937, he was ranked highest among American composers in a Scribner's Record Poll.[35] Farwell's vision of Harris as the protagonist of the "timespirit" appeared to be coming true. Harris had arrived at the forefront of American musical life, and the western iconography that had accompanied him since 1929 had helped prepare the way at every stage of his rapid advance.

9

Manifest Destiny

AMERICAN AUTOGENESIS AND THE THIRD SYMPHONY

Marking the apex of Harris's career was his Third Symphony. Though many listeners single out the Fifth or the Seventh as his finest symphonic achievement, it is the Third and only the Third that remains in the standard repertory. At the time of its first performances, it seemed to represent the fulfillment of all the quasi-messianic hopes that had been vested in the composer. Harris had at last achieved his manifest destiny, uniting his vaunted "personality" with technical innovation in the prestigious genre of symphonic writing. Critics have praised the symphony for its "American flavor" or its organic unfolding, but few have recognized that these two features were intimately linked in Harris's mind through the theory of melodic "autogenesis."

Harris's friends (Farwell included) waxed equally rhapsodic whether describing the natural beauties of his harmonic language, his intuitive mastery of counterpoint, or his scientific principles of orchestration. But it was Harris's handling of melody that most consistently drew wider critical attention. Perhaps recalling Rosenfeld's praise for Harris's "lithe" cowboy gait or Farwell's discovery of corollaries for Harrisian melody in the western landscape, Walter Piston remarked in 1934: "The continual change in length of the rhythmic units making up a melodic line imparts a sense of wandering and seeking which may account in part for the attempts to describe Harris' music in terms of the great open spaces of the West, the American pioneer spirit, and even the distant outline of a mountain range."[1] Copland followed suit: "His melodic gift is his most striking characteristic. His music comes closest to a distinctively American *melos* of anything yet done—in the more ambitious forms. Celtic folksongs and Protestant hymns are its basis, but they have been completely reworked, lengthened, malleated."[2] Together, Piston and Copland allude to the two most important elements of Harris's melodies: the continuous evolution of material and the presence of folklike qualities.

When Harris himself isolated and described each of these aspects of his work, he was responding to the contradictory demands posed by modernism's romantic roots. To cash in on the rhetoric of authenticity that had already marked his reception so prominently, Harris aligned himself with the natural; to maintain this reputation in an age obsessed with technological innovation, he aligned himself with the rational or scientific. The quandaries posed by this dilemma left their traces throughout writings by and about the composer. Take, for example, Slonimsky's account of Harris's melodic habits: "Harris has always emphasized that he is a Man of Nature. His melodic inspiration comes to him from communion with nature, during his solitary walks. . . . In this he is entirely a romantic, with this difference, that he translates his immediate moods into a rational and self-consistent language of rhythms and modes" (CC, 66).

Harris's insistence on the natural or intuitive inspiration behind procedures that might otherwise have seemed overly cerebral was at its most forceful in his descriptions of "autogenetic" melody. We are indebted to Harris's student Sidney Thurber Cox for the clearest explication of Harris's "autogenetic principle," in a 1948 master's thesis that includes examples provided by Harris himself.[3] Among the features Cox cataloged are variously proportioned melodic arch figures, hierarchies in the placement of melodic climaxes, and the manipulation of interval content to suggest gradual expansion or contraction.[4] All of these components work together to create a type of melodic development through variation that should, as Cox observed, "expand and extend the possibilities inherent in the original germ" in such a way that "the process will not strike the auditor as being too facile, or too reminiscent of traditional practice." Distance from tradition was not the only—perhaps not even the primary—target for Harris's autogenetic theorizing. Lest there be any confusion, Cox continued: "This is in direct contrast to the method of Stravinsky and his followers, who prefer to truncate and foreshorten melodic phrases rather than to expand them. They reiterate and vary, and piece together the mosaic bits so formed, and achieve a sort of development by sheer exploitation of the material, but it would seem that any process of diminution such as this could not be so aesthetically satisfying as one which expands from a germ, constantly generating new life from the old."[5]

We find ourselves on a familiar battleground as Cox deploys the "mosaic" metaphor—a cousin of the "tailor-made" aesthetic—to denigrate Stravinskian composition as the "sheer exploitation" of innocent material. Because Harris's own ideas about melody were intimately connected to ideas about form, his theory of autogenetic melody could participate in the fight against the allegedly formalist neoclassicism of the Boulangerie and its favorite Russian icon. With the Third Symphony, Harris attempted to counter Franco-Russian neoclassicism by crafting a single-movement symphony, in a flexible form, with an explicit emphasis on the gradual unfolding of materials. By almost all contemporary evidence, this attempt was successful.

Completed in 1938 but substantially revised in 1939, the symphony was given ten times by the Boston Symphony Orchestra during the 1939–40 season. In 1941–42, American orchestras programmed it on more than thirty occasions.[6] It was the first large-scale American work conducted by Arturo Toscanini, and it won subsequent praise from Thomson, Copland, Leonard Bernstein, Elliott Carter, and Colin McPhee, among others.[7] Olin Downes was famously late to the New York premiere, but even he registered his approval, noting that the symphony displayed "a greater unity of thought and style than any other work of Mr. Harris that we have heard." William Schuman, unsatisfied with the enthusiasm that New York's critical establishment had mustered for his friend and teacher, made his own report to the *New York Times* to catalog the work's virtues: "Its melodic material reveals once again Harris's remarkable gift," he began. "The contrapuntal writing is explicit, the orchestration is original and colorful. The harmonic texture is decidedly on the consonant side, although the combinations are largely polytonal. These materials are successfully wrought into a form, autogenetic in character, wherein each idea is brought to its logical conclusion."[8]

Although Slonimsky later called Harris's Third "the least 'autogenetic'" of the composer's symphonies (CC, 134), autogenesis was a watchword at the time the revised symphony had its premiere. Indeed, Harris seems to be representing its organic processes from the very opening of the score (example 33), where the leisurely low strings intone a series of unpredictable but interrelated phrases. As Copland put it, "Harris—at least in the opening and pastoral sections of this symphony—builds the music out of a seemingly endless succession of spun-out melodies, which, if not remarkable in themselves, together convey a remarkable impression of inexhaustible profusion of melodic invention."[9]

In addition, the work as a whole was meant to convey both self-sufficiency and organic growth in its formal structure, which Harris split into five sections:

SECTION I: Tragic—low string sonorities
SECTION II: Lyric—strings, horns, woodwinds
SECTION III: Pastoral—woodwinds with a polytonal string background
SECTION IV: Fugue—dramatic
SECTION V: Dramatic—tragic

The central pastoral section, replete with triadic woodwind utterances, conjures up a static expanse; the climactic and boisterous fugue quickly succumbs to its own enthusiasm, with brass and percussion evolving or devolving from counterpoint to propulsive exuberance.

EXAMPLE 33. Roy Harris, Symphony No. 3, mm. 1–38 (New York: G. Schirmer, 1940)

As was to be expected, pastoral references and brassy fanfares carried American connotations for the "Log Cabin Composer," as Elliott Carter observed: "The emphasis is prevailingly on qualities of American pioneer life, physical strength, unflinching courage, strong conviction and the grand, lonely bleakness of certain stretches of the natural scene."[10] The program notes made it generally known

EXAMPLE 33 *(continued)*

that there was "an air of the West" in Harris's music and stated that the symphony showed "our persisting racial self-consciousness and root-seeking."[11] Other critics were more geographically specific, referring to "the bleak and barren expanses of Western Kansas" or "the endless rolling plains of the pioneer west and its vast wilderness."[12]

Interestingly, however, when called upon to recount his own narrative of this, his most famous work, Harris chose to emphasize the west of "western music" rather than the trans-Mississippi West. Stretching his World War II chronology a bit in retrospect, he recalled that "just about that time":

> Hitler was taking over one country after another, my students began to be drafted, and we were at war. I wrote the Third Symphony because I didn't know what was going to happen. I thought maybe this would be the last one. And I remember I wrote it as a kind of survey of the evolution of western music. Instead of writing about it, you know, I wrote the actual music, starting with monody and organum, and going on into fauxbourdon harmony, gradually into polytonal counterpoint, and then into fugue. The whole thing was a kind of survey. . . . that's the way it was conceived, but I also wanted to write a work which had a large Gothic arch, which began at the beginning and never did stop until the end. That was what Koussevitzky got so excited about.[13]

Confronted with Harris's musico-historical exegesis and the composer's lingering western connotations, British critic Wilfrid Mellers managed a remarkable fusion of the two:

It resembles Bruckner if one could imagine a Bruckner with no past . . . with nothing, indeed, but the American wilderness. Like a Bruckner symphony, it starts with the emergence of life from the void. . . . The sense of growth and endeavor in the length of the melody, powerfully suggest man alone in the prairies: the music is "religious" in that the continuously evolving monody sounds like a rudimentary, open-air plainchant, a spontaneous, God-given creativity; while it is modern, and perhaps specifically American, in the speech-inflected plasticity of its phrasing and in its harmonic fluidity.

Embracing the "naïvety" that allowed Harris to "substitute for Bruckner's heaven the empty prairie," Mellers continued, arguing that "the music enacts the growth of a civilization." Starting from "the primitive identity between man and nature," the symphony "imaginatively re-enacts man's apparent conquest of nature and his achievement of civilization." With the onset of the pastoral section, woodwind instruments "begin to pick out brief, comparatively fragmentary *tunes* which are derived from the long, plainsong-like melodies, but which become progressively more rhythmic, perky and assertive, less lyrical and 'religious.' Ultimately they turn into American hill-billy and shanty-tune: the crude music the pioneer makes to assert his humanity *against* Nature." Finally, we reach the brusque fugue subject, which "sounds like a fusion of a late medieval hocket or hiccup (which has disrupted the continuity of plainsong line and rhythm) with the fuguing hymn, and with the music of Middle West dance-hall and honky-tonk. The cruelty within the American wilderness comes to the surface as the creative spontaneity of religious lyricism is defeated. The broken rhythms are savage, the scoring harsh. . . . this is the only part of Harris's score which reminds us of the urban idiom of Copland."[14] Though the symphony might have moved from the mythic unity of man and nature to the fractured sounds of the American city, it could not, in Mellers's view, close on Copland's urban turf; the "innate heroism of the pioneer re-establishes itself" in the tragic coda that caused Koussevitzky to claim that Harris's magnum opus was the first "tragic" American symphony.[15]

Harris clearly felt the "weight of history" in this work—whether that history was American history, "western" history, music history, or personal history. As an exercise in autogenesis, the symphony took a stance against the twin poles of Stravinsky and Schoenberg. The slow movement and the boisterous fugue were worlds away from Stravinskian austerity; the consonant and often triadic harmonies also flew in the face of Schoenbergian serialism.[16] In a more intimate realm, the symphony was the first major orchestral work Harris wrote after gaining the critical spotlight, and the first since his marriage to Johana Harris (née Beula Duffey), an event he often credited with boosting his confidence. In retrospect, Harris also allotted to the audiences of the American West a special, and perhaps not entirely justified, role in solidifying the reputation of his "Lucky Third." "Let's not kid ourselves," he reminisced:

The Third Symphony happened to come along when it was needed. The first season it was greeted with all the same boos and bravos as have been all my works. Then because Koussevitzky was completely sold on it, he took it on his Western tour where it was much more warmly received by the public. So it was recorded. Then within a few weeks it was featured by the Chicago Symphony, the Cleveland Symphony, and broadcast by Toscanini over N.B.C. In the same week Victor released the Koussevitzky recordings and *Time* magazine hailed the work as the most important American symphony. From then on, the Third Symphony was in. That's the way things happen in America, and there's nothing anybody can do about it.[17]

WESTWARD EXPANSION—TRAGIC:
FAREWELL TO PIONEERS

By the year of the Third Symphony, then, "autogenetic melody" was a sufficiently established concept to form part of Harris's pedagogical and professional arsenal. The ambiguity in the prefix "auto" would continue to serve him well. It could invoke both the highly personal *auto* of *autobiography* (or, for that matter, *autodidact*) and the impersonal *auto* of the *autochthon*." The origin of the efficacious term *autogenesis* remains shrouded in mystery, but it may once again have been music critics who laid the foundation for this part of Harris's aesthetic platform—this time with Mendel leading the way. As early as 1932, not long after Rosenfeld's influential essay, Mendel attempted to clarify the Harris agenda: "Roy Harris is trying to work out an idiom in which the structure shall be based on the self-determined growth of the melodic material, not on any superimposed form. . . . It must grow as a plant or an animal grows, along lines dictated by its own inner necessity, not imposed on it from above."[18] The parallel between Mendel's "self-determined" and Harris's "autogenetic" is suggestive, but not conclusive in a critical environment saturated with organic theorizing. More striking is the fact that Harris's first documented use of the word seems to have occurred scarcely a year after Mendel's article appeared, explicitly in reference to the "big symphony from the West."[19]

Surprisingly, in his program note for the *Symphony 1933*, Harris uses the term to refer not to the sinuous unfolding of the first movement's lyrical second theme, but to the rather more mechanical, contrapuntal third movement in which most of the thematic material is apparently generated from an opening three-note motive. In his widely disseminated review of the symphony, Henry Taylor Parker picked up the autogenetic idea (though not the term) and put a slightly different spin on it. Rather than focusing on motivic economy, Parker praised Harris's expansive, even long-winded melodic utterances, and it is this sense of the term that Harris (and Cox) would later employ. Couching his description of Harrisian melody between two references to the composer's westernness, the effusive Parker wrote: "From a germ his themes broaden and lengthen in a fashion strange to the short-breathed musical hour. From the themes develops melody long-lined, plastic, outspringing, upswinging, down-turning, unpredictable in its variety."[20] "Autogenesis" thus may have played a role, albeit a murkier one, in Harris's identification with the American West. From the beginning it may have carried a weakly western tinge.

The hypothetically western connotations of "autogenesis" seem still more plausible when one takes into consideration Harris's *Farewell to Pioneers*. Written in September 1935, three years before the Third Symphony, it is Harris's first overtly western work and one of his most extensive essays in "autogenesis." In fact, one might say that the evocatively titled *Farewell to Pioneers* (Symphonic Elegy) takes ideas of "autogenesis" as its musical and programmatic subject matter. What could have offered a stronger invitation to experiment with the idea of autogenesis than a depiction of self-made men and women? Indeed, what could have allowed a more tangible expression of the western heritage that had lately brought Harris such rewards? *Farewell to Pioneers*, Harris maintained, "is a tribute to a passing generation of Americans to which my own father and mother belong. Theirs was the last generation to affirm and live by the pioneer standards of frontiersmen. They were born of and taught by a race of men and women who seemed to crave the tang of conquering wildernesses and wresting abundance from virgin soil."[21] Not everyone was convinced by Harris's tribute. In fact, the 1936 premiere received reviews that were at best lukewarm. Colin McPhee, for example, lamented that Harris had decided to publish the work before it had been heard, noting that "much will have to be done before it can sound. . . . The orchestra is once more the 'voice' of the composer, holding the unwilling listener with its personal tale."[22] Even Harris's much-vaunted "personality" could not save him here—on the contrary, McPhee condemned the work in part because he disliked being manipulated by the nineteenth-century leanings of its composer's "voice."

Although the premiere was a critical disappointment, it seems likely that *Farewell to Pioneers* earned a place in Harris's teaching canon, for this brief work supplied one of the primary exhibits in Cox's discussion of "autogenetic" melody. Though he opened his thesis with a passage from a more sophisticated work, Harris's Fifth Symphony, Cox turned to the *Farewell to Pioneers* for his very next illustration (example 34). As Cox observed, the "fundamental idea" generating the passage is a systematic scheme of widening intervals. The first bar (m. 71) yields first a semitone, then a major second, minor third, and major third. The second bar continues the expansion in a less systematic way, touching on a tritone and a perfect fourth and stretching the range of this measure as a whole to the perfect fifth B–F♯.

In this and other passages, Harris aimed (or so he told Cox) for "a gentle variation of both pitch and rhythm design so subtly conceived that the auditor is gradually and almost imperceptibly led onward and onward into fresh and new fields of melody."[23] Yet these fertile melodic fields eluded listeners. McPhee was

EXAMPLE 34. *Farewell to Pioneers*, mm. 71–85 (as it appears in Cox, "The Autogenetic Principle in the Melodic Writings of Roy Harris" [Master's thesis, Cornell University, 1948]).

not the only critic to reject the work; it had very few performances and was never recorded.[24] Something was obscuring the endless possibilities for development that its themes were supposed to have promised.

At least two explanations for the failure of *Farewell to Pioneers* come to mind, each reflecting a concept of autogenesis different from the melodic autogenesis that Cox painstakingly described. The difficulties seem to stem not from Harris's melodic techniques, but rather from the historical self-fashioning evoked by his title: the odyssey of the American pioneers. In the first place, Harris purposefully eschewed technical sophistication because, according to the program note for *Farewell to Pioneers*, any overrefinement would have been out of place: "this last generation inherited social and economic standards which were direct and simple. They abhorred subtlety and nuance as evidence of an urbanity which could not survive the rigors of Nature's laws."[25] The melody has none of the rhythmic interest and delightful flexibility that had characterized parts of the *Symphony 1933*. Its design is intentionally stark, the changing articulations only emphasizing the driving insistence of nearly incessant eighth notes.

Second and more importantly, Harris placed this theme—and all the others in *Farewell to Pioneers*—in a barren environment where "organic" melody could hardly be expected to thrive. The piece unfolds over a series of ostinato figures (one of the few techniques that both of his teachers, Farwell and Boulanger, would have approved). There are four main sections (example 35), based on four

EXAMPLE 35. Ostinati in *Farewell to Pioneers* (New York: G. Schirmer, 1935)

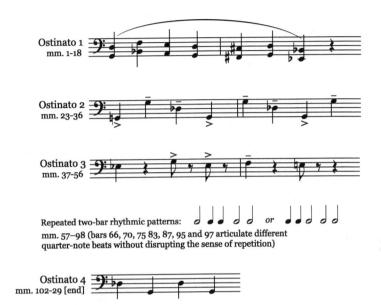

ostinati, the third of which dissipates into a repeated rhythmic motto after nine repetitions. The first and third ostinati are rhythmically and intervallically related; the second and fourth ostinati are based on tritone alternation. Rather than molding the piece into a sonata form, Harris chose an additive structure without prescribed section lengths or thematic functions.

Harris did make a few gestures toward linking the four sections—the five-bar transition between ostinati one and two and the gradual dissolution of ostinato three, for example. But the cumulative result remains blocklike and impenetrable, suggesting a series of static backdrops more than an evolving scene. In his thesis on autogenesis, Cox actually chose for his example the only measures in the piece where ostinati do not absolutely dominate the texture. For these fifteen bars, the lower strings rest from their reiterations, though after one measure's pause, their rhythmic work is dutifully carried on by the entire brass section, *molto marcato*. The sheer accumulation of ostinato patterns led McPhee to observe: "The orchestra labored along far more wearily than did any of the most fatigued pioneers." Incessant repetition undoubtedly also contributed to the displeasure of reviewers for the Philadelphia papers, who called the piece "a bit relentless in its monotony" and a "cheerless journey" that "begins at nothing and ends at nothing."[26]

EXAMPLE 36. *Farewell to Pioneers*, mm. 1–10

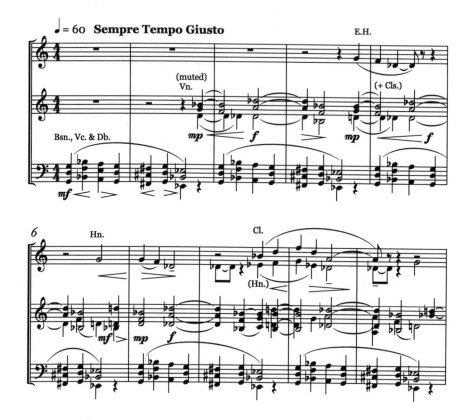

The beginning of *Farewell to Pioneers* in particular betrays the contradiction between autogenesis and musical landscape painting. Its opening melody shares some of the autogenetic traits Cox described: fragments that are recognizably—even crudely—related to one another, and a sense of progression created by the melody's gradually lengthening phrases and slowly rising register. Any perceptible "organic growth" in this melody remains stunted, however, by frequent rests, limited pitch content, and the restrictive space in which the melody travels (example 36). The initial ostinato figure, with its parallel perfect fifths in low registers, precisely recalls the ostinati of the Indianists. For Farwell and Cadman, such ostinati had served to depict the picturesque vastness of nearly empty spaces and to project onto indigenous peoples the qualities of "the primitive": a heroic but ultimately doomed persistence, the tragic inability to change. Such connotations are in fact well suited to *Farewell to Pioneers*. The work was, after all, both elegy and eulogy—not for a "vanishing race," but for a "passing generation." "Time has called them," Harris's program note proclaimed, "and Industrialism has relegated their ideals to the shelves of *the impractical*."

Paradoxically, autogenetic melody and the pioneer program were put at odds in this context. It is not so much that autogenetic procedures cannot be found in the score, but that such procedures are audibly overwhelmed by the persistent ostinati. Melodies, whether autogenetic or not, are dwarfed in this hostile soundscape; or, as Mendel might have put it, the melody was not allowed to dictate the form. The autogenetic process was ultimately thwarted by a setting in which the individuals supposedly central to the program were granted less sonic presence than the imaginary landscape engulfing them. At the same time, Harris seems to have neglected the timbral considerations that usually play such a key role in the evocation of musical landscapes. Compared to the varied palette that Debussy used to color his "Nuages"—or, closer to home, the one that Copland would use in his *Appalachian Spring*—the sonorities of *Farewell to Pioneers* are bleak indeed. This lack of timbral differentiation may have been an unintentional side effect of Harris's concentration on melodic matters, or even a simple miscalculation, since, as McPhee noted, the work was published before it had been performed. On the other hand, it may have faithfully reflected Harris's own views about the stark difficulties of pioneer life, collective difficulties that—at least at first—seemed incongruous with his own heroic individualism.

WESTWARD EXPANSION—TRIUMPHANT: *CIMARRON*

Harris retained both autogenetic and ostinato techniques, but he soon identified himself with a more colorful array of western ancestors, both real and imaginary. The culmination of this process, and Harris's closest approach to western autobiography, can be seen and heard in *Cimarron* (1941). Dedicated to his natal state of Oklahoma and named for one of the regions of Indian Territory opened for white settlement by the land runs that began in 1889, *Cimarron* was a generous gesture by a composer whom Oklahomans were proud to claim as a "native son."[27] As the first of Harris's pieces for symphonic band, the work represents another milestone in Harris's career that was marked by a western reference, and it shows the composer experimenting with an ensemble that was self-consciously distant from the European symphony orchestra.[28]

In his choice of title, Harris did more than reference the Oklahoma land runs. As Denise von Glahn has pointed out, he evoked a web of cultural references loosely linked to the Spanish *cimarrón*, meaning "wild," "untamed," or sometimes "escaped": a parched southwestern river, an infamous city in Kansas, numerous dime novel place names and characters, and especially the northwest portion of Indian Territory, crossed by the Santa Fe Trail and home to battles of resistance by Plains Indian tribes—the Osage, Arapaho, Kiowa, and Comanche.

Von Glahn observes: "The name was synonymous with images of the frontier—open land, rugged men, strong women, brave scouts, resourceful settlers, dangerous natives, lonesome cowboys—America at its earliest."[29] What's more, no less an authority than Paul Rosenfeld had called Harris a "Cimarron" in the first paragraph of a review from the mid-1930s.[30]

Of all the "manifestations of cimarron" that von Glahn describes, Edna Ferber's novel *Cimarron* (1929), adapted for film in 1931, offers by far the most dramatic encapsulation of the land runs that shaped Harris's piece. "It was History made in an hour," declares Ferber's frontier protagonist, Yancey Cravat:

> They came like a procession—a crazy procession—all the way to the Border, covering the ground as fast as they could, by any means at hand. . . . It takes generations of people hundreds of years to settle a new land. This was going to be made livable over night—was made—like a miracle out of the Old Testament. Compared to this, the Loaves and Fishes and the parting of the Red Sea were nothing—mere tricks. . . . A wilderness one day—except for an occasional wandering band of Indians—an empire the next. If that isn't a modern miracle.[31]

With a combination of biblical prophecy and contemporary know-how, Yancey Cravat's fellow settlers tumbled into what appeared to be "promised land." In most respects Harris's Cimarron story was not so very different.

Harris himself was born after the Oklahoma land runs, and his family spent their Oklahoma years many miles east of Cimarron County. Yet the program note printed in the score unsurprisingly smacks of autobiography. Though technically anonymous, it includes a substantial paragraph "in the words of the composer" and gives an outline of events: "The work tells the story of the beginning of a sleeping, uncivilized land—nature undisturbed by man—gradually becoming intensified to an utmost height of excitement." At the climax, "the percussion with the resounding staccato of a shotgun, lets loose a drum shot report, representing the firing of a ten-gauge shotgun, to release those men on horseback, foot and wagons lined along the Cimarron banks at noontime prepared to make a dash for the land on which to build their homesteads." After the mad rush, there emerges a "steady sonorous idealistic march representing the progress of pioneering toward an established civilization."[32]

This is a far cry from the pessimistic program of *Farewell to Pioneers*. Rather than eulogizing the passing of the pioneer family, *Cimarron* ennobles the advancing forces of white civilization committed to settling previously "undisturbed" land. It presents an invasion, not a retreat. Even the initial evocation of landscape illustrates some of these differences. Instead of symmetrical whole-tone wanderings or tritone-driven ostinati, *Cimarron* offers directional diatonic melodic fragments over a static but consonant bass (example 37). As a whole, with its combinations of gong, vibraphone, and tenor saxophone, the opening possesses considerably more timbral

EXAMPLE 37. *Cimarron*, mm. 1–14 (New York: Belwin Mills Music, 1941)

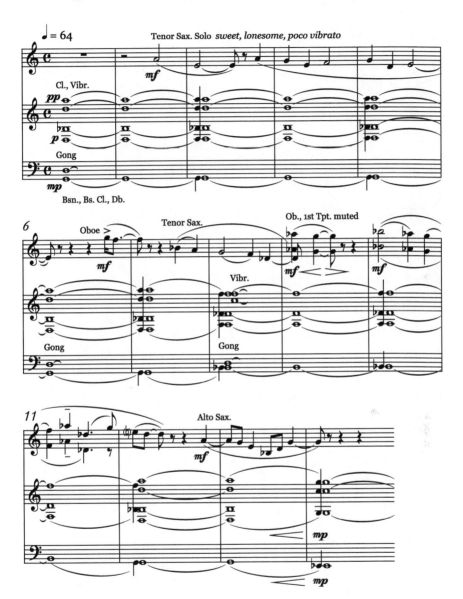

EXAMPLE 38A. *Cimarron,* mm. 62–65

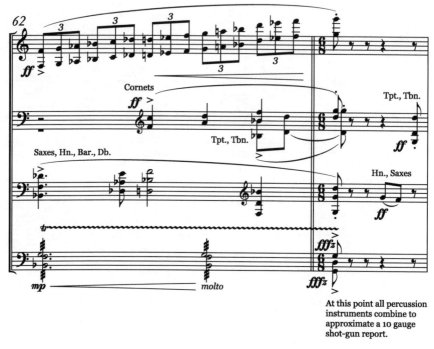

At this point all percussion
instruments combine to
approximate a 10 gauge
shot-gun report.

interest than does the parallel passage in *Farewell to Pioneers,* even though Harris
had recourse to fewer instrumental families. Interjections by oboe and muted trumpet enliven the otherwise bleak texture, suggesting the region's gradual awakening.
Von Glahn has linked the opening tenor saxophone solo, marked "sweet, lonesome"
with the western's "lonesome cowboys," and she aptly observes that the echoes offered up by oboe and other winds recall the "bucolic duets" of earlier pastoral pieces;
the "Open Prairie" of Copland's 1938 ballet *Billy the Kid* may also be hovering in the
background as Harris's *Cimarron* crescendos toward its climax.

   A simulated shotgun blast (example 38a) sets off a flurry of galloping ostinato
patterns, but none dominates the texture and all quickly dissolve into irregular

EXAMPLE 38B. *Cimarron*, mm. 135–42

repetition. The hymnlike melody that emerges from this texture just after figure 10 enters one phrase at a time, in the manner of a chorale prelude, while the racing gestures associated with the land run continue above and brassy fanfare fragments lend what von Glahn calls "a martial air" to the pioneers' journey. As the movement comes to rest, a woodwind chorale intones a complete statement of the hymn (example 38b); neither autogenetic nor folksy, this melody represents a melodic and programmatic culmination—in Harris's words it is "the very broad but simple and warm harmony of the march of progress." As von Glahn puts it, "A listener can almost imagine an 'amen' after the final chord."[33]

Who were the participants in this "march of progress"? Adroitly sidestepping the fact that Harris was too young to have participated in the land run himself, the program note for *Cimarron* nonetheless conveyed the relevant facts: "Of Scotch-Irish parentage, [Harris] spent his early childhood in the productive atmosphere of the farm in this Cimarron country listening to his parents retelling stories of the last frontier land-rush." By placing himself and his family in the pioneering vanguard, he changed the emphasis of his engagement with western history, flipping backward in the story to focus on the triumph, not the tragedy, of the pioneer way. He dispensed with the valorization of industrialism that had condemned pioneer ideals as "impractical" in *Farewell to Pioneers*. Instead, he focused on the role of the frontier in the mythical process of civilization: conquest of the unknown and victory over the "uncivilized."

"THE WHITE HOPE OF AMERICAN MUSIC"

In Edna Ferber's *Cimarron*, Yancey Cravat is adamant about the diversity of the land run, listing participants from every class and many states; an aristocratic surrey with a black coachman runs side by side with a poor, old homesteader with "a face dried and wrinkled as a nutmeg."[34] Like many Indian advocates, Yancey is rumored to be half Indian himself, with "an Indian wife somewhere, and a lot of papooses," and though his wife and some of his in-laws are quick to declare his whiteness, his status remains dubious, especially after his son "Cim" takes an Osage bride. In his (implied but denied) racial liminality, Yancey resembles Cooper's Deerslayer, the legendary Daniel Boone, and all the other "white scouts" (including Buffalo Bill) who were racially white but sufficiently attuned to Indian ways that they could harness the wilderness and teach its secret joys and healing virtues to the overcivilized. As we have seen, Harris and his music were expected to have a similar effect on their own overcivilized surroundings. Yet no one was interested in calling Harris a "half-breed."

In tracing the origins, consolidation, and dissemination of the Harris myth, we have already encountered repeated references to Harris's parentage. These were not innocent remarks. On the contrary, they served to set up certain expectations about style. Whether the fact was hidden behind elaborate metaphor or revealed with alarming candor, it was terribly important that Harris was white. Rosenfeld's concern to demonstrate the Scotch-Irish lineage of cowboy song when outlining the sources of Harris's style betrays an anxiety about matters of race. Farwell, too, made sure that his readers recognized Harris's heritage when he proclaimed: "From old Anglo-Saxon stock, with Scotch and Irish ingredients, he arises not out of the mechanistic tumult of the times, but out of the broad metaphysical movement which gave birth to Emerson and Whitman." Even Slonimsky participated in this campaign in his own way—it is hard to imagine what else he might have intended when, while writing up the pre-performance publicity for the *Symphony 1933*, he described Harris as if advertising livestock: "thirty-five, white, and healthy"![35] Slonimsky was known for writing tongue-in-cheek, but others were all too serious about the importance of Harris's racial background.

In a sense, the most significant legacy of Downes's 1934 diatribe against the *Symphony 1933* may have been that he transmitted John Tasker Howard's salient characterization of Harris as a "white hope" to a national audience far larger than Howard's specialized readership. It is no coincidence that the adjective is racially charged, and no coincidence that the phrase met with such widespread delight in both critical and popular provinces. Originally coined in anticipation of the white boxer who could dethrone black heavyweight champion Jack Johnson, the "white hope" carried a similar mandate in musical circles. In simplest terms, the issue was jazz.

Harris's reception cannot be dissociated from the sometimes violent debates of the 1920s and 1930s about the proper relationship between jazz and American composition. Henry Cowell treated these questions explicitly in his 1930 contribution to the *New Freeman*, entitled "Three Native Composers." In describing Harris, Cowell employed some of the same images that Rosenfeld had used—more evidence that links between Harris and the West had spread very rapidly: "Roy Harris . . . has a personal approach bristling with originality and cowboy punch. He is a real Westerner and has both the direct vehemence and the crudity characteristic of Westerners."[36] The vocabulary is familiar; more telling is the way Cowell chose to frame his discussion. The essay begins with a long paragraph on jazz, arguing against the idea—"based on the curious bias of the Parisian's concept of America"—that using jazz elements is the best path for "sophisticated" American composers. The paragraph closes with a categorical assertion: "The Anglo-Saxon American has no more talent for writing or playing jazz than the European. Both of them are more than bungling at it."

Having set forth his opinions on jazz, Cowell made an abrupt critical swerve. As if suddenly recollecting the "Three Native Composers" of his title, he confessed that "misconceptions concerning jazz" were not the main focus of his article. Rather, they "serve to clarify the issue which is this: What have Anglo-Saxon Americans done in the way of original composition?" The problem, Cowell indicated, was that the public did not usually perceive Anglo-Saxons as a well-defined American group. Thus Cowell's version of Harris's westernness is much more than a recycling of Rosenfeld's terms. Harris's "pronounced Western American breeziness," his combination of "commonplace" and new approaches to melody and form, his "gaunt angularity seeming to spring from plains and sharp mountains"—these things were now part of the catalog for a certain kind of composery whiteness. Such whiteness was not available to everyone—Protestant Anglo-Americans were the favored candidates—and even among this elite group, a cultivated provincialism was necessary insurance against the pitfalls of oversophistication and rootlessness.

It had long been understood by music critics of many nations that a composer's proclivities could be explained by race. The reception of Dvořák's "New World" Symphony provides ample evidence that racial rhetoric was an important component of music criticism in the United States at the turn of the century. Farwell's fascination with Spengler shows that ideas about the different creative capacities of the races continued to hold their appeal through the 1920s. So critics of the 1930s who received Harris's efforts as representative of the Anglo-Saxon in music were participants in an older, larger discourse of racial-musical determinism. In Howard's seminal monograph *Our American Composers* (1941), for example, we find one of the clearest and most casual explanations of the musical results of racial difference: "While racially Harris seems to derive definitively from the Scotch-Irish element of his ancestry, Aaron Copland embodies the Russian-Jewish element transplanted to American soil. Thus we find that while Harris reflects the prairies and vastness of the West, Copland brings us the sophistication of the cosmopolitan cities on the seaboard."[37] Did anyone flinch at Howard's matter-of-fact binarisms? Were any eyebrows raised at his choice of the forceful conjunction "thus"? Probably not at the time, for he was only restating generally accepted truths. Perhaps more than any other single factor, one's race was supposed to determine what could be authentically reflected in one's art—that is to say, what could be considered genuine and what had to be dismissed as artificial or contrived.

In his book *Yankee Blues*, MacDonald Smith Moore examines the racial politics of American musical life between the world wars, focusing on three categories: Yankees, blacks, and Jews. Making extensive comparisons with Copland and Gershwin—two prominent Jews whose works were unmistakably influenced by African American musical traditions during the 1920s—Moore notes that Harris was a favorite choice to take up the "the torch of culture" from New England's musical patriarchs and to carry it through the midcentury: "Proponents of an Anglo-Saxon redemptive culture preferred to pass the Yankee torch into non-Jewish hands. Shunning New York, and in the spirit of Winthrop, Emerson, and Whitman, New England's advocates sought their star of hope in the West. A broad range of critics nominated Roy Harris to be American Music's 'Great White Hope.' Though not a Yankee, he of Lincolnesque bearing hailed from the plains. Ebulliently Harris accepted the nomination."[38] Harris was not the only logical candidate. As Moore points out, certain prominent New Englanders such as Daniel Gregory Mason and Charles Ives promoted other young composers, including Cowell, Hanson, and Douglas Moore, to carry Anglo-American musical culture forward. Nevertheless, as *Yankee Blues* narrates, "their selections fell by the wayside as Roy Harris was chosen by acclamation in the early thirties."[39]

During this period, Harris's whiteness was an asset because it allowed him to claim as his natural (read: racial) inheritance certain compositional practices which were gaining popularity, most notably a reliance on Anglo-American folk music. Through his acknowledged westernness and strong rural ties, Harris bore a unique mantle of musical and moral authority when it came to incorporating folk music into large-scale pieces. Cowboy songs, in particular, fell within Harris's jurisdiction by virtue of their supposedly Scotch-Irish lineage and because of the persistent cowboy imagery that had infiltrated the composer's reception.

Harris's association with the potent images of the American West gave him an edge over other potential "torchbearers." It was indeed crucial that Harris be white, but his popularity grew in part because he also set himself so visibly apart from "Eastern" culture. In an atmosphere of American exceptionalism, a New England pedigree counted for less than a genuine western accent. A "prophet from the Southwest" had more to offer than a Yankee gentleman.[40] As Howard had observed, it was to be expected that Harris's music would reflect "the prairies and vastness of the West" because of his ancestry; as Rosenfeld wrote in 1929, Harris had grown up hearing the "peasant tunes preserved by his stock." Harris had open access to an abundant rhetoric of authenticity that was only reinforced by his western ties. All the usual strategies lay open to him: recollection of childhood experiences and recognition of blood ties, inspiration by nature and justification by race.

Harris shared the critical establishment's underlying assumptions about race and authenticity. He was fully convinced of the connections between race and composition; he had no trouble linking creativity with awareness of one's racial heritage. In a quasi-autobiographical article for *Musical Quarterly* (1934), Harris spoke of the young composer's desire to create "music that will be true to his race, to his time, to himself." The article begins with a Farwellian proclamation: "Call it romantic fervor, call it a longing for truth, call it the atavistic burgeonings from the depth of the race-soul. Always it is a lonesome hunger that gnaws within the human heart, forcing us to search for an understandable race-expression."[41] Harris did not openly proclaim himself an Anglo-American culture hero, but he was well aware of the racial component of his appeal, frequently mentioning—in program notes, articles, and interviews—both his parents' Anglo ancestry and his own musical debts to their favorite folk melodies. As we shall soon see, protestations of authenticity would become the foundation for his later insinuations that he was more entitled to dip into folk sources than his colleagues were.

Harris couched his musings about personal artistic authenticity in extensive discussions of what it meant to be American in music. Association with the West was powerful, but it never replaced the overarching sense of national identity that Harris cultivated before, during, and after his most famous western works. Like many intellectuals grappling with the problem of identity in the United States, Harris tried to make the national character conform to a racial character, outlining its inherent traits and describing its quasi-biological origins. According to Harris, the "characteristic American" had certain typical moods and habits: "Our dignity lies in direct driving force; our deeper feelings are stark and reticent; our gaiety is ribald and our humor ironic. These are moods which young indigenous American composers are born and surrounded with, and from these moods come a unique valuation of beauty and a different feeling for rhythm, melody, and form." In particular, Harris argued, American composers possessed a distinct and asymmetrical sense of rhythm: "This asymmetrical balancing of rhythmic phrases is in our blood; it is not in the European blood. . . . We do not employ unconventional rhythms as a sophistical gesture; we cannot avoid them. To cut them out of our music would be to gainsay the source of our spontaneous musical impulses."[42] By this logic, composers who lacked this typically American rhythmic accent either were trying too hard to make their music sound European or were simply deaf to the rhythms of life around them.

Harris participated fully in the confusion of biological and environmental factors that has typically enabled Americans to discuss their national identity without abandoning models based on the older, more ethnically uniform nations of Europe. He described the mysterious process through which typically "American" traits—behavior patterns, characteristic moods, and even peculiar physical features—were slowly becoming apparent in American life: "Wonderful, young, sinewy, timorous, browbeaten, eager, gullible American society, living in a land of grandeur, dignity, and untold beauty, is slowly kneading consistent racial character from the sifted flour of experience and the sweat of racial destiny. Slowly, surely, there are emerging American types, with characteristic statures, facial expressions, and temperament." In explaining the evolution of the "characteristic American," Harris was careful to disengage the terms of his discussion from mere blood inheritance: "Our climate plus our social, political, and economic customs have produced this characteristic American by the same biological process that characteristic Frenchmen, Germans, and Englishmen were molded from the same Aryan race-stream."[43] In Harris's view, people (like plants) must draw nourishment from the soil and must evolve in response to the environment if they are to survive. The confluence of organicism and nationalism is in itself hardly surprising, for the two have been intertwined since the eighteenth century. What is peculiar to the American context, with its political union of so many ethnic and cultural groups, is that environmental factors are seen as actively uniting disparate groups rather than explaining already acknowledged national or racial differences.

Harris never proposed a time frame according to which these imagined processes might mold the "characteristic American," nor did he maintain that the American continent could somehow erase the color line. Harris was no racist. On the contrary, he was politically liberal and was sympathetic to the political and economic struggles of black Americans. Over the course of his career, he supported integrated education and spoke out against racial prejudice, particularly during his brief tenure at Peabody College for Teachers in Nashville (1950–51), where he cancelled a summer festival after a black student was denied admission. But when it came to race and music, whether as a calculated strategy or by unconscious oversight, Harris tended to drop African Americans from his discussions. He stopped short of calling his "asymmetrical" rhythms "jazzy," and even if he had recognized a connection between his own syncopation and "jazz," he might not have had black music in mind, as Cowell's strictly Parisian purview for jazz made clear.

Among his many folk song settings, Harris did treat a number of black spirituals with great success, occasionally in freestanding pieces but more often—as Farwell had—in collections that defused racial implications by grouping movements drawn from diverse regions or ethnic groups, such as the *Folksong Symphony*, the *Folk Fantasy for Festivals*, or the piano suite *American Ballads*. More telling is his film score for *One Tenth of a Nation* (1941). Here Harris simultaneously lamented the lack of educational facilities for blacks in America and apparently managed to avoid using much African American music in his score. For some on the American music scene, the decision was easily justified. Paul Bowles reviewed the score in his column for *Modern Music*, finding it "satisfactory" in both musical quality and political ideology: "I don't even reproach the composer with having chosen not to include one Negroism in his score, even if he did decide to use folk-music and had to get it in the British Isles. The film was made by Whites for Whites; it is without ethnographic overtones. And since it was only a sociological plea to the White population, its creators were esthetically free to use whatever idioms they thought most effective, provided that each element was completely subservient to the discipline essential in a propaganda film."[44] In the political arena, one ought to act on one's social obligations, but the creative artist had to write from within. According to this philosophy, Harris had little choice but to rely on Anglo music—that was how white composers effectively communicated to white audiences. Aesthetics and politics were equal, but separate.

10

The Composer as Folk Singer

FOLK SONG HERITAGE AND
THE PROVINCIAL COWBOY

At the same time Harris was experimenting with autogenesis in *Farewell to Pioneers,* he was also making forays into a more accessible musical language based on folk song. In response to a commission by RCA Victor—apparently the first American work commissioned specifically for recording—Harris produced the orchestral overture *When Johnny Comes Marching Home* (1935), which took one of Harris's favorite tunes as its basis. This was not his first attempt at folk-based composition. Dan Stehman observes that ten years earlier he had used the tune "Peña Hueca" in his *Fantasy for Trio and Chorus,* almost certainly working from materials provided by Farwell.[1] But *When Johnny Comes Marching Home* did give Harris his first chance to discuss folk song before a national audience. In explaining his reliance on borrowed material, Harris had to transmute his emphasis on organic, self-expressive melody almost completely. Folk songs could hardly be made to fit his autogenetic models (though Harris sometimes pretended that they could). More persuasively, Harris grounded his use of folk material in a different kind of naturalness—not the organic unfolding of autogenesis, but the authenticity of autobiography.

Though not literally a folk song (it was published by Patrick Gilmore in 1863), "When Johnny Comes Marching Home" had honorary folk-song status for Harris, and its rousing tune was something like a theme song early in his career. Although his emerging western aura shed no special light on the song, Harris managed to wrest it from its original Civil War context and insert it into his own, as indicated in the program note appended to the score:

I chose an American theme which is not only well known and loved but capable of extended development: "When Johnny Comes Marching Home." This was one of my father's favorite tunes, and it was he who planted in me the unconscious realization of its dual nature. He used to whistle it with jaunty bravado as we went to work on the farm in the morning and with sad pensiveness as we returned at dusk behind the slow, weary plodding of the horses. These impressions have undoubtedly influenced me in determining the use of this theme; yet the same realization of the dual character of this peculiarly fertile theme might have been arrived at by observing that it is very minor in its tonality and gay in its rhythm.[2]

For Harris, it almost went without saying that the tune should be American. Beyond that, the best reasons for incorporating folk song were personal ones, grounded in biographical experience and (if at all possible) family history. The strange combination of agricultural and psychological vocabulary in this description—according to which this "fertile" tune was "planted" in Harris's subconscious by his father—is less strange than what Harris neglected to mention at all: its Irish background and Civil War connotations. The tune's more general military associations may well have added to the overture's public appeal; such associations certainly received ample attention from other quarters when Harris used the tune again in 1940 in the *Folksong Symphony*.[3] But Harris did not mention them in 1935. Even during the 1940s, when it came to folk song, Harris preferred to let the personal overshadow the political.

It was the plausibility of personal identification with folk song that continued to set Harris apart when American composers began turning to folk song in droves during the Depression. Harris's most famous folk-based works appeared at precisely the time when American artists left and right (but especially left) were scrambling to acquaint or reacquaint themselves with American folklore.[4] The New Deal was blanketing the country with populist propaganda idealizing rural life. The nation's most intellectual flirtation with socialist thinking was making it respectable to aspire toward accessibility. Writers like John Steinbeck were valorizing the working man, Carl Sandburg was publishing Americana song and verse, and Charles Seeger was urging composers to leave the ivory tower and "discover America." In 1934, Seeger had issued a challenge: "If . . . a composer is going to sing the American people anything new . . . he must first get upon a common ground with them, learn their musical lingo, work with it, and show he can do for them something they want to have done and cannot do for themselves."[5] Harris approached these tasks with a special kind of authority and a significant head start. Through good fortune and good publicity, he was well positioned to make a run on this "common ground."

By the early 1940s, however, the common ground that Seeger had in mind was getting crowded. Composers like Thomson and Douglas Moore had already written acclaimed works incorporating hymn tunes and folk materials; Copland, Elie

Siegmeister, and Ruth Crawford Seeger were radically simplifying their musical languages; Morton Gould and Ross Lee Finney were producing a *Cowboy Rhapsody* and choral settings of cowboy songs. In this newly competitive context, Harris took steps to improve his claim on American folklore, particularly western folklore. With a somewhat exaggerated adherence to the adage "good fences make good neighbors," he questioned his compatriots' right to set up camp in this valuable territory, partly through remarkable reconstructions of his own westernness and partly through less palatable attempts to deny others access to the authentic font of folk wisdom. Both strategies are illustrated in Harris's 1940 article published in *Modern Music* under the provocative heading "Folksong—American Big Business." Harris began this contribution without facts and figures and without the elaborate economic analogies his title might have supported. He postponed making any impassioned pleas for fidelity to folk music or preservation of this national resource. Instead, he chose to relate an autobiographical fantasy: a first-person account of a western episode in which he gets to "play cowboy," rubbing shoulders with the imaginary buckaroos "Idaho Bill" and "Shorty Kelsey." Rather than offering a paler paraphrase of Harris's fanciful scenario, or attempting to convey the suddenness with which he lurches into a more objective enumeration of folk song's virtues, I quote the opening of his essay at length:

> We had been dancing all night—putting the finishing touches to three of the most exciting days in my life. The Cowboy's Reunion came to an abrupt end as the pale blue-green dawn crept over the little Western town nestling into the foothills.
> . . . Nostalgia as lonesome as the prairies, and as old, too, led me back to the Fair Grounds. There was old Idaho Bill, well over sixty, directing his outfit. . . . Idaho Bill figured he wouldn't come to any more Cowboy Reunions. The last time he went to Pendleton, Oregon he had felt the same way. The thing was getting a little too professional. ". . . It's getting to be cut and dried. When the boys ride hell-for-leather because their pardners, the old man or their girls and all the folks are a lookin' on— well that's one thing. That's real cowhide. When they calculate to make it pay for a livin'—that's a white horse of different color. You know there's somethin' cussed-ornery about that, somehow. Taint decent to be ridin' your heart out for pay."
> Now that's what folksong is all about. Singing and dancing your heart out for yourself and the people you were born among—whose daily lives you share through the seasons, through thick and thin. From the hearts of our people they have come— our people living, loving, bearing, working, dying. These songs are as the people whom they express—salty, hilarious, sly, vulgar, gay, sad, weary, heroic, witty, prosaic, and often as eloquent as the silent poor burying their dead. They constitute a rich legacy of time-mellowed feelings and thoughts chosen through usage from the experiences of people who lived here and helped make America what she is today.[6]

It is a testament to Harris's national fame in 1940 that this detailed fiction came to grace the pages of America's most prestigious contemporary music journal. Though expressed in a surprisingly whimsical way, Harris's intentions were unabashedly earnest. Even these opening paragraphs betray his motivating concern. Like Bacon, he wanted to protect the "rich legacy" of folk music from the encroaching dangers of commercialism. Rodeo riding (like composing with folk materials) was acceptable as a sincere vocation but not as a mere occupation. Harris framed the folk song question explicitly as an issue of legacy and inheritance. Despite the vast size of the American "folk," it produced very few chosen sons; Harris was lucky enough to have been acknowledged as one such heir.

Of course, it was no accident that Harris chose to focus his fantasy on the cowboy rather than some other folk figure. Harris had already acquired a long history of cowboy associations, from Rosenfeld and Cowell right on down the line. The Columbia Broadcasting System certified this designation when they invited Harris to participate in their "American School of the Air" series on folk music, which aired weekly from late October 1939 until early April 1940. For the inaugural episode, Harris contributed an orchestral arrangement of cowboy tunes to share the program with songs collected by Alan Lomax.[7] Though Harris was a farmer's son, he was a cowman in the popular mind; in fact, when he chose to focus on the farmer's self-sufficiency and independence from social constraint, he himself was emphasizing precisely those traits exaggerated by the stereotypical cowboy, with all his distinctly American vices and virtues.

The cowboy's continued hold on the American imagination has been in no way discouraged by the fact that actual range-riding cowboys were only prominent in this country for about twenty-five years, from the end of the Civil War until around 1890. The cowboy's career was spurred by the westward-reaching railroad, but quickly curtailed by drought and by changes in ranching and transportation technologies. His pay was low; his life was difficult and often subservient. Yet his reputation rests on such attributes as independence (punctuated by moments of gallant camaraderie), bravado, and an expert command of both animals and nature. The nurseries of the cowboy character type were the artworks of Frederic Remington and Charles M. Russell and the pulp fiction of the 1880s-1910s.[8] Just as Buffalo Bill had interlaced his Wild West performances with dime novel characters and plots, so artists in other media blurred the lines between the popular perception and the historical realities of the cowboy West.

Each genre had its own cowboy-and-western heyday and its own heroes: the chivalric Virginian of Owen Wister's 1902 best seller, the melodramatic Bronco Billy of silent films, and the mysterious masked man of the Lone Ranger radio and television series. In the era of the singing cowboy, Gene Autry and Roy Rogers crooned down trail after trail in American theaters, keeping comic and sentimental cowboys in circulation. By 1946, Lawrence Morton could write that "a plaintive ditty is often as essential a part of a cowboy's heroism as are his horse and his gun, as necessary to his virtue as a righteous cause and an unblemished bride."[9] As often as not in all these media, the cowboy was emancipated from the dirty work of driving cattle and recreated as a cunning tracker, patriotic Indian fighter, or glamorous rodeo star. Perhaps most striking is the pervasive whitening of the cowboy image, particularly at the hands of moviemakers but also in other cultural realms: rare indeed is the Mexican vaquero (buckaroo) from whom the cowboy learned his rope tricks, and rarer still the black cowboy, who went the way of the Buffalo soldier, bleached out by the Hollywood spotlight.

Although John Lomax's 1910 collection *Cowboy Songs and Frontier Ballads* had appeared in four editions before 1920 and had exerted a strong influence on the repertory and character of Hollywood's singing cowboys, cowboy songs and characters had been strikingly absent from American composition before the 1930s, as Virgil Thomson was quick to point out. Sandburg's 1927 anthology, *An American Songbag,* earned some interest; Charles Seeger and Henry Cowell's edition of a new Lomax collection *(American Ballads and Folk Songs)* in 1932 fanned the flames. It may seem odd that the rugged individualism of the cowboy should have received such support from members of the radical Composers' Collective, but even uncooperative folk figures could be made to serve the cause of "proletarian music" as the cowboy reached wider and wider segments of the working class.[10]

The great wave of Depression-era interest in folk song drew attention to cowboy materials, but other elements in American culture made the western wrangler America's wartime and postwar hero. As Thomson and his *Plow That Broke the Plains* suggest, New Deal thinking tended to underwrite the agricultural pioneer. But Harris was correct when he noted in his *Farewell to Pioneers* that the ways of the farmer's frontier were hard to reconcile with modern industrial society. Cowboy life, on the other hand, offered robust and assertive individualism. With the burgeoning of Hollywood, representations of cowboys saturated stage and screen to such an extent that the sheer increase in quantity brought about a change in quality: the cowboy's characteristics—aggression, humor, alienation, independence—were intertwined with American self-fashioning. As William Goetzmann has observed: "The early motion pictures had succeeded in molding for all time and for all places on the planet the archetypal cowboy as the archetypal American."[11] This transformation in the cultural significance of the western brought new seriousness to the genre: character development in *Stagecoach* (1939), historical pretensions in countless examples—*The Plainsman* (1936), *Wells Fargo, Destry Rides Again* (1939), *My Darling Clementine* (1946), and others—and cinematic prowess in *High Noon* (1952). While these developments were under way, the contrasting cowboy types enacted by Gene Autry and John Wayne rubbed shoulders as Americans tried to decide which cowboys should represent them at home and abroad.

Thus, it was timely and strategic for Harris to don a cowboy costume when he did in 1940. In "Folksong—American Big Business," Harris led with his strongest suit, reasserting his inimitable westernness in the most vivid way possible. Even those who might have questioned his detailed rodeo narrative could not impugn his cowboy guise. After this memorable opening move, however, Harris cautiously universalized his discussion of folk song, either by avoiding specific mention of the West or by cushioning western references in longer, more geographically diverse lists. Through a careful filtering of the folk spirit into his own biography and somewhat less careful swipes at composers without his fortunate folk affinities, he arranged to claim a genuine connection to folk song regardless of the geographical source of particular tunes: "America," he lamented, "will have many folksong vendors in the next few years. Some city boys may take a short motor trip through our land and return to write the Song of the Prairies—others will be folksong authorities after reading in a public library for a few weeks."[12]

Whether the paraphrase of Copland's *Music for Radio: Saga of the Prairies* (1937) was intentional or subconscious, the sentiment is the same. In contrast to these urban charlatans, Harris presented his vision of an alternative. Though his protagonist remained unnamed, his text carried all the rhetorical force of a credo:

> But all this mushroom exploitation of folksong will neither greatly aid nor hinder it. After the era has run itself out there will remain those composers who have been deeply influenced by the finest, clearest, strongest feeling of our best songs. Because these songs are identified with emotions deeply implicit in themselves, such composers will be enriched and stimulated. . . . They will absorb and use the idioms of folk music as naturally as the folk who unconsciously generated them. They will have learned that folksong is a native well-spring, an unlimited source of fresh material; that it can't be reduced to a few formulas to stir and mix to taste. Those composers who are drawn to and richly satisfied with folksong will inherit the privilege of using it with the professional's resources and discipline and the amateur's enthusiasm and delight.[13]

This was a multifaceted manifesto. It reiterated Harris's understanding of folk song as a legacy to be inherited. It asserted by fiat (and through a judicious use of the future and future-perfect tenses) that the worrisome "exploitation" of folk idioms would prove inconsequential. It reaffirmed the basic criterion that Harris had espoused for the composition of autogenetic melodies: the composer's work should be instinctive. Once the composer had absorbed enough of "the best" songs to radiate folk feeling from sources that were "deeply implicit" within him, he could do no wrong. Harris also took this opportunity to inoculate himself against potential charges that his folk-based works might be less imaginative than pieces with no borrowed material. Harris would not lose his own voice when he chose to sing cowboy songs. On the contrary, because of his faith in folk song, Harris would find an inexhaustible natural resource where others encountered only dry formulas. The professional's tools would be transfigured by the amateur's delight.

HOME ON THE RANGE

These attitudes are exemplified in Harris's largest folk-based work, the *Folksong Symphony* (1939–40). The symphony stands as a musical counterpart to the credo cited above, both in its attention to the cowboy and in its aspiration to an Americanness not limited to a single geographic region. In fact, the symphony corresponds so neatly to the concerns expressed in "Folksong—American Big Business" that the two must be considered companion pieces: the polemical article served as an artistic justification for the new work immediately after its premiere on 25 April and as publicity for its upcoming performances in Cleveland on 26 December 1940 and in Boston, under Koussevitzky, on 21 February 1941.[14]

The *Folksong Symphony* took shape as a set of four folk-song settings for chorus and orchestra commissioned by Howard Hanson for the American Spring Festival at the Eastman School of Music in April 1940. The vocal writing reflected Harris's commitment to composing music that could be used by nonprofessional ensembles, especially high schools, but also university groups, following on his teaching stint at Westminster Choir College (1934–38).[15]

Sometime later that year, Harris offered Carl Engel and the publishing house of G. Schirmer an expanded manuscript, entitled *Folksong Jamboree*. The work now contained five folk-song settings for chorus and orchestra and two instrumental interludes, based on what some reviewers heard as "western" fiddle tunes. Engel pushed him to modify his folksy title, and the composer acquiesced: the resulting *Folksong Symphony* seemed a more suitable (though perhaps less accurate) designation for Harris's next magnum opus.[16] Although only the vocal score was published, the work stands as Symphony No. 4, cataloged between the two purely instrumental single-movement symphonies that are most frequently praised as noteworthy examples of Harris's more abstract melodic and formal innovations.

With the 1940 issue of *Modern Music* still readily available, the *Folksong Symphony* needed no elaborate explanation. Yet, as the years went by, Harris was not content to let the music stand on its own; he wrote a substantial program note for the piece when it was recorded almost two decades later.[17] Perhaps feeling it necessary in retrospect to justify the *Folksong Symphony*'s accessibility and appeal to the amateur, Harris reiterated his strong folk ties: his association with prominent folk musicians of the 1930s and 1940s, his scrupulous attention to the ethics of using folk materials, and above all the influential presence of folk song in his family:

> In those days [the late 1930s] in New York, famous folk singers used to gather in our house, amongst them Alan Lomax, Burl Ives, "Lead Belly," the singers of The Golden Gate Quartet. . . . Questions often arose about folk music—what is it—who makes it—who owns it—what can one do with it—how can it be best used. We never grew weary of discussing and illustrating our diverse points of view. . . . As a composer, I felt that folk songs were like The Good Earth, to be cultivated by musi-

cians according to their tastes and skills. Most of us agreed that folk songs were all things to all people, an inexhaustible source out of which music of many conflicting styles could be fashioned, from cheap assembly-line commercial routine to the latest specimens of transient sophistication.

I was brought up with simple folk attitudes by my pioneer parents. Folk music was as natural to our way of life as corn bread and sweet milk. My mother played the guitar and we hummed along with her after supper on the front porch or in the kitchen. We whistled folk songs as we worked on the farm. When I began to study music I decided that composers were folk singers who had learned to write down the songs that took their fancy; and that therefore folk songs could be recast to suit a composer's purpose, and that they could be legitimately used to generate symphonic forms.[18]

Harris here identified the composer as a folk singer while at the same time publicly accepting Engel's hint that what was really wanted from him was a "symphonic form." Moreover, he continued to assert that the legitimate right to folk song was based on a composer's affinities rather than technical expertise or region of origin. This gave him the geographic breadth necessary to encompass the symphony's diverse choral movements: "The Girl I Left Behind Me" (based on a Civil War song), "Western Cowboy" (based on two cowboy songs), "Mountaineer Love Song" (based on the Appalachian tune "He's Gone Away"), "Negro Fantasy" (based on the spirituals "Little Boy Named David" and "De Trumpet Sounds It in My Soul"), and the "Welcome Party" (based on Harris's old favorite, "When Johnny Comes Marching Home").[19]

Of the three regionally or ethnically specific movements—the "Western Cowboy," the "Mountaineer Love Song," and the "Negro Rhapsody"—the "Western Cowboy" gets top billing. It is the longest and in many ways the simplest of the seven movements. Harris chose three cowboy songs for elaboration: "The Lone Prairie," "Streets of Laredo" (or "The Cowboy's Lament"), and "The Old Chisholm Trail." The first two songs are used as the main melodic basis for a clearly defined ABA' form, where A and B are extended strophic settings and A' is abbreviated to only a few bars. From "The Old Chisholm Trail," Harris extracted the opening sequence of pitches (A–G, A–E–D) and used them as a punctuating device.

As a whole, the movement is consistent with Harris's claim that folk song was his natural inheritance and with his characterization of the composer as a folk singer happily in possession of symphonic training. For this reason, it is important—however obvious—that Harris's work is sung and not merely played. By requiring the actual singing of the song, he guards against potentially "formulaic" manipulation, and by retaining the melodic intervals and phrase structures of the original tunes, Harris seems to invite the audience to sing along. Any listener who arrives unfamiliar with the melodies will surely know them by the end.

Harris's chief contributions lie in the realms of orchestration and harmonic inflection. The movement's opening shows two of his favorite techniques (example 39).

EXAMPLE 39. *Folksong Symphony,* "Western Cowboy," mm. 8–19 (New York: G. Schirmer, 1940)

The melody is presented in straightforward dialogue between sopranos and altos over a gentle harmonic framework of root position and second-inversion triads in A♭ major. The sopranos' second entrance contains the first melodic alteration: C♭ replaces C♮ in a turn toward the minor mode, which recasts the harmony but barely disturbs the tune. The following phrase, however, is presented in an entirely new key (F major), almost as if the altos have suddenly lost track of the original tonic, although the sense of aural disjunction quickly vanishes. Such modest adjustments, which occur throughout the movement as Harris explores varied ways of inflecting the tune, actually enhance the tune's apparent autonomy rather than disrupting it. They encourage the audience to listen for melodic phrasing and contour instead of relying on harmony to provide a sense of direction. Indeed, the regularity of the melodic structure—completely at odds with Harris's autogenetic theorizing—forms one of the movement's most striking features.

The only fragmentation of the tune occurs after more than four minutes of unbroken folk song; moreover, this instance is clearly motivated by the text. After the men's voices trail off—"Oh bury me not"—leaving a six-beat gap in the tune, the sopranos enter both to complete the melodic phrase and to provide a textual explanation—"and his voice died there." The men introduce a single phrase of material unrelated to the tune; their monotone F is answered by a reprise, first in the orchestra and then in the chorus, of the now-familiar melody. Instead of confusing (or amusing) the listener, Harris's alterations reinforce the significance and stability of the folk material.

Harris's concern for a different kind of continuity is apparent in his transition to the second part of the movement's ternary form (example 40). Underneath the chorus's last verse of "Oh Bury Me Not," Harris introduces the "Laredo" tune into the orchestral texture, allowing the new section to emerge "naturally," as if the tune that takes over the foreground had actually been present all along. During the eighteen-measure instrumental introduction to the B section, more complicated, loosely contrapuntal writing holds sway, but the choral entrance brings a return to simpler textures. Though this folk melody is eventually used in canon, it undergoes less harmonic recasting than "Oh Bury Me Not," and it remains both audible and singable through its first four verses, after which modifications in verse five help ease the return to A'.

In general, Harris's treatment of each tune signals his reverence for the folk product and his unwillingness to trifle with its outline. Rather than distancing himself from accessible melodies or sentimental lyrics, he embraced them wholeheartedly and he seemed to expect that audiences would do the same. The fact that the texts of both songs focus on dying cowboys only deepens the suffusion of nostalgia. The slow tempo and piquant harmonies of the outer sections of the movement ably convey his wistful idealization of life and death on the range; the sprightly gait of the "Streets of Laredo" suddenly slows to a funeral procession

EXAMPLE 40. "Western Cowboy," mm. 117–27

as the young cowboy's recollections of past exploits give way to the details of his last rites. The cowboys of the *Folksong Symphony,* then, correspond less to the emerging aggressive western hero than to the sentimental singing cowboys impersonated by Gene Autry and Roy Rogers.

According to his program note, Harris chose the tunes for his "Western Cowboy" because they displayed "the lonesomeness, hilarity, and tragedy which the early Western cowboys lived with every day."[20] But Harris was not primarily concerned with the historical realities of day-to-day life on the cattle trail. Having bid a fond but firm farewell to the pioneers in 1935, Harris might have been ready to dispense with the elegy, but he clung to his nostalgic attitudes about the past and especially about the West. In his autobiographical fiction about the "Cowboy's Reunion," it was "nostalgia as lonesome as the prairies" that had led him back to the fair grounds and to wise old Idaho Bill.

In a literal sense, Harris's compositional output and his actual biography show deep traces of a pervasive and recurring nostalgia. His sojourns to Europe and the eastern United States were punctuated by returns to Los Angeles and Utah; his wandering from one teaching position to another finally ended in 1961 as he settled in California, not far from the farms of his childhood. In the oral history interviews of the 1960s, Harris enjoyed looking backward at the forces that had impelled his westward homecoming. Upon leaving Pittsburgh in the late 1950s, Harris recalled that he "felt a tremendous yen to get out further west": "I needed to go where I could see the sky again in a great big bowl. I needed to go where I could see a moon come up that wasn't always red. I needed to see some harvests. . . . It simply is that primarily, I guess, I am a farmer boy. At least, I am a Western boy. This is something that I can't escape. . . . [While in France] I longed to see those Western plains, deserts, and all those things. . . . So, it's very difficult for me to stay away very long" (OH, 529–30). For Harris, the West and the past represented the goals of two kinds of homecoming, one literal and one figurative. In the *Folksong Symphony,* the cowboy presented Harris with a figure that united the irretrievable past and the ever-receding West in a single nostalgic icon. His longing for the past was, of course, doomed to remain unfulfilled, but Harris continued searching for the West in which he was supposed to have been born.

AFTER THE *FOLKSONG SYMPHONY*

The reception of the *Folksong Symphony* gave Harris conflicting directions about how best to continue pursuing musical counterparts for his mythic westernness. The symphony's early performances (1940–43) received a motley assortment of reviews. In the minds of many critics and composers the work represented a tragic abdication of Harris's heroic role in American music. Rosenfeld, Cowell, Mendel, and Slonimsky remained (perhaps tactfully) silent. Those who did comment usually felt obliged to comment on the work's misleading title; many also expressed reservations about Harris's treatment of folk tunes. Olin Downes, for one, praised Harris's intention to link the high school chorus and the professional symphony orchestra, but he found the symphony unsatisfactory, dismissing its music as "an example of what should not rather than what should, can, and will be done by native educated composers." He thought Harris had failed to reconcile the folk idiom with his own symphonic language.[21] Copland lodged a related complaint, arguing that the symphony lacked variety because of Harris's overbearing approach: It "shows no real feeling for the individuality of the songs given symphonic investiture. Each of the sharply contrasted tunes is approached from the same angle and given a typical Harris workout."[22]

Harris still had some friends in the high places of American music criticism. Arthur Cohn, writing for *Modern Music*, called this work "music for the masses, from the masses," offering a view of Harris's adoption of folk materials that was diametrically opposed to Copland's: "The folk melodies are not patchy, spasmodic fragments developed à la textbook, but full and complete, spun out healthily and organically."[23] Herbert Elwell, a former member of the Boulangerie, registered another early vote of confidence. After a series of disclaimers about the title of the piece and about the length and voicing of specific passages, he wrote:

> There are a half-dozen first rate American folksongs in the work, from *Johnny Comes Marching Home* to *The Gal I Left Behind Me*. To assimilate this material, words and all, and to give it out as sounding fresh and momentous as it does in this music, is to meet a supreme artistic challenge comparable to the decorative problem of the chorale prelude. . . . It almost involves nourishing the exalted conviction, *le peuple, c'est moi.* Yet I find nothing presumptuous about such an attitude in Harris, because his expression of it shows too deep a reverence for emotional realities to bear any symptoms of megalomania.[24]

By evoking the chorale prelude, Elwell also alludes to J. S. Bach—an homage that had considerable force for Boulanger's students and a gesture that Harris would certainly have appreciated.[25] Furthermore, in Elwell's view, Harris's willingness to speak for the people and his "reverence" for their "emotional realities" could atone for a multitude of potential sins, including occasionally exaggerated sentiment or temporary breaches of symphonic decorum.

Quite apart from critical squabbles about the uses and abuses of folk song, the symphony was a stunning popular success, inspiring enormous enthusiasm and a media field day involving substantial articles in both *Newsweek* (6 May 1940) and *Time* (6 January 1941).[26] Harris would later recollect with delight the spontaneous outpourings of support from audiences in New York City, Boston, Detroit, Cincinnati, and especially Cleveland, where the work had its first complete (seven-movement) hearing at a performance for the Music Teachers' National Association (OH, 415–16, 404–5). "That Saturday night they just filled Severance Hall," he remembered. "There wasn't even standing room. And they shouted, and the drummer got so excited that he beat on the big bass drum. We went to a place to have beer afterwards, a big place, and when we came in the people who were there started singing folk songs to us from the symphony. It was wonderful. That's when *Time* magazine said that my music was like the nation standing up and shouting hello" (OH, 389–90).[27] The *Folksong Symphony* allowed Americans to stage their national unity. Its song selections were multiethnic and multiregional; it could and did accommodate massive performing forces, including citywide conglomerate high school choirs. Moreover, with special free performances under the auspices of the Works Progress Administration's Federal Music Project and eventually radio broadcasts to U.S. troops overseas, the symphony reached a wide American audience in a patriotic mood. Throughout the early 1940s, Harris reworked material from the *Folksong Symphony* in other media, most notably in his collaborations with Hanya Holm's ballet company during his residence at Colorado College.[28]

Harris's next treatment of cowboy song, however, abandoned the already old-fashioned, nostalgic cowboy crooner in favor of a more aggressive western hero. "Streets of Laredo" is the opening selection in an inviting group of piano pieces entitled *American Ballads* (1945). The work may have had its origins in musical interludes for a series of broadcasts on a Denver radio station.[29] The resulting suite is similar to the *Folksong Symphony* in that a movement on a western theme takes pride of place in an otherwise geographically diverse collection. Moreover, at least in this movement, Harris remains faithfully committed to presenting folk material completely and recognizably. "Streets of Laredo" takes as its basis one of the same tunes that constituted the "Western Cowboy" of the *Folksong Symphony*, but the piano miniature reverses a number of the symphonic movement's traits (example 41). Harris dropped the mournful tune "Oh Bury Me Not on the Lone Prairie" and elaborated only the more energetic "Laredo" tune. The pace is upbeat—the headlong introduction begins at dotted-half note = 72 before slowing to dotted-half note = 66. The spiky chordal homophony of the opening features stark sonorities of stacked fourths (upbeats to bars 1 and 4) and the grit of major-seventh chords on prominent downbeats (mm. 1, 3, 4, and 6). After the tune enters in bar 13, a dotted rhythm borrowed from the first measure of the melody gently propels it along. The piece shares the ternary structure of the symphony movement, but the jaunty outer sections more than balance a quasi-funereal middle section whose tempo and thumping bass line illustrate the unsung phrase "Beat the drum slowly" from the original song text. Jocular ribaldry and exaggerated pathos have replaced nostalgic sentiment as the cowboy's primary colors.

OF MEN AND MUSTANGS

Harris did not outgrow his cowboy inclinations. On the contrary, even when other American composers retreated from descriptive content into greater and greater abstraction, Harris kept up his assertive Americanism and his western ties. As late as the 1950s, Harris and his wife, Johana, produced a remarkable

EXAMPLE 41. *American Ballads,* "Streets of Laredo," mm. 1–10, 33–41 (New York: Carl Fischer, 1947)

cowboy episode for the television station WQED in Pittsburgh, sponsored by the Pennsylvania College for Women, where Harris was employed (1952–56). In an audiotape of this fifteen-minute broadcast, the second in a series entitled "Sing a Song of Folk," the Harris couple conjure up a Wild West show of their own. Johana provides wonderful piano improvisations on cowboy songs during the entire program; she sings verses of "Chisholm Trail" interspersed within a narrative of Harris's own invention, a revisiting of the Cowboys' Reunion that he had described in 1940 in "Folksong—American Big Business." He reencounters the fictional cowpokes Idaho Bill and Shorty Kelsey, this time in a scenario with far stronger autobiographical implications. Again, Harris's retelling brooks no paraphrase:

> I remember I was on my way to go back East, and a fellow came up to see me, I was standing there, and he says: "Are you the Harris boy?" and I said, "Yes." He said, "I hear you're going East to go to college," and I said, "Yeah, that's right." And he says, "Well, uh, Idaho Bill wants to talk to you." And so I went over, and here was old Idaho Bill. He'd been a friend of Buffalo Bill. And Idaho was down there—I might tell you he raises horses for Uncle Sam. He's got an enormous ranch up there in Idaho. And he shipped down a whole trainload of mustangs, real mustangs. If you've never seen a real wild mustang that's been born and raised on the range and never been in a barn or had a saddle on his back or a bit in his mouth, you ain't seen nothing I can tell you that. He had a whole trainload of 'em.
>
> So I went over to see Buffalo Bill, I mean Idaho Bill, and here he sat on a bale of hay, smokin' a cigar, and he says, "Young fella, I hear you're goin' back to [get an] education, back in the East. Whaddaya wanna do that [for]?" He says, "There's plenty goin' on out here. We need young fellas like you, and I'll tell you what I'll do if you'll stay with me. I'll give you a string to ride for yourself." Some of you folks here in Pittsburgh don't know that a string means a whole bunch of ponies that you ride on the range.
>
> He says, "I tell you what I'll do with you, young fella," he said. "You guard one of the gates for this Cowboys' Reunion anyhow and see [how] you like it. Maybe you'll get some of that in your blood. Maybe you'll stay here with us anyhow," and I did. . . .
>
> That was some Cowboys' Reunion. Of course it was done for the cowboys themselves. It wasn't much of a fair like you'd see, well let's say, in Madison Square Gardens [sic], wasn't professional, but it sure was rough. I remember that probably the most, the most fierce, the roughest one I saw of all was the wild horse race, where a man and his wrangler had to go and rope a wild horse out of a corral, put a saddle on him, and ride him around the track. And I saw some of those horses rise up and buck and fight until the blood ran out of their nose.[30]

Harris here aligns the various elements of his artistic stance with the rodeo: disdain for education and the East, respect for the solitary wrangler working for Uncle Sam, fascination with the instinctive or untamed, concern for the continuity of tradition, personal worthiness to inherit valuable resources (in this case ponies rather than folk songs), and mistrust of all things professional. Running through the allusive account of these aesthetic elements is a curious, concrete, and sometimes violent obsession with wild horses. Considering that Harris had already used these mustangs as a metaphor for his own creative impulses—Boulanger had failed to give him "the machinery with which to release and harness the wild horses within him"[31]—the television fantasy takes on a significance far greater than fiction. The composer was a cowpuncher, and the wild horse race held dangers for both rider and steed.

It should not be overlooked that Harris's characteristic cowpuncher presents a certain stance toward gender and sexuality. Cowgirls, no matter what their talents or aspirations, were considered comic figures in the mass media—and in Agnes de Mille's *Rodeo*. And for all the historically homosocial activity of the cowboy, he remained throughout the twentieth century the staunch symbol of a particular brand of heterosexual machismo, as literary critic Jane Tompkins has observed: "Westerns . . . emphasiz[e] the importance of manhood as an ideal. It is not one ideal among many, it is *the* ideal, certainly the only one worth dying for." She notes that the typical western takes place "in a period and in an environment where few women are to be found and where conditions are the worst possible for their acquiring any social power."[32] Although nothing in Harris's music suggests the stereotypical vices of the western hero, many aspects of his life resonate with the aggressive masculinity that the western hero represented. He broadcast widely his commitment to conventionally masculine habits and hobbies. His love of fast cars (see figure 7) resulted in an accident that nearly left him lame. His lifelong enthusiasm for professional sports was spiced with the claim that he was almost signed by the Chicago White Sox as a young man, and (second only to farming) sports provided Harris with a favorite stockpile of metaphors for music and creativity.[33]

Concern with masculinity had its impact on Harris's private life as well. His four marriages resulted in at least seven children.[34] His last marriage, to the talented pianist Beula Duffey (whom he renamed Johana, in honor of J.S. Bach), counts as his longest and most productive relationship. Their "Sing a Song of Folk" broadcasts were only one of their many collaborations, and it has long been argued that Johana exerted a pronounced influence on Harris's writing for piano. Harris readily acknowledged Johana's expert musicianship and interpretive gifts; his recollections of their married life, however, focus on Johana's role as a willing wife cheerfully performing such domestic duties as keeping the kids quiet during his working hours. Louise Spizizen has shown in detail how Harris arranged a divorce from his third wife while simultaneously supervising the "erasure" of the successful and glamorous Beula, transforming her into his ideal helpmate, Johana, through obvious modifications of her appearance and behavior.[35] Harris's preoccupation with control is, of course, not necessarily a gendered trait; however, in the familial contexts which were so important to him, it resulted in exaggerations of the traditional roles for husband and father.

Although we cannot know for sure, Harris's emphasis on mature male heroes may have been a conscious or unconscious reaction against a critical establish-

FIGURE 7. Roy Harris during his time in Colorado in the 1940s, posing with his favorite car, "Golden Boy." Courtesy of Patricia Harris

ment that frequently portrayed him as childlike or naive. As early as 1926 Copland had characterized Harris as "a child of nature with a child's love for his native hills and a child-like belief in the moral purpose of music."[36] Such portrayals became more and more typical as the composer got older, and even Johana endorsed them. When asked to offer a "personal note" for David Ewen's entry on Harris in *The Book of Modern Composers* (1942), she responded by deftly tying together this and other strands of Harris reception:

> Most people think of my husband as a good-natured, easy-going Westerner. And so he is. But he is many other people as well. To me he is a child—always eager—always ready to believe in everyone, always expecting miracles to happen, always being hurt and enraged by the social and economic injustices that he sees and feels everywhere he goes. And yet, he is an unquenchable optimist who loves beauty in every phase of living. In his creative life he is a priest and a devil rolled into one bundle of uncompromising drive.[37]

The American primitive, the Western naïf, the authentic artistic voice waiting for the proper trigger to release creative impulses already fully formed within him—these were powerful variants on familiar mythologizing constructions, perhaps newer to American music than to American painting or literature, but still based on commonplace romantic views of artistic creation. They were not, however, the only such devices available to American composers in the 1930s and 1940s, and in the long run they were not the most successful ones.

THE LONESOME COWBOY

Harris reveled in the characterizations bestowed upon him by factions of the critical establishment. In some cases he helped to create and shape these characterizations. He remained committed to spreading them, and he continued to believe them, it seems, until the end of his life. From around 1930 until World War II, he was able to adopt or adapt them with relative reliability and great success, yet there were troubling clouds on the horizon for American music's western hero. The essentialism that bolstered his reputation also cast some distorting shadows, and it was not long before the images he had carefully promoted were turned against him.

The first signs that the edges of the Harris myth had started to fray can be seen in a reevaluation of Harris's supposed "earnestness," "sincerity," and "genuineness." These adjectives had clung to him since his pre-Paris days, and at first they were usually benevolent. Henry Cowell, writing in 1933, opened with a celebration of genuineness as it described the composer: "serious, writing only in the larger forms; continually improving his style; deadly earnest, with a devoted sincerity to musical ideals and high standards and with boundless enthusiasm as to his own possibilities." The ambivalence of Cowell's final phrase blossoms into a more pointed suggestion that it was the composer's charisma, not his talent, that listeners found appealing, but for the most part Cowell was content to welcome Harris as a rising star.[38]

The cosmopolitan critics who had been Harris's uneasy comrades in the Boulangerie were less generous in addressing Harris's supposed sincerity. After all, Harris had always been eager to distance himself from them; they seem to have returned the favor with equal grace. Writing less than a year after Cowell—and just before the *Symphony 1933* premiere—Walter Piston amiably congratulated Harris for "surviving the trying experience of being hailed as a genius." Piston, like Cowell, noted Harris's contagious confidence in his own work, praising this enthusiasm as honest and refreshing. But only a few lines later, he introduced an eventually devastating trope into Harris reception. Before beginning his discussion of Harris's music, Piston planted the image of Harris as a musical innocent, working in happy obliviousness: "It is doubtful whether Harris is aware of the exact nature of the most expressive and telling qualities in his music. The slightly uncouth awkwardness, the nervous restlessness, he would undoubtedly consider defects rather than qualities. If these characteristics are due, as some think, to a lack of technic, let us hope the man can in some way be prevented from acquiring a technic which would rob his musical language of some of its most valuable attributes."[39] Piston implied not only that Harris's music might be technically weak, but also that the composer had to be protected from himself if his endeavors were to remain artistically valuable.

Copland noticed this passage in Piston's article and latched onto it, even quoting it in some of his own writings.[40] By 1941, when he published a longer assessment of Harris's life and works in *Our New Music*, he had taken this view of Harris several degrees further. Copland agreed with Cowell and Piston that Harris had real personality. "You can punch that personality full of holes," he proclaimed. "You can demonstrate to your own satisfaction that the man doesn't know the first thing about composing—but the fact will remain that his is the most personal note in American music today." Copland coolly observed that Harris's "essential personality" had hardly changed at all since his years in Paris—a remarkable artistic consistency that he viewed as a mixed blessing.[41] But having raised the question of whether Harris's consistency should be considered a strength or a weakness, the article abruptly dismisses the question:

> Whatever one may think, it is useless to wish Harris otherwise than he is. One may show how much better his work might have been. And one can fervently hope that it will become continually more integrated. But there is no gainsaying that, such as it is, with all its faults and qualities, it is enormously important to us in the immediate scene. This is true, above all, because it is music of vitality and personality. Plenty of Americans have learned how to compose properly, and it has done us little good. Here is a man who, perhaps, may not be said to compose properly but who will do us lots of good.[42]

Copland assigned Harris a specific and significant historical role, but it was a role that Harris played in spite of himself, and a role that nearly required his music to be seen as flawed. In this formulation, Harris's stylistic consistency might indeed reflect the genuineness of his composer's voice, but it also advertised his incorrigible mediocrity and prophesied his eventual obscurity.

There were protests, too, about the substance and spread of the Harris myth. Already in 1934, Piston had wryly joked about the "blasphemy" of discovering any French influence in Harris's harmonic language; in speaking of Harrisian melody, he had made the obligatory references to the West, the pioneer spirit, and the craggy contours of mountain ranges, but he added an acerbic disclaimer: "References to elements not considered characteristic of the 'good old U.S.A.' are carefully avoided in this connection, for Harris is, above all, the accepted one hundred per cent American composer."[43] The next year, Blitzstein complained about Harris's overblown gestures: "Can he do nothing about the insistent mood of 'Olympian' ostentation which has crept in? How often, when a real contour and 'face' begins to appear in a movement, it becomes dimmed and blotted out by vague rhetorical repetitiousness and posturing, gloomy-grand, or American-sinewy, or what-not!"[44]

Others began to question whether Harris's long-standing profession of authenticity could be taken at face value or whether it might have served merely to attract attention—or worse, to make money. By 1940, Virgil Thomson had (suavely, of course) lost his temper:

> No composer in the world, not even in Italy or Germany, makes such shameless use of patriotic feelings to advertise his product. One would think to read his prefaces, that Harris had been awarded by God, or at least by popular vote, a monopolistic privilege of expressing our nation's deepest ideals and highest aspirations. And when the piece so advertised turns out to be a mostly not very clearly orchestrated schoolish counterpoint and a quite skimpy double fugue (neither of which has any American connotation whatsoever), one is tempted to put the whole thing down as insincere and a bad joke.[45]

Thomson tried to strip Harris of his sincerity, allying him with marketing monopolies, and alluding to fascism rather than some more benign form of patriotism.

Finally, Harris's whiteness and his fervent Americanism took on devastating lives of their own, haunting him in contexts where they were unlikely to win him critical or popular support. Harris had openly accepted prevalent racial theories, embracing his Anglo-Saxon heritage absolutely as an artistic asset. But, with the outbreak of World War II, not everyone retained his conviction that racial awareness was so sound a key to creativity. While composers were fleeing the anti-Semitic policies of Nazi Germany, Harris's rosy view of the direct linkage between race and music was quickly becoming unfashionable and in some circles morally suspect.

Within the influential circles of *Modern Music,* for example, voices were being raised against nationalisms of all sorts, but especially against any nationalism that resembled German fascism in its emphasis on race. The refugee musicologist Alfred Einstein, writing in 1939, felt justified in proclaiming that "the greatest foe of freedom, independence and truth in art—and in science—is Nationalism. . . . Blood and soil do not make the creative spirit; it is rather the spirit . . . that makes blood and soil. The whole future of America's music will stand or fall by this truth."[46] Later in the same issue (in the article immediately preceding Mendel's essay on Harris's quintet), Rosenfeld drew bleak portraits of "regionalism and racialism," accusing the regionalist of wanting to keep the "city boys" and the "country boys" carefully separated and equating the racialist's concern for "purity" and "the true folk manner" with a kind of fascism.[47] In the subsequent issue of the journal, Roger Sessions expressed his concern about "the present trend toward nationalism and cultural isolationism among American musicians" in equally powerful terms: "A certain number of our musicians, together with a not negligible part of our musical press, is demanding with a voice quite reminiscent of various totalitarian phrases which we have heard, that music which shall 'express the national feeling,' 'reflect the American scene,' 'establish an American style.'"[48]

Harris was not the direct target of these attacks—in fact, he might not have acknowledged any similarities between his innocent love of nation and the rabid nationalism decried by the critics cited above. Yet Harris's Americanism was falling ever further out of step with the attitudes of his colleagues, and his racially charged rhetoric began to invoke unpleasant analogies. In a quarterly report for *Modern Music* (April–May 1940), Conlon Nancarrow condemned one of Harris's radio broadcasts on these chilling grounds: "WQXR has recently given two recorded programs of Harris' music. On one of them, the composer in person presented his 'rhythm-of-race' theory. I wonder if he feels that it 'can't happen here' and that therefore, because of immunity, all this doesn't really matter; or that it can happen here and would be a fine thing. . . ."[49] Few dared to be this blunt in 1940, but the damning implications of Nancarrow's scenario show how quickly the territory on which Harris had built his reputation could become precarious.

During the 1930s and into the 1940s, Harris had many sympathetic compatriots who were also engaged in producing the kind of all-American music he espoused. Copland, William Schuman, and others joined Harris in writing wartime fanfares, symphonies, ballets, and choral works devoted to patriotic themes. As late as 1945, when Cowell hired Harris to work for the Office of War Information, many other prominent American composers could have filled the bill. Yet Harris's heartfelt justifications of the differences between American and European music lasted much longer, and eventually worked against the growing internationalism and valorization of abstraction that would take hold in the 1950s and 1960s. Swimming upstream, Harris remained true to his patriotic (and programmatic) beginnings by writing the "Gettysburg" Symphony in 1944, *Kentucky Spring* in 1949, the cantata *Abraham Lincoln Walks at Midnight* in 1953, a *Folk Fantasy for Festivals* in 1956, the "Abraham Lincoln" Symphony in 1965, and even the *Bicentennial Symphony 1976*, shortly before his death. Ultimately, these works suffered from a critical neglect that betrays embarrassment with their insistent Americanism, as much as their consonant musical style or questionable counterpoint.

After Harris's death in 1979, numerous obituaries addressed these accumulated questions about Harris's music and his career trajectory. Among the most extensive and thoughtful such treatments is an article-length reflection on the composer entitled, "Roy Harris: In Memoriam (But Keep Your Hats On)." Here, Marshall Bialosky adds Harris's name to a roster of tragic figures in the history of American music: "What is the tragedy of Roy Harris? It is the tragedy of a man who was declared at the very outset of his career—by important composers and critics alike, not to mention himself—capable of great achievements in composition, but who was able in the end only to acquire the trappings and the publicity of a great composer. Then he was robbed of even that by onrushing musical history, which in an age of high technical achievement, atonalism, serialism, indeterminate and chance music, electronic and computer music, made nationalism suddenly obsolete."[50]

Harris was not exceptional in being both an advocate and a victim of certain kinds of racial and national determinism, but he was more profoundly, and in the end more adversely, affected by them than most of his white colleagues. The national and ethnic characterizations that had gathered around him were too strongly established and too publicly sanctioned to be politely overlooked after the cataclysmic racialist-nationalist debacle of World War II and the changes it brought to American musical life. Unlike Cowell, Harris did not balance his overt Americanisms with radically experimental abstract works. Unlike Copland, he took no radical steps to dissociate himself from his supposed racial heritage; on the contrary, he continued to celebrate it, though not exclusively, all his life. Unlike Gershwin, Harris survived well into the second half of the century, by which point such strong ethnic associations and accessible content (at least in American art music) were often more a liability than a strength. For the forty years that stretched from the symphonic triumphs of 1939–40 to his death, driven and encumbered by a legend he had helped to create, Harris held his ground.

PART FIVE

Aaron Copland

From Orient to Occident

Jody lay in his bed and thought of the impossible world of Indians and buffaloes. . . . He wished he could have been living in the heroic time, but he knew he was not of heroic timber. . . . A race of giants had lived then, fearless men, men of a staunchness unknown in this day. Jody thought of the wide plains and of the wagons moving across like centipedes. He thought of Grandfather on a huge white horse, marshaling the people. Across his mind marched the great phantoms, and they marched off the earth and they were gone.

—JOHN STEINBECK, *THE RED PONY*

1111

The Saga of the Prairies

THE MEDIUM AND THE MESSAGE

Late in September 1936, the Columbia Broadcasting System offered Aaron Copland his first radio commission. Along with five other composers—Louis Gruenberg, Howard Hanson, Roy Harris, Walter Piston, and William Grant Still—Copland crafted a piece to fit the network's basic guidelines for length (less than thirty minutes) and instrumentation (fewer than thirty-seven players).[1] Many years after the fact, Copland recalled his excitement at composing for this new medium, claiming to have written "in a style designed to bridge the gap between modern composition and the need for a wider public."[2] His initial title for the work, *Radio Serenade,* was abruptly altered to the even more neutral *Music for Radio,* thanks to a clever public relations move by radio officials: to increase audience interest, listeners would be asked to send in their suggestions for more descriptive subtitles. Over a thousand entries were collected from across the country, including "Cliff Dwellers," "The Inca's Prayer to the Sun," "Machine Age," "Marconi's World Message," "Subway Traveler," "Oriental Phantasy," "Boy Scout Jamboree," "Journey of the British Patrol Across Arabia," "Adventures in the Life of a Robot," and "Futile Search for Order Out of Chaos." The composer telegraphed his response to CBS: "HAVE READ ALL TITLE SUGGESTIONS STOP ASTONISHED AND DELIGHTED BY NUMBER AND VARIETY STOP NO ONE TITLE COMPLETELY SATISFACTORY STOP ACCEPT GLADLY AS IMAGINATIVE SUBTITLE SAGA OF THE PRAIRIE STOP CLOSE RUNNERS UP PRAIRIE TRAVEL STOP JOURNEY OF THE EARLY PIONEERS STOP AMERICAN PIONEER" (VPAC1, 255). Thus did Aaron Copland christen his first work for national broadcast, one of his first with a descriptive

293

title invoking Americana. After all, he reflected, "I had used a cowboy tune in the second of the four sections, so the western titles seemed most appropriate. (The piece, of course, had been composed entirely on West 63rd Street in New York City)" (VPAC1, 255).

There is more to this story than Copland's recollections suggest. The folklike melody that serves as the work's second theme was not originally identified as a cowboy song, and Copland scholars have not found this tune in any of the composer's usual folk music sources.[3] Although the composition of the piece may have taken place mostly in New York, Copland had already left for Mexico (apparently via Hollywood) before it was complete (VPAC1, 255, 265, 270–71). He also neglected to mention that some of the material for the work was drawn from a piece with a definite (and politically controversial) program. Indeed, the real saga of *Music for Radio* draws together a number of the narrative strands that will inform this discussion of Copland: his ambivalent stance toward folk music; the promises and perils of populism during the 1930s; the curious circumstances that allowed his westernness to emerge almost exclusively in response to outside influences instead of personal inclinations; and the ironies that surface when one attempts to map biographical or geographical fact onto popular and critical reception.

Here we will examine the process by which Copland's westernness replaced his more contentious leftism, overshadowed his overt engagement with African American musical materials, and won nationwide popularity for a composer who might otherwise have been marginalized on the basis of his Russian-Jewish heritage or his homosexuality. The conjunction of whiteness, masculinity, and the West that was so significant a part of Harris's appeal had different but still powerful implications for Copland. The aggressive heroes and rugged landscapes of the West helped balance (veiled) allusions to his homosexual preferences, deflecting interest away from his Jewish, cosmopolitan background and focusing it on an Anglo, western mythology that was rapidly becoming a favorite arena for representations of American identity in the mass media. Stylistically speaking, Copland's westward turn softened his jazzy modernism into an all-purpose Americanism steeped in nostalgia and helped recuperate the left-wing overtones of his "pioneer" populism by channeling them into domestic settings more acceptable to the conservative establishment and the listening public. The musical vocabulary associated with Copland's idealizations of frontier America, though in part shared with (or borrowed from) his contemporaries, also offered a disarmingly concrete resolution to those pursuing the chimeric "Copland style."

THE "BROOKLYN STRAVINSKY"

The ready availability today of diverse musical idioms may make it difficult for us to recapture the angst with which Copland and his contemporaries addressed questions of personal style. Though trends in composition had changed radically since the fin de siècle, the rhetoric used to describe the creative process was slow to catch up, clinging instead to romantic notions of originality, creative consistency, and an easily recognizable individual "voice."

As we have seen, faith in the tremendous value of "personality" had spurred the early acclamation of Harris, by Copland and others, despite concerns about his technique. George Antheil's revealing, if somewhat eccentric, recollections further suggest how strongly Copland's appreciation of Harris was linked to the question of individuality. Antheil recalled Copland's admiring words for Harris's Third Symphony: "It is honest, sincere.... you can open any page of it and say, 'Here is Roy Harris.' His music is always written in his own style, nobody else's.... You must always know whether or not this page of music belongs to this or that composer; that comes before everything—excepting, of course, sincerity."[4] Antheil distanced himself from these views, comparing the presence of an individual idiom to an irritating radio advertisement. But Copland remained committed to audible individuality when making aesthetic judgments. Even when his opinion of Harris cooled, his faith in "personality" remained. Such strong feelings from the typically reserved Copland are an indication that by 1941 he bore the scars of his own battles between style and technique. While Harris had been described as possessing an incorrigible sincerity, simultaneously in need and in danger of acquiring technique, Copland's early reception marked him as a skilled craftsman still searching for his own personal voice.

From the start, Copland may have been susceptible to charges of stylistic imitation because of his famous teachers: Rubin Goldmark and especially Nadia Boulanger. Even if he avoided bringing more adventurous compositions to Goldmark, Copland seems to have adopted certain aspects of the older composer's outlook, including an appreciation for craftsmanship and an openness to outside stimulus. True to the Germanic and central European heritage of his musical family, Goldmark emphasized the importance of rigorous study and polished technique, especially when it came to form. In fact, when Copland revealed his hope of joining his friend Aaron Schaffer in France, Goldmark urged him to remain in New York to solidify his technique and to perfect his mastery of sonata form. Even after his protégé had left the New York nest, Goldmark continued to advocate his views on the saving grace of form: "I hope you will make some more progress in the Sonata form. Don't get to despise this, even if you should fall into the hands of some radicals." In Goldmark's musical universe, acquiring the basics through careful study was the proper preparation for "doing anything you like afterwards."[5]

Goldmark encouraged his students to broaden their realm of experiences and to gain competence in a (limited) plurality of compositional styles. While Farwell urged Harris to write from within, Goldmark favored European study, "especially when taken at an impressionable age." "I am sure it will broaden you and be of great value to you," he wrote, "particularly if you make use of all your faculties to absorb and digest."[6] Goldmark was particularly delighted when his pupil wrote from Paris that he was planning to spend the summer in Germany. "You are certainly making the best of your European sojourn," he wrote. "I think it was very wise of you to go into Germany for a while, even tho' its musical lustre may be dimmer for one who has sat at the feet of 'Les Six.' . . . It is a good thing for a well-rounded musician to gain experience in many lands, and absorb what they can give him."[7]

If Germany and France were the sanctioned sites for the "impression," "absorption," and "digestion" that Goldmark favored, what of the United States? When questioned about this in 1914, Goldmark protested: "I believe that too much stress is laid on the negro and Indian aspects of the question."[8] But no matter what he chose to preach, Goldmark practiced a musical nationalism that he may well have learned while studying with Dvořák at the National Conservatory. African American materials inform Goldmark's *"Gettysburg" Requiem* (1919) and *Negro Rhapsody* (1923); Native American references are prominent in the *Hiawatha Overture* (1900) and *The Call of the Plains* (1916, orch. 1925). Copland was ambivalent about Goldmark's potential influence, especially in the realm of Americana. "I never remember his discussing the subject of nationalism or folklorism," he recalled, "and he certainly never suggested them to me as possible influences" (VPAC1, 27–28).[9] Yet he could hardly have helped but notice that a New Yorker could profitably imagine the American heartland in works like Goldmark's piano suite *Prairie Idylls* (1915).[10]

Copland's recollections of Goldmark remained mostly fond, but when it came to Boulanger, Copland was a real American disciple. Dozens of composers—Harris among them—went to study with Boulanger at Copland's recommendation, and he was proud of this legacy. Like Harris, Copland was profoundly impressed by Boulanger's musical facility, but unlike the self-proclaimed "autodidact," he also affirmed the importance of "technical mastery" and the relatively benign influence of having models to follow. He recalled: " 'To study music, we must learn the rules,' she would say. 'To create music, we must forget them' " (VPAC1, 62–63). In the summer of 1932, more than a decade after encountering Boulanger, Copland had occasion to voice his continued approval for his mentor's methods as he argued with Virgil Thomson about whether their friend Paul Bowles should study composition with Boulanger or Paul Dukas. Copland defended Boulanger's sometimes overbearing approach in a letter to Thomson: "I'm all for the teacher influencing the pupil . . . the pupil should swallow it whole for a time and if he has any guts he'll throw them overboard soon enough" (HP, 184).

Scholars have identified several resonances of Boulanger's teaching in Copland's music. First is the pedagogue's concept of *la grande ligne*, or as Copland later described it, "the sense of forward motion, of flow and continuity in the musical discourse" (VPAC1, 67)—ideals that have much in common with Harris's concept of "autogenetic" or organic melody. By contrast, Copland seems to have considered this aspect of Boulanger's pedagogy worthy but perhaps a bit old-fashioned.[11] Later in the paragraph cited above, he observed that "much has happened in music since those years, and perhaps Boulanger's theories seem outdated" (VPAC1, 67). Second, and more important for Copland's stylistic trajectory, was the value Boulanger placed on fluency in a broad range of musical idioms. Many members of the Boulangerie have spoken of the historical breadth they gained from her commitment to contemporary music—not just the works of her friend Stravinsky, but also Les Six, Mahler, and to a certain extent, Bartók. At the same time, Boulanger's historical-analytical teaching style fostered an intimacy with the music of the past through weekly assignments that included orchestrating older works, experimenting with the formal conventions of different eras, and participating in concerts of early music. Hard on the heels of Copland's contrapuntal *Passacaglia* (1922), a genre that Boulanger required of her students, came the asymmetrical meters of his *Rondino* for string quartet (1923), and the ballet *Grohg* (1924–25), which combines impressionist and expressionist elements, Stravinskian octatonicism and polytonality, microtones, and jazz polyrhythms (HP, 85).

Perhaps the most significant of Boulanger's bequests to Copland was his engagement with the music of Stravinsky.[12] Critics of every decade have commented on the Russian composer's influence. In 1953, Arthur Berger wrote dismissively of this tendency: "One sometimes spoke in [the 1920s] of a 'Brooklyn Stravinsky.' Today this seems curious, with both composers better known."[13] Yet in his memoirs of the 1980s, Copland endorsed and intensified the comparison with candor and sophistication. Characterizing Stravinsky as "the hero of my student days," he readily admitted an influence in such areas as "rhythmic virtuosity," "bold use of dissonance," and "unusual instrumental combinations." More significantly, Copland claimed: "I was particularly struck by the strong Russian element in his music. He borrowed freely from folk materials, and I have no doubt that this strongly influenced me to try to find a way to a distinctively American music." But Copland reserved his most powerful rhetoric for a different evaluation of the Stravinskian legacy: "The most important thing for me," he wrote, "was that Stravinsky proved it was possible for a twentieth-century composer to create his own tradition" (VPAC1, 72–73). While Copland's rhythmic ingenuity and free adaptation of folk materials were crucial to the success of his music during the 1930s and 1940s, it is this sense that a composer could "create his own tradition" that had the greatest impact on Copland's western works.

"ECLECTIC IN ALL THE REST"

Creating his own tradition was not something that Copland could accomplish overnight. In contrast to Harris, who had substantial critical help in identifying his musical mission, Copland encountered many obstacles. The diversity apparent in his early works left friends and critics wondering which musical elements were evidence of imitation and artistic immaturity and which ones could be considered "sincere."[14] Immediately after his Symphony for Organ and Orchestra (in which stylistic ties to Boulanger were reinforced by the work's dedication and by Boulanger's physical presence as the soloist) came a work in a radically different vein: *Music for the Theatre* (1925). Copland had returned to New York in June 1924, a mere three months after Paul Whiteman's notorious "Experiment in Modern Music" had given birth to George Gershwin's *Rhapsody in Blue,* and although *Music for the Theatre* did not have the same kind of advertising, it represented a related but less popular "experiment." The first work commissioned by the League of Composers, it was premiered by members of the Boston Symphony Orchestra under Koussevitzky, to whom the work was dedicated. In addition to exhibiting one of the composer's first allusions to an existing popular melody ("The Sidewalks of New York"), the work remains remarkable for its brash use of jazz idioms, especially in the "Dance" and "Burlesque" movements. Together with the Piano Concerto (1926), *Music for the Theatre* provides the musical embodiment of Copland's early writings on jazz, which reveal both his fascination with jazz rhythms and his limited appreciation for the emotional scope of African American music.[15]

Not everyone was pleased with Copland's solution. Some praised his inventiveness, but Copland also drew fire from conservative critics, who disparaged his flouting of concert hall decorum, and more surprisingly, from many of his friends, who worried that he might appear too "commercial" or too narrowly identified with New York.[16] Harris, for one, cautioned Copland against these dangers in a letter written while the Piano Concerto was still in progress: "A word of warning to you—dear brother Aaron—the Jazz idiom is too easily assumed and projected[—]as a serious expression it has nearly burned out already I believe. Either you must chuck it or carry it to ad infinitum—or ad nauseam (which shall I say)—Beware for that new piano concerto which so many Copeland [sic] enthusiasts are waiting for—Don't disappoint us with jazz—(Have I been harsh—if it might seem so—it is only because I have such belief in your integrity—*outside* the *jazz idiom*)" (emphasis in the original).[17] That same year, Roger Sessions expressed similar concerns, objecting vehemently to Copland's claim that *Music for the Theatre* was his most "characteristic" work. It was that assertion, Sessions wrote, "combined with what you said about being a 'New York composer' etc. [that] led me to wonder whether you were not—temporarily, no doubt—going off on a vein which was smaller than your truest one."[18]

Copland's answers to these letters were circumspect, but his subsequent scores may represent a response in their own right.[19] After the Piano Concerto, his next large-scale composition was the 1928 piano trio *Vitebsk (Study on a Jewish*

Theme), and it was dedicated to Harris. While *Vitebsk* preserved and even intensified the dissonant language of his jazz-based works, Copland changed the
frame of reference by aligning its quarter tones not with the jazzy realm of the
"blue note," but with the vocal inflections of Hasidic song. *Vitebsk* won approval
from Harris, but its overt Jewishness remained rare in Copland's oeuvre. Instead, Copland's next compositions—including the *Symphonic Ode* (1929), *Piano
Variations* (1930), and *Short Symphony* (1933)—sported a style that Sessions would
have endorsed: dissonant, tightly constructed, and arguably free of explicit national or ethnic markers.

By the early 1930s, the advice that Copland had been receiving privately from
his colleagues began to find its way into print. In 1930, Theodore Chanler, a fellow member of the Boulangerie, undertook one of the first substantial articles
devoted to the composer. After Copland sent Chanler scores of his most recent
works, he received a letter of thanks and a glib warning: "I finally started writing
the article yesterday. Having no idea what I was going to say it came as something of a shock to me when I found myself positively *roasting* you. I hope you
won't be annoyed. I've decided that your style is full of impurities. So there."[20]
This accusation became the negative refrain in Chanler's otherwise complimentary text, initially published in *The Hound and Horn* (1930) and later antholo-
gized in Henry Cowell's collection *American Composers on American Music*
(1933). Stating from the outset that Copland's "architectural sense is in advance of
his sense of style, which is still impure," Chanler deflated even his most enthusiastic praise with expressions of regret that Copland's own voice was insufficiently
audible: "The zest which he manages to instill into certain rather jaded jazz
motifs, the skilful disposition of the material, the humor and perfect timing of
contrasts . . . save [the Piano Concerto] from being in any sense a *pastiche*,
though one is aware of potentialities in Copland, not realized here, of achieving
a more fruitfully personal style."[21]

Chanler's objections soon found a more potent mouthpiece in Virgil Thomson, whose contribution on Copland for *Modern Music*'s "American Composers"
series began with a notable overstatement: "Aaron Copland's music is American
in rhythm, Jewish in melody, eclectic in all the rest." Later passages expand and
clarify this pithy opening without retracting it:

> Today we ape Stravinsky. Yesterday it was Debussy. Before it was Wagner. Cop-
> land's best recommendation is that he is less eclectic than his confrères. I reproach
> him with eclecticism all the same. . . . He has truth, force, and elegance. He has not
> quite style. There remain too many irrelevant memories of Nadia Boulanger's les-
> sons, of the scores of Stravinsky and Mahler and perhaps Richard Strauss. . . . It is
> a source of continual annoyance to me that his usefulness and his beauty are not
> fully achieved because he has not yet done the merciless weeding out of his garden
> that any European composer would have done after his first orchestral hearing.[22]

In Thomson's eyes, Boulanger's careful curriculum had left Copland with an awkward multiplicity of idioms. If Harris ignored his teachers and struck out prematurely on his own, Copland was too diligent. Finishing off his article with a ringing reversal of Harris's reception, Thomson declared: "The music is all right but the man is not clearly enough visible through it. An American certainly, a Hebrew certainly. But his more precise and personal outline is still blurred by the shadows of those who formed his youth."[23]

In addition to the implications of artistic immaturity or unnecessary reliance on European models, there may have been another specter haunting some of those critics who focused on stylistic eclecticism as Copland's most significant shortcoming. As much of Thomson's acerbic essay makes clear, Copland's jazzy eclecticism resonated with certain perspectives on American Jewish cultural identity—embraced by some and disparaged by others.[24] Rosenfeld and Sessions mention Copland's religious background rather casually when explaining his melodic habits and his receptiveness to jazz (HP, 518–31). Copland himself participated in similar stereotyping; he referred to Darius Milhaud's "profound nostalgia" and "a deep sense of the tragedy of all life" as evidence of his "Jewish blood" and cited the composer's "violence" and "logic" as indications of his "Jewish spirit."[25] Thomson made even heavier weather of Copland's Jewish melos ("When he sings it is as wailing before the wall") and stern Hebraic nature: "He is a prophet calling out her sins to Israel. His God is the god of battle, the Lord of Hosts, the jealous, the angry, the avenging god. . . . The gentler movements of his music are more like an oriental contemplation of infinity than like any tender depiction of the gentler aspects of Jehovah."[26]

Many writers had less flattering agendas when they discussed Jewishness in the arts. Commercial and cosmopolitan connotations plagued Jewish creators trying to succeed in an age devoted to authenticity. Associated in the popular press with the music of Tin Pan Alley and Hollywood, Jewish composers' efforts could easily be branded as inauthentic (or insidious) attempts to assimilate (or to corrupt). In the 1920s, for example, at the height of American anti-Semitism, Henry Ford's *Dearborn Independent* voiced this view: "In this business of making the people's songs, the Jews have shown, as usual, no originality but very much adaptability . . . which is a charitable term used to cover plagiarism, which in its turn politely covers the crime of mental pocket-picking. The Jews do not create; they take what others have done, give it a clever twist, and exploit it."[27] Such brazen accusations still resonate very faintly in Harris's later condemnations of the city composer, the arranger, the musical journalist.

Though speaking from a profoundly different perspective—as a practicing Jew and an authority on Jewish music—Lazare Saminsky reiterated many of these themes in his treatment of composers like Copland, whom he considered contemptibly "Judaic" rather than rooted in the ancient "Hebraic" tradition. Defining the "Judaic" as an assimilationist idiom, "folksong born in the latest ghetto," "orientalized," and "showing an abundance of borrowed and neutralized traits," he observed: "It has emanated from an alien corner, acquired by the Jewish racial psyche; it flows from the mental agility, the calamitous gift of alert self-adaptation to a new cultural quarter."[28] In Copland's case, "self-adaptation" betrayed itself in the composer's chameleon style. By 1934, Saminsky admitted that he had made up his mind, at least temporarily: "I am sorry to profess an eradicable conviction that Copland is of an observing, an absorbing nature, rather than a creative one."[29]

The concept of absorption took on more frightening resonances than creative bankruptcy for those critics worried about the national love affair with African American music. In the United States, there was no more intense locus for anxiety about stylistic eclecticism than the noisy collision of black and white represented by jazz. MacDonald Smith Moore has identified a broad spectrum of writers who linked Jews with "the success of jazz" and "the fusion of jazz and classical music," primarily for racial reasons.[30] As "rootless" cosmopolitans, Jews shared jazz's urban taint; as "Orientals," their racial profile fell between Negro and Anglo. They were cultural middlemen, uniquely situated to perform the anarchic alchemy between "high" and "low" art so well represented by Gershwin's *Rhapsody in Blue* or Copland's *Music for the Theatre*. John Tasker Howard was only one among dozens of contemporary critics who saw both Tin Pan Alley and jazz as "Jewish interpretation[s] of the Negro." Rosenfeld and, later, Wilfrid Mellers echoed Isaac Goldberg's hypothesis that "the ready amalgamation of the American Negro and the American Jew goes back to something Oriental in the blood of both."[31]

As we saw in Henry Cowell's approach to Harris's music, many observers held strong views about the detrimental effects of mingling jazz and classical composition. Though Cowell would later espouse friendship with Copland based on their shared commitment to modern music, in 1930 he was ready to dismiss Copland and Gershwin in a single breath. In a series of articles written for *Melos*, he claimed that it was "a pair of sophisticated Parisians" who had led young American composers to cast their lot with jazz—an amalgam of the Negro's syncopation and rhythmic accents as modernized by "'Tin-Pan-Alley'-Jews."[32] Cowell contended that Copland's Piano Concerto had improved jazz by analyzing and experimenting with its musical elements. But he remained convinced that such music could never fully represent the "true America" because it lacked the Anglo-Saxon character represented by Charles Ives or Carl Ruggles. Daniel Gregory Mason—more vehement in his condemnations of jazz and more virulent in his rhetoric—openly discussed "the insidiousness of the Jewish menace to our artistic integrity." In labeling Copland "a cosmopolitan Jew," Mason meant to position him on the dark side of a battle between "Oriental extravagance" and "the poignant beauty of Anglo-Saxon restraint." Incensed by Jewish "eroticism," "pessimism," and "superficiality," Mason sounded an alarm: "Our public taste is in danger of being permanently debauched . . . by the intoxication of what is, after all, an alien art."[33] For him, Copland's jazzy modernism and stylistic wandering represented more serious sins than youthful epigonism: they were the sounding embodiment of racial miscegenation.

Whether Copland's Jewish identity served as a banner or a stigma, it was not an identity that could be easily escaped. Perhaps this is what Nadia Boulanger meant when she apparently remarked that Harris would go further than Copland as a composer because he was not "handicapped" by being a Jew.[34] Whether her words reflect a sober awareness of prejudice in the world or a sobering reflection of the anti-Semitic attitudes prevalent in interwar Paris, they nonetheless show the power of race and religious creed to determine attitudes even among friends.[35] Copland was well aware of the potential limitations of being a "Jewish composer." In 1939 he warned the young Leonard Bernstein about the dangers of sounding too Jewish: "People are certain to say—'Bloch'" (HP, 522), he wrote, citing perhaps the most potent example of the ways in which racial/religious stereotypes could shape a composer's reputation.[36] But unlike Ernest Bloch, Copland was not, in the end, trapped by his Jewish identity. On the contrary, while never disavowing his heritage, he sidestepped it so completely that audiences today are often unaware that Copland did not begin his career as a "common man."

With this in mind, let us return to one of the most pregnant passages in Thomson's 1932 article, his striking assertion that "[Copland's] music is all right but the man is not clearly enough visible through it." This compositional disappearing act stands in sharp contrast to Harris, who won praise or blame for allowing his "personality" to overshadow his attention to musical detail. With such comparisons in mind, it is tempting to read even more into Thomson's claim. Not only did Copland lack Harris's imposing physicality, he also lacked Harris's aggressive masculinity. This masculinity, so important to the self-image Harris fostered and so much a part of the Depression-era mythology of the American West, would have been hard for many to reconcile with the conceptions of Copland-as-Jew or Copland-as-homosexual. If Copland's music indeed rendered his physical person invisible, one may legitimately wonder (as Thomson does not) whether this obfuscation is a sign of success or failure—whether concealing one's personality or background might sometimes be strategic. Harris eagerly invited the concertgoing public to hear autobiography in his works, but Copland had myriad reasons for discouraging such attempts, especially after he turned toward rural Americana. For Copland, identification with the American folk was at best implausible; instead, he claimed the populist's privilege of appealing to, and even serving them through his music.[37]

MUSIC FOR RADIO

Copland's first populist scores arrived in the mid-1930s with *El Salón México,* the children's opera *The Second Hurricane,* and the radio piece that CBS asked him to write as part of their Columbia Composers' commissions. Together, they illustrate the stylistic turning point that would become the most significant of Copland's changes in musical vocabulary, one that he once described as an "imposed simplicity"—a newly accessible style inspired by the desire to reach new audiences through new media. Though he came to regret the label, the ideals behind it were part and parcel of Copland's aesthetic, as Elizabeth Bergman Crist has aptly observed: they were part of the composer's lifelong commitment to progressive politics encapsulated in "the cultural work of the left-wing social movement known as the Popular Front."[38]

Curiously, Copland was not among those composers originally chosen by CBS to participate in their project. George Gershwin apparently turned down the job, leaving a slot open for Copland, who found the commission attractive for reasons that were not merely monetary. As he famously remarked in his autobiographical essay "Composer from Brooklyn,"

> During these years I began to feel an increasing dissatisfaction with the relations of the music-loving public and the living composer. . . . It seemed to me that we composers were in danger of working in a vacuum. Moreover, an entirely new public for music had grown up around the radio and phonograph. It made no sense to ignore them and to continue writing as if they did not exist. I felt that it was worth the effort to see if I couldn't say what I had to say in the simplest possible terms.[39]

Though Copland put his own spin on composing for the general public, he had substantial help in framing composition for radio as a uniquely populist genre. In an outpouring of public comment similar to that which greeted the advent of the phonograph, composers and commentators speculated on the role the new medium would play in American musical life. Few advocates were more impassioned than Davidson Taylor, the head of CBS's music division and the man responsible for the network's commissioning scheme. Writing in 1936, Taylor hailed radio's emerging role as music patron: "Potentially, indeed, the radio companies are the Brandenburgs, the Haffners, and the Esterhazys of today, since they have the funds, the orchestras and the audiences."[40] In his article, "Coming—The Mass Audience," Marc Blitzstein presented the other side of the cultural coin, positioning radio and other new media at the forefront of an audience-driven socio-musical revolution: "The great mass of people enter at last the field of serious music. Radio is responsible, the talkies, the summer concerts, a growing appetite, a hundred things; really the fact of an art and a world in progress. You can no more stop it than you can stop an avalanche."[41] For his part, Copland offered a more practical message about the responsibilities that composers owed to their expanding public. Speaking on the air in 1940, he observed: "The radio and the phonograph and the movies have broadened the democratic bases of music so suddenly that composers have been taken by surprise.... It is our job to give these new listeners a music that is fresh, direct, simple and profound. I can think of no better program for the composer of today."[42]

It was no accident, then, that the CBS commissions were slated for performance on a series titled "Everybody's Music"[43]—and no accident that this series was chosen as the site for a unique experiment in audience participation. Even before Copland was asked to change the name of his *Radio Serenade* to *Music for Radio,* CBS was already contemplating how best to exploit the public relations potential of its commissioning project. "One caution," wrote Deems Taylor (then the network's "Consultant on Music") in the letter offering Copland the job, "Please do not release any publicity on this thing that we are doing. We want to wait until we have all the acceptances in and then break a big story all over the country."[44] Copland's name was not at the top of the commissioning list, yet a two-page advertisement in *Radio Daily* featured his score as its chief exemplar shortly after the premiere: "This is a final rehearsal, in a CBS studio, for the world-premiere of Aaron Copland's work, 'Music for Radio.' Its first performance wrote a new chapter in the history of serious music. For it belonged entirely to the radio audience; *coming immediately to the whole of our people.*"[45]

The project was a staggering success for CBS, eliciting more than a thousand responses from every part of the United States—a scope that is all the more startling given that the sole prize offered was the composer's manuscript score. Copland's piece had been framed as an homage to modern technology, and it exhibited twentieth-century timbres ranging from vibraphone, saxophones, and unusual brass mutes to solos at the microphone. But apart from its association with the radio medium, Copland's piece was a virtual Rorschach test for audience members. At least two intrepid listeners seem to have grasped the peculiarity of the task at hand. One apparently preferred to retain the title "Music for Radio." Another felt it necessary to explain his suggestion, "Notes in Search of a Program"; according to a letter from Davidson Taylor to Copland, his analysis went something like this: "a bunch of notes get together, deciding to be music. They go along enthusiastically for a while, then consternation overcomes them: my God, they have no program! What are they doing, being a piece of music without a program? They try several programs, none of which seems to fit. Then they strike out again without having found one, and at length they are satisfied just to be a piece of music."[46] In addition to these self-conscious responses, more than 150 suggestions were sent to Copland in Mexico. A representative selection of these entries reveals their striking diversity.[47]

Journey of the British Patrol across Arabia	The Melting Pot	Indecision
A Song of the Mechanical Age	Thoughts while Strolling	A Day's Work
Trip through a National Park	Lilacs in the Rain	Farewell Amelia
New Mexican Village	The Seraphic Triumph	Airline Fantasy
Adventures in the Life of a Robot	Dawn in the Jungle	Sedative
An American Pippa Passes	Sundayschool Carnival	Oriental Fantasy
Early Morn in Bagdad	The Peasant's Fantasy	Gypsy Caravan
Sunday Night in Manhattan	On Set in Hollywood	Metropolis
Futile Search for Order out of Chaos	Commuters' Odyssey	Cliff Dwellers
The Majestic Mississippi	Caprices of the Sea	Urban Nocturne
Autumn of the American Pioneer	Agitation of the Masses	The Jungle Storm
Marconique Melody in the Air	Peace Conference	San Francisco
The Inca's Prayer to the Sun God	A May of Victory	Subway Traveller
Marconi's World Message	A Psalm of Modern Life	The Attack
Tower and Turrets of the Mystic City of Sound	Calling All Nations	Driving the Herd
Whims and Cries from the Great Tribulation	Night in the City	1938
Sylvan Midsummernights Meditations	Escape from the City	Equinox
Transatlantic Liner Ascending Ambrose Channel	Music for Radio	Spiritual Ecstasy

The possibilities ranged from total abstraction to astonishing specificity, encompassing both rural and urban imagery from around the globe. Copland could hardly have wished for a greater range of choices, yet he was not entirely satisfied. After selecting "Saga of the Prairie" as the winning entry, Copland and Taylor decided to retain *Music for Radio* as the main title, giving the colorful caption the status of "subtitle."[48] The eventual designation *Music for Radio: Saga of the Prairie* thus encapsulates quite nicely the tension between modern technology and romantic nostalgia inherent in both the rhetoric of the commissioning process and the expressive and melodic surface of the piece.

One week before the premiere, CBS issued a press release announcing that the piece "had a program, or scenario, that not even its composer . . . ventured to interpret" and that the composer was "putting it up to the audience" to name the composition. In fact, the network noted, the winning title would be the one that "is most successful in telling Mr. Copland what his music is" (HP, 311). This peculiar view of artistic agency might be explained away as savvy advertising. But in the strange case of *Music for Radio*, the advertisement itself could be considered "amazing but true." Although it is unlikely that any listener could truly have told Copland "what his music is," the piece actually did have a scenario that Copland chose not to interpret.

Many of the melodies and textures that eventually found their way into *Music for Radio* appear in sketches (preserved at the Library of Congress) for a choral setting of Langston Hughes's poem "The Ballad of Ozie Powell." The text appeared in the short-lived left-wing journal *The American Spectator* in April 1936, and it pays tribute to one of the so-called Scottsboro Boys: nine black boys falsely accused of raping two itinerant white prostitutes on a train in northern Alabama in 1931.[49] They barely escaped the lynch mob before entering the judicial system: eight were sentenced to death, and the various legal battles that ensued left them in prison anywhere from six to nineteen years before they were released. During the trials, obtaining the release of the Scottsboro boys became a rallying cry for Communists worldwide, but especially for the American Communist Party, which raised money and wrangled with the NAACP over control of the legal defense. Hughes visited Ozie Powell and the rest of the Scottsboro Boys in prison and wrote the "Ballad of Ozie Powell" when his name resurfaced in the news after an altercation in which he slashed a sheriff's throat and was shot in the head.[50]

Copland began sketching his setting of Hughes's poem in mid-December 1936 (about eight months after the poem was published and almost three months after receiving the CBS commission). The most complete, and presumably latest, layer of sketches include at least some vocal parts and scattered piano accompaniment for most of the couplets. The sketches exhibit a refrain structure clearly drawn from the poem, but modified by omitting some of the refrain lines ("Ozie, Ozie Powell") in the latter half of the poem in several places where they are not required by sentence syntax.

COPLAND: BALLADE OF OZZIE POWELL

Red is the Alabama road
Ozzie, Ozzie Powell
[Redder now where your blood has flowed][51]
Ozzie, Ozzie Powell
Strong are the brass and steel the gates
Ozzie, Ozzie Powell
The high sheriff's eyes are filled with hate
Ozzie, Ozzie Powell
The high sheriff shoots And he shoots to kill
Ozzie, Ozzie Powell
The laws a Klansman with an evil will,
Nine old men in Washington
never saw the Sheriff's gun
        aimed at Ozzie Powell

EXAMPLE 42. Copland's sketches for "Ballade of Ozzie Powell" (December 1936–January 1937, Copland Collection, Library of Congress)

> Nine old men so rich and wise
> Never saw the Sheriff's eyes
>   stare at Ozzie Powell
> But nine black boys they know full well
>   What it is to live in Hell
> Don't they Ozzie Powell

The condensed refrain structure dictated the form of Copland's choral setting: each instance of the text "Ozzie, Ozzie Powell" is declaimed using a particular melodic contour and echoing texture (example 42), suggesting a religious litany or ritual incantation. In addition, the constricted marchlike theme introduced in bar nine of the sketches seems to take its inspiration from the tragic traveler on the "Alabama road" whose real imprisonment finds a haunting homology in the melody's inability to break free from the narrow confines of a minor third. Both these motifs are strongly tied to the text and the message of the poem, and both appear prominently in both the sketches and the published score of *Music for Radio* (example 43). Although the material associated with the repeated cry "Ozzie, Ozzie Powell" has lost its function as a refrain, it still punctuates *Music for Radio* periodically and audibly. Some of these references are quite literal, even replicating the quasi-antiphonal texture of the "Ballade" sketches. While other instances may be more subtle—for example, when the "Ozzie" motif infiltrates the violin line at measures 264–70—Ozie Powell remains a palpable presence in Copland's *Music for Radio*.

As Howard Pollack has observed in his biography of Copland, "It seems significant that [*Music for Radio*], widely considered the first of the composer's Western works, should have in its background, if not in its very genesis, a choral work about racial injustice in the rural south" (HP, 313). The significance of this transformation is worth exploring in greater detail. What did it mean when Copland shifted his attention away from Ozie Powell? Copland neither finished the choral setting nor made any allusion to Hughes or Scottsboro in the title or program note for the radio commission. Perhaps he became frustrated by the rigid refrain structure of Hughes's poem. Maybe the pressure of the radio commission did not allow him to complete this piece as he would have liked; although he

EXAMPLE 43. *Music for Radio* (published as *Prairie Journal*), mm. 75–86, woodwinds and brass (London: Boosey & Hawkes, 1967; with annotations from the "Ozzie Powell" sketches)

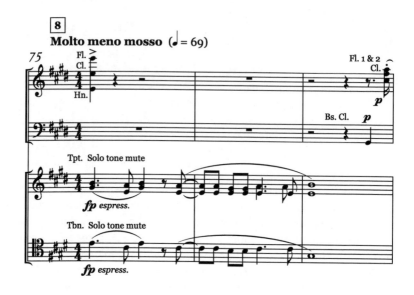

EXAMPLE 43 *(continued)*

started the "Ozzie Powell" sketches after receiving the network's offer, it cannot be determined whether he began the "Ballade" with CBS in mind. But one thing can be said for certain: as the network's deadline came and went, the "Ozzie Powell" sketches were absorbed into *Music for Radio* in such a way that a thousand listeners could devise a thousand wildly divergent interpretations of the work, their imaginations unfettered by inconvenient texts or uncomfortable political references.

Looking back on the rapidly changing politics of the 1930s, one might think that the Scottsboro case would have proved too historically contingent or too ideologically charged to be an effective program for the radio. Copland does not seem to have shared this view. In his essay "The Composer and Radio," he devoted his most effusive language to the idea that radio was an ideal medium for exactly this kind of potent message. The impetus to communicate with "the widest possible audience," he noted, "is not without its political implications . . . for it takes its source partly from that same need to reaffirm the democratic ideal that already fills our literature, our stage, and our screen. It is not a time for poignantly subjective lieder but a time for large mass singing. We are the men who must embody new communal ideals in a new communal music. And the radio is the natural outlet for that new music." Copland knew that even such lofty aims were not guaranteed to be above critical reproach, and he felt compelled to point out that his interest in connecting with audiences "should by no means be confused with mere opportunism. On the contrary, it stems from a healthy desire in every artist to find his deepest feelings reflected in his fellowman."[52]

Copland's continued commitment to progressive politics has been expertly documented by Bergman Crist, and his leftist ties easily spanned the years before and after *Music for Radio*. His own mass song, and his review of the first *Workers' Songbook* were unabashed in their embrace of proletarian sentiments. And *The Second Hurricane*, which actually kept Copland from finishing his radio commission on time, carried a strong didactic message about cooperative brotherhood. But when Copland turned his attention to *Music for Radio*, he effectively erased a far more controversial program—one that had been openly co-opted by communist agitators—in favor of imagery dictated neither by his own aesthetic intent nor by his political conscience. Literally (through the title contest) and figuratively (through the melting away of racial tension into a nostalgic national unity), *Music for Radio* gained a different kind of radical import through its deference to its listeners. In a way that Copland could never have imagined, it became a work that told the public precisely what it wanted to hear.

The fact that the erasure of Ozie Powell coincided with a westward reorientation and an embrace of rural Americana reveals several things about the cultural cachet of westernness during the Great Depression. When Ruth Leonhardt of Grosse Pointe, Michigan, sent in the winning subtitle, she was reacting to what she called the "typically American" sound of Copland's score, and as the symbol of that American sound she chose "the intense courage—the struggles and the final triumphs—of the early settlers, the real pioneers."[53] It was not the dreary Dust Bowl migrations, and certainly not the "Ballad of Ozie Powell," but the experience of pioneering that captured Leonhardt's imagination, and eventually Copland's too. With his move from "Ballade" to "Saga" came a transformation in storytelling mode—from lamenting an individual or regional plight to celebrating a triumph of nation building, from the actual Ozie to the legendary pioneers, from the urban to the rural, from a contemporary climate of racial and political conflict to an imaginary era of unity and resolve. This interpretation situates *Music for Radio* as one moment among many in American history when a turn toward the West coincides with a turn away from black-white racial tension. Just as westward expansion was driven in part by the antebellum desire to keep a balance of free and slave states, so western imagery and the myth of conquest could serve as a positive replacement for unsettling depictions of civil strife and the realities of interracial coexistence.

Given this history, it is not hard to hear "Ozie Powell" whispering from within the pages of *Music for Radio*, offering an eerie counterpoint to the "saga of the prairie." But of course no one was in a position to hear it this way in 1937—with the possible exception of Copland himself and any friends who might have seen his sketchbook. Instead casual listeners and committed critics were faced with a piece that displayed two fairly distinct moods: the kinetic energy of its opening bars could easily be linked to Copland's existing modernist works, but the pastoral strains of its midsection seemed to suggest something new.

For those reviewers inclined to view Copland as the "Brooklyn Stravinsky," the subtitle "Saga of the Prairie" was merely a distraction. The initial bars (example 44) would have confirmed the expected Stravinskian echoes through their superimposition of mildly irregular accent patterns over a steady pulse and layered texture above a bass ostinato (mm. 18–23). In one of the earliest reviews, before the "saga" subtitle was added, critic Moses Smith argued that passages like these represented the young composer at his best: "For this listener the more characteristically Coplandesque (or should it be 'Coplandish'?) portions are the fast parts, except for a few sequences that are a little too baldly Stravinskian and even Respighian. Particularly striking were the very opening measures. The nervous, fitful intensity of the rhythm . . . [is] quite worthy of the composer of 'Music for the Theater' and the Piano Variations."[54] Certain members of the general public responded to such musical features with urban titles, but neither they nor Smith could have noticed that the melodic skeleton of the first two bars [D–C–D–A] is identical to the motivic contour originally associated with the utterance "Ozzie Powell."

Instead, many listeners took note of the gentle tune that marks the work's central section.[55] They suggested such titles as "Lilacs in the Rain" or (one of Davidson Taylor's least favorite entries) "Sedative." Once the "saga" subtitle was in place, however, the narrow range and regular unfolding of the melody began to garner meanings more appropriate to the western backdrop that had suddenly fallen behind it. In retrospect, it became a cowboy song (example 45). If its cowboy origins were verifiable, the tune would be the first memento of Copland's cowboy career and powerful evidence that the composer's interest in the West

EXAMPLE 44. *Music for Radio*, mm. 1–5

EXAMPLE 45. *Music for Radio*, mm. 96–106

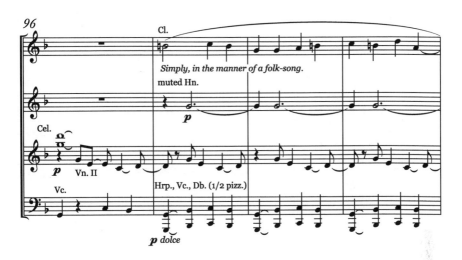

arose independently of Lincoln Kirstein or Agnes de Mille. But the cowboy pedigree is at best unlikely. Though never an entirely reliable witness, the eccentric Oscar Levant was probably on the mark in 1940 when he remembered Copland's surprise at the work's apparently western connotations.[56]

The melody appears without text or comment in the sketches of the "Ballade of Ozzie Powell" and the first draft of *Music for Radio*. In Copland's pencil and

EXAMPLE 45 *(continued)*

ink manuscripts, it appears with the designation "Cl[arinet] 1, subtone (at the mike)"—marking one of the few moments where modern technology might have come to the forefront of the soundscape. After the title contest had reached its Americana conclusion, a program note for the piece (almost certainly by Copland) posited that "the second theme . . . has an American folk-song quality" and that the work's subtitle "emphasized a certain frontier atmosphere derived from the nature of the themes themselves." The published score indicated that the melody should be played "simply, in the manner of a folk song." By the mid-1950s, when Copland's name could not be dissociated from his successful frontier ballets, Julia Smith remarked in her biography that the "folklike" theme of the central section was "presented in the manner of a cowboy song."[57] Thus granted the authority of print, the cowboy allusion stuck, and even though Copland protested against the "corny" title in a letter to Eugene Ormandy in 1958, he dubbed the score *Prairie Journal* some ten years later.[58]

In evaluating the contrast between the folklike central section and the motoric opening, Moses Smith noted: "The quieter parts are more sentimental. This is not written with any derogatory intent, but simply to question the lasting qualities of the music, which would not be apparent on first hearing."[59] Ironically, it is exactly these "sentimental" parts that seem to have had the staying power Smith valued. Whether folk-based or not, the pastoral central section foreshadows Copland's later and most famous works. At the time, however, its melodic warmth clearly took many of his contemporaries by surprise. Judging from his repeated protestations, even Davidson Taylor seems to have been a little uneasy about Copland's new tunefulness: "Did you actually try to be popular?"

he queried. "It's none of my affair, but I'm curious about it. Did you actually try to be popular in 'The Second Hurricane'? Anybody who can write as good tunes as you can ought to write good tunes. Your tunes sound sincere to me. 'Music for Radio' sounds sincere. I believe it is. I think you have imposed upon yourself some limitations of simplicity in both works, but I believe that you really care about simplicity. Am I near the facts?" Taylor also conveyed a reaction from his friend Vittorio Giannini: "He was much interested and said, 'It doesn't sound as Aaron Copland use[d] to sound. I am not sure, but perhaps he is more natural now and more himself than he has ever been before.' He liked the piece. Maybe you'd prefer for him not to like it, but he's in what I consider good company."[60]

Like Taylor, some critics readily convinced themselves of Copland's change of heart. Especially after 1938 and the success of *Billy the Kid*, reviewers confronting *Music for Radio* saw the earlier work as a turning point. In 1939, for example, Marion Bauer could look back at the "amiable effects" and "straightforward melodies" of *Music for Radio* as signs that "Copland's new style may have been creeping up gradually on the public."[61] The critical unease had apparently not been laid to rest even in 1942, when Charles Mills hastened to reassure the readers of *Modern Music* that this "popular and amusing score, commonly supposed to be a concession to mass appeal" was really "a completely honest and natural expression of the composer."[62]

Of course others would never be convinced by Copland's assimilation of the pastoral, and it is no surprise to find Lazare Saminsky among them. Given his deep-seated distrust of Copland's "Judaic" tendencies, he remained skeptical of the composer's sincerity and withering in his critique of what he considered blatant commercialism. Reviewing a concert performance of *Music for Radio* in the summer of 1941, he ridiculed the "prairie" subtitle and complained: "[Copland] everlastingly changes his style, his palette, his composer's technique and his advertising technique, too; and although he is always on the rostrum in one capacity or another, no one knows what it is he really stands for. His orchestral *Music for the Radio*, sometimes given a patriotic name as Saga of the Prairies, which it is not, is painted in faint Slavonic colors. It is far below Copland's best."[63] From Saminsky's perspective, the "pranks of polytonal jazz" and the "wistful, earnest and delicate slow melos of [*Music for the Theatre*]" represented "the best and the Jewish Copland."[64]

Saminsky's voice was extreme, but that does not mean that his objections were ignored—or that his opinions found no echo in more moderate voices. Recall John Tasker Howard's assertion that Harris's Scotch-Irish ancestry enabled him to depict "the prairies and vastness of the West" while Copland's "Russian-Jewish" heritage allied him with "the sophistication of the cosmopolitan cities on the seaboard."[65] The fact that so many listeners today associate the "Copland sound" with America's wide open spaces tells us something about the success of the overtly western works treated in the chapters that follow. Copland's astonishing ability to escape the stereotypes that vexed his early career also suggests a fundamental change in both critical and popular understanding of stylistic "authenticity." For unless one is willing to exaggerate the influence of his mother's early years in Texas, Copland made his mark on the West with little recourse to autobiography or "heritage."[66] Instead, his approach to this brand of Americana was channeled through the media of modern technology and guided by the rhetoric of the political left.

12

Communal Song, Cosmopolitan Song

COPLAND ON THE LEFT

At a time when Russian-Jewish immigrants were considered America's most likely Bolsheviks, Copland's voluntary association with the left probably came as no surprise. Elizabeth Bergman Crist has detailed the prevalence of communist and socialist ideals among Copland's associates and has persuasively situated Copland's own activities within the purview of the Popular Front.[1] For my purposes, the most notable aspects of Copland's political engagement are the geographical settings that agitated his political conscience and the impact that leftism had on his views about folk music. As Bergman Crist has shown, Copland seems to have developed many of his populist ideals while visiting Mexico in the fall of 1932. He was deeply influenced by the example of his friend and colleague Carlos Chávez and by the opportunities offered under the country's quasi-socialist government, confiding in Chávez that he was "a little envious of the opportunity you had to serve your country in a musical way" and praising the Mexican composer's rapport with audiences.[2] Equally distant from factories and sweatshops, Copland's most active engagement with communism occurred in rural Minnesota, where he gave an impromptu speech at a meeting of farmers near Bemidji. Copland's friend Harold Clurman noted this as a departure from the usual pattern when he wrote to congratulate Copland on his political awakening: "Some people go east to the U.S.S.R. to become 'radicalized' but you went west to the U.S.A."[3]

Back in New York, Copland's musical attitudes were shaped in part by his involvement with the Composers' Collective (established by Cowell and Charles

317

Seeger as a branch of the American Communist Party's Workers' Music League). He shared their early ambivalence toward folk sources, considering the "large mass singing" of the international workers' chorus (not the folk song of rural localities) to be the appropriate proletarian antidote to the "poignant subjective lieder" of the bourgeoisie. When Copland's setting of "Into the Streets May First!" won the *New Masses* song contest in 1934, folk qualities were far from the judges' list of criteria. And although the title of *The Young Pioneers* (1935)—Copland's contribution to a collection of children's piano pieces—might seem in retrospect to be crying out for a folk interpretation, Copland was probably motivated less by the title's pastoral connotations than by its association with the Soviet youth organization of the same name. Gradually, however, under the revised Popular Front slogan "Communism is twentieth-century Americanism," Copland joined most of his leftist contemporaries in embracing folk song as the true music of the people.[4]

The advocacy of Seeger and Elie Siegmeister solidified Copland's already substantial interest in popular culture and folk song. As Pollack has noted, it may also have channeled this interest in new directions: "The Popular Front's emphasis on Anglo-American folklore undoubtedly fostered a growing familiarity with and receptivity toward that particular repertoire" (HP, 280). Copland's first experiment with Anglo folklore appeared in *The Second Hurricane*, when high school students, stranded during their rescue mission, muster their courage by singing "The Capture of Burgoyne." Copland borrowed the eighteenth-century song almost literally from S. Foster Damon's *Series of Old American Songs* (1936), making few changes to the tune or the text (HP, 308). More interesting is the song's placement in the operetta shortly after the solo for the only African American character, Jeff. Jeff's jazzy number and the rousing British ballad sung by the teenagers are separated by a memorable soprano solo sung by Queenie, a student selected for the trip because of her nursing skills. Despite this lyric interlude, the musical contrast between "Jeff's Song" and "The Capture of Burgoyne" strongly suggests that Copland was more comfortable with the syncopated idiom that had characterized his earlier music than with the foursquare rhythms of the British tune.

Copland had already tried to reconcile his interest in African American music with the rhetoric of folk-based musical nationalism. In 1925, around the time of *Music for the Theatre* and the Piano Concerto, one such attempt was documented in a newspaper report given the telling title "Jazz as Folk-Music." Here, the writer conveyed Copland's belief that "distinctively national" music required "a literature of folk music as a background."

> "If we haven't a folk-song foundation, we must invent one," he said. "I began by thinking—what is a folk-song after all? And I came to the conclusion that in my case it was the songs I heard when I was a child—rather commonplace jazz tunes

and music of the "Old Black Joe" variety. These, then, are my material, and I must accept them for what they are. If we have only these elements as essentially American, our music must make the best of it and do the work so well that something worth while will come from the effort."[5]

Judging from Copland's emphasis on the effort needed to refine this raw material, building a national music on such rudimentary material was no easy task. By 1929, he was even more pessimistic. With an air of resignation, he dismissed the possibility that jazz could solve the problem of an American composing style: "Five years ago I felt the need of some tradition and at that time I used jazz in my compositions. But no matter what one does with jazz, it is essentially limited. . . . Jazz, at most, means either the excitement of New York City or the supersensuality of the Negro blues."[6] Noting that the United States could neither build upon the centuries-old musical traditions of a nation like France nor rely on the indigenous folk traditions of a country like Russia, he voiced his frustration: "And so one comes to a cul de sac. . . . We have Indian songs, Kentucky mountain songs, the Negro songs, jazz," he observed, "and we have had many attempts to use these songs in our music. But what, for example, do the songs of the Indians mean to me, an American of New York and the twentieth century?"[7]

With attitudes like these, Copland's stint with Anglo or any other folklore might have been a passing fancy had it not been for an earlier but more substantial (and far more successful) foray into the folk sphere. Fortunately, he did discover folk materials that spoke to him—but he found them south of the border. After a trip in 1932 to Mexico City's most famous dance hall, El Salón México, he began thinking about how to shape his sonic impressions of the nightclub and the nation. The resulting work, El Salón México, was not completed until 1934 and not orchestrated until his second trip to Mexico in 1936. This long gestation period gave Copland ample time to ponder his approach. He later recalled: "It seemed natural to use popular Mexican melodies for thematic material; after all, Chabrier and Debussy didn't hesitate to help themselves to the melodic riches of Spain. There was no reason I should not use the tunes of the hispanic land on our southern doorstep. My purpose was not merely to quote literally, but to heighten without in any way falsifying the natural simplicity of Mexican tunes" (VPAC1, 245).

Acquiring appropriate Mexican tunes was the easy part: though his inspiration was the live music of the dance hall, Copland found the melodies for the work in two published collections: Rubén Campos's El Folklore y la Música Mexicana of 1928 and Frances Toor's Cancionero Mexicano of 1931 (HP, 299). The more difficult stages involved finding ways to "heighten" the tunes without corrupting their "natural simplicity." The resulting struggle helped him formulate his ideas about using folk materials: "If quotation of folk tunes is a sure way for a composer to translate the flavor of a foreign people into musical terms, it also presents a formal problem when used in a symphonic composition. Most composers have found that there is little that can be done with such material except repeat it. In *El Salón México* I decided to use a modified potpourri in which the Mexican themes or fragments and extensions thereof are sometimes inextricably mixed" (VPAC1, 246). The potpourri approach outlined here would prove typical of Copland's treatment of folk song in his instrumental music. Its most obvious corollary was the notion that simple quotation or literal repetition was aesthetically insufficient: fragments, extensions, motivic work, and musical mixture were part of his recipe for success. Underlying this surface consideration, one can still sense a palpable insecurity about melodic borrowing. Copland was well aware of the many, many precedents for such borrowing in his own work and elsewhere— Debussy and Chabrier were hardly the most famous precedents he could have cited—but he could not ignore the fact that a wide spectrum of music reviewers (including some of his harshest critics and some of his dearest friends) already thought he was overly inclined toward borrowing.

While Bergman Crist understands Copland's *El Salón México* as a successful rendering of "communitarian vision," I find equally striking the anxiety that the piece seemed to provoke in Copland about his status as a musical outsider.[8] "Despite Chávez' enthusiasm," he recalled, "I still felt nervous about what the Mexicans might think of a 'gringo' meddling with their native melodies" (VPAC1, 246). In this instance, Copland was soon reassured by the warm applause he received from Chávez's orchestra at a rehearsal before the premiere and the appreciative critical reception that followed. "They seemed to agree," he later remarked, "that *El Salón México* might well be taken for Mexican music—'as Mexican as the music of Revueltas,' which was like saying at that time, 'as American as the music of Gershwin'" (VPAC1, 247).

Copland's apparent satisfaction in his role as the Gershwin of Mexico offers an unexpected but instructive vantage point on the vagaries of musical nationalism. However curious, the analogy is apt: like *Porgy and Bess,* for example, *El Salón México* involved a cross-cultural engagement that was far deeper than voyeurism but was still captivated by the exotic nature of the subjects it depicted. Copland freely confessed that he would have considered it "foolish for me to attempt to translate the more profound sides of Mexico into musical sounds—the ancient civilizations or the revolutionary Mexico of our own time—for that, one really had to know a country well" (VPAC1, 245). He would find no such relief back home, for it was abundantly clear that being "as American . . . as Gershwin" would do Copland little good. If Copland was troubled by his "gringo" status in Mexico, he had equal but opposite reasons for concern at home. South of the border, his whiteness marked him as a foreigner; in his native land, his non-whiteness was the greater source of concern.

It is no wonder, then, that Copland was cautious when he cast his lot with Anglo folklore and crossed the Rio Grande. His Norton lectures at Harvard (1951–52) are circumspect, acknowledging that "the composer must have in his background some sense of musical culture and, if possible, a basis in folk or popular art," but balancing this desideratum against the importance of technique.[9] Departing from his brief historical survey to speculate on larger aesthetic questions, Copland wrote: "What, after all, does it mean to make use of a hymn tune or a cowboy tune in a serious musical composition? There is nothing inherently pure in a melody of folk source that cannot be effectively spoiled by a poor setting. The use of such materials ought never to be a mechanical process. They can be successfully handled only by a composer who is able to identify himself with, and reexpress in his own terms, the underlying emotional connotation of the material."[10] Harris could only have seconded Copland's denigration of the mechanical and his call for identification with the material. Yet he might have bristled at the emphasis on professionalism that emerged as Copland continued: "A hymn tune represents a certain order of feeling: simplicity, plainness, sincerity, directness. It is the reflection of those qualities in a stylistically appropriate setting, imaginative and unconventional and not mere quotation, that gives the use of folk tunes reality and importance. In the same way, to transcribe the cowboy tune so that its essential quality is preserved is a task for the imaginative composer with a professional grasp of the problem."[11]

The composer must identify with the material, but he must also refashion it in a way that is "imaginative and unconventional." Inventing autobiographical connections with the American folk would have been impractical for the "Brooklyn Stravinsky." Instead of mourning this separation, he chose to treat the folk sphere with a professional's detached respect. Copland's biographical and emotional distance from western Americana thus opened up space for irony, comedy, and nostalgic displacement in such works as *Billy the Kid, Rodeo,* and *The Red Pony.*

AN AMERICAN ALLEGORY

Though the idea bears a certain geographic neatness, it would oversimplify matters to suggest that cowboy song provided the perfect compromise between the Mexican music Copland found so moving and the Anglo American songs that had won approval from Seeger and others back home. For one thing, Copland had other musical models to follow when it came to cowboy materials, including, of course, Thomson's *Plow That Broke the Plains.* For another, Copland's initiation into the world of western heroes came courtesy of other artists. While it is not common knowledge that *The Saga of the Prairie* got its title from an audience member, it is well known that both his "cowboy ballets" were commissions from prestigious urban ballet companies with East Coast or European ties: *Billy the*

Kid for Lincoln Kirstein in 1938, and *Rodeo* for Agnes de Mille in 1942. Racial and ethnic considerations surely prevented Copland from claiming cowboy songs as his artistic inheritance, but so did the circumstances under which he wrote his western works.

The western United States was by and large unfamiliar ground for Copland. As Jessica Burr has pointed out, Copland had in fact visited the American West long before undertaking such works as *Billy the Kid*.[12] Having written to Boulanger in 1928, "I suppose it is good for me to see America a little," he made a brief stopover in Santa Fe while en route to the Hollywood Bowl in Los Angeles, where he was to perform his Piano Concerto.[13] But his first impressions of the region make it seem unlikely that he would ever return to the West—either musically or in person. Burr uncovered correspondence between Copland and his friend Gerald Sykes that reveals just how strongly he reacted against this unfamiliar territory: "What a country this is!" he exclaimed. "Sickly looking parched earth inhabited by he-men cow-punchers. I should have gone to Finland." Though he later expressed a cautious admiration for the region's diverse people, for him the scenery left much to be desired: "Whatever it was I expected reality proved different—very. I am still trying to acquire a taste for the landscape—it still seems frightfully austere. I can't get used to these barren hills—they remind me of the war-scarred battlefields I saw in France."[14] So remote were the western deserts from Copland's idea of natural beauty, that he did not even venture an analogy between their lonely expanses and other naturally desolate landscapes. Instead, his experiences called to mind a wasteland of human invention, emptied by modern technology and brutal warfare. After almost two months in this new environment, Copland came to admire its impressive vistas and diverse inhabitants, but he still bore a powerful sense of the western landscape's foreignness. He wrote to Serge and Natalie Koussevitzky: "Here I am after seven weeks in Santa Fe, New Mexico. It's certainly far from Paris! But this country is truly magnificent with tall mountains practically without vegetation—which give the country an austere and somewhat horrifying effect. The people are also extremely curious and very diverse—there are Mexicans, cowboys, Redskins, artist-painters, American-pioneers, tourists, etc. In Santa Fe, you get the impression of being more in Spain than in America."[15] As these letters make plain, Europe was still the primary playground for Copland's imagination.

One can only guess how daunting it must have been when Lincoln Kirstein approached Copland with the scenario for *Billy the Kid* in 1938. Though Kirstein may have approached Copland in part because of the popularity of *El Salón México*, there were significant differences in the challenges presented by the two scores. In Mexico City, despite his anxiety about musical borrowing, Copland had felt a real sense of identification with the Mexican people. His descriptions of Santa Fe reveal instead his powerful impressions of sterility and social alienation. To make matters worse, the disclaimers he had been able to make for *El Salón México* were not ones he wished to repeat in his native land. Though not necessarily "profound," *Billy the Kid* still represents an adventure in mythmaking with serious historical and national implications.

When Kirstein showed choreographer Eugene Loring a copy of Walter Noble Burns's *Saga of Billy the Kid* (1925) and exhorted him to "make a ballet out of it," he was asking him to create in dance a legend that had already been recounted in many different formats.[16] Burns's treatment of the subject was new in its sympathy for the outlaw hero—an aspect that Loring and Copland chose to reinforce. Paraphrasing historian Robert Utley, Pollack writes that "Burns's popular *Saga* appealed to readers as a coming-of-age story twice told: as a study in the development from adolescence to manhood and from frontier wilderness to industrial society. Indeed, Billy emerges as a barely disguised symbol for America; his frontier lawlessness must be crushed by a changing world. Unlike previous books about Billy, Burns struck an interwar note of nostalgia for a lost innocence and a bygone America."[17] Given this allegorical potential, it is not surprising that none of the ballet's creative contributors were overly concerned with accuracy of historical detail. The true identity of the outlaw-hero is a fundamental case in point. Although Kirstein was mistaken when he identified Billy by his outlaw alias "William H. Bonney" rather than his given name, William Henry McCarty, the happy coincidence that both "Bonney" and Copland were born in Brooklyn seems to have outweighed any desire to set the record straight. (McCarty grew up in Indiana, Kansas, and Colorado before ending up in the desert Southwest.) Copland later went so far as to suggest that knowing the facts of Billy's life was not merely superfluous, but that it might actually have hindered his creative response. "I didn't think of the story in a realistic sense," he remarked. "If I had, I would never have touched it as I wouldn't have considered it a proper musical subject. Anyway, my knowledge of the actual historical facts was rather vague, and I thought of Billy the Kid as a legendary character, a young innocent who went wrong, part of the picturesque folklore of the Far West."[18]

Loring shared Copland's preconceptions about the West, but he had even less firsthand knowledge. To make matters worse, the standard fare of western literature and film was difficult to translate into dance, and Loring recalled being unable to envision staging *Billy* without horses, guns, and other frontier paraphernalia. The solution he crafted to this balletic impossibility was ingenious: "I thought if you did it like a child playing make-believe that you had guns and horses and cards and all that—that would be a feasible way to do it. But I wasn't sure that adult audiences would take to that."[19] Like Loring, Copland located his personal experience of the West in childhood recollections, justifying his attraction to western folklore by recalling that, like most youngsters, he had enjoyed playing "cowboys and Indians" with his friends.

Given the absence of concrete props, direct personal experience, or detailed historical information, *Billy the Kid* instead staged a regression into childhood and the world of make-believe in ways that many critics found illuminating. In his dance column for the *New York Times,* John Martin readily identified the ballet's paradoxical union of realism and abstraction. "There is no scenery," he commented.

> Jared French has designed a simple back cloth which serves simply to hide the back wall and to suggest a region of sand and cactus. For the rest the dancers themselves make the locales of the many episodes out of their movement and their mood. No scenery of paint and canvas was ever half so genuine. Similarly, when Billy and his bandits crouch with their open hands in front of their faces, it is quite certain that nobody else on stage can see them. It is the stuff of legend, freer and far more eloquent than fact.[20]

Though Loring had wondered about their suitability for "adult audiences," his mimetic choreography appealed to viewers of all ages. For Edwin Denby (dance critic and the librettist for *The Second Hurricane*), these were the most innovative and effective elements of the ballet's choreography: "Looking at the pantomime movements that Loring invented for *Billy,* I find them more interesting when they tend to be literal than when they tend to be symbolic. The storytelling gestures— those of the cowboys riding or strolling, the gun play, the sneaking up on the victim, Billy's turning away from his sweetheart or lying down—all this has more life as dancing than gestures meant as 'modern dance.'"[21] From this perspective, the power of *Billy the Kid* lay not in what was self-consciously "modern" but in its attitude toward representation; its message was best conveyed through a type of imaginary or remembered realism. As Martin put it, "Above all [Loring] has wooed his spectators into the technique of make-believe, where with the genuine, basic magic of the theatre he has led them into creating for themselves the Billy and the Old West that they would like to believe."[22] Like *Music for Radio, Billy the Kid* gained at least some of its success by allowing listeners room for make-believe. In this case, though, traces of the creators' own attitudes are readily visible. By aligning their spectacle with a remembrance of things past, Loring and his cocreators reinforced their psychologically sympathetic portrayal of the youthful Billy and the popular conception of the West as a site of irrecoverable innocence.

THE OPEN PRAIRIE

Compassion for the outlaw hero and an impetus toward allegory were not the only things Loring and his collaborators drew from Burns's *Saga of Billy the Kid.* The ballet's striking initial sequence also takes as its model the evocative descriptions of westward expansion that serve as a leitmotif in Burns's book. In situation after situation, his text launches into a litany of city names, each successively more remote from refined East Coast culture. The perilous migration of a family piano from the Atlantic Seaboard to its new home in New Mexico forms one of the comic episodes in the text. Even passages that could be static description take on the narrative function of signaling westward travel: "Mockingbirds still sing in the towering branches of the survivors of these old trees that have seen pass beneath them, as along a king's highway, the pageantry of the frontier past— pioneers, Indians, soldiers of the old army, descendants of Spanish conquerors, Kit Carson, Billy the Kid and his outlaws, Pat Garrett and his man-hunters, John Chisum the cattle king, and the multitude of forgotten men who played their part in building civilization in the Southwest."[23] Such pomp and circumstance was too good to be true, but too hard to resist, and a similar parade found its way into the ballet. Loring's scenario calls for an opening processional designated "Introduction: March into a new Frontier from an old, Gone are the days. . . . (empty stage fills with men and women pioneers, Indians, Mexicans)" [ellipsis in the original]. The scenario also specifies a "Coda: based on Introduction . . . March on."[24]

The frontier processional in the coda frames the ballet's action in significant ways. According to the scenario, "What takes place between the introduction and the coda. . . . is merely a single episode typical of many on the long westward push to the Pacific" (HP, 318). Among the many reviewers who also picked up this interpretation, Walter Terry of the New York Herald Tribune offered the most evocative summation:

> "Billy" commenced with a powerful dance procession, a stream of humanity which hastens toward the sunlight of the West. There are pioneers and their wives, prospectors, homesteaders, adventurers. Their movements are quick and strong, space-covering, and they are movements which tell of a vast, uncrowded land and of the sturdy, questing citizens, American citizens, who are searching for new thresholds, new frontiers to cross. Out of this westward march comes a story, an episode in the march itself, the story of Billy the Kid. It is a tale of romance, of danger, of lawlessness and of death and when it is over, the march resumes and the beholder again views the westward procession heading toward yet another frontier.[25]

With its motley crew of participants and its mingling of optimism and nostalgia, the frontier processional allows its diverse participants to be unified chiefly by their westward momentum.

The actions of the westering crowd further enhance its allegorical potential, for as dance historian Marcia Siegel has pointed out, they engage in "canonic movements abstracted from frontier activities like roping and riding, scouting, cradling babies, praying."[26] Denby made similar remarks about the historical pretensions of the opening March: "The energetic horizontal arm thrusts with open palms look as if our ballet dancers were mimicking 'pushing back the frontier.'

The 'Come on out West' gestures back to the electricians offstage, the praying, digging, running, housekeeping, ever westward, ever westward are meant as a frieze of history; but it is history like that shown us in the slick-paper ads."[27] Linking the processional to ancient Greece and modern mass media in a single breath, Denby recognized this moment's power to overstep the boundaries of the stage, as the invisible electricians are invited to join in the history-transcending action of westward migration.

But the flat frieze and the glossy magazine covers that Denby called to mind also suggest another, more modern media reference: the silver screen. Siegel notes the ballet's evocation of specific film techniques such as close-up, montage, flash-forward, and even slow motion, and she argues that Loring's cinematic vision shaped the opening frontier processional as well. Loring had the dancers move straight across the stage rather than taking a more typical (and longer) diagonal route. As a result, "their figures remain flat, in the same perspective, like the flat images on film or an unfurling olio in a music hall. They can use only a few feet of the stage depth, and that way their numbers look dense, crowded, and by inference, desperately in need of elbow room."[28] The peculiar flatness of perspective gives the participants in the procession a striking but potentially alienating aspect. Unlike the offstage electricians Denby envisioned, actual audiences remain removed from the ballet's westering impulse. The dancers, with their mechanical gestures, do not approach us, and we can only watch from a distance.

Copland's "maestoso" soundtrack for this epic march remains a haunting model for musical evocations of the Great Plains (example 46). It has become a critical commonplace to link Copland's stark intervals with America's wide open spaces.[29] But of course there is more at work here than the famous open fifths: registral range, sparse scoring, and (only in the original two-piano score) echo effects that Copland seems to have transplanted from the mountains to the prairies. As Jessica Burr has noted, the unusual timbre of the opening bars—low oboe underneath high clarinets—suggests the tremendous loneliness that Copland experienced so viscerally on his first trip to Santa Fe.[30]

The downstage dancers loom large against this sonic horizon. While timbre is a key element in the score's suggestion of alienated observation, its rhythmic and metric elements mirror the dancers' gestures, and by extension suggest the actions of the westering crowd. When he called their opening procession a "march," Loring seems to have been aiming for a patriotic tone. But Copland's frontier-bridging march sports a number of atypical features—most notably its triple meter. According to Pollack, Loring was taken aback by the composer's decision, but apparently Copland reassured him by citing "My Country 'Tis of Thee" as an example. This may seem a less than inspired rejoinder, but at least it reflects the Americanist aspirations of their project. From a somewhat more speculative angle, one might argue that the rhythmic asymmetry of a march in triple time makes

EXAMPLE 46. *Billy the Kid*, "The Open Prairie," arranged for two pianos, mm. 1–24 (London: Boosey & Hawkes, 1946)

EXAMPLE 46 *(continued)*

the dancers' progress seem unusually labored or unwieldy—as if they were limp-
ing or needed an extra beat to catch their breath after each pace.

Working in tandem with the march's peculiar meter is the rhythmic ostinato
that characterizes most of the "Open Prairie" music. Introduced gradually, the
ostinato is fully in place by bar nine and continues unrelieved through the entire
section, except for a four-measure respite at rehearsal number 2. As noted in previous chapters, such ostinato figures were a favorite space-generating mecha-

nism for both Harris and the Indianists (as well as for composers with other geographical preoccupations). Insistent repetition heightens our awareness of the passage of time and, metaphorically, suggests the extent of a vast space devoid of distinguishing topographical features. Harris had put these associations to bleak use in his 1935 elegy *Farewell to Pioneers,* in which autogenetic melody is dwarfed in the hostile environment of repetitive figuration. Copland's prairie ostinato operates a bit differently. First, its mechanical regularity and the fact that it involves the small-scale repetition of measure-long units make it more intense and less leisurely than Harris's landscape painting. Second and more importantly, in *Billy the Kid,* the opening ostinato is linked, by analogy to the dancers' repetitive gestures, as much to people and their epic efforts as to the wilderness in which they wandered. Copland's layered ostinato produces contrasting accents on and off the beats; horns and upper strings are echoed by bass, piano, and percussion as if the lower group were out of step or staggering along behind.

A tune of sorts frames and enlivens this stark ostinato. In its first incarnation, this material seems to function as an introductory figure (mm. 1–7). Its division of the measure into two dotted quarter notes foreshadows the ostinato's rhythmic limp; its halting phrases are divided between oboe, clarinet, and bassoon, rather than forming a single melodic utterance. In bar 14, once the ostinato is in place, this tune takes flight to a more conventional melodic register and scoring (for flute), clearly distinguished from the repetitive accompaniment below. One might expect this melody to be associated with the pioneer processional since it is the aspect of the soundscape with the greatest forward momentum, but Copland has reversed the usual division of labor which would make the ostinato responsible for landscape depiction and use the melody to signal subjective human presence. Instead, the melody seems strangely impassive, like the landscape out of which it emerged.

This emotional detachment becomes easier to explain as the movement continues, for when the melody comes to a cadence (m. 20), it is interrupted by birdsong. Strident woodwind figures (mm. 20–22) rupture the ostinato, suggesting that even the laboring marchers have finally stopped to listen to their surroundings. What they hear sheds new light on the preceding melody and its remarkable preoccupation with thirds. The cuckoo call of the opening bars may have gone unrecognized up to this point, but in retrospect its avian connotations seem all but confirmed. The striking low oboe/high clarinet sonority that resurfaces here suggests that the birds may have been singing all along.

The interjection of birdsong brings the grinding ostinato of the march to a temporary halt, causing a startling orchestral silence and offering up the opportunity for an echo effect. A solo French horn sounds the call, but the only response is a gradual resumption of the familiar melody as the ostinato-laden mass of humanity parades impassively toward the Pacific. The break in the ostinato at measures 23 through 26 also marks the beginning of a twofold orchestral crescendo that shapes the rest of the section to great dramatic effect. This intensification seem at odds with Loring's processional, however, in which the marchers do not actually approach the audience. While the dance emphasizes the uniformly distant march of history, the music gives this journey direction, moving it not only westward (stage right) but also toward the audience, preparing us for the scene change and opening up the possibility of emotional identification with these characters, and ultimately with Billy himself.

"SOMETHING DIFFERENT ABOUT A COWBOY SONG IN PARIS"

At the climax of the prairie processional, the ominous mood is shattered like a shot. The weary ostinato falls away like a curtain to reveal the bustling activity of the "Street in a Frontier Town" and Copland's very first quotation of a bona fide cowboy song. Freed from the historical burden of embodying westward expansion, the dancers leap into action, accompanied by the tune "Great-Granddad," which Copland borrowed from Lomax's *Cowboy Songs and Other Frontier Ballads*. With the benefit of hindsight, it is all too easy to spot the varied forces (Lincoln Kirstein chief among them) making cowboy song Copland's folklore of choice.[31] Nonetheless, the western turn came as something of a surprise for the composer and his contemporaries.

Copland may have enjoyed both roles while playing "cowboys and Indians" as a child, but where music was concerned, he thought that the "wranglers" had a clear advantage over the "redskins." In his Norton lectures, he quickly dismissed Indianism as ineffective: "Despite the efforts of Arthur Farwell and his group of composer friends, and despite the *Indian Suite* of Edward MacDowell, nothing really fructifying resulted. It is understandable that the first Americans would have a sentimental attraction for our composers, especially at a time when the American composer himself was searching for some indigenous musical expression. But our composers were obviously incapable of identifying themselves sufficiently with such primitive source materials as to make these convincing when heard out of context."[32] Copland believed that Native American music's strangeness kept even well-meaning composers from achieving the requisite level of identification with the material. He recognized—in ways that Cadman and Farwell did not—the paradox of building a national music through exotic borrowing. Furthermore, he seems to have realized that using Indian material might entail unwelcome anthropological burdens. "The Indians of today," he commented, "produce a music that is difficult to authenticate. How much of what they do is the result of oral tradition and how much acquired from the circumstances of their post-Conquest environment is difficult to say."[33] This concern for the purity of indigenous materials stands in sharp contrast to the freedom and flexibility with which he approached jazz and other folk musics.

Although in 1929 Copland had posed the rhetorical query "What do the songs of the Indians mean to me?" it was evidently unnecessary to repeat the question with regard to cowboy tunes in 1938. Like most Americans of his generation, he had plenty of exposure to cowboy heroes. Copland's problem with cowboy song was not so much a matter of sympathy as of musical substance. His first impressions were decidedly lukewarm: "I have never been particularly impressed with the musical beauties of the cowboy song as such. The words are usually delightful, and the manner of singing needs no praise from me. But neither the words nor the delivery are of much use in a purely orchestral ballet score, so I was left with the tunes themselves, which, I repeat, are often less than exciting" (VPAC1, 279). What sacrilege such words must have seemed to Harris! But for Copland, using western folk song was not a foregone conclusion, even in a cowboy ballet. "As far as I was concerned," Copland claimed,

> this ballet could be written without benefit of the poverty-stricken tunes Billy himself must have known. Nevertheless, in order to humor Mr. Kirstein, who said he didn't really care whether I used cowboy material or not, I decided to take his two little collections with me when I left for Paris in the summer of 1938. . . . Perhaps there is something different about a cowboy song in Paris. But whatever the reason may have been, it wasn't very long before I found myself hopelessly involved in expanding, contracting, rearranging and superimposing cowboy tunes on the rue de Rennes in Paris.[34]

With an ocean separating Copland from Billy's natural habitat, the composer developed a new fondness for American folk song. Pollack has pointed out the parallel between this passage and Copland's claim that he only warmed up to American jazz after his arrival in France. Taken together, these instances suggest it was not personal proximity but certain kinds of distance that allowed him to feel "at home" with his material.

Although he admitted eventually becoming enthralled by western folk song, Copland still chose to emphasize the technical tinkering required to bring a cowboy ballet to life: "It's a rather delicate operation—to put fresh and unconventional harmonies to well-known melodies without spoiling their naturalness. . . . one must expand, contract, rearrange and superimpose the bare tunes themselves, giving them something of one's own touch. That, at any rate, is what I tried to do."[35] Copland's rhetoric suggests that he would find ways of calling attention to his creative manipulation of borrowed materials. While Harris chose to let the folk songs he borrowed emerge in a seemingly natural or unimpeded manner, Copland preferred to make his cowboy songs sound comic, surprising, or strange. This is not to say that Copland was incapable of keeping a tune intact; his virtually verbatim orchestration of the square dance tune "Bonyparte" for the "Hoedown" dance episode from *Rodeo* is a case in point.[36] The most literal quotation in *Billy the Kid* features "The Dying Cowboy" from John White and George Shackley's *The Lonesome Cowboy*—a different version of the tune that Harris used in his *Folksong Symphony* (1940). Copland retained both the meter and (for the most part) the melody in Billy's nocturnal scene "Prairie Night" ("Card Game at Night").[37] Even in this case, however, Copland alters the rhythmic values of the melody—lengthening certain notes and calling for relaxed duple eighth notes against the underlying triplet pulse.

Copland's relatively elaborate approach to folk materials in *Billy the Kid* led some reviewers to claim that the ballet used no borrowed material at all. In reality, Copland's quotations are obscured (perhaps even disguised) through two main procedures: first, he placed borrowed materials in contexts full of contrasts and rapid juxtapositions. No tune holds the spotlight for very long, and cowboy songs or their fragments intermingle with newly composed material. Like Cadman, Copland did not make a strong distinction between original and borrowed melodies—Virgil Thomson later remarked that *Billy the Kid* "even has folklore in it that doesn't stick out like a sore thumb and that doesn't make the original melodies sound silly either."[38] Second and somewhat less frequently, Copland altered the original tunes—not just through fragmentation, but also through melodic, rhythmic, and timbral changes.

Both procedures are present in full force from the beginning of Copland's cowboy career and his initial western adventure on the "Street in a Frontier Town." As befits the stage action depicting the hubbub of frontier life, the music is a pastiche of new and borrowed material. To set the whole western carnival in motion, Copland chose a clear reference to the cowboy sphere—the tune "Great-Granddad" played "nonchalantly" on piccolo (and tin whistle in staged performances). At first his treatment of the melody is relatively literal, with only rhythmic alterations and occasional note substitutions, usually to eliminate repeated notes—C–B♭ instead of B♭–B♭ in bar 3, F instead of E♭ in bar 4, and so on (see examples 47a and 47b). The tune's ending is more substantially altered to avoid closing on the tonic.

After this initial statement, Copland begins what might be considered a catalog of the many available options for folk song manipulation. As the tune reaches its natural close in the piccolo, Copland inserts a transitional episode or extension based on a three-note fragment of the tune (drawn from bar 2). When the tune reasserts itself in measure 16, it has gained the support of clarinet and plucked strings, but after two of its four phrases it suffers the first of the many interruptions that Copland has in store for it (and for us). Muted trumpet and oboe enter with a phrase that the composer modified from "Whoopee Ti Yi Yo,

EXAMPLE 47A. "Great-Granddad" (from Lomax, *Cowboy Songs and Other Frontier Ballads*, 1938)

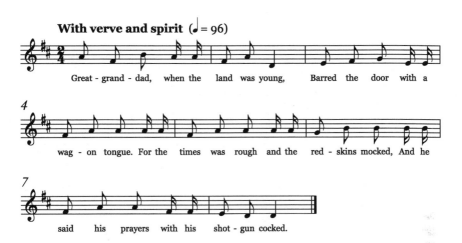

Git Along Little Dogies." Though the melodic rise and fall are preserved, the rhythmic and harmonic character are so altered that it seems like new material—as if Copland wanted to provide his own answer to the open-ended phrases of "Great-Granddad." The cycle repeats itself, but this time the "Whoopee Ti Yi Yo" material infects other sections of the orchestra and begins to gain momentum before lurching into a jaunty volley of grace-note figures that become static enough to serve as the accompaniment for the next entry of "Great-Granddad," which appears in a humorous guise—perhaps a harmonica or street organ—harmonized à la *Petrushka* in parallel triads for flute, piccolo, and clarinet.

The brusque jostling between "Great-Granddad" and "Whoopee Ti Yi Yo" is but a foretaste of the many kinds of visual and musical mixture essential to the tumult of the frontier town. At first, this hybridity takes the form of awkward and usually humorous juxtapositions, but as the scene continues, its cross-fertilizations take on greater significance. After an aggressive rendering of "The Old Chisholm Trail" (readily recognizable despite being truncated and rhythmically altered), the "Great-Granddad"/"Whoopee Ti Yi Yo" complex returns—this time with its comedic potential enhanced by cartoonish semitone clashes between trumpet and oboe and a reprise with sleigh bells of the grace-note-based rhythmic vamp heard earlier. The brief buildup that begins at rehearsal number 19 leads not to more cowboy tunes, but to an episode of Copland's own invention. He called this sequence a "Mexican Dance." Evidently Loring had suggested a *jarabe,* and Copland complied with one of the catchiest tunes in the ballet—a 5/8 trumpet melody over rustling accompaniment of muted winds and *col legno*

EXAMPLE 47B. *Billy the Kid,* "Street in a Frontier Town," opening (London: Boosey & Hawkes, 1941)

EXAMPLE 47B *(continued)*

strings. This moment is a visual as well as a musical climax at which point the chaotic stage action coalesces into an ensemble number for "Mexican women" (or, in some reviewers' minds, "dance-hall girls"). Thus the folk potpourri presented by the scene is an openly multiethnic one. For those who hear submerged jazz idioms in the ballet's rhythmic language, the musical evidence of cultural mixing runs deeper still. It is not unusual for listeners today to discern an African American influence in its pervasive syncopation—from the opening ostinato to the ragtime inflections in the treatment of "The Old Chisholm Trail." Copland's contemporaries, however, were less inclined to hear things this way; Irving Kolodin surely had a different agenda when he cited *Billy the Kid* as proof that "not all the dance impulse in this country originated below the Mason and Dixon line."[39] Whatever its proportion of black, white, and Latino elements, *Billy the Kid* involved cultural collisions. In Copland's hands, even a frontier town could sound cosmopolitan.

BOY BANDIT KING

As the Mexican women end their dance, our attention is drawn to a young boy and his mother. According to Copland's "Notes on a Cowboy Ballet," Billy is about twelve years old when he enters the frontier town and commits his first murder. Documentary evidence of the famous outlaw confirms this age—which together with his unusually boyish appearance earned him his nickname "the Kid"—but different authors have attached different meanings to the early inception of his life in crime. While some portrayed him as innately depraved, others saw his youth as a mitigating factor. Burns's *Saga of Billy the Kid* belongs emphatically to the latter camp, and his attitude rubbed off on Loring. Burns informed his readers that Billy was not "an inhuman monster revelling in blood," but rather "a boy of bright, alert mind, generous, not unkindly, of quick sympathies."[40]

Burns's extravagant language gained both literary and musical admirers, helping to spread his forgiving view of the outlaw to audiences across the country. When he claimed that "a rude balladry in Spanish and English" had already surrounded Billy the Kid, his words actually helped stimulate this ongoing process. For example, one fan commissioned the Reverend Andrew Jenkins to compose a song that took Burns's characterizations to heart:

> Fair Mexican maidens play guitars and sing
> A song about Billy their boy-bandit king;
> How ere his young manhood had reached its sad end
> Had a notch on his pistol for twenty-one men.[41]

Whether they had encountered Jenkins's song or not, Loring and company were nothing if not captivated by the boy hero. They took further steps to generate good feeling toward Billy and to arouse spectators' sympathy for his unique psychology. Most importantly, as Pollack and others have observed, the killing of Billy's mother triggers his lethal act in the ballet (in the book she was only insulted)—giving added justification to his aberrant and perhaps compulsive talent for murder. The ballet's explicit identification between Billy's Mexican sweetheart and his absent mother adds depth to his inner life and makes the devastating death of his mother central to all aspects of his character. A single dancer performs as both Mother and Sweetheart; likewise, all Billy's victims are danced by the same man, Alias, who was responsible for her accidental death in the frontier town. Thus, a maternal shadow falls not only on his murderous acts, but also on his most visible attempts to enter into human relationships—with the (quasi-paternal) sheriff Pat Garrett, and with his (probably fantasized) sweetheart.

Copland's music plays a significant role in arousing and maintaining sympathy for Billy as a child, an outcast, and ultimately as a tragic hero. Though Billy and his mother have been on stage for some time, at rehearsal number 24 a shift in musical material alerts us to their new importance (example 48). At the close of the *jarabe,* Copland inserts a lovely moment of metric disorientation, reinterpreting the already irregular meter in preparation for the prominent pickup notes of the next cowboy tune on his list: "I Ride an Old Paint." "Old Paint" is the third cowboy song to appear on the scene, and it stands apart from the others in the tenderness with which Copland treats the melody. Gentle string brushstrokes and rocking figures in the flute and harp envelop it in sweet lullaby sounds. After a complete iteration of the melody, he crafts a circling accompaniment

EXAMPLE 48. *Billy the Kid,* "Street in a Frontier Town," end of *jarabe*

figure for upper woodwinds from the song's last four notes. Together with the glockenspiel entrance, this whirring figuration lends the clockwork sounds of a music box to the second statement of "Old Paint," completing the nursery rhyme mood and making Billy seem even more childlike than his twelve years would require.

Potent as this musical characterization might be, there is more at stake here than our compassion for Billy. Copland and Loring did not need much prompting to absorb Burns's "nostalgia for a bygone America" or to recognize Billy as a symbol of lost innocence (HP, 317). For them, Billy's lethal coming of age transcended the personal to take on universal and national implications. As the stage action becomes more menacing, the statements of "Old Paint" become more dissonant. In the midst of what Pollack has called an evolution "from pastoral innocence to mechanistic violence" (HP, 321), the cowboy song persists over an ostinato that combines grinding semitones in the bass with the same rhythmic profile of the pioneer processional. The allusions to the opening processional remind us that somehow the process by which Billy loses his carefree childhood parallels the movement of the westering crowd—and that the violence that creates and destroys him is an inescapable consequence of nation building.

Stopped cold by the twin murders that bring the scene to its dreadful end, the ostinato and the townspeople freeze, and all our attention must focus on Billy. Loring described the gestures he devoted to Billy's dastardly deeds: "In *Billy* I worked out a sequence—double pirouette, then double air tour—just before Billy shoots each victim. This is followed by an almost pantomimic gesture of revulsion and sickness. Those steps relay how Billy feels emotionally before he kills, because I believe that Billy *did* care that he was killing, that he was revolted."[42] Through this choreographic inspiration, Billy manages to express both excitement and revulsion at the behaviors to which he has been driven.

The emotional understanding Loring musters for his hero stands in sharp contrast to the ballet's caricature of the townspeople rejoicing after Billy's capture. Their justifiable feeling of triumph is effectively quashed by a musical and choreographic treatment presenting them as utterly unnatural. While the inchoate milling of the frontiersmen during the earlier street scene was harmless enough, when they unite in pursuit of Billy, they become less human than the criminal himself. Loring suggested a "macabre dance" at this point in the action, and Copland rose to the occasion with stilted rhythms, shrieking piccolos, and wrenching bitonality. In response to such sounds, the posse engages in what Siegel describes as "a sort of Virginia reel, a very mechanical, doll-like, and completely unnatural barn dance."[43] With such raucous revelry in the background, it becomes easier to believe Denby's interpretation that "Billy's real enemy is the plain crowd of frontiersmen, who being a crowd can ignore him and whom he ignores by an act of pride."[44]

Apart from Billy's soliloquy, the pas de deux for Billy and the Sweetheart represents the longest and most coherent episode characterizing our antihero. Both of these set pieces were omitted from the orchestral suite, though the waltz tune (based on the cowboy song "Trouble for the Range Cook (Come Wrangle Yer Bronco)" appears in the two-piano version as well as the cello showpiece that Copland excerpted from the work. Even more than the "Card Game at Night," this is an episode devoted to seemingly straightforward melody and the lyrical depiction of Billy and his girlfriend. Yet a number of factors problematize the couple's closeness. Most important is the status of the Sweetheart. Is she real or a fantasy? Though the scenario is somewhat ambiguous on this point, most viewers have interpreted the various disjunctions of the duet as signs that Billy is dreaming. Does this enigmatic female figure represent lover or mother? Because they are represented on stage by the same dancer, the duet would appear to carry both innocent and oedipal connotations.

In keeping with this mood, Copland's score reflects a surreal wistfulness. It gives little flesh to the rhythmic skeleton of oom-pah-pah waltz accompaniment, except in passages where brief countermelodies intertwine, suggesting the physical proximity of the two dancers. The cowboy song that circles above this indifferent figuration is a peculiar choice; Pollack has noted a certain irony in the mismatch between the humorous "Trouble for the Range Cook" and the serious purpose that it serves in the ballet (HP, 322–23). Subsequent solos for bassoon and trombone hardly reinforce the timbral expectations for a traditional love scene. Mosaic rearrangement of the tune's phrases superimposed over harmonic vagaries or cul-de-sacs introduce what Arthur Berger deemed "fruitful distortions" comparable to cubism.[45] The dream state of Copland's music finds ample support in Loring's choreography. The Sweetheart is the only dancer in toe shoes, which sets her apart from the rough and ready "real" characters. Moreover, her interaction with Billy is curiously otherworldly, as Siegel observes: "At first they dance back to back, and during much of his supporting action she is in a position where they can't make eye contact. Even when they can see each other, they have a far-off look, their contacts are remote."[46] The ever-present possibility that Billy is dancing with his dead mother makes the waltz a more than plausible candidate for the ballet's true "danse macabre." Yet the contrast between the disjointed sweetness of Billy's waltz and the jarringly mechanical reel of the frontiersmen could hardly be greater, and Billy is clearly one who deserves our sympathy.

Westerns in other media had already confirmed that the American West was the natural habitat for the badman who is good at heart, the hero who resists societal norms. Already in 1925, Burns had recognized this potential in Billy, calling him "the hero of a Southwestern Niebelungenlied" and noting that "he is destined eventually to be transformed by popular legend into the Robin Hood of New Mexico—a heroic outlaw endowed with every noble quality fighting the battle of the common people against the tyranny of wealth and power."[47] Equally typical of the western are the conflicting feelings Billy engenders toward progress as a cultural imperative. In Billy the Kid, this tension resides somewhere between the gritty optimism of the frontier processional and the cruel jubilation of the "civilized" townspeople after Billy's capture. Reading through a rather grand historical lens, Burns claimed that "[Billy's] life closed the past; his death opened the present. . . . After him came the great change for which he involuntarily had cleared the way. Law and order came in on the flash and smoke of the six-shooter that with one bullet put an end to the outlaw and to outlawry."[48] Copland, Loring, and many of the critics who praised the ballet fed on the western's tremendous nostalgia for an older social order (or disorder) in which chivalrous outlawry remained a viable option.

Despite these stereotypical features, the psychological complexity that music and gesture lend to Billy is remarkable among westerns. With him, we see how the freedom of outlawry brings a fracturing of human relationships. Not all western heroes are so unlucky in love; in Copland's and Loring's hands, however, the boy bandit eschews the heterosexual masculinity of Hollywood cowboys in favor of something decidedly more complicated. The ballet still pays its own variety of homage to the traditionally central (if often silent) role of women in the western. What has changed in *Billy the Kid* is the female figure around which the hero is constructed. When the eternal feminine migrates from lover to mother, the sexual valences of the typical western go awry, changing what should be a crucial present-day relationship (between lovers) into a remembered one. And with this shift in temporal priority comes a sense of distance or disjunction that persistently drives the ballet into surrealism and fantasy. Always poetic in his treatment of such themes, Denby recognized the contemporary motivations of the ballet's move toward myth. He wrote: "*Billy* is about the West as it is dreamed of, as it is imagined by boys playing in empty lots in the suburbs of our cities. And for this reason *Billy* is unreal in its local description, but real in its tragic play. An anthropologist would recognize it as an urban puberty ritual."[49] In *Billy the Kid*, the western hero has himself become nostalgic, making him at once more poignant and, strangely, more modern.

ANOTHER COWBOY BALLET?

Denby appreciated the subjective distance and ritual tone of *Billy the Kid*, and his review encapsulates much of what set the ballet apart from the few existing Americana dance productions (most notably Virgil Thomson's *Filling Station*). At the time of his writing, he was particularly interested in distinguishing the ballet from its closest sibling in the dance world: Agnes de Mille's *Rodeo*, for which Copland wrote the score in 1942. Denby considered the later work far removed from Billy's panoramic West, asserting that "*Rodeo* is about the West as it is lived in" not "as it is dreamed of."[50] Though his description of *Billy the Kid* seems uncannily on the mark, his claims for the "realism" of *Rodeo* are harder to swallow. The ballet is a virtual Cinderella story with no historical antecedent, but it did rely on more naturalistic dance gestures, and it did abandon at least some of *Billy*'s epic and psychological pretensions.

When a second cowboy ballet appeared while *Billy* was still in the active repertory—again produced by a company with prominent East Coast or European ties, again relying on Copland and cowboy song—invidious comparisons were inevitable. It required no special genius to predict this reaction, and Copland himself was understandably concerned. Nor could he have been oblivious to the fact that, although he had rarely been west of the Mississippi, he might be risking permanent identification as a cowboy composer. These factors may help explain Copland's initial reluctance to take on the project. Looking back on his first discussion with de Mille, the composer recalled: "When she started to tell me about it being a cowboy ballet, I immediately said, 'Oh no! I've already composed one of those. I don't want to do *another* cowboy ballet! Can't you write a script about Ellis Island?'" (V PAC1, 355–56). Though perhaps offered in jest, there is a poignancy in Copland's question that reflects more than a fear of self-repetition or typecasting. De Mille's own writings from the 1950s give us a glimpse of the other issues at stake: "I detailed the scenario.... There was a pause. 'Well,' I said, 'it isn't *Hamlet*.' He giggled. '—but it can have what Martha Graham calls an "aura of race memory."'' At this Copland's glasses flashed and gleamed. His body began to vibrate all over with great explosive laughs. 'Couldn't we do a ballet about Ellis Island?' he asked, his glasses opaque with light. 'That I would love to compose.'"[51] Regardless of the possible pitfalls, writing a score for the Ballet Russe de Monte Carlo was an opportunity not to be missed, and Copland was soon at work on his second cowboy commission.

Copland and de Mille may have professed their amusement at the notion of "race memory," but it is easy to imagine a nervousness behind their laughter. In her 1991 memoir *Blood Memory,* Graham speaks of "ancestral footsteps" pushing her to create and of moments when "your body [becomes] something else and ... takes on a world of cultures from the past."[52] De Mille was not especially interested in such transhistorical transubstantiation; and if she were listening for ancestral footsteps, the loudest might have belonged to her uncle Cecil B. Agnes was a child of Hollywood; her early life was far removed from the world of ranching and roping. And as for Copland, he still considered horseback "a dangerous place to be."

By the time Copland sat down to write *Rodeo,* after the outbreak of World War II, he had joined many of his compatriots in composing pieces that abandoned regional references altogether or subsumed them into the all-encompassing Americanism of the *Fanfare for the Common Man.* In de Mille's case, although it marked her debut as director of the Ballet Russe de Monte Carlo (the first American choreographer the troupe had ever employed), *Rodeo* was not her first or last experiment in Americana. Her reputation stemmed from works like *American Street* (1938), in which she had employed stylized horseback-riding gestures independently of Loring (HP, 363–64). In fact, her "big break" coincided with the company's desire to make a patriotic statement during wartime.

Few if any moments in the ballet reflect the seriousness of its time. The scenario's lightheartedness—the fact that it was no *Hamlet*—may also have contributed to the collaborators' unease. One dance sequence (which was later scrapped) in which the men all rush off to take care of ranch business during the dance seems to have sprung from de Mille's awareness of the many separations suffered by military families (HP, 365). For the most part, however, *Rodeo* escapes the gravity of wartime, and this left its creators open to a certain type of critique.[53] Yet the ballet's ebullience at least had the advantage of obvious contrast with *Billy the Kid*. De Mille may even have had this in mind when describing her own scenario: "It is not an epic, or the story of pioneer conquest. It builds no empires. It is a pastorale, a lyric joke."[54] From the beginning, Copland was reassured by the differences in the artistic personalities behind the two cowboy ballets. He recalled: "I came to the conclusion that since de Mille was a very different person from Eugene Loring, it was bound to be a very different ballet. Loring was interested in legendary figures and grandiose effects, while Agnes was after something lighter and more bouncy" (VPAC1, 356). After the birth of the younger cowboy ballet, Copland further separated his western progeny by making analogies to dramatic genres and operatic types. He claimed that *Billy the Kid* had "a certain 'grand opera' side," while *Rodeo* was "closer to musical comedy."[55] Though Copland had a tendency to protest too much, when it came to evaluating his western scores, his near-dismissal of *Rodeo* was not merely retrospective. In 1942, he wrote to Benjamin Britten: "I'm doing a frothy ballet for the Monte Carlo people on the usual wildwest subject—full of square dances and Scotch tunes and the like" (VPAC1, 364–65).

Hamlet was out of the question. Even *A Midsummer Night's Dream* would have been a stretch, but de Mille chose her own Shakespearean precedent by referring to *Rodeo* as "the Taming of a Shrew—cowboy style."[56] The parallel is apt for a ballet in which traditional gender roles are violently reinforced under the guise of comedy. De Mille had originally wanted the title "The Courting at Burnt Ranch," and according to the scenario, the ballet "deals with the problem that has confronted all American women, from earliest pioneer times, and which has never ceased to occupy them throughout the history of the building of our country: how to get a suitable man." Though lonely and infatuated with the Head Wrangler, the tomboy-cowgirl fails to make an impression until she dons a dress and puts a bow in her hair. Suddenly both the Wrangler and the Champion Roper are vying for her affections. The Roper proves quicker on his feet, and she takes up his challenge to dance the hoedown—a dance that the choreographer linked to the sexually charged flamenco (HP, 364). These would-be lovers reach their denouement when he takes her firmly in hand. As de Mille originally put it,

"He grabs her, forces her to dance his way and wears her out by sheer brute strength. That's all she wanted. She has met her master." In later versions of the scenario, a Hollywood-style kiss replaces this aggressive dance duet as the gesture that seals their union.

Rodeo's gender stereotyping and emphasis on conformism drew strong words from Marcia Siegel, who condemned the ballet's values as "absurd" and "pernicious" and used a comparison with *Billy the Kid* to drive home her point: "Loring's characters are types, even archetypes. They don't develop or change during the ballet. But what a varied population these types comprise. Loring distinguished them in several ways, by their occupations, their temperaments, their racial origins. . . . De Mille's community, on the other hand, is entirely homogeneous. In fact, the moral purpose of her ballet is to show the error in being a nonconformist. All the cowboys do the same movements, usually in tight, unison floor patterns." The heroine's eccentricity is bound to stand out in such a rigid context for, as Siegel relates, "The Cowgirl is the worst sort of misfit, a sexual misfit, and in a highly conformist society she must be shunned until she gives up her peculiar notions."[57]

Why would de Mille choose this view of society for her Monte Carlo debut? Comic considerations aside, it is tempting to link *Rodeo*'s emphasis on conformity with its historical context. Though this interpretation received scant recognition at the time, the ballet's celebration of unity at the expense of self-expression would have been an appropriate wartime message. More particularly, its dramatic crux involves a woman trying to enter a predominantly male profession. Though the Cowgirl ultimately fails to shed her domestic femininity, her attempt to do a "man's job" might have seemed familiar to the many American women who took up factory positions while their husbands and brothers were mobilized for war. Pollack points out that de Mille was preoccupied with the changing gender roles brought on by the conflict. She recalled thinking of "the men leaving, leaving everywhere—generation on generation of men leaving and falling and the women remembering" (HP, 365). But de Mille's Cowgirl does more than remember. In less than half an hour, she acts out one of the country's most striking demographic shifts during the 1940s, when women temporarily swelled the workforce.[58]

A more widespread interpretation of the ballet's social philosophy draws directly from de Mille's own biography. Siegel is not the only critic to have suggested that de Mille's sympathy for the Cowgirl's predicament had autobiographical roots—especially in the early 1940s, when the young choreographer was frustrated and isolated, struggling to make a place for herself in the male-dominated dance world and to carve out her own niche between ballet and modern or popular dance styles. Like the Cowgirl and the courting couples on the ranch, de Mille's aspirations could be realized only through dance. (The fact that de Mille had married a Texan only the year before she began drafting "The Courting at Burnt Ranch" adds yet another layer to the self-portrait.)[59]

Rodeo was de Mille's signature work in more ways than one—she wrote the scenario, invented and rehearsed the choreography, and prepared the lead role for herself. Her controlling presence in the work had serious consequences for Copland. Perhaps with so much of de Mille in the ballet, there was little room left for him—at any rate, he hardly strayed from the detailed scenario she provided and used folk songs and fiddle tunes where she had suggested them.[60] Whether because of these constraints or not, Copland invented less music for *Rodeo* than he had for *Billy the Kid,* and according to some reviewers, his most "original" contribution to the ballet was an episode with no music at all—where he required the men in the orchestra to clap and tap their instruments in time with the dancing.

The opening "Buckaroo Holiday" is by far the most elaborate of the episodes Copland contributed to the score. Pollack and others agree that this movement rivals anything in *Billy the Kid* for its sophisticated handling of borrowed material. Even more than the "Street in a Frontier Town," it shows the degree to which Copland was willing to alter his folk songs for dramatic effect. This section of the ballet draws upon two tunes taken from *Our Singing Country,* although only one of them features cowboys. In addition to the topical tune "If He'd Be a Buckaroo," Copland chose "Sis Joe," a railroaders' work song notable for its change of meter and irregular speech rhythms. It seems likely that these features attracted Copland, for they are the ones he exaggerated (examples 49a and 49b). In the initial statement of this melody, the middle five bars are omitted and rhythmic values (especially lengths of rests) are altered. As the movement unfolds, these two tunes appear in canon and in counterpoint with one another, and together they provide a host of punctuating devices, characteristic rhythms, and melodic motives.

If any moment in the ballet could single-handedly justify *Rodeo*'s designation as the comic counterpart to *Billy the Kid,* it would be the first appearance of the cowboy tune "If He'd Be a Buckaroo" (example 50). After a full stop and a change of key, the arrival of the new tune is staged in a manner worthy of Dukas's *Sorcerer's Apprentice.* The trombone seems to awaken and reconstitute its melody phrase by phrase with prolonged, unpredictably humorous silences between the tune's phrases, making it seem awkward and out of kilter. Presumably the comic revivification of "If He'd Be a Buckaroo" originated as a musical pun accompanying the Cowgirl's masculine posturing and misguided efforts to mount her bronco. (One reviewer responded: "The note of humor runs its telling course . . . and not infrequently some one or other of the instruments does a rubbery-legged walk-on, Leon Errol style.")[61]

Throughout the cowboy ballets, ironic touches serve to denature the folk material, thwarting efforts to "sing along" and continually reminding the listener of

EXAMPLE 49A. "Sis Joe" (from Lomax, *Our Singing Country,* 1941)

the composer's active, "professional" manipulation and recasting of whatever he borrows. In both ballets as well there is often a dramatic aptness in the tunes Copland selected and deployed. Just as the subdued strains of "The Dying Cowboy" had accompanied Billy's lonely card game on the prairie, so the riotous rhythmic energy of "Sis Joe" marks the moment in *Rodeo* when the cowboys rush onto the stage "like thunder."

Rodeo's other dance episodes are actual dances (figure 8). As befits their dramatic function, they quote folk songs more literally than almost anything else in Copland's oeuvre (with the possible exception of "Simple Gifts" from *Appalachian Spring*). For the second episode, the "Corral Nocturne," Copland wrote his own melody in a style that could pass for folk, but in the others he borrowed liberally. After some clever written-out tuning effects in the strings, the third movement, "Saturday Night Waltz," preserves even the metrical and melodic variants of the version of "Old Paint" that de Mille had provided from memory.[62] And as noted above, the final movement is primarily an orchestration of the square dance tune "Bonyparte" whose melody the composer lifted from Ira Forbes's *Traditional Music of America.*

No one could blame de Mille for exploiting the strengths of her medium or Copland for allowing his tuneful material to perform its traditional function. Yet Siegel senses an insidious side to the ballet's square dances: "The floor patterns are straight and orderly. Every person has a partner of the opposite sex, and the dance requires the participation of each couple in order to be accomplished. The steps are prescribed in advance and are simple enough so that with a little practice any energetic person could perform them."[63] Like the social dances of other

EXAMPLE 49B. *Rodeo,* "Buckaroo Holiday," arranged for piano solo, mm. 114–27
(London: Boosey & Hawkes, 1962)

nations and eras, *Rodeo*'s choreographing of conformity puts the values of its
participants into motion and on display. Edwin Denby said as much—in more
words—when he reacted to the work and its many conventional attitudes: "The
effect of the ballet . . . is like that of a pleasant comic strip. You watch a little coy
and tear-jerky cowgirl-gets-her-cowboy story, and you don't get upset about it.

EXAMPLE 50. *Rodeo*, "Buckaroo Holiday," mm. 167–93

What you are really recognizing is what people in general do together out West. Somehow the flavor of American domestic manners is especially clear in that peculiar desert landscape."[64]

What was it about the "peculiar desert landscape" that brought *Rodeo*'s relationships into such sharp relief? In a way, the simple barrenness of the

FIGURE 8. Square-dancing couples in *Rodeo,* set against a backdrop that suggests both the spaciousness and the energy of Agnes de Mille's West. Courtesy of Boosey and Hawkes/ArenaPAL

surrounding terrain foregrounds the actions of its human inhabitants. Reading de Mille's scenario for *Rodeo* also suggests some psychological corollaries to western desolation. Before launching into the details of the ballet's plot, de Mille explained to Copland: "There are never more than a very few people on the stage at a time, and while they generate a lot of excitement between themselves, they are always dwarfed by space and height and isolation. One must always be conscious of the enormous land on which these people live and of their proud [loneliness]."[65] It is a tall order to portray such a complex relationship between land and people in dance, but judging from reviewers' reactions, de Mille seems to have managed it. The profound isolation that she had in mind struck a responsive chord in part because of its resonance with the angst of modern industrial society.

Later in the scenario, de Mille described the solo piece that was to fall between the opening rodeo antics and the boisterous collective dancing that fills the rest of the ballet—a contemplative moment that was apparently intended to occur without orchestral accompaniment:

The show is over, the men dismount. The girls saunter off to meet them.... The cowgirl sits on a post of the corral forgotten. The men and their sweethearts stroll in the evening. The twilight deepens. The sky goes green. They walk in the dusk. (This is a dance entirely of mood, lyric, quiet, almost mystic, a dance of courting, but abstracted, impersonal. It is more a dance between people and darkness than between people and people.) The few stragglers move like moths in the darkness. They are barely visible, outlined only against the deepening sky. The girl still sits. She is lonely. But she is in love with the land around and the great glowing night sky, and the smells and the sounds. She leaves the fence and moves across the moonlit space. Someone hurries by with an oil lantern. She run[s] through the empty corrals intoxicated with space, her feet thudding in the stillness. She stops spell-bound. A coyote calls.[66]

The changing light at sunset reveals the couples' courtships as mystic and abstract—more about their relationship to the natural world than to each other. The Cowgirl alone exults in the self-sufficiency of her relationship with her surroundings. The fact that her moment of self-discovery happens in silence and social isolation—apart from the rough physicality of the ranch house—calls into question the ballet's emphasis on conformity and temporarily inverts its sexual politics. Suddenly, if only for a moment, finding a "suitable man" has become less important than the opportunity for self-realization and the possibility of intoxication by space.

Though the subversive potential of this self-discovery remains, the Cowgirl's moonlit reverie is short-lived. Her solo is well contained by the episodes of communal dancing that push her back into the comic flux of social relations, redress her in conventionally feminine attire, and drive her toward the expected "happy" ending. Despite its moment of freedom, the plot of *Rodeo* and its success as a ballet show that there is much to be gained by playing societally sanctioned roles—a moral that is particularly relevant to the biographies of its creators. For de Mille, casting herself as a foolishly romantic heroine offset the fact that she was breaking new ground as a female choreographer. For Copland, who had little if any control over the details of the work's plot and characterization, the situation is harder to pin down.

Though analogies between Copland and his ballet characters must remain speculative, they are nonetheless worth exploring, especially in light of recent scholarship on Copland and sexuality. Pollack has posited a loose link between Copland's homosexuality and his attraction to the themes of loneliness and liberation.[67] In a more provocative analysis, David Metzer has identified a homoerotic strain in Copland's early works (often masked by allusions to the sensuality of the Orient or the physicality of black Africa). Metzer argues that Copland "later backed away from this erotic-racial play," retreating to abstraction in works like the *Piano Variations* and replacing sexually charged references to other cultures with the supposedly straightforward use of Anglo folk materials. As he points out, references to homosexual desire "appear remote from the American frontier celebrated in *Appalachian Spring, Rodeo,* and *Billy the Kid,* the popular ballets of the 1930s and 1940s with which the composer is almost exclusively associated."[68] The apparent gulf Metzer identifies between Copland's sexuality and his western works is interesting in its own right, but its distance is all too easy to collapse if one takes the details of the cowboy ballet plots seriously.

It is surely striking that both of his cowboy ballets center on individuals who are visibly alienated from the communities around them: the outlaw Billy and the misfit Cowgirl. Each protagonist is marked by the frustration or displacement of desire, each plot hinges on a sudden change in the direction or expression of sexual energy, and each community reasserts itself in such a way that deviance (sexual or otherwise) is suppressed. The Cowgirl's sexual awakening is endangered—or at least forestalled—by her blatant disregard for gender roles and her unwillingness to conform to social norms. And as for that incorrigible adolescent, Billy the Kid, although he is a favorite with the Mexican girls, his fantasies are fixated on his mother—an unattainable and unacceptable object of desire. He is betrayed at the moment he surrenders to his Sweetheart's reassurances and allows himself to be "disarmed." Billy's relationship cannot bring him to sexual adulthood, nor can it save him from social ostracism.

These are not really the standard character types of the Wild West dime novel or the Hollywood western. In fact, their remarkable divergence from the typical, sexually powerful heroes of western genres suggests that Copland and his collaborators viewed western settings as an appropriate backdrop for the exploration (and arguably the expansion) of acceptable sexual mores and gender roles. Whatever Copland's role in shaping our sympathies toward these atypical western heroes may have been, his own biography offers supporting evidence for the idea that the imagery of the American West offered a haven for social and sexual aberrance, but also a site where patriarchal visions of social and moral order could be vigorously upheld.

13

Copland and the Cinematic West

COMING OF AGE IN ELDORADO

Alienation and self-discovery (sexual or otherwise) are major themes in all of Copland's western scores. *Billy the Kid* and *Rodeo* made these themes visible through dance, but they withheld definitive answers about Copland's own attitudes. His authorial voice is even harder to tease out of his western film scores: *Of Mice and Men* (1939) and *The Red Pony* (1949). Both are based on previously published works of John Steinbeck, and in both cases the screenplays were substantially complete before anyone thought to approach Copland for the music. Nevertheless, the resulting scores represent his most direct engagement with western character types, gender roles, and the idea of westward expansion. They also represent the realm in which Copland's identity as a "western" composer was most influential on future generations.

In some ways, film was a natural medium for a composer like Copland. His preferences had always tended toward the pictorial and the dramatic, and his love of rapid juxtapositions was well suited to screen action. He often articulated the view that accommodating other artists' needs did not preclude creative expression. "Having to compose music to accompany specific action," he wrote, "is a help rather than a hindrance, since the action itself induces music in a composer of theatrical imagination."[1] As Sally Bick and Elizabeth Bergman Crist have shown, working for film also had special resonance for left-leaning artists who saw in the movie theater a mass audience attuned to a medium with great persuasive power. In short, film was enticing to Copland for political and aesthetic reasons, as well as social ones, and he praised Hollywood as a site where musicians were actually needed, calling it "a composer's Eldorado."[2]

Despite the encouragement of Harold Clurman and George Antheil, Copland's first stab at a Hollywood contract in the spring of 1937 resulted only in weeks of frustration. Instead, he began his film career two years later and on more familiar ground: at the World's Fair in New York City. Like Thomson before him, Copland got his "big break" courtesy of a documentary film written in support of a civic agenda. In this case, Ralph Steiner and Willard Van Dyke approached him on behalf of the American City Planning Institute to score *The City*, a film portraying the evils of unregulated urban growth.[3] Though Steiner recalled his qualms about engaging a composer of Copland's markedly "modern" tendencies, he was eventually won over by some of the composer's more popular scores.[4] With its evocations of small-town America, horrific industrial slums, and the improvements enabled by conscientious urban planning, Copland's contribution to *The City* won praise from Paul Bowles, Henry Cowell, and Stravinsky; it also had the desired impact on Hollywood producers and directors, including Lewis Milestone, the man behind three of the most important film projects that Copland subsequently scored.[5]

The most immediate result of the Copland-Milestone connection was *Of Mice and Men* (1939). Its shocking, realistic plot and lean, dissonant score made it a watershed work for Copland and for Hollywood—one that would, in Sally Bick's words, both challenge and inspire industry norms, "establishing what would eventually become identified as an American nondiegetic style."[6] David Raksin, for one, praised Copland's contribution in retrospect, pointing to its transforming influence on later Westerns: "Not only was the score wonderful," he told the aging composer, "you began something with that from which none of us have ever escaped: you created a definite style having to do with the Western film. Before that they used to think they were doing all right if they played 'Bury Me Not on the Lone Prairie.' And then all of a sudden we were face to face with this absolutely clear and pure and wonderful style."[7] Yet the "purity" of Copland's western style was not something that could be taken for granted in 1939. On the contrary, the soundtrack for *Of Mice and Men* was notable for its mixing of the folksy and the contemporary and for the sheer variety of sound sources it employed: a Jew's harp during the main title music, solo guitar, a jazzy song on the radio, the honky-tonk piano at a saloon, and a snippet from an "authentic" hymn tune that the producers selected in consultation with the Farm Security Administration.[8] If Copland's stylistic choices later appeared natural and straightforward, this may be traced in part to the simplifying powers of hindsight but also to the character and influence of his intervening film scores, especially *The Red Pony*.

FATHERS AND SONS

When Copland moved to California early in 1948 to begin work on *The Red Pony,* many things had changed. Although he had three more movie credits to his name—*Our Town* (1940), *North Star* (1943), and his score for the Office of War Information's documentary *The Cummington Story* (1945)—it had been a number of years since he had worked in Hollywood. He had received several offers from movie producers, but he was preoccupied with such wartime works as *Appalachian Spring* (1944) and the massive Symphony no. 3 (1944–46). The end of World War II and the revelation of its man-made horrors rendered the patriotic tone of such pieces difficult to sustain, and the postwar years instead saw the reevaluation of concepts like race and nation and a renewed sense of social alienation among artists and intellectuals.

In the wake of such widespread cultural upheaval, Copland may have sensed the strangeness of his situation when he was invited by the same man who had approached him eight years earlier (Milestone) to score a story by the same author (Steinbeck), to be filmed on exactly the same site as *Of Mice and Men* (figure 9). Steinbeck and Milestone had actually begun planning for the production shortly after the release of *Of Mice and Men,* but the project was delayed until 1947 by the war and by financial considerations—*Of Mice and Men* had been a critical success, but a box office failure. The two films share more than their local color. Each deals with the connections between maturity and violence or death, and each stresses personal responsibility in the face of impersonal and often hostile environmental forces. But while the migratory workers in *Of Mice and Men* have relatively contemporary plights and aspirations, the turn-of-the-century characters in *The Red Pony* move in different psychological realms: the daydreams of childhood and the reminiscences of old age. The later film lacks the extroverted action scenes and the threats of violence in the earlier film, and perhaps as a result, Copland confessed that the film had the potential to seem dull. "The picture is a nice one but no epic or path-breaker," he wrote to Irving and Verna Fine shortly after his arrival. "The trouble from my angle is that it was shot on the same ranch that 'Of Mice and Men' was shot on. Now I ask you: if you had to look at the same landscape every day could you think up different music? (Note, I'm getting my alibis all set up in advance.)"[9]

When it came time to write program notes for the orchestral suite drawn from the film score, however, the composer had found a silver lining in the film's quietude, using it to explain the story's susceptibility to musical treatment. "There is a minimum of action of a dramatic or startling kind," he admitted. "The story gets its warmth and sensitive quality from the character studies of the boy Jody, Jody's grandfather, the cow-hand Billy Buck and Jody's parents, the Tiflins [Alice and Fred]. The kind of emotions that Steinbeck evokes in his story

FIGURE 9. Copland with Peter Miles on the set of *The Red Pony*. Courtesy of Paramount Pictures Corporation

are basically musical ones since they deal so much with the unexpressed feelings of daily living."[10]

Steinbeck created his film scenario from materials originally published in four distinct but thematically interrelated short stories: "The Gift," "The Great Mountains," "The Promise," and "The Leader of the People."[11] These stories were originally self-sufficient snapshots of life on the Tiflin Ranch, but the screenplay omits the second story and interweaves the remaining events into a single narrative. From the beginning, there were autobiographical overtones. As he completed the stories, Steinbeck was preparing for the death of his mother and remembering his own childhood joy at receiving his first pony. In the later screenplay, produced while he was in the midst of his own domestic strife, he escalated the unspoken tension between Fred and Billy and pushed the Tiflins' unhappy marriage to the brink of disaster. In addition, the child protagonist, originally "Jody," was renamed "Tom"—perhaps after Steinbeck's own son, or perhaps to avoid confusion with the child protagonist "Jody" in *The Yearling* (1947). Tom (played by Peter Miles) gains a gang of schoolyard friends and a Technicolor dreamworld for his heroic fantasies. Grandfather (Louis Calhern), who appears only in the last of the four stories, becomes a central presence in the movie, providing occasional comic relief and genuine pathos.

Neither a straightforward children's film nor a conventional western, *The Red Pony* offers an essay on conflicting models of masculinity, with the warm but flawed ranchman Billy Buck replacing Tom's distant schoolteacher father, Fred (Sheppard Strudwick), as mentor and confidant. From the very first scene, when Fred burns himself while trying to help Alice with the breakfast dishes, we are faced with illustrations of his physical and emotional impotence. Most important to the unfolding plot is his ill-timed outburst over Alice's father's rambling anecdotes about "Indians and crossing the plains." Domestic meltdown is followed by lame attempts at apology and Fred's eventual departure for his parents' home in San Jose to "think things out" alone. Fred is hardly more successful in his attempts to connect with his son. He quashes his moment of paternal glory—when he gives Tom the pony—by immediately threatening to sell off the animal if Tom falls behind in his chores. In similar fashion, Fred has erected barriers between himself and his neighbors; to his chagrin, none of the other ranchers ever call him by his first name. As Alice observes, he has made himself "a stranger." By contrast, Billy Buck is competent and approachable. Naturally, the Tiflins rely on his expert horsemanship, but his nurturing attitude toward Tom is what sets him most starkly apart from Fred. It is from Billy that Tom learns the ways of the ranch, and it is by recognizing Billy's limitations that Tom gains a more mature understanding of the ways of the world.

Like the short stories, the film shows little affectionate interaction between Alice and Fred—a lack that seems more acute on screen because of Hollywood genre expectations (even a family drama might be expected to have a glimmer of romance). The fact that Billy was played by the charismatic Robert Mitchum makes an even greater issue of Fred's masculinity by suggesting, probably unintentionally, a covert love interest between Billy and Alice, played by Myrna Loy. To make matters worse, Billy's active sexuality is discreetly but clearly apparent during a comic dialogue in the bunkhouse when he explains away his pinup pictures of attractive women by telling Tom they are his "cousins."

Musically, Copland's sympathies are clear. Fred has no recognizable music of his own, apart from a repetitive (and probably intoxicated) song that he and Billy sing on their way home from town. As Pollack points out, "For much of the film, Copland leaves Fred in chilly silence, thus emphasizing his presence as a distant husband and father" (HP, 432). By contrast, Billy Buck moves easily to the music that accompanies the daily activities of rural life. He is the first human we see after the main title music merges into the musical cue labeled "Morning on the Ranch." Simple and triadic, the irregular but repetitive melodic strains make a flexible and effective background accompaniment to the long sequence of stage actions that introduces the characters. As Copland described it, "The daily chores begin. A folk-like melody suggests the atmosphere of simple country living." The small range, circular tendencies, and potential motivic monotony of this folklike music also underscore the routine nature of the actions on-screen, as if to say that this "morning on the ranch" is much like any other. While Fred and Tom struggle to get out of bed, Billy's chores in the barn and Alice's kitchen duties show that they are the ones in charge of this gentle morning choreography.

Billy becomes the primary agent of Tom's initiation into adulthood as the child's innocent faith is tested by the death of his beloved pony. Indeed the film's preoccupation with life-and-death matters occasionally outweighs its schoolyard antics and heroic daydreams. Tom's brutal battle with the buzzards drew numerous critiques from viewers expecting a lighthearted family film. Steinbeck himself, however, emphasized the story's weighty implications in a narration he wrote and recorded for Copland's orchestral suite. Here the eminent author refers to "the twisted and lovely and tortured path up the Hill of the Skull which every boy must travel to become a man."[12] Nonetheless, for much of the movie, Tom's childlike side prevails. Joseph Millichap has noted that one response to the poor box office return on *Of Mice and Men* was to market *The Red Pony* as a "kiddy western about a boy and his horse."[13] The most serious casualty of this transformation is the poorly prepared climax, which betrays all previous foreshadowing in favor of the Hollywood "Happy Ending" that gives the last movement of Copland's orchestral suite its title. Avoiding the gruesome birth/death scene that ends Steinbeck's story "The Promise," the movie shows Billy's willingness to sacrifice his horse Rosie in order to deliver her colt to Tom, but then ends with smiles and relieved laughter: Fred and Alice are reunited; Tom and Billy are reconciled; both mare and foal survive.

The movie enacts its creators' reluctance to let carefree childhood be overshadowed by the awareness of death, and this is nowhere more apparent than in the memorable sequences illustrating Tom's daydreams. Caught in the routine events and awkward family dynamics of the Tiflin household, Tom escapes into a fantasy world that seems extremely remote from the western ranch. Our first glimpse of his vibrant inner life comes during his long walk to school. Using a stick to beat out a march rhythm on his metal lunch bucket, he is magically transformed into a knight in shining armor, riding at the head of a stately processional in the company of Billy Buck. When this fantasy is dispelled by the shouts of his approaching classmates, Tom reappears in his familiar overalls, kicking up dust from the dirt road at his feet. His next adventure occurs as he does his after-school chores. While feeding the chickens gathered in a circle around him, Tom suddenly finds himself the ringmaster of a cartoon circus. These daydream sequences have been roundly criticized for their lack of integration into the film; nevertheless, each one provided an opportunity to explore the newest frontiers in cinematic technology. The *Red Pony* was Milestone's first color film, and the fantasy sequences let him make the most of Technicolor. For his part, Copland used a click track in Tom's "Dream March," and the circus fantasy allowed him to experiment with mixing two different source tracks, "overlapping incoming and outgoing music tracks when the daydreaming imagination of a little boy turns white chickens into white circus horses."[14]

Although the fantasy sequences were drastically curtailed during the production process, the movie retained its status as a kids' film, thanks to inserted schoolroom sequences, numerous lines for child actors, and Tom's almost continuous presence on screen. Copland, too, allowed childlike qualities to infiltrate portions of the score both inside and outside of Tom's imagination. As he put it in his program note for the orchestral suite, "I decided to call it a children's suite because so much of the music is meant to reflect a child's world."[15] In addition to the nursery rhyme march rhythms of the knights' parade or the giddy bitonal play of the "Circus March," Copland made frequent recourse to the "toy" timbres of celesta, glockenspiel, and string harmonics and devised a static shimmer (courtesy of vibraphone and divisi strings) to accompany Tom's wide-eyed wonder when he first sees his pony.

Yet the *Red Pony*'s picture of childhood is complicated by nostalgia. Jarring shifts between the serious and the comic, between the violent and the pastoral, create the occasional impression that what we see on the screen is somehow clouded by the passing of time—an adult's memory of past innocence. Arguably, this stance exists from the very beginning of the film, when the opening credits emerge as if from the pages of a child's picture book, which has appeared inexplicably on the Tiflins' front porch. Like Grandfather's anecdotes about crossing the plains, this is a story that can be told again and again, but only to an audience with childlike qualities. Confronted with Fred's angry indifference, Grandfather proclaims: "It was a job for men. Now only little boys want to hear about it." His words capture the intergenerational conflict within the Tiflin family, but he also speaks of the forces that transformed *The Red Pony* into a "kiddy western."

THE GREAT CROSSING

Tom does not play "cowboys and Indians," and at first glance his fantasies appear far removed from his western surroundings. Nonetheless his parade with the knights on horseback has many parallels to his Grandfather's experience as "Leader of the People," and his circus dream shows him firmly in command of animals (white horses, in fact), practicing postures that he will soon assume in real life as he trains the red pony. A screenplay housed at the Library of Congress further suggests that Steinbeck might not have meant to exclude Indians from the ranks of Tom's imaginary friends and adversaries; this document (presumably an early version since it identifies the protagonist both as "Paddy" and as "Tom") refers to a "wild Indian cry," which startles Tom out of his "circus dream" and alerts him to his Grandfather's approach.[16] This scene is substantially shorter in the film, and no Indian connotations remain to color Grandfather's piercing call. Shortly after his arrival, however, the old man compares the boy's plans for a "mouse hunt" in the haystack to the latter years of the Indian wars, when soldiers stooped to killing children and burning tepees.

More than Copland's other projects, *The Red Pony* tackles the complexities of westward expansion overtly, through Grandfather's reminiscences and Tom's reactions to them. Although Copland had disclaimed any "epic" pretensions in his letter to Irving and Verna Fine, both his score and Steinbeck's screenplay carry moderately epic overtones from the start. As the camera pans across the Californian landscape, a narrative voice-over situates the Tiflin ranch geographically and makes sure we are aware of regional history: "In central California many small ranches sit in the hollows of the skirts of the Coast Range Mountains. Some, the remnants of old and gradually disintegrating homesteads; some the remains of Spanish grants. To one of them in the foothills to the west of Salinas Valley, the dawn comes, as it comes to a thousand others."[17] Prefacing this narration, Copland's main title music features aggressive upward leaps, rhythmic unisons, and the brassy timbres of a fanfare. Perfect fourths and fifths in the melody and a strong harmonic emphasis on C within the ostensible framework of F major lend the score an open-air quality that makes its woodwind birdsong seem right at home.[18]

After this opening fanfare, however, Copland's background music becomes unobtrusive; instead our attention is arrested by the overloud crowing of roosters heralding the dawn. Other sounds from the natural world intrude on the pleasant background music. An owl hoots and we see a rabbit run for cover. The owl swoops down upon its prey (politely hidden from view), the rabbit screams, and we see the family dog react to its death cry. It is typical to see the dissonance between the rabbit's shriek and Copland's cheerful score as an illustration of Steinbeck's message about the interdependence of life and death. While this interpretation may be correct, the disjunction between the "live" sounds and the underscoring also raises questions about the function of Copland's music. The harsh sounds of the natural world are the more potent reflection of the violent "reality" unfolding before our eyes; we observe their effect on the animals. At these moments, the composed score seems somehow "unreal," something added, imagined, or remembered. What better way to symbolize this stance than that picture book on the Tiflins' front porch? It frames the events we are about to witness as often told or distantly remembered. This is not an unusual choice in the context of forties filmmaking, but it carries special meaning in a movie so desperately concerned with storytelling and recollection.

At the heart of *The Red Pony*'s engagement with storytelling are Grandfather's incessant reminiscences about his long-lost role on the front lines of westward expansion. All the adult characters find them irritating, and when Fred's bitter complaints about the garrulous old man are overheard, the tension among the dysfunctional Tiflins reaches its peak. After Fred's awkward exit, young Tom insists that he is always ready to listen to the old man's stories of the "Great Crossing" to the Pacific. At first, Grandfather remains unmoved, but he eventually opens up to his grandson in one of Hollywood's most remarkable reflections on Manifest Destiny:

> I tell those old stories, but they're not what I want to tell. I only know how I want people to feel when I tell them. It wasn't Indians that were important, nor adventures, nor even getting out here. It was a whole bunch of people made into one big crawling beast. And I was the head. It was westering and westering. Every man wanted something for himself, but the big beast that was all of them wanted only westering. I was the leader, but if I hadn't been there, someone else would have been the head. The thing had to have a head.[19]

Steinbeck abridged Grandfather's narrative from "Leader of the People" only slightly when writing his screenplay, leaving it open to the same charge that many critics leveled at the literary original: that the speech is merely propaganda for Steinbeck's so-called phalanx theory of human behavior, which holds that "a group is a living entity with desires, hungers, and strivings of its own."[20] Applying the "phalanx theory" to American pioneering calls attention to westward expansion's potential to unify across social or class lines. Yet for the Tiflin family, the repeated recounting of western history actually becomes a divisive force, bringing their divergent perspectives into sharp relief—differences between the impatient, cosmopolitan Fred and the ranch-born Alice, and the generational conflicts between Grandfather, young Tom, and the adult characters. Although westward expansion gave the Tiflins their ranch, the tensions involved in remembering it threaten to break up their home.

Perhaps this gulf between memory and experience explains why Grandfather's heroic narration seems in so many ways to fall flat. He speaks with melancholy fervor: "We carried life out here and set it down and planted it the way ants carry eggs, and I was the leader. The westering was big as God, and the slow steps that made the movement piled up and piled up until the continent was crossed. Then we come down to the sea, and it was done." But ten-year-old Tom is the only visible audience, and for him Grandfather's tales of adventure are precisely as real as his own fantasies about leading knights in shining armor or showing off the white horses of his circus dream. Though he may comprehend that Grandfather's glory days have passed away forever, he has a harder time accepting that no pioneering role remains for him:

> *Tom:* Maybe I could lead the people someday.
>
> *Grandfather:* No, there's no place to go. There's the ocean to stop you. And there's a line of old men along the shore hating the ocean because it stopped them.
>
> *Tom:* In boats I might, sir.

> *Grandfather:* No, Thomas, there's no place to go. Every place is taken. But that isn't
> the worst—no, that isn't the worst. Westering has died out of the
> people. Westering isn't a hunger any more. It's finished. Your father's
> right. It's all done.

Tom quickly scampers off to join Billy Buck in the barn, but listening to Grandfather's stories brings the boy closer to understanding his own place in the West.
As much as he might like to try, Tom cannot continue westward expansion's
legacy of conquest. With the Christlike proclamation "It's finished," Grandfather
has closed a chapter on western history, and when Tom tries to reopen the book,
it has become a children's story—"an impossible world of Indians and buffaloes,
a world that had ceased to be forever."[21]

An ambivalence about narration, a complicated perspective on the "progress"
of westward expansion, and a feeling of irretrievable nostalgia—remarkably, Copland manages to capture all these things in the music he wrote for "Grandfather's
Story." First, a chorale-like texture of strings, clarinets, and pensive English horn
plods with sentimental calm (example 51). Compared with other passages in the
film score, it is wrenchingly slow, without the jocular saunter of the "Walk to the
Bunkhouse" or the shimmer of "The Gift." Moreover, Copland's score must vie
with the old man's words and copious natural noises for our attention, making
the action of narration far more complicated on screen than it is in print. A
change in orchestral register marks the camera's move from the interior of the
Tiflin home to the bright sunlight of the front porch. The camera settles on
Grandfather in his rocking chair, stretching his tired hands and looking out toward the horizon. As soon as we begin to associate the poignant underscoring
with his bittersweet reflections, two hawks interrupt his reverie with harsh cries
as they fight over a moth. He looks up distracted, the camera follows his gaze,
and Tom, too, looks upward to witness one of the film's thematic life-and-death
encounters. By comparison, Grandfather's memories are distant indeed. Again
there is a palpable tension between the sounds we hear and the sounds that impact the characters in the film, making the underscoring less a mirror of their
emotions than a reminder of our own.

As the truly narrative portion of Grandfather's speech begins ("It wasn't the
Indians that were important . . ."), Copland responds with suitably narrative music (example 52). This passage is unusual in the context of the film, for it reflects
neither the characters' emotions nor the on-screen action. Instead, it depicts the
unrepeatable progress of westward expansion. The cluster chords of imagined
Indians and desolate landscapes gain shape and direction in a rhythmic ostinato
while muted trumpets evoke space in dissonant antiphony. Although the trumpets' music might be called a fanfare, it is a fanfare wholly denatured by its subdued tone color and clashing counterpoint. Even the underlying ostinato is dis-

EXAMPLE 51. *The Red Pony,* film suite, "Grandfather's Story," mm. 1–8 (London: Boosey & Hawkes, 1951)

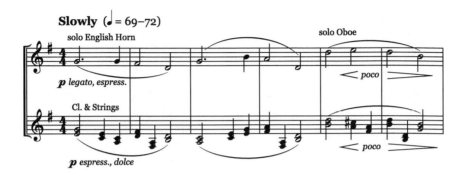

torted with the strings playing "at the frog" to achieve Copland's expressive (or antiexpressive) marking "thud like." Yet both ostinato and fanfare are nearly drowned out by twittering songbirds as Grandfather's narration nears its close, again allowing the natural world of the present to take precedence over the past.

Like Tom's "Dream March," Grandfather's westward processional gradually builds to a climax over its obsessive figuration. While we could see the boy's daydream vividly, no such Technicolor assistance attends the old man's memories. On the contrary, everything seems calculated to enhance the remoteness of a spectacle that we can neither see nor hope to experience. Though far closer in time and space than any knight in shining armor, the vision of Grandfather on his white horse marshaling the people is just as unattainable. When Grandfather speaks of times past, we are not allowed to forget that the story he tells is over—and has been over for some time: "Westering has died out of the people."

Grandfather's narrative is indeed a lonely one. In Steinbeck's and Copland's hands, it evokes an emptiness that can sound unsatisfying. Virgil Thomson seems to have felt this way, for he argued that this movement might be cut from the orchestral suite because it appeared "less intensely conceived" than the others.[22] But like the flatness of the western landscape, the old man's isolation bears the traces of many meanings. Although Grandfather is the sole representative of his generation in the movie, this need not have been the case. When Steinbeck excised

EXAMPLE 52. *The Red Pony,* film suite, "Grandfather's Story," mm. 29–46, woodwinds, trumpet, and strings

EXAMPLE 52 *(continued)*

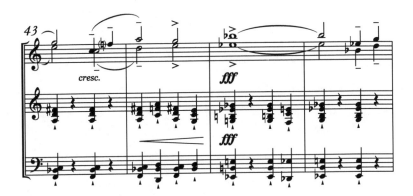

his third short story ("The Great Mountains") from the screenplay, he also lost the old Chicano laborer, Gitano, who returns, ghostlike, to the Tiflin ranch in order to die on the land where he was born. His absence is palpable. The disembodied narrator mentions Spanish land grants during the main title music, and Grandfather has instilled in the family a serious preoccupation with Indians. But apart from that, at least to the casual observer, *The Red Pony*'s West appears to be a white West.

Living as he does at the end of the frontier, Tom cannot cross the plains. He need not cross the Pacific. But in the "Walk to the Bunkhouse," he does make a crossing of his own, one that bears its own more modest associations with personal maturity and western history. After the atmospheric "Morning on the Ranch" music fades away, the first specifically action-oriented cue underscores young Tom and Billy on their way to retrieve a newspaper clipping that documents Billy's rodeo-riding days. According to Copland's program note for the suite, "Billy Buck 'was a fine hand with horses,' and [Tom's] admiration knew no bounds. This is a scene of the two pals on their walk to the bunkhouse." The horsemanship to which Tom aspires is already integral to Billy's character and to the jaunty musical language that accompanies him. The first four measures of the orchestral suite set up a jaunty rhythmic vamp based on the simplest of harmonic progressions (I, IV⁶, IV, V, I) and a regular alternation between 3/4 and 2/4.

As soon as this rhythmic vamp is in place, the violins enter with a sweetly meandering melody that Pollack has aptly called "bow-legged" (HP, 431). The falling contour of its single leisurely phrase gives it an air of relaxation that is reinforced by its utter disregard for the rhythmic precision of the accompaniment (example 53). Its second note stretches easily beyond the five beats of the first note, tumbling comfortably out of sync with the underlying two-bar unit; the subsequent string

EXAMPLE 53. *The Red Pony,* film suite, "Walk to the Bunkhouse," mm. 1–12

of half notes and quarter notes further disrupts the phrase structure suggested by Copland's bar lines and eventually causes a momentary hiccup in the regular pattern of the vamp. A picture of relaxed assuredness, Billy's melody could hardly be more different from Fred's anxious silence or formal speech.

As the scene reaches its close, Copland calls attention to another, more pointed difference between the two men: Fred's romantic repression is upstaged by Billy's more obvious sexuality. In the film, when Billy puts an end to Tom's questions about his pinups by swiftly shutting his trunk, gaps in the background music ensure that his thinly veiled spoken allusions to his romantic life can be clearly heard. In the orchestral suite, Copland preserves the space originally left for dialogue but fills it in with clarinet figuration. Though retaining the original phrase structure was surely convenient, the decision to replace the spoken dialogue with a cartoonish cascade for solo clarinet is a significant one. Grace notes, nonharmonic tones, and improvisatory flourishes give the impression that this particular clarinet has wandered in from a jazz band to make a guest appearance. Here, however, connotations of sexual freedom trump any urban associations. A few "nights on the town" are not enough to compromise Billy's rural status. His heterosexual prowess does not result in inconvenient progeny or the potentially emasculating responsibilities of domestic life. Like so many western heroes, he remains both sexually active and permanently unattached.

If the soundtrack for the "Walk to the Bunkhouse" suggests something about male sexuality in the West, it has even more to say about the "progress" of westward expansion. Though they traverse only the distance from breakfast table to bunkhouse, Billy and Tom together enact Manifest Destiny's characteristic conflation of the modern and the nostalgic, and at least some of its troubling erasure of ethnic diversity. Given Copland's prior experiences, the distinctive rhythmic and timbral profile of Billy Buck's barnyard walk has a genealogy bearing further investigation. Many scholars have noted that syncopation, layered textures, and jazz harmonies are unifying elements in Copland's oeuvre—evidence of his thorough absorption of African American materials or his lingering debt to Stravinsky. The 3+3+2+2 gait of the "Walk to the Bunkhouse" resembles the syncopation of Copland's Piano Concerto and his later Four Piano Blues (especially the third), and it reflects his understanding of jazz's rhythmic language as essentially additive.[23] It is not surprising to find syncopation in a western setting laden with roping, riding, and laid-back humor. But recognizing possible connections between African Americans and the West—links so often obscured by the absence of black characters in western Americana—makes audible a facet of westward expansion that American culture has been more than willing to ignore.

More precisely in tune with The Red Pony's California setting are the Hispanic elements of Billy Buck's ranch walk. Its asymmetrical meter and folkloric melodies for solo trumpet link it to traditional Mexican music, to the topoi of El Salón México, and to passages from Billy the Kid (examples 54a and 54b). El Salón México made no secret of its national origin. And in Billy the Kid, these musical elements were associated with the jarabe of the Mexican women visible on stage, dancing in a potent spectacle of interaction between races. In The Red Pony, such stylistic allusions serve a different purpose. Although they stop short of transforming the American ranch back into a Spanish "rancho," they solidify Billy's identification with the land and (perhaps inadvertently) with its changing meanings during western history. In this way, Billy's walk across the barnyard has a

EXAMPLE 54A. *The Red Pony,* film suite, "Walk to the Bunkhouse," mm. 24–33

EXAMPLE 54B. *Billy the Kid,* beginning of the *jarabe*

more accurate soundtrack for Manifest Destiny than Grandfather's recollections of the Great Crossing to the Pacific.

While Billy the Kid was a great favorite with the Mexican girls, Billy Buck has no such colorful associates to complicate our perception of the region. Instead it is young Tom who shares Billy's barnyard migration. He is practically following in Billy's footsteps, confirming that the future of the western ranch lies in his innocent hands—whatever its complicated past might have been. This excerpt might be said to enact western history—by placing Latin and African American elements in the service of the white ranchman and his metaphorical descendants. But whether anyone hears this history, whether these elements signify, depends on us. Within the world of the movie, circumstances conspire to make such a historically conscious reading difficult. When Grandfather speaks explicitly about "westering," multicultural allusions are absent, filtered out by his fading memory, silenced by official history, or factored out of social theorizing. ("It wasn't the Indians that were important.") When Tom imagines the West, he envisions an "impossible world" not a historical one—a "heroic time" inhabited by a "race of giants." Surely the real West must lie somewhere between the child's play and the old man's remembering. But when Fred and Billy are on screen, it is the implied conflict between them that comes to the fore: Billy's expertise with horses, his closeness to Tom, and his active sexuality—all these things call attention to Fred's inadequacies, not to regional history. In *The Red Pony*, as in so much of western Americana, conflicts between generations and different types of masculinity overshadow any interracial interaction more complicated than the stereotyped play of cowboys and Indians.

EAST MEETS WEST

Though *The Red Pony* engages most directly with the idea of westward expansion, Copland's other western works also rehearse the theme of conquest in subtle and unsubtle ways. With the "Saga of the Prairies," Copland launched his own westward migration as if by accident. Looking backward, he transferred the optimism of contemporary leftist politics onto a mythic vision of pioneering that had captured his listeners' imagination. In *Billy the Kid*, westward expansion became an abstract and alienating process, which united its participants but rendered them mechanical and grotesque. Even *Rodeo* made a statement about power relations in the West, though here the stakes of its "conquest" are personal rather than national. When the Cowgirl yields to her man, she fulfills a social contract that remains central to western mythology.

The Red Pony picks up on these themes in ways that reflect profound changes both in the political and cultural life of the United States and within the narrower scope of Copland's life and works. What sounded like progress in 1937 had become lonely nostalgia in 1947. The isolation that set the outlaw Billy the Kid apart from civilized society has penetrated to the very core of the Tiflin family, separating husband from wife and leaving the most engaging character, Billy Buck, with no family of his own. There is a world of distance between *Rodeo*'s cheerful social dancing and the uncomfortable silences and fractured fantasies of *The Red Pony*.

By choice or chance, *The Red Pony* contains Copland's last musical thoughts on the West. As he worked on the film score, looking out on the ranch that served as a backdrop for *Of Mice and Men*, he might have taken a moment to ponder the turn his career had taken. It meant something quite different for him to write a western score in the late 1940s than it had a decade earlier. In 1939, Steinbeck and Milestone were taking a chance on Copland's western credentials; when they were preparing *The Red Pony*, after the resounding successes of *Rodeo* and *Appalachian Spring*, Copland had become the logical man for the job.

Much has been made of Copland's later ambivalence about his populist scores—their fraught reception and his supposedly wavering faith in their artistic and social worth. Yet given the degree of critical angst about style and audience exhibited by most of his contemporaries, Copland's confidence in his stylistic flexibility seems all the more remarkable. Rather than endorsing his colleagues' sometimes awkward attempts to view his diverse oeuvre as the product of a single-minded artistic sincerity, Copland hit upon a solution that was more radical and, in a quiet way, more courageous. Recall his admission of the audience's role in the formation of his so-called simple style: "It made no sense to ignore them and to continue writing as if they did not exist. I felt that it was worth the effort to see if I couldn't say what I had to say in the simplest possible terms."[24] Building on this candid confession, Arthur Berger took the argument a step further, noting that Copland's individual style "has undergone a series of striking transformations, partly determined by a rare critical faculty and partly by a sense of responsibility to musical audiences. Copland is not of the line of artists who, after following a dubious creative urge, justify their course by saying merely that they 'felt that way.' "[25]

By departing from the rhetoric of sincerity, naturalness, and isolated inspiration (all code words for different kinds of authenticity), Copland allowed himself to be a man of many conversions—from modernism to populism, from urban to rural, from East to West and back again. The imagery of the American West provided a suitable sacrament for Copland's cultural conversions, for it has always been a favorite backdrop for journeys of self-discovery. Like the cowgirl heroine of *Rodeo* or the outlaw Billy the Kid, Copland found himself in the West. But unlike them, he had to travel to get there.

Conclusion

On the Trail

Along his path from orient to occident, Aaron Copland shed old identities and invented new ones. It is this symbolic flexibility that best identifies him as a hero of the mythic West we still know today—a world in which aspirations toward authenticity so often dissolve into souvenirs and simulacra. Mediated by the History Channel and Hollywood, by education and entertainment, by travel and tourism and television, the souvenirs of westward expansion are all around us, and the simulacra too: in the rhetoric of our politicians and the attractions at our theme parks, in our highway system and on our restaurant menus, in the names of our athletic teams and our sports utility vehicles, and in our visions of conservation and multiculturalism.

The cultural mythology that has consistently linked the West with opportunities, both lost and found, takes its particular force from the land and its resources, whether those resources are understood as natural or human, economic or spiritual. More important still, the mythology of the West takes the abstract telos of opportunity and infuses it with both motion and direction. As a replication or "false copy," the simulacrum points toward a nonexistent original, carrying with it a sense of impossible distance to be traversed. Even the souvenir, which might be supposed to fix our attention on some particular time and place, gains its true significance only through movement and migration—only as a remembrance of things passed.

Motion and direction. How else to explain the trails and travelers that have figured in every chapter of this book? Arthur Farwell gave us the unnamed traveler of his *Domain of Hurakan,* the seeker of "The Old Man's Love Song," and above all the Seer who forges a path to the divine in *The March of Man.* Charles

Wakefield Cadman began his western career with an evocation of displacement ("From the Land of the Sky Blue Water") and continued to commemorate travel in all its forms: *The Sunset Trail*, "The New Trail," *The Golden Trail*, and *The Pageant of Colorado* with its epochs—"The Coming of the Runner," "The Coming of the Horse," and "The Coming of the Wheel." We have seen how the American pastoral featured trailblazers whose pioneering energy could not be contained in the Arcadian pastoral frame—Sandburg's farmer-soldiers, the caravan of dusty Okie autos in *The Plow That Broke the Plains*, and Ernst Bacon's frontier family reunited but ultimately fractured by planes, trains, and automobiles. Roy Harris represented both the tragedies and triumphs of Manifest Destiny, bidding farewell to his trudging pioneer parents and celebrating the gunshot conquest of the Cimarron. The frontier processional of *Billy the Kid* unfolds as a chapter of western history that pits the colorful outlaw against a motley but mechanical crowd. Yet, echoing Steinbeck, Copland's *Red Pony* also reminds us that the Great Crossings of the West are largely past, codified in stories for recollection and reenactment.

Given this extensive travelogue, it is hardly surprising that the most famous orchestral evocation of the West bears the title "On the Trail." This central movement of Ferde Grofé's *Grand Canyon Suite*, premiered by Paul Whiteman in 1931, has for generations represented the quintessential western soundtrack. In typical occidental fashion, its popularity springs from at least three sources: the colorful and pictorial surface of the score, the "real-life" connotations of its ersatz cowboy song; and the influence of new media and clever marketing. Over the course of two decades, it reached millions of radio listeners courtesy of the Philip Morris Company's tobacco advertisements (perhaps spurring a later cigarette spokesman and rodeo hero, the Marlboro Man, into action).

More than any other portion of Grofé's suite, "On the Trail" celebrates the human presence in the West.[1] The other movements trace a day in the life of the West, from "Sunrise" and the broad light of day shimmering on the "Painted Desert," to "Sunset," and a dramatic nighttime "Cloudburst." As a whole, then, the suite rehearses the natural cyclical passage of time in ways that we have encountered in other western scores: in the pioneer's diurnal routine, the cowboy's weary day and sleepless night-herding songs, and above all in the logic of racial inevitability that shaped Indianism, freighting it with the sunset ideology of "the vanishing race" or the sunrise impulse meant to mark the dawning of a New Age. While the basic facts of celestial motion clearly link the western horizon with twilight hours and the closing of a day or an era, the tenets of terrestrial history have more often focused on the West as a site of renewal.

In Grofé's suite, "Sunrise" and "Sunset" both give way to companion movements devoted to landscape painting in the most vivid of orchestral traditions: the flat, hot, crystalline noontime desert, and the sudden thunderstorm. Instead of marking the liminal moments of dawn and twilight, these picture postcard movements capture the extremes of light and dark, weather and topography in a pattern entirely typical of western works both before and since. Recall the "Crags" of Farwell's *Mountain Song*, the melodramatic storm of Cadman's *Daoma*, the "Open Prairie" of *Billy the Kid*, or the silent desert reverie of *Rodeo*'s Cowgirl. In 1938, Grofé tallied his own "recollections of grandiose Nature" in an expansive program note called "Story of the *Grand Canyon Suite*": "Vast areas of eloquent solitudes, towering heights, silent deserts, rushing rivers, wild animal life; of health-giving ozone, magic dawns and resplendent sunsets, silvery moonshine, iridescent colorings of skies and rocks; and before all else, of a stock of men and women who breathe deeply and freely, live bravely and picturesquely, speak their minds in simplicity and truth, and altogether represent as typical and fine a human flowering as this land of ours has inherited from its pioneer days."[2] By including the "human flowering" of pioneer stock in his catalog of the West's natural resources, Grofé recaps more than a century of rhetoric about the evolution of an American "type" based on the mingling of racial and botanical metaphor. He also goes some way toward explaining why, in the decades after its premiere, "On the Trail" became, as he put it, "the 'best-seller' of the series."

"On the Trail" places man and animal front and center. More specifically, it shows burro and cowboy in motion, jostling down their dusty way. Presumably, they are descending to the canyon floor, but their destination seems less important than their iconic gait: a jaunty common-time clip-clop, achieved by using coconut shells "muffled on leather" and set into relief by the prevailing 6/8 meter of the melody associated with the braying burro.[3] Like the reeling cowboys that Rosenfeld associated with Roy Harris or the multiethnic clockwork of *The Red Pony*'s "Walk to the Bunkhouse," Grofé's signature rhythm is neither a dance nor a straightforward march. Lively but mechanical (the composer claimed to have modeled it on the off-kilter pile drivers that he heard at a Chicago construction site), it carries the obstinate momentum of the Indian double drumbeat without the menace.

More important still, Grofé introduces his cowboy protagonist onto a musical stage just as aptly framed as the parlor where Mrs. Everton hosts Shanewis or the self-referential "Hoedown" dancing of *Rodeo*. A sweeping "hee-haw" from the ensemble alerts us to the burro, but what comes next is neither onomatopoetic nor folksy. It is a violin cadenza. Though obviously an elaboration of the disjunct "burro theme," the gesture is utterly incongruous unless understood as a celebration of performance itself or perhaps a moment of suspense before some musicodramatic arrival. Indeed a new character enters right on cue: the cowboy. Supported (appropriately enough) on the back of the burro's characteristic clip-clop, a mellow brass melody typically identified as a "cowboy song" enters in nonchalant counterpoint (example 55).

EXAMPLE 55. Grofé, *Grand Canyon Suite*, "On the Trail," mm. 78–88 (New York: Robbins Music, 1932)

This is not the last we will hear of its leisurely unfolding. As musicologist Brooks Toliver has observed, the *Grand Canyon Suite* is full of reflexive moments—music-about-music. In addition to transforming the burro melody into a violin cadenza, Grofé dresses both donkey and cowboy in new costumes. First, when the traveling companions stop to rest at "a lone cabin," they encounter, of all things, "a music box" programmed to play the burro theme (a close cousin of the *Red Pony* pic-

EXAMPLE 55 *(continued)*

ture book on the Tiflins' cinematic front porch). Impersonated by the celesta, its magical timbres suggest a wistful reminiscence related to Thomson's ironic doxology, Harris's cowboy recollections, or the fatal nostalgia of *Billy the Kid*. Second, as Toliver points out, the cowboy melody is transfigured in Grofé's "Cloudburst," opening the movement with sentimental pathos but ending in a blaze of glory that puts even the sunset to shame.[4]

When Farwell had visited the Grand Canyon in December 1903, he despaired of finding a musical language that could capture this "wonderworld." Whether out of reflexive optimism or genuine foresight, he nevertheless heard in his mind's ear "the unwritten symphonies of the ages past and the ages to come." Presumably Farwell and Grofé would have agreed that the "ages past" belonged to the Indian. Although the *Grand Canyon Suite* is pointedly free of Native American references, Grofé himself recalled how he had "hobnobbed with Indians" during his time as a gold prospector.[5] Hearing the music of "ages to come" is a trickier business, and yet all the composers in this book believed that they could do it. They had a claim both on the "music of the future" and on "the music of the people"— whether this meant community pageants, folk song symphonies, or film scores. In this respect they played the role of trailblazing pioneers, the middle term omitted from the child's play of cowboys and Indians.

This artistic pioneer holds a precarious position, needing to be both ahead of the current time and a voice arising from within the crowd, emblematic not of timeless tribal identity or gunslinging individualism, but of something in between, defined by relationship to community and sense of direction. Walt Whitman called upon such artists to "take up the task eternal" as the "elder races . . . droop and end their lesson, wearied over there beyond the seas":

> Minstrels latent on the prairies!
> (Shrouded bards of other lands, you may rest, you have done your work,)
> Soon I hear you coming warbling, soon you rise and tramp amid us,
> Pioneers! O pioneers![6]

Whether it came courtesy of Whitman or Whiteman, the invitation to imagine the American West produced music that can barely contain the frontier figures that populate its colorful landscapes. For all their descriptive power, depictions of sunrise or sunset, desert or storm, mountain or prairie cannot situate themselves with any certainty in the West. Perhaps we may someday develop a musical language capable of speaking for rocks and plants—although this seems unlikely given that music can best describe sound and motion. In the meantime, the most specific musical mile-markers will refer to people. This musical truth in fact reflects one of the defining ironies of western history and its representations of place. Patricia Limerick observes that, in popular parlance, the West has always represented freedom, openness, and emptiness: "The theory was the same: the West is remote and vast; its isolation and distance will release us from conflict; this is where we can get away from each other. But the workings of history carried an opposite lesson. The West was not where we escaped each other, but where we all met."[7] The varied figures in this book were shaped as they met and moved along frontiers of history, mythology, geography, ethnicity, and style. On these trails all are in transit. All are transformed.

INTRODUCTION

1. Cited in Charles Hamm, "Dvořák, Nationalism, Myth, and Racism," in *Rethinking Dvořák: Views from Five Countries*, ed. David Beveridge (Oxford, UK: Clarendon Press, 1996), 278.

2. Joseph Horowitz, "Dvořák and Boston," *American Music* 19, no. 1 (2001): 3–17; and Adrienne Fried Block, "Boston Talks Back to Dvořák," *I. S. A. M. Newsletter* 18, no. 2 (May 1989): 10, 11, 15.

3. For a detailed exposition of Dvořák's reliance on Longfellow, see Michael Beckerman, "Dvořák's 'New World' Largo and *The Song of Hiawatha*," *19th-Century Music* 16, no. 1 (1992): 35–48; and Beckerman, "The Dance of Pau-Puk-Keewis, the Song of Chibiabos, and the Story of Iagoo: Reflections on Dvořák's 'New World' Scherzo," in *Dvořák in America, 1892–1895*, ed. John C. Tibbetts (Portland, OR: Amadeus Press, 1993), 210–27.

4. Richard Crawford, "Dvořák and the Historiography of American Music," in Beveridge, *Rethinking Dvořák*, 257–63.

5. James Huneker, "Dvořák's New Symphony: The Second Philharmonic Concert," *Musical Courier*, 20 December 1893; reprinted in *Dvořák and His World*, ed. Michael Beckerman (Princeton, NJ: Princeton University Press, 1993), 160.

6. William J. Henderson, review in the *New York Times*, 17 December 1893; cited in Horowitz, "Dvořák and Boston," 6–7.

7. William Apthorp, review in the *Boston Evening Transcript*, 1 January 1894; cited in Horowitz, "Dvořák and Boston," 8.

8. Philip Hale, 1910 Program Notes, cited in Horowitz, "Dvořák and Boston," 16.

9. Block, "Boston Talks Back," 10.

10. Dvořák, "Music in America," *Harper's New Monthly Magazine* 90, no. 537 (February 1895), 433; reprinted in Tibbetts, *Dvořák in America*, 377.

11. See Michael Beckerman, "In Search of Czechness in Music," *19th-Century Music* 10 (1986–87): 61–73.

12. Michael Beckerman, "The Master's Little Joke: Antonín Dvořák and the Mask of Nation," in *Dvořák and His World*, 134–54. See also John Clapham, "Dvořák and the American Indian," in Tibbetts, *Dvořák in America*, 113–22.

13. Block, "Boston Talks Back," 11; and Block, "Dvořák, Beach, and American Music," in *A Celebration of American Music: Words and Music in Honor of W. Wiley Hitchcock*, ed. Richard Crawford, R. Allen Lott, and Carol Oja (Ann Arbor: University of Michigan Press, 1990), 260. See also Block, *Amy Beach, Passionate Victorian: The Life and Work of an American Composer, 1867–1944* (New York: Oxford University Press, 1998).

14. Block, "Dvořák, Beach," 260. For explication of the changing status of various immigrant groups vis-à-vis whiteness, see Matthew Frye Jacobson, *Whiteness of a Different Color: European Immigrants and the Alchemy of Race* (Cambridge, MA: Harvard University Press, 1998).

15. Cited in Lawrence Gilman, *Edward MacDowell* (New York: John Lane, 1908), 84.

16. Frederick Jackson Turner, "The Significance of the Frontier in American History," reprinted in Martin Ridge, ed., *Frederick Jackson Turner: Wisconsin's Historian of the Frontier* (Madison: State Historical Society of Wisconsin, 1986), 26.

17. Ibid., 27–28.

18. Kerwin Lee Klein, *Frontiers of Historical Imagination: Narrating the European Conquest of Native America, 1890–1990* (Berkeley and Los Angeles: University of California Press, 1997), 129.

19. Ibid., 144–45.

20. Turner, "The Significance of History" (1891), reprinted in Ridge, *Frederick Jackson Turner*, 53.

21. Turner, "Significance of the Frontier," 27.

22. Ibid., 47.

23. Klein, *Frontiers of Historical Imagination*, 7.

24. Henry Krehbiel, "Dr. Dvořák's Reception," *New York Daily Tribune*, October 1892; reprinted in Beckerman, *Dvořák and His World*, 157–59.

25. Richard Taruskin, "'Nationalism': Colonialism in Disguise?" *New York Times*, Arts and Leisure, 22 August 1993; reprinted in Taruskin, *The Danger of Music and Other Anti-Utopian Essays* (Berkeley and Los Angeles: University of California Press, 2009), 25–29.

26. Louis Warren, *Buffalo Bill's America: William Cody and the Wild West Show* (New York: Alfred A. Knopf, 2005); Richard Slotkin, "The White City and the Wild West," chapter 2 of Slotkin, *Gunfighter Nation: The Myth of the Frontier in Twentieth-Century America* (Norman: University of Oklahoma Press, 1992), 63–87; Frederick Nolan, *The Wild West: History, Myth, and the Making of America* (London: Arcturus, 2003); and especially Richard White, "When Frederick Jackson Turner and Buffalo Bill Cody Both Played Chicago in 1893," in *Frontier and Region: Essays in Honor of Martin Ridge*, ed. Robert C. Ritchie and Paul Andrew Hutton (Albuquerque: University of New Mexico Press, 1997), 201–12.

27. See, among others, Robert Rydell, *All the World's a Fair: Visions of Empire and American International Expositions, 1876–1916* (Chicago: University of Chicago Press,

1984); and Robert Muccigrosso, *Celebrating the New World: Chicago's Columbian Exposition of 1893* (Chicago: Ivan R. Dee, 1993).

28. Introduction to the Wild West program of 1899, as cited in Michael Lee Masterson, "Sounds of the Frontier: Music in Buffalo Bill's Wild West Shows" (PhD diss., University of New Mexico, 1990), 56.

29. Slotkin, *Gunfighter Nation*, 87.

30. On the intertwining of the Buffalo Bill of the dime novel and the real William Cody, see Henry Nash Smith, *Virgin Land: The American West as Symbol and Myth* (New York: Vintage Books, 1957), 113–25.

31. On Buffalo Bill's veracity, see Warren, *Buffalo Bill's America;* and Perry Meisel, *The Cowboy and the Dandy: Crossing Over from Romanticism to Rock and Roll* (New York: Oxford University Press, 1999), 42–43.

32. Warren, *Buffalo Bill's America*, 72–73.

33. Ibid., 264.

34. Slotkin, *Gunfighter Nation*, 278–343. See also Jacobson, *Whiteness of a Different Color.*

35. Warren, *Buffalo Bill's America*, 270, 97. Despite similarities between Buffalo Bill's ideology of racial progress and Turner's frontier line, Warren is right to link Cody's views to the older strain of racial theorizing known as Anglo-Saxonism: "Anglo-Saxonism was, of course, a variant of Aryanism, which was itself a theory of westering race history. . . . In all these myths, the racial energies of white people aged in the East and were renewed through bloody encounters with barbarians in the West." Warren, *Buffalo Bill's America*, 316–17. See also Reginald Horsman, *Race and Manifest Destiny: The Origins of American Racial Anglo-Saxonism* (Cambridge, MA: Harvard University Press, 1981).

36. Warren, *Buffalo Bill's America*, 332, 357.

37. Slotkin, *Gunfighter Nation*, 81–82.

38. Ibid., 83.

39. See, for example William T. Hagan, *Theodore Roosevelt and Six Friends of the Indian* (Norman: University of Oklahoma Press, 1997); G. Edward White, *The Eastern Establishment and the Western Experience: The West of Frederic Remington, Theodore Roosevelt, and Owen Wister* (Austin: University of Texas Press, 1989). Elizabeth Bergman Crist discusses Roosevelt's attitudes toward the West in *Music for the Common Man: Aaron Copland during the Depression and War* (New York: Oxford University Press, 2005), 114–16.

40. Slotkin, *Gunfighter Nation*, 86.

41. See, among others, Robert F. Berkhofer, *The White Man's Indian: Images of the American Indian from Columbus to the Present* (New York: Alfred A. Knopf, 1978); Philip J. Deloria, *Playing Indian* (New Haven, CT, and London: Yale University Press, 1998); and Deloria, *Indians in Unexpected Places* (Lawrence: University Press of Kansas, 2004).

42. Recent scholars have confirmed that the labels *Native American* and *Indian* each carry traces of colonialism. *Indian* bears witness to the prejudices of the age of discovery, and *Native American* not only elides human beings with flora and fauna but also inscribes the assumptions of an externally imposed multiculturalism. Nonetheless, for lack of a better alternative, I will use the two terms more or less interchangeably.

43. For a brief treatment of these two figures, see my article "'In the Glory of the Sunset': Arthur Farwell, Charles Wakefield Cadman, and Indianism in American Music," *repercussions* 5, nos. 1–2 (1996): 124–83.

44. Throughout this book, I use the terms *cosmopolitan* and *provincial* in the sense outlined by Richard Crawford in *The American Musical Landscape* (Berkeley and Los Angeles: University of California Press, 1993).

45. Amid the vast literature on the topic, a good place to begin is Edward Said, *Orientalism* (New York: Pantheon Books, 1978). Of special interest here is that early twentieth-century writers frequently identified Native American tribes as "oriental" immigrants. See Klein, *Frontiers of Historical Imagination*, 143–44.

46. Michael Rogin, *Blackface, White Noise: Jewish Immigrants in the Hollywood Melting Pot* (Berkeley and Los Angeles: University of California Press, 1998), 47.

1. THE WA-WAN AND THE WEST

1. *California: A Masque of Music* (typescript), Arthur Farwell Collection, Sibley Library, Eastman School of Music, Box 24, Folder 8 (hereafter cited as AFC, 24/8). The Farwell family allowed copyright on the materials in this collection to expire in 2003; I am extremely grateful to them for their generosity in preserving and disseminating his work.

2. *California*, AFC, 24/8.

3. "Note by Arthur Farwell," *Spanish Songs of Old California* (1923), published by Charles F. Lummis.

4. *California*, AFC, 24/8.

5. Arthur Farwell, *"Wanderjahre of a Revolutionist" and Other Essays on American Music*, ed. Thomas Stoner (Rochester, NY: University of Rochester Press, 1995), 90–91 (hereafter cited as WJ).

6. Farwell, "A Letter to American Composers," 1903; cited in Gilbert Chase's introductory essay, "The Wa-Wan Press: A Chapter in American Enterprise," in *The Wa-Wan Press, 1901–11*, ed. Vera Brodsky Lawrence (New York: Arno Press, 1970), ix–xix.

7. Gilman, "Some American Music," *Harper's Weekly*, 7 March 1903. John Tasker Howard echoed Gilman in 1931, ascribing credit to the press for the "awakening of American interest in the folk-song on our soil." Howard, *Our American Music* (New York: Thomas Y. Crowell, 1931), 441–42.

8. From 1901 to 1906, issues appeared twice quarterly; 1907 saw a brief increase to a monthly schedule coupled with a determination to take a more populist tone. After this, the publication schedule was erratic.

9. Edward Waters, "The Wa-Wan Press: An Adventure in Musical Idealism," in *A Birthday Offering to C[arl] E[ngel]*, ed. Gustave Reese (New York: G. Schirmer, 1943), 219; WJ, 89.

10. Farwell, "Introduction," *The Wa-Wan Press* 3, no. 19 (1904) (hereafter cited as Wa-Wan, 3/19); reprinted in *The Wa-Wan Press, 1901–11*, ed. Lawrence (hereafter cited as WWP), 2:153; WJ, 88.

11. Farwell, "Letter to American Composers," xvii–xix. See also Farwell, "National Work vs. Nationalism," *The New Music Review* (July 1909): 432: "Let me affirm and reiterate that I am not working for an obvious nationalism in music."

12. *Wa-Wan*, 1/7 (1902); WWP, 1:127.

13. *Wa-Wan*, 2/15 (1903); WWP, 2: 64–65.

14. Farwell, "The Struggle Toward a National Music," *North American Review* 186 (1907): 567, 569.

15. *Wa-Wan*, 2/15 (1903); WWP, 2:67.

16. *Wa-Wan*, 2/15 (1903); WWP, 2:66.

17. Farwell, "An Affirmation of American Music," *Musical World* (January 1903): 11; reprinted in Gilbert Chase, ed., *The American Composer Speaks* ([Baton Rouge]: Louisiana State University Press, 1966), 88–93.

18. Evelyn Davis Culbertson, *He Heard America Singing: Arthur Farwell, Composer and Crusading Music Educator* (Metuchen, NJ: Scarecrow Press, 1992), 13–14 (hereafter cited as EDC).

19. Alice Fletcher, preface to *Indian Story and Song from North America* (Boston: Smalls Maynard and Company, 1900), vii–ix.

20. For more information on Fletcher, see Joan Mark, *A Stranger in Her Native Land* (Lincoln and London: University of Nebraska Press, 1988). Fillmore's work is discussed in James McNutt, "John Comfort Fillmore: A Student of Indian Music Reconsidered," *American Music* 2, no.1 (1984): 61–70.

21. Farwell, "Aspects of Indian Music," *Southern Workman* 31 (1902): 212. See also WJ, 77; and *Wa-Wan*, 1/2 (1901); WWP, 1:23–30.

22. John Comfort Fillmore, *The Harmonic Structure of Indian Music* (New York: G. Putnam's Sons, 1899).

23. *Wa-Wan*, 1/2 (1901); WWP, 1:23–30.

24. Farwell, "Aspects of Indian Music," 216.

25. *Wa-Wan*, 3/20 (1904); WWP, 2:154.

26. *Wa-Wan*, 1/4 (1902); WWP, 1:76.

27. According to the *Seattle Post Intelligencer*, 2 February 1904, "From the Press": "The original Indian melody is supported with another melody which gives a broad expression of day." A neatly handwritten copy appears in AFC, 31/6, labeled "Otoe Tribe" but with no text underlay.

28. *Wa-Wan*, ¼ (1902); WWP, 1:77.

29. *Wa-Wan*, 2/10 (1902); WWP, 1:182.

30. Fletcher and Gilman as quoted in EDC, 371, 372.

31. *Musical Courier*, 24 January 1904; cited in EDC, 370. Benjamin Lambord praised the orchestral "Hurakan" for its "great impressiveness and brilliant color" in Arthur Farwell and W. Dermot Darby, eds., *Music in America*, vol. 4 of *The Art of Music*, ed. Daniel Gregory Mason (New York: National Society of Music, 1915), 411.

32. AFC, 23/15.

33. See Fletcher, *Indian Story and Song*, 70–71.

34. *Wa-Wan*, 3/19 (1904); WWP, 2:151.

35. *Wa-Wan*, 2/12 (1903); WWP, 2:18, 20.

36. *Wa-Wan*, 1/7 (1902); WWP, 1:128.

37. Farwell, "Pioneering for American Music," *Modern Music* 12 (1935): 119.

38. WJ, 90–91. The "Wa-Wan" rubric had its detractors from the beginning, but Farwell felt that "the moment demanded a striking and curiosity-provoking title." Farwell, "Pioneering for American Music," 118.

39. *Wa-Wan*, 4/25 (1905); WWP, 3:2.

40. *Wa-Wan*, 3/17 (1904); WWP, 2:105.

41. *Wa-Wan*, 3/17 (1904); WWP, 2:105–6.

42. A fifth trip was planned for the summer of 1907, at which point Farwell did travel as far west as Evanston, Illinois, but illness prevented him from venturing farther. The publicity for the fourth "western tour" advertised a "TOUR TO CALIFORNIA next summer 1907." AFC Scrapbook.

43. "Music for Americans. Arthur Farwell Believes Indian Themes Offer Material," unsigned article from a Portland newspaper, January 1904, clipping from the AFC Scrapbook.

44. AFC Scrapbook.

45. Brochure titled "Western Tour, October 1903–February 1904." AFC Scrapbook.

46. For an excellent discussion of Farwell's and Loomis's lecture-recitals, see Michael Pisani, *Imagining Native America in Music* (New Haven, CT, and London: Yale University Press, 2005), 177–80.

47. Pisani, *Imagining Native America*, 364.

48. AFC, 39/29; reprinted in EDC, 372.

49. Cadman's brochure is preserved in the AFC Scrapbook, as are a variety of programs and reviews of other Indianist concerts and lecture-recitals.

50. Cadman to La Flesche, 10 February 1909; cited in Harry D. Perison, "Charles Wakefield Cadman: His Life and Works" (PhD diss., Eastman School of Music, University of Rochester, 1978), 83–84.

51. *Wa-Wan*, 2/12 (1903); WWP, 2:18.

52. *Wa-Wan*, 1/4 (1902); WWP, 1:76–77. *Wa-Wan*, 3/17 (1904); WWP, 2:106.

53. Pisani, *Imagining Native America*, 7.

54. *Wa-Wan*, 1/7 (1902); WWP, 1:128.

55. Publicity brochure for "Two Lecture Recitals. II. The Wa-Wan Ceremony of the Omahas." Loose insert to AFC Scrapbook.

56. Ibid.

57. Alice Fletcher, *Study of Omaha Indian Music*, published in the Archaeological and Ethnological Papers of Harvard's Peabody Museum, 1893.

58. See Pisani, *Imagining Native America*, 179, 266, 278.

59. Edgar Lee Kirk, "Toward American Music: A Study of the Life and Music of Arthur George Farwell" (PhD diss., Eastman School of Music, University of Rochester, 1958), 201.

60. *Wa-Wan*, 5/37 (1906); WWP, 3:229.

61. Ibid.

62. "Indian Melody Starts New Cult—Art Society, Charmed by Music of the Tepees, Favors Original Song—Science Corners Tunes," *Pittsburgh Gazette*, April 1905. AFC Scrapbook.

63. Stoner clarifies this matter in WJ, 123. The other war dance (in compound meter with a key signature of C major) was conceived slightly later, in 1905, but it is now simply called "Navajo War Dance." It was published in the Wa-Wan Press (vol. 4, no. 28) as part of the collection *From Mesa and Plain,* before being revised for republication by G. Schirmer in 1912. My analysis of "Navajo War Dance no. 2" is based on John Kirkpatrick's 1947 edition (Music Press).

64. The provenance of the original Navajo material is uncertain. Farwell justified his use of parallel fourths by stating that "I have heard the Navajos sing this dance in 4ths" (EDC, 384), and if this is the case, then he must have either witnessed a live performance or listened to a wax cylinder in Lummis's or Fletcher's collections.

65. Lambord in Farwell and Darby, *Music in America,* 4:412.

66. David Ewen, *American Composers Today* (New York: H. W. Wilson, 1949), 92.

67. Farwell to Arnold Schwab, 3 February 1951; cited in EDC, 393.

68. *Three Indian Songs* was published by G. Schirmer in 1912; EDC suggests a publication date of 1908, but I have not found supporting evidence for this.

69. Farwell made choral arrangements of "The Old Man's Love Song" and "Song of the Ghost Dance" for the *Laurel Songbook* in 1901. His first four choruses were intended for conductor John Finley Williamson at Westminster Choir College and were published in 1937. Two others were stymied by disagreements between Farwell and Carl Fischer, and they remain unpublished. See EDC, 387–91.

70. Arthur Farwell to Sara Farwell, 5 May 1946; cited in EDC, 390.

71. Fletcher, *The Hako: A Pawnee Ceremony* (1904); reprinted as *The Hako: Song, Pipe, and Unity in a Pawnee Calumet Ceremony* (Lincoln and London: University of Nebraska Press, 1996), 20; see also Helen Myers's introduction to *The Hako* (reprint edition), 6–7.

72. Farwell to Arthur Cohn, 17 October 1935, AFC, 35/30.

73. Ibid.

74. Fletcher, *The Hako,* 101–2. Ron Erickson, preface to *The Hako* (San Francisco: Erickson Editions, 1997). See also EDC, 377–82.

75. *Wa-Wan,* 5/37 (1906); WWP, 3:226.

2. WESTERN DEMOCRACY, WESTERN LANDSCAPES, WESTERN MUSIC

1. Charles Lummis, "New Mexican Folk-Songs," *Cosmopolitan,* October 1892, 720. John Koegel, "Mexican-American Music in Nineteenth-Century Southern California: The Lummis Wax Cylinder Collection at the Southwest Museum, Los Angeles," PhD diss., Claremont Graduate School, 1994.

2. Lummis lived at Isleta Pueblo from 1888 to 1892, recuperating from a paralytic stroke brought on by overwork. This was some three and a half years after his "Tramp Across the Continent," a cross-country walk from Ohio to Los Angeles, during which he sent dispatches to newspapers back East.

3. Martin Padget, "Travel, Exoticism, and the Writing of Region: Charles Fletcher Lummis and the 'Creation' of the Southwest," *Journal of the Southwest* 37, no. 3 (1995): 431–32.

4. Lummis, "Catching Our Archaeology Alive," *Out West* 22, no. 1 (January 1905): 35–47.

5. After an initial rebuff, Farwell met with the president of the American Archaeological Institute, Thomas Day Seymour, a professor of classics at Yale. Lummis approved, writing to Farwell that although Seymour was an "Easterner," he could still be "converted" to their cause. Lummis to Farwell, 16 May 1904, AFC, 39/60.

6. "Boston Man to Help the Archaeological Society." AFC Scrapbook. Lummis, by contrast, described Farwell's "transliteration" work as "most difficult, and wholly beyond the average trained musician who has not had this specific experience." Lummis, "Catching Our Archaeology Alive," 45.

7. Curtis was also impresario of an Indianist "picture-opera" called *The Vanishing Race,* featuring music by Henry Gilbert, who managed the Wa-Wan Press while Farwell traveled. See Valerie Daniels, "Edward Curtis: Selling the North American Indian," June 2002, accessed August 2006, http://xroads.virginia.edu/~MA02/daniels/curtis/vanishing.html.

8. When he admired the Indian music of the Southwest, with its "rhythmic irregularities and complexities of the most extraordinary nature," (WJ, 122), he was gathering ammunition to counter critics who asserted that Native music was uniform and undistinguished. Critic Henry Krehbiel had welcomed the *American Indian Melodies* (*New York Times,* 31 August 1902), but more recently he had panned Farwell's "Dawn," saying that "any cool-headed student of the music of the American aborigine ought to be able to duplicate it fifty times in an hour." "Music: A Concert of American Compositions," *New York Daily Tribune,* 19 April 1909, 7.

9. Farwell, *Folk-Songs of the West and South: Negro, Cowboy, and Spanish-Californian* (Newton Center, MA: Wa-Wan Press, vol. 4, no. 27, 1905). The "Bird Dance Song" is reprinted with critical commentary in Victoria Lindsay Levine, *Writing Indian Music: Historic Transcriptions, Notations, and Arrangements,* vol. 11 of *Music in the United States of America* (Middleton, WI: A-R Editions, 2002), 38–39.

10. Farwell, "Toward American Music," *Boston Evening Transcript,* 1905, p. 6.

11. Little is known about Alice Haskell, whom Farwell credits as the collector of the spirituals he set. According to EDC, 155–56, she was a composer who had submitted music to the Wa-Wan Press in 1904. Together with her sister Mary, she introduced Farwell to Kahlil Gibran, author of *The Prophet.*

12. Describing this work in 1909 (WJ, 134–35), Farwell adopted the more familiar text: "Oh, bury me not. . . ." The accompaniment won approval from Phillips Barry, a ballad scholar recently from Harvard. In fact, Barry may have suggested the analogy between the tremolo and the prairie. In a letter of 29 October 1905, he compared Farwell's melody and accompaniment to the wind passing over the plains. AFC, 35/9.

13. *Wa-Wan,* 2/15 (1903); WWP, 2:67.

14. Lambord in Farwell and Darby, *Music in America,* 4:311–12.

15. Farwell to J. L. Hubbell, 18 August 1908, AFC, 36/18.

16. Among the cowboy sketches in Farwell's papers are "Wunct [sic] in My Saddle" (or "Cowboy's Lament"); a very simple setting of "Up on the Trail"; and a slightly more elaborate treatment of "It Was a Long and a Tiresome Go," which appears ready for publication.

17. Farwell, introduction to Farwell and Lummis, *Spanish Songs of Old California* (Los Angeles: Lummis, 1923).

18. Neither Thomas Stoner nor I have been able to trace the source of Farwell's peculiar identification of Spanish origins for African American song. He may have been referring to an Old World exchange between Spain and North Africa or to the Caribbean contexts of the New World. Farwell, "Toward American Music," *Out West* 20 (May 1904): 454–58; reprinted in WJ, 188.

19. *Wa-Wan*, 2/12 (1903); WWP, 2:20.

20. Farwell, "Toward American Music," *Boston Evening Transcript*, 1905, p. 5.

21. AFC Scrapbook; clippings indicate that sometimes the order was switched or only one of the two lecture recitals was given. For more detail, see WJ, 140–42.

22. AFC brochures.

23. Ibid.

24. Farwell, "Community Music and the Music Teacher," *M.T.N.A. Proceedings* (1916): 195.

25. Farwell, address to the Canadian Club Meeting, 21 March 1914 (typescript)], AFC, 24/31.

26. John Graziano, "Community Theater, *Caliban by the Yellow Sands,* and Arthur Farwell," in *Vistas of American Music: Essays and Compositions in Honor of William K. Kearns,* ed. John Graziano and Susan Porter (Warren, MI: Harmonie Park, 1999), 306–7.

27. "Kaiser's Defeat by Singing Army Seen," *Los Angeles Times,* 18 June 1918, 112.

28. George Boosinger Edwards, undated clipping reporting a lecture Farwell gave on 2 April 1919; also cited in EDC, 199.

29. *Berkeley Times,* 9 September 1919, front page.

30. *Musical America,* 24 January 1920, page 13; cited in EDC, 203. Mary Louise Overman to Farwell, 19 October 1919, AFC 36/58. Postcard from Julia M. Platt to Mrs. Linn, dated 2 January 1920, AFC, 31/15.

31. Koegel, "Mexican-American Music," 39–43. "Report on Folk Song work for Southwest Society A.I.A.," 1 October 1905, AFC, 31/12.

32. According to "Drama of 'Ramona' with a Local Star," *Los Angeles Times,* 13 January 1905, B1, Farwell's incidental music consisted of arrangements of "Cachuca," "La Golondrina," and "La Paloma," as well as a "Sunrise Hymn" and a "Navajo War Dance."

33. On the plan to devote a Wa-Wan issue to Spanish California song, see "Music and Musicians," *Los Angeles Times,* 24 July 1904, B2.

34. Farwell to Carl Fischer, 26 February 1922, Charles F. Lummis Collection; cited in Koegel, "Mexican-American Music," 42.

35. "A Note by Arthur Farwell," prefatory material to *Spanish Songs of Old California.* Spanish songs are also singled out in his "Outline of the Principles of A NEW MUSICAL EPOCH and Ideas Concerning MUSIC SERVICE as a Vehicle for the Manifestation of These Principles," 1926 (typescript), page 12, AFC, 24/40.

36. Lummis, "Flowers of Our Lost Romance," preface to Farwell and Lummis, *Spanish Songs of Old California.*

37. Farwell, "The Riddle of the Southwest, II," *Los Angeles Times,* 27 September 1926, A4. See also "The Riddle of the Southwest, I," "The Riddle of the Southwest, III," "The Message of the Southwest, I," and "The Message of the Southwest, II," *Los Angeles Times,* 26 September, 29 September, 24 October, and 25 October 1926.

38. Farwell, "Outline of the Principles."

39. See Farwell, "America's Gain from a Bayreuth Romance: The Mystery of Anton Seidl," *Musical Quarterly* 30 (1944): 448–57.

40. Farwell, "Outline of the Principles."

41. Farwell's orchestration of his early Indianist piano score "The Domain of Hurakan" was performed at the Hollywood Bowl in 1922 under Alfred Hertz. See also Catherine Parsons Smith, "Founding the Hollywood Bowl," *American Music* (1997): 206–42; Isabel Morse Jones, *Hollywood Bowl* (New York: G. Schirmer, 1936); and Grace G. Koopal, *Miracle of Music* (Los Angeles: Charles E. Toberman, 1972).

42. Isabel Morse Jones, who worked for Artie Mason Carter and chronicled the Hollywood Bowl's early history, stated that "Farwell's community music work . . . inspired the financing and building of the Hollywood Bowl" (EDC, 218).

43. Bruno David Ussher, [*Pacific Coast Musician?*], 12 September 1925, p. 10; AFC, 23/35.

44. Wayne Carr Willis interprets *The March of Man* in light of Farwell's early vision experiences and later writings on intuition in "The 'Apocalyptic' Visions of Arthur Farwell: Music for a World Transfigured," delivered at the annual meeting of the Society for American Music in 2002 (Lexington, KY). I am grateful to him for providing me with a longer version of this paper.

45. Ussher, [*Pacific Coast Musician?*], 10.

46. Charles H. Gabriel Jr., "Music and Colored Lighting Glorify Natural Theater," *Musical America*, 21 November 1925, 3; Ussher, [*Pacific Coast Musician?*], 10.

47. The precise relationship of "Big Country" to *In the Tetons* is unclear. Farwell planned to write two suites of five movements each. In the end, only seven movements were finished. "Big Country" bears no number, but its texture resembles the etudelike "Wind Play," which Farwell indicated should be inserted as the fifth movement of an expanded six-movement suite, ending with "The Peaks at Night."

48. Farwell, "People's Musical Movement" (typescript), AFC, 25/2.

49. Program note, AFC; reprinted in Brice Farwell, ed., *A Guide to the Music of Arthur Farwell and to the Microfilm Collection of His Work: A Centennial Commemoration Prepared by His Children* (Briarcliff Manor, NY: The Estate of Arthur Farwell, 1972), 45.

50. Edwin Schallert, "Music: Revives Modes: Arthur Farwell Believes in Their Future," *Los Angeles Times*, 15 October 1922, p. III-42.

51. Farwell to Roy Harris, 8 or 9 January 1931, AFC, 36/6.

52. As cited in Ron Erickson, "Arthur Farwell (1872–1952) and the Quintet for Piano and Strings," foreword to *Quintet in E minor, Opus 103 (1937) for Two Violins, Viola and Violoncello and Piano* (San Francisco: Erickson Editions, 1997). For more detailed analysis of the quintet, see Linda Sue Richer, "Arthur Farwell's Piano Quintet: Aspects of Form and Thematic Development," MA thesis, San Francisco State University, 1987.

53. Program for the Composers' Forum-Laboratory Concert, 13 December 1939, AFC Scrapbook; Farwell, program note, as cited in Erickson, "Arthur Farwell."

54. The reminiscences of Farwell's first wife can hardly be considered objective, but she was probably on the mark when she said that her former husband's "quality of creativity was very dictatorial." She continued: "When the task was done, the project in a com-

munity on a fair way to being realized, the same energy that used him to create and build, then would use him to destroy his own usefulness with the group and send him else-where." "Gertrude Farwell's memories, presented by Brice, 12/54," AFC, 35/55.

55. Farwell, "The Music Teacher and the Times" (typescript), AFC, 24/32.

56. Farwell, "The Artist as a Man of Destiny" (typescript), AFC, 24/5.

57. Farwell to Harris, 8 or 9 January 1931, AFC, 36/6. MacDonald Smith Moore discusses the influence of Spengler's *Decline of the West* in *Yankee Blues: Musical Culture and American Identity* (Bloomington: Indiana University Press, 1985), 91–92, 165.

58. Farwell, "The Riddle of the Southwest, I," *Los Angeles Times,* 26 September 1926, B4; and "The Riddle of the Southwest, II," *Los Angeles Times,* 27 September 1926, A4. For the relevant passage of Whitman's "Facing West," see the epigraph to the introduction to this volume.

59. Farwell, "Riddle of the Southwest, II," *Los Angeles Times,* 27 September 1926, A4.

60. "Music for Americans. Arthur Farwell Believes Indian Themes Offer Material," AFC Scrapbook.

3. ENCOUNTERING INDIANS

1. Arthur Farwell and Edna Kingsley Wallace, libretto for *Cartoon, or Once Upon a Time Recently* (typescript), AFC, 10/6, 11/1.

2. Patricia Nelson Limerick, *The Legacy of Conquest: The Unbroken Past of the American West* (New York: W. W. Norton, 1987), 290, 292.

3. Farwell, "Jazz and the Fourth Dimension" (typescript), AFC, 24/25.

4. Cadman wrote to Fletcher in 1907: "Mr. Farwell is broadly known as an extremist and his *methods* are not altogether legitimate tho' his object is always noteworthy"; Cadman to La Flesche, 1908; cited in Harry D. Perison, "Charles Wakefield Cadman: His Life and Works" (PhD diss., Eastman School of Music, University of Rochester, 1978), 67–68 (hereafter cited as Perison CWC).

5. See Arlouine Goodjohn Wu, *Constance Eberhart: A Musical Career in the Age of Cadman* ([Oxford, MS]: National Opera Association, 1983), 18; and Grace Overmyer, "Charles Wakefield Cadman," in *Famous American Composers* (New York: Thomas Y. Crowell, 1944), 164–65.

6. Cadman, "The 'Idealization' of Indian Music," *Musical Quarterly* (1915): 388.

7. Ibid., 391, 390. Cadman reviewed the slow movement of MacDowell's "Indian" Suite when it was performed at the Pittsburgh Sesquicentennial under the title "Music of the Iroquois Echoes in Expo Hall During Sesqui Program: Weird Melodies of MacDowell Applauded by Great Audience at the Exercises," *Pittsburgh Dispatch,* Charles Wakefield Cadman Collection, Pennsylvania State University, Scrapbook G.

8. Cadman, "'Idealization' of Indian Music," 394, 390.

9. Ibid., 391, 394–95.

10. Ibid., 389–90.

11. Perison CWC, 62–71, 416–17.

12. Cadman to Fletcher, 8 October 1907, 18 March 1908, and 13 March 1908; cited in Perison CWC, 67, 73, 68.

13. For a complete catalog, see the works list provided by the Cadman Collection at Pennsylvania State University, http://www.libraries.psu.edu/speccolls/FindingAids/cadman.frame.html.

14. Cadman to Fletcher, 13 March 1908; cited in Perison CWC, 68.

15. Lulu Sanford-Tefft, *Little Intimate Stories of Charles Wakefield Cadman* (Hollywood: Graham Fischer Corp., 1926), 23.

16. As cited in Wu, *Constance Eberhart*, 20.

17. Cadman was mortified at the illustrator's inaccurate representation of the flute itself (which is drawn and positioned more like an oboe than an Indian flageolet), but he also objected to the relegation of this handsome artwork to the inside title page instead of the outside cover. See Cadman's letters of 4 December 1908 and 20 January 1909, Perison CWC, 79.

18. Perison CWC, 98.

19. *Poia* was also presented in illustrated lecture form at the White House at Roosevelt's invitation in 1907. See also "Explains Berlin's Attack upon *Poia*," *Musical America* 12, no. 2 (1910): 25; and Elise K. Kirk, *American Opera* (Urbana and Chicago: University of Illinois Press, 2001), chap. 8, 139–59.

20. Perison CWC, 99.

21. Eberhart to Cadman, 20 May 1909; cited in Perison CWC, 97.

22. Eberhart to La Flesche, 27 April 1910; as cited in Perison CWC, 104. Perison sums up: "From time to time La Flesche objected to what he considered unrealistic . . . but in every case he seems to have acceded finally to the judgment of his collaborators." Harry D. Perison, "The 'Indian' Operas of Charles Wakefield Cadman," *College Music Symposium* 22, no.2 (1982): 23.

23. Cadman to Eberhart, 15 April 1911; cited in Perison CWC, 118.

24. Perison, "'Indian' Operas," 26. Details of the opera's structure are also taken from this source. The Pennsylvania State University Cadman Collection holds a typescript titled *Daoma*, dividing the action into four acts; the score, revised as *Ramala*, combines the rescue and death of Nemaha into a single Act 3.

25. Cadman to La Flesche, 3 October 1909; cited in Perison CWC, 102.

26. Perison CWC, 102–3.

27. Stokowski led a Hollywood Bowl performance in August 1946, which was broadcast on the Standard Hour—the last major performance of Cadman's work during his lifetime. Perison, "'Indian' Operas," 35.

28. Cadman to Eberhart, 1 March 1917; cited in Perison CWC, 134.

29. Perison, "'Indian' Operas," 24–25; Perison CWC, 174–76. The watercolor drawings survive at the New York Public Library, but it is not known whether Cadman ever used them. The opera was revised throughout Cadman's lifetime and was eventually retitled *Ramala*.

30. Perison, "'Indian' Operas," 30–31.

31. Cadman to Eberhart, 1 March 1917; cited in Perison CWC, 134.

32. Cadman's lapses in racial sensitivity had strained his relationship with Fletcher and La Flesche from the start. His name kept cropping up in the press next to distinctly unflattering statements about Native America. An account of his first trip to the reservation, published in the *Pittsburgh Dispatch*, described an Omaha pow wow in language that the

ethnologists considered insulting. Cadman also had occasion to apologize for one of Leonard Liebling's columns in the *Musical Courier,* in which he was reported to have said that Indian music "sounds as uncouth to us as the tone poems that come out of Japan, China, and Tibet" and that most Indian melodies "are not even melodies until after the adapter has given them form, symmetry, and rhythmical cohesion." Perison CWC, 99–100.

33. For details, see Perison CWC, 118–19.

34. G. Edward White, *The Eastern Establishment and the Western Experience: The West of Frederic Remington, Theodore Roosevelt, and Owen Wister* (New Haven, CT, and London: Yale University Press, 1968), 82–83; John Koegel, "Mexican-American Music in Nineteenth-Century Southern California: The Lummis Wax Cylinder Collection at the Southwest Museum, Los Angeles" (PhD diss., Claremont Graduate School, 1994), 30, citing Lummis Correspondence Files, 12 April 1904, Braun Research Library, Southwest Museum. Lummis and Cadman were also acquainted, but their surviving correspondence deals mostly with plans for in-person visits.

35. Cadman to [unidentified, possibly Alice Nielsen], 6 February 1919, Pennsylvania State University Rare Materials.

36. Cadman to the Eberharts, 30 October 1911; cited in Perison CWC, 400.

37. Cadman to Eberhart, 28 January 1935; cited in Perison CWC, 400–401. Cadman's assumption in both letters is that some responsibility for his "tendencies" should rest with his neglectful and alcoholic father. In 1935, he wrote, "I feel sure my childhood wasnt just what it should have been and the queer twists in me physically etc. etc. must have come from away back or NOT so far back." Perison CWC, 401–2, reports one near-marriage—in early 1915, to a pianist, composer, and teacher; Tsianina [Blackstone] reports another, later love interest, without divulging further details of time or place. Tsianina, *Where Trails Have Led Me,* 2nd ed. (Santa Fe: Vergara, 1970), 115–16.

38. Catherine Parsons Smith observes that Cadman's homosexuality "was well known in Southern California and was generally ignored." Smith, *Making Music in Los Angeles: Transforming the Popular* (Berkeley and Los Angeles: University of California Press, 2007), 317.

39. Tsianina, *Where Trails Have Led Me,* 13–14, 23.

40. Cadman to Eberhart, 1 May 1913; cited in Perison CWC, 147.

41. Tsianina, *Where Trails Have Led Me,* 26–27.

42. Perison CWC, 145, 406, 206–7.

43. Perison CWC, 93, 74.

44. Tsianina, *Where Trails Have Led Me,* 41–42.

45. At its premiere, it was billed with two other ethnically charged works: a ballet set to Henry Gilbert's symphonic poem "Dance in the Place Congo" and Franco Leoni's *L'Oracolo,* an opera set in San Francisco's Chinatown. See Irving Kolodin, *The Metropolitan Opera, 1883–1966* (New York: Alfred A. Knopf, 1966), 269–74; and Quaintance Eaton, *The Miracle of the Met* (New York: Meredith Press, 1968), 193–95, 201, 233.

46. While Lulu Sanford-Tefft credits Tsianina with suggesting the opera subject, Perison argues that the suggestion came from several Denverites, including Wilcox. It is noteworthy that "Shanewis" was also the name of the Indian maiden in Cadman's first song on a text by Eberhart, "The Tryst."

47. Cadman to Eberhart, 1 March 1917; cited in Perison CWC, 134.

48. Cadman, "Some Confessions about Shanewis," *Violinist* (July 1918): 354; cited in Gary William Mayhood, "Charles Wakefield Cadman and His Opera *Shanewis*" (MA thesis, Kansas State University, 1991), 95.

49. Cadman, foreword to *The Robin Woman (Shanewis): An American Opera* (Boston: White-Smith, 1918).

50. Foreword and "Argument" in *The Robin Woman (Shanewis)*.

51. *Musical Courier*, 28 March 1918, 8.

52. This passage was cut when *Shanewis* was produced in Denver on 5 December 1924.

53. Cadman, foreword to the Piano Suite "Thunderbird" (Boston: White-Smith, 1917), 3. This technique resembles and may even have been borrowed from Frederick Burton's music for the *Hiawatha* pageant, held at Kensington Point on Lake Huron. See Pisani, *Imagining Native America*, 247.

54. *Musical Courier*, 28 March 1918, 8; *Evening Sun*, as reprinted in *Musical Courier*, 4 April 1918, 13.

55. *New York Times* review, cited in *Musical Courier*, 4 April 1918, 13.

56. *The Evening World*, cited in *Musical Courier*, 4 April 1918, 13.

57. Tsianina recalled: "[The conductor] had me sing the opening aria, *The Spring Song of the Robin Woman*, on the stage for him, so that he could get the feel of Indian rhythm. He was wonderful and wanted to take steps to have me sing the part of 'Shanewis,' but the very thought frightened me terribly." Tsianina, *Where Trails Have Led Me*, 123.

58. Chicago's American Grand Opera Company announced *Shanewis* for a spring 1920 tour, but then postponed it. It was finally featured in 1922, as part of the company's "American" season, to generally favorable reviews. See Perison CWC, 228–31. During this time, a petition to have *Shanewis* heard in Philadelphia was circulated but came to nothing. Pennsylvania State University Cadman Collection, Scrapbook I.

59. See Wu, *Constance Eberhart*, 44–45, for descriptions of some of these events.

60. Upon her return, when Tsianina sang excerpts from *Shanewis* on a tour of the Pacific Northwest, one reviewer called Shanewis's final monologue "Into the Forest Near to God I Go" a "formidable arraignment of the pale-face civilization," continuing: "Tsianina lived and suffered in every note. . . . lived the age-old anguish, felt the fierce indictment, and so made her hearers live and feel the same emotion." Tsianina, *Where Trails Have Led Me*, 114, 115.

61. Tsianina, *Where Trails Have Led Me*, 125.

62. One later letter in this vein can be found in AFC, 39/12, in which Cadman announces the recent completion of his Pennsylvania Symphony and apologizes for not phoning Farwell when he was in New York City for his Composers Forum-Laboratory concert. Farwell, too, seems cordial, but he took pains to protest the "misconception" that he was "some sort of follower of my good friend Charley Cadman" when Quaintance Eaton asked him for biographical information in 1935: "I had been composing Indian music, playing it and lecturing on it . . . before Cadman began sending me his compositions, and those were not Indian music at all. I advised him to tackle the Indian music or other American folk music sometime about 1902 to 1904. This is what started him on it. . . . What I told you above about Cadman's beginning is of course not to be published. That is,

not unless it should come from Cadman himself." Farwell to Eaton, 12 June 1935, AFC, 35/49.

4. STAGING THE WEST

1. On the forest as wilderness, see, among others, Roderick Nash, *Wilderness and the American Mind* (New Haven, CT, and London: Yale University Press, 1982). On the evolution from Cooper's Leatherstocking figure Natty Bumppo into the late nineteenth-century gunslinger, see Henry Nash Smith, *Virgin Land*, 106–12.

2. In *Imagining Native America*, Pisani chronicles over seventy-five "Hiawatha" works. On Longfellow's choice of the name "Hiawatha" and on the later pageant plays that recreate the Iroquois hero's deeds, see Alan Tractenberg, *Shades of Hiawatha* (New York: Hill and Wang, 2004), 81–82, 86–97.

3. Before it was imported to *Shanewis*, Burton's "My Bark Canoe," was originally included in a suite of music composed for the Lake Huron *Hiawatha Pageant*. Pisani, *Imagining Native America*, 248.

4. Cadman assigns actual Indian tunes to only two points in the score; each emphasizes superstition and death: Wokomis's recitation of "The Legend of Niagara" uses an Osage tune in its background music, and Shungela's stoic "Death Song" is based on a Vancouver Indian melody collected by Fletcher.

5. Program preserved in the Pennsylvania State University Cadman Collection, 16/16.

6. Pennsylvania State University Cadman Collection Scrapbook.

7. Burrill Phillips, "History of Colorado Is Idealized in Brilliant Pageant," *Musical America*, May [1927], clipping in the Pennsylvania State University Cadman Collection, Scrapbook H. All citations from the libretto come from the program included in this scrapbook. Music from the pageant and related materials are held in the Lillian White Spencer Papers at Denver Public Library.

8. Kaspar Monahan, "Colorado Pageant Proves Grand Epic," [Denver] E[vening] *News*, 3 May [1927], clipping in the Pennsylvania State University Cadman Collection, Scrapbook H.

9. Ibid.

10. This proclamation reads, in part: "WHEREAS, Our sturdy, fearless PIONEERS ... have wrought MIRACLE [sic] in hollowing a mighty mountain, and making therein a *great road* from vast new realms of plenty; a road whose bonds of steel unite the eastern and the western *seas;* therefore BE IT RESOLVED, That we, *sons and daughters of the* PIONEERS, pause a moment in the busy rush of life, to voice our gratitude and to offer praise for blessings that have been, and are, and WILL BE in this dear land of COLORADO."

11. Guelfo Civinini and Carlos Zangarini, *La Fanciulla del West* [libretto], English version by R. H. Elkin (Milan, Italy: Ricordi, 1910), 4; cited in Annie Randall and Rosalind Gray Davis, *Puccini and the Girl: The History and Reception of "The Girl of the Golden West"* (Chicago: University of Chicago Press, 2005), 10.

12. See Allan Atlas, "Belasco and Puccini: 'Old Dog Tray' and the Zuni Indians," *Musical Quarterly* 75, no. 3 (1991): 362–98.

13. Randall and Davis, *Puccini and the Girl*, 32.

14. Kathryn Kalinak interprets the role of Foster's songs in the movie western in *How the West Was Sung: Music in the Westerns of John Ford* (Berkeley and Los Angeles: University of California Press, 2007), 57–59, 89–90, 117, 136.

15. Catherine Parsons Smith and Cynthia S. Richardson, *Mary Carr Moore, American Composer* (Ann Arbor: University of Michigan Press, 1987), 69–72. All three productions of *Narcissa* took place on the West Coast (Seattle, 1912; San Francisco, 1925; and Los Angeles, 1945). See also Mary Carr Moore, "Writing and Producing an Opera," *Pacific Coast Musician,* 7 July 1915, 51.

16. Score excerpt reprinted by permission in Smith and Richardson, *Mary Carr Moore,* 74–77.

17. Smith and Richardson, *Mary Carr Moore,* 71–72.

18. Ibid., 79, 72, 74.

19. Sydney Strong, "Whitman in Grand Opera," *Chicago Advance,* n.d.; and "Narcissa," *Argonaut,* 19 September 1925, 10; cited in Smith and Richardson, *Mary Carr Moore,* 80, 104.

20. Edward N. Waters, *Victor Herbert: A Life in Music* (New York: Macmillan, 1955), 385.

21. "Grand Opera Written by Americans to be Given Here," *New York Times,* 22 January 1911, SM13. Farwell praised Herbert's score: "His Indian themes, whether borrowed entire or simulated, are authentic in their quality. He has shown remarkable sympathy in devising a scheme of development for these themes which retains their peculiar character and 'color.'" "American Opera on American Themes," *American Review of Reviews,* April 1911, 445.

22. "Grand Opera Written by Americans to be Given Here," *New York Times,* 22 January 1911, SM13.

23. Pisani (*Imagining Native America,* 264–66) offers a detailed discussion of the Dagger Dance, noting its later uses and its characteristic tropes (tom-tom rhythms, tetratonic melody, descending contours, and parallel harmonization).

24. In addition to his brilliant analysis of Natoma's "theme of fate," Pisani (*Imagining Native America*) also identifies a "Natoma chord" (the minor-seventh F♯, A, C♯, E) and documents its prior occurrence in Dvořák "New World" Symphony and Henry Gilbert's music for Curtis's "Vanishing Race."

25. Waters, *Victor Herbert,* 374–75.

26. My interpretation here differs slightly from James Parakilas's in his excellent article "The Soldier and the Exotic: Operatic Variations on a Theme of Racial Encounter, Part II," *Opera Quarterly* 10, no. 3 (1994): 43–69, esp. 55–59. Parakilas notes: "The racial difference between Yankee and Native American . . . is treated as so great that Natoma cannot even play the role of exotic to Paul. A representative of an intermediate race [Barbara] is needed for that role" (p. 55).

27. Waters (*Victor Herbert,* 562) cites Herbert's 1924 response to an article in *Musical America.*

28. Lee Shippey, "The Lee Side O' L.A.: Personal Glimpses of World-Famed Southlanders," *Los Angeles Times,* 1 September 1929, A4.

29. Cadman to Eberhart, 27 September 1937; cited in Perison CWC, 334.

30. Cadman appears to have written his own textual prefaces for *From Hollywood.* Two of its movements evoke silent film stars: the second movement scherzo is titled "To a

Comedian" and is dedicated to Charlie Chaplin, and the first movement ("June on the Boulevard") celebrates Mary Pickford.

31. Perley Poore Sheehan, *Hollywood as a World Center* (Hollywood Citizen Press, 1924), 44. A list of Sheehan's screenplays can be found at the Internet Movie Database (www.imdb.com).

32. Sheehan, *Hollywood as a World Center,* 43, 58. Sheehan's claim that the Bowl had "never been touched by greed or strife" is definitively countered by Catherine Parsons Smith, *Making Music in Los Angeles,* chap. 10.

33. Farwell, "The Riddle of the Southwest, I," *Los Angeles Times,* 26 September 1926, B4.

34. Sheehan, *Hollywood as a World Center,* 99–100, 2. See also similar rhetoric on pages 35, 41, 44, and 50, where the Hollywood Bowl is described as the "highest expression" of "the community life of these Aryan migrants."

35. Smith, *Making Music in Los Angeles,* 235.

36. Ibid., 231–33.

37. Smith and Richardson, *Mary Carr Moore,* 180–81.

38. Ives was persuaded to join the Society of Native American Composers by Adolph Weiss, but in March 1943 he wrote that he had received a report "that this Society is against all Jews, and also pro-Fascist. I cannot believe that this is true—but, if it is, accept my resignation immediately." Charles Ives to Henri Lloyd Clement (Ethel Dofflemeyer). See also Mary Carr Moore to Charles Ives, 22 March 1943; cited in Smith and Richardson, *Mary Carr Moore,* 184, 259.

39. Jerome Moross, "Hollywood Music without Movies," *Modern Music* 18 (May–June 1941), 262.

40. Cadman to Eberhart, 11 February 1936; cited in Perison CWC, 323. See also Cadman's letter to the *New York Times,* 12 February 1936.

41. Cadman had already written some film music for *The Vanishing American* (1925), in addition to his incidental music for Earle's *Rubaiyat.* His best-known work for Fox was the theme song for *The Sky Hawk,* reportedly finished a mere three hours after he received the text by telegram. He also appeared on screen performing "From the Land of the Sky-blue Water" in the 1930 film *Harmony at Home.* Perison CWC, 253–63.

42. Cadman, "The Musical Enigma of the Soundies," *The Music World* (September 1930): 9, 20; (October 1930): 6, 21. Cadman's most notorious article of this period was "Musicus Quo Vadis?" written for the *London Chesterian* in 1931 but reprinted in *The Music World* in March 1932. His linking of "radical" tendencies with communism and fascism required numerous apologies, one of which appeared in the *New York Times,* 6 March 1932, section VIII, p. 8. See also Cadman, "Evolutionary Versus Revolutionary Music," *Music News,* 20 May 1937, 3, 15.

43. Quoted in Shippey, "Personal Glimpses."

44. Robert Kimball and Alfred Simon, *The Gershwins* (New York: Atheneum, 1973), 125; Pollack, *George Gershwin: His Life and Music* (Berkeley and Los Angeles: University of California Press, 2006), 468.

45. Charles Schwartz, *Gershwin: His Life and Music* (Indianapolis and New York: Bobbs-Merrill, 1973), 196.

46. Pollack (*George Gershwin,* 445ff., 478) discusses "I Got Rhythm" as a jazz standard. He also provides a detailed account of the intriguing relationships between several of *Girl Crazy*'s most popular tunes and the unproduced Gershwin-Ziegfeld show *East Is West.*

47. Pollack, *George Gershwin,* 466. See also Andrea Most, *Making Americans: Jews and the Broadway Musical* (Cambridge, MA: Harvard University Press, 2004), 56–66; and Deena Rosenberg, *Fascinating Rhythm: The Collaboration of George and Ira Gershwin* (New York: Dutton, 1991), 167.

5. WEST OF EDEN

1. Cadman, "The Thresher," *How Constance & Donald Spent the Summer: Eight Studies without Octaves* (Boston: Ditson, 1909).

2. Examples include the piano suite *Prairie Sketches* (1906) and a 1928 song called "Prairie Night."

3. Cadman to Eberhart, 1 March 1939; cited in Perison CWC, 348–49.

4. Cadman to Eberhart, 21 March 1939; cited in Perison CWC, 350.

5. Program for the Chicago Symphony Orchestra, 19–20 February 1942, Pennsylvania State University Cadman Collection 16/14. The notes state that "authoritative information . . . has been provided by Mr. Cadman" describing "a long line of Pennsylvania pre-revolutionary ancestors on his mother's side. His father's father hailed from England. Both the Cadmans and the Wakefields are particularly Anglo-Saxon and have been prominent in British and Colonial affairs throughout the centuries."

6. Perison CWC (362–63) identifies performances in Harrisburg, Kansas City, Detroit, Chicago, and reports of performances in Cleveland and Chile.

7. Cadman to Constance Eberhart, 27 December [1946]; cited in Perison CWC, 364.

8. See, among others, Limerick, *Legacy of Conquest;* and T. J. Jackson Lears, *No Place of Grace: Antimodernism and the Transformation of American Culture, 1880–1920* (New York: Pantheon Books, 1981).

9. Leo Marx, *The Machine in the Garden: Technology and the Pastoral Ideal in America* (New York: Oxford University Press, 1964), 25.

10. Ibid., 88, 141, 159.

11. Ibid., 99, 111, 122, 127.

12. Ibid., 246. Marx observes that these American hunters are often "impelled to restrict or even renounce their hunting. I am thinking of Natty Bumppo, Melville's Ishmael, Faulkner's Ike McCaslin, and Thoreau himself."

13. Henry Nash Smith, *Virgin Land,* 173.

14. Ibid., 138.

15. Willa Cather, *My Ántonia* (1918; repr. New York: Quality Paperback Book Club, 1995), 156.

16. In 1917, the Chicago Symphony devoted an entire concert to Sowerby's works. See B. Wayne Hinds, "Leo Sowerby: A Biography and Descriptive Listing of Anthems," EdD thesis (George Peabody College for Teachers, 1972), 21–22; and Dena J. Epstein, "Frederick Stock and American Music," *American Music* 10 (1992): 20–52.

17. Burnet C. Tuthill, "Leo Sowerby," *Musical Quarterly* 24 (1938): 250.

18. Hinds, "Leo Sowerby," 58.

19. Sowerby, *Musical News,* responding to the idea that his *Eight Little Pieces* were imitative of Schoenberg and futurism; W. L. Hubbard, "America Will Lose Its Greatest Composer If Sowerby Goes Abroad," *Chicago Daily Tribune,* 6 March 1920; cited in Hinds, "Leo Sowerby," 29, 63–64.

20. Hinds, "Leo Sowerby," 35.

21. Sowerby, *From the Northland,* piano suite (Boston: Boston Music Company, 1926); and *From the Northland,* orchestra (New York: G. Schirmer, 1927).

22. Margie A. McLeod, "Apathy Drawing Us Back Under Foreign Domination, Says Sowerby," *Musical America,* 12 February 1921.

23. Carl Sandburg, *The American Songbag* (New York: Harcourt Brace Jovanovich, 1927).

24. Ibid., x. Sandburg's introduction devotes paragraphs to four arrangers, including Sowerby, elevating them above the pro forma list of contributors that includes Arthur Farwell, Charles Farwell Edson, and "Ruth Porter Crawford," soon to be Ruth Crawford Seeger.

25. Tuthill, "Leo Sowerby," 252–53.

26. Daniel Gregory Mason, writing in an unidentified publication called "The Berkshire Festival of Music," from the scrapbook of Bertha Wiersma Nolton; as cited in Hinds, "Leo Sowerby," 62.

27. Marx, *Machine in the Garden,* 23.

28. For more on the pastoral topic in eighteenth-century music, see, among others, Leonard Ratner, *Classic Music: Expression, Form, Style* (New York: Schirmer, 1980); and Wye Jamison Allanbrook, *Rhythmic Gesture in Mozart* (Chicago: Chicago University Press, 1983).

29. Sandburg, "The Prairie," in *Poems of the Midwest* (contains *Chicago Poems* [1916] and *Cornhuskers* [1918]) (Cleveland: World Publishing, 1946). Subsequent quotations and references to line numbers in the poem correspond to this edition.

30. "Champagne & Cornbread," *Time,* 29 January 1945.

31. Sandburg, "The Prairie," 164.

32. Sandburg, "Youth and Pioneers: An Ode," 14 June 1927; reprinted in Carl Sandburg, *Home Front Memo* (New York: Harcourt Brace, 1940), 291–94.

33. Sowerby, "The Folk Element—The Vitalizer of Modern Music," *Musical Scrap Book* 1 (October 1927): 11; cited in Hinds, "Leo Sowerby," 132.

34. Cadman, letter printed in the *Pacific Coast Musician,* 7 August 1943, p. 5.

35. Critic Moses Smith faced a similar confusion two years later, and he approved when the Boston Symphony Orchestra classified Foss as a "native" composer rather than a "foreigner" because he had spent his "formative years amid American influences." "Boston Goes All Out for Premieres," *Modern Music* 21 (January–February 1944): 103–4. Smith heard the "symphonic synthesis" that Koussevitzky performed in Boston in 1943. The choral version of *The Prairie,* premiered by Robert Shaw, won a New York Music Critics Circle Award for 1944, and the following year Artur Rodzinski performed it with the Westminster Choir and the New York Philharmonic.

36. *New Yorker* (30 January 1965): 23. See also Raymond Yiu, "Renaissance Man: A Portrait of Lukas Foss," *Tempo* 221 (July 2002): 15–23.

37. Foss, "*The Prairie, A Parable of Death,* and *Psalms,*" in *The Composer's Point of View: Essays on Twentieth-Century Choral Music by Those Who Wrote It,* ed. Robert Stephan Hines (Norman: University of Oklahoma Press, 1963), 10.

38. Thomson, *New York Herald Tribune,* 16 May 1944. Though he praised Foss's musicianship, he noted that "Mr. Foss's language is elegant, scholastic, dainty. It is dry and clean and pleasant, and it is adjusted for precise depiction rather than for emotional excitement."

39. Donald Fuller, "Stravinsky's Visit; New Music in 1945," *Modern Music* 22 (March–April 1945): 178; Irving Fine, "Young America: Bernstein and Foss," *Modern Music* 22 (May–June 1945): 243. See also Arthur Berger's review of *The Prairie* score, "Scores and Records," *Modern Music* 22 (March–April 1945): 199–201.

40. Fine, "Young America," 242.

41. "A Word from Lukas Foss," printed as record jacket program note of *Lukas Foss: The Prairie,* Brooklyn Philharmonic Orchestra, Lukas Foss, conductor, VOX, TV-S 54649, 1976; Foss, "*The Prairie, A Parable of Death,* and *Psalms,*" 6.

42. Foss, "*The Prairie, A Parable of Death,* and *Psalms,*" 65.

43. Ibid., 7.

44. Foss reordered the text in such a way that a reader of the poem would encounter the texts of Foss's movements in the following order: I, VIa, II, III(part1), III(part4), IV, V, III (parts 2–3), VIc, VIb, IX.

45. Lukas Foss, comment on *Prairie,* originally published in Robert Bagar and Louis Biancolli, eds., *The Concert Companion* (New York: McGraw-Hill, 1947), 267–68.

46. Richard Dyer, CD liner notes for Lukas Foss, *The Prairie,* (BMOP/sound 1007).

47. "Champagne & Cornbread," *Time,* 29 January 1945.

48. Foss, comment on *Prairie.*

49. Marx, *Machine in the Garden,* 225.

50. Berger, "Scores and Records," 200.

51. Fine, "Young America," 243. On page 242, Fine remarked on a tendency "to resort to construction of themes by symmetrically repeated fragments, which are in turn extended by sequence . . . not only for phrase extension but also for climactic effects, in the manner of the romantics. In his most recent work Foss has aggravated this sequential tendency by the addition of ostinato rhythms."

52. Foss, comment on *Prairie.*

53. Ibid.

54. Two fleeting echo moments also begin movement VIb, "O prairie girl," where trumpet answers the vocal call "Spring slips back with a girl face" and then the soprano soloist repeats herself as if listening: "Any new songs for me? Any new songs?"

55. Foss, "The Prairie," 4.

56. Berger continues: "When he is not so impelled . . . he shows a soft lyric inspiration and a personal style of which we may expect him to become more keenly aware in the future." Berger, "Scores and Records," 200.

6. POWER IN THE LAND

1. Lukas Foss, interview with Vivian Perlis (1986). *Oral History of American Music* project at Yale University; as cited in Richard Dyer, CD liner notes for *Lukas Foss: The Prairie,* Boston Modern Orchestra Project and Providence Singers, dir. Andrew Clark (BMOP/sound 1007), 8.

2. Steven Watson, *Prepare for Saints: Gertrude Stein, Virgil Thomson, and the Mainstreaming of American Modernism* (New York: Random House, 1998), 50.

3. Thomson, *Virgil Thomson* (New York: Alfred A. Knopf, 1966), 91–92.

4. On Thomson's exposure to chant and early polyphony, see, among others, Carol J. Oja, "Virgil Thomson's Harvard Years," in *A Celebration of American Music,* ed. Crawford, Lott, and Oja, 327–32.

5. Nadine Hubbs, *The Queer Composition of America's Sound: Gay Modernists, American Music, and National Identity* (Berkeley and Los Angeles: University of California Press, 2004), 20.

6. Watson, *Prepare for Saints,* 53.

7. Thomson, *Virgil Thomson,* 105.

8. Thomson, program note, cited in the liner notes for *Music of Virgil Thomson* (CRI SRD 398), 1979.

9. Watson, *Prepare for Saints,* 12.

10. Anthony Tommasini, *Virgil Thomson: Composer on the Aisle* (New York: W. W. Norton, 1997), 22.

11. Watson, *Prepare for Saints,* 26; Tommasini, *Virgil Thomson,* 58.

12. Thomson to Ruby Gleason, 30 September 1917; see also Thomson to Clara May Gaines Thomson (his mother), 10 October 1917; reprinted in *Selected Letters of Virgil Thomson,* ed. Tim Page and Vanessa Weeks Page (New York: Summit Books, 1988), 19–22. Thomson, *Virgil Thomson,* 35.

13. Thomson, *Virgil Thomson,* 33. He continued: "Neither then nor later did I have much interest in whether any country involved in the war, including my own, was right or wrong. . . . I could only think of it as myth-in-action; and acting out myths was a mystery that I had as much right as any other man to get involved in."

14. Oja, "Thomson's Harvard Years," 328–35.

15. Samuel L. M. Barlow, "Virgil Thomson," *Modern Music* 18 (May–June 1941): 248.

16. See, among others, Victor Fell Yellin, "The Operas of Virgil Thomson," in Thomson, *American Music since 1910* (London: Weidenfeld and Nicolson, 1970), 91–109.

17. Paul Rosenfeld, *An Hour with American Music* (Philadelphia: J. B. Lippincott, 1929), 98–99.

18. Michael Meckna, "Sacred and Secular America: Virgil Thomson's *Symphony on a Hymn Tune,*" *American Music* 8 (1990): 474.

19. For more on *The River,* see Neil William Lerner, "The Classical Documentary Score in American Films of Persuasion: Contexts and Case Studies, 1936–1945," PhD diss., Duke University, 1997; and Claudia Jean Widgery, "The Kinetic Temporal Interaction of Music and Film: Three Documentaries of 1930s America," PhD diss., University of Maryland, 1990.

20. Meckna, "Sacred and Secular America," 471, 476.

21. Tommasini, *Virgil Thomson,* 33, 57.

22. Thomson, "A Little about Movie Music," *Modern Music* 10 (May–June 1933): 188–91.

23. Lerner ("Classical Documentary," 160) also notes similarities between one motive in the *Symphony on a Hymn Tune* and a repeated melody in the *Plow* score.

24. Lerner, "Classical Documentary," 90. Lorentz refers to the steady drumbeat of a later sequence as "a distant tom tom" (as the first fence post is driven into baked-out ground), and Thomson includes one in his menagerie of percussion, but in this earlier instance the ostinato is played by the timpani.

25. Lorentz, *FDR's Moviemaker: Memoirs and Scripts* (Reno: University of Nevada Press, 1992), 28. Lorentz's left-wing credentials were substantial, but he was no radical; see William Alexander, *Film on the Left: American Documentary Film from 1931 to 1942* (Princeton, NJ: Princeton University Press, 1981), 97–109.

26. Sidney Baldwin, *Poverty and Politics: The Rise and Decline of the Farm Security Administration* (Chapel Hill: University of North Carolina Press, 1968).

27. Lorentz, *FDR's Moviemaker,* 37. J. P. McEvoy, "Young Man with a Camera," *Reader's Digest,* August 1940, 74; cited in Robert L. Snyder, *Pare Lorentz and the Documentary Film* (Norman: University of Oklahoma Press, 1968), 24. "Documented Dust," *Time,* 25 May 1936, 47.

28. Lorentz, *McCall's,* August 1939; reprinted in *Lorentz on Film: Movies 1927–1941* (Norman: University of Oklahoma Press, 1986), 170–71.

29. *Study Guide: "The Plow That Broke the Plains" U.S. Documentary Film,* (Washington, DC: United States Film Service, Division of the National Emergency Council, 1938), 2, 4–5; Snyder, *Pare Lorentz,* 26.

30. Thomson, *Virgil Thomson,* 259.

31. Lerner, "Classical Documentary," esp. chaps. 2, 3, and 6. On page 57, Lerner documents the authors' fluctuations between the British spelling *Plough* and the American *Plow.*

32. Snyder, *Pare Lorentz,* 14–15. Virgil Thomson papers, Irving S. Gilmore Library, Yale University, Box 29A/90, Folder 14 (hereafter cited as VTP, 29A/90/14).

33. Thomson to Robert Snyder, 14 December 1961; quoted in Thomson, *Selected Letters,* 304–5. Lorentz (*FDR's Moviemaker,* 39) concurs with this version of events: "I had finally cut the footage of *The Plow That Broke the Plains* down to the running time of Virgil Thomson's full-length score, which was approximately thirty minutes."

34. Lorentz, *FDR's Moviemaker,* 39.

35. Thomson, *Virgil Thomson,* 260.

36. Robert L. Snyder, introduction to *Lorentz on Film,* xiv–xv.

37. Lorentz, *McCall's,* July 1936; reprinted in *Lorentz on Film,* 135. W. L. White provides a colorful but sometimes inaccurate vision of the film's collaborative process in "Pare Lorentz," *Scribner's Magazine,* January 1939, 7–11, 42.

38. For comparison of the section titles in three of Lorentz's scenarios to Thomson's full score, see Lerner, "Classical Documentary," 76. For the concert suite, Thomson selected six movements (Prelude, Grass, Cattle, Blues, Drought, Devastation); the piano suite bears the titles Prelude, Cowboy Songs, Blues, and Devastation. *The Plow That Broke*

the Plains: Suite for Orchestra (Music Press, Inc., 1942); *Suite from The Plough That Broke the Plains: Four Pieces for Piano* (New York: G. Schirmer, 1942, 1980).

39. Lorentz, *McCall's*, July 1936; reprinted in *Lorentz on Film*, 135–36.

40. Lerner, "Copland's Music of Wide Open Spaces: Surveying the Pastoral Trope in Hollywood," *Musical Quarterly* 85 (2001): 477–515.

41. *Variety*, 12 May 1936; cited in Snyder, *Pare Lorentz*, 30–31. The notoriety of Strand's and Hurwitz's interest in Soviet models is apparent in *Time*, 25 May 1936, 27; and in W. L. White, "Pare Lorentz," 8. One might speculate that Lorentz's reservations about "radicals" also affected his selection of Thomson to score *The Plow* and *The River*—certainly Aaron Copland and Roy Harris (two composers whom Lorentz had passed over) had stronger pro-Soviet sympathies during the mid-1930s.

42. W. L. White, "Pare Lorentz," 9. In his article "The Plow That Broke the Plains" (*New Theatre* [July 1936]: 18), Peter Ellis [Irving Lerner] presents a possibly more accurate version of this episode, claiming that the original scenario "embodied a concept of epic implications: capitalism's rape of the land, and—by extension—the impoverishment of all the natural resources of America: mines, forests, men." In this account, after the RA became uneasy with this scenario, Lorentz modified the narration but not the image track; the photographers did not go "on strike," but disclaimed responsibility for anything but the photography.

43. VTP, 29A/145/6.

44. Tommasini, *Virgil Thomson*, 283; W. L. White, "Pare Lorentz," 10.

45. Lorentz, *McCall's*, April 1940; reprinted in *Lorentz on Film*, 184.

46. *Study Guide*, 35. Lorentz took two lines of his narration from Lange's photograph captions: "Blown out, baked out and broke" and "No place to go . . . and no place to stop."

47. *Literary Digest*, 16 May 1936, 22–23; *Variety*, 13 May 1936; preserved in VTP, 29A/145/6.

48. *Study Guide*, 5; *Literary Digest*, 16 May 1936, 22; Copland's lecture on film music is cited in Lerner. "Music of Wide Open Spaces," 485. See also Edwin Denby, "Thomson Scores for a New Deal Film," *Modern Music* 13 (May–June 1936): 47.

49. VTP, 29A/90/14; Lerner, "Classical Documentary," 68; Margaret Larkin, *The Singing Cowboy: A Book of Western Songs* (New York: Oak Publications, 1931).

50. Lorentz's notes to Thomson, pages 3–4. VTP, 29A/51/542.

51. *Study Guide*, 8. The *Study Guide* includes the Turner thesis on its list of recommended reading, along with novels by Rölvaag, Cather, and Hamlin Garland, and numerous government publications.

52. Lorentz's notes to Thomson. VTP, 29A/51/542.

53. *Study Guide*, 28. Though the promotional materials for *The Plow* do not mention it, Lerner ("Classical Documentary, 125) cites A. J. Smithers, *A New Excalibur: The Development of the Tank, 1909–1939* (London: Leo Cooper, 1986), on the shared technology of tractors and early tanks.

54. VTP, 29A/51/542; see also Lerner, "Classical Documentary," 127.

55. See, among others, "George Stoney on *The Plow* and *The River*," special feature on *The Plow That Broke the Plains* and *The River*, Post-Classical Ensemble, directed by Angel

Gil-Ordóñez (Naxos DVD 2.110521). Karel Reisz treats this sequence in *The Technique of Film Editing* (London: Focal Press, 1953), 164.

56. Snyder (*Pare Lorentz*, 38) gives the final cost of the film as over nineteen thousand dollars—well over the initial budget of six thousand dollars, but still so far below the typical Hollywood budget that the *New York Herald Tribune*, 26 May 1936, called *The Plow* "a wheezy, badly handicapped little effort," and "far too crude, too amateurish and too painfully poor in its skeleton frame to offer entertainment."

57. See George Stoney in conversation with Joseph Horowitz (2 December 2005), "*The Plow That Broke the Plains*" and "*The River*," Naxos DVD 2.110521; and Widgery, "Kinetic Temporal Interaction," 204–5. John Cage attempted to explain away the aptness of Thomson's hymn texts: "The ironical appropriateness of these [hymn tune] titles need not be taken to mean that they have been chosen for their topical references. Quite the contrary. It is simply that tunes which have an expressive or characteristic quality usually end by getting themselves words of the same character." Kathleen O'Connell Hoover and John Cage, *Virgil Thomson: His Life and Music* (New York: Thomas Yoseloff, 1959; Freeport, NY: Books for Libraries Press, 1970), 180–81.

58. The "Buffalo Skinners" was one of Sandburg's favorite ballads. He considered its lyrics "blunt, direct, odorous, plain and made-to-hand, having the sound to some American ears that the Greek language of Homer had for the Greeks of that time." Sandburg, quoted in Larkin, *Singing Cowboy*, 83.

59. Larkin, *Singing Cowboy*, 85.

60. VTP, 29A/51/542; see also Lerner, "Classical Documentary," 138–41.

61. Lerner, "Classical Documentary," 138.

62. Denby, "Thomson Scores," 46–47. Denby's final adjective finds some unexpected support in Lorentz's instructions to Thomson for the "Devastation" scene: "The music I vaguely hear is a movement for bassoon and kettle drum—the bassoon mocking and the kettle drum warning and saying 'I told you so.'" VTP, 29A/51/542.

63. *Variety*, 13 May 1936, suggests that the plan to remove the epilogue originated shortly after the premiere: "Last reel is marred by inexcusably obvious boost for various government agencies involved in rehabilitating farmers in duststorm areas. . . . Sequence, which is completely out of keeping with the rest of the film, is being cut and may be revised along softer lines before film gets into general circulation." William Alexander (*Film on the Left*, 140) states that the epilogue was removed "in the second or third year after *The Plow*'s appearance."

64. The epilogue can be viewed among the appendixes on "*The Plow That Broke the Plains*" and "*The River*" (Naxos DVD 2.110521).

65. Frank Nugent, "Raw Deal for the New Deal," *New York Times*, 24 May 1936.

66. VTP, 29A/51/542; see also Lerner, "Classical Documentary," 77.

67. Undated report by Addison Foster, held in the National Archives, Entry 266, Box 1446, A-Br; cited in Lerner, "Classical Documentary," 80.

68. VTP, 29A/51/542.

69. *Study Guide*, 6.

70. Lorentz, *McCall's*, July 1936; reprinted in *Lorentz on Film*, 136.

71. "Says Film Loses a State," *New York Times*, 4 August 1936; "Dust Bowl Film Brings Threat to Punch Tugwell," *New York Times*, 10 June 1936.

72. Mrs. R.L. Duke to Pare Lorentz; cited in Snyder, *Pare Lorentz*, 49.

73. Francis Parkman, *Oregon Trail: Sketches of Prairie and Rocky-Mountain Life* (Boston: Little, Brown, 1892), xi.

74. Lerner, "Classical Documentary," 249.

75. Lorentz continued: "If you feel you can build storm more completely without hymn then ignore cue at one minute—but the hymn still seems a natural part of the sequence to me." VTP, 29A/51/542.

76. Olin Downes, *New York Times*, 6 January 1943. In Downes's defense, one might observe that each tune contains a prominent four-note descent from tonic to dominant.

77. VTP, 29A/51/542.

78. Thomson, *Virgil Thomson*, 5.

79. Joseph Horowitz, liner notes for *"The Plow That Broke the Plains" and "The River"* (Naxos DVD 2.110521); Lerner, "Classical Documentary," 152.

80. Lorentz, "Lorentz on Film," Program I; cited in Snyder, *Pare Lorentz*, 32.

81. Text and details taken from Austin E. Fife and Alta S. Fife, eds., *Cowboy and Western Songs: A Comprehensive Anthology*, music edited by Mary Jo Schwab (N.p.: Clarkson N. Potter, 1969), 179–82.

82. John Steinbeck, *Grapes of Wrath* (1939; repr. New York: Penguin Books, 1992), 272.

83. "The Trail to Mexico" appears in Larkin, *Singing Cowboy*, but with no reference to Texas.

84. Thomson, "Swing Music," *Modern Music* 13 (May–June 1936): 12–17; see also "Swing Again," *Modern Music* 15 (March–April 1938): 160–66.

85. Thomson, "Swing Music," 13.

86. *Study Guide*, 31.

7. HARVEST HOME

1. Tommasini, *Virgil Thomson*, 289. Apparently, Kirstein also considered a ballet based on Thomson's film scores, but to my knowledge this never came to fruition. Kirstein to Thomson, 28 January [1950], VTP, 29/57/19.

2. Wilfrid Mellers, *Music in a New Found Land: Themes and Developments in the History of American Music* (New York: Alfred Knopf, 1965), 87.

3. Thomson, *American Music since 1910* (New York: Holt, Rinehart and Winston, 1971), 53–55. This and other excerpts of Thomson's writing on Copland are conveniently collected in *Virgil Thomson: A Reader, Selected Writings, 1924–1984*, ed. Richard Kostelanetz (New York: Routledge, 2002), 167–81.

4. Lerner, "Music of Wide Open Spaces," 510. After receiving Thomson's *American Music since 1910*, Lorentz wrote that Thomson's remarks on Copland were "quite justified": "I have been irked over the years hearing some of your music coming out of his scores." Lorentz to Thomson, 18 March 1971; VTP, 29A/154/79.

5. Thomson, "Two Ballets," *New York Herald Tribune,* 20 May 1945; reprinted in *The Art of Judging Music* (New York: Greenwood Press, 1969), 162.

6. See Daniel E. Mathers, "Expanding Horizons: Sexuality and the Re-zoning of *The Tender Land,*" in *Copland Connotations: Studies and Interviews,* ed. Peter Dickinson (Rochester, NY: Boydell Press, 2002).

7. Moore wrote to critic Harold C. Schonberg, "There's no Norwegian blood in me. . . . Sundgaard, though, is the son of Norwegian parents." *New York Times,* 25 March 1951, 83. Sundgaard also wrote the libretto for Kurt Weill's *Down in the Valley* (1948).

8. Sara Eddy, "'Wheat and Potatoes': Reconstructing Whiteness in O. E. Rølvaag's Immigrant Theory," *MELUS* 26, no. 1 (spring 2001): 129–49; Eric Haugtvedt, "Abandoned in America: Identity Dissonance and Ethnic Preservation in *Giants in the Earth,*" *MELUS* 33, no. 3 (fall 2008): 147–68.

9. Some of his impressions of these trips are recorded in diary form. Ernst Bacon Collection, Library of Congress, Box 36, Folder 23 (hereafter cited as EBC, 36/23): "Notebooks, 1912 June 27."

10. For details, see Leta E. Miller and Catherine Parsons Smith, "Playing with Politics: Crisis in the San Francisco Federal Music Project," *California History* 86, no. 2 (2009): 26–47, 68–71.

11. See, among others, Paul Griffiths, "Tribute to a Neglected Composer," *New York Times,* 17 September 1998.

12. Bacon's tribute reconciles Sandburg's love for nature with his evocations of industry by noting that he "sang the praise of smoke and steel (that was some time ago)." Bacon, "A Tribute in Reverse" (typescript), EBC, 40/33.

13. Horgan to Bacon, 1934?, EBC, 45/61.

14. Bacon, "Native Soil" (typescript), in the unpublished collection "The Honor of Music," EBC, 32/24. A shorter and more carefully edited version of this material appears under the same title in the *Sonneck Society Bulletin* 14, no. 1 (spring 1988): 9–10.

15. Bacon, notes for a "Talk on Regional Music," EBC, 40/19.

16. Horgan to Bacon, 1 May 1941, 12 August 1941, EBC, 45/61.

17. Bacon, "Has the Native Opera a Future?" *Musical Courier,* 22 February 1944.

18. Bacon, "Notebooks, misc., n.d. EBC, 39/1.

19. Bacon, "Has the Native Opera a Future?"

20. Wallace Stegner, "Living Dry," in *Where the Bluebird Sings to the Lemonade Springs: Living and Writing in the West* (New York: Penguin Books, 1992), 61.

21. Prologue to *A Tree on the Plains* as it appears in the program notes for City Summer Opera's world premiere (1991) of the 1963 revision of the opera, City College, San Francisco.

22. Horgan to Bacon, 1 July 1958, EBC, 45/61.

23. Bacon, "Comments and Problems," *The Argonaut,* 9 November 1934. Ernst Bacon Papers, Music Library, University of California, Berkeley.

24. Bacon, preface to *From These States (Gathered Along Unpaved Roads)* (New York: Associated Music Publisher, 1951); Bacon also collected eight folk song arrangements for voice and piano under the title *Along Unpaved Roads: Songs of a Lonesome People* (Los Angeles: Delkas Music Publishing Company, 1944).

25. In another typescript essay, he noted: "A million Sequoia seeds scattered over Death Valley will not do what one acorn will, properly nourished in the Sierra ramparts. What is needed is *a true regionalism, of time and place, even a little insularity*." Ernst Bacon, "How a Major Career . . . ," EBC, 33/2.

26. Bacon, "Folk Song" (typescript), EBC, 32/14.

27. Ibid.

28. While some of the opera's association between jazz and sex must be attributed to Horgan, Bacon later endorsed and exaggerated the association, in an undated essay called "Jazz and the Like": "Jazz is youth, impatience, irresponsibility, irrepressibility, sex, often pornography, impertinence, and a compulsive return to barbarity. . . . It is the supreme equalizer, giving us a taste at once of the virtue and the vice of commonality." EBC, 34/10.

29. Bacon, "The Singer," in *Words on Music* (Syracuse, NY: Syracuse University Press, 1960), 41.

30. Like many pianist-composers before him, most notably Liszt and Ravel, Bacon's scalar experiments were often linked to generating chords. The notes of any octatonic scale may be conceptualized as the combination of two diminished seventh chords, for example, or otherwise distributed into a combination of major and minor triads linked by a root progression of minor thirds. For details, see Arthur Berger, "Problems of Pitch Organization in Stravinsky," *Perspectives of New Music* 2 (fall-winter 1963–64): 11–42; and chapter 2 of Pieter van den Toorn, *The Music of Igor Stravinsky* (London and New Haven, CT: Yale University Press, 1983), 31–72.

31. Bacon's "Our Musical Idiom," is discussed in Severine Neff, "An American Precursor of Non-tonal Theory: Ernst Bacon (1898–1990)," *Current Musicology* 48 (1991): 5–26.

32. Bacon also provides octatonic music for the neighbors' frenzied fight, for Buddy's description of running water in town, and for parts of Mom's rebuke.

33. Bacon, "Teaching and Learning" (aphorisms), EBC, 30/19.

34. Horgan, "Ernst Bacon: A Contemporary Tribute," in the typescript catalog *Ernst Bacon* (Orinda, CA): January 1974.

35. Bacon, "An Honorable Science," April 1988, EBC, 32/26.

36. Harris and Adams as quoted in the typescript catalog *Ernst Bacon* (Orinda, CA): January 1974. The Adams quotation is taken from a letter dated 24 May 1963, EBC, 43/2. Bacon acknowledged his long friendship with Adams in the typescript "On Ansel Adams," 28 April 1989, EBC, 39/9.

37. Bacon, "Notes on Style," from *Works to 1969*, reprinted in program notes for the City Summer Opera.

38. Commissioned by the Louisville Orchestra and performed by the New York Philharmonic in 1949, *Wheat Field at Noon* is part of Thomson's *Three Pictures for Orchestra*.

39. Bacon, untitled, handwritten essay, n.d. A related typescript, "Too Much Music," states that the "queen of the arts" has become "a ubiquitous, strident slattern, a stench to the ear, a major pollution of the atmosphere. That it is sweet rather than sour makes it no better. Would you swim in a lake of Coca-Cola?" Though this typescript is also undated, it appears to be the near-final draft of "How Much Music," April 1988. EBC, 40/28, 33/5.

40. Bacon to the magazine *True West,* 7 April 1988; EBC, 40/34. See also "The New Hideousness," in which Bacon states: "It is all in the spirit of *pioneering,* [crossed out: (call it progress if you like)], a tradition too glorious to reveal its historical underside."

41. Stegner, "Variations on a Theme by Crèvecoeur," in *Where the Bluebird Sings,* 105–6.

8. HOW ROY HARRIS BECAME WESTERN

1. Copland, "The American Composer Gets a Break," *American Mercury* 34 (April 1935): 490; "Log Cabin Composer," *Time,* 11 November 1935, 36–37. I have explored this myth in " 'The White Hope of American Music'; or, How Roy Harris Became Western," *American Music* 19, no. 1 (1999): 131–67.

2. John Tasker Howard, *Our Contemporary Composers* (New York: Thomas Y. Crowell, 1941), 133. Many of these ingredients were already present in Howard's earlier book, *Our American Music* (New York: Thomas Y. Crowell, 1931), 572: "In some respects Roy Harris is the white hope of the nationalists, for this raw-boned Oklahoman has the Southwest in his blood. And he puts it in his music."

3. Copland, "Roy Harris," in *Our New Music* (New York: McGraw Hill, 1941), 164; reprinted with a postscript in *The New Music, 1900–1960* (New York: W.W. Norton, 1968).

4. Nicolas Slonimsky, "Roy Harris: Cimarron Composer," unpublished manuscript (1951), Music Library, Special Collections, University of California, Los Angeles (hereafter cited as CC); "Roy Harris, Composer of American Music," Oral History Program, University of California, Los Angeles, typescript (1983) in the Bancroft Library, University of California, Berkeley (hereafter cited as OH).

5. Barbara A. Zuck, *A History of Musical Americanism* (Ann Arbor: University of Michigan Research Press, 1980), 222.

6. Dan Stehman, *Roy Harris: An American Musical Pioneer* (Boston: G. K. Hall, 1984), 13; EDC, 254–85.

7. For a concise treatment of this aesthetic reorientation, see Alan Howard Levy, *Musical Nationalism: American Composers' Search for Identity* (Westport, CT: Greenwood Press, 1983).

8. Harris, "Perspective at Forty," *Magazine of Art* 32, no. 11 (1939): 639, 667.

9. Excerpts from Slonimsky's manuscript are published in "Roy Harris: The Story of an Oklahoma Composer Who Was Born in a Log Cabin on Lincoln's Birthday," in Crawford, Lott, and Oja, eds., *Celebration of American Music,* 311. See also Slonimsky, "Roy Harris," *Musical Quarterly* 33 (1947): 17–37.

10. See Robert Evett, "The Harmonic Idiom of Roy Harris," *Modern Music* 23 (January–February 1946): 100–107.

11. Harris, "Sources of a Musical Culture," *New York Times,* 1 January 1939, part ix, 7–8.

12. Copland, "America's Young Men of Promise," *Modern Music* 3 (March–April 1926): 13–20.

13. Ibid., 17.

14. Paul Rosenfeld, *An Hour with American Music* (Philadelphia: J.B. Lippincott, 1929), 107–25 (hereafter cited as PR).

15. PR, 118–19. The work in question is the Concerto for String Quartet, Piano, and Clarinet (1927), the first large-scale work Harris completed in Paris.

16. Farwell, "Roy Harris," *Music Quarterly* 18 (1932): 18.

17. Ibid., 20–21.

18. Ibid., 24.

19. Ibid., 31–32.

20. Ibid., 25.

21. Ibid., 19.

22. This version is from OH, 371–72. Other incarnations include Stehman, *American Musical Pioneer,* 52; CC, 38–39; and OH, 222–23. Harris also related this anecdote (complete with faux-Russian accent) in the first part of a lecture series entitled "Roy Harris Speaks on Contemporary Music" and in a video interview from the 1970s held at the Roy Harris Collection, California State University, Los Angeles (hereafter cited as RHC).

23. Dan Stehman, "The Symphonies of Roy Harris: An Analytical Study of the Linear Materials and of Related Works" (PhD diss., University of Southern California, 1973), 81, footnote 4.

24. Slonimsky, "From the West Composer New to Bostonians. Background for Roy Harris, About to Be Heard at Symphony Hall," *Boston Evening Transcript,* 24 January 1934, pt. 1: 7, col. 1.

25. Ibid., col. 2. Punctuation as in the original.

26. Stehman, "Symphonies of Roy Harris," 95. Stehman gives the following probable distribution of the extensive borrowed material in the first movement of the *Symphony 1933*: mm. 1–10, from *American Portrait,* "Speed"; mm. 11–57 and mm. 123–33 from a String Quartet (first movement); mm. 58–113, mm. 174–279, and mm. 300–378 from a lost orchestral Toccata.

27. Harris, "Symphony: 1933," Boston Symphony Orchestra *Programme,* ed. John B. Burk, 26–27 January 1934; cited in Stehman, "Symphonies of Roy Harris," 82.

28. Moses Smith, "Stravinsky's Ballet Feature of Program at Symphony," *Boston Evening American,* 27 January 1934; and George S. McManus, "Music," *Boston Herald,* 27 January 1934, 4; cited in Dan Stehman, *Roy Harris: A Bio-bibliography* (Westport, CT: Greenwood, 1991), 377–78.

29. H[enry] T[aylor] P[arker], "Manifold, Abundant, Individual," *Boston Evening Transcript,* 27 January 1934, pt. iii: 4.

30. Olin Downes, "Harris Symphony Has Premiere Here," *New York Times,* 3 February 1934, 9; Theodore Chanler was somewhat kinder in "New York, 1934," *Modern Music* 11 (March–April 1934): 142–47, but he had similar reservations: "It gave me the intuitive assurance that beneath all this composer's erratic inadequacies and undiscipline there flows a deep current of music."

31. Irving Kolodin names Harris as the first in his list of "false prophets" for American music in "Wanted—An American Composer," *The New Republic,* 16 January 1935, 273. Two indignant responses appear in *The New Republic,* 13 February 1935, 19–20.

32. According to Robert Stevenson, "Roy Harris at UCLA: Neglected Documentation," *Inter-American Music Review* 2, no. 1 (1979): 59–73, the biography was written "under the

composer's eye" in Tennessee; Harris's departure from that state in 1951 might help explain why the manuscript remained unfinished.

33. CC, 42. Slonimsky says that a thousand copies of this document were printed. I have found none extant, but the fact that *Time* magazine's article "Log Cabin Composer" cites excerpts from exactly these two reviews may provide indirect evidence for its existence.

34. David Ewen, *Composers Since 1900* (New York: H. W. Wilson, 1969), 263.

35. See Robert Strassburg, *Roy Harris: A Catalog of His Works* (Los Angeles: California State University, 1973), 29.

9. MANIFEST DESTINY

1. Walter Piston, "Roy Harris," *Modern Music* 11 (January–February 1934): 74.

2. Copland, "American Composer," 490.

3. Sidney Thurber Cox, "The Autogenetic Principle in the Melodic Writing of Roy Harris," MA thesis, Cornell University, 1948. Cox studied with Harris at Cornell and at Colorado College.

4. Stehman adduces similar examples in his dissertation, "Symphonies of Roy Harris," and more briefly in *American Musical Pioneer*, 26–29.

5. Cox, "Autogenetic Principle," 5.

6. See Zuck, *History of Musical Americanism*, 221–43, esp. 226–27.

7. Elliott Carter, "Season of Hindemith and Americans," *Modern Music* 16 (May–June 1939): 250–51; Thomson, "Harris and Shostakovich," in *The Musical Scene* (New York: Alfred A. Knopf, 1945), 123–24.

8. Olin Downes, "New Work Given by Koussevitzky," *New York Times*, 12 March 1939, p. 60; William Schuman, "Letter to the Music Editor," *New York Times*, 12 March 1939, sec. 3, p. 6. For more information on the Harris-Schumann relationship, see Steven R. Swayne, *Orpheus in Manhattan: William Schuman and the Shaping of American Musical Life* (New York: Oxford University Press, 2010).

9. Copland, "Composers in America," in *The New Music*, 124–25.

10. Elliott Carter, "American Music in the New York Scene," *Modern Music* 17 (January–February 1940): 94.

11. Boston Symphony Orchestra *Programme*, ed. John N. Burk, 24 February 1939, 780; cited in Zuck, *History of Musical Americanism*, 237.

12. George Henry Lovett Smith, "American Festival in Boston," *Modern Music* 42 (October–November 1939): 44; Strassburg, *Catalog*, 13.

13. OH, 387. This story is repeated with varying amounts of detail in Evett, "Harmonic Idiom," 102–3; Strassburg, *Catalog*, 13; and in interviews preserved at the RHC.

14. Mellers, *Music in a New Found Land*, 73–75.

15. Harris's first attempt at an ending in 1938 avoided the tragic collapse of the final, successful 1939 version. For details, see Stehman, *American Musical Pioneer*, 67–68; and Stehman, "Symphonies of Roy Harris," part 5.

16. Autogenesis represented not just an attack on neoclassicism but also a correction of twelve-tone technique, as Arthur Mendel noted in 1939. An early Harris advocate, he

praised the Passacaglia theme of the composer's Piano Quintet for its "free, asymmetrical, 'autogenetic' growth" and its pitch content: "The theme is so eminently singable, so strongly diatonic and tonal in feeling, that one is surprised to realize that it contains every note of the twelve-note scale." *Modern Music* 17 (October–November 1939): 25–36. See also the description of this Passacaglia theme preserved on cassette H1555, RHC.

17. CC, 64–65; a shorter explanation appears in Slonimsky, "Roy Harris," 315.

18. Mendel, "Music: A Change in Structure," *The Nation* 134, no. 3470 (6 January 1932): 26.

19. Stehman cites Harris's program note for the *Symphony 1933* as the earliest instance of the term *autogenetic* that he has encountered in his extensive research. Stehman, "Symphonies of Roy Harris," 84n8. Perhaps misreading some advance publicity, an anonymous writer for *American Music Lover* called the symphony "autogenuous" in 1938: "Roy Harris—American Composer," 3, no. 11 (March 1938): 409.

20. H[enry] T[aylor] P[arker], "Manifold, Abundant, Individual," part 3, p. 4.

21. Roy Harris, program note for *Farewell to Pioneers, Journal of the Philadelphia Orchestra*, 27 March 1936, 813; cited in the preface to Stehman, *American Musical Pioneer.*

22. Colin McPhee, "New York's Spring Season, 1936," *Modern Music* 13 (May–June 1936): 39–42.

23. Cox, "Autogenetic Principle," 13–14, 5.

24. Stehman, *Bio-bibliography*, 73, 334.

25. Stehman, preface to *American Musical Pioneer.*

26. McPhee, "New York's Spring Season." See also Edwin H. Schloss, "Chavez Makes Bow as Guest Maestro," *Philadelphia Record*, 28 March 1936; and Henry Pleasants, "Music in Review," *Philadelphia Evening Bulletin*, 28 March 1936; cited in Stehman, *Bio-bibliography*, 334.

27. CC, 1, 70. The Cimarron land run of 1893 opened the panhandle of Indian Territory, not the area of the Harris farm (near Tulsa). Stehman (*American Musical Pioneer*, 1) notes that there is some uncertainty about when the family moved to Oklahoma (and thus about the location of Roy's birth in 1898). His father's claim is dated 1901, but territorial records may simply be incomplete.

28. *Cimarron* was written for the Tri-State Band Festival in Enid, Oklahoma. Harris may have been aware of Edwin Gerschefski's article "To the Brass Band," *Modern Music* 14 (May–June 1937): 188–92, which extols the band as an ensemble uniquely "in touch" with the people and as a "more lively and vital factor" in the West and Midwest than in the East.

29. Denise von Glahn, *The Sounds of Place: Music and the American Cultural Landscape* (Boston: Northeastern University Press, 2003), 180–97.

30. Paul Rosenfeld, "Harris," in *Discoveries of a Music Critic* (New York: Vienna House, 1972), 325; orig. Harcourt Brace Jovanovich, 1936.

31. Edna Ferber, *Cimarron* (Garden City, NY: Doubleday, 1930), 14, 16; cited in von Glahn, *Sounds of Place*, 191–93.

32. Program note in the published score (Mills Music, 1941). Von Glahn observes that the mixing of fact and fiction is key to Ferber's novel as well. Ferber made a short research trip to the Oklahoma State Historical Library, and she framed her book by saying: "Only the more fantastic and improbable events contained in this book are true." See Ferber, *Cimarron*, ix–x; and von Glahn, *Sounds of Place*, 190.

33. Von Glahn (*Sounds of Place*, 197) hears the Indians of Oklahoma Territory in the accented timpani strokes on beats 1 and 2 of measures 48–54. While I find her suggestion both attractive and plausible, for me this association is undermined by the 5/4 meter, the interruptive rests, and the fact that the melody, too, appears "stuck" at this point, making the percussion seem part of a more general attempt to create tension and anticipation.

34. Ferber, *Cimarron*, 15. The film exaggerates the racial and class diversity of the novel, showing a variety of vehicles in the land run and featuring Indians and a Jew more prominently than in the original book.

35. PR, 117, 119–20; Farwell, "Roy Harris," 31–32; Slonimsky, "From the West," 7.

36. Henry Cowell, "Three Native Composers," *New Freeman*, 3 May 1930, 184–86.

37. John Tasker Howard, *Our Contemporary Composers*, 145. See also Paul Rosenfeld, "Current Chronicle: Copland–Harris–Schuman," *Musical Quarterly* 25 (1939): 372–81; and Rosenfeld, "The Newest American Composers," *Modern Music* 15 (March–April 1938): 153–59.

38. MacDonald Smith Moore, *Yankee Blues: Musical Culture and American Identity* (Bloomington: Indiana University Press, 1985), 71–72. See especially Chapter 5, the final section of which treats Harris under the subtitle "The Great White Hope"—an adaptation of Howard's "white hope of the nationalists."

39. Copland, "American Composer," 490; Howard, "Contemporary Composers," 145; PR, 120–21.

40. Moore, *Yankee Blues*, 161.

41. Harris, "The Growth of a Composer," *Musical Quarterly* 20 (1934): 188.

42. Harris, "The Problems of American Composers," in *American Composers on American Music*, ed. Henry Cowell ([Stanford, CA]: Stanford University Press, 1933), 150–51. This article is modified from "Does Music Have to Be European?" *Scribner's Magazine* 91, no. 4 (1932): 204–9. Many of the ideas in these essays seem to have taken shape in Harris's first public lectures, given at the Los Angeles Public Library in 1931. *Los Angeles Times*, 5 July 1931, iii: 17.

43. Harris, "Problems of American Composers," 150.

44. Paul Bowles, "On the Film Front," *Modern Music* 18 (January–February 1941): 134.

10. THE COMPOSER AS FOLK SINGER

1. Stehman, "Symphonies of Roy Harris," 265. According to CC, 14, Farwell himself conducted Harris's arrangement of "Peña Hueca" in 1920 with the Pasadena Community Chorus.

2. Harris, "Notes" for *When Johnny Comes Marching Home* (New York: G. Schirmer, 1935).

3. According to Slonimsky ("Roy Harris," 317), during World War II "the notorious 'Tokyo Rose' paid Harris the dubious tribute of featuring his overture *When Johnny Comes Marching Home* on one of her propaganda broadcasts. 'Stand for democracy as Roy Harris does in his music,' she coaxed. 'Go marching home!'"

4. Barbara Zuck (*History of Musical Americanism*) notes the widespread use of folk songs in the 1930s-40s and discusses some of the political implications of this trend. See

also Mark Fenster, "Preparing the Audience, Informing the Performers: John A. Lomax and *Cowboy Songs and Other Frontier Ballads,*" *American Music* 7 (1989): 260–77; and Crist, *Music for the Common Man.*

5. Charles Seeger, "Grass Roots for American Composers," *Modern Music* 16 (March–April 1939): 143–49. See also Paul Rosenfeld's response, "Variations on the Grass Roots Theme," *Modern Music* 16 (May–June 1939): 214–19.

6. Harris, "Folksong—American Big Business," *Modern Music* 18 (November–December 1940): 8–9.

7. The Harris scores are in manuscript at the New York Public Library. For an early reaction to the broadcasts, see Conlon Nancarrow, "Over the Air," *Modern Music* 12 (November–December 1939): 55.

8. Henry Nash Smith, *Virgin Land,* chaps. 9 and 10.

9. Lawrence Morton, "On the Hollywood Front," *Modern Music* 23 (1946): 141.

10. The cowboy's anti-industrial connotations, along with his marked tendency to keep to himself, made him an unlikely hero for Marxist theorizing. Nonetheless, some made the attempt, particularly after the failed strike among cowhands in 1883. See Don D. Walker, "The Left Side of the American Ranges: A Marxist View of the Cowboy," in *Clio's Cowboys* (Lincoln: University of Nebraska Press, 1981), 131–46.

11. William H. Goetzmann, *The West of the Imagination* (New York: W.W. Norton, 1986), 310.

12. Harris, "Folksong—American Big Business," 11.

13. Ibid.

14. A later performance on 31 December 1942 with the New York Philharmonic under Dimitri Mitropoulos was recorded by the Office of War Information for broadcast to American troops during the war.

15. Stehman, *American Musical Pioneer,* 72–79.

16. Ibid., 73; Nicolas Slonimsky, program note for *Folksong Symphony 1940,* Vanguard Classics, OVC 4076.

17. Stehman ("Symphonies of Roy Harris," 271) calls this "the most complete and up-to-date program note" and suggests that it was written around 1960.

18. Harris, program note for *Folksong Symphony,* American Festival Chorus and Orchestra, conducted by Vladimir Golschmann, Vanguard: VSD 2082, 1960.

19. See Stehman, "Symphonies of Roy Harris," 265–359. The last movement was originally the first of the four choral settings; its overture-like title, "Welcome Party," is thus sometimes omitted, as is the case in the G. Schirmer vocal score.

20. Harris, program note for *Folksong Symphony.*

21. Olin Downes, "Unusual Program by Mitropoulos," *New York Times,* 1 January 1943, p. 26, col. 1.

22. Copland, "Roy Harris," in *Our New Music,* 171.

23. Arthur Cohn, "Americans at Rochester," *Modern Music* 17 (May–June 1940): 257.

24. Herbert Elwell, "Harris' *Folksong Symphony,*" *Modern Music* 18 (January–February 1941): 113–14.

25. Apparently following suit, Harris's student Robert Evett called the *Folksong Symphony* the equal of *Christ Lag in Todesbanden* (and an improvement upon Hindemith's

Schwanendreher and Bartók's *Improvisations*). Evett, "Harmonic Idiom," 101. On Harris's obsession with Bach, see Slonimsky, *Perfect Pitch: A Life Story* (Oxford: Oxford University Press, 1988), 246.

26. "Symphony in Folk Songs: New Roy Harris Opus the Hit of Eastman Music Festival," *Newsweek*, 6 May 1940, 44–45; "Folk-Song Symphony," *Time*, 6 January 1941, 34.

27. The unsigned article to which Harris refers attributes these words to Herbert Elwell. "Folk-Song Symphony," *Time*, 6 January 1941.

28. Harris began teaching summer sessions at Colorado College in 1941 and joined the full-time faculty in 1943. He taught there for five years, with a one-year leave of absence in 1945 while he was Director of Music for the Office of War Information. Holm devoted many ballets to western themes and included music by Harris, Cowell, and others. See Edwin Denby, "With the Dancers," *Modern Music* 18 (May–June 1941): 269–70; and James Sykes, "Native Notes in Colorado," *Modern Music* 20 (November–December 1942): 49–50.

29. David Hall, liner notes for Composers Recordings, CD 818. Fifteen interludes were planned, but only five were published by Carl Fischer. Two others were edited in 1987 by Dan Stehman and the RHC.

30. Roy Harris and Johana Harris, "Sing a Song of Folk," WQED Television, Pittsburgh, n.d. An audio recording is preserved as cassette H2025A in the RHC. Used by permission of Patricia Harris.

31. Slonimsky, "Oklahoma Composer," in Crawford, Lott, and Oja, *Celebration*, 311.

32. Jane Tompkins, *West of Everything: The Inner Life of Westerns* (New York: Oxford University Press, 1992), 17–18, 44–45; see also pp. 127–28.

33. For a description of Harris's car accident, see OH, 526–28.

34. Harris was extremely secretive about his second and third wives; there is no mention of them in the oral history interviews. Scholars are not even certain of their full names. Stehman, *American Musical Pioneer*, 14–15. He may also have fathered an illegitimate son while in Paris; see Stehman, *Bio-bibliography*, 5.

35. Louise Spizizen, "Johana and Roy Harris: Marrying a Real Composer," *Musical Quarterly* 77 (1993): 579–606.

36. Copland, "America's Young Men of Promise," 17.

37. Johana Harris, "Personal Note," in *The Book of Modern Composers*, ed. David Ewen (New York: Alfred A. Knopf, 1942), 451.

38. Cowell wrote that Harris "often convinces his friends and listeners of the extreme value of his works by his own indefatigable enthusiasm for them, when in reality they are only mildly interesting and would not be very highly regarded by these selfsame people if they heard them in performances without the stimulating presence of their creator." Cowell, "Roy Harris," 64–65.

39. Piston, "Roy Harris," 73, 74.

40. Copland, "American Composer," 490.

41. Copland, "Roy Harris," in *Our New Music*, 162–64.

42. Ibid., 174–75.

43. Piston, "Roy Harris," 73.

44. Marc Blitzstein, "Composers as Lecturers and in Concerts," *Modern Music* 13 (November–December 1935): 50.

45. Thomson, *New York Herald Tribune*, 21 November 1940; cited in MacDonald Smith Moore, *Yankee Blues*, 167.

46. Alfred Einstein, "War, Nationalism, Tolerance," *Modern Music* 17 (October–November 1939): 3, 4.

47. "For the racialist . . . the spiritual and economic salvation of the unhappy region is identical with its bloodstream's retention of its 'purity.' He introduces into the Virginia House of Burgesses bills illegalizing marriage between whites and blacks, and is all for 'the true folk manner.' East Side boys it is clear to him can never sing in it: also, he proclaims the doctrine that American expressions to be 'American' must base themselves on the Anglo-Saxon tradition. Noteworthy is the fact that this fascist deems the ribald songs beloved of the people and their 'songs of social significance,' not in the 'true folk' manner." Rosenfeld, "Folksong and Culture-Politics," *Modern Music* 17 (October–November 1939): 23.

48. Roger Sessions, "On the American Future," *Modern Music* 17 (January–February 1940): 72.

49. Conlon Nancarrow, "Over the Air," *Modern Music* 17 (May–June 1940): 265. The final ellipsis is present in the original.

50. Marshall Bialosky, "Roy Harris: In Memoriam (But Keep Your Hats On)," *College Music Symposium* 22, no. 2 (1982): 8.

11. THE SAGA OF THE PRAIRIES

1. Margaret Susan Key, "'Sweet Melody over Silent Wave': Depression-Era Radio and the American Composer" (PhD diss., University of Maryland, College Park, 1995), 166–67, 182.

2. Aaron Copland and Vivian Perlis, *Copland: 1900 through 1942* (New York: St. Martin's Press, 1984), 254–55 (hereafter cited as VPAC1).

3. Howard Pollack, *Aaron Copland: The Life and Work of an Uncommon Man* (New York: Henry Holt, 1999), 312 (hereafter cited as HP).

4. George Antheil, *Bad Boy of Music* (Garden City, NY: Doubleday, 1945), 324–25.

5. Rubin Goldmark to Copland, 26 April 1921, Copland Collection, Library of Congress, Box 255, Folder 17 (hereafter cited as CCLC, 255/17).

6. Ibid.

7. Goldmark to Copland, 21 August 1922, CCLC, 255/17.

8. Cited in H. F. P., "Advice on Composition from Rubin Goldmark," *Musical America*, 16 May 1914, 6.

9. Copland, "Rubin Goldmark: A Tribute," *Juilliard Review* 3, no. 3 (fall 1956): 15. In 1977, Copland told Leo Smit that Goldmark "really should get more credit than he has been given for my early training." Cited in David Beveridge, "Dvořák's American Pupil Rubin Goldmark," in *Dvořák-Studien*, ed. Klaus Döge and Peter Jost (Mainz, Germany: Schott, 1994), 237. See also David J. Tomatz, "Rubin Goldmark, Postromantic: Trial Balances in American Music," PhD diss., Catholic University of America, 1966.

10. Surprisingly, Goldmark spent far more time in the West than Copland did. He moved to Colorado Springs in 1894 for his health and taught at Colorado College until 1900. After returning to New York, he continued to spend summers at a cabin in the Rockies, which he described to Copland in a letter of 26 April 1921, CCLC, 255/17.

11. Copland, "Gabriel Fauré, a Neglected Master," *Musical Quarterly* 10 (1924): 573–86. Gayle Minetta Murchison also emphasizes the relationships between *la grande ligne* and Copland's clarity of musical form in "Nationalism in William Grant Still and Aaron Copland between the Wars: Style and Ideology," PhD diss., Yale University, 1998, 62–63.

12. See, among others, David Matthews, "Copland and Stravinsky," *Tempo* 95 (Winter 1950): 10–14; and Arthur Berger, "Stravinsky and the Younger American Composers," *Score and I.M.A. Magazine* 12 (June 1955): 39–40.

13. Arthur Berger, *Aaron Copland* (New York: Oxford University Press, 1953), 42.

14. These questions grew more urgent as Copland became a prominent exponent of "modern music"—both in the journal of that name and in his work as a concert organizer. See David Metzer, "The League of Composers: The Initial Years," *American Music* 15 (1997): 45–69; and the writings of Carol Oja, especially "The Copland-Sessions Concerts and Their Reception in the Contemporary Press," *Musical Quarterly* 65 (1979): 212–29; and Oja, *Making Music Modern: New York in the 1920s* (New York: Oxford University Press, 2000).

15. Copland's writings on jazz include "Jazz Structure and Influence," *Modern Music* 4 (January–February 1927): 9–14; and "The Jazz Interlude," in *Our New Music* (New York: McGraw-Hill, 1940). See also David Schiff, "Copland and the 'Jazz Boys,'" in *Copland Connotations: Studies and Interviews*, ed. Peter Dickinson (Woodbridge, UK: Boydell Press, 2002), 14–21; Stanley V. Kleppinger, "On the Influence of Jazz Rhythm in the Music of Aaron Copland," *American Music* 21, no. 1 (2003): 74–111; and Murchison, "Nationalism."

16. See Nicholas Slonimsky, *Lexicon of Musical Invective* (New York: Colemann-Ross, 1953), 86–87.

17. Harris to Copland, 26 July [1926], CCLC. Courtesy of Patricia Harris. Harris had apparently reacted strongly to the jazz idiom of *Music for the Theatre*. Pollack suggests that the "grotesco" music in the midsection of the aptly named "Burlesque" movement inspired Harris's outburst at an early informal hearing of the score: "It's whorehouse music! It's whorehouse music!" HP, 130. See also Leo Smit, "A Conversation with Aaron Copland on His 80th Birthday," *Contemporary Keyboard* 6, no. 11 (1980): 12.

18. Andrea Olmstead reprints the surviving letter exchange in *The Correspondence of Roger Sessions* (Boston: Northeastern University Press, 1992), 65–71, 73–77. See also Olmstead's overview and excerpts from the correspondence between these two men in "The Copland–Sessions Letters," *Tempo* 175 (1990): 2–5.

19. From later letters, we can see that Copland took pains to reassure Sessions that his jazz days were over. On March 18, 1927, he wrote: "I'm glad you liked the Jazz article. It has helped considerably to get the whole business out of my system," and in a postscript to his letter of 18 August 1927, he exclaimed: "The Irony of Fate. Now that I am done with jazz an article by I. Goldberg is to appear in the Sept. 'Mercury' on 'A.C. and his Jazz.'" *The Selected Correspondence of Aaron Copland*, ed. Elizabeth [Bergman] Crist and Wayne Shirley (New Haven, CT, and London: Yale University Press, 2006), 54, 57.

20. Theodore Chanler to Copland, 16 August 1930, CCLC, 249/21.

21. Chanler, "Aaron Copland," in *American Composers on American Music*, ed. Henry Cowell, 51. The essay originally appeared as "Aaron Copland up to Now," in 1930 in *The Hound and Horn*. In his editorial postscript to Chanler's article, Cowell felt compelled to

comment on Copland's recent growth: "Since the foregoing article was written, Aaron Copland has produced a number of new works, and has materially broadened his tendencies in composition. For one thing, he no longer relies on jazz themes to animate his auditors" (55–56).

22. Virgil Thomson, "Aaron Copland," *Modern Music* 9 (January–February 1932): 71–72.

23. Ibid., 72.

24. On Copland and Judaism, see especially Howard Pollack, "Copland and the Prophetic Voice," *Aaron Copland and His World*, ed. Carol J. Oja and Judith Tick (Princeton, NJ: Princeton University Press, 2005), 1–14.

25. Copland, "The Lyricism of Milhaud," *Modern Music* 6 (January–February 1929): 16.

26. Thomson, "Aaron Copland," 67.

27. *Jewish Influences in American Life, vol. III: International Jew: The World's Foremost Problem* (reprints from the *Dearborn Independent*, 1921), 65, 70, 75–78; cited in MacDonald Smith Moore, *Yankee Blues*, 146.

28. Lazare Saminsky, *Music of the Ghetto and the Bible* (New York: Bloch Publishing, 1934), 67–69.

29. Ibid., 123, 125.

30. MacDonald Smith Moore, *Yankee Blues*, 131.

31. Howard, *Our Contemporary Composers*, 3. Isaac Goldberg, "Aaron Copland and His Jazz," *American Mercury*, September 1927, 63–64. See also HP, 518; and David Metzer, "'Spurned Love': Eroticism and Abstraction in the Early Works of Aaron Copland," *Journal of Musicology* 15 (1997): 419–43.

32. Henry Cowell, "Bericht aus Amerika: Amerikanische Musik?" trans. Hanns Gutman, *Melos* 9, nos. 8–9 (August–September 1930): 362–65, 363; "Die beiden wirklichen Amerikaner: Ives und Ruggles," trans. Hanns Gutman, *Melos* 9, no. 10 (October 1930): 417–20; and "Die kleineren Komponisten," trans. Hanns Gutman, *Melos* 9, no. 12 (December 1930): 526–29, esp. 527.

33. Daniel Gregory Mason, ". . . And a Moral," in *Tune In, America: A Study of Our Coming Musical Independence* (New York: Alfred A. Knopf, 1931), 160–61.

34. Copland's longtime friend Harold Clurman recalls this episode in *All People Are Famous (Instead of an Autobiography)* (New York: Harcourt Brace Jovanovich, 1974), 33.

35. For more on prejudice against Jews in France, see Jane F. Fulcher, "The Preparation for Vichy: Anti-Semitism in French Musical Culture between the Two World Wars," *Musical Quarterly* 79 (1995): 458–75. Fulcher endorses and provides a broader intellectual context for Léonie Rosenstiel's claim that Boulanger considered Jews a less creative race. Rosenstiel, *Nadia Boulanger: A Life in Music* (New York: W. W. Norton, 1982), 198–99. It is important to note that many Boulanger pupils, including Copland himself, vehemently disagreed with Rosenstiel's characterization: "[Boulanger] and I became close friends, and there were other Jewish students who were Nadia's friends. It is impossible that one of us would not have noticed anti-Semitism in her behavior. Especially during the war years, we were very much aware of such things." VPAC1, 65.

36. See Klára Móricz, *Jewish Identities: Nationalism, Racism, and Utopianism in Twentieth-Century Music* (Berkeley and Los Angeles: University of California Press, 2008).

37. For further discussion of these themes in relation to *Music for Radio,* see my chapter "From Orient to Occident: Aaron Copland and the Sagas of the Prairies," in *Aaron Copland and His World,* ed. Oja and Tick, 307–49.

38. Crist and Shirley, *Selected Correspondence,* 5–9.

39. Copland, "Composer from Brooklyn," in *Our New Music,* 228–29.

40. Davidson Taylor, "Tomorrow's Broadcast," *North American Review* 241 (March 1936): 51.

41. Marc Blitzstein, "Coming—The Mass Audience," *Modern Music* 13 (May–June 1936): 25.

42. Cited in Key, " 'Sweet melody,' " 136–37. In "The Composer and Radio," Copland offered the utopian suggestion that networks should employ ten "staff composers" and that a radio audience free of concert-hall prejudices would be more receptive to new music. *Our New Music,* 233–42.

43. Key, " 'Sweet melody,' " 138–39.

44. Deems Taylor to Copland, 28 September 1936, CCLC, 335/9.

45. Cited in Key, " 'Sweet melody,' " 131. Emphasis in the original.

46. Davidson Taylor to Copland, 30 July 1937, CCLC, 335/9.

47. This typescript is preserved in CCLC, 406/10. Jessica Burr has discussed this document and other important matters in "Copland, the West and American Identity," in *Copland Connotations,* ed. Dickinson, 22–28. In the list presented here, I have attempted to roughly preserve the relative proportions of urban versus rural and American versus non-American titles while also conveying some of the more colorful entries.

48. Davidson Taylor to Copland, 30 July 1937, CCLC, 335/9.

49. See Dan T. Carter, *Scottsboro: A Tragedy of the American South* (Baton Rouge: Louisiana State University Press, 1969); and James Goodman, *Stories of Scottsboro* (New York: Pantheon Books, 1994). "The Ballad of Ozie Powell" was later included in Hughes's collection *A New Song* (1938).

50. Copland was not the only composer whose conscience was caught by the plight of the Scottsboro Boys. L. E. Swift (a.k.a. Elie Siegmeister) penned a mass song "The Scottsboro Boys Shall Not Die" for the first *Workers' Song Book,* which Copland reviewed for *New Masses* in 1934. HP, 276. Aaron Copland, "Workers Sing!" *New Masses* 11, no. 9 (1934): 28–29; reprinted in *Aaron Copland, A Reader: Selected Writings, 1923–72,* ed. Richard Kostelanetz (New York: Routledge, 2004), 88–90. Although it is possible that Copland intended his "Ballad" as a "correction" of Siegmeister's song, I find no compelling links in their music. See also Carol J. Oja, "Marc Blitzstein's *The Cradle Will Rock* and Mass-song Style in the 1930s," *Musical Quarterly* 73 (1989): 445–475; Zuck, *History of Musical Americanism;* and Elizabeth [Bergman] Crist, *Music for the Common Man: Aaron Copland during the Depression and War* (New York: Oxford University Press, 2005), 27–31.

51. Although, the text underlay is missing for this line in the most complete version of the sketches, these words are present in other sketches.

52. Copland, "The Composer and Radio," 241–42.

53. "Copland Decides He Likes Own Name Best" (unsigned), *Boston Evening Transcript,* 21 August 1937. Leonhardt's justification for the "Saga of the Prairie" title appears in a slightly different form in a telegram from Copland to Davidson Taylor, 12 August

1937. CCLC, 406/10. I am grateful to Elizabeth Bergman for pointing out the likelihood that Leonhardt was inspired by the subtitle of Ole Rölvaag's novel *Giants in the Earth: A Saga of the Prairie* (New York: Harper & Row, 1927).

54. Moses Smith, "Music for the Radio," *Boston Evening Transcript,* 26 July 1937, 8, col. 5.

55. This material appears on the penultimate page of the "Ballade of Ozzie Powell" sketches. Although there is neither text underlay nor any indication of where the passage might fit in to the "Ballade," the motivic and physical connections (the page is attached to the rest of the sketch) strongly suggest that the material was conceived at the same time as the choral setting.

56. Oscar Levant, *A Smattering of Ignorance* (Garden City, NY: Garden City Publishing, 1940), 241: "To Copland's surprise, the piece had distinctly Western overtones for a good many of his listeners, the winning title, eventually, being 'Saga of the Prairee' [*sic*]."

57. Julia Smith, *Aaron Copland: His Work and Contribution to American Music* (New York: E. P. Dutton, 1955), 178.

58. Aaron Copland to Eugene Ormandy, 23 September 1958: "As you can imagine, I don't at all like the idea of being difficult about a mere title of a piece. After all, the music is the same whatever it is called. On the other hand, I must confess that I never liked the title 'Saga of the Prairie,' for the simple reason that it sounds too corny to me, and was not my idea in the first place." Crist and Shirley, *Selected Correspondence,* 222.

59. Moses Smith, "Music for the Radio."

60. Davidson Taylor to Copland, 30 July 1937, CCLC, 335/9.

61. Marion Bauer, "Aaron Copland: A Significant Personality in American Music," *American Music Lover* 4, no. 12 (April 1939): 429.

62. Charles Mills, "Over the Air," *Modern Music* 20 (November–December 1942): 63.

63. Lazare Saminsky, "'American' Phase of International Music Festival Revealed New Talent," *Musical Courier,* July 1941, 19.

64. Saminsky, *Music of the Ghetto,* 124.

65. Howard, *Our Contemporary Composers,* 145.

66. It is unclear when his mother's early residence in Texas became important to Copland's representation of his heritage. Although it goes unmentioned in "Composer from Brooklyn," his later autobiographical memoirs take up this theme. See VPAC1, 3: "Aaron Copland's mother, Sarah Mittenthal, born in Russia, grew up in Illinois and Texas, where cowboys and Indians were a natural part of her life. Perhaps this is at least a partial answer to that question so often asked the composer: 'How could a Jewish boy, born and raised in Brooklyn, write "cowboy" music?'"

12. COMMUNAL SONG, COSMOPOLITAN SONG

1. Crist, *Music for the Common Man,* chaps. 1 and 2.

2. Copland to Carlos Chávez, 16 December 1933; Crist and Shirley, *Selected Correspondence,* 103.

3. Harold Clurman to Copland, 16 August 1934; cited in HP, 277. Copland recounts the inspiration he derived from this experience in a letter to Israel Citkowitz (September 1934): "When S. K. Davis, Communist candidate for Gov. in Min., came to town and spoke

in the public park, the farmers asked me to talk to the crowd. Its one thing to think revolution, or talk about it to ones friends, but to preach it from the streets—OUT LOUD— Well, I made my speech (Victor [Kraft] says it was a good one) and I'll probably never be the same!" Crist and Shirley, *Selected Correspondence*, 106.

4. For more detailed discussion, see Zuck, *History of Musical Americanism*, 103–53; R. Serge Denisoff, *Great Day Coming: Folk Music and the American Left* (Urbana: University of Illinois Press, 1971); Robbie Lieberman, *"My Song Is My Weapon": People's Songs, American Communism, and the Politics of Culture, 1930–1950* (Urbana: University of Illinois Press, 1989); Richard A. Reuss with JoAnne C. Reuss, *American Folk Music and Left-Wing Politics, 1927–57* (Lanham, MD: Scarecrow Press, 2000); and Benjamin Filene, *Romancing the Folk: Public Memory and American Roots Music* (Chapel Hill: University of North Carolina Press, 2000).

5. Copland, "Jazz as Folk-Music," *Musical America*, 19 December 1925, 18.

6. As cited in Martha Dreiblatt, "Lack of Tradition Blocks Musical Progress Here: Personalities of Composers One Solution, Says Aaron Copland," *World* [New York], 7 July 1929, Metropolitan Section, 3. Copland's attitudes here prefigure his more infamous assessment of jazz in "Composer from Brooklyn," in *Our New Music*, 227: "All American music could not possibly be confined to two dominant jazz moods—the 'blues' and the snappy number."

7. Copland as quoted in Dreiblatt, "Lack of Tradition."

8. Crist, *Music for the Common Man*, 48–59.

9. See, for example, Copland's treatment of Farwell's friend and Wa-Wan associate Henry Gilbert: "What he did was suggestive on a primitive and pioneering level, but the fact is that he lacked the technique and musicianship for expressing his ideals in a significant way." Copland, "Musical Imagination in the Americas" and "The Composer in Industrial America," in *Music and Imagination* (Cambridge, MA: Harvard University Press, 1952), 79, 103.

10. Copland, "Composer in Industrial America," 103–4.

11. Ibid.

12. Burr, "Copland, the West and American Identity," in Dickinson, *Copland Connotations*, 23–24.

13. Copland to Nadia Boulanger, 1 June 1928, CCLC; Crist and Shirley, *Selected Correspondence*, 64. Apparently, the fact that Copland went "out West" on his own irritated Harris, who had been coaxing Copland to visit California with him. Harris wrote from Paris: "Dearly Beloved: So this is what you do when my back is turned—Just like that he ups and goes West without me—It's perfectly [ridiculous?]—and I am seriously considering taking the next Boat home—Why, Aaron, you can't go all alone out in that wild and woolly west. One of these heavy-breasted real estate salesmen might mistake you for a buck from Missouri and try to sell you a sand lot—and Good Lord there might be all sorts of complications—I just won't hear of it, that's all [punctuation added]." Harris to Copland, 1928 (penciled), CCLC, 256/8. Courtesy of Patricia Harris.

14. Copland to Gerald Sykes, 20 May 1928; cited in Burr, "American Identity," in Dickinson, *Copland Connotations*, 23.

15. Copland to Serge and Natalie Koussevitzky, 2 July 1928, CCLC (my translation from the French); accessed online through the Library of Congress American Memory Project (http://memory.loc.gov/ammem/index.html), digital ID: copland corro109.

16. Pollack describes Kirstein's manner of commissioning the scenario from Loring based on an interview with Richard Schottland. HP, 316. See also Frederick Nolan, *The West of Billy the Kid* (Norman: University of Oklahoma Press, 1998), 291–99.

17. Robert Utley, *Billy the Kid: A Short and Violent Life* (Lincoln: University of Nebraska Press, 1989), 200; cited in HP, 317.

18. Copland in an interview with Philip Ramey, cited by Richard Freed in the liner notes to *Aaron Copland: Billy the Kid, Rodeo* (Leonard Slatkin and the Saint Louis Symphony Orchestra), Angel DS-37357, 1986. See also Philip Ramey, "Copland and the Dance," *Ballet News* 2, no. 5 (1980): 11.

19. Pollack cites an undated interview with Loring. HP, 318.

20. John Martin, "The Dance: 'Billy': Loring Ballet Restored to the Repertoire," *New York Times*, 11 April 1948.

21. Edwin Denby, "*Billy the Kid* and Its Dance Faults," *New York Herald Tribune*, 31 October 1943; reprinted in Denby, *Dance Writings and Poetry*, ed. Robert Cornfield (New Haven, CT: Yale University Press, 1998), 102.

22. Martin, "The Dance."

23. Walter Noble Burns, *The Saga of Billy the Kid* (Garden City, NY: Garden City Publishing, 1925), 173.

24. CCLC, 395/10. Kirstein attributed the opening action of *Billy the Kid* to the influence of Martha Graham, who had a penchant for processionals. VPAC1, 284. As Pollack points out, Burns's *Saga of Billy the Kid*, seems a more immediate and likely source. HP, 319. Though Graham's *Frontier* (1935) was surely familiar to Kirstein and others on the New York ballet scene, Louis Horst's score does not involve an ensemble processional.

25. Walter Terry, "The Ballet," *New York Herald Tribune*, 7 April 1948. Terry expands on sentiments from his earlier review, "The Ballet," *New York Herald Tribune*, 23 April 1942; CCLC, 395/3.

26. Marcia B. Siegel, *The Shapes of Change: Images of American Dance* (Boston: Houghton Mifflin, 1979), 119.

27. Denby, *Dance Writings and Poetry*, 102.

28. Siegel, *Shapes of Change*, 121, 119. A nine-page typescript (CCLC, 63/33-F) signed "Eugene Loring & Lemuel Ayers" illustrates Loring's cinematic preoccupations. It gives camera and lighting instructions for the entire action of the ballet, in a total of sixty distinct shots. It may have been crafted in preparation for a 1976 Dance in America production for National Educational Television, in which, according to Siegel, "Loring and the telecast producers converted [the ballet] into the Western it had so carefully tried not to be" by adding film footage of frontier action ("chopping down of trees," "watching for possible dangers," etc.).

29. Neil Lerner provides a history of such gestures in "Music of Wide Open Spaces."

30. Burr, "American Identity," in *Copland Connotations*, ed. Dickinson. Burr spoke about the opening of *Billy the Kid* in her paper "Open Fifths, Open Prairie, and the Opening

of *Billy the Kid*," presented at the annual meeting of the Sonneck Society (Seattle, 1997); cited in HP, 629.

31. Kirstein provided Copland with two collections of folk tunes: Ira Sires's *Songs of the Open Range* and *The Lonesome Cowboy: Songs of the Plains and Hills,* edited by John White and George Shackley. A third collection was sent to the composer in Paris. According to Pollack, Jessica Burr discovered the Sires collection in Copland's library, and Elizabeth Bergman Crist found assorted sheet music edited by John Lomax and Oscar J. Fox stitched into his copy of *The Lonesome Cowboy.* From these sources, Copland selected six tunes: "Great-Granddad," "Whoopee Ti Yi Yo, Git Along Little Dogies," "The Old Chisholm Trail," "Old Paint," "The Dying Cowboy (Oh, Bury Me Not on the Lone Prairie)," and "Trouble for the Range Cook (Come Wrangle Yer Bronco)." HP, 316, 320, 628.

32. Copland, *Music and Imagination,* 90–91.

33. Ibid., 90.

34. HP, 320, citing CCLC, "Notes on a Cowboy Ballet."

35. "Composer Aaron Copland Says: 'Billy the Kid' Is a Big Boy Now," *RCA Victor Picture Record Review,* January 1950. CCLC, 395/3.

36. See Stephen Wade, "The Route of 'Bonyparte's Retreat': From 'Fiddler Bill' Stepp to Aaron Copland," *American Music* 18 (2000): 343–69.

37. Larry Starr offers an intelligent discussion of this passage in "Copland's Style," *Perspectives of New Music* 19, nos. 1–2 (1980–81): 69–89.

38. Virgil Thomson and Walter Terry, "The Ballet and Music," *New York Herald Tribune,* 14 February 1941; CCLC, 395/2. Halsey Stevens makes a similar observation in his liner notes for *Aaron Copland: . . . Billy the Kid (Complete Ballet),* Antal Dorati and the London Symphony Orchestra, Mercury, MG 50246.

39. Irving Kolodin, "Billy the Kid Is Danced by Kriza," CCLC, 395/5.

40. Burns, *Saga of Billy the Kid,* 56. 53. Burns writes: "In every *placeta* in New Mexico, Mexican girls sing to their guitars songs of Billy the Kid. A halo has been clapped upon his scapegrace brow. The boy who never grew old has become a sort of symbol of frontier knight-errantry, a figure of eternal youth riding for ever through a purple glamour of romance" (p. 53).

41. D. K. Wilgus, "The Individual Song: 'Billy the Kid,'" *Western Folklore* 30, no. 3 (July 1971): 226–34. This stanza of text (only slightly varied) eventually found its way into the Philadelphia Orchestra program of 1943 and an undated publicity sheet from Boosey & Hawkes. CCLC, 395/5.

42. Loring as quoted by Lisa Anne Sabatini in her program notes for the Oakland Ballet performance of *Billy the Kid* (with Loring's choreography), November 1998.

43. Siegel, *Shapes of Change,* 122.

44. Denby, *Dance Writings and Poetry,* 103.

45. Berger, *Aaron Copland,* 62–63.

46. Siegel, *Shapes of Change,* 123.

47. Burns, *Saga of Billy the Kid,* 69.

48. Ibid., 54–55.

49. Denby, *Dance Writings and Poetry,* 101.

50. Ibid.

51. Agnes de Mille, *Dance to the Piper* (Boston: Little, Brown, 1952; repr., New York: Da Capo Press, 1980), 275.

52. Martha Graham, *Blood Memory* (New York: Doubleday, 1991), 13.

53. HP, 373.

54. Agnes de Mille's scenario, CCLC, 253/18.

55. Richard Freed, record jacket liner notes for *Billy the Kid: Complete Ballet; Rodeo: Complete Ballet* (Leonard Slatkin and the Saint Louis Symphony Orchestra), Angel DS-37357, 1986.

56. Agnes de Mille's scenario, CCLC, 253/18.

57. Siegel, *Shapes of Change*, 128.

58. For information on American employment during World War II and the rise of "Rosie the Riveter" as a mythic character, see David M. Kennedy, *Freedom from Fear: The American People in Depression and War, 1929–1945* (New York: Oxford University Press, 1999), 776–82.

59. Siegel, *Shapes of Change*, 126, 131; HP, 365–66.

60. The other tunes Copland used are "I Ride an Old Paint"(in the "Saturday Night Waltz") and the fiddle tunes "Bonyparte" and "McLeod's Reel" (in the "Hoedown"). Jessica Burr also discovered traces of the fiddle tunes "Gilderoy" and "Tip, Toe, Pretty Betty Martin" in the "Hoedown."

61. Robert Bagar, "Smallens in Debut at Stadium," *Evening Telegram*, [18?] June 1947, CCLC, 415/14. Leon Errol was a vaudeville and early film comedian known as "Rubberlegs" for his trademark staggering walk.

62. Pollack notes the metric and structural similarities between de Mille's transcription and Copland's music, for example, the presence of a "bridge" section between the melodic variants of the tune. HP, 367, 370.

63. Siegel, *Shapes of Change*, 130.

64. Edwin Denby, "With the Dancers," *Modern Music* 20 (November–December 1942): 53; reprinted in *Dance Writings,* ed. Robert Cornfield and William MacKay (New York: Alfred A. Knopf, 1986), 96.

65. Agnes de Mille, "American Ballet" (penciled: "original script of Rodeo–1942"); CCLC, 253/18. The final word is printed "loliness"; "lowliness" is a possible correction, but "loneliness" seems to me more likely.

66. De Mille, "An American Ballet," CCLC, 253/18.

67. Howard Pollack, "The Dean of Gay American Composers," *American Music* 18 (2000): 39–49. See also the chapters "Personal Affairs" and "Identity Issues," HP, 234–56, 518–31.

68. Metzer, " 'Spurned Love,' " 418. For a broader discussion of sexuality among composers in Copland's generation, see Hubbs, *Queer Composition.*

13. COPLAND AND THE CINEMATIC WEST

1. Copland, "Film Music," in *What to Listen for in Music* (New York: McGraw-Hill, 1957), 259. Writing in 1940, Copland was more pointed: "The man who insists on complete self-expression had better stay home and write symphonies. He will not be happy

in Hollywood." Copland, "Second Thoughts on Hollywood," *Modern Music* 17 (March–April 1940): 141–43. Sally Bick discusses Copland's writings on film music in "Copland on Hollywood," in *Copland Connotations,* ed. Dickinson, 39–54.

2. Copland, "Film Music," 260–61.

3. Crist, *Music for the Common Man,* 92–110.

4. Alfred Cochran, "Style, Structure and Tonal Organization in the Early Film Scores of Aaron Copland" (PhD diss., Catholic University of America, 1986), 11.

5. Milestone was responsible for *Of Mice and Men* (1939), *North Star* (1943), and *The Red Pony* (1949). Copland's other film projects were *Our Town* (1940), the documentary *Cummington Story* (1945), *The Heiress,* for which he won an Academy Award in 1949, and the avant-garde *Something Wild* (1961).

6. Sally Bick, "Copland, Hollywood, and American Musical Modernism," *American Music* 23 (2005): 426, 438. See also Bick, "Composers on the Cultural Front: Aaron Copland and Hanns Eisler in Hollywood" (PhD diss., Yale University, 2001).

7. HP, 347, quoting David Raksin, Los Angeles Philharmonic intermission tribute, broadcast 11 February 1986, courtesy of Philip Ramey.

8. Cochran, "Style, Structure," 354–58, 443–46.

9. Copland to [Irving and Verna Fine], 4 March 1948, in Crist and Shirley, *Selected Correspondence,* 187. I treat the nostalgia and family dynamics of the film at somewhat greater length in "The Great Crossing: Nostalgia and Manifest Destiny in Aaron Copland's *The Red Pony,*" *Journal of Film Music* 2, nos. 2–4 (2009): 201–23.

10. Aaron Copland, *The Red Pony: Film Suite for Orchestra* (London: Boosey & Hawkes, 1951).

11. Two of the short stories were published in 1933, giving Steinbeck his first national success. Another was written in 1937. All four appeared in the 1938 collection *The Long Valley,* but only the first three were grouped under the title *The Red Pony.* "The Leader of the People," which shares the characters and setting of the other three stories, was included in *The Red Pony* for the first time in the "first illustrated" edition of 1945.

12. Steinbeck insisted that he have veto power over any performances of the suite using another narrator's voice and any alterations to his own tape-recording. Steinbeck to Copland, as transcribed in a letter from Lucile Sullivan at Annie Laurie Williams, Inc., to Copland, 15 September 1964, CCLC, 415/7. See also Aaron Copland and Vivian Perlis, *Copland since 1943* (New York: St Martin's Press, 1989), 90–91.

13. Joseph Millichap, *Steinbeck and Film* (New York: Frederick Ungar, 1983), 109.

14. See Copland, *What to Listen For in Music,* 259–60. On Milestone's openness to new sonic possibilities, see Bick, "Copland, Hollywood," 430–31.

15. Copland, "Notes on the *Children's Suite* from *The Red Pony,*" CCLC, 415/7. The suite was dedicated to Copland's lover Erik Johns and was created for Efrem Kurtz, who wanted a world premiere at his opening concert with the Houston Symphony. It was completed in August 1948 and was eventually published without the "for children" designation.

16. CCLC, 415/4.

17. Cited in Millichap, *Steinbeck and Film,* 113.

18. Alfred W. Cochran, "*The Red Pony,*" *Cue Sheet* 11, no. 2 (April 1995), 26.

19. Steinbeck, "The Leader of the People," in *The Red Pony* (New York: Bantam Books, 1976), 90–91.

20. R.S. Hughes, *Beyond the Red Pony: A Reader's Companion to Steinbeck's Complete Short Stories* (Metuchen, NJ: Scarecrow, 1987), 101.

21. Steinbeck, "Leader of the People," 86.

22. Thomson, "Music: Philharmonic Normal," *New York Herald Tribune,* 14 October 1949. Thomson also reviewed the film itself at great length: "Copland's Score for 'The Red Pony' Hollywood's Best, but Still Hollywood," 10 April 1949; reprinted as "Hollywood's Best" in *Music Right and Left* (New York: Henry Holt, 1951), 120–23.

23. Copland, "Jazz Structure and Influence."

24. Copland, "Composer from Brooklyn," in *Our New Music,* 228–29.

25. Arthur Berger, "The Music of Aaron Copland," *Musical Quarterly* 31 (1945): 420.

CONCLUSION

1. The complexities of the relationship between man and nature in the suite are intriguingly explored by Brooks Toliver in "Eco-ing in the Canyon: Ferde Grofé's *Grand Canyon Suite* and the Transformation of Wilderness," *Journal of the American Musicological Society* 57 (2004): 325–67.

2. Ferde Grofé, "Story of the *Grand Canyon Suite,*" 1938; reprinted in *Arizona Highways* 71, no. 4 (1995): 5.

3. Toliver, "Eco-ing in the Canyon," esp. 344–46.

4. For discussion of this passage and of Grofé's geographical suites more generally, see von Glahn, *Sounds of Place,* 198–215.

5. Grofé contended that when he wrote the suite he considered himself "almost a native Arizonan"—yet another instance of mingled biography and myth. In the published score he states: "I lived in Arizona, roaming the desert and mountain country as an itinerant pianist." In the 1938 "Story of the *Grand Canyon Suite,*" he expands on this theme, identifying himself with a variety of western pursuits, including both mining and cattle ranching.

6. Walt Whitman, "Pioneers! O Pioneers!" in *Leaves of Grass: "Death-bed" Edition* (New York: Barnes and Noble, 2004), 383, 386.

7. Limerick, *Legacy of Conquest,* 291.

SELECTED BIBLIOGRAPHY

ARCHIVAL MATERIALS

Arthur Farwell Collection, Sibley Library, Eastman School of Music, Rochester, NY.

Charles Wakefield Cadman Collection, Historical Collections and Labor Archives, Special Collections Library, the Pennsylvania State University, University Park.

Copland Collection, Library of Congress, Washington, DC.

Ernst Bacon Collection, Library of Congress, Washington, DC.

Ernst Bacon Papers, Music Library, University of California, Berkeley.

Lillian White Spencer Papers, Denver Public Library.

Nicolas Slonimsky, "Roy Harris: Cimarron Composer," unpublished manuscript (1951), Music Library, Special Collections, University of California, Los Angeles.

Roy Harris Collection, California State University, Los Angeles.

"Roy Harris, Composer of American Music," Oral History Program, University of California, Los Angeles, interviewed by Donald Schippers (1962) and Adelaide G. Tusler (1966, 1968, and 1969). Regents of the University of California, 1983. Transcript in the Bancroft Library, University of California, Berkeley.

Steinbeck Papers, Bancroft Library, University of California, Berkeley.

Virgil Thomson Papers, Irving S. Gilmore Music Library, Yale University.

PUBLISHED SCORES AND FILMS

Bacon, Ernst. *From These States (Gathered Along Unpaved Roads)*. New York: Associated Music Publishers, 1951.

Cadman, Charles Wakefield. *Bells of Capistrano*. Chicago: H.T. FitzSimons Co., 1928.

———. *Four American Indian Songs: Founded upon Tribal Melodies*. Boston: White-Smith, 1909.

———. "God Smiled Upon the Desert (A California Poppy Song)." Boston: White-Smith, 1917.

———. *The Golden Trail: Adventures of the Pioneers of '49.* Cincinnati: Willis Music, 1929.

———. *Hollywood Extra.* C.C. Birchard & Co., 1938.

———. *Indian Love Charm: An Amerindian Choral Work.* Cincinnati: Willis Music Co., 1932.

———. *Lelawala: The Maid of Niagara.* Cincinnati: Willis Music Co., 1926.

———. *Meet Arizona.* Boston: C.C. Birchard & Co., 1947.

———. "The New Trail." Boston: White-Smith, 1928.

———. *Prairie Sketches.* Cincinnati: Willis Music Co., 1906.

———. *The Robin Woman (Shanewis): An American Opera.* Boston: White-Smith, 1918.

———. *South in Sonora.* Boston: Oliver Ditson Company, 1932.

———. *The Sunset Trail.* Boston: White-Smith, 1925.

———. *Three Songs from the West.* Boston: White-Smith, 1916.

———. *Thunderbird,* piano suite. Boston: White-Smith, 1917.

Copland, Aaron. *Appalachian Spring: Ballet for Martha,* for thirteen instruments. New York: Boosey & Hawkes, 1972.

———. *Billy the Kid.* New York: Boosey & Hawkes, 1941.

———. *Billy the Kid,* arranged for two pianos. New York: Boosey & Hawkes, 1946.

———. *Four Dance Episodes from Rodeo.* London: Boosey & Hawkes, 1946.

———. *Prairie Journal* [*Music for Radio: Saga of the Prairie*]. London: Boosey & Hawkes, 1967.

———. *The Red Pony: Film Suite for Orchestra.* London: Boosey & Hawkes, 1951.

———. *Rodeo,* arranged for piano solo. London: Boosey & Hawkes, 1962.

———. *El Salón México.* London: Boosey & Hawkes, 1939.

———. *The Second Hurricane.* New York: Boosey & Hawkes, 1938.

———. *The Tender Land.* New York: Boosey & Hawkes, 1956.

Farwell, Arthur. *The Hako.* Edited by Ron Erickson. San Francisco: Erickson Editions, 1997.

———. *Navajo War Dance, No. 2.* Edited by John Kirkpatrick. New York: Music Press, Inc., 1947.

———. *Piano Quintet.* Edited by Ron Erickson. San Francisco: Erickson Editions, 1997.

Farwell, Arthur, and Charles Fletcher Lummis. *Spanish Songs of Old California.* Los Angeles: Lummis, 1923.

Foss, Lukas. *The Jumping Frog of Calaveras County.* New York: Carl Fischer, 1951.

———. *The Prairie.* New York: G. Schirmer, 1944.

Gershwin, George. *Girl Crazy.* New York: New World Music Corp., 1954.

Grofé, Ferde. *Grand Canyon Suite.* New York: Robbins Music Corp., 1932.

Harris, Roy. *American Ballads.* New York: Carl Fischer, 1947.

———. *Cimarron.* New York: Belwin Mills, 1941.

———. *Farewell to Pioneers.* New York: G. Schirmer, 1935.

———. *Folksong Symphony.* New York: G. Schirmer, 1940.

———. *Symphony No. 3.* New York: G. Schirmer, 1940.

———. *When Johnny Comes Marching Home.* New York: G. Schirmer, 1935.

Herbert, Victor. *Natoma*. G. Schirmer, 1911.

Of Mice and Men. Directed by Lewis Milestone. Rereleased on DVD: Chatsworth, CA: Image Entertainment, 2001.

Moore, Douglas. *The Ballad of Baby Doe*. Winona, MN: Hal Leonard Publishing Co., 1958.

Nevin, Arthur. *Poia*. Berlin: A. Fürstner, 1909.

The Plow That Broke the Plains. Directed by Angel Gil-Ordóñez. 1936. Naxos DVD 2.110521.

Puccini, Giacomo. *Fanciulla del West*. Milan and New York: G. Ricordi, 1910.

The Red Pony. Directed by Lewis Milestone. Los Angeles, CA: Republic Pictures, 1949. Rereleased on DVD: Santa Monica, CA: Artisan Entertainment, 2003.

Sowerby, Leo. *From the Northland*, piano suite. Boston: The Boston Music Company, 1926.

———. *From the Northland*, orchestra. New York: G. Schirmer, 1927.

———. *Prairie*. Boston: C. C. Birchard & Co., 1931.

Thomson, Virgil. *Four Saints in Three Acts*. New York: Music Press, Inc., 1948.

———. "Persistently Pastoral: Aaron Copland." In *Thirteen Portraits*, for piano. New York: Boosey & Hawkes, 1981.

———. *The Plow That Broke the Plains: Suite for Orchestra*. New York: Mercury Music Corporation, 1942.

———. *Suite from The Plough That Broke the Plains: Four Pieces for Piano*. New York: G. Schirmer, 1942, 1980.

———. *Wheat Field at Noon*. New York: G. Schirmer, 1949.

The Wa-Wan Press, 1901–11, edited by Vera Brodsky Lawrence. Reprint, New York: Arno Press, 1970.

BOOKS AND ARTICLES

Alexander, Charles C. *Here the Country Lies: Nationalism and the Arts in Twentieth-Century America*. Bloomington: University of Indiana Press, 1980.

Alexander, William. *Film on the Left: American Documentary Film from 1931 to 1942*. Princeton, NJ: Princeton University Press, 1981.

Anderson, Benedict. *Imagined Communities*. 2nd ed. London: Verso, 1991.

Ashley, Patricia. "Roy Harris." *Stereo Review* 21, no.6 (December 1968): 63–73.

Athearn, Robert G. *The Mythic West in Twentieth-Century America*. Lawrence: University Press of Kansas, 1986.

Atlas, Allan W. "Belasco and Puccini: 'Old Dog Tray' and the Zuni Indians." *Musical Quarterly* 75 (1991): 362–98.

Bacon, Ernst. "Comments and Problems." *The Argonaut*, 9 November 1934.

———. "Has the Native Opera a Future?" *Musical Courier*, 22 February 1944.

———. "Native Soil." *Sonneck Society Bulletin* 14, no. 1 (spring 1988): 9–10.

Barg, Lisa. "Black Voices/White Sounds: Race and Representation in Virgil Thomson's *Four Saints in Three Acts*." *American Music* 18 (2000): 121–61.

Barlow, Samuel L. M. "Virgil Thomson." *Modern Music* 18 (May–June 1941): 248.

Bazelon, Irwin. *Knowing the Score: Notes on Film Music*. New York: Van Nostrand Reinhold, 1975.

Beckerman, Michael, ed. *Dvořák and His World*. Princeton, NJ: Princeton University Press, 1993.

———. "Dvořák's 'New World' Largo and *The Song of Hiawatha*." *19th-Century Music* 16 (1992): 35–48.

———. "Henry Krehbiel, Antonin Dvořák, and the Symphony 'From the New World.'" *Notes* 49 (1992): 447–74.

Berger, Arthur. *Aaron Copland*. New York: Oxford University Press, 1953.

———. "The Music of Aaron Copland." *Musical Quarterly* 31 (1945): 420–47.

———. *Reflections of an American Composer*. Berkeley and Los Angeles: University of California Press, 2002.

Berkhofer, Robert F. *The White Man's Indian: Images of the American Indian from Columbus to the Present*. New York: Alfred A. Knopf, 1978.

Beveridge, David, ed. *Rethinking Dvořák: Views from Five Countries*. Oxford, UK: Clarendon Press, 1996.

Bialosky, Marshall. "Roy Harris: In Memoriam (But Keep Your Hats On)." *College Music Symposium* 22, no. 2 (1982): 7–19.

Bick, Sally. "Composers on the Cultural Front: Aaron Copland and Hanns Eisler in Hollywood." PhD diss., Yale University, 2001.

———. "Copland, Hollywood, and American Musical Modernism." *American Music* 23 (2005): 426–72.

Bindas, Kenneth J. *"All of This Music Belongs to the Nation": The Federal Music Project of the WPA and American Cultural Nationalism*. Knoxville: University of Tennessee Press, 1995.

Blitzstein, Marc. "Composers as Lecturers and in Concerts." *Modern Music* 13 (November–December 1935): 47–51.

Block, Adrienne Fried. *Amy Beach, Passionate Victorian: The Life and Work of an American Composer, 1867–1944*. New York: Oxford University Press, 1998.

———. "Amy Beach's Music on Native American Themes." *American Music* 8 (1990): 141–66.

———. "Boston Talks Back to Dvořák." *I. S. A. M. Newsletter* 18, no. 2 (May 1989): 10, 11, 15.

Brancaleone, Francis. "Edward MacDowell and Indian Motives." *American Music* 7 (1989): 359–81.

Briggs, Harold. "Indians! A Whole Movement of Native Opera Romanticized the American Savage." *Opera News* 40, no. 23 (June 1976): 22–24, 51.

Browner, Tara. "'Breathing the Indian Spirit': Thoughts on Musical Borrowing and the 'Indianist' Movement in American Music." *American Music* 15 (1997): 265–84.

Burns, Walter Noble. *The Saga of Billy the Kid*. Garden City, NY: Garden City Publishing, 1925.

Cadman, Charles Wakefield. "The American Indians' Music Idealized." *Etude Magazine*, October 1920, 659.

———. "The 'Idealization' of Indian Music." *Musical Quarterly* 1 (1915): 387–96.

———. Foreword to *The Robin Woman (Shanewis): An American Opera*. Boston: White-Smith, 1918.

———. Foreword to *Thunderbird*. Boston: White-Smith, 1917.

Carter, Tim. *Oklahoma! The Making of an American Musical.* New Haven, CT, and London: Yale University Press, 2007.

"Champagne and Cornbread." *Time,* 29 January 1945.

Chanler, Theodore. "New York, 1934." *Modern Music* 11 (March–April 1934): 142–47.

Chase, Gilbert. *America's Music: From the Pilgrims to the Present.* 3rd ed. Urbana: University of Illinois Press, 1987.

———, ed. *The American Composer Speaks.* [Baton Rouge]: Louisiana State University Press, 1966.

Cochran, Alfred W. "*The Red Pony.*" *Cue Sheet: Journal of the Society for the Preservation of Film Music* 11, no. 2 (April 1995): 25–35.

———. "Style, Structure, and Tonal Organization in the Early Film Scores of Aaron Copland." PhD diss., Catholic University of America, 1986.

Cole, Hugo. "Popular Elements in Copland's Music." *Tempo* 95 (1970–71): 4–10.

Cone, Edward T. "Conversation with Aaron Copland." *Perspectives of New Music* 6, no. 2 (1968): 57–72.

Copland, Aaron. "The American Composer Gets a Break." *American Mercury* 34 (April 1935): 488–92.

———. "America's Young Men of Promise." *Modern Music* 3 (March–April 1926): 13–20.

———. *Copland on Music.* New York: Da Capo, 1976.

———. "From the 20s to the 40s and Beyond." *Modern Music* 20 (January–February 1943): 78–82.

———. "Jazz as Folk-Music." *Musical America,* 19 December 1925, 18.

———. "Jazz Structure and Influence." *Modern Music* 4 (January–February 1927): 9–14.

———. *Music and Imagination.* Cambridge, MA: Harvard University Press, 1952.

———. *Our New Music.* New York: McGraw-Hill, 1940. Reprinted as *The New Music, 1900–1960.* New York: W. W. Norton, 1968.

———. "Second Thoughts on Hollywood." *Modern Music* 17 (March–April 1940): 141–47.

———. "What Is Jewish Music?" *New York Herald Tribune,* 2 October 1949, sec. 7, 14.

Copland, Aaron, and Vivian Perlis. *Copland: 1900 through 1942.* New York: St. Martin's Press, 1984.

———. *Copland since 1943.* New York: St. Martin's Press, 1989.

"Copland Decides He Likes Own Name Best." *Boston Evening Transcript,* 21 August 1937, IV: 4.

Cowell, Henry, ed. *American Composers on American Music.* [Stanford, CA]: Stanford University Press, 1933.

———. "Bericht aus Amerika: Amerikanische Musik?" Translated by Hanns Gutman. *Melos* 9, nos. 8–9 (August–September 1930): 362–65.

———. "Die beiden wirklichen Amerikaner: Ives und Ruggles." Translated by Hanns Gutman. *Melos* 9, no. 10 (October 1930): 417–20.

———. "Die kleineren Komponisten." Translated by Hanns Gutman. *Melos* 9, no. 12 (December 1930): 526–29.

———. "Three Native Composers." *New Freeman* 1 (3 May 1930): 184–86.

Cox, Sidney Thurber. "The Autogenetic Principle in the Melody Writing of Roy Harris." MA thesis, Cornell University, 1948.

Crawford, Richard. *The American Musical Landscape*. Berkeley and Los Angeles: University of California Press, 1993.

———. *America's Musical Life: A History*. New York: W. W. Norton, 2001.

———. "Edward MacDowell: Musical Nationalism and an American Tone Poet." *Journal of the American Musicological Society* 49 (1996): 528–60.

Crawford, Richard, R. Allen Lott, and Carol Oja, eds. *A Celebration of American Music: Words and Music in Honor of H. Wiley Hitchcock*. Ann Arbor: University of Michigan Press, 1990.

Crist, Elizabeth B[ergman]. *Music for the Common Man: Aaron Copland during the Depression and War*. New York: Oxford University Press, 2005.

Crist, Elizabeth B[ergman], and Wayne Shirley, eds. *The Selected Correspondence of Aaron Copland*. New Haven, CT, and London: Yale University Press, 2006.

Culbertson, Evelyn Davis. "Arthur Farwell's Early Efforts on Behalf of American Music, 1889–1921." *American Music* 5 (1987): 156–75.

———. *He Heard America Singing: Arthur Farwell, Composer, and Crusading Music Educator*. Metuchen, NJ: Scarecrow Press, 1992.

Curtis, Natalie. *The Indians' Book*. 2nd ed. New York: Harper and Brothers, 1923. Reprint, New York: Dover, 1968.

Deloria, Philip J. *Indians in Unexpected Places*. Lawrence: University Press of Kansas, 2004.

———. *Playing Indian*. New Haven, CT, and London: Yale University Press, 1998.

de Mille, Agnes. *Dance to the Piper*. Boston: Little, Brown, 1952. Reprint, New York: Da Capo Press, 1980.

Denby, Edwin. *Dance Writings*. Edited by Robert Cornfield and William Mackay. New York: Alfred A. Knopf, 1986.

———. *Dance Writings and Poetry*. Edited by Robert Cornfield. New Haven, CT: Yale University Press, 1998.

———. "Thomson Scores for a New Deal Film." *Modern Music* 13 (May–June 1936): 46–47.

Dickinson, Peter, ed. *Copland Connotations: Studies and Interviews*. Rochester, NY: Boydell Press, 2002.

Dippie, Brian W. *The Vanishing American: White Attitudes and U.S. Indian Policy*. Middletown, CT: Wesleyan University Press, 1982.

"Documented Dust." *Time*, 25 May 1936, 47.

Downes, Olin. "Harris Symphony Has Premiere Here." *New York Times*, 3 February 1934, 9.

DuPree, Mary Herron. "The Failure of American Music: The Critical View from the 1920s." *Journal of Musicology* 2 (1983): 305–15.

Easton, Carol. *No Intermissions: The Life of Agnes de Mille*. Boston: Little, Brown, 1996.

Ellis, Peter [Irving Lerner]. "The Plow That Broke the Plains." *New Theatre* (July 1936): 18.

Elwell, Herbert. "Harris' Folksong Symphony." *Modern Music* 18 (January–February 1941): 113–14.

Erickson, Ron. Preface to *Quintet for Piano and Strings*, by Arthur Farwell. San Francisco: Erickson Editions, 1997.

Etulain, Richard W., ed. *The American West in the Twentieth Century: A Bibliography*. Norman: University of Oklahoma Press, 1994.

Evett, Robert. "The Harmonic Idiom of Roy Harris." *Modern Music* 23 (January–February 1946): 100–107.

Ewen, David. *American Composers.* New York: H. W. Wilson, 1949.

Farwell, Arthur. "Aspects of Indian Music." *Southern Workman* 31 (1902): 211–17.

———. "Community Music and the Music Teacher." *Proceedings of the Music Teachers' National Association* 11 (1916): 191–98.

———. "National Work vs. Nationalism." *New Music Review* 8, no. 92 (July 1909): 432–34.

———. "Pioneering for American Music." *Modern Music* 12 (March–April 1935): 116–22.

———. "The Riddle of the Southwest, I, II, III." *Los Angeles Times,* 26 September, 27 September, and 29 September, 1926.

———. "Roy Harris." *Musical Quarterly* 18 (1932): 18–32.

———. "The Struggle Toward a National Music." *North American Review* 186 (December 1907): 565–70.

———. "*Wanderjahre of a Revolutionist*" *and Other Essays on American Music.* Edited by Thomas Stoner. Rochester, NY: University of Rochester Press, 1995.

Farwell, Brice, ed. *A Guide to the Music of Arthur Farwell and to the Microfilm Collection of His Work: A Centennial Commemoration Prepared by His Children.* Briarcliff Manor, NY: The Estate of Arthur Farwell, 1972.

Fenster, Mark. "Preparing the Audience, Informing the Performers: John A. Lomax and *Cowboy Songs and Other Frontier Ballads.*" *American Music* 7 (1989): 260–77.

Fife, Austin E., and Alta S. Fife, eds. *Cowboy and Western Songs: A Comprehensive Anthology.* Music edited by Mary Jo Schwab. N.p.: Clarkson N. Potter, 1969.

Filene, Benjamin. *Romancing the Folk: Public Memory and American Roots Music.* Chapel Hill: University of North Carolina Press, 2000.

Fine, Irving. "Young America: Bernstein and Foss." *Modern Music* 22 (May–June 1945): 238–43.

Fletcher, Alice. *The Hako: Song, Pipe, and Unity in a Pawnee Calumet Ceremony.* Lincoln and London: University of Nebraska Press, 1996.

———. *Indian Story and Song from North America.* Boston: Small Maynard and Company, 1900.

"Folk-song Symphony." *Time,* 6 January 1941, 34.

Foss, Lukas. "*The Prairie, A Parable of Death,* and *Psalms.*" In *The Composer's Point of View: Essays on Twentieth-Century Choral Music by Those Who Wrote It,* edited by Robert Stephan Hines. Norman: University of Oklahoma Press, 1963.

Fry, Stephen M., ed. *California's Musical Wealth: Sources for the Study of Music in California.* Music Library Association, Southern California Chapter, 1988.

Gabriel, Charles H., Jr. "Music and Colored Lighting Glorify Natural Theater." *Musical America,* 21 November 1926, 3.

Gann, Kyle. *American Music in the Twentieth Century.* New York: Prentice-Hall, 1997.

Gibbs, L. Chesley, and Dan Stehman. "The Roy Harris Revival." *American Record Guide* 42, no. 7 (May 1979): 8–13; 42, no. 8 (June 1979): 4–8, 57–59.

Glassberg, David. *American Historical Pageantry: The Uses of Tradition in the Early Twentieth Century.* Chapel Hill: University of North Carolina Press, 1990.

Goetzmann, William H., and William N. Goetzmann. *The West of the Imagination*. New York: W.W. Norton, 1986.

Goldberg, Isaac. "Aaron Copland and His Jazz." *American Mercury*, September 1927, 63–65.

——. "Roy Harris." *Musical Record* 1, no. 7 (December 1933): 253–56.

——. "Roy Harris's Symphony: 1933–Again Americanism in Music." *Musical Record* 1, no. 10 (March 1934): 354–56.

Graziano, John. "Community Theater, *Caliban by the Yellow Sands,* and Arthur Farwell." In *Vistas of American Music: Essays and Compositions in Honor of William K. Kearns,* edited by John Graziano and Susan Porter, 293–308. Warren, MI: Harmonie Park, 1999.

Green, Douglas B. "The Singing Cowboy: An American Dream." *Journal of Country Music* 7 (May 1978): 4–62.

Grofé, Ferde. "Story of the *Grand Canyon Suite.*" 1938. Reprinted in *Arizona Highways* 71, no. 4 (1995): 5.

Gruen, Jason Philip. "Manifest Destinations: Tourist Encounters in the Urban American West, 1869–1893." PhD diss., University of California, Berkeley, 2004.

Hall, Roger A. *Performing the American Frontier, 1870–1906.* Cambridge: Cambridge University Press, 2001.

Hanson, Howard. "Twenty Years' Growth in America." *Modern Music* 20 (January–February 1943): 95–101.

Harris, Johana. "Personal Note." In *The Book of Modern Composers,* edited by David Ewen, 451. New York: Alfred A. Knopf, 1942.

Harris, Roy. "American Music Enters a New Phase." *Scribner's Magazine* 96 (October 1934): 218–21.

——. "Folksong—American Big Business." *Modern Music* 18 (November–December 1940): 8–11. Reprinted in *Contemporary Composers on Contemporary Music,* edited by Elliott Schwartz and Barney Childs, 160–64. New York: Holt, Rinehart and Winston, 1967.

——. "The Growth of a Composer." *Musical Quarterly* 20 (1934): 188–91.

——. "Perspective at Forty." *Magazine of Art* 32, no.11 (1939): 638–39, 667–71.

Hinds, B. Wayne. "Leo Sowerby: A Biography and Descriptive Listing of Anthems." EdD thesis, George Peabody College for Teachers, 1972.

Hollinger, David A. *Postethnic America*. New York: Harper Collins, 1995.

"Home-Grown Composer." *Time,* 8 April 1940, 45–46.

Hoover, Kathleen O'Connell, and John Cage. *Virgil Thomson: His Life and Works.* New York: Thomas Yoseloff, 1959; repr. Freeport, NY: Books for Libraries Press, 1970.

Horowitz, Joseph. *Classical Music in America: A History of Its Rise and Fall.* New York: W.W. Norton, 2005.

——. "Dvořák and Boston." *American Music* 19 (2001): 3–17.

Horsman, Reginald. *Race and Manifest Destiny: The Origins of American Racial Anglo-Saxonism.* Cambridge, MA: Harvard University Press, 1981.

Howard, John Tasker. *Our American Music.* New York: Thomas Y. Crowell, 1931.

——. *Our Contemporary Composers.* New York: Thomas Y. Crowell, 1941.

Hubbs, Nadine. *The Queer Composition of America's Sound: Gay Modernists, American Music, and National Identity.* Berkeley and Los Angeles: University of California Press, 2004.

Hyde, Anne Farrar. *An American Vision: Far Western Landscape and National Culture, 1820–1920*. New York: New York University Press, 1990.

Jacobson, Matthew Frye. *Whiteness of a Different Color: European Immigrants and the Alchemy of Race*. Cambridge, MA: Harvard University Press, 1998.

Jones, Isabel Morse. *Hollywood Bowl*. New York: G. Schirmer, 1936.

Kalinak, Kathryn. *How the West Was Sung: Music in the Westerns of John Ford*. Berkeley and Los Angeles: University of California Press, 2007.

Kay, Norman. "Aspects of Copland's Development." *Tempo* 95 (1970–71): 23–29.

Kendall, Alan. *The Tender Tyrant, Nadia Boulanger: A Life Devoted to Music*. London: Mac-Donald, 1976.

Kennedy, David M. *Freedom from Fear: The American People in Depression and War, 1929–1945*. New York: Oxford University Press, 1999.

Key, Margaret Susan. "'Sweet melody over silent wave': Depression-Era Radio and the American Composer." PhD diss., University of Maryland, College Park, 1995.

Kingman, Daniel. *American Music: A Panorama*. Foreword by Virgil Thomson. New York: Schirmer Books, 1979.

Kirk, Edgar Lee. "Toward American Music: A Study of the Life and Music of Arthur George Farwell." PhD diss., Eastman School of Music, University of Rochester, 1958.

Kirk, Elise. *American Opera*. Urbana: University of Illinois Press, 2001.

Klein, Kerwin Lee. *Frontiers of Historical Imagination: Narrating the European Conquest of Native America, 1890–1990*. Berkeley and Los Angeles: University of California Press, 1997.

Kleppinger, Stanley V. "On the Influence of Jazz Rhythm in the Music of Aaron Copland." *American Music* 21 (2003): 74–111.

Koegel, John. "Mexican-American Music in Nineteenth-Century Southern California: The Lummis Wax Cylinder Collection at the Southwest Museum, Los Angeles." PhD diss., Claremont Graduate School, 1994.

Kolodin, Irving. "Wanted—An American Composer." *The New Republic*, 16 January 1935, 272–74.

Larkin, Margaret. *The Singing Cowboy: A Book of Western Songs*. New York: Oak Publications, 1931.

Lears, T. J. Jackson. *No Place of Grace: Antimodernism and the Transformation of American Culture, 1880–1920*. New York: Pantheon Books, 1981.

Lerner, Neil William. "The Classical Documentary Score in American Films of Persuasion: Contexts and Case Studies, 1936–1945." PhD diss., Duke University, 1997.

———. "Copland's Music of Wide Open Spaces: Surveying the Pastoral Trope in Hollywood." *Musical Quarterly* 85 (2001): 477–515.

Levant, Oscar. *A Smattering of Ignorance*. Garden City, NY: Garden City Publishing, 1940.

Limerick, Patricia Nelson. "Disorientation and Reorientation: The American Landscape Discovered from the West." In *Discovering America: Essays on the Search for an Identity*, edited by David Thelen and Frederick E. Hoxie, 187–215. Urbana: University of Illinois Press, 1994.

———. *Legacy of Conquest: The Unbroken Past of the American West*. New York: W. W. Norton, 1987.

———. *Something in the Soil: Legacies and Reckonings in the New West*. New York: W. W. Norton, 2000.

"Log Cabin Composer." *Time* 26, 11 November 1935, 36–37.

Lomax, John A., and Alan Lomax. *Cowboy Songs and Other Frontier Ballads*. Rev. ed. New York: Macmillan, 1938.

Lorentz, Pare. *FDR's Moviemaker: Memoirs and Scripts*. Reno: University of Nevada Press, 1992.

———. *Lorentz on Film: Movies 1927 to 1941*. Norman: University of Oklahoma Press, 1986.

Lummis, Charles. "Catching Our Archaeology Alive." *Out West* 22, no. 1 (January 1905): 35–47.

———. "New Mexican Folk-Songs." *Cosmopolitan*, October 1892, 720.

Mark, Joan. *A Stranger in Her Native Land*. Lincoln: University of Nebraska Press, 1988.

Martin, John. "The Dance: 'Billy': Loring Ballet Restored to the Repertoire." *New York Times*, 11 April 1948.

Marx, Leo. *The Machine in the Garden: Technology and the Pastoral Ideal in America*. New York: Oxford University Press, 1964.

Mason, Daniel Gregory. *Music in My Time and Other Reminiscences*. Westport, CT: Greenwood Press, 1938.

———. *Tune In, America: A Study of Our Coming Musical Independence*. New York: Alfred A. Knopf, 1931.

Masterson, Michael Lee. "Sounds of the Frontier: Music in Buffalo Bill's Wild West Shows." PhD diss., University of New Mexico, 1990.

McNutt, James C. "John Comfort Fillmore: A Student of Indian Music Reconsidered." *American Music* 2 (1984): 61–70.

McWilliams, Carey. "Myths of the West." *North American Review* 232 (November 1931): 424–32.

Meckna, Michael. "The Rise of the American Composer-Critic: Aaron Copland, Roger Sessions, Virgil Thomson and Elliott Carter in the Periodical *Modern Music*." PhD diss., University of California, Santa Barbara, 1984.

———. "Sacred and Secular America: Virgil Thomson's *Symphony on a Hymn Tune*." *American Music* 8 (1990): 465–76.

Mellers, Wilfrid. *Music in a New Found Land: Themes and Developments in the History of American Music*. New York: Alfred A. Knopf, 1965.

Mendel, Arthur. "Music: A Change in Structure." *The Nation* 134, no. 3470 (6 January 1932): 26.

———. "The Quintet of Roy Harris." *Modern Music* 17 (October–November 1939): 25–28.

Metzer, David. "'Spurned Love': Eroticism and Abstraction in the Early Works of Aaron Copland." *Journal of Musicology* 15 (1997): 419–43.

Miller, Leta E., and Catherine Parsons Smith. "Playing with Politics: Crisis in the San Francisco Federal Music Project." *California History* 86, no. 2 (2009): 26–47, 68–71.

Millichap, Joseph R. *Steinbeck and Film*. New York: Frederick Ungar, 1983.

Moore, MacDonald Smith. *Yankee Blues: Musical Culture and American Identity*. Bloomington: Indiana University Press, 1985.

Morton, Lawrence. "*The Red Pony:* A Review of Aaron Copland's Score." *Film Music Notes* (February 1949): 2–8.

Most, Andrea. *Making Americans: Jews and the Broadway Musical.* Cambridge, MA: Harvard University Press, 2004.

Murchison, Gayle Minetta. "Nationalism in William Grant Still and Aaron Copland between the Wars: Style and Ideology." PhD diss., Yale University, 1998.

Nancarrow, Conlon. "Over the Air." *Modern Music* 17 (May–June 1940): 263–65.

Nash, Gerald D. *Creating the West: Historical Interpretations, 1890–1990.* Albuquerque: University of New Mexico Press, 1991.

Nash, Roderick. *Wilderness and the American Mind.* New Haven, CT: Yale University Press, 1967.

Neff, Severine. "An American Precursor of Non-tonal Theory: Ernst Bacon (1898–1990)." *Current Musicology* 48 (1991): 5–26.

Nicholls, David, ed. *The Cambridge History of American Music.* Cambridge: Cambridge University Press, 1998.

Oja, Carol. *Making Music Modern: New York in the 1920s.* New York: Oxford University Press, 2000.

Oja, Carol, and Judith Tick, eds. *Aaron Copland and His World.* Princeton, NJ: Princeton University Press, 2005.

Olmstead, Andrea. "The Copland–Sessions Letters." *Tempo* 175 (1990): 2–5.

———, ed. *The Correspondence of Roger Sessions.* Boston: Northeastern University Press, 1992.

Padget, Martin. "Travel, Exoticism, and the Writing of Region: Charles Fletcher Lummis and the 'Creation' of the Southwest." *Journal of the Southwest* 37, no. 3 (1995): 421–49.

Parakilas, James. "The Soldier and the Exotic: Operatic Variations on a Theme of Racial Encounter, Part II." *Opera Quarterly* 10, no. 3 (1994): 43–69.

P[arker], H[enry] T[aylor]. "Manifold, Abundant, Individual." *Boston Evening Transcript,* 27 January 1934, pt. 3: 4 (review of Harris, *Symphony 1933*).

Perison, Harry D. "Charles Wakefield Cadman: His Life and Works." PhD diss., Eastman School of Music, University of Rochester, 1978.

———. "The 'Indian' Operas of Charles Wakefield Cadman." *College Music Symposium* 22, no. 2 (1982): 20–48.

Perlis, Vivian, and Libby Van Cleve. *Composers' Voices from Ives to Ellington: An Oral History of American Music.* New Haven, CT, and London: Yale University Press, 2005.

Perlove, Nina. "Inherited Sound Images: Native American Exoticism in Aaron Copland's *Duo for Flute and Piano*." *American Music* 18 (2000): 50–77.

Perspectives of New Music 19, nos. 1–2 (1980–81). [Special Copland issue.]

Pisani, Michael. "Exotic Sounds in the Native Land." PhD diss., Eastman School of Music, University of Rochester, 1996.

———. "From Hiawatha to Wa-Wan: Musical Boston and the Uses of Native American Lore." *American Music* 19 (2001): 39–50.

———. *Imagining Native America in Music.* New Haven, CT, and London: Yale University Press, 2005.

———. "'I'm an Indian too': Creating Native American Identities in Nineteenth- and Early Twentieth-Century Music." In *The Exotic in Western Music,* edited by Jonathan Bellman, 218–57. Boston: Northeastern University Press, 1998.

Piston, Walter. "Roy Harris." *Modern Music* 11 (January–February 1934): 73–83.

Pollack, Howard. *Aaron Copland: The Life and Work of an Uncommon Man.* New York: Henry Holt, 1999.

———. "The Dean of Gay American Composers," *American Music* 18 (2000): 39–49.

———. *George Gershwin: His Life and Music.* Berkeley and Los Angeles: University of California Press, 2006.

Prevots, Naima. *American Pageantry: A Movement for Art and Democracy.* Ann Arbor: University of Michigan Research Press, 1990.

Prown, Jules David, Nancy K. Anderson, William Cronon, Brian W. Dippie, Martha A. Sandweiss, Susan P. Schoelwer, and Howard R. Lamar. *Discovered Lands, Invented Pasts: Transforming Visions of the American West.* New Haven, CT: Yale University Press, 1992.

Randall, Annie, and Rosalind Gray Davis. *Puccini and the Girl: The History and Reception of "The Girl of the Golden West."* Chicago: University of Chicago Press, 2005.

Ridge, Martin, ed. *Frederick Jackson Turner: Wisconsin's Historian of the Frontier.* Madison: State Historical Society of Wisconsin, 1986.

Robertson, Marta Elaine. "'A gift to be simple': The Collaboration of Aaron Copland and Martha Graham in the Genesis of *Appalachian Spring.*" PhD diss., University of Michigan, 1992.

Robertson, Marta, and Robin Armstrong. *Aaron Copland: A Guide to Research.* New York: Routledge, 2001.

Rogin, Michael. *Blackface, White Noise: Jewish Immigrants in the Hollywood Melting Pot.* Berkeley and Los Angeles: University of California Press, 1996.

Rosenfeld, Paul. "Aaron Copland's Growth." *New Republic,* 27 May 1931, 46–47.

———. "Current Chronicle: Copland–Harris–Schuman." *Musical Quarterly* 25 (1939): 372–81.

———. "Folksong and Culture-Politics." *Modern Music* 17 (October–November 1939): 18–24.

———. "Harris before the World." *New Republic,* February 1934, 364–65.

———. *An Hour with American Music.* Philadelphia: J. B. Lippincott, 1929.

———. "Tragic and American." *New Republic,* November 1934, 147.

Rosenstiel, Léonie. *Nadia Boulanger: A Life in Music.* New York: W. W. Norton, 1982.

Rundell, Walter, Jr. "The West as Operatic Setting." In *Probing the American West,* edited by K. Ross Toole, John Alexander Carroll, Robert M. Utley, and A. R. Mortensen, 49–61. Santa Fe: Museum of New Mexico Press, 1962.

Saminsky, Lazare. *Living Music of the Americas.* New York: Howell, Soskin and Crown, 1949.

———. *Music of the Ghetto and the Bible.* New York: Bloch Publishing, 1934.

Sandburg, Carl. *The American Songbag.* New York: Harcourt Brace Jovanovich, 1927.

———. *Poems of the Midwest.* Cleveland: World Publishing Company, 1946.

Sanford-Tefft, Lulu. *Little Intimate Stories of Charles Wakefield Cadman.* Hollywood: David Graham Fischer Corporation, 1926.

Savage, William W., Jr. *The Cowboy Hero: His Image in American History and Culture.* Norman: University of Oklahoma Press, 1979.

Schwartz, Stephen. *From West to East: California and the Making of the American Mind.* New York: The Free Press, 1998.

Sheehan, Perley Poore. *Hollywood as a World Center.* Hollywood Citizen Press, 1924.

Shull, Paul, ed. "Music in the West." *Journal of the West* 22 (1983): 4–9; "Music in the West: II." *Journal of the West* 28 (1989): 3–51.

Siegel, Marcia B. *The Shapes of Change: Images of American Dance.* Boston: Houghton Mifflin, 1979.

Slonimsky, Nicolas. "From the West Composer New to Bostonians." *Boston Evening Transcript,* 24 January 1934, pt. 1: 7, col. 1.

———. *Perfect Pitch: A Life Story.* New York: Oxford University Press, 1988.

———. "Roy Harris." *Musical Quarterly* 33 (1947): 17–37.

Slotkin, Richard. *Gunfighter Nation: The Myth of the Frontier in Twentieth-Century America.* Norman: University of Oklahoma Press, 1992.

Smith, Catherine Parsons. *Making Music in Los Angeles: Transforming the Popular.* Berkeley and Los Angeles: University of California Press, 2007.

Smith, Catherine Parsons, and Cynthia S. Richardson. *Mary Carr Moore, American Composer.* Ann Arbor: University of Michigan Press, 1987.

Smith, Henry Nash. *Virgin Land: The American West as Symbol and Myth.* Cambridge, MA: Harvard University Press, 1950. Reprint, New York: Vintage Books, 1957.

Smith, Julia. *Aaron Copland: His Work and Contribution to American Music.* New York: E. P. Dutton, 1955.

Smith, Moses. "Music for the Radio." *Boston Evening Transcript,* 26 July 1937, 8.

Snyder, Robert L. *Pare Lorentz and the Documentary Film.* Norman: University of Oklahoma Press, 1968.

Speaking of Roy Harris. Los Angeles: Friends of Roy Harris: University of California, Los Angeles, 12 February 1966.

Spizizen, Louise. "Johana and Roy Harris: Marrying a Real Composer." *Musical Quarterly* 77 (1993): 579–606.

Stanfield, Peter. *Horse Opera: The Strange History of the 1930s Singing Cowboy.* Urbana: University of Illinois Press, 2002.

Starr, Lawrence. "Copland's Style." *Perspectives of New Music* 19, nos. 1–2 (1980–81): 69–89.

———. "Ives, Gershwin, and Copland: Reflections on the Strange History of American Art Music." *American Music* 12 (1994): 167–87.

Stegner, Wallace. *Where the Bluebird Sings to the Lemonade Springs: Living and Writing in the West.* New York: Penguin Books, 1992.

Stehman, Dan. *Roy Harris: A Bio-bibliography.* Westport, CT: Greenwood, 1991.

———. *Roy Harris: An American Musical Pioneer.* Boston: G. K. Hall, 1984.

———. "The Symphonies of Roy Harris: An Analytical Study of the Linear Materials and of Related Works." PhD diss., University of Southern California, 1973.

Sternfeld, Frederick W. "Copland as Film Composer." *Musical Quarterly* 37 (April 1951): 161–75.

Stevenson, Robert. "Roy Harris at UCLA: Neglected Documentation." *Inter-American Music Review* 2, no. 1 (1979): 59–73.

Stoner, Thomas. "'The New Gospel of Music': Arthur Farwell's Vision of Democratic Music in America." *American Music* 9 (1991): 183–208.

Stoney, George. "George Stoney on *The Plow* and *The River*." *"The Plow That Broke the Plains" and "The River."* Post-Classical Ensemble, directed by Angel Gil-Ordóñez. Naxos DVD 2.110521.

Strassburg, Robert. *Roy Harris: A Catalog of His Works.* Los Angeles: California State University, 1973.

Struble, John Warthen. *The History of American Classical Music: MacDowell through Minimalism.* New York: Facts on File, 1995.

Study Guide: "The Plow That Broke the Plains" U.S. Documentary Film. Washington, DC: United States Film Service, Division of the National Emergency Council, 1938.

Swan, Howard. *Music in the Southwest, 1825–1950.* New York: Da Capo, 1977.

Taruskin, Richard. *The Danger of Music and Other Anti-Utopian Essays.* Berkeley and Los Angeles: University of California Press, 2009.

Taylor, Davidson. "Tomorrow's Broadcast." *North American Review* 241 (March 1936): 49–56.

———. "Why Not Try the Air?" *Modern Music* 15 (January–February 1938): 86–91.

Thomson, Virgil. *American Music since 1910.* New York: Holt, Rinehart and Winston, 1971.

———. *Selected Letters of Virgil Thomson.* Edited by Tim Page and Vanessa Weeks Page. New York: Summit Books, 1988.

———. "Swing Music." *Modern Music* 13 (May–June 1936): 12–17.

———. *Virgil Thomson.* New York: Alfred A. Knopf, 1966.

———. *Virgil Thomson: A Reader, Selected Writings 1924–1984.* Edited by Richard Kostelanetz. New York: Routledge, 2002.

Tibbetts, John C., ed. *Dvořák in America, 1892–1895.* Portland, OR: Amadeus Press, 1993.

Tischler, Barbara L. *An American Music: The Search for an American Musical Identity.* New York: Oxford University Press, 1986.

Toliver, Brooks. "Eco-ing in the Canyon: Ferde Grofé's *Grand Canyon Suite* and the Transformation of Wilderness." *Journal of the American Musicological Society* 57 (2004): 325–67.

Tommasini, Anthony. *Virgil Thomson: Composer on the Aisle.* New York: W.W. Norton, 1997.

Tompkins, Jane. *West of Everything: The Inner Life of Westerns.* New York: Oxford University Press, 1992.

Trachtenberg, Alan. *Shades of Hiawatha: Staging Indians, Making Americans, 1880–1930.* New York: Hill and Wang, 2004.

———. "The Westward Route." In *The Incorporation of America: Culture and Society in the Gilded Age*, 11–37, 236–38. New York: Hill and Wang, 1982.

Tsianina [Blackstone]. *Where Trails Have Led Me*, 2nd ed. Burbank, CA: T. Blackstone, 1970.

Tuthill, Burnet C. "Leo Sowerby." *Musical Quarterly* 24 (1938): 249–64.

Ussher, Bruno David, ed. *Who's Who in Music and Dance in Southern California*. Holly-wood: Bureau of Musical Research, 1933.

Utley, Robert. *Billy the Kid: A Short and Violent Life*. Lincoln: University of Nebraska Press, 1989.

von Glahn, Denise. "Charles Ives, Cowboys, and Indians: Aspects of the 'Other Side of Pioneering.'" *American Music* 19 (2001): 291–314.

———. *The Sounds of Place: Music and the American Cultural Landscape*. Boston: North-eastern University Press, 2003.

Wade, Stephen. "The Route of 'Bonyparte's Retreat': From 'Fiddler Bill' Stepp to Aaron Copland." *American Music* 18 (2000): 343–69.

Warren, Louis. *Buffalo Bill's America: William Cody and the Wild West Show*. New York: Alfred A. Knopf, 2005.

Waters, Edward N. *Victor Herbert: A Life in Music*. New York: Macmillan, 1955.

———. "The Wa-Wan Press: An Adventure in Musical Idealism." In *A Birthday Offering to C[arl] E[ngel]*, edited by Gustave Reese, 214–33. New York: G. Schirmer, 1943.

Watson, Steven. *Prepare for Saints: Gertrude Stein, Virgil Thomson, and the Mainstream-ing of American Modernism*. New York: Random House, 1998.

White, G. Edward. *The Eastern Establishment and the Western Experience: The West of Frederic Remington, Theodore Roosevelt, and Owen Wister*. New Haven, CT: Yale University Press, 1968.

White, John. *Git Along, Little Dogies: Songs and Songmakers of the American West*. Urbana: University of Illinois Press, 1975.

White, John, and George Shackley. *The Lonesome Cowboy*. New York: George T. Worth, 1930.

White, Richard. *"It's Your Misfortune and None of My Own": A New History of the American West*. Norman: University of Oklahoma Press, 1991.

———. "When Frederick Jackson Turner and Buffalo Bill Cody Both Played Chicago in 1893." In *Frontier and Region: Essays in Honor of Martin Ridge*, edited by Robert C. Ritchie and Paul Andrew Hutton, 201–12. Albuquerque: University of New Mexico Press, 1997.

White, W. L. "Pare Lorentz." *Scribner's Magazine*, January 1939, 7–11, 42.

Willis, Wayne Carr. "The 'Apocalyptic' Visions of Arthur Farwell: Music for a World Transfigured." Paper presented at the Society for American Music Conference, Lexington, KY, 2002.

Worster, Donald. *Under Western Skies: Nature and History in the American West*. New York: Oxford University Press, 1992.

Wrobel, David M., and Patrick T. Long, eds. *Seeing and Being Seen: Tourism in the American West*. Lawrence: University Press of Kansas, 2001.

Wu, Arlouine Goodjohn. *Constance Eberhart: A Musical Career in the Age of Cadman*. NOA monograph series, vol. 4. (Oxford, MS): National Opera Association, 1983.

Yiu, Raymond. "Renaissance Man: A Portrait of Lukas Foss." *Tempo* 221 (July 2002): 15–23.

Zuck, Barbara A. *A History of Musical Americanism*. Ann Arbor: University of Michigan Research Press, 1980.

Paine, John Knowles, 3, 4
Parker, Charlie, 151
Parker, Henry Taylor, 244, 252–53
Parker, Horatio, 237
Parkman, Francis, 200
Pasadena, Composer's Fellowship of, 70
pastoral imagery, 16, 156–59, 161, 164–66, 172, 173–74, 178, 180, 183, 188–89, 191–94, 197–99, 204–6, 211–13, 220, 222–23, 338, 397n40; and the "machine in the garden," 16, 156, 157–58, 166, 171, 178, 183, 194, 216, 217; and the "middle landscape," 158, 161, 166, 173, 181, 194, 208; and military associations, 159–60, 162, 166, 194–97, 205, 212; and religious associations, 164, 200–201, 203, 205, 210–12
pastoral music, 314, 326–30, 338, 358; woodwind timbres, 164, 174, 188–89, 196, 205, 248, 251, 260, 329, 358. See also echo effects; ostinato or drone figures
pentatonic, 42, 51, 78, 125, 166, 174
Perison, Harry, 99, 100
Perlis, Vivian, 179
phonograph. See recording technology
pioneers, images of, 2, 16, 18–19, 69–70, 129–30, 131–34, 152, 155–57, 158–59, 167–68, 179, 181, 185–88, 190–94, 203, 205, 206, 211–13, 222–23, 228, 229–30, 236, 249, 251, 253–57, 258, 261–62, 293, 294, 304, 305, 310–11, 325–26, 329, 342, 359, 367, 370, 371; as Anglo, 156, 201, 203, 261; as Protestant, 156, 200–201, 203, 211, 212
Pisani, Michael, 37, 38–39, 42, 126
Piston, Walter, 233, 246–47, 286–87, 293
plow. See farm machinery
Plow That Broke the Plains, The. See Thomson, Virgil
Pocahontas, 114, 144
Pollack, Howard, 150, 307, 318, 323, 326, 331, 336, 338, 343, 344, 349, 355, 363
Pony Express, 11, 131, 134, 167
Popular Front, 303, 317, 318
populism, 16, 19, 228, 240, 269, 294
Powell, Ozie, 306–7, 310–11
pow wow, 74, 110, 114–15, 122, 123, 127, 151
progress, rhetoric of, 2, 10, 129–30, 156, 157, 158, 173, 176, 178, 194, 223, 240, 250, 258, 261–62, 303, 325–26, 338–40, 360, 365, 373
propaganda, 178, 189–90, 198, 211, 240, 267, 406n3
Puccini, Giacomo, 89, 100, 117, 130–31; Fanciulla del West, 130–31, 131–32
Puritans, 124, 134, 213

racial determinism, 148, 264–66, 288–89, 290, 300–302, 315, 409n47
radio, 14, 17, 150, 208, 216, 271, 281, 289, 293, 303–7, 309–10, 352, 370, 409n1
ragtime, 36, 62, 204, 214, 335
railroads, 57, 129, 130, 158, 171, 172, 181, 183, 190, 192, 194, 211, 271, 306, 344–45
Raksin, David, 352
Randall, Annie, 131
RCA Victor Records, 245, 252, 268
real estate market, 72, 74, 138, 141, 144, 156
recording technology, 56–59, 99, 103, 127, 268, 303, 304, 356–57
Redding, Joseph Deighn, 136, 137
Redfeather, Tsianina. See Tsianina
Red Pony, The. See Copland, Aaron; Steinbeck, John
Remington, Frederic, 200, 271, 387n34
Resettlement Administration, 185, 186, 188, 189, 190, 198, 199, 200, 397n42
Revueltas, Silvestre, 319
Richardson, Cynthia S., 134–35
River, The. See Thomson, Virgil
rodeo, 271–73, 283–84, 325, 348, 363, 370
Rogers, Roy, 271, 278
Rogin, Michael, 19
Rölvaag, Ole, 159, 206, 397n51, 400n8, 412–13n53
Roos, Charles and Juanita, 142
Roosevelt, Franklin Delano, 185, 189
Roosevelt, Theodore, 12–13, 104, 387n34
Rosenfeld, Paul, 183, 204, 237–38, 241, 243, 244, 246, 252, 258, 262, 263, 265, 271, 279, 288, 300, 301, 371, 409n47
Rough Riders, 12–13, 13fig
Rubaiyat of Omar Khayyam, 147
Rudhyar, Dane, 147
Ruggles, Carl, 148, 301
Russell, Charles Marion, 14, 271
Russell, Henry, 103
Russian music, 46, 82, 90, 297, 319

Salsbury, Nate, 10
Saminsky, Lazare, 300–301, 315
Sandburg, Carl, 16, 69, 161, 166–74, 176, 178, 179, 187, 188, 207, 222, 269, 272, 370, 398n58, 400n12; American Songbag, 161, 191, 272; on pioneering, 167
Santa Fe Opera, 208
Santa Fe Trail, 181, 257
Satie, Erik, 180
Schaffer, Aaron, 295

THE AUTHORS IMPRINT ENDOWMENT FUND

University of California Press gratefully acknowledges the following generous donors to the Authors Imprint Endowment Fund of the University of California Press Foundation.

Wendy Ashmore

Clarence & Jacqueline Avant

Diana & Ehrhard Bahr

Nancy & Roger Boas

Robert Borofsky

Beverly Bouwsma

Prof. Daniel Boyarin

Gene A. Brucker

William K. Coblentz

Joe & Wanda Corn

Liza Dalby

Sam Davis

William Deverell

Frances Dinkelspiel & Gary Wayne

Ross E. Dunn

Carol & John Field

Phyllis Gebauer

Walter S. Gibson

Jennifer A. González

Prof. Mary-Jo DelVecchio Good & Prof. Byron Good

The John Randolph Haynes & Dora Haynes Foundation / Gilbert Garcetti

Daniel Heartz

Leo & Florence Helzel / Helzel Family Foundation

Prof. & Mrs. D. Kern Holoman

Stephen & Gail Humphreys

Mark Juergensmeyer

Lawrence Kramer

Mary Gibbons Landor

Constance Lewallen

Raymond Lifchez

David & Sheila Littlejohn

Dianne Sachko Macleod

TEXT
10/12.5 Minion Pro

DISPLAY
Minion Pro

COMPOSITOR
Westchester Book Group

PRINTER AND BINDER
IBT Global